WINNING WAYS

WINNING WAYS

for your mathematical plays

VOLUME 1: GAMES IN GENERAL

Elwyn R. Berlekamp
John H. Conway
Richard K. Guy

ACADEMIC PRESS

(Harcourt Brace Jovanovich, Publishers)

London   Orlando   San Diego   New York
Toronto   Montreal   Sydney   Tokyo

ACADEMIC PRESS INC. (LONDON) LTD
24/28 Oval Road,
London NW1 7DX

United States Edition published by
ACADEMIC PRESS INC.
Orlando,
Florida 32887

British Library Cataloguing in Publication Data

Berlekamp, E. R.
  Winning Ways, Vol. 1
  1. Mathematical recreations
  I. Title II. Conway, J. H. III. Guy, R. K.
  793.7′4   QA95   LCCCN 81-66678
ISBN 0-12-091101-9

Text set in 10/12pt Times, printed
in Great Britain by Page Bros (Norwich) Ltd.
Mile Cross Lane, Norwich

To Martin Gardner

*who has brought more mathematics
to more millions than anyone else*

Elwyn Berlekamp was born in Dover, Ohio, on September 6, 1940. After spending two years as Assistant Professor at the University of California, Berkeley, and five years at the Bell Telephone Laboratories, in 1971 he became Professor of Mathematics and Electrical Engineering–Computer Science at Berkeley.

His book *Algebraic Coding Theory* received the best research paper award of the IEEE Information Theory Group. Eta Kappa Nu named him the "Outstanding Young Electrical Engineer" of 1971 in the US, and he has been President of the IEEE Information Theory Society. In 1977 he was elected to membership of the US National Academy of Engineering.

John Conway was born in Liverpool, England, on December 26, 1937. He is a Fellow of Gonville and Caius College and a former Fellow of Sidney Sussex College, Cambridge, and is Reader in Pure Mathematics at the University of Cambridge. He has held visiting professorships at several universities and has made original contributions to many branches of mathematics, notably transfinite arithmetic, the theory of knots, many-dimensional geometry and the theory of symmetry (group theory).

He has published two previous books, *Regular Algebra and Finite Machines* and *On Numbers and Games*. He has recently been made a Fellow of the Royal Society.

Richard Guy was born in Nuneaton, England, on September 30, 1916. He has taught mathematics at many levels and in many places—England, Singapore, India, Canada. Since 1965 he has been Professor of Mathematics at the University of Calgary and he is a member of the Board of Governors of the Mathematical Association of America.

He edits the Unsolved Problems section of American Mathematical Monthly; he wrote the volume on Number Theory for the series *Unsolved Problems in Intuitive Mathematics* and is preparing another on Combinatorics, Graph Theory and Game Theory. He is a keen member of the Alpine Club of Canada.

Preface

Does a book need a Preface? What more, after fifteen years of toil, do three talented authors have to add?

We can reassure the bookstore browser, "Yes, this is just the book you want!"

We can direct you, if you want to know quickly what's in the book, to the last page of this preliminary material. This in turn directs you to pages 1, 255, 427 and 695.

We can supply the reviewer, faced with the task of ploughing through nearly a thousand information-packed pages, with some pithy criticisms by indicating the horns of the polylemma the book finds itself on. It is not an encyclopedia. It is encyclopedic, but there are still too many games missing for it to claim to be complete. It is not a book on recreational mathematics because there's too much serious mathematics in it. On the other hand, for us, as for our predecessors Rouse Ball, Dudeney, Martin Gardner, Kraitchik, Sam Loyd, Lucas, Tom O'Beirne and Fred. Schuh, mathematics itself is a recreation. It is not an undergraduate text, since the exercises are not set out in an orderly fashion, with the easy ones at the beginning. They are there though, and with the hundred and sixty-three mistakes we've left in, provide plenty of opportunity for reader participation. So don't just stand back and admire it, work of art though it is. It is not a graduate text, since it's too expensive and contains far more than any graduate student can be expected to learn. But it does carry you to the frontiers of research in combinatorial game theory and the many unsolved problems will stimulate further discoveries.

We thank Patrick Browne for our title. This exercised us for quite a time. One morning, while walking to the university, John and Richard came up with "Whose game?" but realized they couldn't spell it (there are three tooze in English) so it became a one-line joke on line one of the text. There isn't room to explain all the jokes, not even the fifty-nine private ones (each of our birthdays appears more than once in the book).

Omar started as a joke, but soon materialized as Kimberly King. Louise Guy also helped with proof-reading, but her greater contribution was the hospitality which enabled the three of us to work together on several occasions. Louise also did technical typing after many drafts had been made by Karen McDermid and Betty Teare.

Our thanks for many contributions to content may be measured by the number of names in the index. To do real justice would take too much space. Here's an abridged list of helpers: Richard Austin, Clive Bach, John Beasley, Aviezri Fraenkel, David Fremlin, Solomon Golomb, Steve Grantham, Mike Guy, Dean Hickerson, Hendrik Lenstra, Victor Meally, Richard Nowakowski, Anne Scott, David Seal, John Selfridge, Cedric Smith and Steve Tschantz.

No small part of the reason for the assured success of the book is owed to the well-informed and sympathetic guidance of Len Cegielka and the willingness of the staff of Academic Press and of Page Bros. to adapt to the idiosyncrasies of the authors, who grasped every opportunity to modify grammar, strain semantics, pervert punctuation, alter orthography, tamper with traditional typography and commit outrageous puns and inside jokes. We have taken the opportunity of re-printing to make some slight additions and corrections.

Thanks also to the Isaak Walton Killam Foundation for Richard's Resident Fellowship at The University of Calgary during the compilation of a critical draft, and to the Natural Sciences and Engineering Research Council of Canada for a grant which enabled Elwyn and John to visit him more frequently than our widely scattered habitats would normally allow.

And thank you, Simon!

University of California, Berkeley, CA 94720   *Elwyn Berlekamp*

University of Cambridge, England, CB2 1SB   *John Conway*

University of Calgary, Canada, T2N 1N4   *Richard Guy*

Contents

Biography   ix

Preface   xi

Contents of Volume 2   xxiii

♠

SPADE WORK!

Chapter 1 **Whose Game?**   3

BLUE-RED HACKENBUSH   4
THE TWEEDLEDUM AND TWEEDLEDEE ARGUMENT   5
HOW CAN YOU HAVE HALF A MOVE?   6
. . . AND QUARTER MOVES?   8
SKI-JUMPS FOR BEGINNERS   10
DON'T JUST TAKE THE AVERAGE!   12
WHAT IS A JUMP WORTH?   13
TOADS-AND-FROGS   14
DO OUR METHODS WORK?   15

Extras
WHAT IS A GAME?   16
WHEN IS A MOVE GOOD?   17
FIGURE 8(d) IS WORTH $\frac{3}{4}$ 18
REFERENCES AND FURTHER READING   19

Chapter 2 **Finding the Correct Number is Simplicity Itself**   21

WHICH NUMBERS ARE WHICH?   21
SIMPLICITY'S THE ANSWER!   23
SIMPLEST FORMS FOR NUMBERS   24
CUTCAKE   26
MAUNDY CAKE   28
A FEW MORE APPLICATIONS OF THE SIMPLICITY RULE   29
POSITIVE, NEGATIVE, ZERO AND FUZZY POSITIONS   30
HACKENBUSH HOTCHPOTCH   31
SUMS OF ARBITRARY GAMES   32
THE OUTCOME OF A SUM   33
THE NEGATIVE OF A GAME   35
CANCELLING A GAME WITH ITS NEGATIVE   36
COMPARING TWO GAMES   37
COMPARING HACKENBUSH POSITIONS   38

THE GAME OF COL   39
A STAR IS BORN!   40
COL CONTAINS SUCH VALUES   41
GAME TREES   42
GREEN HACKENBUSH, THE GAME OF NIM, AND NIMBERS   42
GET NIMBLE WITH NIMBERS!   44
CHILDISH HACKENBUSH   45
SEATING COUPLES   46

Extras
WINNING STRATEGIES   48
THE SUM OF TWO FINITE GAMES CAN LAST
FOREVER   48
A THEOREM ABOUT COL   49
COL-LECTIONS AND COL-LAPSINGS   50
MAUNDY CAKE   53
ANOTHER CUTCAKE VARIANT   53
HOW CHILDISH CAN YOU GET?   54
REFERENCES AND FURTHER READING   54

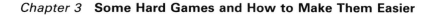

Chapter 3   Some Hard Games and How to Make Them Easier   **55**

POKER-NIM   55
NORTHCOTT'S GAME   56
BOGUS NIM-HEAPS AND THE MEX RULE   57
THE SPRAGUE-GRUNDY THEORY FOR IMPARTIAL GAMES   58
THE WHITE KNIGHT   59
ADDING NIMBERS   60
WYT QUEENS   61
REVERSIBLE MOVES IN GENERAL GAMES   62
DELETING DOMINATED OPTIONS   64
TOADS-AND-FROGS WITH UPS AND DOWNS   65
GAME TRACKING AND IDENTIFICATION   67
WHAT ARE FLOWERS WORTH?   68
A GALLIMAUFRY OF GAMES   69
WHO WINS SUMS OF UPS, DOWNS, STARS AND NUMBERS?   70
A CLOSER LOOK AT THE STARS   71
THE VALUES $\{\uparrow \mid \uparrow\}$ and $\{0 \mid \uparrow\}$ 71
THE UPSTART EQUALITY   73
GIFT HORSES   74

Extras
THE NIM-ADDITION RULE IN SEVERAL VARIATIONS   75
WYT QUEENS AND WYTHOFF'S GAME   76
ANSWERS TO FIGS. 8, 9 AND 11   77
TOAD VERSUS FROG   77
TWO THEOREMS ON SIMPLIFYING GAMES   78
BERLEKAMP'S RULE FOR HACKENBUSH STRINGS   79
REFERENCES AND FURTHER READING   80

Chapter 4 **Taking and Breaking**   **81**

KAYLES 82
GAMES WITH HEAPS 82
$\mathcal{P}$-POSITIONS AND $\mathcal{N}$-POSITIONS 83
SUBTRACTION GAMES 83
FERGUSON'S PAIRING PROPERTY 86
GRUNDY SCALES 87
OTHER TAKE-AWAY GAMES 87
DAWSON'S CHESS 88
THE PERIODICITY OF KAYLES 90
OTHER TAKE-AND-BREAK GAMES 91
DAWSON'S KAYLES 92
VARIATIONS 93
GUILES 93
TREBLECROSS 93
OFFICERS 94
GRUNDY'S GAME 96
PRIM AND DIM 97
REPLICATION OF NIM-VALUES 97
DOUBLE AND QUADRUPLE KAYLES 98
LASKER'S NIM 99

Extras
SOME REMARKS ON PERIODICITY 100
STANDARD FORM 100
A COMPENDIUM OF OCTAL GAMES 101
ADDITIONAL REMARKS 101
SPARSE SPACES AND COMMON COSETS 109
WILL GRUNDY'S GAME BE ULTIMATELY PERIODIC? 111
SPARSE SPACE SPELLS SPEED 111
GAMES DISPLAYING ARITHMETIC PERIODICITY 112
A NON-ARITHMETIC-PERIODICITY THEOREM 114
SOME HEXADECIMAL GAMES 116
REFERENCES AND FURTHER READING 116

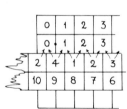

Chapter 5 **Numbers, Nimbers and Numberless Wonders**   **117**

DOMINEERING 117
SWITCH GAMES 119
CASHING CHEQUES 120
SOME SIMPLE HOT GAMES 123
THE TINIEST GAMES 123
MODERN MANAGEMENT OF CASH FLOW 124
TINY TOADS-AND-FROGS 125
THE OPENING DISSECTION OF TOADS-AND-FROGS 126
SEATING BOYS AND GIRLS 130

Extras
TOADS-AND-FROGS COMPLETELY DISSECTED 132
TOADS-AND-FROGS WITH TWO SPACES 135
MORE DOMINEERING VALUES 137
REFERENCES AND FURTHER READING 140

Chapter 6   The Heat of Battle   **141**

SNORT 141
A GRAPHIC PICTURE OF FARM LIFE 142
DON'T MOVE IN A NUMBER UNLESS THERE'S
NOTHING ELSE TO DO! 144
WHAT'S IN IT FOR ME? 144
THE LEFT AND RIGHT STOPS 146
COOLING—AND THE THERMOGRAPH 147
COOLING SETTLES THE MEAN VALUE 148
HOW TO DRAW THERMOGRAPHS 149
WHEN A PLAYER HAS SEVERAL OPTIONS 150
FOUNDATIONS FOR THERMOGRAPHS 151
EXAMPLES OF THERMOGRAPHS 152
WHO IS TO MOVE FROM THE FINAL STOP? 154
A FOUR-STOP EXAMPLE 154
THE CHEQUE-MARKET EXCHANGE 155
EQUITABLE GAMES 156
EXCITABLE GAMES 156
THE EXTENDED THERMOGRAPH 157
GETTING THE RIGHT SLANT 159
THE THERMOSTATIC STRATEGY 159
THERMOSTRAT'S NOT OFTEN WRONG! 162
HEATING 163
DOES THE EXCITEMENT SHOW? 166
HOW TO SELL INFINITESIMAL VALUES TO YOUR
PROFIT-CONSCIOUS FRIENDS 167
NIM, REMOTENESS AND SUSPENSE IN HOT GAMES 169
OVERHEATING 170
COOLING THE CHILDREN'S PARTY 174
BUT HOW DO YOU COOL A PARTY BY ONE DEGREE? 175

Extras
THREE SNORT LEMMAS 176
A SNORT DICTIONARY 179
PROOF OF THE NUMBER AVOIDANCE THEOREM 179
WHY THERMOSTRAT WORKS 179
REFERENCES 182

Chapter 7   Hackenbush   **183**

GREEN HACKENBUSH 184
GREEN TREES 184

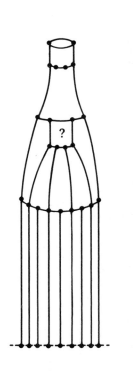

FUSION 186
PROVING THE FUSION PRINCIPLE 187
A MORE COMPLICATED PICTURE 189
IMPARTIAL MAUNDY CAKE 190
BLUE-RED HACKENBUSH 191
HACKENBUSH HOTCHPOTCH 191
FLOWER GARDENS 192
THE BLUE FLOWER PLOY 193
ATOMIC WEIGHTS 194
ATOMIC WEIGHT OF JUNGLES 196
MAKING TRACKS IN THE JUNGLE 199
TRACKING DOWN AN ANIMAL 200
AMAZING JUNGLE 203
SMART GAME IN THE JUNGLE 204
UNPARTED JUNGLES 205
BLUE-RED HACKENBUSH CAN BE HARD, TOO! 206
REDWOOD FURNITURE 206
REDWOOD BEDS 210
HOW BIG IS A REDWOOD BED? 211
WHAT'S THE BOTTLE? 213

Extras
ORDINAL ADDITION, THE COLON PRINCIPLE, AND
NORTON'S LEMMA 214
BOTH WAYS OF ADDING IMPARTIAL GAMES 214
MANY-WAY MAUNDY CAKE 215
SOLUTION TO FIGURE 15 215
TRACKS CLEARED THROUGH THE AMAZING JUNGLE 216
HOW HARD WAS THE BED? 216
NP-HARDNESS 218
THE BOTTLE AT THE END OF CHAPTER SEVEN 220
REFERENCES AND FURTHER READING 220

Chapter 8 **It's a Small, Small, Small, Small World**   **221**

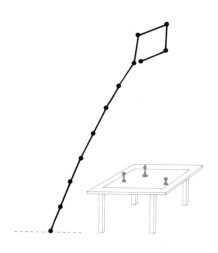

UPPITINESS AND UNCERTAINTY 222
COMPUTING ATOMIC WEIGHTS 223
EATCAKE 225
SPLITTING THE ATOM 226
TURN-AND-EATCAKE 227
ALL YOU NEED TO KNOW ABOUT ATOMIC
WEIGHTS BUT WERE AFRAID TO ASK 228
CHILDISH HACKENBUSH HOTCHPOTCH 229
ATOMIC WEIGHTS OF LOLLIPOPS 230
PROVING THINGS ABOUT ATOMIC WEIGHTS 232
PLAYING AMONG THE FLOWERS 232
WHEN IS g AS UPPITY AS h? 233
GO FLY A KITE! 234
ALL REMOTE STARS AGREE 235
LARGE AND SMALL FLOWERBEDS 236
PLAYING UNDER A LUCKY STAR 237
GENERAL MULTIPLES OF UP 238
PROOF OF THE REMOTE STAR RULES 239

CONTENTS

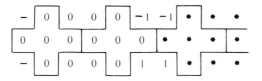

PROOF THAT ATOMIC WEIGHT = UPPITINESS 240
THE WHOLENESS OF HACKENBUSH HOTCHPOTCH 242
PROPER CARE OF THE ECCENTRIC 242
GALVINIZED GAMES 243
TRADING TRIANGLES 244

Extras
MULTIPLES OF POSITIVE GAMES 246
MULTIPLES WORK! 246
FIRST FOR THE "WITH" RULE: 247
NOW FOR THE "WITHOUT" RULE: 248
SHIFTING MULTIPLES OF UP BY STARS 249
A THEOREM ON INCENTIVES 249
SEATING FAMILIES OF FIVE 251
REFERENCE 253

CHANGE OF HEART!

Chapter 9 **If You Can't Beat 'Em, Join 'Em!** **257**

ALL THE KING'S HORSES 257
WE CAN JOIN ANY GAMES 258
HOW REMOTE IS A HORSE? 258
WHAT IF THE FIRST HORSE TO GET STUCK WINS? 261
A SLIGHTLY SLOWER JOIN 263
MOVING HORSES IMPARTIALLY 263
CUTTING EVERY CAKE 264
EATCAKES 266
WHEN TO PUT YOUR MONEY ON THE LAST HORSE 266
SLOW HORSES JOIN THE ALSO-RANS 266
LET THEM EAT CAKE! 269

Extras
ALL THE KING'S HORSES ON A QUARTER-INFINITE BOARD 272
CUTTING YOUR CAKES AND EATING THEM 272
REFERENCES AND FURTHER READING 278

Chapter 10 **Hot Battles Followed by Cold Wars** **279**

HOTCAKES 279
UNIONS OF GAMES 280
COLD GAMES—NUMBERS ARE STILL NUMBERS 280
HOT GAMES—THE BATTLE IS JOINED! 280
TOLLS, TIMERS AND TALLIES 280
WHICH IS THE BEST OPTION? 283

CONTENTS   xix

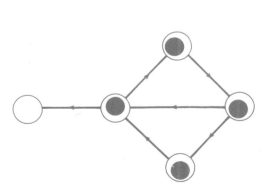

HOT POSITIONS 284
COLD POSITIONS 284
TEPID POSITIONS 286
TALLY TRUTHS TOTALLY TOLD 288
A TEPID GAME 288
SELECT BOYS AND GIRLS 290
MRS. GRUNDY 290
HOW TO PLAY MISÈRE UNIONS OF PARTIZAN GAMES 292
URGENT UNIONS (SHOTGUN WEDDINGS?) 292
PREDECIDERS—OVERRIDERS AND SUICIDERS 292
FALADA 292
ONE FOR YOU, TWO FOR ME, NOTHING FOR BOTH OF US 299
TWO MORE FALADA GAMES 300
BAKED ALASKA 301

Extras
A FELICITOUS FALADA FIELD 304
THE RULES FOR TALLIES ON INFINITE TOLLS 305
TIME MAY BE SHORTER THAN YOU THINK 306

Chapter 11   **Games Infinite and Indefinite**   **307**

INFINITE HACKENBUSH 307
INFINITE ENDERS 309
THE INFINITE ORDINAL NUMBERS 309
OTHER NUMBERS 310
INFINITE NIM 310
THE INFINITE SPRAGUE–GRUNDY AND SMITH THEORIES 313
SOME SUPERHEAVY ATOMS 313
LOOPY GAMES 314
FIXED, MIXED AND FREE 315
ONSIDES AND OFFSIDES, UPSUMS AND DOWNSUMS 316
STOPPERS 317
on, off AND **dud** 317
HOW BIG IS **on**? 318
IT'S BIGGER THAN ALL OF THEM! 318
SIDLING TOWARDS A GAME 318
SIDLING PICKS SIDES 320
STOPPERS HAVE ONLY ONE SIDE 320
'TIS! – 'TISN'! – 'TIS! – 'TISN'! – . . . 322
LOOPY HACKENBUSH 323
DISENTANGLING LOOPY HACKENBUSH 323
LOOPILY INFINITE HACKENBUSH 324
SISYPHUS 326
LIVING WITH LOOPS 328
COMPARING LOOPY GAMES 328
THE SWIVEL CHAIR STRATEGY 329
STOPPERS ARE NICE 330
PLUMTREES ARE NICER! 332
TAKING CARE OF PLUMTREES 334

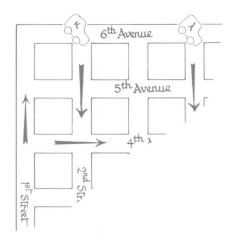

WORKING WITH UPSUMS AND DOWNSUMS 335
on, off AND hot 336
A SUMMARY OF SOME SUM PROPERTIES 337
THE HOUSE OF CARDS 337
THE DEGREE OF LOOPINESS 341
CLASSES AND VARIETIES 342
NO HIGHWAY 344
BACKSLIDING TOADS-AND-FROGS 347

Extras
BACH'S CAROUSEL 349
PROOF OF THE SIDLING THEOREM 351
ANSWER TO EXERCISE ONE 354
tis AND tisn 354
upon 355
BACKSLIDING TOADS-AND-FROGS 355
REFERENCES AND FURTHER READING 357

Chapter 12   Games Eternal—Games Entailed   359

FAIR SHARES AND VARIED PAIRS 359
HOW SOON CAN YOU WIN? 361
THERE MAY BE OPEN POSITIONS (ⓞ-POSITIONS) 362
DE BONO'S *L*-GAME 364
ADDERS-AND-LADDERS 366
JUST HOW LOOPY CAN YOU GET? 371
CORRALL AUTOMOTIVE BETTERMENT SCHEME 371
SHARING OUT OTHER KINDS OF NUT 373
FAIR SHARES AND UNEQUAL PARTNERS 374
SWEETS AND NUTS, AND MAYBE A DATE? 374
THE ADDITIONAL SUBTRACTION GAMES 375
HORSEFLY 375
SELECTIVE AND SUBSELECTIVE COMPOUNDS OF
IMPARTIAL GAMES 376
ENTAILING MOVES 376
SUNNY AND LOONY POSITIONS 377
CALCULATING WITH ENTAILED VALUES 378
NIM WITH ENTAILING MOVES 380
GOLDBACH'S NIM 381
WYT QUEENS WITH TRAINS 382
ADDING TAILS TO PRIM AND DIM 384
COMPLIMENTING MOVES 385
ON-THE-RAILS 387

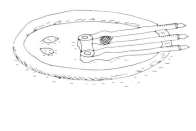

Extras
DE BONO'S *L*-GAME 388
PROVING THE OUTCOME RULES FOR LOOPY POSITIONS 388
FAIR SHARES AND UNEQUAL PARTNERS 390
WERE YOUR WAYS WINNING ENOUGH? 390
DID YOU MOVE FIRST IN HORSEFLY? 391
REFERENCES AND FURTHER READING 392

Chapter 13 **Survival in the Lost World** 393

MISÈRE NIM 393
REVERSIBLE MOVES 395
THE ENDGAME PROVISO 396
THE AWFUL TRUTH 396
WHAT'S LEFT OF THE OLD RULES? 398
AS EASY AS TWO AND TWO? 399
THE MISÈRE FORM OF GRUNDY'S GAME 399
ANIMALS AND THEIR GENUS 402
WHAT CAN WE DO WITH THE GENUS? 403
FIRM, FICKLE AND TAME 403
WHICH ANIMALS ARE TAME . . . 405
. . . AND WHICH ARE RESTIVE? 405
SOME TAME ANIMALS IN THE GOOD CHILD'S ZOO 407
MISÈRE WYT QUEENS 407
JELLY BEANS AND LEMON DROPS 408
STALKING ADDERS AND TAKING SQUARES 409
"BUT WHAT IF THEY'RE WILD?" ASKS THE BAD CHILD 410
MISÈRE KAYLES 411
THE NOAH'S ARK THEOREM 412
THE HALF-TAME THEOREM 415
GUILES 416
DIVIDING RULERS 416
DAWSON, OFFICERS, GRUNDY 418

Extras
ALL SUBTRACTION GAMES REDUCE TO NIM 422
PRIM AND DIM 422
PROOF OF THE NOAH'S ARK THEOREM 423
MISÈRE OCTAL GAMES 423
STOP PRESS: EVEN MORE GAMES ARE TAMEABLE 426
REFERENCES AND FURTHER READING 426

Index **I**

Contents of Volume 2

Biography   ix

Preface   xi

Contents of Volume 1   xxiii

♣
GAMES IN CLUBS!

Chapter 14 **Turn and Turn About**   **429**

TURNING TURTLES 429
MOCK TURTLES 431
ODIOUS AND EVIL NUMBERS 431
MOEBIUS, MOGUL AND GOLD MOIDORES 432
THE MOCK TURTLE THEOREM 432
WHY MOEBIUS? 434
MOGUL 435
MOTLEY 437
TWINS, TRIPLETS, ETC. 437
THE RULER GAME 437
CIRCUMSCRIBED GAMES 438
TURNIPS (OR TERNUPS) 438
GRUNT 440
SYM 441
TWO-DIMENSIONAL TURNING GAMES 441
ACROSTIC TWINS 441
TURNING CORNERS 441
NIM-MULTIPLICATION 443
SWIRLING TARTANS 444
THE TARTAN THEOREM 445
RUGS, CARPETS, WINDOWS AND DOORS 446
ACROSTIC GAMES 450
STRIPPING AND STREAKING 451
UGLIFICATION AND DERISION 451

Extras
UNLOCKING DOORS 456
SPARRING, BOXING AND FENCING 456
COINS (OR HEAPS) WITH INFINITELY
MANY (OR 2^{2^N}) "SIDES" 456
REFERENCES AND FURTHER READING 456

Chapter 15 **Chips and Strips**   **457**

THE SILVER DOLLAR GAME 457
PROFIT FROM GAMING TABLES 458
ANTONIM 459
SYNONIM 460
SIMONIM 462
STAIRCASE FIVES 465
TWOPINS 466
CRAM 468
WELTER'S GAME 472
FOUR-COIN WELTER IS JUST NIM 473
AND SO'S THREE-COIN WELTER! 473
THE CONGRUENCE MODULO 16 473
FRIEZE PATTERNS 475
INVERTING THE WELTER FUNCTION 477
THE ABACUS POSITIONS 478
THE ABACUS STRATEGY 479
THE MISÈRE FORM OF WELTER'S GAME 480
KOTZIG'S NIM 481
FIBONACCI NIM 483
MORE GENERALLY BOUNDED NIM 483
EPSTEIN'S PUT-OR-TAKE-A-SQUARE GAME 484
TRIBULATIONS AND FIBULATIONS 486
THIRD ONE LUCKY 486
HICKORY, DICKORY, DOCK 487
D.U.D.E.N.E.Y. 487
STRINGS OF PEARLS 488
SCHUHSTRINGS 489
THE PRINCESS AND THE ROSES 490
ONE-STEP, TWO-STEP 495
MORE ON SUBTRACTION GAMES 495
MOORE'S NIM_k 498
THE MORE THE MERRIER 499
MOORE AND MORE 499
NOT WITH A BANG BUT A WHIM 500

Extras
DID YOU WIN THE SILVER DOLLAR? 501
HOW WAS YOUR ARITHMETIC? 501
IN PUT-OR-TAKE-A-SQUARE, 92 IS AN $\mathcal{N}$-POSITION 501
TRIBULATIONS AND FIBULATIONS 501
OUR CODE OF BEHAVIOR FOR PRINCES 503
REFERENCES AND FURTHER READING 505

Chapter 16 **Dots-and-Boxes**   **507**

DOUBLE-DEALING LEADS TO DOUBLE-CROSSES 509
HOW LONG IS "LONG"? 512
THE 4-BOX GAME 513
THE 9-BOX GAME 515
THE 16-BOX GAME 515

OTHER SHAPES OF BOARD 516
DOTS-AND-BOXES AND STRINGS-AND-COINS 516
NIMSTRING 518
WHY LONG IS LONG 520
TO TAKE OR NOT TO TAKE A COIN IN NIMSTRING 521
SPRAGUE-GRUNDY THEORY FOR NIMSTRING GRAPHS 522
ALL LONG CHAINS ARE THE SAME 527
WHICH MUTATIONS ARE HARMLESS? 528
CHOPPING AND CHANGING 530
VINES 530

Extras
DOTS + DOUBLECROSSES = TURNS 537
HOW DODIE CAN WIN THE 4-BOX GAME 538
WHEN IS IT BEST TO LOSE CONTROL? 540
COMPUTING THE VALUES OF VINES 541
LOONY ENDGAMES ARE NP-HARD 543
SOLUTIONS TO DOT-AND-BOXES PROBLEMS 544
SOME MORE NIMSTRING VALUES 546
NIMBERS FOR NIMSTRING ARRAYS 548
REFERENCES AND FURTHER READING 550

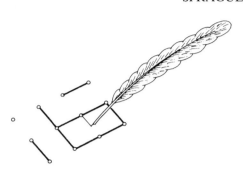

Chapter 17 Spots and Sprouts   **551**

RIMS 551
RAILS 552
LOOPS-AND-BRANCHES 552
CONTOURS 553
LUCASTA 554
A CHILD'S GUIDE TO NORMAL LUCASTA 555
THE MISÈRE FORM OF LUCASTA 556
THE POSITIONS (7, 3, 1) AND (11, 1, 1) 560
CABBAGES; OR BUGS, CATERPILLARS
AND COCOONS 563
JOCASTA 563
SPROUTS 564
BRUSSELS SPROUTS 569
STARS-AND-STRIPES 569
BUSHENHACK 570
GENETIC CODES FOR NIM 571
BUSHENHACK POSITIONS HAVE GENETIC CODES! 572
VON NEUMANN HACKENBUSH 572

Extras
THE JOKE IN JOCASTA 573
THE WORM IN BRUSSELS SPROUTS 573
BUSHENHACK 573
REFERENCES AND FURTHER READING 573

Chapter 18   The Emperor and His Money   575

$\{16\}, \{18\}, \{24\}, \{27\}, \{32\}, \{36\}, \ldots\ ?$

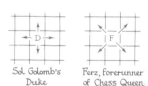

SYLVER COINAGE 576
HOW LONG WILL IT LAST? 576
SOME OPENINGS ARE BAD 577
ARE ALL OPENINGS BAD? 579
NOT ALL OPENINGS ARE BAD 581
STRATEGY STEALING 582
QUIET ENDS 583
DOUBLING AND TRIPLING? 586
HALVING AND THIRDING? 586
FINDING THE RIGHT COMBINATIONS 587
WHAT SHALL I DO WHEN g IS TWO? 592
THE GREAT UNKNOWN 595
ARE OUTCOMES COMPUTABLE? 596
THE ETIQUETTE OF SYLVER COINAGE 597

Extras
CHOMP 598
ZIG-ZAG 598
MORE CLIQUES FOR SYLVER COINAGE 602
5-PAIRS 602
POSITIONS CONTAINING 6 602
SYLVER COINAGE HAS INFINITE NIM-VALUES 606
A FEW FINAL QUESTIONS 606
REFERENCES AND FURTHER READING 606

Chapter 19   The King and the Consumer   607

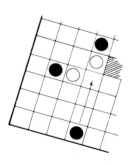

Sol Golomb's
Duke

Ferz, forerunner
of Chess Queen

CHESSGO, KINGGO AND DUKEGO 607
QUADRAPHAGE 608
THE ANGEL AND THE SQUARE-EATER 609
STRATEGY AND TACTICS 609
DUKEGO 610
THE GAME OF KINGGO 611
THE EDGE ATTACK 611
THE EDGE DEFENCE 613
A MEMORYLESS EDGE DEFENCE 613
THE EDGE-CORNER ATTACK 617
STRATEGIC AND TACTICAL STONES 618
CORNER TACTICS 618
DEFENCE ON LARGE SQUARE BOARDS 622
THE 33 × 33 BOARD 623
THE CENTRED KING 624
LEAVING THE CENTRAL REGION 624
THE CORNERED KING 627
THE SIDELINED KING 627
HOW CHAS. CAN WIN ON A 34 × 34 BOARD 629
RECTANGULAR BOARDS 630

Extras
MANY-DIMENSIONAL ANGELS 631

GAMES OF ENCIRCLEMENT 631
WOLVES-AND-SHEEP 631
TABLUT 632
SAXON HNEFATAFL 632
KING AND ROOK VERSUS KING 633
REFERENCES AND FURTHER READING 634

Chapter 20 **Fox and Geese**   **635**

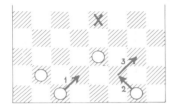

SOME PROPERTIES OF OUR STRATEGY 638
THE SIZE OF THE GEESE'S ADVANTAGE 639
THE PARADOX 642
PUNCHING THE CLOCK 644

Extras
MAHARAJAH AND SEPOYS 646
REFERENCES AND FURTHER READING 646

Chapter 21 **Hare and Hounds**   **647**

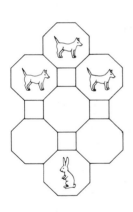

THE FRENCH MILITARY HUNT 647
TWO TRIAL GAMES 649
HISTORY 649
THE DIFFERENT KINDS OF PLACE 649
THE OPPOSITION 650
WHEN HAS THE HARE ESCAPED? 651
LOSING THE OPPOSITION 652
A STRATEGY FOR THE HARE 654
ON THE SMALL BOARD 657
ON THE MEDIUM AND LARGER BOARDS 658

Extras
ANSWERS TO QUESTIONS 661
A SOUND BOUND FOR A HOUND? 661
ALL IS FOUND FOR THE SMALL BOARD HOUND 661
PROOF OF THE THIRTY-ONE THEOREM 665
REFERENCES AND FURTHER READING 665

Chapter 22 **Lines and Squares**   **667**

TIT-TAT-TOE, MY FIRST GO, THREE JOLLY
BUTCHER BOYS ALL IN A ROW 667
MAGIC FIFTEEN 668
SPIT NOT SO, FAT FOP, AS IF IN PAN! 668

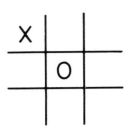

JAM 668
HOW LONG CAN YOU FOOL YOUR FRIENDS? 669
ANALYSIS OF TIC-TAC-TOE 669
OVID'S GAME, HOPSCOTCH, LES PENDUS 672
SIX MEN'S MORRIS 673
NINE MEN'S MORRIS 673
THREE UP 673
FOUR-IN-A-ROW 673
FIVE-IN-A-ROW 674
GO-MOKU 676
SIX, SEVEN, EIGHT, NINE, . . ., IN A ROW 676
n-DIMENSIONAL k-IN-A-ROW 678
STRATEGY STEALING IN TIC-TAC-TOE GAMES 679
HEX 680
BRIDGIT 680
HOW DOES THE FIRST PLAYER WIN? 680
THE SHANNON SWITCHING GAME 680
THE BLACK PATH GAME 682
LEWTHWAITE'S GAME 683
MEANDER 683
WINNERS AND LOSERS 684
DODGEM 685
DODGERYDOO 687
PHILOSOPHER'S FOOTBALL 688

Extras
REFERENCES AND FURTHER READING 692

SOLITAIRE DIAMONDS!

Chapter 23 **Purging Pegs Properly**   **697**

CENTRAL SOLITAIRE 698
DUDENEY, BERGHOLT AND BEASLEY 699
PACKAGES AND PURGES 701
PACKAGES PROVIDE PERFECT PANACEA 703
THE RULE OF TWO AND THE RULE OF THREE 705
SOME PEGS ARE MORE EQUAL THAN OTHERS 706
REISS'S 16 SOLITAIRE POSITION CLASSES 708
THE CONTINENTAL BOARD 711
PLAYING BACKWARDS AND FORWARDS 711
PAGODA FUNCTIONS 712
THE SOLITAIRE ARMY 715
MANAGING YOUR RESOURCES 717
UNPRODUCTIVITY AND THE PRODIGAL SON 719
DEFICIT ACCOUNTING AND THE G.N.P. 720
ACCOUNTING FOR TWO-PEG REVERSAL PROBLEMS 720
FORGETTING THE ORDER CAN BE USEFUL 721
BEASLEY'S EXIT THEOREMS 723

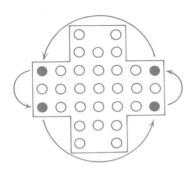

A STOLID SURVIVOR PROBLEM 723
ANOTHER HARD PROBLEM 725
THE SPINNER 727

Extras
OUR FINE FINALIST 728
DOING THE SPLITS 728
ALL SOLUBLE ONE-PEG PROBLEMS ON THE
CONTINENTAL BOARD 729
THE LAST TWO MOVES 729
A 20-MAN SOLITAIRE ARMY 729
FOOL'S SOLITAIRE, ETC. 729
BEASLEY PROVES BERGHOLT IS BEST 731
THE CLASSICAL PROBLEMS 733
REFERENCES AND FURTHER READING 734

Chapter 24　**Pursuing Puzzles Purposefully**　　　　**735**

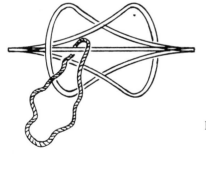

SOMA 735
BLOCKS-IN-A-BOX 736
HIDDEN SECRETS 736
THE HIDDEN SECRETS OF SOMA 737
HOFFMAN'S ARITHMETICO-GEOMETRIC PUZZLE 739
COLORING THREE-BY-THREE-BY-THREE BY THREE, BAR THREE 740
WIRE AND STRING PUZZLES 741
THE MAGIC MIRROR METHOD 741
BARMY BRAID 745
THE ARTFUL ARROW 746
THE MAGIC MOVIE METHOD 746
PARTY TRICKS AND CHINESE RINGS 748
CHINESE RINGS AND THE GRAY CODE 750
THE TOWER OF HANOÏ 753
A SOLITAIRE-LIKE PUZZLE AND SOME COIN-
SLIDING PROBLEMS 755
FIFTEEN PUZZLE AND THE LUCKY SEVEN PUZZLE 756
ALL OTHER COURSES FOR POINT-TO-POINT 759
THE HUNGARIAN CUBE—BÜVÖS KOCKA 760
JUST HOW CHAOTIC CAN THE CUBE GET? 761
CHIEF COLORS AND CHIEF FACES 761
CURING THE CUBE 763
A: ALOFT, AROUND (ADJUST) AND ABOUT 764
B: BOTTOM LAYER CORNER CUBELETS 764
C: CENTRAL LAYER EDGE CUBELETS 764
D: DOMICILING THE TOP EDGE CUBELETS 764
E: EXCHANGING PAIRS OF TOP CORNERS 766
F: FINISHING FLIPS AND FIDDLES 766
EXPLANATIONS 766
IMPROVEMENTS 767
ELENA'S ELEMENTS 768
ARE YOU PARTIAL TO PARTIAL PUZZLES? 768
OTHER "HUNGARIAN" OBJECTS 768
A TRIO OF SLIDING BLOCK PUZZLES 769
TACTICS FOR SOLVING SUCH PUZZLES 770

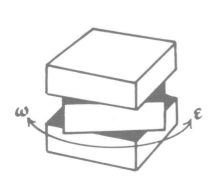

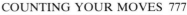

COUNTING YOUR MOVES 777
PARADOXICAL PENNIES 777
PARADOXICAL DICE 778
MORE ON MAGIC SQUARES 778
THE MAGIC TESSERACT 783
ADAMS'S AMAZING MAGIC HEXAGON 784
THE GREAT TANTALIZER 784
POLYOMINOES, POLYIAMONDS AND SEARCHING POLICY 786
ALAN SCHOEN'S CYCLOTOME 789
MACMAHON'S SUPERDOMINOES 791
QUINTOMINAL DODECAHEDRA 792
THE DOOMSDAY RULE 795
. . . AND EASTER EASILY 797
HOW OLD IS THE MOON? 799
JEWISH NEW YEAR (ROSH HASHANA) 800

Extras
BLOCKS-IN-A-BOX 801
THE SOMAP 801
SOLUTIONS TO THE ARITHMETICO-GEOMETRIC
PUZZLE 804
. . . AND ONE FOR "THREE" TOO! 807
HARES AND TORTOISES 807
THE LUCKY SEVEN PUZZLE 807
TOP FACE ALTERATIONS FOR THE HUNGARIAN CUBE 808
THE CENTURY PUZZLE 810
ADAMS'S AMAZING MAGIC HEXAGON 810
FLAGS OF THE ALLIES SOLUTION 811
ANSWER TO EXERCISE FOR EXPERTS 811
WHERE DO THE BLACK EDGES OF MACMAHON
SQUARES GO? 812
THE THREE QUINTOMINAL DODECAHEDRA 813
DOOMSDAY ANSWERS 813
REFERENCES AND FURTHER READING 813

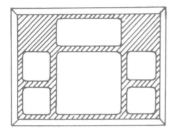

Chapter 25   **What is Life?**   **817**

STILL LIFE 819
LIFE CYCLES 820
THE GLIDER AND OTHER SPACE SHIPS 821
THE UNPREDICTABILITY OF LIFE 824
GARDENS OF EDEN 828
LIFE'S PROBLEMS ARE HARD! 829
MAKING A LIFE COMPUTER 830
WHEN GLIDER MEETS GLIDER 831
HOW TO MAKE A NOT GATE 832
THE EATER 833
GLIDERS CAN BUILD THEIR OWN GUNS! 837
THE KICKBACK REACTION 837
THINNING A GLIDER STREAM 837

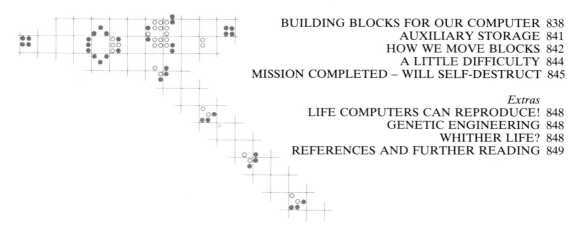

BUILDING BLOCKS FOR OUR COMPUTER 838
AUXILIARY STORAGE 841
HOW WE MOVE BLOCKS 842
A LITTLE DIFFICULTY 844
MISSION COMPLETED – WILL SELF-DESTRUCT 845

Extras
LIFE COMPUTERS CAN REPRODUCE! 848
GENETIC ENGINEERING 848
WHITHER LIFE? 848
REFERENCES AND FURTHER READING 849

Index   **I**

You are
now here

If you want to know roughly what's elsewhere,
turn to the little notes about our four main themes:

Adding Games ... ... ♠ page 1
Bending the Rules ... ... ♡ page 255
Case Studies ... : ... ... ♣ page 427
Doing It Yourself ... ... ◇ page 695

There are a number of other connexions between various chapters of the book:

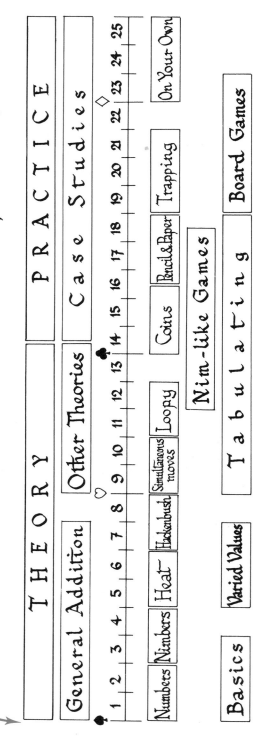

However, you should be able to pick any chapter and read almost all of it
without reference to anything earlier, except perhaps the basic ideas at the start of the book.

SPADE-WORK!

Let spades be trumps! she said, and trumps they were.
Alexander Pope, *The Rape of the Lock,* c.iii, l.46.

CECILY: When I see a spade I call it a spade.
GWENDOLEN: I am glad to say I have never seen a spade.
Oscar Wilde, *The Importance of Being Earnest,* II.

Our first few chapters do the spade-work for the rest by telling how to add games together and how to work out their values.

Chapters 1 and 2 introduce these ideas and show that some simple examples have ordinary numbers for values while others don't.

In Chapter 3 you'll see how the special values called nimbers, that arise in the game of Nim, suffice for *all* impartial games, and lots of examples are tackled in Chapter 4.

Chapter 5 has some very small games, and some others which, because they are both big (unlike nimbers) and hot (unlike numbers), really need the theory of Chapter 6.

Finally, Chapter 7 discusses the small games to within an atom or two, and Chapter 8 shows how such values arise along with ordinary numbers in the game of Hackenbush.

Chapter 1

'Begin at the beginning,' the King said, gravely, 'and go on till you come to the end; then stop.'
Lewis Carroll, *Alice in Wonderland*, ch. 12

It is hard if I cannot start some game on these lone heaths.
William Hazlitt, *On Going a Journey*

Whose Game?

Who's game for an easy pencil-and-paper (or chalk-and-blackboard) game?

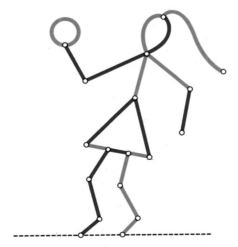

Figure 1. A Blue-Red Hackenbush Picture.

3

BLUE-RED HACKENBUSH

(or Red-Blue Hackenbush) is played with a picture such as that of Fig. 1. We shall call the two players **Left** and **Right**. Left moves by deleting any bLue edge, together with any edges that are no longer connected to the ground (which is the dotted line in the figure), and Right moves by deleting a Red edge in a similar way. (Play it on a blackboard if you can, because it's easier to rub the edges out.) Quite soon, one of the players will find he can't move because there are no edges of his color in what remains of the picture, and whoever is first trapped in this way is the loser. You must make sure that doesn't happen to you!

Well, what can you do about it? Perhaps it would be a good idea to sit back and watch a game first, to make quite sure you understand the rules of the game before playing it with the professionals, so let's watch the effect of a few simple moves. Left might move first and rub out the girl's left foot. This would leave the rest of her left leg dangling rather lamely, but no other edges would actually disappear because every edge of the girl is still connected to the ground through her right leg. But Right at his next move could remove the girl completely, if he so wished, by rubbing out her right foot. Or Left could instead have used his first move to remove the girl's upper arm, when the rest of her arm and the apple would also disappear. So now you really understand the rules, and want to start winning. We think Fig. 1 might be a bit hard for you just yet, so let's look at Fig. 2, in which the blue and red edges are separated into parts that can't interact. Plainly the girl belongs to Left, in some sense, and the boy to Right, and the two players will alternately delete edges of their two people. Since the girl has more edges, Left can survive longer than Right, and can therefore win no matter who starts. In fact, since the girl has 14 edges to the boy's 11, Left ends with at least $14 - 11 = 3$ spare moves, if he chops from the top downwards, and Right can hold him down to this in a similar way.

Figure 2. Boy meets Girl.

Tweedledum and Tweedledee in Fig. 3 have the same number of edges each, so that Left is $19 - 19 = 0$ moves ahead. What does this mean? If Left starts, and both players play sensibly from the top downwards, the moves will alternate Left, Right, Left, Right, until each player has made 19 moves, and it will be Left's turn to move when no edge remains. So if Left starts, Left will lose, and similarly if Right starts, Right will lose. So in this **zero position**, whoever starts loses.

Figure 3. Tweedledum and Tweedledee, about to have a Battle.

THE TWEEDLEDUM AND TWEEDLEDEE ARGUMENT

In Fig. 4, we have swapped a few edges about so that Tweedledum and Tweedledee both have some edges of each color. But since we turn the new Dum into the new Dee exactly by interchanging blue with red, neither player seems to have any advantage. Is Fig. 4 still a zero position in the same sense that whoever starts loses? Yes, for the player second to move can copy any of his opponent's moves by simply chopping the corresponding edge from the other twin. If he does this throughout the game, he is sure to win, because he can never be without an available move. We shall often find games for which an argument like this gives a good strategy for one of the two players—we shall call it the **Tweedledum and Tweedledee Argument** (or **Strategy**) from now on.

Figure 4. After their first Battle: Ready for the Next?

The main difficulty in playing Blue-Red Hackenbush is that your opponent might contrive to steal some of your moves by cutting out of the picture a large number of edges of your color. But there are several cases when even though the picture may look very complicated, you can be sure he will be unable to do this. Figure 5 shows a simple example. In this little dog, each player's edges are connected to the ground via other edges of his own color. So if he chops these in a suitable order, each player can be sure of making one move for each edge of his own color, and plainly he can't hope for more. The value of Fig. 5 is therefore once again determined by counting edges—it is $9 - 7 = 2$ moves for Left. In pictures like this, the correct chopping order is to take first those edges whose path to the ground via your own color has most edges—this makes sure you don't isolate any of your edges by chopping away any of their supporters. Thus in Fig. 5 Left would be extremely foolish to put the blue edges of the neck and head at risk by removing the dog's front leg; for then Right could arrange that after only 2 moves the 5 blue edges here would have vanished.

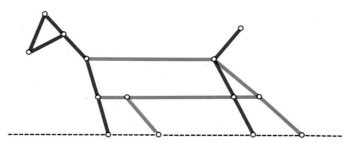

Figure 5. A Dog with Leftward Leanings.

HOW CAN YOU HAVE HALF A MOVE?

But these easy arguments won't suffice for all Hackenbush positions. Perhaps the simplest case of failure is the two-edge "picture" of Fig. 6(a). Here if Left starts, he takes the bottom edge and wins instantly, but if Right starts, necessarily taking the top edge, Left can still remove the bottom edge and win. So Left can win no matter who starts, and this certainly sounds like a positive advantage for Left. Is it as much as a 1-move advantage? We can try counterbalancing it by putting an extra red edge (which counts as a 1-move advantage for Right) on the ground, getting Fig. 6(b). Who wins now?

(a)   (b)   (c)   (d)

Figure 6. What do we mean by Half a Move?

If Right starts, he should take the higher of his two red edges, since this is clearly in danger. Then when Left removes his only blue edge, Right can still move and win. If Left starts, his only possible move still leaves Right a free edge, and so Right still wins. So this time, it is Right that wins, whoever starts, and Left's positive advantage of Fig. 6(a) has now been overwhelmed by adding the free move for Right. We can say that Left's advantage in Fig. 6(a), although positive, was strictly less than an advantage of one free move. Will it perhaps be one-half of a move?

We test this in Fig. 6(c), made up of *two* copies of Fig. 6(a) with just *one* free move for Right added, since if we are correct $\frac{1}{2}+\frac{1}{2}$ for Left will exactly balance 1 for Right. Who wins Fig. 6(c)? Left has essentially only one kind of move, leading to a picture like Fig. 6(b), which we know Right wins. On the other hand, if Right starts sensibly by taking either of his two threatened edges, Left will move to a picture like Fig. 6(d) and win after Right's next move. If Right has used up his free move at the outset, Left's reply would take us to Fig. 6(a), which we know he wins.

We've just shown that Right wins if Left starts and Left wins if Right starts, so that Fig. 6(c) is a zero game. This seems to show that *two* copies of Fig. 6(a) behave just like *one* free move for Left, in that together they exactly counterbalance a free move for Right. So it's really quite sensible to regard Fig. 6(a) as being a half-move's advantage for Left.

Putting Right's red edge partly under Left's control made Fig. 6(a) worse for him than Fig. 6(d). So perhaps Fig. 7(a) should be worth less to Right than Fig. 7(b) in which Right's edge is threatened by only one of Left's?

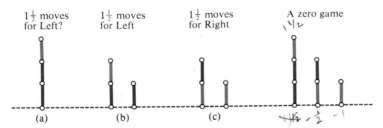

Figure 7. Is Right's Edge even more under Left's Control?

We are asking whether Fig. 7(a) is worth exactly $1\frac{1}{2}$ moves to Left like Fig. 7(b). We can test this by adding $1\frac{1}{2}$ free moves for Right to Fig. 7(a). Since Fig. 7(c) is the opposite of Fig. 7(b), we produce the required allowance by adjoining it to Fig. 7(a), giving Fig. 7(d).

Who wins this complicated little pattern? Here each player has just one risky edge partly in control of his opponent, and if a player starts by taking his risky edge, his opponent can remove the other, leaving two unfettered moves each. If instead he takes the edge just below his opponent's risky edge, the opponent can do likewise, now leaving just one free move each. The only other starting move for Left is stupid since it leaves only red edges touching the ground and indeed Right can now win with a move to spare.

What about Right's remaining move? Since this is to remove the isolated red edge, it *must* be stupid, for surely it would be better to take the middle red edge and so demolish a blue edge at the same time? And indeed Left's reply of chopping the middle edge of the chain of three proves perfectly adequate. So *every* first move loses, and once again the game is what we called a zero game. This seems to show that contrary to our first guess, Figs. 7(a) and 7(b) confer exactly the same advantage upon Left, namely one and a half free moves.

... AND QUARTER MOVES?

In Fig. 8(a), Right's topmost edge is partly under Left's control, but also partly under Right's as well, so it should perhaps be worth more to him than his middle one? Since we found that the middle edge was worth half a move to Right, the pair of red edges collectively would then be worth at least a whole move to him, counteracting Left's single edge. So maybe Right has the advantage here?

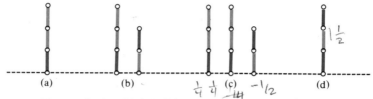

Figure 8. Are Right's Edges worth more than Left's?

This naive opinion is dispelled as soon as play starts, for Left's only move wins the game as soon as he makes it, showing that Fig. 8(a) gives a positive advantage to Left. But when we adjoin half a move for Right as in Fig. 8(b). Right can win playing first, by removing the topmost edge, or playing second, by removing the highest red edge then remaining. So Fig. 8(a), though a positive advantage for Left, is worth even less to him than half a move. Is it perhaps, being three edges high, worth just one-third of a move? No! We leave the reader to show that two copies of Fig. 8(a) exactly balance half a move for Right, by showing that the second player to move wins Fig. 8(c), so that Fig. 8(a) is in fact a quarter move's advantage for Left.

And how much is Fig. 8(d) worth?

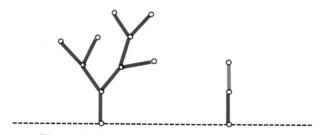

Figure 9. A Hackenbush Position worth $9\frac{1}{2}$.

Figure 9 shows a Hackenbush position of value $9\frac{1}{2}$, since the tree has value 9, and the rest value $\frac{1}{2}$. What are the moves here? Right has a unique red edge, and so a unique move, to a position of value $9 + 1 = 10$, but Left can move either at the top of the tree, leaving $8\frac{1}{2}$, or by removing the $\frac{1}{2}$ completely, which is a better move, since it leaves value 9. Since Left's best move is to value 9, and Right's to 10, we express this by writing the equation

$$\{9 | 10\} = 9\frac{1}{2} \qquad \text{(``9 slash 10 equals } 9\frac{1}{2}\text{'')}.$$

In a similar way, we have the more general equation

$$\{n \,|\, n+1\} = n+\tfrac{1}{2},$$

of which the simplest case is

$$\{0|1\} = \tfrac{1}{2},$$

with which we began. We also have the simpler equation

$$\{n| \ \} = n+1$$

for each $n = 0,1,2,\ldots$, for if Left has just $n+1$ free moves, he can move so as to leave just n free moves, while Right cannot move at all. The very simplest equation of this type is

$$\{ \ | \ \} = 0$$

which expresses the fact that if neither player has a legal move the game has zero value.

Figure 10. A Game of Ski-Jumps.

SKI-JUMPS FOR BEGINNERS

Figure 10 shows a ski-slope with some skiers in the pay of Left and Right, about to participate in our next game. In a single move, Left may move any skier a square or more Eastwards, or Right any one of his, Westwards, provided there is no other active skier in the way. Such a move may take the skier off the slope; in this case he takes no further part in the game. No two skiers may occupy the same square of the slope. Alternatively a skier on the square immediately *above* one containing a skier of the opposing team, may jump over him onto the square immediately below, provided this is empty. A man jumped over is so humiliated that he will never jump over anyone else—in fact he is demoted from being a *jumper* to an ordinary skier, or *slipper*!

No other kind of move is permitted in this game, so that when all the skiers belonging to one of the players have left the ski-slope, that player cannot move, and a player who cannot move when it is his turn to do so, loses the game. Let's examine some simple positions. Figure 11(a) shows a case when Left's only jumper is already East of Right's, so that no jump is possible. Since Left's man can move 5 times and Right's only 3, the value is $5 - 3 = 2$ spare moves for Left.

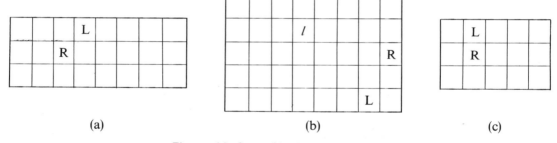

Figure 11. Some Ski-Jumps Positions.

We can similarly evaluate any other position in which no further jumps are possible. Thus in Fig. 11(b) Left has one man on the row above Right's, and another lower down, but still no jump will be possible, for Left's upper man has been demoted to a mere slipper (hence his lower case name, *l*), while his lower man, being two rows below Right's, is not threatened. Left's two men have collectively $2 + 5$ moves to Right's 8, so the value is

$$2 + 5 - 8 = -1$$

moves to Left, that is, 1 move in favor of Right.

Now let's look at Fig. 11(c), in which Left's man may jump over Right's, if he wishes. If he does so, the value will be $4 - 2 = 2$, which is better than the value $3 - 2 = 1$ he reaches by sliding one place East. If, on the other hand, Right has the move, it will be to a position of value $4 - 1 = 3$. So the position has value

$$\{2|3\} = 2\tfrac{1}{2}$$

moves to Left. More generally, if Left has a single man on the board, with a spaces (and hence $a + 1$ moves) before him, and Right a single man with b spaces before *him*, and one of the two men is now in position to jump over the other, the value will be

$$a - b + \tfrac{1}{2} \quad \text{or} \quad a - b - \tfrac{1}{2}$$

according as it is Left's or Right's man who has the jump. We can think of an imminent jump as being worth half a move to the player who can make it.

Figure 12 shows all the positions on a 3 × 5 board in which there are just two men, of which Left's might possibly jump Right's either at his first move or later.

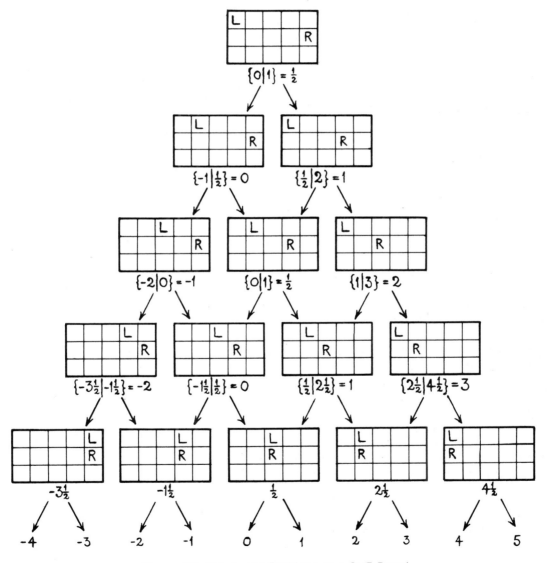

Figure 12. Ski-Jumps Positions on a 3×5 Board.

DON'T JUST TAKE THE AVERAGE!

The positions in the bottom two lines are those we have just analyzed, in which the jump is imminent or past. From any of the other positions, Left has just one move, to the position diagonally down and left from the given one, and Right similarly has a unique move, to the position diagonally rightwards. We have appended the values of all these positions, measured as usual in terms of free moves for Left, and there are some surprises. We have evaluated the rightmost position on the fourth row as

$$\{2\tfrac{1}{2}|4\tfrac{1}{2}\} = 3.$$

Surely this is wrong? Anyone can see that the average of $2\tfrac{1}{2}$ and $4\tfrac{1}{2}$ is $3\tfrac{1}{2}$, can't they?

Well yes, of course $3\tfrac{1}{2}$ is the *average*, but it turns out that the *value* is 3, nevertheless. You *don't* simply evaluate positions in games by averaging Left's and Right's best moves! Exactly how you *do* evaluate them is the main topic of this book, so we can't reveal it all at once. But we *will* explain why the second position on the fourth row has value 0, rather than $-\tfrac{1}{2}$, as might have been expected.

If the value were $-\tfrac{1}{2}$ or any other negative number, Right ought to win, no matter who starts. But in this position, if Right starts, Left can jump him immediately, after which they will each have just two moves, and Right will exhaust his before Left. In fact neither player can win this position if he starts, for if Left moves first, Right can slip leftwards past him to avoid the threatened jump, leaving Left with but one move to Right's two. A position in which the first player to move loses *always* has value zero.

We could have seen the same thing from the symbolic expression $\{-1\tfrac{1}{2}|\tfrac{1}{2}\}$ for the position, for since Left's best option has negative value he cannot move to it and win (if Right plays well), and since Right's best move is positive, he cannot move to win either. It does not matter exactly *how much* each of these moves favors the second player, so long as he is assured of a win. So for exactly the same reason, the game $\{-\tfrac{1}{2}|17\} = 0$, since the starter loses, even though 17 is much further above 0 than $-\tfrac{1}{2}$ is below it.

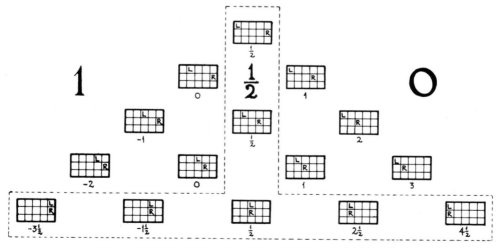

Figure 13. The Value of a Potential Jump is 1, $\tfrac{1}{2}$, or 0.

WHAT IS A JUMP WORTH?

We do not explain the other values here. The reader can verify for example, that $\{2\frac{1}{2}|4\frac{1}{2}\} = 3$, by playing the position $\{2\frac{1}{2}|4\frac{1}{2}\}$ together with an allowance of just 3 moves for Right, and checking that the starter loses. We can summarize the results of Fig. 12 as follows: a potential jump is worth half a move only if it is either imminent or the two players are the same distance from the central column. It is worth a whole move (just as if it were a sure thing) if the potential jumper is nearer to the central column than the jumpee and worth nothing (just as if it were impossible) otherwise (Fig. 13).

We can now predict who will win the more complicated Ski-Jumps positions of Fig. 10. Because the pairs of rows A,B,C are so far apart, moves made by the skiers in one of these pairs will not affect the play in others, so we can just add up the values for the three pairs A,B,C (Fig. 14).

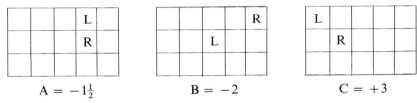

$$A = -1\tfrac{1}{2} \qquad\qquad B = -2 \qquad\qquad C = +3$$

Figure 14. Values of Ski-Jumps Positions in Figure 10.

The values for A and C can be read off from Fig. 12 as $-1\frac{1}{2}$ and $+3$, while that for B is

(value 2) with the roles of Left and Right reversed, and so has value -2.

The total value is therefore

$$-1\tfrac{1}{2} - 2 + 3 = -\tfrac{1}{2},$$

and so Right is half a move ahead and should be able to win, no matter who starts. It will be harder for him if he starts himself, since then he must use up a move. What move should he make? His three choices are from

$$-1\tfrac{1}{2} \text{ to } -1 \text{ (in A)}, \qquad -2 \text{ to } -1 \text{ (in B)}, \qquad \text{and} \quad 3 \text{ to } 4\tfrac{1}{2} \text{ (in C)}$$

which lose him

$$\tfrac{1}{2}, \qquad\qquad\qquad 1, \qquad\qquad\qquad 1\tfrac{1}{2}$$

moves respectively. So he can only guarantee to retain his win if he moves his A man, so as to avoid the otherwise imminent jump by Left.

TOADS-AND-FROGS

Left has trained a number of Toads (*Bufo vulgaris*) and Right a number of Frogs (*Rana pipiens*) to play the following game. Each player may persuade one of his creatures either to move one square or to jump over an opposing creature, onto an empty square. Toads move only Eastward, Frogs only to the West (*toads to, frogs fro*). The game is to be played according to the normal play rule that a player unable to move loses. Verify the values in Fig. 16. Who wins Fig. 15 and by how much?

Figure 15. A Game of Toads-and-Frogs.

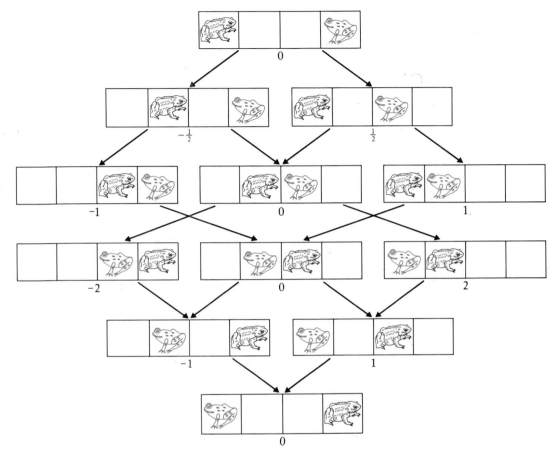

Figure 16. Values of Positions in 4-place Toads-and-Frogs.

DO OUR METHODS WORK?

Several questions will have entered the reader's mind. Can we really evaluate positions by adding up numbers of moves advantage, even when they are fractions? Is it wise to regard all positions in which the starter loses as having zero value? The answers are yes. For the pragmatic reader perhaps the best proof of this pudding will be in the eating—if he works out who has more moves advantage this way he'll be sure to pick the winner. Mathematical unbelievers must await our later discussion.

EXTRAS

Under this heading we shall occasionally insert additional detail and examples which will interest some readers, but might interrupt the general flow of ideas for others.

WHAT IS A GAME?

Our games of Hackenbush and Ski-Jumps are typical of almost all discussed in the first part of *Winning Ways* in that:

1. There are just two players, often called Left and Right.
2. There are several, usually finitely many, **positions**, and often a particular **starting position**.
3. There are clearly defined **rules** that specify the **moves** that either player can make from a given position to its **options**.
4. Left and Right move alternately, in the game as a whole.
5. In the **normal play** convention a player unable to move **loses**.
6. The rules are such that play will always come to an end because some player will be unable to move. This is called the **ending condition**. So there can be no games which are drawn by repetition of moves.
7. Both players know what is going on, i.e. there is **complete information**.
8. There are no **chance moves** such as rolling dice or shuffling cards.

The reader should see how far his own favorite games satisfy these conditions. He will also see from some of the comments below that many games not satisfying all of the conditions are also treated later in this book. But all the games we *do* treat satisfy 7 and 8.

Tic-Tac-Toe (Noughts-and-Crosses) fails 5. because a player unable to move is not necessarily the loser, since ties are possible. We will give a complete analysis in Chapter 22, and will discuss various generalizations, such as **Go-Moku**.

Chess also fails 5. and contains positions that are *tied* by stalemate (in which the last player does *not* win) and positions that are *drawn* by infinite play (of which perpetual check is a special case). We reserve the complete analysis for a later volume.

The words "tied" and "drawn" are often used interchangeably, though with slight transatlantic differences, for games which are neither won nor lost. We suggest that **drawn** be used for cases when this happens because play is drawn out indefinitely and **tied** for cases when play definitely ends but the rules do not award a win to either player.

Ludo, **Snakes-and-Ladders** and **Backgammon** all have complete information, but contain chance moves, since they all use dice.

Battleships, **Kriegspiel**, **Three-Finger Morra** and **Scissors-Paper-Stone** have no chance moves but the players do not have complete information about the disposition of their opponent's pieces or fingers. In both the finger games, moreover, the players move simultaneously rather than alternately.

Monopoly fails on several counts. Like Ludo, it has chance moves and may have more than two players. The players don't have complete information about the arrangement of the cards and the game could, theoretically, continue for ever.

Solitaire (Patience) played with cards and **Peg Solitaire** (Chapter 23) are one-person games and in the first the arrangement of the cards is determined by chance.

The game of **Life** which we discuss in Chapter 25, is a no-player, never-ending game!

In **Poker** much of the interest arises from the incompleteness of the information, the chance moves and the possibility of **coalitions** which arises in games with three or more players.

Bridge is peculiar in that it has two players, each a team of two persons, and a "player" does not even have complete information about "his" own cards.

Tennis, **Hockey**, **Baseball**, **Cricket**, **Lacrosse** and **Basketball** are also "two-person" games, but there are difficulties in the definitions of appropriate "positions" and "moves".

Nim (Chapter 2), **Wythoff's Game** (Chapter 3) and **Grundy's Game** (Chapter 4) satisfy all our conditions and indeed a further one, that from any position exactly the same moves are available to either player. Such games are called **impartial**. Games in which the two players may have different options we shall call **partizan**. Red-Blue Hackenbush is partizan because Left may only remove blue edges and Right only red ones; Ski-Jumps because different players control different skiers.

Dots-and-Boxes is usually won by the player scoring the larger number of boxes, so that it does not satisfy the normal play convention. However, we shall see in Chapter 16 that in practice it can almost always be treated as an impartial game, satisfying our normal play convention, part of whose theory is closely related to **Kayles** and **Dawson's Kayles** (see Chapter 4).

Sylver Coinage, which we discuss in Chapter 18, is an impartial game which violates the normal play convention because the last player to move is the *loser*. In Chapter 13 we show you how to play sums of impartial games subject to this **misère play** convention.

Fox-and-Geese is a pursuit game which doesn't satisfy the ending condition, but in Chapter 20 we are able to compare its value with those of other partizan games which *do* satisfy the condition. It is a loopy game in the sense of Chapter 11.

The French Military Hunt and other partizan pursuit games also yield to analysis in Chapter 21.

Go is not analyzed in this book, but provides an interesting example of a "hot" partizan game. Go players might find the thermographic techniques of Chapter 6 useful in their game.

WHEN IS A MOVE GOOD?

We usually call a move "good" if it will win for you, and "bad" if it will not, and throughout most of the book we regard it as sufficient analysis to find any good move, or show that none exists.

But in real life games there are many other criteria for choosing between your various options. If you're *losing*, then all your options are bad in the above sense, but in practice they're not all equal, and you might prefer one that makes the situation too complicated for your opponent to analyze (the **Enough Rope Principle**).

There are even cases where you should prefer a bad move to a good one! Your opponent might be learning how to play a game which you're already familiar with. In this case you'll probably be able to win a few times despite the bad moves you deliberately make so as not to give your strategy away. Or one move, though theoretically the best, might gain you only a dollar, while another, which theoretically *loses* a dollar, might actually get you a hundred if your opponent fails to find the rather subtle winning reply. And of course you might be a card sharp who's playing badly now so as to win more later when the stakes are raised.

FIGURE 8(d) IS WORTH $\frac{3}{4}$

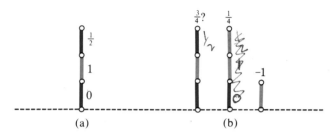

Figure 17. How we can have Three-Quarters of a Move.

The Blue-Red Hackenbush position of Fig. 8(d) may be evaluated as follows. Write against each edge (Fig. 17(a)) the value of the position when that edge is removed. Then the greatest number against a blue edge (here $\frac{1}{2}$) is Left's best option, and the least number against a red edge is Right's. So in the given case we obtain the expression

$$\{\tfrac{1}{2}\mid 1\}$$

suggesting a value of $\frac{3}{4}$. So if we add $\frac{1}{4}$ and subtract 1 as in Fig. 17(b) we should obtain a zero position. Check that whoever starts loses.

Verify that the Blue-Red Hackenbush positions in Fig. 18 have the indicated values, in terms of moves advantage to Left.

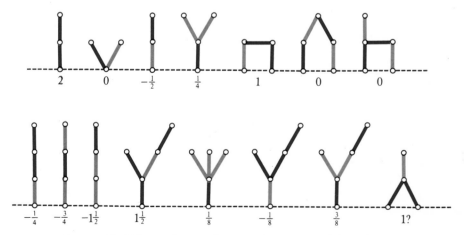

Figure 18. Values of some Blue-Red Hackenbush Positions.

REFERENCES AND FURTHER READING

J.H. Conway, "On Numbers and Games", Academic Press, London and New York, 1976.

J.H. Conway, All games bright and beautiful, Amer. Math. Monthly, **84** (1977) 417–434.

J.H. Conway, A gamut of game theories, Math. Mag. **51** (1978) 5–12.

Martin Gardner, Mathematical Games, Sci. Amer., each issue (monthly).

Donald Knuth, "Surreal Numbers", Addison-Wesley, Reading, Mass., 1974.

Chapter 2

Finding the Correct Number is Simplicity Itself

Simplicity, simplicity, simplicity. I say let your affairs be
as two or three, and not a hundred or a thousand; instead of a
million count half a dozen and keep your accounts
on your thumbnail.
> Henry David Thoreau, *Walden*.

And calculate the stars.
> John Milton, *Paradise Lost*, VIII, 80.

We have seen that positions in Hackenbush and Ski-Jumps are often composed of several non-interacting parts, and that then the proper thing to do is to add up the values of these parts, measured in terms of free moves for Left. We have also seen that halves and quarters of moves can arise. So plainly we'll have to decide exactly what it means to add games together, and work out how to compute their values.

WHICH NUMBERS ARE WHICH?

Let's summarize what we already know, using the notation

$$\{a,b,c,\ldots|d,e,f,\ldots\}$$

for a position in which the options for Left are to positions of values $a,b,c,\ldots$ and those for Right to positions of values $d,e,f,\ldots$. In this notation, the whole numbers are

$$0 = \{\ |\ \}, \qquad 1 = \{0|\ \}, \qquad 2 = \{1|\ \}, \qquad \ldots, \qquad n+1 = \{n|\ \},$$

for from a zero position, neither player has a move, and from a position with $n+1$ free moves for Left, he can move so as to leave himself just n moves, whereas Right cannot move at all.

The negative integers are similarly

$$-1 = \{\ |0\}, \qquad -2 = \{\ |-1\}, \qquad -3 = \{\ |-2\}, \qquad \ldots, \qquad -(n+1) = \{\ |-n\}.$$

We also found values involving halves:

$$\tfrac{1}{2} = \{0|1\}, \qquad 1\tfrac{1}{2} = \{1|2\}, \qquad 2\tfrac{1}{2} = \{2|3\}, \qquad \ldots,$$

$$-\tfrac{1}{2} = \{-1|0\}, \qquad -1\tfrac{1}{2} = \{-2|-1\}, \qquad \ldots \quad \text{and so on.}$$

21

Our proof that $\{0|1\}$ behaves like half a move was contained in the discussion of the Hackenbush position of Fig. 6(a) in Chapter 1.

We also discussed a Hackenbush position (Fig. 8(a) of Chapter 1) whose value was $\{0|\frac{1}{2}\}$ and showed that it behaved like one quarter of a move. So we can guess that we have all the equations

$$\{0|1\} = \tfrac{1}{2}, \qquad \{0|\tfrac{1}{2}\} = \tfrac{1}{4}, \qquad \{0|\tfrac{1}{4}\} = \tfrac{1}{8}, \quad \text{and so on,}$$

and leave a more precise discussion of what these equations mean until later.

Will there be any game with a position of value $\frac{5}{8}$? Yes, of course! All we have to do is add together two positions of values $\frac{1}{2}$ and $\frac{1}{8}$ as in the Hackenbush position of Fig. 1.

Figure 1. A Blue-Red Hackenbush Position Worth Five-Eighths of a Move.

What are the moves from the position $\frac{1}{2} + \frac{1}{8}$, that is from the position

$$\tfrac{1}{2} \quad + \quad \tfrac{1}{8}$$

which we write

$$\{0|1\} + \{0|\tfrac{1}{4}\}$$

in the new notation?

Each player can move in either the first or second component, but must then leave the other component untouched, so Left's options are the positions

$$0 + \tfrac{1}{8} \quad \text{(if he moves in the first), and}$$

$$\tfrac{1}{2} + 0 \quad \text{(if he moves in the second).}$$

He should obviously prefer the latter, which leaves a total value of half a move, rather than one-eighth of a move, to him. Right's options are similarly

$$1 + \tfrac{1}{8} \quad \text{and} \quad \tfrac{1}{2} + \tfrac{1}{4}$$

of which he should prefer the second, since it leaves Left only three-quarters of a move, rather than one-and-one-eighth. We have shown that the best moves from $\frac{5}{8}$ are to $\frac{1}{2}$ (Left) and $\frac{3}{4}$ (Right), or in our abbreviated notation, we have demonstrated the equation

$$\frac{5}{8} = \left\{\frac{1}{2} \,\middle|\, \frac{3}{4}\right\}.$$

In a precisely similar way, we can add various fractions $1/2^k$ so as to prove that

$$\frac{2p+1}{2^{n+1}} = \left\{\frac{2p}{2^{n+1}} \,\middle|\, \frac{2p+2}{2^{n+1}}\right\} = \left\{\frac{p}{2^n} \,\middle|\, \frac{p+1}{2^n}\right\}$$

or in words, that each fraction with denominator a power of two has as its Left and Right options the two fractions nearest to it on the left and right that have smaller denominator which is again a power of two. For example

$$3\tfrac{57}{128} = \{3\tfrac{56}{128}|3\tfrac{58}{128}\} = \{3\tfrac{7}{16}|3\tfrac{29}{64}\}.$$

SIMPLICITY'S THE ANSWER!

The equations we've just discussed are the easy ones. What number is the game $X = \{1\tfrac{1}{4}|2\}$? We have already seen in our discussion of Ski-Jumps that we should not necessarily expect the answer to be the mean of $1\tfrac{1}{4}$ and 2, that is, $1\tfrac{5}{8}$. Why not? We can test this question by playing the sum

$$X+(-1\tfrac{5}{8}) = \{1\tfrac{1}{4}|2\}+\{-1\tfrac{3}{4}|-1\tfrac{1}{2}\}$$

since we already know that $-1\tfrac{5}{8} = \{-1\tfrac{3}{4}|-1\tfrac{1}{2}\}$. Only if neither player has a winning move in this sum will we have $X = 1\tfrac{5}{8}$.

The two moves from the component X are certainly losing ones, because $1\tfrac{5}{8}$ is strictly between $1\tfrac{1}{4}$ and 2, so that Left's move leaves the total value $1\tfrac{1}{4}-1\tfrac{5}{8}$ which is negative, while Right's leaves it $2-1\tfrac{5}{8}$ which is positive. But Right nevertheless has a good move, namely that from $-1\tfrac{5}{8}$ to $-1\tfrac{1}{2}$. Why is this?

The answer is that in the new game

$$X+(-1\tfrac{1}{2}) = \{1\tfrac{1}{4}|2\}+\{-2|-1\}$$

it is still true that neither player will want to move in the component X, *for essentially the same reason as before*, since $1\tfrac{1}{2}$ still lies strictly between $1\tfrac{1}{4}$ and 2. So Left's only hope for a reply is to replace $-1\tfrac{1}{2}$ by -2 which Right can neatly counter by moving from X to 2, leaving a zero position.

So the reason that $\{1\tfrac{1}{4}|2\}$ is *not* $1\tfrac{5}{8}$ is that $1\tfrac{5}{8}$ is not the *simplest* number strictly between $1\tfrac{1}{4}$ and 2, because it has the Left option $1\tfrac{1}{2}$ with the same property, and we therefore find ourselves needing to discuss $X+(-1\tfrac{1}{2})$ before we can evaluate $X+(-1\tfrac{5}{8})$.

Now $1\tfrac{1}{2}$ must be the simplest number between $1\tfrac{1}{4}$ and 2, because the immediately simpler numbers are its options 1 and 2, which don't fit. We shall use this to prove that in fact $X = 1\tfrac{1}{2}$.

It is still true for the position

$$X+(-1\tfrac{1}{2}) = \{1\tfrac{1}{4}|2\}+\{-2|-1\}$$

that neither player has a good move from the component X, so that we need only consider their moves from $-1\tfrac{1}{2}$. After Right's move the total is $X+(-1)$, to which Left can reply by moving from the component X so as to leave the positive total $1\tfrac{1}{4}-1$, because 1 is not *strictly between* $1\tfrac{1}{4}$ and 2, but *less than* $1\tfrac{1}{4}$. After Left's move from $-1\tfrac{1}{2}$, the total is $X+(-2)$ and Right's response is to the zero position $2-2$, because 2 is no longer *strictly between* $1\tfrac{1}{4}$ and 2, but this time *equal to* 2.

The argument can be used in general to prove the **Simplicity Rule**, which we shall use over and over again:

> If there's *any* number that fits,
> the answer's the *simplest* number that fits.

THE SIMPLICITY RULE

If the options in

$$\{a,b,c,\ldots \,|\,d,e,f,\ldots\}$$

are all numbers, we'll say that the number x **fits** just if it's

strictly greater than each of $a,b,c,\ldots$, and
strictly less than each of $d,e,f,\ldots$,

and x will be the **simplest** number that fits, if none of its options fit. For the options of x you should use the particular ones we found in the previous section.

For example, if the best Left move from some game G is to a position of value $2\frac{3}{8}$, and the best Right move to one of value 5, we can show that G itself must have value 3, which we found before in the form $\{2|\ \}$, for in this form 3 has only one option, 2, which does *not* lie strictly between $2\frac{3}{8}$ and 5, while 3 *does*. Note that the Simplicity Rule still works when one of the players, here Right, has no move from the number c. It also works for games of the form $\{a|\ \}$ or $\{\ |b\}$ in which again one of the two players is deprived of a move. For example, $\{a|\ \}$ is a number c which is greater than a, but has no option with this property. This is in fact the smallest whole number 0 or 1 or 2 or ... which is greater than a. Thus $\{2\frac{1}{2}|\ \} = 3$, $\{-2\frac{1}{2}|\ \} = 0$.

SIMPLEST FORMS FOR NUMBERS

Figure 2 displays most of what we've learnt so far. The central ruler is the ordinary real number line with bigger marks for simpler numbers, while below it are the corresponding Hackenbush strings; the simpler the number, the shorter the string.

The binary tree of numbers appears upside-down above the ruler, although we can't draw all of it on our finite page with finite type—for more details see ONAG, pp. 3–14.† Each fork of the tree is a number whose best options are the nearest numbers left and right of it that are higher up the tree. For example 1 and 2 are the best options for $1\frac{1}{2}$. For $\frac{13}{16}$ we find $\frac{3}{4}$ and $\frac{7}{8}$, so

$$\tfrac{13}{16} = \{\tfrac{3}{4}|\tfrac{7}{8}\}$$

as a game. (The numbers on the leftmost branch have no Left options and those on the rightmost branch no Right ones.)

The options of a number that we find in this way define its canonical or **simplest form**. Here are the rules for simplest forms:

$$0 = \{\ |\ \}$$
$$n+1 = \{n|\ \}$$
$$-n-1 = \{\ |-n\}$$
$$\frac{2p+1}{2^{q+1}} = \left\{\frac{p}{2^q}\,\middle|\,\frac{p+1}{2^q}\right\}$$

SIMPLEST FORMS FOR NUMBERS

e.g.

$$79 = \{78|\ \},\quad -53 = \{\ |-52\},\quad \text{and}\quad \tfrac{47}{64} = \{\tfrac{23}{32}|\tfrac{24}{32}\} = \{\tfrac{23}{32}|\tfrac{3}{4}\}.$$

The simpler the number, the nearer it is to the root (top!) of the tree.

† Throughout the book, ONAG refers to J.H. Conway, "On Numbers and Games", Academic Press, London and New York, 1976

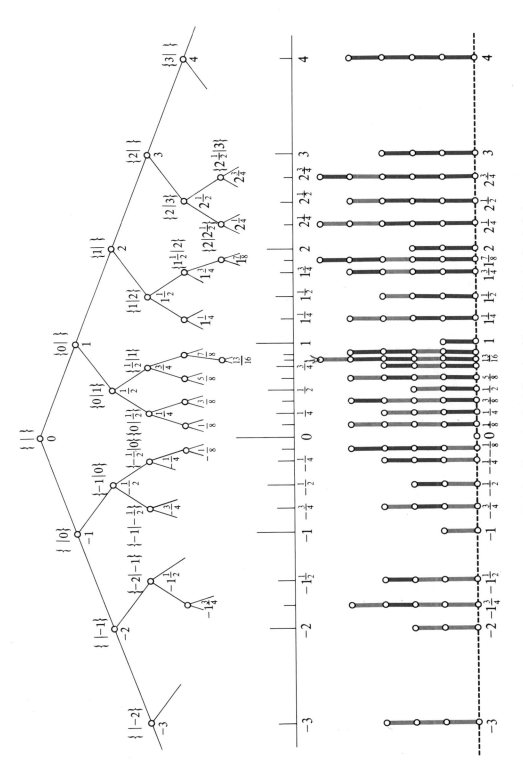

Figure 2. Australian Number Tree, the Real Number Line, and Hackenbush Strings.

CUTCAKE

Mother has just made the oatmeal cookies shown in Fig. 3. She hasn't yet broken them up into little squares, although she has scored them along the lines indicated. Rita and her brother Lefty decide to play a game breaking them up. Lefty will cut any rectangle into two smaller ones along one of the North–South lines, and Rita will cut some rectangle along an East–West line. When one of the children is unable to move, the game ends, and that child is the loser.

Figure 3. Ready for a Game of Cutcake.

We'll evaluate the positions in this game using the Simplicity Rule. Plainly a single square ☐ leaves no legal move for either player, and so is a zero position. The 1×2 rectangle ☐☐ gives just a single free move for Lefty, the 1×3 rectangle ☐☐☐ two free moves for him, and so on. When these rectangles are turned through a right angle, they yield the corresponding numbers of free moves for Rita instead.

The 2×2 square is the zero position $\{-2|2\}$, for when Lefty starts, he leaves two moves for Rita, and if she starts, she must leave two moves for him. So let's consider the 2×3 rectangle

. Since this has more vertical lines than horizontal ones, it should perhaps be a win for Lefty? No! If he starts, he must leave a 2×1 rectangle, which is one move in favor of Rita, together with a 2×2 square, which we can ignore as having value zero. But Rita can't win either, for her only opening move gives Lefty four free moves. So the 2×3 rectangle is the zero position $\{-1|4\}$.

But the 2×4 rectangle $\qquad$ *is* long enough to favour Lefty, for if he chops it into two 2×2 squares at his first move, he wins, and he plainly wins if Rita is made to start. In fact, we have

$$\square\!\square\!\square = \left\{ \square + \square\!\square\!\square \, , \, \square\!\square + \square\!\square \; \middle| \; \begin{matrix} \square\!\square\!\square \\ + \\ \square\!\square\!\square \end{matrix} \right\}$$

$$= \{-1 + \quad 0 \quad , \quad 0 + 0 \quad | \quad 3 + 3\}$$
$$= \{-1,0 \,|\, 6\},$$

which the Simplicity Rule tells us is worth one move for Lefty.

		Breadth														
	1	2	3	4	5	6	7	8	9	10	11	12	13	14	15	16
1	0	1	2	3	4	5	6	7	8	9	10	11	12	13	14	15
2	−1	0		1		2		3		4		5		6		
3	−2															
4	−3	−1		0				1				2				
5	−4															
6	−5	−2														
7	−6															
8	−7	−3														
9	−8			−1												
10	−9	−4						0								
11	−10															
12	−11	−5														
13	−12			−2												

Depth

Table 1. Values of Rectangles in Cutcake.

Using arguments like these, we can draw up a table (Table 1) showing the values of rectangles of various sizes in Cutcake. We see that there is an interesting pattern—the border of the table is divided into 1×1 squares holding a different integer, corresponding to the values of strips of width 1. But then there's a second border of 2×2 squares which is a bit harder to explain. Thus all the four rectangles of breadth 2 or 3 and depth 4 or 5 have the same value, -1, meaning that they count as one free move for Rita. (We already saw that the 2×2 and 2×3 rectangles had the same value, namely 0.) Then the table continues with a third border of 4×4 squares, followed by a fourth of 8×8 squares, and so on. So all rectangles whose depth is 4, 5, 6, or 7, and breadth 8, 9, 10, or 11 have value 1, and behave like a single free move for Lefty, despite their variable shapes.

Let's consider a fairly complicated example, the 5×10 rectangle. Lefty can split 10 into $1+9$, $2+8$, $3+7$, $4+6$ or $5+5$ and we can read the values of the corresponding rectangles 5×1 and 5×9, etc. from Table 1 to see that Lefty's options have values

$$-4+1, \quad -1+1, \quad -1+0, \quad 0+0, \quad 0+0$$

Rita can split 5 into $1+4$ or $2+3$ yielding pairs of breadth 10 rectangles of values $9+1$ or $4+4$. So the 5×10 rectangle has value

$$\{-3,0,-1,0,0 \mid 10,8\} = \{0 \mid 8\} = 1,$$

and Table 1 is continued in this way.

MAUNDY CAKE

Every Maundy Thursday Lefty and Rita play a different cake-cutting game, in which Lefty's move is to divide one cake into *any* number of *equal* pieces, using only vertical cuts, while

	1	2	3	4	5	6	7	8	9	10	11	12	13	14	15	16	17	18
1	0	1	1	3	1	4	1	7	4	6	1	10	1	8	6	15	1	13
2	-1	0	0	1	0	1	0	3	1	1	0	4	0	1	1	7	0	4
3	-1	0	0	1	0	1	0	3	1	1	0	4	0	1	1	7	0	4
4	-3	-1	-1	0	-1	0	-1	1	0	0	-1	1	-1	0	0	3	-1	1
5	-1	0	0	1	0	1	0	3	1	1	0	4	0	1	1	7	0	4
6	-4	-1	-1	0	-1	0	-1	1	0	0	-1	1	-1	0	0	3	-1	1
7	-1	0	0	1	0	1	0	3	1	1	0	4	0	1	1	7	0	4
8	-7	-3	-3	-1	-3	-1	-3	0	-1	-1	-3	0	-3	-1	-1	1	-3	0
9	-4	-1	-1	0	-1	0	-1	1	0	0	-1	1	-1	0	0	3	-1	1
10	-6	-1	-1	0	-1	0	-1	1	0	0	-1	1	-1	0	0	3	-1	1
11	-1	0	0	1	0	1	0	3	1	1	0	4	0	1	1	7	0	4

Table 2. Maundy Cake Values.

Rita does likewise, but with horizontal cuts. Once again the cuts must follow Mother's scorings, so that all dimensions will be whole numbers.

This game was proposed and solved by Patrick Mauhin—can you see the general pattern in his table of values (Table 2)? We worked them out as follows:

$$
\begin{array}{l}
\text{value of} \\
5 \times 12
\end{array}
= \left\{
\begin{array}{ccccc|c}
\text{twelve of} & \text{six of} & \text{four of} & \text{three of} & \text{two of} & \text{five of} \\
5 \times 1 & 5 \times 2 & 5 \times 3 & 5 \times 4 & 5 \times 6 & 1 \times 12
\end{array}
\right\}
$$

$$
= \left\{
\begin{array}{ccccc|c}
\text{twelve of} & \text{six of} & \text{four of} & \text{three of} & \text{two of} & \text{five of} \\
-1 & 0 & 0 & 1 & 1 & 10
\end{array}
\right\}
$$

$$
= \{\ -12\ ,\ 0\ ,\ 0\ ,\ 3\ ,\ 2\ \mid\ 50\ \} = 4.
$$

If you haven't guessed a general rule, you'll find ours in the Extras. If you have, try it out on the 999×1000 cake, or the 1000×1001 one.

A FEW MORE APPLICATIONS OF THE SIMPLICITY RULE

The more questionable values for Ski-Jumps and Hackenbush positions are easily understood in terms of the Simplicity Rule. For example the Ski-Jumps position

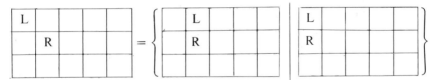

has value $\{2\frac{1}{2}|4\frac{1}{2}\}$ which the Simplicity Rule requires to be 3, just as we said. The last Hackenbush position

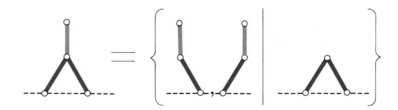

of Fig. 18 in the Extras to Chapter 1 can be seen to have $\{\frac{1}{2},\frac{1}{2}|2\} = 1$ by another application of the Rule. Values of more complicated positions such as the horse of Fig. 4 can be found by repeated applications. We have followed the recommended practice of writing against each edge the value of the position which would result if that edge were deleted. These positions will either be found later in the figure or are sums of the simple positions discussed in Chapter 1.

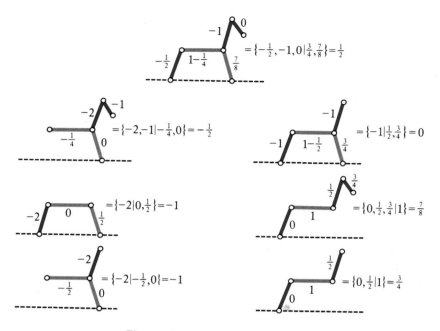

Figure 4. Working Out a Horse.

POSITIVE, NEGATIVE, ZERO AND FUZZY POSITIONS

We can classify all games into four *outcome classes*, which specify who has the winning strategy when Left starts and who has the winning strategy when Right starts, as in Table 3. It may happen that Left can win no matter who starts—in this case we shall call G **positive**, since we are in favor of Left. Conversely, if Right wins whoever starts, we shall call G **negative**. In the other two cases, the player who wins may be Left or Right depending on who starts. If the player who starts is the *loser*, we have already called the game a **zero game**, and if the player who starts is the *winner*, we shall call it a **fuzzy** one.

		If Left starts:	
		Left wins	Right wins
If Right starts	Left wins	positive (L wins)	zero (2 wins)
	Right wins	fuzzy (1 wins)	negative (R wins)

Table 3. The Four Possible Outcomes.

A handy way of remembering these four cases is just to describe the player who has the winning strategy—this is either *Left*, *Right*, or the *first*, or the *second* player to move from the start. In symbols, we have

$$G > 0 \text{ or } G \text{ is \textbf{positive} if player L (Left) can always win}$$
$$G < 0 \text{ or } G \text{ is \textbf{negative} if player R (Right) can always win}$$
$$G = 0 \text{ or } G \text{ is \textbf{zero} \quad if player 2 (second) can always win}$$
$$G \parallel 0 \text{ or } G \text{ is \textbf{fuzzy} \quad if player 1 (first) can always win}.$$

In Blue-Red Hackenbush we've already seen that a picture with only blue edges is positive (if there are any), and one with only red edges is negative. A picture having no edges is zero, but there are also other zero pictures, for example any picture with as many red edges as blue in which each edge is connected to the ground by its own color, or the rather simple picture of Fig. 6(c) in Chapter 1, which has two blue edges and three red.

There are no *fuzzy* positions in Blue-Red Hackenbush, which makes it rather unusual, because in most games it is some advantage to be the first player. So to get more varied behavior, we introduce a new kind of edge.

HACKENBUSH HOTCHPOTCH

This game is played as before except that there may also be some *green* edges, which either player may chop. But blue edges are still reserved for Left, and red ones for Right and we continue to use the normal play rule, that when you can't move, you lose.

The pretty flower of Fig. 5(a) is an example of a fuzzy position in Hackenbush Hotchpotch, for since its stalk is green, either player may win the game at the first move by chopping this edge.

(a)   (b)

Figure 5. Two Fuzzy Flowers make a Positive Posy.

It might be thought that, like a zero game, a fuzzy game confers no particular advantage on either player, and so should also be said to have value 0. But this would be a misleading convention, because often a fuzzy game can be more in favor of one player than the other, even though either player can win starting first. For example, the flower of Fig. 5(a) has more blue petals than red ones, and this favors Left by just enough to ensure that the sum of two such flowers, as in Fig. 5(b), is positive. For no matter who starts in Fig. 5(b), Left has enough spare moves to arrange that Right is first to take a stalk, whereupon Left wins by taking the other.

In fact a fuzzy game is neither greater than 0, less than 0, nor equal to 0, but rather *confused* with 0. Figure 6 shows a good mental picture, illustrating a fuzzy game *G* whose place in the number scale is rather indeterminate, being represented by the cloud. Since this covers 0 and stretches some way on either side, we can't tell exactly where *G* is. It's probably buzzing about under the cloud, so that it seems positive at some times, and negative at others, according to its environment.

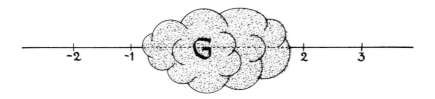

Figure 6. How Big is a Fuzzy Game?

SUMS OF ARBITRARY GAMES

Now that we've learned how to work with numbers and how to find when games are positive, negative, zero, or fuzzy, we should learn what it means to add two games in general. Being very clever, Left and Right may play a sum of *any* pair of games *G* and *H* as in Fig. 7. We shall refer to the two games *G* and *H* as the **components** of the compound game *G + H*, which is played as follows. The players move alternately in *G + H*, and either player, when it is his turn to move, chooses one of the components *G* or *H*, and makes a move legal for him in that component.

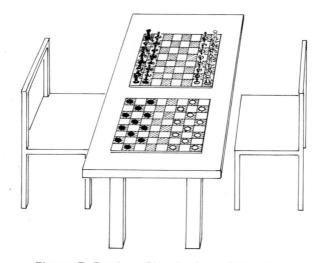

Figure 7. Ready to Play the Sum of Two Games.

The turn then passes to his opponent, who plays in a similar manner. The game ends as usual when some player finds himself unable to move (this will only happen when there is no component in which he has a legal move) and that player loses.

Symbolically we shall write G^L for the typical Left option (i.e., a position Left can move to) from G, and G^R for the typical Right option, so that

$$G = \{G^L | G^R\}.$$

We use this notation even when a player has more than one option, or none at all, so that the symbol G^L need not have a unique value. Thus if $G = \{a,b,c,\ldots | d,e,f,\ldots\}$, G^L means a or b or c or $\ldots$ and G^R means d or e or f or $\ldots$. In the game $2 = \{1 | \}$, G^L has only the value 1, but G^R has no value. In this notation the definition of sum is written

$$G + H = \{G^L + H, G + H^L \,|\, G^R + H, G + H^R\}$$

since Left's options from $G + H$ are exactly the sums $G^L + H$ or $G + H^L$ in which he has moved in just one component, and Right's are the similar sums $G^R + H$, $G + H^R$.

It should be made clear that there is no restriction on the component a player moves in at any time other than his ability to move in that component. You need not follow your opponent's move with another move in the same component, nor need you switch components unless you want to. Indeed in many games (e.g. Blue-Red Hackenbush and Cutcake) a move may produce more than one component.

THE OUTCOME OF A SUM

The major topic of this book is the problem of finding ways of determining the outcome of a sum of games given information only about the separate components, so we cannot expect to answer this question instantly. But we should at least expect that if both G and H are in favor of Left, so is $G + H$ and this turns out to be the case. In fact we can strengthen the assertion a little, by allowing zero games.

If G and H are greater than or equal to 0, so is $G + H$.

What does it mean for G to be greater than or equal to 0? From Table 3, we see that these are just the two cases in which Left has a winning strategy *provided Right starts*. If this is true of G and H, it is also true of $G + H$, for if Right starts, he must make a move in one of G and H, say G, and Left can reply with the responses of his winning strategy in G for as long as Right continues to move in that game. Whenever Right switches to H, Left responds in H with the moves of his winning strategy in that game, and so on. If he plays like this, Left will never be lost for a move in $G + H$, for he can always respond in whatever component Right has just played in, so he cannot lose.

Now we have another principle, which covers some fuzzy games:

> If G is positive or fuzzy, and
> H is positive or zero, then
> $G + H$ is positive or fuzzy.

For we see from Table 3 that the positive or fuzzy games are just those from which Left has a winning strategy *provided Left starts*. So what we have to show is that if Left has a winning strategy in G with Left starting, and one in H with Right starting, he has one in $G + H$ with Left starting.

This is easy. He starts in $G + H$ by making the first move of his winning strategy for G, and then always replies to any of Right's moves with another move in the same component, so that the sequence of moves played in G is begun by Left and that in H by Right. If Left follows his two winning strategies in the two components he will therefore win their sum.

We can summarize these results, and those obtained by interchanging the roles of Left and Right, in symbols.

> If $G \geqslant 0$ and $H \geqslant 0$ then $G + H \geqslant 0$,
> If $G \leqslant 0$ and $H \leqslant 0$ then $G + H \leqslant 0$,
> If $G \rhd 0$ and $H \geqslant 0$ then $G + H \rhd 0$,
> If $G \lhd 0$ and $H \leqslant 0$ then $G + H \lhd 0$.

Here "$\geqslant$" means "$>$" or "$=$", "$\lhd$" means "$<$" or "$\parallel$", etc.

In particular if H is a zero game, it may be used in all four lines, and then $G + H$ will have the same outcome as G in all circumstances.

> Adding a zero game never affects the outcome.

We've already seen some of these principles in action in Blue-Red Hackenbush. But now we know that they work for arbitrary games, and did not depend on the fact that the positions we evaluated in Hackenbush turned out to be numbers. Table 4 shows the possibilities for the outcome of $G + H$, given those of G and H.

	$H = 0$	$H > 0$	$H < 0$	$H \parallel 0$
$G = 0$	$G + H = 0$	$G + H > 0$	$G + H < 0$	$G + H \parallel 0$
$G > 0$	$G + H > 0$	$G + H > 0$	$G + H \ ? \ 0$	$G + H \rhd 0$
$G < 0$	$G + H < 0$	$G + H \ ? \ 0$	$G + H < 0$	$G + H \lhd 0$
$G \parallel 0$	$G + H \parallel 0$	$G + H \rhd 0$	$G + H \lhd 0$	$G + H \ ? \ 0$

Table 4. Outcomes of Sums of Games. The entries $G + H \ ? \ 0$ are unrestricted.

Any Hackenbush picture in which only blue edges touch the ground is positive, for plainly the last move will be Left's. In particular the house of Fig. 8 is positive. But the garden is also positive, for it is made from two of the positive posies of Fig. 5(b). So the whole picture can be won by Left, no matter who starts.

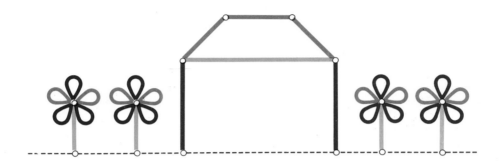

Figure 8. A Positive House and Garden.

THE NEGATIVE OF A GAME

In our examples of Blue-Red Hackenbush we found that whenever we interchanged the colors red and blue throughout, the number representing the value changed sign. This suggests that in general we define the negative of a game by interchanging the roles of Left and Right throughout. So, from no matter what position of G, the moves that once were legal for Left now become legal for Right, and vice versa. If G is the position

$$G = \{A,B,C,\ldots|D,E,F,\ldots\},$$

then $-G$ will be the position

$$-G = \{-D,-E,-F,\ldots|-A,-B,-C,\ldots\}.$$

For the general game $G = \{G^L|G^R\}$ we have

$$\boxed{-G = \{-G^R|-G^L\}.}$$

This definition works even when applied to fuzzy positions. Let's see what it means in practice. The negative of any Hackenbush position is obtained by interchanging the colors red and blue. Any green edges are unaltered. So for example the negative the flower of Fig. 5(a) is a similar flower, but with three red and two blue petals instead of three blue and two red. A Hackenbush picture made entirely of green edges will therefore be its own negative. This means in particular that the little forest of Fig. 9 is a zero game, for it consists of the sum of two trees and their negatives (which have the same shape).

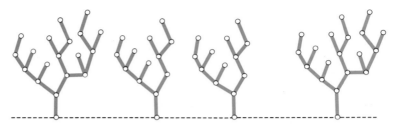

Figure 9. Under the Greenwood Trees.

But no single tree of this forest is zero (the first player could win by chopping its trunk), and in fact the sum of one large and one small tree from Fig. 9 is also non-zero (chop the larger one's horizontal branch). So $G + G$ can be zero without G's being zero. In fact we'll meet the commonest such game, Star, in just a few pages. Star is its own negative.

CANCELLING A GAME WITH ITS NEGATIVE

Is the negative of a game properly defined? Is it really true that the sum of a game and its negative is a zero game? How does the second player win the compound game $G + (-G)$?

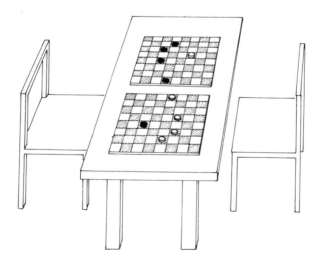

Figure 10. Playing a Game with its Negative.

The answers are fairly obvious. The first player must move in some component—let's suppose he moves from G to H, making the total position $H + (-G)$. Then by the definition of $-G$, the move from $-G$ to $-H$ will be legal for his opponent, who can therefore convert the whole position to $H + (-H)$. The first player might then move to $H + (-K)$, but this the second player can convert to $K + (-K)$, and so on. In other words, the second player can always mimic his opponent's previous move by making an exactly corresponding move in the other component. If he does this, he will never be lost for a move, and so will win the game. This is, of course, simply the Tweedledum and Tweedledee Argument, which we learned in Chapter 1.

> For any game G, the game $G + (-G)$ is a zero game.

We are only discussing finite games, so the ending condition prevents draws by infinite play.

COMPARING TWO GAMES

We shall say that G is greater than or equal to H, and write $G \geqslant H$, to mean that G is at least as favorable to Left as H is. What exactly does this mean? We can get a hint from ordinary arithmetic, when $x \geqslant y$ if and only if the number $x - y$ is positive or zero. Let's take this as the definition for games:

> $G \geqslant H$ means that $G + (-H) \geqslant 0$.

Then it's easy to see that if $G \geqslant H$ and $H \geqslant K$, we have $G \geqslant K$. For $G + (-K)$ has the same outcome as $G + (H + (-K)) + (-H)$, since $H + (-H)$ is a zero game, and this can be written as the sum of $G + (-H)$ and $H + (-K)$, which are both $\geqslant 0$. Appealing to our results on sums of games, we see that $G + (-K) \geqslant 0$, that is, $G \geqslant K$. In a similar way, from Table 4 we derive Table 5, showing what we can deduce about the order relation between G and K from those between G and H and H and K.

	$H = K$	$H > K$	$H < K$	$H \parallel K$
$G = H$	$G = K$	$G > K$	$G < K$	$G \parallel K$
$G > H$	$G > K$	$G > K$	$G\ ?\ K$	$G \rhd K$
$G < H$	$G < K$	$G\ ?\ K$	$G < K$	$G \lhd K$
$G \parallel H$	$G \parallel K$	$G \rhd K$	$G \lhd K$	$G\ ?\ K$

Table 5. What Relation is G to K?

Here $G = H$ means that G and H are *equally favorable* to Left
  $G > H$ means that G is *better* than H for Left
  $G < H$ means that G is *worse* than H for Left
  $G \parallel H$ means that G is *sometimes better*, *sometimes worse*, than H for Left.

Once again "$\rhd$" means "$>$" or "$\parallel$", etc.

COMPARING HACKENBUSH POSITIONS

The comparisons we made between Blue-Red Hackenbush positions in Chapter 1 are still valid, but more general things can happen when we meet fuzzy positions. Let's discuss the flower of Fig. 5(a). This is fuzzy as it stands. How much do we have to add to it before it becomes positive? It's not too hard to see that adding one free move for Left is already enough, since Left can win no matter who starts, by chopping the flowerstalk if this is still available, and using his free move if not.

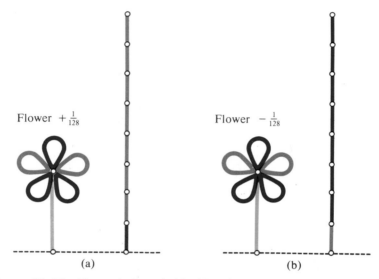

Figure 11. The Flower is Dwarfed by Very Small Hollyhocks of Either Sign.

Is half a move still enough? The answer again turns out to be "yes", and in fact Fig. 11 shows that even a very small fraction of a move is ample. Figure 11(a) adds only $\frac{1}{128}$ of a move to the flower, but it is clear that Left still wins by essentially the same strategy, giving first preference to chopping the flowerstalk, and if the flower has already gone, chopping the blue edge of his allowance. In Fig. 11(b) we have subtracted $\frac{1}{128}$ of a move, and this time Right wins by a similar strategy.

This means that the flower must be very small indeed—we have just proved that

$$-\tfrac{1}{128} < \text{flower} < +\tfrac{1}{128}$$

and of course our argument is actually enough to show that the flower is greater than all negative numbers and less than all positive ones, although still not zero. So the only number its cloud covers is 0 itself (see Fig. 12).

Figure 12. The Cloud Hides the Flower, but Covers only one Number.

The same kind of argument proves a much more general result, that any Hackenbush picture in which all the ground edges are green has a value which lies strictly between all negative and all positive numbers. Right can win when we subtract $\frac{1}{128}$ from such a picture by giving first priority to chopping any ground edge of the picture, and removing his free move allowance only when the rest of the picture has vanished. So the house of Fig. 13 is less than every positive number.

Figure 13. A Small but Positive House.

But Left can win in this picture by itself, so although the house is small, it's quite definitely positive (compare Fig. 5(b)). (The fight is about who first chops one of the walls, for his opponent will win by chopping the other. If Left works down the edges available to him from the chimney, he can make at least 5 moves to Right's at most 4 before a wall need be chopped.)

THE GAME OF COL

Colin Vout has invented the following map-coloring game. Each player, when it is his turn to move, paints one region of the map, Left using the color blue and Right using red. No two regions having a common frontier edge may be painted the same color. Whoever is unable to paint a region loses. Let us suppose that Right has made the first move in the very simple map with three regions shown in Fig. 14(a). What is the value of the resulting position?

The effect of Right's move has been to reserve the central region for Left so that we can think of it as being already *tinted* blue (Fig. 14(b)). In general any unpainted region next to a painted one automatically acquires a tint of the opposite color, indicating that only one player may use it thereafter. In the figures tinting is represented by hatching. Figure 14(c) shows the results of

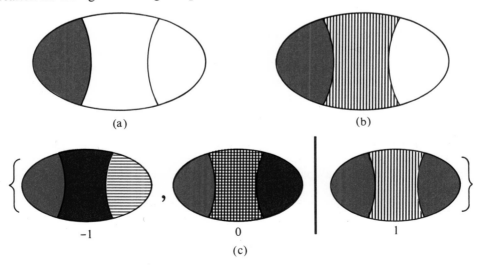

Figure 14. A Simple Game of Col.

each possible move from Fig. 14(b). If Left exercises his first option, there will remain one unpainted region, but this will be tinted red and so have value -1. After his second option, the unpainted region is tinted both red *and* blue, so neither player may use it and the value is zero. Right's only possible move leaves a blue tinted region, value 1. The value of Fig. 14(a) is therefore $\{-1,0|1\} = \frac{1}{2}$.

A STAR IS BORN!

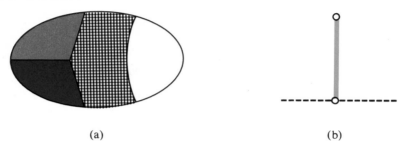

(a)   (b)

Figure 15. A Startling Value.

In Fig. 15(a) the only available region is not restricted in any way. Either player may therefore paint it and so move to a position of value zero. The value of Fig. 15(a) is therefore $\{0|0\}$. How should we interpret this? The Simplicity Rule will not help us, for there is no number strictly between 0 and 0, but we should expect the value to be less than or equal to each of

$$\{0|1\}, \ \{0|\tfrac{1}{2}\}, \ \{0|\tfrac{1}{4}\}, \ \ldots,$$

since Right's option 0 is less than or equal to each of

$$1 \ , \quad \tfrac{1}{2} \ , \quad \tfrac{1}{4} \ , \ \ldots$$

In other words the value is less than or equal to each of

$$\tfrac{1}{2} \ , \quad \tfrac{1}{4} \ , \quad \tfrac{1}{8} \ , \ \ldots$$

Since it is also greater than or equal to the negatives of these, one might guess the value 0. But is Fig. 15(a) a zero position? No! For whoever starts is the winner, not the loser. In fact, the position is fuzzy. Since the value $\{0|0\}$ arises in many games, it deserves a proper name, and we write it $*$, pronounced **Star**. A solitary green stalk in Hackenbush has a value $*$ (Fig. 15(b)), since again each player must end the game with his first move.

Although the value $*$ is not a number it can perfectly well be added to any other positions, whether their values are numbers or not. For instance the entire Fig. 15 can be regarded as a compound position in the sum of a Col game with a Hackenbush one, and has value $*+*$. Who wins this compound position? If you start and paint the region, I shall take the stalk and finish. If you take the stalk, I shall paint the region. In either case the second player wins and so the value is zero!

$$\boxed{*+* = 0.}$$

More generally, we consider positions of value $\{x|x\}$ for any number x. This is strictly greater than every number $y < x$ and strictly less than every number $z > x$, but neither greater than, less than nor equal to x itself. We can also add such values to other values of the same kind or to numbers.

Let us add $\frac{3}{4}$ to $*$, that is $\{\frac{1}{2}|1\} + \{0|0\}$. Left has two options $\frac{1}{2}+*$ (moving from $\frac{3}{4}$) and $\frac{3}{4}+0$ (moving from $*$), and Right has the two options $1+*$, $\frac{3}{4}+0$. Since $* < \frac{1}{4}$, Left's best option is $\frac{3}{4}$, and this is also Right's best option for the same reason. So we have

$$\tfrac{3}{4}+* = \{\tfrac{3}{4}|\tfrac{3}{4}\}$$

and more generally

$$x+* = \{x|x\}$$

for any number x.

THE VALUE $x*$

This type of value occurs so often that we'll use an abbreviated notation

$$x* \qquad \text{for} \qquad x+*$$

just as people write $2\frac{1}{2}$ for $2+\frac{1}{2}$. You must learn not to confuse $x*$ with x times $*$, just as you don't confuse $2\frac{1}{2}$ with 2 times $\frac{1}{2}$.

COL CONTAINS SUCH VALUES

For example, in the position of Fig. 16(a), which has tints as in Fig. 16(b), the players have the options shown in Fig. 16(c). It therefore has the value $\{*, -1, 1|1\}$. Since the values $*$ and -1 are both less than 1, this simplifies to $\{1|1\} = 1*$.

You'll find more about Col in the Extras.

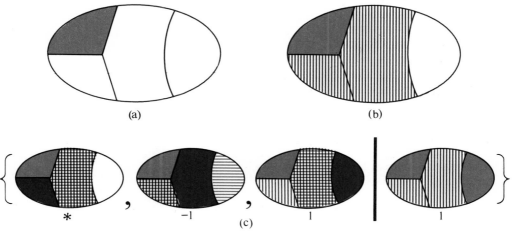

Figure 16. The Value of a Col Position.

GAME TREES

We usually display games by trees, with nodes for positions and edges for moves, as in the examples

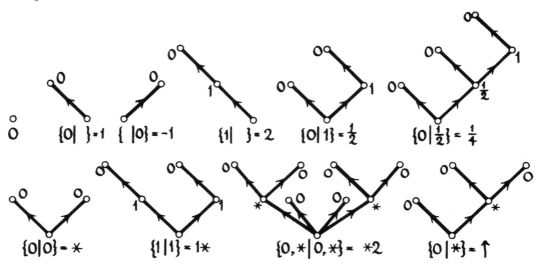

Of course we use edges slanting to the left for Left's moves and to the right for Right's. This can help you to see that games that superficially look very different may have the same essential structure (e.g. Figs. 15(a) and (b)). In complicated positions we often combine nodes to avoid repetitions and we sometimes draw the diagrams upside-down as we did for Ski-Jumps and Toads-and-Frogs in Figs. 12 and 16 of Chapter 1.

GREEN HACKENBUSH, THE GAME OF NIM, AND NIMBERS

In Chapter 7 we shall give a complete theory for Hackenbush pictures that are entirely green, containing neither blue nor red edges. Of course the game represented by a green Hackenbush picture is an **impartial** one, in the sense that from any position exactly the same moves are legal for each player. There are several of our chapters (4, 12–17) devoted to impartial games, which make it clear that the game of **Nim** plays a central role in the theory of such games. We shall introduce this game by analyzing some particularly simple green Hackenbush positions.

A very simple kind of green Hackenbush picture is the green snake, which consists of a chain of green edges with just one end touching the ground. It will not affect the play to bend some of the topmost edges into loops, so allowing our snakes to have heads. Figure 17 illustrates a number of snakes, those of length 1 being perhaps better called blades of grass. How shall we play such a game?

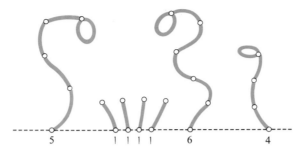

Figure 17. *Latet anguis in herba* (Virgil, Eclogue, III, 93).

Plainly any move will affect just one snake, and will replace that snake by a strictly shorter one. This means that if we write ∗*n* for the value of a snake with *n* edges (counting the head loop, if present), then we have

$$*0 = \{ \ | \ \} = 0,$$
$$*1 = \{*0|*0\} = \{0|0\}, \quad \text{the game we called } *,$$
$$*2 = \{*0,*1|*0,*1\} = \{0,*|0,*\},\dots,$$
$$*n = \{*0,*1,*2,\dots,*(n-1)|*0,*1,*2,\dots,*(n-1)\}.$$

These special values are called **nimbers** and you'll hear about them incessantly from now on. The fact that the same options appear on both sides of the | emphasizes the impartiality of the game.

It might be safer to play the game with heaps of counters instead of snakes. In this form, the general position has a number of heaps, and the move is to remove any positive number of counters from any one heap. In the normal play version, the winner is the person who takes the last counter. So this is the same as the snake game, with an *n*-edge snake replaced by a heap of *n* counters, and Fig. 17 becomes Fig. 18.

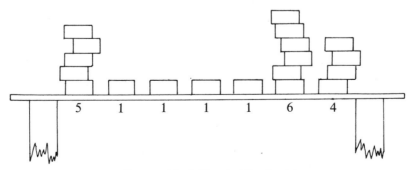

Figure 18. A Simple Nim Position.

The game is the celebrated game of Nim, analyzed by C.L. Bouton, and we shall meet it again and again, for R.P. Sprague and P.M. Grundy showed (independently) that it implicitly contains the additive theory of all impartial games. For the moment, we refrain from giving the theory in general (see the Extras to Chapter 3), and just describe a few simple positions and equalities.

GET NIMBLE WITH NIMBERS!

Firstly, note that a single non-empty heap is fuzzy, for the first player to move can take the whole heap. In the Hackenbush form, he chops the bottom edge of the snake. Next, two heaps of equal size add up to zero, for the impartiality ensures that a position is its own negative. So any pair of equal heaps in a position may be neglected—this allows us to neglect all four blades of grass in Fig. 17. On the other hand, the sum of two unequal heaps is a fuzzy game, for the first player can equalize them by reducing the larger one.

These remarks show that in a three-heap game, the player who first (fatally) equalizes two of the heaps or empties any heap is the loser, for in the first case his opponent can remove the third heap, and in the second, equalize the two non-empty heaps. But in the position $*1 + *2 + *3$, every move of the first player loses for one of these reasons, and so $*1 + *2 + *3 = 0$. Since nimbers are their own negatives this can also be written in any of the forms

$$*1 + *2 = *3, \qquad *1 + *3 = *2, \qquad *2 + *3 = *1,$$

which are very useful in simplifying positions. For example, any situation in which there is one heap of size 2 and another of size 3 may be simplified by regarding these as a single heap of size 1.

From the position $*1 + *4 + *5$, if either player reduces one of the larger heaps to 2 or 3, the other player can reduce the other to 3 or 2 respectively. Since all other moves are fatal for one of our two reasons, this shows that $*1 + *4 + *5 = 0$, enabling us in general to replace two heaps of any two distinct sizes from 1,4,5 by one heap of the third size.

The equality $*2 + *4 + *6 = 0$ can be checked in a similar way. If either player reduces one of the larger heaps to 1 or 3, his opponent can reduce the other to the other, getting $*2 + *1 + *3$. The only other moves not obviously fatal are to reduce 2 to 1 or 6 to 5, and these counter each other, since $*1 + *4 + *5 = 0$.

We can now do some rather clever nimber arithmetic:

$$*3 + *5 = *2 + *1 + *5 = *2 + *4 = *6,$$

so we have another equality, representable in any of the ways

$$*3 + *5 = *6, \qquad *3 + *6 = *5, \qquad *5 + *6 = *3, \qquad *3 + *5 + *6 = 0.$$

Later on we shall show that the sum of *any* two nimbers is another nimber, and give rules for working out which one it will be. But we have already more than enough to work out who wins the game of Figs. 17 and 18, and how. Since the four blades of grass can be neglected, the value of this is $*5 + *6 + *4 = *3 + *4$, which, being fuzzy, is a first-player win by reducing 4 to 3. So one winning move is to chop the head off the third snake, reducing his value from $*4$ to $*3$. The diligent reader should check that the only other two winning first moves are to reduce $*5$ to $*2$ and $*6$ to $*1$. Our Most Assiduous Reader will prepare an extended nim-addition table using our examples as basis.

CHILDISH HACKENBUSH

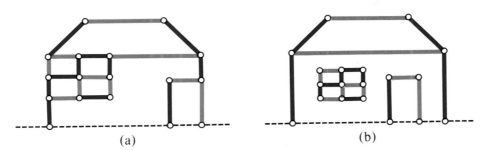

(a)   (b)

Figure 19. Childish and Grown-Up Pictures.

We call a Hackenbush picture *childish* because every edge is connected to the ground, perhaps via other edges. For example, the house of Fig. 19(a) is childish, but that of Fig. 19(b) is not, because the window will fall down and no longer be part of the position. The rule in ordinary Hackenbush is that edges which might make a picture non-childish are deleted as soon as they arise. However, in **Childish Blue-Red Hackenbush** (J. Schaer) you are only allowed to take edges which leave all the others connected to the ground; nothing may fall off. It might be thought that this is not a very interesting game. However Childish Blue-Red Hackenbush is far from trivial and the reader may like to verify the values of the positions in Fig. 20, and to compare them with the values of ordinary Blue-Red Hackenbush in Fig. 16 of Chapter 1.

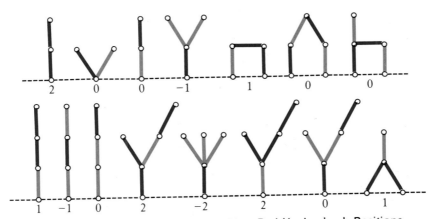

Figure 20. Values of Childish Blue-Red Hackenbush Positions.

Some Childish Hackenbush positions with non-integer values can be found in the Extras.

SEATING COUPLES

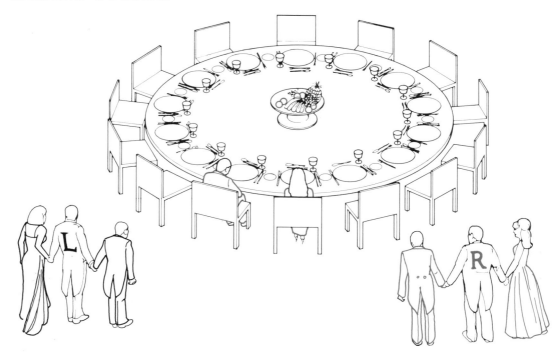

Figure 21. A Dinner to Celebrate the End of Chapter 2.

Figure 21 shows the dining table around which Left and Right are taking turns to seat couples for a dinner to celebrate the end of this chapter. Left prefers to seat a lady to the *left* of her partner, while Right thinks it proper only to seat her to the *right*. No gentleman may be seated next to a lady other than his own partner. The player, Left or Right, who first finds himself unable to seat a couple, has the embarrassing task of turning away the remaining guests, and so may be said to *lose*.

Of course the rules have the effect of preventing either player Left or Right from seating two couples in four adjacent chairs, for then the gentleman from one of his two couples will be next to the lady from the other. So when either player seats a couple, he effectively reserves the two seats on either side for the use of his opponent only. So after the game has started, the available chairs will form rows of three types:

LnL,   a row of n empty chairs between two of Left's guests,

RnR,   a row of n empty chairs between two of Right's, and

LnR or RnL, a row of n empty chairs between one of Left's guests and one of Right's.

Thus Fig. 21 is R 12 R. It is convenient to start the numbering from $n = 0$, but of course disallowing the positions L 0 L and R 0 R in which one player has illegally seated two adjacent couples. When we do this, we have

$$LnL = \{LaL + LbL \mid LaR + RbL\}$$
$$RnR = \{RaL + LbR \mid RaR + RbR\} \quad (= -LnL)$$
$$LnR = \{LaL + LbR \mid LaR + RbR\} \quad (= \quad RnL)$$

where a and b range over all pairs of numbers adding to $n-2$, but excluding the disallowed positions $L0L$ and $R0R$. Of course this is because whenever a player seats a couple they occupy 2 of the n seats.

As an example, we have

$$R5R = \begin{Bmatrix} R3L + L0R & \\ R2L + L1R & R2R + R1R \\ R1L + L2R & R1R + R2R \\ R0L + L3R & \end{Bmatrix} = \begin{Bmatrix} *+0 & \\ 0+0 & 1+0 \\ 0+0 & 0+1 \\ 0+* & \end{Bmatrix}$$

which simplifies to $\{0,*\mid1\}$. What value is this? To find out, we use the inequalities $-\frac{1}{4} \leqslant * \leqslant \frac{1}{4}$, which tells us that

$$\{0,-\tfrac{1}{4}\mid1\} \leqslant R5R \leqslant \{0,\tfrac{1}{4}\mid1\},$$

and so we must have $R5R = \frac{1}{2}$, since the Simplicity Rule tells us that this is the value of both $\{0,-\frac{1}{4}\mid1\}$ and $\{0,\frac{1}{4}\mid1\}$. Verify in like manner the first few entries of Table 6. Who wins Fig. 21?

n	0	1	2	3	4	5	6	7	8	9	10	11	12	13	14	$\ldots$
LnL	$-$	0	-1	-1	$*$	$-\frac{1}{2}$	$-\frac{1}{2}$	0	$-\frac{1}{4}$	$-\frac{1}{4}$	$*$	$-\frac{1}{8}$	$-\frac{1}{8}$	0	$-\frac{1}{16}$	$\ldots$
$LnR = RnL$	0	0	0	$*$	$*$	$*$	0	0	0	$*$	$*$	$*$	0	0	0	$\ldots$
RnR	$-$	0	1	1	$*$	$\frac{1}{2}$	$\frac{1}{2}$	0	$\frac{1}{4}$	$\frac{1}{4}$	$*$	$\frac{1}{8}$	$\frac{1}{8}$	0	$\frac{1}{16}$	$\ldots$

Table 6. Values of Positions in Seating Couples.

EXTRAS

WINNING STRATEGIES

It is not hard to see that for games which satisfy the eight conditions given in the Extras to Chapter 1, with a given player to start, say Right, there must be a winning strategy for either Left or Right. We prove this as follows.

Suppose first that there is a Right option G^R of G for which Right has a winning strategy supposing that Left starts in G^R. Then of course Right has a winning strategy in G—he moves to that G^R and continues by playing his winning strategy for G^R.

If there is no such Right option, it may happen that all the Right options have winning strategies for Left, supposing Left starts in them. But in this case, Left has a winning strategy in the whole game—he waits until Right has made his first move, which must be to some G^R, and then Left continues play with his winning strategy in that G^R.

So if neither player has a winning strategy from G under the supposition that Right starts, there must be some G^R from which neither player has a winning strategy supposing Left starts. This in turn involves the existence of some Left option G^{RL} of that G^R from which neither player has a winning strategy supposing Right starts, and so on. But we obtain in this way an infinite sequence

$$G \to G^R \to G^{RL} \to G^{RLR} \to \ldots$$

of legal moves in G. This shows that a play of G can last forever, which contradicts the ending condition (6. in the Extras for Chapter 1) for G.

THE SUM OF TWO FINITE GAMES CAN LAST FOREVER

It is possible that two games D and G which individually satisfy the ending condition might have a sum $D + G$ that does not. For instance if Left can make an infinite succession of moves in D:

$$D \underset{L}{\to} D_1 \underset{L}{\to} D_2 \underset{L}{\to} \ldots,$$

and Right an infinite succession of moves in G:

$$G \underset{R}{\to} G_1 \underset{R}{\to} G_2 \underset{R}{\to} \ldots,$$

then even though neither component game might have an infinite sequence of *alternating* Left and Right moves, there is such a sequence in the compound game $D + G$, namely:

$$D + G \underset{L}{\to} D_1 + G \underset{R}{\to} D_1 + G_1 \underset{L}{\to} D_2 + G_1 \underset{R}{\to} D_2 + G_2 \underset{L}{\to} \ldots.$$

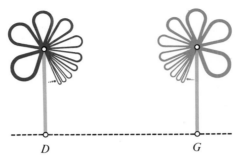

Figure 22. An Infinite Delphinium and an Infinite Geranium.

If we compare the Hackenbush Hotchpotch picture of Fig. 22 with those of Fig. 5, we will see that if play is restricted to the delphinium (or the geranium) *only*, then the first player wins smartly by plucking the flower by its stem. But if *both* flowers are available, then *neither* player will take a stem, lest his opponent grab the other and win the game. So each sits plucking appropriate petals alternately and the compound game goes on forever.

If we want a condition that ensures that all sums of games will end, we should demand that in no game is there any infinite sequence $G \to G_1 \to G_2 \to \ldots$ of legal moves, *alternating or not*. You must look in Chapters 11 and 12 if you want to know how to add games that violate this condition.

A THEOREM ABOUT COL

> Each Col position has a value
>
> z or $\{z|z\} = z*$
>
> for some number z.

To prove this we'll use a notation like that we'll introduce in Chapter 6 for the (contrasting) game of Snort, namely:

●		for a region available to either player,
●	(blue)	for one usable by Left only,
○	(red)	for one usable only by Right, and
◑	(piebald)	for one available to neither;

with edges joining these spots indicating adjacency of regions. The typical Left option is obtained by deleting a node of type ● or ● and adding a red tint to all adjacent nodes; similarly for Right options.

We assert that for any G^L and G^R we must have

$$G^L + * \leqslant G \leqslant G^R + *.$$

As an example, the latter inequality is proved by providing the obvious imitation strategy that wins for Left as second player on the difference game:

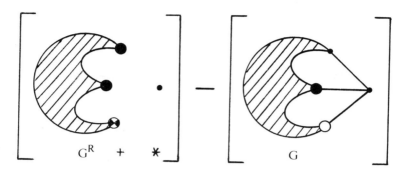

It follows that we have

$$\text{every } G^L \leqslant \text{every } G^R.$$

Since these are simpler positions we know inductively that their values are either numbers or numbers plus star. Call the best Left options x or $x*$, and the best Right ones y or $y*$. If $x < y$. then G's value is a number by the Simplicity Rule. Otherwise G must be one of the two forms

$$\{x|x\} = x* \quad \text{or} \quad \{x+*|x+*\} = x,$$

since the condition $G^L \leqslant G^R$ precludes such forms as

$$\{x|x+*\}.$$

COL-LECTIONS AND COL-LAPSINGS

Here are the values of some Col positions in the above notation (Fig. 23), and some rules, collected from ONAG, for simplifying larger positions.

1. You may omit piebald nodes and edges connecting oppositely tinted nodes without altering the value.
2. The value is unaltered or increased if you either

   tint a node blue, or
   delete an edge ending in a blue tinted node.

   (Similarly with "decreased" and "red".)
3.

4. The positions

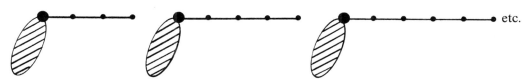

etc.

all have equal value A, say, and the corresponding positions

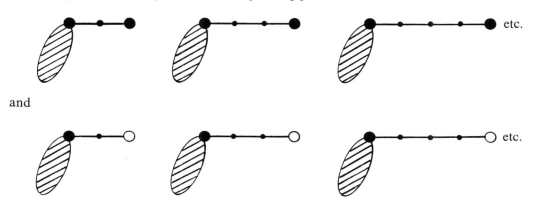

etc.

and

etc.

have values $A + \frac{1}{2}$ and $A - \frac{1}{2}$ respectively.

5. If two joined untinted nodes are each connected to the same set of nodes, you may tint one blue and one red (and then delete their join).

6. If the value of a configuration is unaltered, both when a node is tinted blue and when tinted red, it's **explosive** and you may delete that node, even when it joins the configuration to another. For example

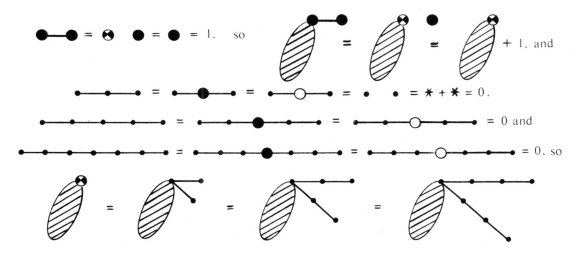

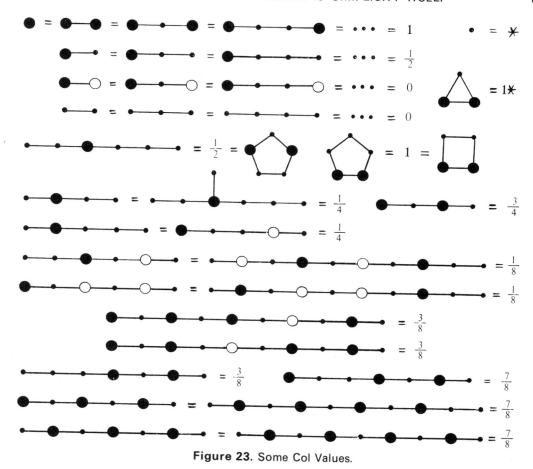

Figure 23. Some Col Values.

7. Other examples of explosive nodes are: any node in an untinted chain with at least three others on each side; and the ones indicated by the lightning bolts in

8. A configuration having a symmetry moving every node and reversing any tints has value 0. For example

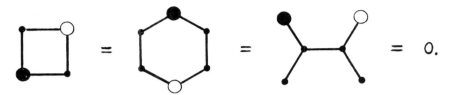

Nick Inglis has shown that there are Col positions with arbitrarily large denominators.

MAUNDY CAKE

Here's how we work out the value $M(r, l)$ of an $r \times l$ cake (r rows, l columns):

$$r = \ \ 999 : 333 : 111 : \ \ 37 : \ 1$$
$$l = 1000 : 500 : 250 : 125 : 25 : 5 : 1$$
$$M(999,1000) = 5 + 1 = 6 \text{ for Lefty, i.e. } +6.$$

$$r = 1000 \ : \ 500 \ : \ 250 \ : \ 125 \ : \ 25 \ : \ 5 \ : \ 1$$
$$l = 1001 \ : \ 143 \ : \ \ 13 \ : \ \ \ 1$$
$$M(1000,1001) = 25 + 5 + 1 \text{ for Rita, i.e. } -31.$$

In every line you divide by the smallest possible prime to get the next number, stopping exactly when you get to 1. You then add the "leftovers" as in the examples, and assign the game to whoever has the longer sequence (so the value is 0 if Lefty's sequence is the same length as Rita's).

ANOTHER CUTCAKE VARIANT

Dean Hickerson, who independently discovered the game of Cutcake, notes that if Lefty must make v vertical cuts at each turn, and Rita h horizontal ones, then the value of an $r \times l$ cake is still the same as one which is

$$\lfloor r/(h+1) \rfloor \quad \text{by} \quad \lfloor l/(v+1) \rfloor.$$

(The broken brackets mean "greatest integer less than or equal to"; Donald Knuth calls this the **floor**.) To calculate the values, start from

$$\lfloor (l-1)/v \rfloor \quad \text{if} \quad 1 \leqslant r \leqslant h \quad \text{and} \quad \lfloor (r-1)/h \rfloor \quad \text{if} \quad 1 \leqslant l \leqslant v.$$

HOW CHILDISH CAN YOU GET?

When you compared the values in Fig. 20 with the ones in Fig. 18 of Chapter 1, you may have thought that not only are the pictures simpler for Childish Hackenbush, but that the values are too. But this isn't always so, as you'll find out if you check the values in Fig. 24. The value at the end of the first row was found by Richard Austin, and for a long time we couldn't find one with a bigger denominator. Then Steve Tschantz came up with the sequence on the second row. Some positions aren't even numbers at all! You'll learn about the values in the third row in the next few chapters, and meet some more Childish Hackenbush positions in Chapters 6 and 8.

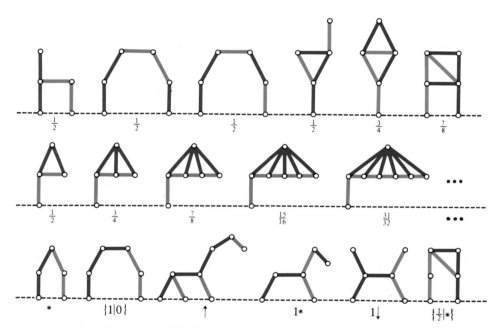

Figure 24. Childish Hackenbush Can Get Quite Playful!

REFERENCES AND FURTHER READING

Richard Austin, Impartial and Partisan Games, M.Sc. Thesis, The University of Calgary, 1976.
C.L. Bouton, Nim, a game with a complete mathematical theory, Ann. Math., Princeton (2), **3** (1902) 35–39.
J.H. Conway, "On Numbers and Games", Academic Press, London and New York, 1976, pp. 3–14.
J.H. Conway, All games bright and beautiful, Amer. Math. Monthly, **84** (1977) 417–434.
Martin Gardner, Mathematical Games, Sci. Amer., each issue (monthly).
P.M. Grundy, Mathematics and games, Eureka, **2** (1939) 6–8; reprinted *ibid.* **27** (1964) 9–11.
R.P. Sprague, Über mathematische Kampfspiele, Tôhoku Math. J. **41** (1935–36) 438–444; Zbl. **13**, 290.

Chapter 3

Some Harder Games and How to Make Them Easier

Our life is frittered away by detail . . . Simplify, simplify.
Henry David Thoreau, *Walden.*

Nim? Yes, yes, yes, let's nim with all my heart.
John Byrom, *The Nimmers,* 27.

Figure 1. A Well Advanced Game of Poker-Nim.

POKER-NIM

This game is played with heaps of Poker-chips. Just as in ordinary Nim, either player may reduce the size of any heap by removing some of the chips. But now we allow a player the alternative move of increasing the size of some heap by adding to it some of the chips he acquired in earlier moves. These two kinds of moves are the only ones allowed.

Let's suppose there are three heaps, of sizes 3,4,6 as in Fig. 1, and that the game has been going on for some time, so that both players have accumulated substantial reserves of chips. It's Left's turn to move, and he moves to 2,4,6 since he remembers from Chapter 2 that this is a good move in ordinary Nim. But now Right adds 50 chips to the 4 heap, making the position into 2,54,6, which is well beyond those discussed in Chapter 2.

55

This seems somewhat disconcerting, especially since Right has plenty more chips at his disposal, and doesn't seem too scared of using them to complicate the position. What does Left do? After a moment's thought, he just removes the 50 chips Right has just added and waits for Right's reply. If Right adds 1000 chips to one of the heaps, Left will remove them and restore the position to 2,4,6 once again. Sooner or later, Right must reduce one of the three heaps (since otherwise he'll run out of chips no matter how many he has), and then Left can reply with the appropriate Nim-move.

So whoever can win a position in ordinary Nim can still win in Poker-Nim, no matter how many chips his opponent has accumulated. He replies to the opponent's reducing moves just as he would in ordinary Nim, and reverses the effect of any increasing move by using a reducing move to restore the heap to the same size again. The new moves in Poker-Nim can only postpone defeat, not avoid it indefinitely. Since the effect of any of the new moves can be immediately reversed by the other player, we call them **reversible moves**.

NORTHCOTT'S GAME

The same sort of thing happens in other games, often in better disguise. Northcott's game is played on a checkerboard which has one black and one white piece on each row, as in Fig. 2. You may move any piece of your own color to any other empty square in the same row, provided

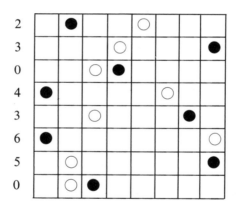

Figure 2. A Position in Northcott's Game.

you do not jump over your opponent's piece in that row. If you can't move (because all your pieces are trapped at the side of the board by your opponent's), you lose.

This can seem an aimless game if you don't see the point, and indeed it usually goes on forever if it is played badly. But when you realize that it's only Nim in disguise once more, you'll soon be able to beat anybody pretty quickly. To the left of the board in Fig. 2 we have shown the numbers of spaces between the two pieces in each row. When someone moves, just one of these numbers will be changed, and might be either increased or decreased, according as the move was retreating or advancing. But just as in Poker-Nim, any moves increasing one of the numbers can be reversed by the next player, and so are not much use.

Who wins in Fig. 2? We can see the zero-position 2,4,6 among the numbers shown, and of course the two numbers 3 together form another zero. Neglecting the two rows that are already 0, the only other number is 5, and we maintain that the first player can win by moving so as to reduce this 5 to 0. Whenever the other player enlarges some gap by retreating, the first player should reduce it again by the same extent. In fact the winner should *always advance* on his opponent, *never retreat*.

It should not be thought that the moves we advise here are the only good ones. For example, from Fig. 2 instead of reducing 5 to 0, we could replace 6 by 3, 4 by 1 or even 3 by 6 in the second row (for White) or 0 by 5 in the last row (for Black). In fact it will help to avoid revealing the strategy if you do *not* always reply to a retreating move by the corresponding advance—for similar reasons occasional retreating moves might be desirable.

BOGUS NIM-HEAPS AND THE MEX RULE

Consider the impartial game

$$G = \{*0,*1,*2,*5,*6,*9|*0,*1,*2,*5,*6,*9\}.$$

This is a new kind of Nim-heap from which either player can move to a heap of size 0, 1, 2, 5, 6, or 9. In other words, we can regard it as a rather peculiar Nim-heap of size 3 (the first missing number), from which, as well as the usual moves to heaps of sizes 0 or 1 or 2, we are allowed to move to a heap of size 5 or 6 or 9. However, the Poker-Nim argument shows that this extra freedom is in fact of no use whatever.

To be more precise, suppose some player has a winning strategy in the game $*3 + H + K + \dots$. Then in the same circumstances, he has one in $G + H + K + \dots$. When his strategy calls for a move from any of $*3, H, K, \dots$, that move is still available, and he need not use the new permitted moves from G to $*5$, $*6$, or $*9$. If his opponent tries to do so, he can immediately reverse the effect of this move by moving back to $*3$ (since 5, 6, and 9 are all greater than 3), and revert to the original strategy. So G can be replaced by $*3$ without affecting either player's chances.

The same argument shows that any game of the form

$$G = \{*a,*b,*c,\dots|*a,*b,*c,\dots\},$$

in which the same numbers appear on both sides, is really a Nim-heap in disguise. For if m is the least number from $0,1,2,3,\dots$ that does *not* appear among the numbers $a,b,c,\dots$, then either player can still make from G any of the moves to $*0,*1,*2,\dots*(m-1)$ that he could make from $*m$. If his opponent makes any other move from G, it must be to some $*n$ for which $n > m$, and can be reversed by moving back from $*n$ to $*m$. So G is really just a bogus Nim-heap $*m$.

We summarize:

> If Left and Right have exactly the same options from G,
> all of which are Nim-heaps $*a,*b,*c,\dots$,
> then G can itself be regarded as a Nim-heap, $*m$,
> where m is the least number 0 or 1 or 2 or $\dots$
> that is *not* among the numbers $a,b,c,\dots$.

THE MINIMAL-EXCLUDED (MEX) RULE

This **minimal-excluded** number is called the **mex** of the numbers $a, b, c, \dots$.

THE SPRAGUE-GRUNDY THEORY FOR IMPARTIAL GAMES

The above result enables us to show that *every* impartial game can be regarded as a bogus Nim-heap. For suppose we have an impartial game

$$G = \{A,B,C,...|A,B,C,...\}.$$

Then $A,B,C,...$ are simpler impartial games, and therefore we can suppose they have already been shown to be equivalent to Nim-heaps $*a,*b,*c,...$. But in this case G can be thought of as the Nim-heap $*m$ defined above. This gives us

THE BOGUS NIM-HEAP PRINCIPLE

> Every impartial game is just a bogus Nim-heap
> (that is, a Nim-heap with reversible
> moves added from some positions).
> The Mex Rule gives the size of the heap for G as
> the least possible number that is not the size of
> any of the heaps corresponding to the options of G.

This principle was discovered independently by R.P. Sprague in 1936 and P.M. Grundy in 1939, although they did not state it in quite this way. This means that provided we can play the game of Nim, we can play *any* other impartial game given only a "dictionary" saying which **nimbers** (i.e. Nim-heaps) correspond to the positions of that game. Here's a game played with a White Knight that gives a simple example of this dictionary method.

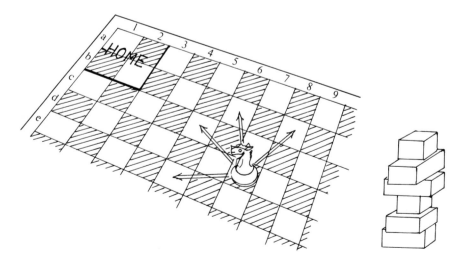

Figure 3. The White Knight and his Baggage.

THE WHITE KNIGHT

has, from any position on the chessboard, the moves shown in Fig. 3. You may recall that he was in the habit of losing his belongings. Alice has kindly boxed them up and the boxes now form the Nim-heap to the right of the figure. Now consider the game in which you can *either* move the Knight to one of the four places shown *or* steal some of the boxes. The game ends only when the Knight is on one of the four home squares and all the boxes have gone.

	1	2	3	4	5	6	7	8	9	10	11	12	13	14	15	16	17	18	19	20
a	0	0	*1	*1	0	0	*1	*1	0	0	*1	*1	0	0	*1	*1	0	0	*1	*1
b	0	0	*2	*1	0	0	*1	*1	0	0	*1	*1	0	0	*1	*1	0	0	*1	*1
c	*1	*2	*2	*2	*3	*2	*2	*2	*3	*2	*2	*2	*3	*2	*2	*2	*3	*2	*2	
d	*1	*1	*2	*1	*4	*3	*2	*3	*3	*3	*2	*3	*3	*3	*2	*3	*3	*3	*2	
e	0	0	*3	*4	0	0	*1	*1	0	0	*1	*1	0	0	*1	*1	0	0		
f	0	0	*2	*3	0	0	*2	*1	0	0	*1	*1	0	0	*1	*1	0	0		
g	*1	*1	*2	*2	*1	*2	*2	*2	*3	*2	*2	*2	*3	*2	*2	*2	*3			
h	*1	*1	*2	*3	*1	*1	*2	*1	*4	*3	*2	*3	*3	*3	*2	*3	*3			
i	0	0	*3	*3	0	0	*3	*4	0	0	*1	*1	0	0	*1	*1				
j	0	0	*2	*3	0	0	*2	*3	0	0	*2	*1	0	0	*1	*1				
k	*1	*1	*2	*2	*1	*1	*2	*2	*1	*2	*2	*2	*3	*2						
l	*1	*1	*2	*3	*1	*1	*2	*3	*1	*1	*2	*1								
m	0	0	*3	*3	0	0	*3	*3	0	0										
n	0	0	*2	*3	0	0	*2	*3												
o	*1	*1	*2	*2	*1	*1														
p	*1	*1	*2	*3																
q	0	0																		

Table 1. Nimbers for the White Knight.

The whole game is the result of adding a Nim-heap *6 to a game with only the Knight. Table 1 shows which nimbers correspond to the game with the Knight in various positions. Let's find the value of the Knight on d7 as in Fig. 3, assuming we already know the values of the four places he can move to. Figure 4 shows that these places can be thought of as bogus Nim-heaps of sizes

$$0, \quad 3, \quad 0, \quad 1 \quad (\text{mex} = 2)$$

and so the present position corresponds to a bogus Nim-heap of size 2, value *2. So the good move in Fig. 3 is to steal all but two of the boxes.

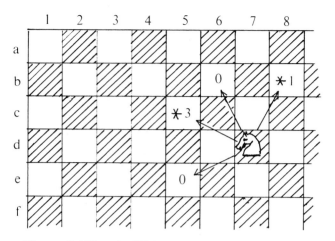

Figure 4. What the White Knight Moves are Worth.

ADDING NIMBERS

0	1	2	3	4	5	6	7	8	9	10	11	12	13	14	15
1	0	3	2	5	4	7	6	9	8	11	10	13	12	15	14
2	3	0	1	6	7	4	5	10	11	8	9	14	15	12	13
3	2	1	0	7	6	5	4	11	10	9	8	15	14	13	12
4	5	6	7	0	1	2	3	12	13	14	15	8	9	10	11
5	4	7	6	1	0	3	2	13	12	15	14	9	8	11	10
6	7	4	5	2	3	0	1	14	15	12	13	10	11	8	9
7	6	5	4	3	2	1	0	15	14	13	12	11	10	9	8
8	9	10	11	12	13	14	15	0	1	2	3	4	5	6	7
9	8	11	10	13	12	15	14	1	0	3	2	5	4	7	6
10	11	8	9	14	15	12	13	2	3	0	1	6	7	4	5
11	10	9	8	15	14	13	12	3	2	1	0	7	6	5	4
12	13	14	15	8	9	10	11	4	5	6	7	0	1	2	3
13	12	15	14	9	8	11	10	5	4	7	6	1	0	3	2
14	15	12	13	10	11	8	9	6	7	4	5	2	3	0	1
15	14	13	12	11	10	9	8	7	6	5	4	3	2	1	0

Table 2. A Nim-Addition Table.

We saw in Chapter 2 that a Nim-heap of size 2 together with one of size 3 is equivalent to one of size 1. We now see that this was no accident, for the sum of *any* two Nim-heaps $*a$ and $*b$ is an impartial game, and so is equivalent to *some* other Nim-heap $*c$. The number c is called the **nim-sum** of a and b, and written $a \overset{*}{+} b$. How can we work out nim-sums in general?

The options from $*a + *b$ are all the positions of the form $*a' + *b$ or $*a + *b'$ in which a' denotes any number (from $0,1,2,...$) less than a, and b' any number (from $0,1,2,...$ again) less than b. So $a \overset{*}{+} b$ is the least number $0,1,2,...$ not of either of the forms

$$a' \overset{*}{+} b, \qquad a \overset{*}{+} b' \qquad (a' < a, \ b' < b)$$

Table 2 was computed using this rule. For example the entry $6 \overset{*}{+} 3$ was computed as follows. The earlier entries $3,2,1,0,7,6$ in column 3 correspond to the options $*6' + *3$ (where $6'$ means one of $0,1,2,3,4,5$) and the earlier entries $6,7,4$ in row 6 correspond to options $*6 + *3'$ ($3'$ means $0,1$ or 2). The least number not observed earlier in either row or column is 5, so $6 \overset{*}{+} 3 = 5$, i.e. $*6 + *3 = *5$. It might help you to follow how the table is computed if you look at the game in which our White Knight is replaced by a White Rook which can only move North or West.

You'll find a general Nim-Addition Rule in the Extras, and will have many opportunities to apply it; for example, in Chapters 4, 12, 14 and 15.

WYT QUEENS

Figure 5. How the Wyt Queens Move.

In the game of Wyt Queens any number of Queens can be on the same square and each player, when it is her turn to move, can move any single Queen an arbitrary distance North, West or North-West as indicated, even jumping over other Queens.

Because the Queens move independently, we can regard the whole game as the sum of smaller ones with just one Queen. The various Queens on the board will therefore correspond to Nim-heaps $*a, *b, *c....$ which we can add using the Nim-Addition Rule. Try computing the nimber dictionary for this game—when you get tired you can look in the Extras for more information.

The one-Queen game is a transformation of **Wythoff's Game** (1905) played with two heaps in which the move is to reduce *either* heap by *any* amount, or *both* heaps by the *same* amount. We'll meet Wyt Queens again in Chapters 12 and 13.

REVERSIBLE MOVES IN GENERAL GAMES

What does it mean for some move to be reversible in an arbitrary game G? We shall suppose Right's move to D is reversible in the game

$$G = \{A, B, C, ... | D, E, F, ...\}.$$

This will mean that there is some move for Left from D to a Left option D^L which is at least as good for Left as G was, i.e. $D^L \geqslant G$. Then if ever Right moves from G to D, Left can at least reverse the effect by moving back from D to D^L, and might even improve his position by doing so. We shall suppose that D^L is the game

$$D^L = \{U, V, W, ... | X, Y, Z, ...\},$$

so that G looks something like Fig. 6(a).

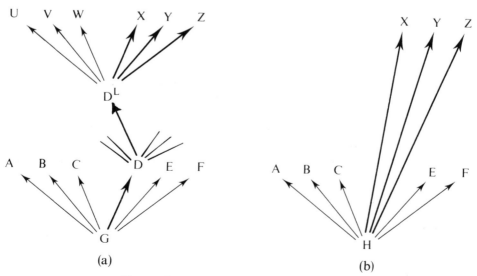

(a)   (b)

Figure 6. Bypassing a Reversible Move.

Now whenever Right plays from G to D, Left will reverse from D to D^L, from which Right can move to any of $X, Y, Z, \ldots$. So we might as well shorten G by omitting Right's move to D and letting him move directly to X or Y or Z or $\ldots$. In this way, we get the game

$$H = \{A, B, C, \ldots | X, Y, Z, \ldots, E.F. \ldots\},$$

shown in Fig. 6(b), which should have the same value as G.

We can easily test this by playing the game $G - H$, that is

$$\{A, B, C, \ldots | D, E, F, \ldots\} + \{-X, -Y, -Z, \ldots, -E, -F, \ldots | -A, -B, -C, \ldots\},$$

shown in Fig. 7, and verifying that there is no good move for either player as follows.

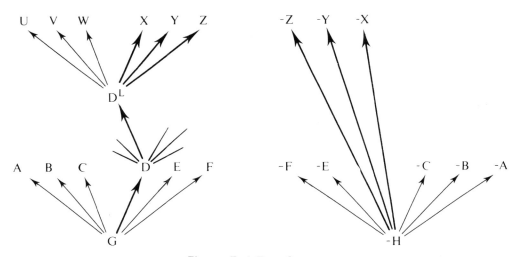

Figure 7. A Zero Game.

Obviously the moves from G to $A, B, C, \ldots$ or $E, F, \ldots$ are exactly countered by moves to their negatives from $-H$, and conversely, so that the only hopeful moves are those for Left from $-H$ to $-X$ or $-Y$ or $-Z$ or $\ldots$, and that for Right from G to D.

Left's hopes are soon dashed. His move from $-H$ to $-X$, say, leaves the total position $G - X$, worse for him than $D^L - X$, which Right can win by moving from D^L to X. There remains Right's move from G to D, which Left will reverse to D^L, leaving the total position $D^L - H$, namely:

$$\{U, V, W, \ldots | X, Y, Z, \ldots\} + \{-X, -Y, -Z, \ldots, -E, -F, \ldots | -A, -B, -C, \ldots\}.$$

Now Right dare not move from D^L to X or Y or Z or $\ldots$, since Left can counter by moving from $-H$ to the corresponding one of $-X$ or $-Y$ or $-Z$ or $\ldots$. So Right's only hope is to move from $-H$, leaving the total position $D^L - A$ or $D^L - B$ or $D^L - C$ or $\ldots$. But since $D^L \geqslant G$ these are at least as bad for Right as $G - A$, $G - B$, $G - C$, $\ldots$, which Left can win by moving in G to the appropriate one of A or B or C or $\ldots$.

Since we have now dealt with all possible first moves, $G - H$ is a zero game, and we can afford to replace G by H in any of our calculations, which will often be a very valuable simplification. We summarize:

> If any Right option D of G has itself a Left option $D^L \geqslant G$, then it will not affect the value of G if we replace D as a Right option of G by all the Right options $X, Y, Z, \ldots$ of that D^L.

BYPASSING RIGHT'S REVERSIBLE MOVE

Of course a move by Left can also be reversible:

> If any Left option C of G has itself a Right option $C^R \leqslant G$, then it will not affect the value of G if we replace C as a Left option by the list of all Left options of that C^R.

BYPASSING LEFT'S REVERSIBLE MOVE

DELETING DOMINATED OPTIONS

Now there is another kind of simplification we've already mentioned, which it would be wise to discuss more precisely here. In the game

$$G = \{A, B, C, \ldots | D, E, F, \ldots\},$$

if $A \leqslant B$ we say that A is **dominated** by B, and if $D \leqslant E$, that E is dominated by D. In other words, given two possible moves for the same player, one dominates the other if it is at least as good for the person making it. Then we can simplify by *omitting dominated moves* (provided we retain the moves that dominate them). In the case discussed, this will mean that G has the same value as the game

$$K = \{B, C, \ldots | D, F, \ldots\}.$$

And indeed, $G - K$ is a zero game, since the moves from G to A or E are countered by those from $-K$ to $-B$ or $-D$, and all other moves in either component are countered by moves to their negatives from the other.

> It won't affect the value of G
> if we delete dominated options
> but retain the options that dominated them.

DELETING DOMINATED OPTIONS

But remember that *reversible* options are *not* deleted, but *bypassed*, i.e. replaced by the list of options, for the appropriate player, from the position his opponent reverses to.

TOADS-AND-FROGS WITH UPS AND DOWNS

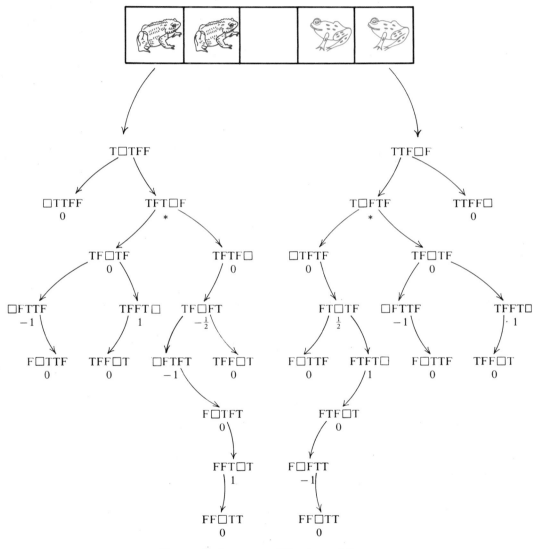

Figure 8. Anatomy of Toads-and-Frogs.

We considered a 4-place version of this game in Chapter 1. The 5-place version we now consider displays more interesting behavior. In any 5-place lane Left may move one of his toads one space right, onto an empty square, or jump over just one frog onto an empty square immediately beyond. Right's moves are similar, moving his frogs leftwards. Figure 8 shows the complete play from the initial position in which two toads are separated by just one space from two frogs. We already know how to evaluate, working upwards, all positions except the top three.

The next position to be considered is

$$T\ \square TFF = \{\square TTFF | TFT\ \square F\} = \{0|*\}.$$

Since 0 is a loss for the player to move from it, Left can win this game by moving to 0, and Right's move to $*$ does not win since Left will reply to 0. So $\{0|*\}$ is a positive game. But since $*$ is less than each of the numbers

$$2,\ 1,\ \tfrac{1}{2},\ \tfrac{1}{4},\ \dots$$

$\{0|*\}$ is less than or equal to each of

$$\{0|2\},\ \{0|1\},\ \{0|\tfrac{1}{2}\},\ \{0|\tfrac{1}{4}\}.\ \dots$$

that is, each of

$$1,\ \tfrac{1}{2},\ \tfrac{1}{4},\ \tfrac{1}{8},\ \dots$$

So we have here a positive value less than every positive number. Since we have not seen such a thing before, we cannot hope to simplify it, and we therefore need a new name, ↑, pronounced "**up**".

Similarly, the position $TTF\ \square F$, obtained by interchanging the roles of Left and Right, has the value $\{*|0\}$ which is negative, but greater than every negative number. Since $*$ is its own negative, $\{*|0\}$ is the negative of $\{0|*\}$ and we call it ↓, pronounced "**down**". By the end of the book we shall have had many ups and downs!

So the starting position of Fig. 8 has value

$$TT\ \square FF = \{T\ \square TFF | TTF\ \square F\} = \{\uparrow|\downarrow\}.$$

Do we need a new name for this? Let's first see if we can simplify it. Since each player has only one option, no move dominates another, so we next look for reversible moves. Is Right's move to ↓ reversible from the game $G = \{\uparrow|\downarrow\}$? This happens only if there is some Left option $\downarrow^L \geqslant G$. Since ↓ $= \{*|0\}$, we are asking if $* \geqslant G$, i.e. if $G - * \leqslant 0$. Has Left a winning move from

$$G - * = \{\uparrow|\downarrow\} + \{0|0\}?$$

His move from $*$ to 0 is parried by Right's reply from G to ↓, and his move from G to ↑ is countered by Right's response from ↑ to $*$, which leaves the total value $* + * = 0$. So indeed if Left starts Right wins, showing that $G - * \leqslant 0$. This means that Right can bypass his move to ↓ by moving directly from G to $\downarrow^{LR} = *^R = 0$, and shows that $G = \{\uparrow|0\}$. In this Left can also bypass his move, so that G simplifies further to $\{0|0\} = *$.

$$\boxed{\{\uparrow|\downarrow\} = \{\uparrow|0\} = \{0|\downarrow\} = \{0|0\} = *.}$$

We could otherwise have seen that $G = *$ by observing that Right also had no winning move from $G - *$. However, for a more complicated G we can ask which moves are reversible even before we have guessed the simplest form of G.

GAME TRACKING AND IDENTIFICATION

Much of this book is about finding out who wins various partizan games from arbitrary positions. **Partizan** games, we recall from the Extras to Chapter 1, are those in which the options available to the two players are not necessarily the same. For example, to find the winner in the 9-lane 5-place Toads-and-Frogs position of Fig. 9, we must work with sums of terms whose values may be $\uparrow$, $\downarrow$, $*$, or various numbers. When stalking other game we shall need to know how to add even more general values and find when the result is positive, negative, zero or fuzzy. We learned how to add *numbers* at school and we can add any small enough *nimbers* using our nim-addition table (Table 2). We also know that $x + * = \{x|x\} = x*$ for any number x. So perhaps the simplest pair of values we have not yet added are $\uparrow$ and $*$. We shall call their sum $\uparrow*$. Is it perhaps equal to $\{\uparrow|\uparrow\}$?

Figure 9. Toads and Frogs make easy Big Game.

We can always test for equality of two values by seeing if their difference is a win for the second player. Is this true of the difference game

$$\{\uparrow|\uparrow\} - \uparrow* = \{\uparrow|\uparrow\} + \overset{\downarrow}{\{*|0\}} + \overset{*}{\{0|0\}},$$

do you think? No! If Left makes his move to $*$ from the component $\downarrow$, the total value becomes $\{\uparrow|\uparrow\} + * + * = \{\uparrow|\uparrow\}$ which is clearly positive, since Left can win and Right can't. In fact it turns out that Right has no good move from $\{\uparrow|\uparrow\} - \uparrow*$ so that $\{\uparrow|\uparrow\}$ is strictly greater than $\uparrow*$.

We shall find a correct formula for $\uparrow*$. From the definition of the sum of two games we have, by considering the moves of Left and Right in the two components,

$$\uparrow* = \uparrow+* = \{0+*, \uparrow+0 \mid *+*, \uparrow+0\} = \{*, \uparrow\mid 0, \uparrow\}$$

using the equation $*+* = 0$. We can simplify this to

$$\uparrow* = \{\uparrow, *\mid 0\}$$

since Right's option $\uparrow$ was dominated by his other option, 0. Neither of Left's options dominates the other, for from their difference $\uparrow-* = \uparrow+*$, Left can win by moving to $\uparrow+0$ and Right by moving to $*+*$.

However, Left's option $\uparrow$ is reversible by Right through $\uparrow^R = *$, for plainly $* \leqslant \uparrow*$. So we can bypass $\uparrow$ by allowing Left to move directly to $\uparrow^{RL} = *^L = 0$, without affecting the value of the game. We therefore have the equation

$$\boxed{\uparrow* = \uparrow+* = \{0, *\mid 0\}}$$

and similarly its negative

$$\boxed{\downarrow* = \downarrow+* = \{0\mid 0, *\}.}$$

We have put these in boxes because they are in fact the simplest forms. They have no dominated or reversible options.

WHAT ARE FLOWERS WORTH?

We can now evaluate some simple Hackenbush Hotchpotch positions:

$$= \{0*\mid 0\} = \uparrow*.$$

$$= \{0\mid 0*\} = \downarrow*$$

A prettier position is the flower of Fig. 5(a) in Chapter 2. More generally we can consider such flowers with any numbers of red and blue petals, as in Fig. 10(a). Which player will win the sum of two flowers of this kind?

Figure 10. Two Flower Shows Ready for Judging.

Here it is easy to see that whoever first chops one of the two green stalks will lose, for his opponent will chop the other. So this kind of game reduces to "She-Loves-Me, She-Loves-Me-Not", this time played on the red and blue colored petals. Whichever of Left and Right is first unable to remove a petal of his color will lose, since his only other options are the stalks. So in a two-flower position the player having the larger number of petals of his color will win, except that if there are as many red as blue petals in all, the second player will win, for his opponent must take the first petal and hence the first stalk.

This argument proves that Fig. 10(b) is a zero game, for each player has three petals in all, and it establishes that the value of the flower of Fig. 5(a) in Chapter 2 is $\uparrow + *$, since the one-petal flower in Fig. 10(b) has value $\downarrow + *$ (the petal can be uncurled without affecting play, like a snake's head).

A GALLIMAUFRY OF GAMES

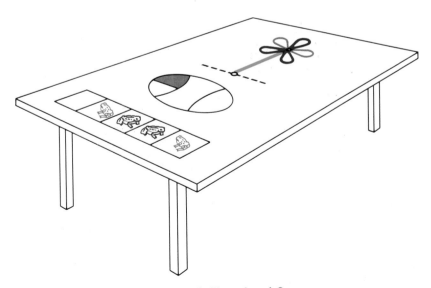

Figure 11. A Gallimaufry of Games.

Left and Right will soon return to the table shown in Fig. 11, on which they have been playing the sum of three games, namely Hackenbush Hotchpotch, Col, and Toads-and-Frogs. You can be sure that they will be unable to agree whose turn it was to move. Will it matter?

WHO WINS SUMS OF UPS, DOWNS, STARS AND NUMBERS?

A 5-place Toads-and-Frogs position with any number of lanes has a value which is the sum of terms from

$$0, \ 1, \ -1, \ \tfrac{1}{2}, \ -\tfrac{1}{2}, \ *, \ \uparrow \text{ and } \downarrow$$

To work out who wins we need rules telling us when such a sum is positive, negative, zero or fuzzy. Using the equations $* + * = 0$, and $\downarrow = -\uparrow$, any such sum reduces to a form $x + n . \uparrow$ or $x + n . \uparrow + *$, where x is a number and n an integer which may be positive, negative or zero. The rules (valid for arbitrary numbers x) are:

If x is any number, then $x + n . \uparrow$ is
positive, if x is positive, *or* x is zero and $n \geqslant 1$;
negative, if x is negative, *or* x is zero and $n \leqslant -1$;
and *zero*, only if x and n are both zero.

If x is any number, then $x + n . \uparrow + *$ is
positive, if x is positive, *or* x is zero and $n \geqslant 2$;
negative, if x is negative, *or* x is zero and $n \leqslant 2$;
and *fuzzy*, if x is zero and $n = -1, 0$ or 1.

In these rules, $n . \uparrow$ denotes the sum of n copies of $\uparrow$, or $-n$ copies of $\downarrow$. We usually abbreviate $2 . \uparrow$ to $\Uparrow$, and write $\Uparrow *$ for $\Uparrow + *$, etc.

The proofs require only the observations we have already made that $*$ is fuzzy and $\uparrow$ positive and that both are dominated by any positive number, together with the observations that $\uparrow *$ is fuzzy but $\Uparrow * = \uparrow + \uparrow + *$ is positive.

To see that $\uparrow *$ is fuzzy we need only observe that from the equivalent form $\{0, * | 0\}$ each player has a (winning) move to 0. From

$$\Uparrow * = \overset{\uparrow}{\{0 | *\}} + \overset{\uparrow}{\{0 | *\}} + \overset{*}{\{0 | 0\}} .$$

Right's only options are to replace a component $\uparrow$ by $*$, leaving a total of $\uparrow + * + * = \uparrow$, or to replace $*$ by 0, leaving $\Uparrow$. Since these are both positive, Right has no winning option, so that $\Uparrow * \geqslant 0$. Since $\Uparrow$ is positive it cannot equal $*$, so $\Uparrow *$ must be strictly positive. In fact Left wins by replacing $*$ by 0, leaving the positive remainder $\Uparrow$.

A CLOSER LOOK AT THE STARS

We have now acquired a better idea of how fuzzy $*$ really is, for we have shown that it is *less than* $\Uparrow = \uparrow + \uparrow$, *greater than* $\Downarrow = \downarrow + \downarrow$, but *confused with* each of $\downarrow, 0, \uparrow$. The cloud under which it is hiding, see Fig. 12, although it covers only one *number*, 0, can now be seen to have a radius of at least $\uparrow$.

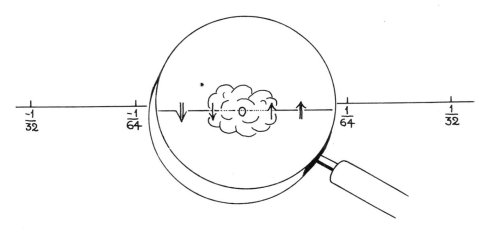

Figure 12. Star, Seen Through a Glass, Darkly.

We can examine other small games using similar devices. Fig. 13(a) shows $\uparrow *$, obtained by adding $\uparrow$ to Fig. 12. Figure 13(b) will serve for any $*n$ with $n \geqslant 2$.

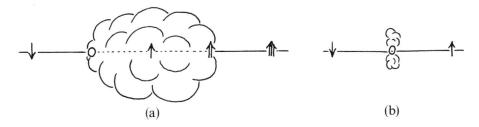

(a)   (b)

Figure 13. The Whereabouts of $\uparrow *$ and of $*n$ ($n \geqslant 2$).

THE VALUES $\{\uparrow|\uparrow\}$ AND $\{0|\uparrow\}$

In more complicated positions, $\uparrow$ and $\downarrow$ frequently arise as options. For example, we have already seen that $\{\uparrow|\downarrow\} = \{\uparrow|0\} = \{0|\downarrow\} = *$, and enquired about the position $\{\uparrow|\uparrow\}$.

The value $\{0|\uparrow\}$ arises from the 7-place Toads-and-Frogs position of Fig. 14, in which the four positions marked 0 may be checked to be second player wins. How big are $\{\uparrow|\uparrow\}$ and $\{0|\uparrow\}$?

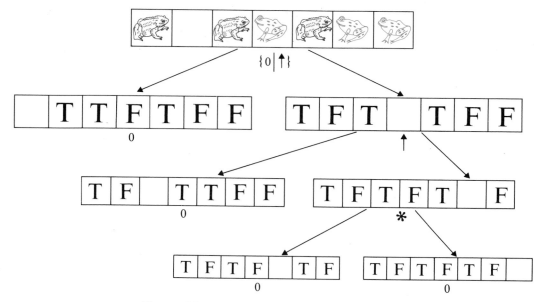

Figure 14. Up Among the Toads and Frogs.

We first examine $\{\uparrow|\uparrow\} = X$, say. Right's option of $\uparrow$ will only be reversible if there is some $\uparrow^L \geqslant X$, i.e. if $0 \geqslant X$, which we know is false. As a Left option, $\uparrow$ will be reversible if there is some $\uparrow^R \leqslant X$, i.e. if $* \leqslant X$, which is true since

$$* = \{0|0\} \leqslant \{\uparrow|\uparrow\} = X.$$

So we can bypass, replacing $\uparrow$ by $*^L = 0$, to obtain $X = \{0|\uparrow\}$, the value of Fig. 14, proving that our two questions were the same. Since 0 has no right option there will be no further simplification.

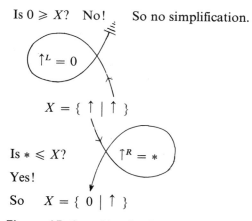

Figure 15. Searching for Reversible Moves.

For a general X, each player must ask if to any one of his opponent's options from X he has a response Y which is at least as good for him as X was. If so, he replaces that option by the list of all his opponent's options from Y. Figure 15 shows a graphical way of asking these questions that we have often found useful. The arrows are curved so as to remind us which players make which of the moves we hope to bypass.

THE UPSTART EQUALITY

How big is $X = \{0|\uparrow\}$ on our microscopic scale? It is certainly less than $4.\uparrow$ (the sum of 4 copies of $\uparrow$), since in the difference $X + 4.\downarrow$, Right can move from X to $\uparrow$ at his first opportunity and there will be at least two $\downarrow$ components, even after cancelling $\uparrow$ with $\downarrow$. By a similar move Right can win $X + 3.\downarrow$ if he moves first. However, Left can also win this moving first if he replaces $\downarrow$ by $*$, leaving

$$
\begin{array}{cccc}
X & \downarrow & \downarrow & * \\
\end{array}
$$
$$
X + \Downarrow* = \{0|\uparrow\} + \{*|0\} + \{*|0\} + \{0|0\}.
$$

To see this, recall that we already know that X, alias $\{\uparrow|\uparrow\}$, is strictly greater than $\uparrow*$, so Left wins if Right replaces a $\downarrow$ by 0, while if Right replaces $*$ by 0, Left can win by replacing a $\downarrow$ by $*$. Right's only other option is from X to $\uparrow$ leaving a fuzzy total of $\downarrow*$.

The argument has shown that X is confused with $3.\uparrow$, and so with $\Uparrow$ and $\uparrow$, since even from $X + \downarrow$ Left has a winning move (to $X + *$). We now know all order relations between X and values of the form $n.\uparrow$. How does it compare with values $n.\uparrow + *$? Since it is greater than $\uparrow*$ we compare it with $\Uparrow*$. In the difference $X + \Downarrow*$, displayed above, we have already dismissed all Right's options. However, Left's option from X leaves the negative total $\Downarrow*$; his option from $\downarrow$ leaves the fuzzy total $X + * + \downarrow + * = X + \downarrow$, while that from $*$ leaves another fuzzy total $X + \Downarrow$, so all Left's options can be dismissed too! This gives us the remarkable identity

$$
\boxed{\{0|\uparrow\} = \uparrow + \uparrow + * = \Uparrow*.}
$$

The theory of partizan games is notable for the occurrence of such surprising identities. Although the pattern in Table 3 extends naturally in both directions, some of the middle entries are far

$3.\downarrow = \{\Downarrow*|0\}$	$3.\downarrow+* = \{\Downarrow|0\}$	$3.\downarrow+*n = \{\Downarrow*m|0\}$
$\Downarrow \;\; = \{\downarrow*|0\}$	$\Downarrow* \;\;\; = \{\downarrow|0\}$	$\Downarrow*n \;\;\; = \{\downarrow*m|0\}$
$\downarrow \;\; = \{*|0\}$	$\downarrow* \;\;\; = \{0|0,*\}$	$\downarrow*n \;\;\; = \{*m|0\}$
$0 \;\; = \{\;|\;\}$	$* \;\;\; = \{0|0\}$	
$\uparrow \;\; = \{0|*\}$	$\uparrow* \;\;\; = \{0,*|0\}$	$\uparrow*n \;\;\; = \{0|*m\}$
$\Uparrow \;\; = \{0|\uparrow*\}$	$\Uparrow* \;\;\; = \{0|\uparrow\}$	$\Uparrow*n \;\;\; = \{0|\uparrow*m\}$
$3.\uparrow = \{0|\Uparrow*\}$	$3.\uparrow+* = \{0|\Uparrow\}$	$3.\uparrow+*n = \{0|\Uparrow*m\}$

Table 3. Simplest Forms for Ups and Stars.

from immediately obvious. In the last column $*n$ denotes the nimber $\{0,*,\ldots,*(n-1)|0,*,\ldots,*(n-1)\}$ for some $n \geqslant 2$ and $m = n \overset{*}{+} 1$; $\uparrow *n$ denotes $\uparrow + *n$, etc.

In particular, these relationships allow us to obtain a tractable expression for Toads-and-Frogs positions of the form

$$(TF)^x T \,\square\,(TF)^n F.$$

Omar will already notice that the Toad move gives a position of value 0; our less assiduous readers will find that this is a consequence of a more general result in Chapter 5. If follows that

$$(TF)^x T \,\square\,(TF)^n F = \{0|(TF)^{x+1} T \,\square\,(TF)^{n-1} F\}$$

which equals $n.\uparrow + (n+1).*$ by induction on n (and doesn't depend on x).

GIFT HORSES

The following principle often makes it easy to check one's guess about the value of a position:

It does not affect the value of G
if we add a new Left option H provided $H \lhd\!| \ G$,
or a new Right option $\overline{H}$ provided $\overline{H} \ |\!\rhd\ G$.

THE GIFT HORSE PRINCIPLE

The new options H or $\overline{H}$ are the **gift horses**; although they may appear to be useful presents, the recipient who looks them in the mouth will find that they have no teeth. For in the difference game

$$\{G^L,H|G^R\}+\{-G^R|-G^L\},$$
$$(-G)$$

if H is a gift horse, Left will find no joy in moving to the difference $H-G \lhd\!| \ 0$, and the other options for Left and Right cancel each other as in the Tweedledum and Tweedledee Argument.

Thus, we know that $\{0|\!\uparrow\} = \Uparrow\!*$ is confused with $\uparrow$, so $\uparrow$ will make a fine gift horse for Left; $\{0|\!\uparrow\} = \{0,\uparrow|\!\uparrow\}$. Since Left's old option 0 becomes dominated in the new form, we can deduce $\{0|\!\uparrow\} = \{\uparrow|\!\uparrow\}$ more simply than we did before. In fact we have $\Uparrow\!* \parallel \Uparrow$ and $\Uparrow\!* \parallel 3.\uparrow$ and so by a similar argument

$$\Uparrow\!* = \{0|\!\uparrow\} = \{\uparrow|\!\uparrow\} = \{\Uparrow|\!\uparrow\} = \{3.\uparrow|\!\uparrow\}.$$

On the other hand $\Uparrow\!* < 4.\uparrow$, so the latter would *not* be a mere gift horse for Left, and indeed $\{4.\uparrow|\!\uparrow\}$ is strictly greater than $\Uparrow\!*$.

EXTRAS

THE NIM-ADDITION RULE IN SEVERAL VARIATIONS

If you think about the way the nim-addition table (Table 2) extends, you'll see that

$$\text{if } a \text{ and } b \text{ are less than } 2^k,$$
$$\text{then so is } a \overset{*}{+} b, \text{ and}$$
$$2^k \overset{*}{+} a = 2^k + a.$$

From this you can deduce that

> the nim-sum of a number of different powers of 2
> is their ordinary sum, and, of course,
> the nim-sum of two equal numbers is zero.

THE BASICS OF NIM-ADDITION

You can use these two basic properties to find the nim-sum of any collection of numbers by writing each of them as a sum of distinct powers of 2 and then cancelling repetitions in pairs. For example,

$$5 \overset{*}{+} 3 = (4+1) \overset{*}{+} (2+1) = 4 \overset{*}{+} \cancel{1} \overset{*}{+} 2 \overset{*}{+} \cancel{1} = 4 \overset{*}{+} 2 = 4+2 = 6,$$

$$11 \overset{*}{+} 22 \overset{*}{+} 33 = (8+\cancel{2}+\cancel{1}) \overset{*}{+} (16+4+\cancel{2}) \overset{*}{+} (32+\cancel{1}) = 8+16+4+32 = 60.$$

These could also be written directly in terms of nimbers,

$$*5 + *3 = *6 \quad \text{and} \quad *11 + *22 + *33 = *60,$$

and you should get used to working in either notation:

$$*9 + *25 + *49 = (*8 + *\cancel{1}) + (*16 + *8 + *\cancel{1}) + (*32 + *\cancel{16} + *1) = *32 + *1 = *33.$$

This way of calculating shows you that

> the nim-sum is less than or equal to the ordinary sum,
> and they differ by an even number.

SEE HOW THE SUMS COMPARE AND HAVE COMMON PARITY

The textbooks usually say "write the numbers in binary and add without carrying" which comes to the same thing:

75

```
            4 2 1                 32 16 8 4 2 1                 32 16 8 4 2 1
           ------                ----------------              ----------------
       5 = 1 0 1           11 =          1 0 1 1          9 =          1 0 0 1
       3 =   1 1           22 =       1  0 1 1 0         25 =       1  1 0 0 1
           ------          33 = 1     0  0 0 0 1         49 = 1     1  0 0 0 1
       6 = 1 1 0                ----------------              ----------------
                           60 = 1     1  1 1 0 0         33 = 1     0  0 0 0 1
```

But since you don't want to be scribbling on bits of paper, you should use our way, which makes it easy to do the sums in your head, and is less prone to error.

WYT QUEENS AND WYTHOFF'S GAME

Table 4 gives the nimbers for various possible positions of Wyt Queens.

	0	1	2	3	4	5	6	7	8	9	10	11	12	13	14	15	16	17
0	0	*1	*2	*3	*4	*5	*6	*7	*8	*9	*10	*11	*12	*13	*14	*15	*16	*17
1	*1	*2	0	*4	*5	*3	*7	*8	*6	*10	*11	*9	*13	*14	*12	*16	*17	*15
2	*2	0	*1	*5	*3	*4	*8	*6	*7	*11	*9	*10	*14	*12	*13	*17	*15	*16
3	*3	*4	*5	*6	*2	0	*1	*9	*10	*12	*8	*7	*15	*11	*16	*18	*14	*13
4	*4	*5	*3	*2	*7	*6	*9	0	*1	*8	*13	*12	*11	*16	*15	*10	*19	*18
5	*5	*3	*4	0	*6	*8	*10	*1	*2	*7	*12	*14	*9	*15	*17	*13	*18	*11
6	*6	*7	*8	*1	*9	*10	*3	*4	*5	*13	0	*2	*16	*17	*18	*12	*20	*14
7	*7	*8	*6	*9	0	*1	*4	*5	*3	*14	*15	*13	*17	*2	*10	*19	*21	*12
8	*8	*6	*7	*10	*1	*2	*5	*3	*4	*15	*16	*17	*18	0	*9	*14	*12	*19
9	*9	*10	*11	*12	*8	*7	*13	*14	*15	*16	*17	*6	*19	*5	*1	0	*2	*3
10	*10	*11	*9	*8	*13	*12	0	*15	*16	*17	*14	*18	*7	*6	*2	*3	*1	*4
11	*11	*9	*10	*7	*12	*14	*2	*13	*17	*6	*18	*15	*8	*19	*20	*21	*4	*5

Table 4. Nimbers for Wyt Queens.

Most of the entries are chaotic, but Wythoff's **Difference Rule** is that the *zero* entries have coordinates

$$(0,0), \quad (1,2), \quad (3,5), \quad (4,7), \quad (6,10), \quad (8,13), \quad (9,15), \quad (11,18), \quad \ldots$$

with differences

$$0, \quad 1, \quad 2, \quad 3, \quad 4, \quad 5, \quad 6, \quad 7, \quad \ldots$$

the first number in every pair being the smallest number that hasn't yet appeared. He also showed that the nth pair is

$$([n\tau], [n\tau^2]) \qquad n = 0,1,2,\ldots$$

where τ is the golden number

$$\frac{1+\sqrt{5}}{2}.$$

ANSWERS TO FIGS. 8, 9 AND 11.

Now that we know that $\{0|*\} = \uparrow$, $\{*|0\} = \downarrow$ and $\{\uparrow|\downarrow\} = *$ we can fill in the values of the positions in the first two rows of Fig. 8. Then in the easy big game of Toads-and-Frogs shown in Fig. 9, the values of the 9 lanes are $*$, 0, $\uparrow$, $\frac{1}{2}$, $*$, -1, $*$, $\frac{1}{2}$ and $\uparrow$, whose total is $\Uparrow*$, a win for Toads. But if Left has to play first, he must be careful and move in one of the star lanes, either in the starting position of lanes 1 or 7 to make the value $3.\uparrow$, or in the middle lane, making the value $\Uparrow$.

In our Gallimaufry of Games (Fig. 11) the Hackenbush position has the value $\uparrow*$; the Col position $1*$; and the Toads-and-Frogs position -1. In their sum, 1 and -1 cancel, as do the two stars, leaving simply $\uparrow$. This is a win for Left, no matter who starts.

TOAD VERSUS FROG

A special case of Toads-and-Frogs which we can analyze completely is when each lane contains just one toad and one frog. After some moves we might find that the toad confronts the frog, so that either could jump over the other into an empty space just beyond. We then have

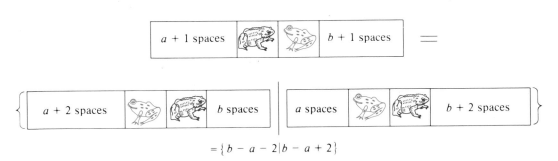

$$= \{b - a - 2 \mid b - a + 2\}$$

since after either jump is made we can see exactly how many moves each creature has left to make. So for such positions the value is $\{d-2 \mid d+2\}$ where d is the difference

(number of spaces to right of frog) $-$ (number of spaces to left of toad).

This rule also works if either of these parentheses is 0. In the general position before confrontation there will be c spaces between the two creatures and a move by either player will shorten this gap to $c-1$ and decrease d by 1, if a toad move, increase it by 1 if a frog move. So in Table 5 the Left and Right options for each entry are the entries left and right of it in the row above, for $c = 1,2,3,\ldots$ while for $c = 0$ they are $d-2$ and $d+2$.

Using this rule to compute the entries it is easy to see that the rows continue to alternate. In the position of Fig. 16 the values of the lanes are, in order, 1, $*$, $-\frac{1}{2}$, 0 and $-\frac{1}{2}$, which add to $*$, so that either player can win by moving in the second lane. Can the reader find Left's only other winning move?

d	...	-4	-3	-2	-1	0	1	2	3	4	...
$c = 0$	...	-3	-2	-1	0	0	0	1	2	3	...
$c = 1$	...	-3	-2	-1	$-\frac{1}{2}$	$*$	$\frac{1}{2}$	1	2	3	...
$c = 2$	...	-3	-2	-1	0	0	0	1	2	3	...
$c = 3$	...	-3	-2	-1	$-\frac{1}{2}$	$*$	$\frac{1}{2}$	1	2	3	...

Table 5. Toad Approaching Frog.

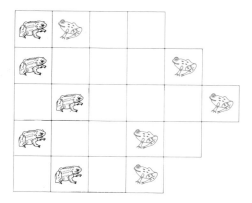

Figure 16. A 5-lane Game of Toad versus Frog.

TWO THEOREMS ON SIMPLIFYING GAMES

We prove that by omitting all dominated options and bypassing reversible ones we really do obtain the absolutely simplest form of any game with finitely many positions. For suppose that G and H are games which have the same value, but that neither of them has any position with dominated or reversible options. Then we shall prove that for every option of G there is an equal option of H, for the same player, and vice versa, so that G and H are not only equal in value, but identical in form.

Since the difference game

$$G - H = \{G^L | G^R\} + \{-H^R | -H^L\}$$

is a second player win, Right must have some winning response

$$G^{LR} - H \leqslant 0 \quad \text{or} \quad G^L - H^L \leqslant 0$$

to any one of Left's options $G^L - H$. The first case would imply $G^{LR} \leqslant H = G$, making G^L a reversible move from G, so that for every G^{L_0} there must be some $H^{L_0} \geqslant G^{L_0}$. By a similar argument there must be some $G^{L_1} \geqslant H^{L_0} (\geqslant G^{L_0})$ and since there are no dominated options, in fact $G^{L_1} = H^{L_0} = G^{L_0}$. The argument works equally well if we interchange G with H or Left with Right.

Our second theorem is that from the simplest form one can obtain any other form by adding gift horses and then perhaps deleting some dominated options. For if $G = \{G^L|G^R\}$ is the simplest form of some game $H = \{H^L|H^R\}$, we can prove as before that Right's winning move from $G^L - H$ must be to some game $G^L - H^L \leqslant 0$ (rather than some $G^{LR} - H \leqslant 0$).

This proves that for each G^L there is some $H^L \geqslant G^L$, and similarly for each G^R, some $H^R \leqslant G^R$. Also for every H^L we must have $H^L \lhd\!| H$ and for every $H^R, H^R |\!\rhd H$, since neither player can have a winning move from $H - H = 0$. The last sentence shows that the options of H will serve as gift horses for G, so that

$$G = \{G^L, H^L | G^R, H^R\}$$

by the Gift Horse Principle. In this form each option G^L or G^R is dominated by some H^L or H^R and so may be omitted.

BERLEKAMP'S RULE FOR HACKENBUSH STRINGS

Here's how to find a Hackenbush string for a given number. The color of the edge which touches the ground is taken from the sign of the number, so that positive numbers start with a blue edge and negative with a red one. We'll just do the positive case.

Write the fractional part of the number in binary; thus

$$3\tfrac{5}{8} = 3{\cdot}101.$$

Then, to find the Hackenbush string, replace the integer part by a string of L's, the point by

$$LR$$

and convert 1's and 0's after the point into L's and R's, but *omitting the final digit*, 1:

$$\begin{array}{cccccccc} 3\tfrac{5}{8} = & 3 & & \cdot & & 1 & 0 & 1 \\ & \text{L} \quad \text{L} \quad \text{L} & & \text{LR} & & \text{L} & \text{R} & \end{array}$$

Of course,

$$-3\tfrac{5}{8} = \text{R} \quad \text{R} \quad \text{R} \qquad \text{RL} \qquad \text{R} \quad \text{L}.$$

The rule actually works even for real numbers which don't terminate, except that there is then no final 1 to be omitted. E.g.,

$$\begin{array}{ccccccccc} \tfrac{1}{3} = & 0 & & \cdot & & 0 & 1 & 0 & 1 & 0 & 1 & \ldots \\ & \text{L} & & \text{R} & & \text{R} & \text{L} & \text{R} & \text{L} & \text{R} & \text{L} & \ldots \end{array}$$

Of course, the rule can be reversed to convert any Blue-Red Hackenbush string to a number. For example:

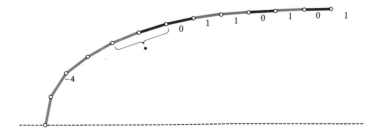

We write this as a string of L's and R's and replace the first pair of adjacent branches of different colors by a point, convert subsequent branches by the rule:

> a color agreeing with the grounded color becomes 1,
> a color opposite to the grounded color becomes 0,

and append an extra 1 bit at the end. Thus

$$\text{R} \quad \text{R} \quad \text{R} \quad \text{R} \qquad \text{R} \quad \text{L} \qquad \text{L} \quad \text{R} \quad \text{R} \quad \text{L} \quad \text{R} \quad \text{L}$$

becomes

$$-4 \qquad\qquad \cdot \qquad\quad 0 \quad 1 \quad 1 \quad 0 \quad 1 \quad 0 \quad 1$$

i.e.

$$-\left(4 \qquad + \qquad \frac{1}{4} + \frac{1}{8} + \frac{1}{32} + \frac{1}{128}\right) = -4\frac{53}{128}.$$

In certain applications when one wishes to store numbers whose distribution is known *a priori*, this Hackenbush number system may have significant advantages over the more conventional computer representations of fixed or floating point numbers.

REFERENCES AND FURTHER READING

Claude Berge, "The Theory of Graphs and its Applications", Methuen, London, 1962, p. 53.

E.R. Berlekamp, The Hackenbush number system for compression of numerical data, Information and Control, **26** (1974) 134–140.

Charles L. Bouton, Nim, a game with a complete mathematical theory, Ann. of Math., Princeton (2), **3** (1901–02) 35–39.

Ian G. Connell, Generalization of Wythoff's game, Canad. Math. Bull. **2** (1959) 181–190.

J.H. Conway, "On Numbers and Games", Academic Press, London and New York, 1976, Chapter 10.

H.S.M. Coxeter, The golden section, phyllotaxis and Wythoff's game, Scripta Math. **19** (1953) 135–143.

A.S. Fraenkel and I. Borosh, A generalization of Wythoff's game, J. Combin. Theory Ser. A, **15** (1973) 175–191.

P.M. Grundy, Mathematics and games, Eureka, **2** (1939) 6–8; reprinted *ibid.* **27** (1964) 9–11.

V.E. Hoggatt, Marjorie Bicknell-Johnson and Richard Sarsfield, A generalization of Wythoff's game, Fibonacci Quart. **17** (1979) 198–211.

V.E. Hoggatt and A.P. Hillman, A property of Wythoff pairs, Fibonacci Quart. **16** (1978) 472.

A.F. Horadam, Wythoff pairs, Fibonacci Quart. **16** (1978) 147–151.

J.G. Mauldon, Num, a variant of Nim with no first player win, Amer. Math. Monthly, **85** (1978) 575–578.

T.H. O'Beirne, "Puzzles and Paradoxes", Oxford University Press, London, 1965, pp. 131–139.

Robert Silber, A Fibonacci property of Wythoff pairs, Fibonacci Quart. **14** (1976) 380–384.

Robert Silber, Wythoff's Nim and Fibonacci representations, Fibonacci Quart. **15** (1977) 85–88.

R.P. Sprague, Über mathematische Kampfspiele, Tôhoku Math. J. **41** (1935–36) 438–444; Zbl. **13**, 290.

W.A. Wythoff, A modification of the game of Nim, Nieuw Archief voor Wiskunde (2), **7** (1905–07) 199–202.

Chapter 4

Taking and Breaking

He's up to these grand games, but one of these days I'll loore him on to skittles—and astonish him.
　　Henry J. Byron, *Our Boys.*

I'll live by Nym and Nym shall live by me; — Is not this just? — for I shall sutler be.
　　William Shakespeare, *King Henry* V, II, i.

KAYLES

In Fig. 1 we see Left and Right playing the old English game of Kayles. They have become so skilful at this game that they can bowl so as to take out any desired pin or any two adjacent ones. The game is played with light and well-spaced pins so that the world champion can do no

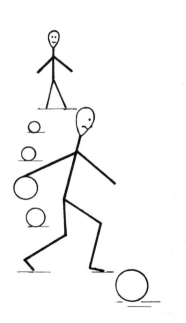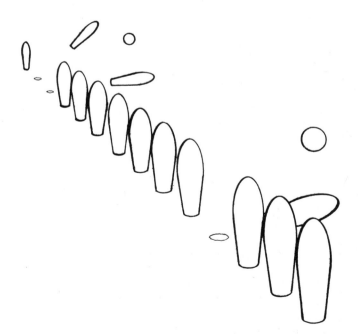

Figure 1. Playing Kayles.

81

better; it is impossible to knock down two pins separated by a greater distance. Whoever is unable to knock down a pin loses.

How shall we analyze this game? In the general position there are several rows of adjacent pins (e.g. rows of lengths 1, 7 and 3 in Fig. 1). Each move affects just one of these rows, of length n, say, and replaces it by two rows, whose lengths $a \geqslant 0$ and $b \geqslant 0$ add to $n-1$ or $n-2$. Rows of length 0 may be ignored. The possible moves from a row K_7 of length 7 are to:

$$K_6, \ K_5+K_1, \ K_4+K_2, \ K_3+K_3$$
$$K_5, \ K_4+K_1, \ K_3+K_2.$$

We can therefore play the same game on a table top with heaps of beans: each player, when it is his turn to move, may take 1 or 2 beans from a heap, and, if he likes, split what is left of that heap into two smaller heaps. We shall analyze Kayles in this form later in the chapter, and discover that Right, bowling in Fig. 1, is in a desperate situation.

Kayles was introduced by Dudeney and also by Sam Loyd, who called it Rip Van Winkle's Game.

GAMES WITH HEAPS

Consider any game played with a number of heaps in which each move affects *just one of the heaps* on the table, and in which exactly the same moves are available to each player. Any position in such a game is therefore the sum of its single heap positions, so the game is solved when we know the value of a heap of n beans for every n. Moreover, since the games are *impartial*, each such value is a Nim-heap, $*m$. In this chapter we'll usually omit the stars, so if heaps of sizes 0,1,2,3,... have values $*a, *b, *c, *d,...$ we shall say that the game has the **nim-sequence**

$$a.bcd...$$

(sometimes we omit the decimal point) and refer to

$$\mathcal{G}(0) = a, \qquad \mathcal{G}(1) = b, \qquad \mathcal{G}(2) = c, \qquad \mathcal{G}(3) = d, \qquad ...$$

as the **(nim-)values**. Using the information contained in the nim-sequence, we can analyze any position.

The nim-value of a sum of heaps of sizes

$$i, \qquad j, \qquad k, \qquad ...$$

is the nim-sum

$$\mathcal{G}(i) \overset{*}{+} \mathcal{G}(j) \overset{*}{+} \mathcal{G}(k) \overset{*}{+} ...$$

and each nim-value, $\mathcal{G}(n)$, is computed as the least one of 0,1,2,3,... that is *not* the nim-value of any option from a heap of size n. As in Chapter 3 we shall call the least number (from 0,1,2,3,...) which is *missing* from a set $\{x,y,z,...\}$ the **mex** (**m**inimal **ex**cluded number) of that set. Thus

$$\text{mex}(0,1,3,7) = 2, \qquad \text{mex}(2,4,5) = 0$$

and the mex of the empty set is 0.

$\mathscr{P}$-POSITIONS AND $\mathscr{N}$-POSITIONS

Impartial games can only have *two* outcome classes which we call

$\mathscr{P}$-positions (Previous player winning), and
$\mathscr{N}$-positions (Next player winning).

In this chapter we'll frequently be working with nimbers, so you'll need to know that

a value of 0   indicates a $\mathscr{P}$-position, while
values $*,*2,*3,\ldots$ indicate $\mathscr{N}$-positions.

No other value is possible for an impartial game. But remember that if you're going to add up your games, you'll need to know the exact value, and not just the outcome class, of each component.

SUBTRACTION GAMES

We might modify the game of Nim by requiring that in any move the number of beans taken is at most three. This will mean that for the nim-values we have

$$\mathscr{G}(n) = \mathrm{mex}(\mathscr{G}(n-1), \mathscr{G}(n-2), \mathscr{G}(n-3)),$$

so that the nim-sequence is

$$n = 0\ 1\ 2\ 3\ 4\ 5\ 6\ 7\ 8\ 9\ \ldots$$
$$\mathscr{G}(n) = 0.1\ 2\ 3\ 0\ 1\ 2\ 3\ 0\ 1\ \ldots$$

and a single heap is a $\mathscr{P}$-position (previous player winning) just if its size is a multiple of 4. We could instead allow a heap to be reduced by any number up to k, when the nim-sequence would be

$$n = 0\ 1\ 2\ \ldots\ k-1\ \ k\ \ k+1\ \ k+2\ \ldots\ \ \ 2k\ \ \ 2k+1\ \ 2k+2\ \ 2k+3\ \ldots$$
$$\mathscr{G}(n) = 0.1\ 2\ \ldots\ k-1\ \ k\ \ \ \ 0\ \ \ \ \ \ 1\ \ \ \ldots\ k-1\ \ \ \ k\ \ \ \ \ \ 0\ \ \ \ \ \ \ 1\ \ \ \ldots$$

and a single heap would be a $\mathscr{P}$-position just if its size were a multiple of $k+1$.

These results are well known and easily discovered so that it might be wise to play a game whose theory is less obvious. For example the game in which a heap may be reduced only by taking 2, 5 or 6 beans from it. In this case

$$\mathscr{G}(n) = \mathrm{mex}(\mathscr{G}(n-2), \mathscr{G}(n-5), \mathscr{G}(n-6))$$

and the nim-sequence is found to be

$$n = 0\ \ 1\ \ 2\ \ 3\ \ 4\ \ 5\ \ 6\ \ 7\ \ 8\ \ 9\ \ 10\ 11\ 12\ 13\ 14\ 15\ 16\ 17\ 18\ldots$$
$$\mathscr{G}(n) = \overset{.}{0}.0\ \ 1\ \ 1\ \ 0\ \ 2\ \ 1\ \ 3\ \ 0\ \ 2\ \ \overset{.}{1}\ \ 0\ \ 0\ \ 1\ \ 1\ \ 0\ \ 2\ \ 1\ \ 3\ \ldots$$

where the dots indicate that the first eleven values repeat indefinitely, so a single heap is a $\mathscr{P}$-position only if its size is congruent to 0, 1, 4 or 8, modulo 11. But of course we can also analyze positions with arbitrarily many heaps. Let us find all winning moves from the position with three heaps of sizes

5, 7, 9   values   2, 3, 2.

In Nim, the winning moves from the position

$$2, \ 3, \ 2$$

are to

$$1, \ 3, \ 2 \quad or \quad 2, \ 0, \ 2 \quad or \quad 2, \ 3, \ 1 \ .$$

So by subtracting 2, 5 or 6 we must achieve a change from

> the 5-heap to one of value 1, that is a 3-heap $(5-2=3)$,
> or the 7-heap to one of value 0, that is a 1-heap $(7-6=1)$,
> or the 9-heap to one of value 1, that is a 3-heap $(9-6=3)$.

More generally, for any **subtraction set**

$$\{s_1, s_2, s_3, \ldots\}$$

we can define the corresponding **subtraction game** $S(s_1, s_2, s_3, \ldots)$ in which a heap may be reduced only by one of the numbers $s_1, s_2, s_3, \ldots$. Table 1 gives the nim-sequences for some of these games.

For the subtraction game $S(2,5,6)$ we find that $\mathscr{G}(n)$ is never equal to $\mathscr{G}(n-9)$, so the game $S(2,5,6,9)$ has the same nim-sequence since adjoining $\mathscr{G}(n-9)$ never alters the mex. More generally, if for the subtraction set $\{s_1, s_2, \ldots, s_k\}$ we find another number s with the property that $\mathscr{G}(n)$ is never equal to $\mathscr{G}(n-s)$ we can adjoin s to the subtraction set without affecting the nim-sequence. Such optional extras are shown in parentheses in Table 1 which therefore displays the nim-sequences for all cases with numbers up to 7.

Table 1. Nim-Sequences for Subtraction Games.

Subtraction set (with optional extras)	nim-sequence	period
1(3 5 7 9 11 …)	0̇101̇…	2
2(6 10 14 18 …)	0̇011̇0011…	4
1 2(4 5 7 8 10 11 …)	0̇12̇012…	3
3(9 15 21 27 …)	0̇00111̇000111…	6
2 3(7 8 12 13 17 18 …)	0̇0112̇00112…	5
1 2 3(5 6 7 9 10 11 13 …)	0̇123̇0123…	4
4(12 20 28 36 …)	0̇0001111̇00001111…	8
1 4(6 9 11 14 16 19 …)	0̇1012̇01012…	5
2 4(3 8 9 10 14 15 16 …)	0̇01122̇001122…	6
3 4(10 11 17 18 24 25 …)	0̇0011120̇0001112…	7
1 3 4(6 8 10 11 13 15 17 …)	0̇1012320̇101232…	7
1 2 3 4(6 7 8 9 11 12 13 14 …)	0̇1234̇01234…	5
5(15 25 35 45 …)	0̇0000111110̇000011111…	10
2 5(9 12 16 19 23 26 …)	0̇0110210̇011021…	7
3 5(4 11 12 13 19 20 21 …)	0̇00111220̇0011122…	8
2 3 5(4 9 10 11 12 16 17 18 19 …)	0̇0112230̇011223…	7
4 5(13 14 22 23 31 32 40 …)	0̇0001111̇2000011112…	9
1 4 5(3 7 9 11 12 13 15 17 19 …)	0̇1012323̇01012323…	8
2 4 5(3 9 10 11 12 16 17 18 19 …)	0̇0112230̇011223…	7
1 2 3 4 5(7 8 9 10 11 13 14 15 16 …)	0̇123455̇012345…	6

Table 1. (*continued*)

Subtraction set (with optional extras)	nim-sequence	period
6(18 30 42 54 ...)	0000001111110000001111...	12
1 6(8 13 15 20 22 27 29 ...)	01010120101012...	7
1 2 6(5 8 9 12 13 15 16 19 20 ...)	01201230120123...	7
3 6(4 5 12 13 14 15 21 22 23 ...)	000111222000111222...	9
1 3 6(8 10 12 15 17 19 21 24 ...)	010101232010101232...	9
2 3 6(7 11 12 15 16 20 21 24 ...)	001120312001120312...	9
4 6(5 14 15 16 24 25 26 34 ...)	00001111220000111122...	10
2 4 6(3 5 10 11 12 13 14 18 19 ...)	0011223300112233...	8
1 2 4 6(7 9 10 12 14 15 17 18 20 ...)	0120123401201234...	8
5 6(16 17 27 28 38 39 49 50 ...)	0000011111200000111112...	11
1 5 6(3 8 10 12 14 16 17 19 21 ...)	0101012323201010123232...	11
2 5 6(9 13 16 17 20 24 27 28 ...)	0011021302100110213021...	11
2 3 5 6(4 10 11 12 13 14 18 19 ...)	0011223300112233...	8
1 4 5 6(3 8 10 12 13 14 15 17 19 ...)	010123234010123234...	9
1 2 4 5 6(8 9 11 12 14 15 16 18 19 ...)	01201234530120123453...	10
1 2 3 4 5 6(8 9 10 11 12 13 15 16 17 ...)	01234560123456...	7
7(21 35 49 63 ...)	0000000111111100000001...	14
2 7(11 16 20 25 29 34 ...)	001100112001100112...	9
3 7(13 17 23 27 33 37 ...)	00011102210001110221...	10
4 7(5 6 15 16 17 18 26 27 28 ...)	000011111222000011111222...	11
1 4 7(9 12 15 17 20 23 25 28 ...)	0101201201012012...	8
2 4 7(10 13 16 19 22 25 28 31 ...)	00112203102102...	3
3 4 7(5 6 13 14 15 16 17 23 24 ...)	00011122230001112223...	10
1 3 4 7(5 9 11 12 13 15 17 19 20 ...)	0101232301012323...	8
2 3 4 7(8 9 13 14 15 18 19 20 24 ...)	0011220314200112203142...	11
5 7(6 17 18 19 29 30 31 41 ...)	0000011111220000011111...	12
→ 2 5 7(11 15 17 20 24 27 29 33 ...)	0011021322031001122332...	22 ←
3 5 7(4 6 13 14 15 16 17 23 24 ...)	00011122230001112223...	10
2 3 5 7(4 6 11 12 13 14 15 16 20 ...)	001122334001122334...	9
2 4 5 7(3 6 11 12 13 14 15 16 20 ...)	001122334001122334...	9
6 7(19 20 32 33 45 46 58 ...)	0000001111112000000111...	13
1 6 7(3 5 9 11 13 15 17 18 19 ...)	0101012323230101012323...	12
2 6 7(11 15 19 20 24 28 32 33 ...)	0011001120312001100112...	13
1 2 6 7(4 9 10 12 14 15 17 18 20 ...)	0120123401201234...	8
3 6 7(4 5 13 14 15 16 17 23 24 ...)	00011122230001112223...	10
1 4 6 7(9 12 14 17 19 20 22 25 ...)	0101201232012010120123...	13
2 4 6 7(3 5 11 12 13 14 15 16 20 ...)	001122334001122334...	9
1 3 4 6 7(5 9 11 13 14 15 16 17 19 ...)	01012323450101232345...	10
2 5 6 7(10 14 17 18 19 22 26 29 ...)	0011021322300011021322...	12
1 2 5 6 7(4 9 10 12 13 15 16 17 18 ...)	0120123453401201234534...	11
1 4 5 6 7(3 9 11 13 14 15 16 17 19 ...)	01012323450101232345...	10
1 2 3 4 5 6 7(9 10 11 12 13 14 15 17 ...)	0123456701234567...	8

The table displays many regularities. For all entries except {2,4,7} the sequence is *exactly* periodic in the sense that $\mathscr{G}(n) = \mathscr{G}(n+p)$ for *all* values of $n \geq 0$. Moreover for every other entry except {2,5,7}, the period p is the sum of two numbers from the subtraction set. We feel that these features deserve explanation even though they occasionally fail. It is easy to prove that they hold for two-element subtraction sets and for sets in which $s_{i+1} \le s_i + s_1$.

There are obviously some new theorems waiting to be discovered. In Chapter 15 we shall analyze subtraction games $S(a,b,a+b)$ and we close here with a surprising result about *all* subtraction games:

FERGUSON'S PAIRING PROPERTY

T.S. Ferguson has observed and proved that there is a remarkable pairing between nim-values 0 and 1 in any subtraction game, namely

$\mathscr{G}(n) = 1$ if and only if $\mathscr{G}(n-s_1) = 0$, where s_1 is the least member of the subtraction set.

For example, the nim-sequence for $S(2,5,6)$,

0 0 1 1 0 2 1 3 0 2 1 0 0 1 1 0 2 1 ...

has its 0's and 1's paired as shown ($s_1 = 2$).

We can prove Ferguson's pairing property by obtaining a contradiction. If n is the *least* number for which the above boxed statement *fails*, we have *either*

$\mathscr{G}(n) = 1$　and　$\mathscr{G}(n-s_1) \ne 0$　　*or*　　$\mathscr{G}(n-s_1) = 0$　and　$\mathscr{G}(n) \ne 1$.

These respectively imply

$\mathscr{G}(n-s_1-s_k) = 0$ for some s_k,
which implies inductively
$\mathscr{G}(n-s_k) = 1$,
which implies
$\mathscr{G}(n) \ne 1$.

or

$\mathscr{G}(n-s_k) = 1$ for some s_k,
which implies inductively
$\mathscr{G}(n-s_k-s_1) = 0$,
which implies
$\mathscr{G}(n-s_1) \ne 0$.

In Chapter 13 we shall show how Ferguson uses this pairing to analyze subtraction games in misère play.

GRUNDY SCALES

Calculation of nim-sequences is often made easier if we use a **Grundy scale**. Figure 2 shows such a scale being used for the subtraction game $S(2,5,6)$. Successive values are written on squared paper and the arrowed entry is computed as the mex of the underlined entries, before the scale is moved on one place. Thus in Fig. 2, $\mathscr{G}(14) = 1$ is about to be computed as the mex of 0, 2 and 0. Boxwood scales like that in the figure are expensive, but a serviceable substitute can be made from a strip of squared paper.

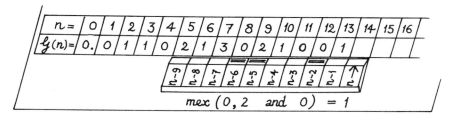

Figure 2. Using a Grundy Scale.

OTHER TAKE-AWAY GAMES

We can modify the rules slightly so as to obtain games with less regular behavior which can still be handled by the same methods, provided the rules are still such that only one heap is affected by any move. In the game called ·**123** the possible moves are to

remove a heap containing just *one* bean,
or remove *two* beans from any heap with *more than* two,
or remove *three* beans from *any* heap.

A heap of one has nim-value 1, since it may be reduced to zero, using the first kind of move. The restriction on the second kind of move implies that a heap of two has nim-value 0, since it cannot be removed. For heaps of three or more we can use the Grundy scale shown in Fig. 3, since either 2 or 3 beans may be removed.

We can see that the sequence has period 5 after the first few terms, and this property will persist: the scale now refers to the same numbers (1,0) as it did five steps ago and so we get the same answer, 2, for $\mathscr{G}(13)$ as we did for $\mathscr{G}(8)$.

$n =$	0	1	2	3	4	5	6	7	8	9	10	11	12	13	14	15
$\mathscr{G}(n) =$	0.	1	0	2	2	1	0	0	2	1	1	0	0			

Figure 3. The Nim-Sequence for ·**123**.

Figure 4. Ready for a Game of Dawson's Chess.

DAWSON'S CHESS

T.R. Dawson invented a game, which, as modified in Guy and Smith, we shall call Dawson's Chess. It is played on a $3 \times n$ chessboard with White pawns on the first rank and Black pawns on the third. Pawns move (forwards) and capture (diagonally) as in Chess; in this game capturing is obligatory and the winner in normal play is the last player to move. We shall see that "queening" can never arise in this game. For example, if White starts on a 3×8 board by advancing has a-pawn, Black must capture this with his b-pawn, White must then recapture with *his* b-pawn and the result is Fig. 5(a) in which the a-pawns are immobilized and it is Black's turn to move. If Black now advances his f-pawn, White must capture with his e- or g-pawn, which Black will recapture, and after two further recaptures we reach Fig. 5(b). Once again a pair of pawns is blocked and the player to move has changed. White may pass the turn back to Black by advancing his h-pawn, and so immobilizing yet another pair of pawns.

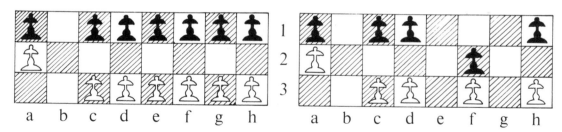

Figure 5. Playing Dawson's Chess on a 3×8 Chessboard.

In general the advance of a pawn is followed by pairs of captures until the neighboring files are empty, isolating an immobilized pair of pawns and passing the turn to the opposing player. So we can imagine the same game played by skilful players with rows of pins like Kayles. This time the rule is that any one pin may be taken out provided that its immediate neighbors, if any, are removed at the same time. The player unable to move because no pin remains is the loser. When recast in this way as a pin game, we can see that the game is impartial, even though the moves in the board game were different for the two players. Moreover as in Kayles the initial row of pins may become separated into independent rows and the value of the whole position will be the sum of the values of these.

The moves from a row of 11 pins leave rows of

$$9, \quad 8, \quad 7 \text{ and } 1, \quad 6 \text{ and } 2, \quad 5 \text{ and } 3, \quad \text{or} \quad 4 \text{ and } 4$$

pins, so that

$$\mathscr{G}(11) = \operatorname{mex}(\mathscr{G}(9), \mathscr{G}(8), \mathscr{G}(7) \overset{*}{+} \mathscr{G}(1), \mathscr{G}(6) \overset{*}{+} \mathscr{G}(2), \mathscr{G}(5) \overset{*}{+} \mathscr{G}(3), \mathscr{G}(4) \overset{*}{+} \mathscr{G}(4)).$$

With the natural conventions $\mathscr{G}(-1) = \mathscr{G}(0) = 0$, we have in general

$$\mathscr{G}(n) = \operatorname{mex}(\mathscr{G}(a) \overset{*}{+} \mathscr{G}(b)) \qquad \text{where} \quad -1 \leqslant a,b \quad \text{and} \quad a+b = n-3.$$

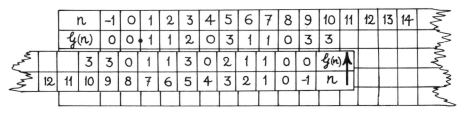

Figure 6. Calculating $\mathscr{G}(11)$ in Dawson's Chess.

A Grundy scale suitable for this calculation appears in Fig. 6. As the nim-values are computed they are entered both on the paper, and, in the reverse order, on the scale. Reading from the figure we see that $\mathscr{G}(11)$ is the mex of the nim-sums $\mathscr{G}(a) \overset{*}{+} \mathscr{G}(b)$ in the table

$$\begin{aligned}
\mathscr{G}(a) &= 0\ 0\ 1\ 1\ 2\ 0\ 3\ 1\ 1\ 0\ 3 \\
\mathscr{G}(b) &= 3\ 0\ 1\ 1\ 3\ 0\ 2\ 1\ 1\ 0\ 0 \\
\mathscr{G}(a) \overset{*}{+} \mathscr{G}(b) &= 3\ 0\ 0\ 0\ 1\ 0\ 1\ 0\ 0\ 0\ 3
\end{aligned}$$

whence $\mathscr{G}(11) = \operatorname{mex}(3,0,1) = 2$.

n	0	1	2	3	4	5	6	7	8	9		11		13		15		17		19		21		23		25		27		29		31		33
0.	**1**	1	2	0	3	1	1	0	3	3	2	2	**4**	0	5	2	2	3	3	0	1	1	3	0	2	1	1	0	4	5	**2**	**7**	**4**
34	0	1	1	2	0	3	1	1	0	3	3	2	2	4	4	5	5	2	3	3	0	1	1	3	0	2	1	1	0	4	5	3	7	4
68	**8**	1	1	2	0	3	1	1	0	3	3	2	2	4	4	5	5	**9**	3	3	0	1	1	3	0	2	1	1	0	4	5	3	7	4
102	8	1	1	2	0	3	1	1	0	3	3	2	2	4	4	5	5	9	3	3	0	1	1	3	0	2	1	1	0	4	5	3	7	4
136	8	1	1	...																														

Table 2. The Remarkable Periodicity of Dawson's Chess.

A persevering reader, armed with a very long Grundy scale, might find sufficient reward in the remarkable pattern that emerges (Table 2). If we disregard the seven exceptional numbers printed bold-face in the table, we find that the nim-values have period 34, and of course if this persists, we can regard ourselves as having solved the game completely.

Does it persist? In Fig. 7 we take a careful look at that very long Grundy scale, set to compute $\mathscr{G}(174)$, which is the first value we *don't* need to compute. As the scale is positioned, we can see two complete periods of 34 regular values between the innermost exceptional ones ($\mathscr{G}(51) = 2$: one is on the scale, the other on the paper). The calculation is exactly the same as it was for

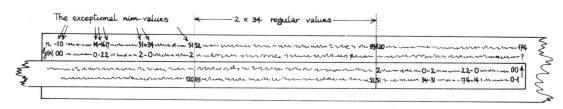

Figure 7. A Finicky Look at a Very Long Grundy Scale.

$\mathscr{G}(140)$, with the scale shifted back 34 places, except that 34 of the nim-sums of regular values are repeated. So the last value we need to compute in order to establish the periodicity, is $\mathscr{G}(173)$. The number 173 is obtained by doubling the last irregularity (51) and adding twice the period (34) together with the number 3, the largest number of pins that may be taken in a single move.

THE PERIODICITY OF KAYLES

It is slightly harder to use the Grundy scale for the original game of Kayles in which one or two adjacent pins may be removed from anywhere in the row, giving the equation

$$\mathscr{G}(n) = \operatorname{mex}(\mathscr{G}(a) \overset{*}{+} \mathscr{G}(b)) \qquad \text{where} \quad 0 \leqslant a,b \quad \text{and} \quad a+b = n-1 \quad or \quad n-2.$$

We could first align the scale and note down the nim-sums for $a+b = n-2$ and then realign it and adjoin those for $a+b = n-1$, before taking the mex. However, by placing the scale in an intermediate position we can read off all the nim-sums with one setting. The small arrows in Fig. 8 indicate exactly which pairs of numbers must be nimmed to calculate $\mathscr{G}(11)$. Reading them from left to right we find

$$\mathscr{G}(11) = \operatorname{mex}(2,4,5,0,3,0,1,0,2,5,0,5,2,0,1,0,3,0,5,4,2) = 6.$$

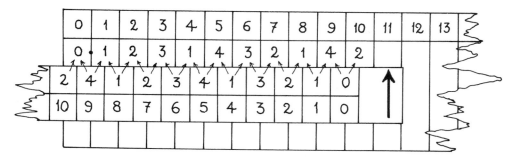

Figure 8. Grundy Skayles?

(The obvious symmetry means we need only examine half of this list, but calculation of the whole list provides a useful check when doing hand calculation.) The nim-values for Kayles also exhibit periodicity (see Table 3). This time we have period 12, but with 14 exceptional values, the last

n	0	1	2	3	4	5	6	7	8	9	10	11
0	**0** .	1	2	3	1	4	3	2	1	4	2	6
12	4	1	2	7	1	4	3	2	1	4	6	7
24	4	1	2	8	**5**	4	7	2	1	8	6	7
36	4	1	2	3	1	4	7	2	1	8	2	7
48	4	1	2	8	1	4	7	2	1	**4**	2	7
60	4	1	2	8	1	4	7	2	1	8	**6**	7
72	4	1	2	8	1	4	7	2	1	8	2	7
84	4	1	2	8	1	4	7	2	1	8	2	7
96	4	1	2	...								

Table 3. The Periodicity of the Nim-Values of Kayles.

of which is $\mathscr{G}(70) = 6$. The periodicity may be checked by verifying that it holds up to

$$n = 166 = 2(70) + 2(12) + 2.$$

since the last irregularity occurs at $n = 70$, the period is 12 and no move takes more than 2 pins.

OTHER TAKE-AND-BREAK GAMES

Let us turn Dawon's Chess into a game with heaps. Recall that in the form with pins a pin may only be removed along with its neighbors, so that:

A *single* pin may be removed just if it is the only pin in its row, and so leaves nothing behind.

Two pins may be removed only if they are the two pins at one end of a longer row or form a whole row by themselves, so their removal leaves either a shorter row or nothing at all.

Any *three* adjacent pins may be removed; their removal will usually leave two shorter rows, but may leave only one or none at all.

So if we play it with heaps of beans, the moves from a single heap must have the effect of replacing that heap by

0 heaps, if just *one* bean is removed,

1 or 0 heaps, if just *two* beans are removed, and

2, 1 or 0 heaps, if just *three* beans are removed.

We can symbolize such conditions by a code digit for each number of beans that may be removed. For Dawson's Chess these digits are

1	2^0	for removal of *one* bean,
3	$2^1 + 2^0$	for removal of *two* beans,
7	$2^2 + 2^1 + 2^0$	for removal of *three* beans,

and so the game may be written symbolically as ·**137**.

More generally, if in some game we remove k beans from a heap provided we partition what remains of that heap into just a or b or c or ... heaps (where $a,b,c,...$ are distinct) we give that game the code digit

$$\mathbf{d}_k = 2^a + 2^b + 2^c + ... \qquad \text{for removal of } k \text{ beans.}$$

In Kayles we can remove 1 or 2 beans in any way so as to replace some heap by 2 or 1 or 0 heaps, so that $d_1 = d_2 = 7$, since $2^2 + 2^1 + 2^0 = 7$. In Dawson's Chess we have seen that $d_1 = 1$, $d_2 = 3$ and $d_3 = 7$. For the game we called $\cdot 123$ we have $d_1 = 1$, $d_2 = 2$ and $d_3 = 3$. In general there is a game

$$\cdot d_1 d_2 d_3 \ldots$$

for any possible sequence of code digits. In this notation, Kayles itself is the game

$$\cdot 77 = \cdot 77000 \ldots$$

while Dawson's Chess is, as we have already seen,

$$\cdot 137 = \cdot 137000 \ldots$$

If the digit $d_k = 0$, there is no move removing exactly k beans. The subtraction games are those in which every code digit is 0 or 3 ($3 = 2^1 + 2^0$); for example $S(2,5,6)$ has the name $\cdot 030033$. Table 4 interprets the smallest values of d_k.

Value of d_k.	Conditions for removal of k beans from a single heap.
0	Not permitted.
1	If the beans removed are the whole heap.
2	Only if some beans remain and are left as a single heap.
3	Provided the remaining beans, if any, are left in one heap.
4	Only if some beans remain and are left as exactly two non-empty heaps.
5	Provided the remaining beans, if any, are left as two non-empty heaps.
6	Only if some beans remain and are left as one or two heaps.
7	Provided the remaining beans are left in at most two heaps.
8	Only if some beans remain and are left in just three non-empty heaps.
etc.	

Table 4. Interpretation of Code Digits for Take-and-Break Games.

DAWSON'S KAYLES

The particular case $\cdot 07$ corresponds to the bowling game in which the only legal move is to knock down *two* adjacent pins. We call this Dawson's Kayles because it is a sort of first cousin to Dawson's Chess ($\cdot 137$). In fact the nim-value, D_n, of a row of n pins in Dawson's Kayles is the same as that of the Dawson's Chess game with $n-1$ pairs of pawns:

$n =$	0	1	2	3	4	5	6	7	8	9	10	11	12	13	14	15	16	17	18	19	20	...
$D_n =$	0	.	0	1	1	2	0	3	1	1	0	3	3	2	2	4	0	5	2	2	3	3	...

Because its rules are slightly simpler than those for Dawson's Chess, it is Dawson's Kayles that arises most naturally in other contexts, and so in Chapters 8, 13, 15 and 16, the notation D_n refers to this variant.

VARIATIONS

The nim-sequences for these take-and-break games are often related to each other in various ways. The nim-values for ·**17**

$$n = \begin{array}{ccccccccccccccccccccc} 0 & 1 & 2 & 3 & 4 & 5 & 6 & 7 & 8 & 9 & 10 & 11 & 12 & 13 & 14 & 15 & 16 & 17 & 18 & 19 & 20 & \ldots \end{array}$$
$$\mathcal{G}(\cdot\mathbf{17}) = \begin{array}{ccccccccccccccccccccc} 0 & . & 1 & 1 & 0 & 2 & 1 & 3 & 0 & 1 & 1 & 3 & 2 & 2 & 3 & 4 & 1 & 5 & 3 & 2 & 2 & 3 & \ldots \end{array}$$

are obtained from those for Dawson's Kayles by nim-adding 1 when n is odd.

Some other cases show duplication or doubling of nim-values, as we'll see later.

GUILES

For many of these games the nim-values are easily calculated, using suitable Grundy scales and taking care with the early values. The possible moves in the game of Guiles are to remove a heap of 1 or 2 beans completely, or to take 2 beans from a sufficiently large heap and partition what remains into two smaller non-empty heaps. In short, it is the game ·**15**.

As usual, $\mathcal{G}(0) = 0$, and since the only moves from heaps of 1 or 2 remove them completely, we have $\mathcal{G}(1) = \mathcal{G}(2) = 1$. A heap of 3 admits no legal move and can take no part in the game; $\mathcal{G}(3) = 0$. For larger heaps we have

$$\mathcal{G}(n) = \operatorname{mex}(\mathcal{G}(a) \stackrel{*}{+} \mathcal{G}(b)) \qquad \text{where} \quad 1 \leqslant a,b \quad \text{and} \quad a+b = n-2,$$

and we can use the Grundy scale shown in Fig. 9. The nim-sequence is

$$0.1101122122110112212221110\ldots$$

in which the values after the point turn out to have period 10.

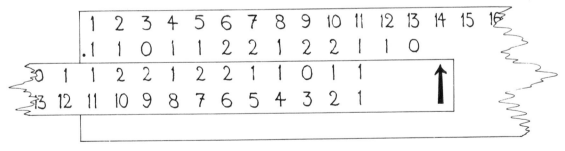

Figure 9. Guiles.

TREBLECROSS

is a Tic-Tac-Toe game played on a $1 \times n$ strip in which both players use the same symbol (X). The first person to complete a line of three consecutive crosses wins. How shall we analyze this game?

It's stupid to move next or next but one to a pre-existing cross, since your opponent wins immediately. If we consider only sensible moves we can therefore regard each X as also occupying

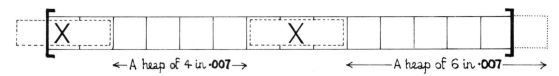

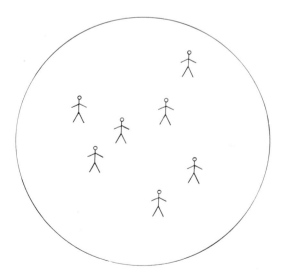

Figure 10. Treblecross is ·007 in Disguise.

the two neighbors of the square in which it lies (one of which may be off the board), and no two of these 3-square regions may overlap. Our treblecrosser is therefore only James Bond (·007) in disguise (see Fig. 10)! So writing X*n*X for a strip of *n* empty squares between X's, and using [and] for the ends of the board we have the values:

			[0]	[1]	[2]	[3]	[4]	[5]	[6]	[7]	[8]	[9]	[10]	[11]	[12]
Treblecross	X0]	X1]	X2]	X3]	X4]	X5]	X6]	X7]	X8]	X9]	X10]	X11]	X12]	X13]	X14]
		X2X	X3X	X4X	X5X	X6X	X7X	X8X	X9X	X10X	X11X	X12X	X13X	X14X	X15X	X16X
·007 heap		0	1	2	3	4	5	6	7	8	9	10	11	12	13	14
nim-value		0	0	0	1	1	1	2	2	0	3	3	1	1	1	0

OFFICERS

The take-and-break games often arise in other unexpected contexts. We shall see that both Kayles and Dawson's Kayles arise naturally in the theory of Dots and Boxes (Chapter 16) and Dawson's Kayles in the game Seating Families of Five (Chapter 8), a variation of the game we called Seating Couples in Chapter 2. Some other cases appear in our Chapter 17 on Spots and Sprouts, and we give a further example here.

Figure 11. A Seven-Man Army in Disarray.

The army has been in disarray and the General has reduced all officers to the ranks and made everyone directly responsible to him. He now intends, on the alternate advice of his military advisers, Left and Right, to recruit, from outside the army, a new hierarchy of officers.

Left and Right will alternately advise that some officer currently in direct charge of four or more officers and men should recruit a new subordinate. The new officer will be directly responsible to the one who appointed him, and will, until further notice, take over direct responsibility for three or more, but not all, of those officers and men previously directly responsible to his appointer. Of course the game must end when every officer has either 2 or 3 direct subordinates, and whichever of Left and Right gave the last advice retains the confidence of the General.

We can play the game with pencil and paper by drawing the men with a circle round them all to represent the General, as in Fig. 11. As each officer is recruited we draw a circle round all his subordinates. Figure 12 shows four different ways in which the first officer can be recruited for the seven-man army.

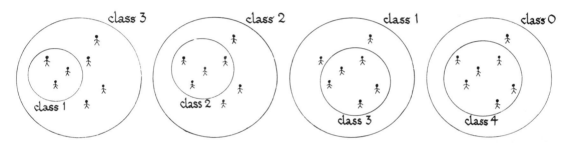

Figure 12. The First Recruit Takes Command of his Men.

For administrative purposes officers are classified, not according to rank, but according to their number of *direct* subordinates. A class n officer is directly responsible for just $n+2$ officers and men. So the General for the army in Fig. 11 is initially a class 5 officer, but after the first move his class will be reduced in one of the four ways indicated in Fig. 12.

Every move reduces the class of some officer from n to a and introduces a new officer of class b, where $a+b = n-1$, and b may not be 0. So the Officers game is equivalent to the take-and-break game ·6, in which one bean is removed from a heap and what remains of that heap must be left in exactly 2 or 1 non-empty heaps ($6 = 2^2 + 2^1$).

The initial nim-values for ·6, namely

```
0.0 1 2 0 1 2 3 1 2 3 4 0 3 4 2 1 3 2 1 0 2 1 4 5 1
4 5 1 2 0 1 2 3 1 2 3 4 2 3 4 2 3 4 2 1 0 2 8 4 5 3
4 5 6 2 5 1 2 3 1 2 3 4 2 3 4 2 3 4 2 3 0 ...
```

after starting with period 3, show a strong inclination towards a period of 26. Richard Austin computed as far as $\mathscr{G}(10342) = 256$; a complete analysis is still to be found.

Should the officers hold a ball in honor of the superb reorganization of their army, the game itself will provide an excellent waltz (N.B. one note spans the 7th and 8th bars).

The ·6 Waltz
(unfinished)

Melody by ·6. Arr. C.A.B. Smith
Key of 𝒢.

Words by Blanche Descartes

If I'm a—lone, all on my own, there I must al—ways st—a—y.

But if I touch an—oth—er such, I may be ta—ken a—wa—y.

And as a boon, this lit—tle tune shows you the right move to pla—y.

The val—ues 𝒢 quite baf—fle me; do they show per—io—di—ci—ty?

Pr'aps they just wan—der a—long aim—less—ly ...

We are indebted to the trustees of the estate of Blanche Descartes and to the publishers of *Eureka* for permission to reproduce The ·6 Waltz, and to make small changes in the words and the arrangement.

GRUNDY'S GAME

is a breaking game in which the only legal move is to split a single heap into two smaller ones of different sizes. Eventually all the heaps will have size 1 or 2 and can no longer be split, and the player who splits the last heap is the winner. You can use a Grundy scale to work out the values, provided you remember *not* to include the move which breaks a heap into two *equal* ones. Here are the first 101 nim-values:

$n =$	0–19	0 0 0 1 0 2 1 0 2 1	0 2 1 3 2 1 3 2 4 3
	20–39	0 4 3 0 4 3 0 4 1 2	3 1 2 4 1 2 4 1 2 4
	40–59	1 5 4 1 5 4 1 5 4 1	0 2 1 0 2 1 5 2 1 3
	60–79	2 1 3 2 4 3 2 4 3 2	4 3 2 4 3 2 4 3 2 4
	80–100	5 2 4 5 2 4 3 7 4 3	7 4 3 7 4 3 5 2 3 5 2 ....

The strong tendency to period 3 continues as far as the values have been calculated, but the series has not been proved to be periodic, despite extensive calculations by many people. In 1973 we computed more than a quarter of a million values and discovered some interesting phenomena we'll tell you about in the Extras. Variations on the game appear in Chapters 10, 13 and 14.

PRIM AND DIM

In **Prim** you may remove m beans from a heap of size n provided m and n are coprime (i.e. no number larger than 1 divides both m and n). In **Dim** you may take d beans from a heap of size n provided d divides n. Each game has two variants:

$$\text{Prim}^+ \text{ if 1 to 0 is legal; Prim}^- \text{ if not.}$$
$$\text{Dim}^+ \text{ if } n \text{ to 0 is legal; Dim}^- \text{ if not.}$$

Here are the nim-values:

n	0	1	2	3	4	5	6	7	8	9	10	11	12	13	14	15	...	$n>0$	...
Prim$^-$	0 .	0	1	2	1	3	1	4	1	2	1	5	1	6	1	2	...	j	...
Prim$^+$	0 .	1	0	2	0	3	0	4	0	2	0	5	0	6	0	2	...	j'	...
Dim$^-$	0 .	0	1	0	2	0	1	0	3	0	1	0	2	0	1	0	...	k	...
Dim$^+$	0 .	1	2	1	3	1	2	1	4	1	2	1	3	1	2	1	...	$k+1$	...

where the jth prime is the least prime divisor of n,

$\quad j'$ is obtained from j by swapping 0 and 1, and

$\quad 2^k$ is the largest power of 2 dividing n.

REPLICATION OF NIM-VALUES

It is easy to see that the subtraction game $S(4,10,12)$ has nim-sequence

$$0.0001111100221133002211000011...$$

obtained by duplicating every digit in the nim-sequence

$$0.0 1 1 0 2 1 3 0 2 1 0 0 1...$$

for the subtraction game $S(2,5,6)$. More generally the nim-sequence for

$$S(ms_1, ms_2, ..., ms_k)$$

is the m-**plicate** of that for

$$S(s_1, s_2, ..., s_k)$$

obtained by repeating each nim-value m times.

Any game, such as ·777077, whose code has only **0**'s and **7**'s and no isolated **7**'s, has an *m*-plicate. Wherever there is a run of **7**'s between $\mathbf{d}_u$ and $\mathbf{d}_{v+1}$ inclusive in the original game, the *m*-plicate game will have a run of **7**'s from $\mathbf{d}_{mu}$ to $\mathbf{d}_{mv+1}$ inclusive, and otherwise has only **0** digits. Games obtained by changing some digits, not at the ends of these runs of **7**'s, will have the same nim-sequence provided that not more than $2m-2$ consecutive digits are changed.

DOUBLE AND QUADRUPLE KAYLES

Double Kayles is the game ·7777 in which any number up to 4 beans may be removed from a heap and what remains is left in at most two heaps. We display its nim-sequence in correspondence with that for Kayles (= ·77).

Double Kayles	0.1	2 3	4 5	6 7	3 2	8 9	7 6	5 4	3 2	8 9	4 5 ...
Kayles	0	1	2	3	1	4	3	2	1	4	2 ...

The reader will see that each nim-value g for Kayles doubles up into a pair of values $2g$, $2g+1$ for ·7777 in either that or the reverse order. Guy and Smith showed that this situation persists indefinitely and that the order is given by the scheme shown in Table 5. The table applies equally to the game Quadruple Kayles (·77777777) except that now g in Kayles is replaced by a sequence $4g$, $4g+1$, $4g+2$, $4g+3$ or its reverse according to the same scheme. The game ·77...7 with 2^{m+1} **7**'s may be called 2^m-**tuple Kayles**. Its nim-sequence is similarly obtained on replacing g by

$$2^m g, \qquad 2^m g + 1, \qquad \ldots, \qquad 2^m(g+1) - 1$$

or the reverse. The rather irregular-looking scheme can be summarized as follows: write the value $\mathscr{G}(n) = g$ for Kayles in binary and ignore the 2's bit (e.g. $7 = 01\not{1}1$); if the sum of the remaining bits is even, and n is even, then the sequence is in its normal order, as it is if both n and the sum of the remaining bits is odd; otherwise the sequence is reversed.

$\mathscr{G}(n)$	n even	n odd	For ·7777 n even	n odd	For ·77777777 n even	n odd
0	up	down	0, 1	1, 0	0, 1, 2, 3	3, 2, 1, 0
1	down	up	3, 2	2, 3	7, 6, 5, 4	4, 5, 6, 7
2	up	down	4, 5	5, 4	8, 9, 10, 11	11, 10, 9, 8
3	down	up	7, 6	6, 7	15, 14, 13, 12	12, 13, 14, 15
4	down	up	9, 8	8, 9	19, 18, 17, 16	16, 17, 18, 19
5	up	down	10, 11	11, 10	20, 21, 22, 23	23, 22, 21, 20
6	down	up	13, 12	12, 13	27, 26, 25, 24	24, 25, 26, 27
7	up	down	14, 15	15, 14	28, 29, 30, 31	31, 30, 29, 28
8	down	up	17, 16	16, 17	35, 34, 33, 32	32, 33, 34, 35

Table 5. Values for Multiple Kayles.

LASKER'S NIM

The standard game of Nim is the subtraction game $S(1,2,3,...)$ and so may be written $\cdot333...$ or $\cdot\dot{3}$. Ed. Lasker has proposed that we adjoin the option of splitting a heap into two smaller non-empty ones without removing any bean. It is natural to denote the new option by the code digit $d_0 = 4$, so that Lasker's Nim is the game $4\cdot333...$ or $4\cdot\dot{3}$. Its nim-sequence is

$$0.\ 1\ 2\ 4\ 3\ 5\ 6\ 8\ 7\ 9\ ...$$

in which the numbers $4m$ and $4m-1$ occur in the reverse of the usual order. This is one of a number of games with infinitely many non-zero code digits, many of which exhibit **arithmetic periodicity**. We will say that $\mathscr{G}(n)$ has (ultimate) **period** p with **saltus** s if (for all sufficiently large n)

$$\mathscr{G}(n+p) = \mathscr{G}(n) + s.$$

Of course, $s = 0$ corresponds to ordinary periodicity. We write the nim-sequence of $4\cdot\dot{3}$ as $0.\dot{1}24\dot{3}(+4)$ where the parenthesis means the saltus 4 is to be added to each successive period, and similarly for other games displaying arithmetic periodicity.

Some other games of this type appear in the Extras.

EXTRAS

SOME REMARKS ON PERIODICITY

When we used our very long Grundy scale to analyze Dawson's Chess (= ·**137**) we were exemplifying a general theorem for all games whose code digits $d_z = 0$ for $z > t$. If the nim-values of an octal game are observed to have period p after the last irregular value $\mathcal{G}(i)$, then the last value that need be computed to verify that the period persists is

$$\mathcal{G}(2i + 2p + t).$$

After this point we can see that the calculations will duplicate earlier ones in the same way as they did for Dawson's Chess. Some of the examples displayed below in Tables 6 and 8 are (ultimately) periodic, but many games of this kind have not yet been shown to be so. It is an open question whether there are games with only a finite number of non-zero code digits which do not ultimately become periodic. We will have more to say on this topic at the end of the Extras.

STANDARD FORM

If we analyze the game ·**4** (take one bean and break the remainder of the heap into two non-empty heaps) we find that its nim-sequence begins

$$0.0011203110332240522330 11302\ldots$$

where $\mathcal{G}(1) = \mathcal{G}(2) = 0$ because we cannot move from heaps of 1 or 2 beans. From here on, the values agree with those for Dawson's Chess, if we have 2 more beans in a heap in ·**4** than we had pairs of pawns in Dawson's Chess. A similar coincidence occurred when we analyzed ·**07** (Dawson's Kayles; take 2 beans from a heap, leaving the rest of it in at most two heaps).

Generally, if d_1 is even, we are not allowed to remove a heap of 1 bean and $\mathcal{G}(1) = 0$, but if d_1 is odd, we can remove isolated beans and $\mathcal{G}(1) = 1$. In the latter case (d_1 odd) we say that the game ·$d_1 d_2 d_3\ldots$ is in **standard form**.

A game $D = $ ·$d_1 d_2 d_3\ldots$ with d_1 *even* can be reduced to standard form by (a sufficient number of) applications of the following rule. Construct a new code name $E = $ ·$e_1 e_2 e_3\ldots$ from ·$d_1 d_2 d_3\ldots$ where

- e_r *contains* **1** (i.e. is odd) if d_{r+1} contains **1**
- e_r contains **3** (i.e. is of form $4m+3$) if d_r contains **2** (is of form $4m+2$ or $4m+3$)
- e_r contains **7** (i.e. is of form $8m+7$) if d_{r-1} contains **4** (is of form $8m+4$, 5, 6 or 7)
- e_r contains **f** ($= 15$, i.e. is of form $16m+15$) if d_{r-2} contains **8**, and generally
- e_r contains $2^{h+2} - 1$ if d_{r-h} contains 2^{h+1} ($h \geqslant -1$).

Then it is not hard to show that

$$\mathcal{G}_E(n) = \mathcal{G}_D(n+1).$$

If e_1 is now odd, E is in standard form and we will call D its **first cousin**. If e_1 is even, we repeat the rule. If t applications of the rule are necessary before the game D is changed to standard form, we say that D is the tth **cousin** of its standard form. For example, Dawson's Kayles is the first cousin and ·4 the second cousin of Dawson's Chess. Again if we apply the rule to $D = $ ·04 or to $D = $ ·042 we obtain $E = $ ·007, and two further applications give ·0137 and ·11337. So ·04 and ·042 are third cousins, ·007 a second cousin and ·0137 a first cousin, to ·11337.

A COMPENDIUM OF OCTAL GAMES

Tables 6 and 7 give information about all **octal games** (i.e. every code digit less than **8**) of the forms $\cdot d_1 d_2$, $4 \cdot d_1$ and $\cdot d_1 d_2 d_3$, $4 \cdot d_1 d_2$. Dots indicate the first complete period. The range is the range of values that has been computed.

If you can't find your game $\cdot d_1 d_2$ or $4 \cdot d_1$ in Table 6(b), use Table 6(a) to locate the appropriate row.

Table 7(a) similarly locates 3-digit octal games in Tables 7(b) and 6(b); the octal points have been omitted. The sign § is a reference to the additional remarks which follow.

d_1 \ d_2	0	1	2	3	4	5	6	7	$4.d_1$
0				·02					·05
1	·01			·02					·51
2	.05	·05		·22	·05	·05		·06	·05
3	·05			·22					
4	·07	·17	·07	·17			·44	·45	·77
5	·05					·51			·51
6	·37	·37	·37	·37		·64	·64	·64	·77
7	·05			·26					·75

Table 6a. Game Locator for Table 6(b).

ADDITIONAL REMARKS

Table 8 gives some periods which were too long for display in Table 7. The later entries actually refer to infinitely many games since each bracket [ ] contains a digit which may be repeated the same number, k, of times ($k \geqslant 0$). Guy and Smith gave a complete analysis of ·177 which may be called $\frac{5}{3}$-plicate Kayles (period 20) whose last exceptional value is $\mathscr{G}(497) = 8$. The last entry in Table 8 is a sort of $(k + 1\frac{2}{3})$-plicate Kayles.

Jack Kenyon discovered the long period, 349, for ·156 and Richard Austin later found periods 142, 148, 442 and 1550 for ·356, ·055, ·644 and ·165. Table 9 exhibits the noteworthy structure in these periods, except the longest, which you can find in Austin's thesis. As you can see, the second half of the period for ·055 is obtained, with few exceptions, by nim-adding 5 to the first half. For similar reasons only half of the periods of ·356 and ·644 are shown; you can get the other halves by nim-adding 7 to every value except the two values $S = 16$ in ·356.

game	cousins 2nd	1st	standard form	nim-sequence, from $\mathscr{G}(1) = 1$	period	range
·01	·001	·01	·1	1̇0̇	1	
·02	·02y	·03y	·13	1̇100̇	4	
·04	·007	·0137	·11337	1112203311 1043332224 4055222330 5011133356		3216
·05		·05W·2YW ·012 4·WY	·U0X ·10U	1̇0̇	2	
·06	·06x	·03T	·1337	1122031122 3344053342 2113022114 4552647581		17999
·07	·4Wx	·07x	·137	1120311033 2240522330 1130211045 2740112031	34	
·11		·011	·11	11̇0̇	1	
·12			·12	1̇001̇	4	
·14			·14	1001021221 0414412212 0104126164 1401021261		35949
·15			·15	1̇101122122̇	10	
·16			·16	1001221401 4214014214 2102142145 1421421423		50174
·17		·4Vy	·17	1102130113 2234153223 1103120114 4264110213	34	
·22		·2Sy	·33	1̇20̇	3	
·26		·2Tx 4·WN	·33U ·73X	1̇230̇	4	
·31		·2y1	·31	120̇1̇	2	
·32			·32y	1̇02̇	3	
·34			·34y	1012010̇312 1203̇	8	
·35			·35	1̇20102̇	6	
·36			·36y	1021021321 3243043241 2312012415 4154152102		17999
·37		·6xy	·37	1201231234 0342132102 1451451201 2312342342		10342
·44	·4Qx	·07Z	·1377	1122331144 3322114422 6644112277 1144332211	24	
·45		·4Rx	·177	1122311443 2211422644 1122711443 2211482744	20	
·51			·5PY 4·PY	1̇	1	
·52			·52x	1022̇103̇	4	
·53			·53y	1122102240 1̇22112241̇	9	
·54			·54x	101̇222411̇	7	
·56			·56x	1022411324 4662117684 11654811T4 56113T6689		49999
·57			·175 ·53z ·57Y 4·1T 4·5N	1̇122̇ (x = 11, T = 12)	4	
·64		·6Zx	·377	1234153215 4268123745 8295476814 6274x23854		1127
·71		·2y3 ·2zV	·31M ·71X	121̇0̇ (X = 10, x = 11)	2	
·72			·32N·72X	1̇023̇	4	
·74			·74x	1012324146 2321517685 1Xx26845X6 2151562681		101
·75		4·7Y	·35R ·75X	1̇2̇	2	
·76			·76x	1023416234 1673216752 89652871X4 371X428613		1875
·77		4·Qx	·77y	1231432142 6412714321 4674128547 2186741231	12	
4·3			·352 4·3Y	1̇20̇	2	

M = 1, 3, 5, 7   R = 5, 7   V = 1, 3   Y = 0, 1, 4, 5
N = 2, 3, 6, 7   S = 2, 3   W = 0, 2   y = 0, 1
P = 1, 5   T = 6, 7   X = 0, 1, 2, 3, 4, 5, 6, 7   Z = 4, 5, 6, 7
Q = 4, 6   U = 3, 5, 7   x = 1, 2, 3   z = 4, 5

Table 6(b). Octal Games with two Code Digits.

d_1d_2	$d_3=1$	2	3	4	5	6	7	d_1d_2	$d_3=1$	2	3	4	5	6	7
00	01	—	002	—	—	—	04	10	—	—	05	—	05	—	05
01	11	05	002	—	024	—	026	11	—	—	002	—	—	—	051
02	02	02	022	—	024	—	026	12	—	—	—	—	—	—	—
03	02	022	022	—	034	06	06	13	—	—	022	—	—	—	07
04	017	04	017	—	—	044	045	14	—	—	—	—	—	—	—
05	—	05	051	—	—	054	055	15	51	—	—	—	51	—	—
06	06	06	06	—	064	064	064	16	—	—	—	—	—	—	—
07	07	07	07	44	44	44	44	17	—	—	—	—	57	—	45
20	31	05	71	—	—	—	—	30	05	05	05	05	05	05	05
21	31	05	71	204	205	206	207	31	71	—	71	31	71	—	71
22	22	26	26	—	224	—	226	32	32	72	72	—	324	72	72
23	22	26	26	224	224	226	226	33	—	—	26	—	26	—	26
24	71	05	71	—	—	244	245	34	34	—	342	—	344	—	346
25	71	05	71	244	245	244	245	35	—	4·3	—	—	75	—	75
26	26	26	26	—	264	264	264	36	36	—	362	—	364	—	366
27	26	26	26	264	264	264	264	37	—	332	—	—	—	—	64
40	07	07	07	—	404	404	404	50	05	05	05	05	05	05	05
41	17	173	173	—	414	—	416	51	51	—	512	51	51	157	157
42	07	07	07	404	404	404	404	52	52	52	52	—	524	524	524
43	17	173	173	414	414	416	416	53	53	—	532	57	57	—	536
44	44	44	44	—	444	444	444	54	54	54	54	147	147	147	147
45	45	45	45	—	454	454	454	55	51	157	157	51	51	157	157
46	44	44	44	444	444	444	444	56	56	56	56	—	564	564	564
47	45	45	45	454	454	454	454	57	57	536	536	57	57	536	536
60	37	373	373	—	604	—	606	70	05	05	05	05	05	05	05
61	37	373	373	604	604	606	606	71	71	71	71	71	71	71	71
62	37	373	373	604	604	606	606	72	72	72	72	72	72	72	72
63	37	373	373	604	604	606	606	73	26	26	26	26	26	26	26
64	64	64	64	—	644	644	644	74	74	74	74	—	744	744	744
65	64	64	64	644	644	644	644	75	75	75	75	75	75	75	75
66	64	64	64	644	644	644	644	76	76	76	76	—	764	764	764
67	64	64	64	644	644	644	644	77	77	—	772	—	774	—	776

$4·d_1$	$d_2=1$	2	3	4	5	6	7
4·0	05	26	26	05	05	26	26
4·1	51	—	4·12	51	51	57	57
4·2	05	26	26	05	05	26	26
4·3	4·3	332	332	4·3	4·3	332	332
4·4	77	77	77	776	776	776	776
4·5	51	57	57	51	51	57	57
4·6	77	77	77	776	776	776	776
4·7	75	—	4·72	75	75	4·72	4·72

Table 7(a). Game Locator in Tables 7(b) and 6(b).

Table 7(b). Octal Games with three Code Digits

game	cousins 2nd	cousins 1st	standard form	nim-sequence, from $\mathscr{G}(1) = 1$				period	range
·002	·003	·013	·113	1̇11000̇				6	
·004	·00137	·011337	·1113337	1111222033	3111104433	3322224440	5552222333		14999
·005	·005	·0107	·10137	1011222033	4110154333	2221601045	2216657010		19999
·006	·0037	·01337	·113337	1112220331	1122433355	2144333222	1114050222		14999
·014		·014	·1007	1001012212	3401051212	5303451211	2303323451		
·015		·015	·1107	1101021223	0142145122	3234014512	5123423401		
·016		·016	·1037	1012220101	4422161604	2127661512	8461210845		19999
·017		·017	·1137	1112023114	0451320211	1402616404	1112026154	60	§
·022	·02S	·03S	·133	1̇1200̇				5	
·024	·02z	·0307	·13137	1122304112	5324115560	3125148142	1967422168		
·026	·02T	·0337	·13337	1122304112	5334112530	4421133442	1156322815		
·034		·03z	·1307	1102231401	4312210514	5632481402	7624584113		
·044	·0077	·01377	·113377	1112223331	1144433322	2111444222	6664441112	36	
·045	·04R	·0177	·11377	1112223311	1444332221	1144222664	4411122277	32	
·051		·05V	·117	1110221340	1113222340	1543222310	1043222010	48	§
·054		·05Q	·1077	1012223441	1163222411	6667344511	1673544187		
·055		·05R	·1177	1112223111	4443222111	4222644411	1222711144	148	§
·064	·06Z	·0377	·13377	1122334115	5332211544	2266841122	3374455872		
·101			·101	101̇0̇				1	
·102			·102	1̇00011̇				6	
·104			·104	1000102212	2410401566	1228104015	6625481010		50000
·106			·106	1000122214	4010621242	1045166512	4510653045		53199
·111			·111	1110̇				1	
·112			·112	1̇10001̇				6	
·114			·114	1100112021	2041104115	2415241120	1120432244		5124
·115			·115	1̇1101112221222̇				14	§
·116			·116	1100212021	1044152411	2041204115	4425202154	96	§
·121			·121y	102̇İ00İ				4	
·122			·122y	İ002İ				5	
·123			·123y	1022İ002İ				5	
·124			·124y	1001102130	2130113023	3223425042	5322332031	62	§
·125			·125y	1021102130	1130234223	4253225320	3110312011		
·126			·126y	1002133210	4250315041	5041304130	2234453722		
·127			·127y	1022104412	2014461770	1226144812	7810726814		17999
·131			·131	1120̇01İ				4	
·132			·132	İ1002̇				5	
·134			·134	1100112031	2031103122	3322435143	5223322130	62	§
·135			·135	1120112031	1031224322	4352235221	3011302110		5112
·136			·136	1100213021	1022334251	4223342011	2031205144		3889
·141			·141y	1011012212	410İ121221	241̇2̇		11	
·142			·142y	1002221103	3241063231	0162240115	3384062355		2039
·143			·143y	1012220104	2215047228	0412228104	2215047228		50000
·144			·144y	100İ222244111İ				10	§
·145			·145y	10İ12222241İ				9	§
·146			·146y	1002224111	3324446662	3111766842	1176534811		2075
·147			·54Zy	10İ2224411İ				8	§

Table 7(b) (*continued*)

game	1st cousins	standard form	nim-sequence, from $\mathscr{G}(1) = 1$	period	range
·152		·152y	1102220104 3231013224 0104223101 3234010222	48	§
·153		·153y	1112221102 2244011222111122244 1	14	
·154		·154y	1101122222411 1	11	
·156		·156y	1102224411 1322444666 2111576688 1112655581	349	§
·157		·157y	111222	6	
·162		·162y	1002231104 2261034266 0542330142 8365142308		3734
·163		·163y	1022310422 6104226104 3221043265 0432610532		54424
·164		·164y	1001223445 1163223415 66738211X7 6675541X82		2099
·165		·165y	1021321344 3623128126 5445182182 136T564812	1550	§
·166		·166y	1002234116 6224411338 5446633118 826441933X		
·167		·167y	1022341162 2441133544 663315866X 44336XX443		
·171		·171y	1122110214 011221122142	11	
·172		·172y	1102230113 2244063224 0163220116 3344110354		4875
·173	·4VS	·173y	1122310432 0112235143 2211023741 3221046274	40	§
·174		·174y	1102132214 4564223115 4128865741 x22688X1xX		
·176		·176y	1102234411 6223441166 332411166334	8	
·204	·2y4	·3007	1012010123 1212314303 1432324323 2452021523		
·205	·2y5	·3107	1201012312 3134034532 3253210202 5473420464		
·206	·2y6	·3037	1012320101 2323451232 3454010342 4217545321		
·207	·2y7	·3137	1212030124 5312124303 0214358213 6304121205		
·224	·2Sz	·3307	1201231231 4304314213 2102142641 6426120123		
·226	·2ST	·3337	1234012345 123451230512345	5	
·244	·2zQ	·3077	1012323451 5673232158 9767654548 232Xx45452		
·245	·2zR	·3177	1212345156 7321289765 64T9212X74 52T73t2183		
·264	·2TZ	·3377	1234516325 1867524816 X45267X518 7F6153861T		
·312		·312y	120201	2	
·316		·316y	120212301030123	12	
·324		·32zy	1021301340 2342132034 1346201253 1678134160		29999
·331		·331	123012	3	
·332		{ ·332y ·372y 4·3N }	1203	4	
·334		·334y	1201203123 1243503426 1241302172 4784206152		
·336		·336y	1203124031 2034123612 3051306413 5246301430		29999
·342		·34Sy	1012320103 2345023254 0102321456 7205476232		2719
·344		·34zy	1012324514 6232145876 7X14123264 1482321X18		
·346		·34Ty	1012324516 7232158676 X548923Xx4 58326X1589		

Table 7(b). (*continued*)

game	cousins 2nd	cousins 1st	standard form	nim-sequence, from $\mathscr{G}(1) = 1$	period	range
·351			·351y	1̇2120102̇		
·353			·353y	12120̇	8	
·354			·354y	1201243123 5243513524 7247864762 786836T742	2	
·356			·356y	1202124516 7512826281 5x79581212 T258561812	142	§
·362			·36Sy	1023410234 1523714237 0123750132 5486254872		
·364			·36zy	1021321345 3423125125 7457482962 968764721X		5101
·366			·36Ty	1023451623 4576891276 85432915x3 284Xx3659X		
·371			·371y	1231032402 3401241632 0123413421 0734162187		
·373		·6xS	·373y	1̇234012341 5231472104 321402640̇		500
·374			·374y	1201243123 5243513524 7247864762 7869369742	28	
·375			·375y	1231243213 4274814812 4814381482 1481481̇248		
·376			·376y	1203124352 4351432645 867X827362 7465392534	18	§
·404	·4WZx	·07x7x	·13737	1122334115 6332211087 7255401122 8845566772		
·414		·4Vzx	·1707y	1102234401 1322344566 3223118763 XX01187644		
·416		·4VTx	·1737y	1122341166 3221066844 5X17833241 66884XXT18		
·444	·4QZx	·0777x	·13777	1122334115 6332211887 7655441122 8845566778		
·454		·4RZx	·1777y	1122341166 3221166844 5X11833447 6688411678		
·512			·51Sy	111̇22210̇		
·524			·52Zy	1̇022104416 7012261446 1870187614 7610781674	6	
·532			·53Sy	1122401̇2241̇	52	§
·536			{·53Ty / ·57Ny}	1̇1224̇	5 / 5	
·564			·56Zy	1022441132 5476823X76 8932T65432 11945XXTF9		
·604		·6xzW	·3707y	1201231234 5345321321 0254754768 9201239674		
·606		·6xTx	·3737y	1234012345 1234562345 6734167891 6789143765		
·644		·6ZZx	·3777y	1234516325 896X5496FX 42367S49FX Ss94Ff19S2	442	§
·744			·74Zy	1012324516 723218967X 45981XxX45 961Xx39896		
·764			·76Zy	1023451623 4576891X76 8543261543 28FXx59SFf		
·772			·77Sy	12341624̇163̇		
·774			·77zy	1231456713 289546T219 645Tt23895 6tT3296XST	4	
·776		4·QZy	·77Ty	1234163216 74581X5476 1236143218 X4FS123416		
4·12			4·1Sy	112204̇21122İ		
4·72			4·7Ny	1̇24̇	7 / 3	

X = 10   x = 11   T = 12   t = 13   F = 14   f = 15   S = 16   s = 17

game	period p	regular nim-values, $\mathscr{G}(n)$, $n \equiv 1, 2, \ldots, p$, mod p.	exceptional nim-values, $\mathscr{G}(0) = 0$. $\mathscr{G}(1) = 1$ and
·017	60	1112026114 0461320211 1402616404 1112026154 0461320211 1802616404	$\mathscr{G}(7) = 3$, $\mathscr{G}(13) = 5$.
·051	48	10102323 40101323 23401043 23231010 43232010 10432340	$\mathscr{G}(6) = \mathscr{G}(16) = \mathscr{G}(26) = \mathscr{G}(36) = 2$, $\mathscr{G}(2) = \mathscr{G}(7) = \mathscr{G}(12) = 1$, $\mathscr{G}(22) = \mathscr{G}(46) = 5$.
·116	96	1120X120 61104415 24112041 50411524 25X0X154 2T582855 24X1X0X5 24251140 51202114 X5142011 20X120X8 18981T20	$\mathscr{G}(3) = 0$, $\mathscr{G}(5) = \mathscr{G}(9) = \mathscr{G}(25) =$ $= \mathscr{G}(35) = \mathscr{G}(37) = \mathscr{G}(47) = 2$, $\mathscr{G}(31) = \mathscr{G}(41) = 4$, $\mathscr{G}(42) = \mathscr{G}(94) =$ $= \mathscr{G}(138) = 8$, $\mathscr{G}(88) = 1$.
·124	62	58411 02130 21301 1302 3322 7465 4455 79633 20311 03120 3120. 1140 5547 5647	$\mathscr{G}(2) = \mathscr{G}(3) = \mathscr{G}(28) = \mathscr{G}(64) = 0$, $\mathscr{G}(24) = \mathscr{G}(32) = \mathscr{G}(121) = 3$, $\mathscr{G}(26) = \mathscr{G}(30) = \mathscr{G}(33) =$ $= \mathscr{G}(34) = \mathscr{G}(59) = \mathscr{G}(95) = 2$.
·134	62	51401 12031 20311 0312 2332 6475 4475 62732 21301 13021 3021 1041 5446 3746	$\mathscr{G}(3) = 0$, $\mathscr{G}(28) = 1$, $\mathscr{G}(24) = \mathscr{G}(32) = \mathscr{G}(59) = 2$, $\mathscr{G}(26) = \mathscr{G}(30) = \mathscr{G}(34) = 3$.
·152	48	01022201 04323101 32240104 22310132 34010222 01043234	no others
·173	40	01223 10462 01122 75147 22110 23741 32210 46274	$\mathscr{G}(9) = \mathscr{G}(16) = \mathscr{G}(20) = 3$.
·375	18	124814 781482 148174	$\mathscr{G}(4) = 1$, $\mathscr{G}(5) = \mathscr{G}(8) = 2$, $\mathscr{G}(3) = \mathscr{G}(7) = \mathscr{G}(10) = \mathscr{G}(25) = 3$, $\mathscr{G}(11) = \mathscr{G}(17) = \mathscr{G}(35) = 4$, $\mathscr{G}(13) = 7$, $\mathscr{G}(18) = \mathscr{G}(36) = 8$.
·524	52	1022104416701 2261446187018 7614761078167 4107210781678	no others
·1[1]5	$4k+10$	11[1]01[1]12[2]21[2]22	none
·1[1]44	$4k+10$	11[1]11[1]22[2]22[2]44	$\mathscr{G}(k+2) = \mathscr{G}(k+3) = 0$.
·1[1]45	$4k+9$	11[1]11[1]22[2]22[2]4	$\mathscr{G}(k+2) = 0$.
·1[1]47	$3k+8$	111[1]22[2]24[4]4	$\mathscr{G}(k+2) = 0$.
·[1]53	$5k+9$	1[1]12[2]21[1]12[2]24[4]	$\mathscr{G}(3k+6) = \mathscr{G}(5k+10) = 0$.
·[1]54	$4k+7$	[1]11[1]12[2]22[2]4	$\mathscr{G}(k+2) = 0$.
·1[1][3]77	$12k+20$	1[1]12[2]28[8]1[1]14[4]47[7] 2[2]21[1]18[8]2[2]27[7]44[4]	many

Table 8. Periods of some Octal Games.

```
1 1           4 4 4   7 2
1 1 1         4 4 4     8
1 1       2   4 4 4
1 1 1   2 7   4 4 4
1 1 1     7 4         7 2
1 1 1         4 4 4 7
1 1     2 8   4 4
1 1 1   2 7   4 4 4
1 1 1     8   4 4             2
1 1 1         4 4 4   7 2
1       2 8
4 4                 1 1 1   2 7
4 4 4               1 1 1   2 8
4 4     7           1 1 1
4 4 4   7 2         1 1 1
4 4 4     2 1                 2 7
4 4                 1 1 1   2 2
4 4     7 8         1 1
4 4 4   7 2         1 1 1
4 4 4     8         1 1           7
4 4 4               1 1 1         7
4       7 8
```

Period of ·055

x = 11	f = 15	τ = 23
T = 12	S = 16	σ = 27
F = 14	V = 20	α = 28

```
S f x   5 1 5 1   T 8   6 2 6 2
S x f   1 5 1 5   8 T   2 6 2 6
x f x   5 1 5 1   T 8   6 2 6 2
f x f   1 5 1 5   8 T   2 6 2 6
x f x   5 1 5 1   T 8   6 2 6 2
f x f   1 5 1
```

Half-Period of ·356

```
T 5 5 5   6           8 1   2 2 2
    T T   6 6         8 1   2 2 2
    T 5   6 6 6 8 8         2 2 2
  5 T     6 6 x          1  8 2 2
    T T   6 6 6 8 8         2 2 2
  5       6 6        8 8 1  2 2 2
    T T   6   f      8 8     2 2 2
    T 5   6 6 6        8 1   2 2 2
    T T   6 6          8 1   2 2 2
    T 5   6 6 6 8 8         2 2 2
  5 5 5   6           8 1 8 2 2
    T T   6 6 6 8 8         2 2 2
  5       6 6        8 8 1  2 2 2
    T T   6   f      8 8 1  2 2
    T 5   6 6 6        8 1   2 2 2
f 5       6 6 6          1   2 2 2
    T 5   6 6 6        8 1   2 2 2
    T T   6 6          8 1   2 2 2
    T T   6 6 6        8 1   1 x 2
  5 T     6 6          8 1   2 2 2
    T T   6 6 6 8 8         2 2 2
  5       6 6 6        8 1   2 2 2
f 5       6 6 6        8     2 2 2
    T 5   6 6 6 8 8         2 2
T   T T   6 6          8 1   2 2 x
    T T   6 6 6 8 8         2 2 2
  5 T     6 6 S          1   2 2 2
    T T   6 6 6 8 8         2 2 2
  5       6 6 6        8 1   1 x 2
    T 5   6 6 6        8     2 2 2
    T 5   6 6 6 8 8         2 2 x
    T T   6 6          8 1   2 2 x
T 5 T     6 6 S       8     2 2 2
  5 T     6 6 x          1  8 2 2
V   T     6 6 6 8 8         2 2 2
  5 T     6 6          8 1   2 2 2
    T T   6 6 6        8     2 2 2
```

Period of ·156

```
S   5 F   τ   9 2
S   5 F       9 2
S   5 F   τ   2 9
S   F 5   τ     2
S   F 5   τ   2 9
S   5 F       2 9
S   σ 5   τ   2 9
S   5 F   τ   2 9
S     5   τ α 2
S   F 5   τ   2 9
    5 F   τ α 2
S   5 F   τ   2 9
S   5 F   τ     2
S   σ 5   τ   9 2
S   5 F   τ   2 9
S     5   τ   2 9
S   F 5       2 9
S   σ 5   τ α 2
S   5 F   τ   2 9
S   5 F   τ     2
S   σ 5   F   2 9
S   5 F   τ   2 9
S     5   τ α 2
S   F 5   τ   2 9
S   σ 5   τ α 2
9   5 F   τ   2 9
S     5   τ α 2
S   F 5   τ   2 9
S     5   τ   2 9
S   F 5   τ   9 2
S   5 F   τ     2
S   σ 5   τ   9 2
S   5 F   τ   9 2
S   5 F       9 2
S   σ 5   τ   2 9
S   F 5   τ   2 9
    F 5   τ α 2
S   5 F
```

Half-Period of ·644

Table 9. Some Long Periods of Octal Games.

The relationship between the structure of the period, if any, and the rules of the game, is an intriguing one. Tom Schaefer has done some investigation into this. Omar will discover numerous features: subperiods, reflexion, repetition, nim-additions, and...

SPARSE SPACES AND COMMON COSETS

In many take-and-break games some nim-values occur much more often than others. For example in Kayles

0 and 5 happen only once each
3 and 6 only four times each, while

$$1, \quad 2, \quad 4, \quad 7, \quad 8$$

all occur infinitely often with frequencies

$$\tfrac{1}{4}, \quad \tfrac{1}{4}, \quad \tfrac{1}{6}, \quad \tfrac{1}{6}, \quad \tfrac{1}{6}.$$

It's not too surprising that the small numbers 1 and 2 happen more often than 4, 7 and 8, but the reason why 0, 3, 5 and 6 occur so rarely is more subtle. Let's look at the binary expansions of the two kinds of value

common values	rare values
....0001 = 1	....0000 = 0
....0010 = 2	....0011 = 3
....0100 = 4	....0101 = 5
....0111 = 7	....0110 = 6
....1000 = 8	....1001 = 9
	....1010 = 10

To help you see the pattern, we've added 9 and 10 (which don't occur) to the rare list. If you've already peeked ahead at Chapter 14 you might recognize that the common values are what we call the *odious* numbers with an odd number of ones in their expansions, while the rare ones are the *evil* ones, with an even number.

However, the property that interests us here is just that for these meanings of the words rare and common, we have

$$\begin{array}{rcccl} \text{rare} \overset{*}{+} \text{rare} & = & \text{rare} & = & \text{common} \overset{*}{+} \text{common}, \\ \text{rare} \overset{*}{+} \text{common} & = & \text{common} & = & \text{common} \overset{*}{+} \text{rare}. \end{array}$$

There are other octal games which have *different* splittings into rare and common values, but in each case the above relations hold, so that the rare values form a closed space under nim-addition (the **sparse space**) and the common ones its complementary set (the **common coset**).

How does this come about? Look at the nim-values

$$\mathscr{G}(0), \mathscr{G}(1), \mathscr{G}(2), ..., \mathscr{G}(n-1)$$

for some take-and-break game. Suppose there is a way of separating all nimbers into rare and common halves so that the rare half is a closed subspace under nim-addition which happens to contain relatively few of the above nimbers. Then

$$\mathscr{G}(n) = \text{mex } \mathscr{G}(i) \overset{*}{+} \mathscr{G}(j) \qquad (i,j < n)$$

taken over certain pairs (i,j) which depend on the rules of the game. In this most of the *excluded* values will be

$$\text{common} \overset{*}{+} \text{common} = \text{rare},$$

while a common value will only be excluded when just one of $\mathscr{G}(i)$ and $\mathscr{G}(j)$ is rare. $\mathscr{G}(n)$, being the first value that *isn't* excluded, is therefore likely to be in the common set.

> A space that's sparse so far
> tends to remain so.

So once the nim-values in a sequence begin to cluster in a suitable coset of common values, this clustering is likely to persist. Often it shows itself much earlier than the ultimate periodicity; for example the first 25 nim-values of Kayles include 19 occurrences of 1, 2, 4 and 7, but only six of 0, 3, 5 and 6, so that the sparse space is already quite well established.

A division of $0,1,2,\ldots,2^n-1$ into a sparse space and its common complement can be extended to the numbers $0,1,2,\ldots,2^{n+1}-1$ in two distinct ways. Thus the division of the first 25 Kayles values into

> sparse: 0,3,5,6 and common: 1,2,4,7

might extend either to

> sparse: 0,3,5,6,9,10,12,15 and common: 1,2,4,7,8,11,13,14

or to

> sparse: 0,3,5,6,8,11,13,14 and common: 1,2,4,7,9,10,12,15.

However the first few values that exceed 7 are likely to be 8 because numbers larger than 8 can occur only when 8 is excluded, which would require a previous value of 8 or more. More generally:

> A new power of two
> is quite likely to
> establish itself as
> a new common value.

So on the basis of the first 25 Kayles values it would be quite reasonable to conjecture that there will be a sparse space containing none of

$$1, \ 2, \ 4, \ 8, \ 16, \ \ldots,$$

explaining the evil–odious division.

WILL GRUNDY'S GAME BE ULTIMATELY PERIODIC?

The sparse space phenomenon was first suggested to us by our computation of the first quarter of a million nim-values for Grundy's Game (divide any heap into two unequal ones). This has a different sparse space, consisting of all numbers whose binary expansions, after deleting the last digit, have an even number of ones. Thus

common	rare
....0010 = 2	....0000 = 0
....0011 = 3	....0001 = 1
....0100 = 4	....0110 = 6
....0101 = 5	....0111 = 7
....1000 = 8	....1010 = 10
....1001 = 9	....1011 = 11
....	....

Mike Guy found no other rare values among the first ten million nim-values; among these, $\mathscr{G}(7250049) = 256$ is the only one with nine binary digits.

The largest of the first quarter million nim-values for Grundy's Game is 230 and among them there are only 1273 rare ones. $\mathscr{G}(82860) = 108$ is the only rare value of $\mathscr{G}(n)$ in the range $36184 < n \leqslant 250000$.

If we suppose that the values remain bounded and that the rare ones die out absolutely, as happened for Kayles and seems to be happening for Grundy's Game, then the values must ultimately become periodic, since the value of $\mathscr{G}(n)$ can be computed from the finitely many nim-values $\mathscr{G}(n-r)$ for which $\mathscr{G}(r)$ is rare. We therefore conjecture that the answer to our section heading is

YES!

SPARSE SPACE SPELLS SPEED

Naively, it would seem that to compute $\mathscr{G}(250001)$ would require 125000 nim-sum calculations, but we can find the first unexcluded common value after only 1273 nim-sums and $\mathscr{G}(250001)$ must be either this number or a smaller rare value. We can now proceed by computing further nim-sums until *either* all the smaller rare values are excluded (which will probably happen fairly quickly) *or* (just possibly) we have computed all 125000 nim-sums and established a new rare value. On average we expect this method to find $\mathscr{G}(n)$ in only a few thousand operations.

We also computed values for the games

·0007, ·00007, ·000007

with the following results:

m	Smallest value of n for which $\mathscr{G}(n) = m$		
	·0007	**·00007**	**·000007**
1	4	5	6
2	8	10	12
4	20	25	30
8	75	95	115
16	157	190	230
32	508	437	530
64	1521	1257	1125
128	5894	3368	2691
256	22337	11776	5425
512	65758	31700	15858
1024	157185	86894	74667
apparent sparse space	...11111000	...???10000	...11011110

GAMES DISPLAYING ARITHMETIC PERIODICITY

If there are infinitely many non-zero code digits in the name of the game, the nim-values are usually unbounded and sometimes display arithmetic periodicity of the kind we saw in Lasker's Nim. In Tables 10(a) and 10(b) we show all games $\cdot\mathbf{d_1\dot{d}_2}$ $(= \cdot\mathbf{d_1 d_2 d_2 d_2}...)$, $\cdot\mathbf{\dot{d}_1\dot{d}_2}$ $(= \cdot\mathbf{d_1 d_2 d_1 d_2}...)$ and $4\cdot\mathbf{\dot{d}_1}$ $(= 4\cdot\mathbf{d_1 d_1 d_1}...)$. *Two entries in the same place of Table 10(a) refer to the games $\cdot\mathbf{d_1\dot{d}_2}$ and $\cdot\mathbf{\dot{d}_1 d_2}$; a single entry refers to both. An asterisk indicates *bounded* nim-values, for example

$\cdot\dot{1}$, $\cdot\dot{5}$, $\cdot1\dot{5}$, $\cdot1\dot{5}$, $\cdot5\dot{1}$, $\cdot\dot{5}\dot{1}$, $4\cdot\dot{1}$ and $4\cdot\dot{5}$ each have nim-sequence $0.\dot{1}$;

$\cdot3\dot{1}$, $\cdot\dot{3}\dot{1}$, $\cdot3\dot{5}$, $\cdot\dot{3}\dot{5}$, $\cdot7\dot{1}$, $\cdot\dot{7}\dot{1}$, $\cdot7\dot{5}$ and $\cdot\dot{7}\dot{5}$ each have nim-sequence $0.\dot{1}\dot{2}$;

$\mathbf{d_1} \backslash \mathbf{d_2}$	0	1	2	3	4	5	6	7	$4\cdot\dot{\mathbf{d}}_1$
0	*	*	$0\dot{2}$	$0\dot{2}$	$0\dot{4}$	$0\dot{5}$,*	$0\dot{2}$	$0\dot{2}$	*
1	*	*	$1\dot{2},\dot{1}\dot{2}$	$0\dot{2}$	$1\dot{4},\dot{1}\dot{4}$	*	$1\dot{6},\dot{1}\dot{6}$	$1\dot{7}$	*
2	*	*	$\dot{2}$	$\dot{2}$	$2\dot{4}$,*	$2\dot{5}$,*	$\dot{2}$	$\dot{2}$	$\dot{2}$
3	*	*	$3\dot{2}$	$\dot{2}$	$3\dot{4}$	*	$3\dot{2}$	$\dot{2}$	$4\cdot3$
4	*,$0\dot{2}$	*,$1\dot{7}$	$0\dot{2}$	$1\dot{7}$	$0\dot{2}$	$1\dot{7}$	$0\dot{2}$	$1\dot{7}$	$\dot{2}$
5	*	*	$5\dot{2},5\dot{6}$	$5\dot{3},5\dot{7}$	$5\dot{4}$	*	$5\dot{6}$	$5\dot{7}$	*
6	*,$\dot{2}$	?,$\dot{2}$	$\dot{2}$	$\dot{2}$	$\dot{2}$	$\dot{2}$	$\dot{2}$	$\dot{2}$	$\dot{2}$
7	*	*	$3\dot{2}$	$\dot{2}$	$7\dot{4}$	*	$3\dot{2}$	$\dot{2}$	$4\cdot\dot{7}$

Table 10(a). Games $\cdot\mathbf{d_1\dot{d}_2}$, $\cdot\mathbf{\dot{d}_1 d_2}$ and $4\cdot\mathbf{\dot{d}_1}$ listed in Table 10(b).

while ·0̇5, ·2̇0, ·2̇1, ·2̇4, and ·2̇5 each have nim-sequence 0.0̇1̇, so they are first cousins of

·1̇0̇7, ·3̇0, ·3̇0̇7, ·5̇0 and ·7̇0, which are each forms of She-Loves-Me, She-Loves-Me-Not;

finally ·4̇1 has nim-sequence 0.0̇1̇12̇2̇.

The ? in Table 10(a) means that the status of ·6̇1 is unknown; it has been analyzed to $n = 14999$; it may have bounded nim-values.

In Table 10(b), ·0̇2̇, ·0̇4̇, ·2̇, ·2̇4̇ and 4·3̇ are respectively Duplicate Nim, Triplicate Nim, ordinary Nim, Double Duplicate Nim and Lasker's Nim.

game	3rd	cousins 2nd	1st	standard form	nim-sequence, from $\mathscr{G}(1) = 1$	p	s
·0̇2̇		·0̇2̇ ·0̇2̇ ·0̇6̇ ·0̇6̇ ·4̇2̇ ·4̇Ẇ ·4̇Q̇ ·4̇Q̇	·0̇3̇ ·0̇3̇ ·0̇7̇ ·0̇7̇	·1̇3̇ ·1̇3̇ }	1̇1̇(+1) i.e. 0.1122334455...	2	1
·0̇4̇	·0̇4̇ ·0̇4̇ }	·0̇0̇7̇	·0̇1̇3̇7̇	·1̇1̇3̇3̇7̇	1̇1̇1̇(+1) i.e. 0.111222333...	3	1
·0̇5			·0̇5	·1̇1̇7	111̇22̇(+2) i.e. 0.11122234445666...	4	2
·1̇2̇				·1̇2̇	100̇2̇2̇(+1)	2	1
·1̇4̇				·1̇4̇	100̇12̇2̇2224444̇(+4)	7	4
·1̇6̇				·1̇6̇	100̇2̇2̇3̇(+2)	3	2
·1̇7			·4̇U̇ ·4̇U̇ ·4̇1	·1̇7 ·1̇7 }	11̇2̇2̇3̇(+2)	3	2
·2̇		·2̇3̇ ·2̇Ṡ ·2̇Ṫ ·2̇Ṫ ·6̇Ṡ ·6̇Ẋ ·6̇Ż 4·2̇ 4·Q̇ }	·3̇ ·7̇ ·3̇7̇ ·3̇7̇ ·7̇3̇ ·7̇3̇	1̇(+1)	1	1
·2̇4̇			·2̇4̇	·3̇0̇7̇	1̇01̇2̇(+2)	4	2
·2̇5̇			·2̇5̇	·3̇1̇7̇	121̇23454̇(+4)	6	4
·3̇2̇				·3̇2̇ ·3̇2̇ ·3̇6̇ ·3̇6̇ ·7̇2̇ ·7̇2̇ ·7̇6̇ ·7̇6̇ }	10̇2̇(+1)	1	1
·3̇4̇				·3̇4̇ ·3̇4̇	101̇23̇2̇(+2)	3	2
·5̇2̇				·5̇2̇	10224433557̇688XX99xxtṪ(+8)	12	8
·5̇3̇				·5̇3̇	112244633557788XXṪ99xxtṫFFSSAffssaaV̇(+8)	13	8
·5̇4̇				·5̇4̇	101̇2̇2̇2444̇(+4)	5	4
·5̇6̇				·5̇6̇	10̇2̇2̇(+2)	2	2
·5̇7̇				·5̇7̇	11̇2̇2̇(+2)	2	2
·7̇4̇				·7̇4̇ ·7̇4̇	101̇232̇45467̇(+4)	5	4
·1̇2				·1̇2	1̇0̇(+1)	2	1
·1̇4				·1̇4	1011212232̇444466̇(+4)	7	4
·1̇6				·1̇6	102132̇445̇(+2)	3	2
4·3̇				4·3̇	1̇243̇(+4)	4	4
4·7̇				4·7̇	12̇(+2)	1	2

X = 10, x = 11, T = 12, t = 13, F = 14, f = 15, S = 16, s = 17, A = 18, a = 19, V = 20.

Table 10(b). Guide to Octal Games ·$d_1 d_2$, ·$\dot{d}_1 \dot{d}_2$ and 4·$\dot{d}_1$.

A NON-ARITHMETIC-PERIODICITY THEOREM

We've just seen a number of take-and-break games with infinite recurring octal definitions, which exhibit arithmetic periodicity,

$$\mathscr{G}(n+p) = \mathscr{G}(n)+s, \qquad s > 0$$

for all large enough n. Jack Kenyon noticed that this didn't seem to happen for *finite* octal games. Here's why!

As usual the rules of the game tell us that $\mathscr{G}(n)$ is the mex of certain values

$$\mathscr{G}(i) \overset{*}{+} \mathscr{G}(j),$$

where $i+j = n-c$ for one of a finite number of values of c. If the nim-values were arithmetico-periodic then the *ordinary* sums

$$\mathscr{G}(i)+\mathscr{G}(j)$$

would also assume only finitely many values, of various forms $\lambda n + \mu$.

But we'll show that the number of different nim-sums

$$x \overset{*}{+} y$$

among the pairs for which

$$x+y = \lambda n + \mu$$

is very small compared with n. It follows that $\mathscr{G}(n)$, the first non-excluded value, would also be small compared with n, contradicting the supposed arithmetico-periodicity.

The number, $f(N)$, of nim-sums corresponding to a given ordinary sum N, can be read from the diagonals of a nim-addition table (Fig. 13).

$$f(N) = 1 \quad 1 \quad 2 \quad 1 \quad 3 \quad 2 \quad 3 \quad 1 \quad 4 \quad 3 \quad 5 \quad 2 \quad 5 \quad 3 \quad 4 \quad 1 \quad 5 \quad \ldots$$
$$\text{for} \quad N = 0 \quad 1 \quad 2 \quad 3 \quad 4 \quad 5 \quad 6 \quad 7 \quad 8 \quad 9 \quad 10 \quad 11 \quad 12 \quad 13 \quad 14 \quad 15 \quad 16 \quad \ldots .$$

It satisfies

$$f(2n+1) = f(n)$$
$$f(2n) = f(n)+f(n-1),$$

and since one of n and $n-1$ is odd, we have

$$f(N) = f(a) \quad \text{or} \quad f(a)+f(b) \qquad \text{where} \quad a \leqslant \tfrac{1}{2}N, \quad b \leqslant \tfrac{1}{4}N.$$

It follows that

$$f(N) \leqslant \tfrac{5}{4}N^\theta \qquad (N = 1,2,3,\ldots)$$

where we define

$$\theta = 0 \cdot 694\ldots \quad \text{by} \quad (\tfrac{1}{2})^\theta = \sigma$$

and

$$\sigma = 0 \cdot 618\ldots \quad \text{by} \quad \sigma^2 + \sigma = 1.$$

For after verifying the inequality at $N = 1$ and 2, we can continue inductively,

$$f(N) \leqslant f(a)+f(b) \leqslant \tfrac{5}{4}[(\tfrac{1}{2}N)^\theta+(\tfrac{1}{4}N)^\theta] = \tfrac{5}{4}(\sigma N^\theta+\sigma^2 N^\theta) = \tfrac{5}{4}N^\theta.$$

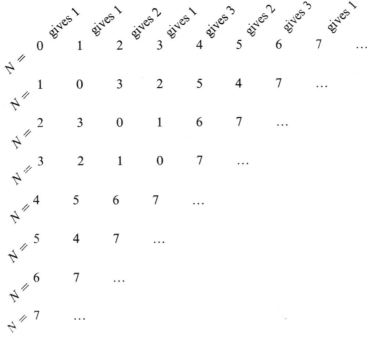

Figure 13. Read the Nim-Addition Table Diagonally for $f(N)$.

Game	Nim-sequence	
·8	$0.\dot{0}0\dot{0}(+1)$	First cousin of Triplicate Nim.
·9	$0.1000122234445666783838XXXT7T7T5F5FS...$	
·X	$0.\dot{0}\dot{1}$	First cousin of She-Loves-Me, She-Loves-Me-Not.
·x ·t ·f	$\dot{0}.\dot{1}$	She-Loves-Me, She-Loves-Me-Not
·T	$0.\dot{0}0\dot{0}(+1)$	First cousin of Duplicate Nim.
·F	$0.01234153215826514...$	$\mathcal{G}(246) = 128.$
·18	$0.10000122223444456666788388...$	
·19	$0.110000222233444455666688889XXXXTTTT77...$	
·1X	$0.1001\dot{2}\dot{2}(+1)$	
·1x	$0.1100\dot{2}\dot{2}(+1)$	
·1T	$0.100\dot{1}02222444466668883333X...$	
·1t	$0.11012222444466668333...$	$\mathcal{G}(240) = 128.$
·1F	$0.1001223445667883...$	
·1f	$0.1102234456673885...$	$\mathcal{G}(207) = 128.$
·38	$0.1010210102323453 43456...$	$\mathcal{G}(301) = 128.$
·39	$0.12010120345343478...$	$\mathcal{G}(164) = 77.$
·3X	$0.1021023453456876...$	$\mathcal{G}(190) = 121.$
·3x	$0.1201203453456786789X...$	$\mathcal{G}(206) = 128.$
·3T	$0.10120103234534547678...$	
·3t	$0.120103453426276...$	
·3F	$0.102102345345768...$	
·3f	$\dot{0}.1201\dot{2}(+3)$	Kenyon's Game: take 1 from a heap, or take 2 and leave the rest in any number of heaps up to 3.

Table 11. Hexadecimal Games are Even More Unruly than Octal Games.

SOME HEXADECIMAL GAMES

The hexadecimal games are those with one or more code digits d_k, $8 \leqslant d_k \leqslant 15$ (compare Table 4). So some moves break a heap into *three* heaps. This usually leads to larger nim-values. Jack Kenyon showed that a few of these games are arithmetico-periodic, including $\cdot 3f$ ($f = 15$) which has period 6 and saltus 3, countering a conjecture of Guy and Smith that the saltus was always a power of 2. Richard Austin found some rather restricted conditions under which such games are arithmetico-periodic, but usually they seem even less disciplined than octal games. A few examples are given in Table 11: the notation is as in Table 10(b). Enough nim-values are given to confound your early guesses about the behavior of the games.

REFERENCES AND FURTHER READING

E.W. Adams and D.C. Benson, Nim-type games, Carnegie Inst. Tech., Report 13, 1956.

R.B. Austin, Impartial and Partisan Games, M.Sc. Thesis, University of Calgary, 1976.

W.W. Rouse Ball and H.S.M. Coxeter, "Mathematical Recreations and Essays", 12th edition, University of Toronto, 1974, pp. 36–40.

J.H. Conway, "On Numbers and Games", Academic Press, London and New York, 1976, Chapter 11.

T.R. Dawson, Fairy Chess Review (Dec. 1934) p. 94, problem 1603.

T.R. Dawson, "Caissa's Wild Roses", 1935, p. 13.

Blanche Descartes, Why are series musical? Eureka, **16** (1953) 18–20; reprinted *ibid.* **27** (1964) 29–31.

H.E. Dudeney, "Canterbury Puzzles", London, 1910, pp. 118, 220.

T.S. Ferguson, On sums of graph games with last player losing, Internat. J. Game Theory, **3** (1974) 159–167.

D. Gale and A. Neyman, Nim-like games, Internat. J. Game Theory, **11** (1982) 17–20.

Richard K. Guy and Cedric A.B. Smith, The *G*-values of various games, Proc. Cambridge Philos. Soc. **52** (1956) 514–526.

John C. Holladay, Cartesian products of termination games, Ann. Math. Studies, Princeton, **39** (1957) 189–199.

J.C. Kenyon, Nim-like Games and the Sprague–Grundy Theory, M.Sc. Thesis, University of Calgary, 1967.

J.C. Kenyon, A Nim-like game with period 349, University of Calgary Math. Research Paper No. 13, Feb. 1967.

E. Lasker, "Brettspiele der Völker", Berlin, 1931, pp. 183–186.

Sam Loyd, "Cyclopedia of Tricks and Puzzles", New York, 1914, p. 232.

Thomas J. Schaefer, Self-sustaining periods in the G-series of Kayles-like games, (unpublished notes, Jan. 1977).

Fred. Schuh, "The Master Book of Mathematical Recreations" (tr. F. Göbel, ed. T.H. O'Beirne). Dover, New York, 1968, Chapters VI, XII.

Neil Y. Wilson, A number problem, Proc. Edinburgh Math. Soc., Vol. II, Part 4 (Nov. 1959) 11–14.

Chapter 5

Numbers, Nimbers and Numberless Wonders

Aquaintance I would have, but when't depends
Not on the number, but the choice of friends.
    Abraham Cowley, *Of Myself.*

To numbers I'll not be confined.
    Sir Charles Hanbury Williams, *A Ballad in Imitation of Martial.*

DOMINEERING

This game has been considered by Göran Andersson and has also been called Crosscram and Dominoes. Left and Right take turns in placing dominoes on a checker-board. Left orients his dominoes North–South and Right East–West. Each domino must exactly cover two squares of

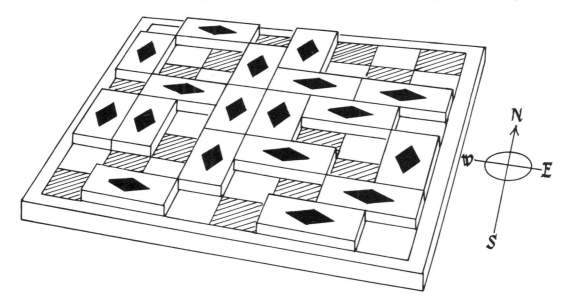

Figure 1. A Game of Domineering.

the board and no two dominoes may overlap. A player who can find no room for one of his dominoes loses.

After a time the available space may separate into several disconnected regions, and then the game for the whole board will be the sum of several smaller games corresponding to these. In Fig. 2 we display values of all regions with five squares or fewer. A square may be added to any *one* of the indicated edges without affecting the value of the region. Some other values are given in the Extras to this chapter.

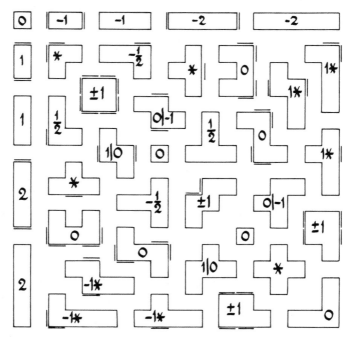

Figure 2. Values of Domineering Positions (±1 means 1|−1).

We discuss some of the more interesting simple cases. The positions

$$\text{⌐|} = \left\{ \text{⌐|} \;\middle|\; \text{|⌐} \right\} = \{0|0\} = *$$

$$\text{⌐|} = \left\{ \text{⌐|} , \text{⌐|} \;\middle|\; \text{|⌐} \right\} = \{-1, 0|1\} = \tfrac{1}{2}$$

yield two old friends, but we also find some new values:

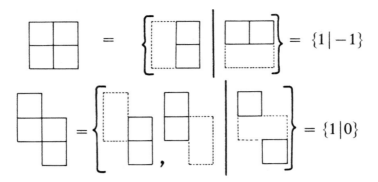

How shall we reckon with these?

SWITCH GAMES

In a position $\{x|y\}$ where x and y are numbers and $x \geqslant y$, each player will be keen to move first, since he prefers the effect of his own move to that of his opponent's. Although this feature is common in real-life games we have tended to avoid it in our carefully chosen examples. How do such **switch values** compare with ordinary numbers? As a more interesting example we consider [grid] $= \{2|-\tfrac{1}{2}\}$ in which Left's best move is to [piece] $+$ [piece] $= 2$, and Right's moves lead to positions like [piece] of value $-\tfrac{1}{2}$, the negative of [piece] $= \tfrac{1}{2}$.

If z is a number, Left's best option from $\{2|-\tfrac{1}{2}\} - z$ is to $2-z$, and so he can win only if $z \leqslant 2$. Right's best option is to $-\tfrac{1}{2} - z$, so that *he* can win only if $z \geqslant -\tfrac{1}{2}$. We conclude that

$$\text{for} \quad z > 2, \qquad z > \{2|-\tfrac{1}{2}\},$$
$$\text{for} \quad z < -\tfrac{1}{2}, \qquad z < \{2|-\tfrac{1}{2}\},$$
$$\text{for} \ -\tfrac{1}{2} \leqslant z \leqslant 2, \qquad z \parallel \{2|-\tfrac{1}{2}\},$$

as illustrated in Fig. 3.

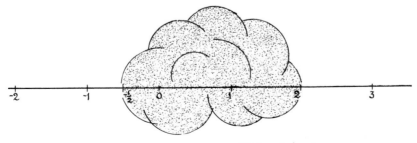

Figure 3. Where is [grid] $= \{2|-\tfrac{1}{2}\}$?

More generally:

> If x and y are numbers and $x \geqslant y$, then for any number z:
>
> $$z > x \text{ implies } z > \{x|y\},$$
> $$z < y \text{ implies } z < \{x|y\},$$
> $$y \leqslant z \leqslant x \text{ implies } z \parallel \{x|y\}.$$

COMPARING NUMBERS WITH SWITCHES

CASHING CHEQUES

Figure 4 shows the usable regions of the Domineering position of Fig. 1 with their values. Who should win?

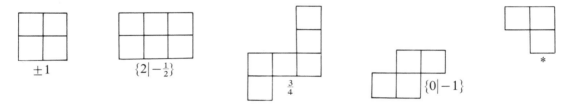

Figure 4. The Available Regions of Figure 1.

More generally, how do we cope with any sum of values each of which is either a number, z, or a switch $\{x|y\}$? In particular, what happens for the game $\{x|y\} + z$? It is easy to guess the answer:

> If x, y and z are numbers, and $x \geqslant y$, then each player
> should prefer to move in $\{x|y\}$ rather than in z.
> In symbols
> $$\{x|y\} + z = \{x+z \mid y+z\}$$

ADDING NUMBERS TO SWITCHES

This is also easy to prove, for since $\{x|y\}$ is less than any number strictly greater than x, Left's other option $\{x|y\} + z^L$ will be less than any number greater than $x + z^L$, and so less than his sensible option $x+z$. So for example, we have

$$\{2|-\tfrac{1}{2}\} + 5 = \{7|4\tfrac{1}{2}\}, \qquad \{2|-\tfrac{1}{2}\} - \tfrac{3}{4} = \{1\tfrac{1}{4}|-1\tfrac{1}{4}\}.$$

We can use this principle to eliminate the bias from any value like $\{x|y\}$:

> If x and y are numbers with $x \geqslant y$, then
> $$\{x|y\} = u + \{v|-v\} = u \pm v, \text{ say,}$$
> where $u = \tfrac{1}{2}(x+y)$, $v = \tfrac{1}{2}(x-y)$.

CENTRALIZING SWITCHES

So any sum of such terms reduces to the sum of a collection of terms of form $\{v|-v\}$ for various v, together with an ordinary number. We shall write $\pm v$ for $\{v|-v\}$, and more generally,

$$z \pm a \pm b \pm c \pm \dots$$

for

$$z + \{a|-a\} + \{b|-b\} + \{c|-c\} + \dots$$

We may think of a position of value $\pm v$ as a cheque for v moves, payable to whoever moves in it, while the ordinary number term represents the difference between the bank balances of Left and Right.

Figure 5. Some Cheques Ready for Cashing.

In the game of Cashing Cheques, each player starts with a sum of money, and there are a number of cheques (or coins) on the table, already made out for various amounts. The players alternately appropriate these cheques, and at the end of the game the winner is whoever has the larger amount of money in all, except that if both have exactly the same amount, the last to cash a cheque is the winner.

No worldly reader will have much difficulty planning his moves in this game. Obviously, whoever goes first will grab the largest available amount, his opponent will grab the next largest, and so on until we find ourselves fighting over the quarters. So the game

$$z \pm a \pm b \pm c \pm \dots \qquad (a \geqslant b \geqslant c \geqslant \dots \geqslant 0)$$

will soon become

$$z + a - b + c - \dots$$

if Left starts, and

$$z - a + b - c + \dots$$

if Right starts. Moreover, we can tell whose turn it is to move next, for the number of moves made so far is simply the total number of terms of form $\pm v$. Knowing this, it is easy to see who wins in any particular case.

There is no need to reduce the switches $\{x|y\}$ to the form $u \pm v$ before applying this method. Since the value of v is $\frac{1}{2}(x - y)$, which we call the **temperature** of $\{x|y\}$, the policy is simply:

In any sum of switches $\{x|y\}$, together possibly with a number,
move in any $\{x|y\}$ having the largest possible temperature $\frac{1}{2}(x - y)$.
When the dust has settled after these moves the result will be
a number which tells us the winner. Of course, when this number is 0,
the outcome depends on whose turn it is to move.

THE TEMPERATURE POLICY FOR SWITCHES

The values in Fig. 4, arranged in decreasing order of temperature, with the number at the end, are

$$\{2|-\tfrac{1}{2}\}, \ \{1|-1\}, \ \{0|-1\}, \ \{0|0\} \text{ and } \tfrac{3}{4}.$$

So if Left starts, after four moves we reach the number

$$2 - 1 + 0 + 0 + \tfrac{3}{4} = 1\tfrac{3}{4}$$

while if Right starts, the opposing four moves lead to

$$-\tfrac{1}{2} + 1 - 1 + 0 + \tfrac{3}{4} = \tfrac{1}{4}.$$

Since both numbers are positive, so is the whole game, and Left can win no matter who starts.

Suppose however that Left stupidly moves in the bottom left-hand corner, so converting the region of value $\frac{3}{4}$ to ⊔, value $\frac{1}{2}$. Will Right be able to win if Left makes no other lapses? No! Although Right is better off, in that the value after the next four moves will be 0 rather than $\frac{1}{4}$, he will still lose because it will be his turn to move. What would have happened had Left instead made his first move in the top right-hand corner, so creating a second region ⊞ of value ± 1?

SOME SIMPLE HOT GAMES

Positions like the ones we've just been discussing, in which both players are eager to move, naturally make for exciting play and so may be called **hot**. Thus ± 1 is hot, but ± 1000 is hotter still; indeed it has a temperature of $1000°$ on the natural scale. Some new hot values appear in

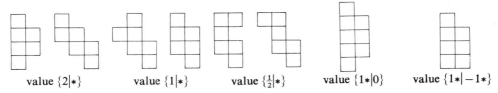

value $\{2|*\}$ value $\{1|*\}$ value $\{\frac{1}{2}|*\}$ value $\{1*|0\}$ value $\{1*|-1*\}$

Figure 6. Heat Associated with Stars.

the positions of Fig. 6. They are all of the form $\{x|y*\}$, $\{x*|y\}$ or $\{x*|y*\}$, with $x \geqslant y$. The temperature policy we laid down for sums of ordinary switches $\{x|y\}$ extends to include these: we still move in the game with greatest temperature $\frac{1}{2}(x-y)$. But some care is needed if two games are equally hot.

We have the identities:

$$\{x|y\} + * = \{x*|y*\} \quad (x \geqslant y)$$
$$\{x|y*\} + * = \{x*|y\} \quad (x > y)$$

So the value of the last region of Fig. 6 can be written in several forms:

$$= \{1*|-1*\} = \pm(1*) = \pm 1 + * = \pm 1*, \text{ say.}$$

THE TINIEST GAMES

The value of the position

$$= \{\quad 0, \quad \{2|0\} \,|\, \{0|-2\}, \{\tfrac{1}{2}|-2\}\}$$

simplifies on bypassing Left's reversible move and omitting Right's dominated one, to

$$\{0|\{0|-2\}\}.$$

It turns out that this value, though positive, is very small indeed, much smaller than $\uparrow$, and we shall write it $+_2$ and pronounce it "**tiny-two**". More generally there is a game "**tiny**-x, namely

$$+_x = \{0|\{0|-x\}\}$$

for any value x, and as x gets larger $+_x$ gets smaller, very rapidly. Indeed, if x and y are numbers with $x > y \geqslant 0$, then $+_x$ is so much smaller than $+_y$ that no matter how many terms $+_x$ we add to each other, the sum will be less than $+_y$. So any multiple of $+_{\frac{1}{4}}$ will be less than $\uparrow$, for we have

$$+_0 = \{0|\{0|0\}\} = \{0|*\} = \uparrow.$$

The negative of $+_x$ is, of course

$$-_x = \{\{x|0\}|0\}.$$

We may pronounce this "**miny**-x"! For sums involving tinies and minies we use natural abbreviations, thus

$$1 +_2 = 1 + (+_2) = 1 + \{0|\{0|-2\}\} = \{1|\{1|-1\}\} = \{1|\pm1\}$$

$$\tfrac{1}{2} -_{\frac{1}{4}} = \tfrac{1}{2} + (-_{\frac{1}{4}}) = \tfrac{1}{2} + \{\{\tfrac{1}{4}|0\}|0\} = \{\{\tfrac{3}{4}|\tfrac{1}{2}\}|\tfrac{1}{2}\}.$$

MODERN MANAGEMENT OF CASH FLOW

The tiny game

$$+_{500} = \{0|\{0|-500\}\}$$

may be interpreted as a clause in the fine print of a contract which reads:

> If Left has not yet filed form XYZ, then Right may issue a formal request that he do so. After such a request has been issued, on any subsequent turn on which Left has still not filed the form, Right may file a decree compelling Left to forfeit a penalty of 500 moves.

The reason that this clause gives no competitive advantage to Right is that issuing the request requires just as much effort (one turn) as filing the form. In fact, careful analysis reveals that the clause gives a tiny positive advantage to Left, because he has the option of filing the form even before it's requested. Not surprisingly, the amount of this tiny advantage decreases rapidly with the increasing value of the penalty which may be imposed for failure to comply with the formal request.

In a sum of tinies and minies, each player emulates the modern businessman who is quick to bill but slow to pay, even though the effort required to issue an invoice is the same as the effort needed to write a cheque. The optimal cash management strategy may be to postpone payment of every bill until the prospect of a penalty is imminent. Every payment is made just prior to its deadline, so no penalties need ever actually be invoked. Thus, issuing a formal request which threatens the opponent with the prospect of a larger penalty always takes precedence over responding to any outstanding smaller threat. In any well-played sum of tinies and minies, the games are completed in order of *increasing* magnitude. The tiniest tinies and minies receive the highest priorities because they are associated with the transactions involving the largest potential penalties. In the end, the outcome of the sum depends only on the sign of the largest component. The winner is the accounts-payable manager who can set the longest record for slow payment while still avoiding any penalty. The explanation for his success is that he holds the purchasing contract on which the penalty for late payment is minimal.

TINY TOADS-AND-FROGS

We return to the game of Toads-and-Frogs and consider some positions in which the numbers of toads and frogs need not be equal, but each lane has just one empty space. The (l,r) game is that whose starting position is

in which Left has l toads and Right r frogs. It turns out that the position

resulting from Right's first move of the (3,2) game has the value $-_{\frac{1}{4}}$ and other tiny and miny values arise from longer Toads and Frogs positions. Let's see how this comes about.

First observe the

DEATH LEAP PRINCIPLE

> If the only legal moves from some position
> are jumps, the value is 0.

This applies just when there is neither a toad immediately to the left of the space, nor a frog immediately to its right. In such positions the first player's later moves are also necessarily jumps and always clear a space for his opponent to reply. Now we can deduce that

> the value of any position of the form
>
>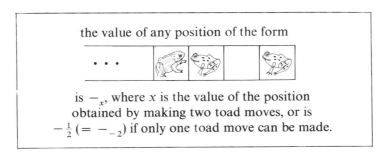
>
> is $-_x$, where x is the value of the position
> obtained by making two toad moves, or is
> $-\frac{1}{2} (= -_2)$ if only one toad move can be made.

Figure 7 illustrates this.

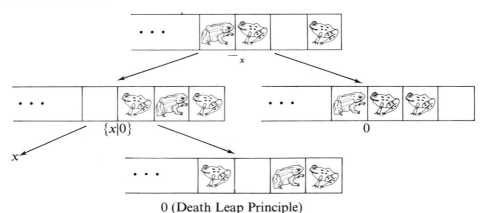

0 (Death Leap Principle)

Figure 7. Miny Toads and Frogs.

THE OPENING DISSECTION OF TOADS-AND-FROGS

We can now evaluate the initial position of any game (l,r) of Toads-and-Frogs with one empty space.

Trivially:

> If $r = 0$, the value is l.

However,

> If $r = 1$ and $l \geqslant 1$, the value is
> $$\{\{l-2 \mid 1\}|0\}.$$

This is proved (for $l \geqslant 2$) by Fig. 8.
In fact the same figure proves the more general result:

> The position
>
>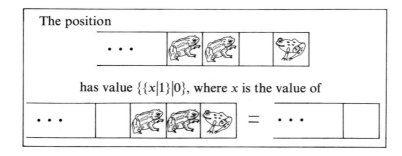
>
> has value $\{\{x|1\}|0\}$, where x is the value of

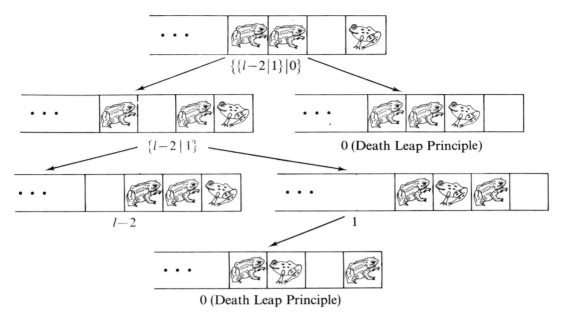

Figure 8. A Lone Frog Faces Toads

The remaining initial positions are covered by

> If $r \geqslant 2$, $l \geqslant 2$, the initial position of (l,r) has value $*$.

The skeptical reader should play the game

 $+ \quad *$

as second player, always playing in the Toads-and-Frogs component if he can. He will find that after a few moves the Death Leap Principle applies.

Our results on initial positions are summarized in Table 1. To save space we have omitted the braces, writing $1*|0$ for $\{1*|0\}$, etc. Since $2|1|0$ would be ambiguous we have introduced $\|$ ("slashes") as a stronger form of $|$. Thus $2|1\|0$ means $\{\{2|1\}|0\}$, whereas $2\|1|0$ would mean $\{2|\{1|0\}\}$.

Table 1. Initial Values for Toads-and-Frogs.

	r = 0	1	2	3	4	5	6
l = 0 0	0	−1	−2	−3	−4	−5	−6
1 1	1	*	$0\mid-\frac{1}{2}$	$0\mid-1*$	$0\parallel-1\mid-2$	$0\parallel-1\mid-3$	$0\parallel-1\mid-4$
2 2	2	$\frac{1}{2}\mid0$	*	*	*	*	*
3 3	3	$1*\mid0$	*	*	*	*	*
4 4	4	$2\mid1\parallel0$	*	*	*	*	*
5 5	5	$3\mid1\parallel0$	*	*	*	*	*
6 6	6	$4\mid1\parallel0$	*	*	*	*	*

In the Extras to this chapter we evaluate a number of other Toads-and-Frogs positions. The position

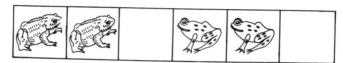

with two empty spaces has value $\{\frac{1}{4}\mid\downarrow\}$. Our policy about playing in the hottest game still applies to sums involving such values, but it can be hard to make the correct choice when several components are equally hot.

Figure 9 shows a Toads-and-Frogs position chosen so as to make these ideas clear. We suppose that it is Left's turn to move. To help him, we have appended the values (see the Extras to this chapter) and arranged the lanes in decreasing order of temperature. What should he do?

grid						value	temperature, $\frac{1}{2}(x-y)$
T	T	F		F	F	$*\mid-1$	$\frac{1}{2}$
	F	T	T		F	$-\frac{1}{2}\mid-1$	$\frac{1}{4}$
T	F	T		F	F	$0\mid-\frac{1}{4}$	$\frac{1}{8}$
T	T			F	F	$\frac{1}{4}\mid\downarrow$	$\frac{1}{8}$
F	T	T		T	F	$1\mid1 = 1*$	0
T		T	F	F	T	$0\mid* = \uparrow$	0

Figure 9. Left to Move and Win.

There is no room for doubt about the first moves of the two players. Left moves from the hottest game, $*\mid-1$, to $*$, and **Right** then converts the next hottest game, $-\frac{1}{2}\mid-1$, to -1. But now

Left faces a dilemma, since the next two games, $0|-\frac{1}{4}$ and $\frac{1}{4}|\downarrow$, are equally hot. If Left moves in $0|-\frac{1}{4}$ and Right in $\frac{1}{4}|\downarrow$, the value will become

$$* - 1 + 0 + \downarrow + 1* + \uparrow = 0,$$

a win for Right, as most recent mover. But if instead Left moves in $\frac{1}{4}|\downarrow$ and Right in $0|-\frac{1}{4}$, the value will be

$$* - 1 + \frac{1}{4} - \frac{1}{4} + 1* + \uparrow = \uparrow,$$

a clear win for Left. We might have guessed this, for since the difference between $\frac{1}{4}$ and $\downarrow$ is greater than that between 0 and $-\frac{1}{4}$, the value $\frac{1}{4}|\downarrow$ is really just a little bit hotter than $0|-\frac{1}{4}$, and should perhaps have been placed above it. But neither of $1|*$ and $0|-1$ can be considered hotter than the other, for in their sum

$$\{1|*\} + \{0|-1\}$$

Left should prefer to move from the latter and Right from the former. Find the best starting move for each player from the 3-lane Toads-and-Frogs position of Fig. 10.

F	T		F	F	F	value	$0|-1*$
T		F		F	T	value	$-1*$
T	T	T		T	F	value	$2|1$

Figure 10. What Are the Best Moves?

Positions involving tinies and minies can be even more difficult, and the temperature policy may suggest the wrong move. If Left starts and both players apply the temperature policy from

	T	T		F	T	value	temperature
T	F	T		F	F	$\frac{1}{2}|0$	$\frac{1}{4}$
T		T	F	F	F	$0|-\frac{1}{4}$	$\frac{1}{8}$
	T	T	F		F	$+_{\frac{1}{4}}$	0
						$-\frac{1}{4}$	0

the value after two moves will be

$$\tfrac{1}{2} - \tfrac{1}{4} + +_{\frac{1}{4}} - \tfrac{1}{4} = +_{\frac{1}{4}},$$

a win for Left. However, if Right had responded to Left's opening by moving from

$$+_{\frac{1}{4}} = \{0|\{0|-\tfrac{1}{4}\}\}$$

to $0|-\frac{1}{4}$, the resulting value would have been

$$\tfrac{1}{2} + \{0|-\tfrac{1}{4}\} + \{0|-\tfrac{1}{4}\} - \tfrac{1}{4},$$

which after two more moves becomes

$$\tfrac{1}{2} + 0 - \tfrac{1}{4} - \tfrac{1}{4} = 0,$$

a win for Right, the last mover. We can say that $+_{\frac{1}{4}}$ possesses **latent heat** since it has the hot option $0|-\frac{1}{4}$. The temperature policy works with games whose options are like

$$x, \quad x + *, \quad x + \uparrow, \quad x + *2, \quad x + \uparrow + *$$

for any number x, since these have no latent heat.

SEATING BOYS AND GIRLS

Let's have a children's party to celebrate the end of this chapter. Left will seat the boys and Right the girls round the table shown in Fig. 11. To preserve decorum no child may be seated next to another of the opposite sex. Whichever of Left and Right is first unable to seat a child must cope with the angry parents.

This is rather like the game of Seating Couples from Chapter 2, with the difference that a player's move effectively reserves the adjacent seats, if empty, for him rather than for his opponent. We use

> LnL for a row of n empty chairs between two boys,
> RnR for a row of n empty chairs between two girls, and
> LnR for a row of n empty chairs between a boy and a girl.

Figure 11. Where Does Left Seat the Next Boy?

The values are computed using the equations

$$LnL = \{LaL + LbL \mid LaR + RbL\}$$

$$RnR = \{RaL + LbR \mid RaR + RbR\} \qquad (= -LnL)$$

$$LnR = \{LaL + LbR \mid LaR + RbR\} \qquad (= RnL)$$

where a and b are any numbers adding to $n-1$ *except* that L0R and R0L are illegal. These look like the equations for Seating Couples (Chapter 2). However, the values are hotter (Table 2).

n	0	1	2	3	4	5	6
LnL	0	1	2	2|0	3|*	$\{4 \mid 0, \pm 1\}$	$\{3 \mid *\} \pm 1$
LnR	—	0	*	± 1	± 2	$\pm 2*$	$\pm 2 \pm 1$
RnR	0	-1	-2	$0\|-2$	*|-3	$\{\pm 1, 0 \mid -4\}$	$\{* \mid -3\} \pm 1$

Table 2. Values of Positions in Seating Boys and Girls.

In Fig. 11 can Left win?

EXTRAS

In Fig. 10 the only good move for Left is in the first lane and the only good move for Right is in the last.

Left cannot win the position R5R, R4L, L3R in Seating Boys and Girls shown in Fig. 11. The value is

$$\{\pm 1,0\,|-4\} \pm 2 \pm 1.$$

If Left plays in the first component (seats a boy on the far side of the table) Right seats a girl by the near jug of lemonade, while if he seats a boy anywhere else, Right seats a girl opposite the far jug, securing four more seats for the girls.

TOADS AND FROGS COMPLETELY DISSECTED

Figure 12 represents the moves from the general initial position (l,r) in 1-space Toads-and-Frogs.

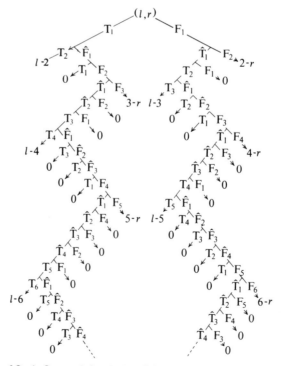

Figure 12. A General Analysis of 1-space Toads-and-Frogs.

132

Each edge is labelled so as to show exactly which creature makes the corresponding move (the creatures of each species being numbered from the initial space outwards); a circumflex indicates that the move is a jump. There are only two ways of leaving the main zig-zags of the figure: the positions marked 0 are instances of the Death Leap Principle, and those marked with the integers

$$l-2, l-3, l-4, \ldots \quad \text{or} \quad 2-r, 3-r, 4-r, \ldots$$

are cases in which only toads or only frogs are able to move from now on. The values in any particular case can be found by omitting moves which would be made by non-existent animals. Figures 13 to 16 illustrate the cases $(l,r) = (2,2), (3,2), (4,2)$ and $(3,3)$, which together with $(l,1)$ (which we have already discussed) and their negatives suffice for positions with up to 7 places and only 1 space. **Dead** animals, no longer able to move, are indicated by lower case letters. Positions where further application of the Death Leap Principle has been made are boxed.

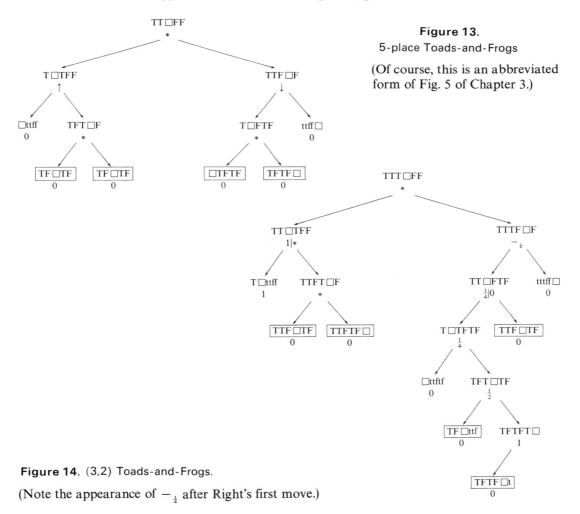

Figure 13.

5-place Toads-and-Frogs

(Of course, this is an abbreviated form of Fig. 5 of Chapter 3.)

Figure 14. (3,2) Toads-and-Frogs.

(Note the appearance of $-\frac{1}{4}$ after Right's first move.)

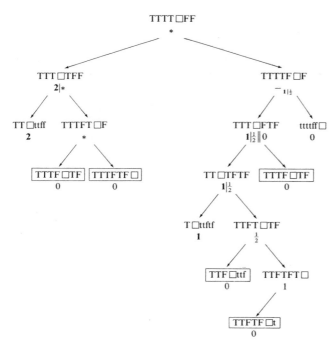

Figure 15. (4,2) Toads-and-Frogs.

(We obtain the figure for the position $(l,2)$ with larger l on replacing the bold figures **2** and **1** by $l-2$ and $l-3$ respectively.)

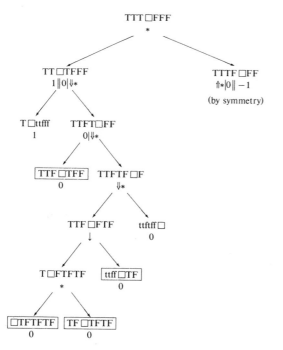

Figure 16. (3,3) Toads-and-Frogs.

(The value $\Uparrow*|0$ will occur again in Bynum's game of Eatcake in Chapter 8).

TOADS-AND-FROGS WITH TWO SPACES

In general one can play $(l+c+r)$-place Toads-and-Frogs from the starting position in which l toads are separated by c spaces from r frogs; we call this the $(l,r)_c$ game, where we have omitted c when it is 1. Figures 17, 18 and 19 show the positions arising in one lane of each of the 2-space games $(2,1)_2$, $(2,2)_2$ and $(3,1)_2$. Options are shown except where values, or their negatives, can be quoted from elsewhere, e.g. from Fig. 16 of Chapter 1 (the $(1,1)_2$ game), Fig. 8 of Chapter 3 (the $(2,2)$ game), or Figs. 13 to 16 in this chapter.

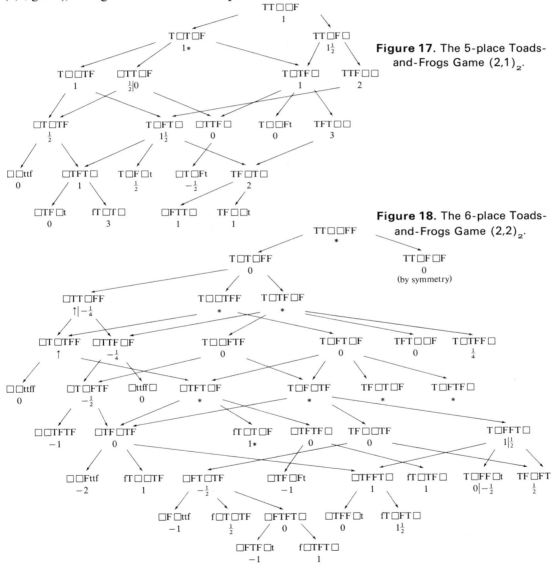

Figure 17. The 5-place Toads-and-Frogs Game $(2,1)_2$.

Figure 18. The 6-place Toads-and-Frogs Game $(2,2)_2$.

136

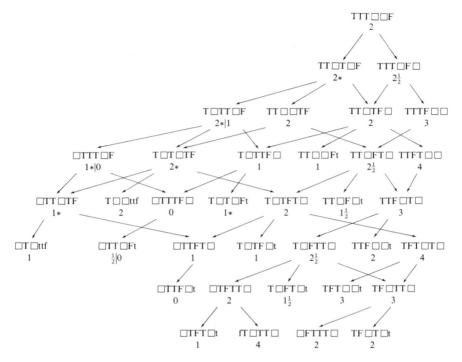

Figure 19. The 6-place Toads-and-Frogs Game $(3,1)_2$.

Omar might like to confirm and extend the results of Table 3 which gives the values of the starting positions for some $(l,r)_2$ games.

$r = 0$	1	2	3	4	5	6
$l = 0$ 0	-2	-4	-6	-8	-10	-12
1 2	0	-1	-2	-3		
2 4	1	$*$	$0\|-\frac{1}{2}$			
3 6	2	$\frac{1}{2}\|0$	$\pm\frac{1}{8}$			
4 8	3					
5 10						

Table 3. Values of Starting Positions in $(l,r)_2$ Toads-and-Frogs.

MORE DOMINEERING VALUES

Values for all positions with six and seven squares are shown in Figs. 20 and 21 and values for some larger positions in Fig. 22. These results are partly quoted from ONAG where some of them are explained. The following ideas are useful:

(i) If from some position, Left has an option of value n and it is impossible to pack $n+1$ vertical dominoes into the region, then n is Left's best option.

(ii) The value of a position is unaltered or increased by cutting it along some vertical lines; it is unaltered or decreased by cutting it along horizontal lines.

(iii) If

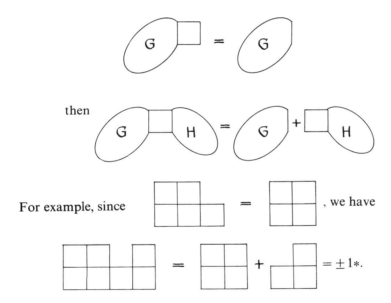

Care must be exercised in making *multiple* use of this principle; a square may be added to any *one* of the double edges in each position of Figs. 2 and 20 without affecting the values of the position (there are 3 cases where a square may be added to two double edges *simultaneously*).

Figure 20 gives the values of all the 35 6-square regions; note that if a region is turned through a right angle its value changes sign. There are 108 7-square regions. The values of 30 of these are the same as those of appropriate 6-square regions, the 7-square regions being obtained by adjoining a square to any one of the double edges in Fig. 20. Figure 21 gives the values of 58 other 7-square regions. The remaining 20 are obtained by rotating the sets of squares marked with circles about the axis drawn through one of the circles.

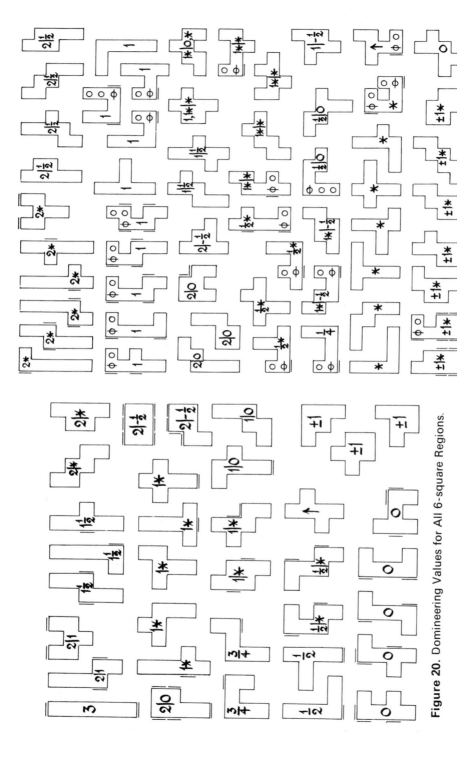

Figure 21. Domineering Values for 7-square Regions.

Figure 20. Domineering Values for All 6-square Regions.

Table 4 gives the values of $m \times n$ rectangles in Domineering.

n	1	2	3	4	5	6	7	8
m								
1	0	-1	-1	-2	-2	-3	-3	-4
2	1	± 1	$2\vert-\frac{1}{2}$	$-_2$	$\frac{1}{2}$	$1-_2\vert-1$	$1\frac{1}{2}\vert-\frac{1}{2}$	$2-_2\vert 0\Vert-\frac{1}{2}\vert-2\frac{1}{2}$
3	1	$\frac{1}{2}\vert-2$	± 1	$-1\frac{1}{2}$	-1			
4	2	$+_2$	$1\frac{1}{2}$					
5	2	$-\frac{1}{2}$	1		0			
6	3	$1\vert-1+_2$						
7	3	$\frac{1}{2}\vert-1\frac{1}{2}$						
8	4	$2\frac{1}{2}\vert\frac{1}{2}\Vert 0\vert-2+_2$						

Table 4. Values of Rectangular Regions in Domineering.

Figure 22 gives values for some miscellaneous regions with eight or more squares, while Fig. 23 shows some interesting sequences.

The impartial version of Domineering, in which either player may place his domino in either orientation, is discussed in Chapter 15 under the name of Cram.

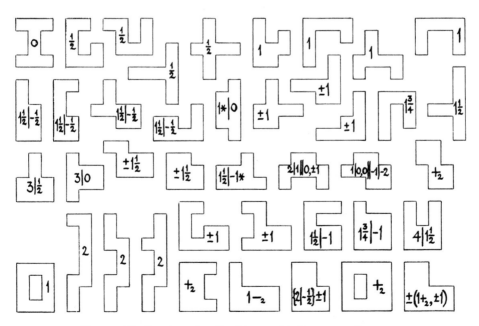

Figure 22. Domineering Positions with 8 or more Squares.

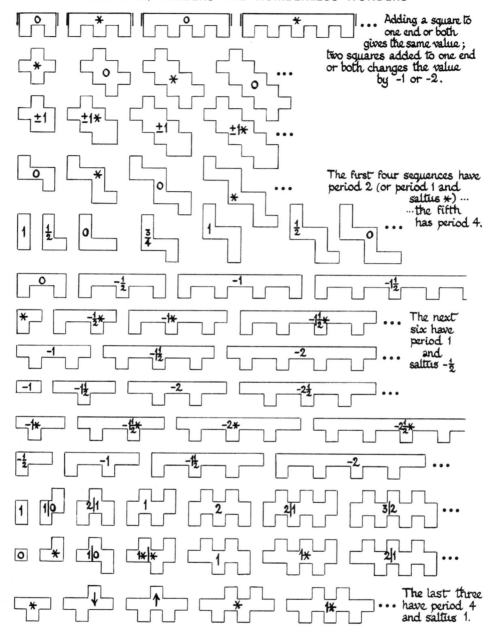

Figure 23. Some Sequences of Domineering Positions.

REFERENCES AND FURTHER READING

J. H. Conway, "On Numbers and Games", Academic Press, London and New York, 1976, pp. 74–77, 114–121.
Martin Gardner, Mathematical Games: Cram, crosscram and quadraphage: new games having elusive winning strategies, Sci. Amer. **230** #2 (Feb. 1974) 106–108.

Chapter 6

The Heat of Battle

When the hurly-burly's done
When the battle's lost and won.
      William Shakespeare, *Macbeth,* I.i, 1.

. . . not without dust and heat.
      John Milton, *Areopagitica.*

When you're playing a sum of cold games there's not much of a problem. Their values will be numbers, every move gives something away and you just have to tot up the numbers to find the least disadvantageous move. When the hot games are switches with only cold options, as in Cashing Cheques, you just move in the hottest game. But when you're in a really complicated battle, and things are likely to stay hot for quite some time, then you'll have a hard job deciding what to do. This chapter will give you some help in coping with the heat.

SNORT

This is a game introduced by S. Norton in which there are many hot and complicated positions. On alternate weeks Farmer Black is in the bull market buying black bulls, and in the intervening week Farmer White will be found buying white cows. They jointly rent a certain farm and intend to put each herd in a separate field. Of course they mustn't put bulls and cows in adjoining fields. That farmer loses who is first unable to find a suitable open field for his latest purchase.

You can play this game like the map-coloring game of Col, introduced in Chapter 2. The difference is that in Snort adjacent fields may not be used by *opposing* players, whereas adjacent regions of the maps in Col were not available to the *same* player.

A GRAPHIC PICTURE OF FARM LIFE

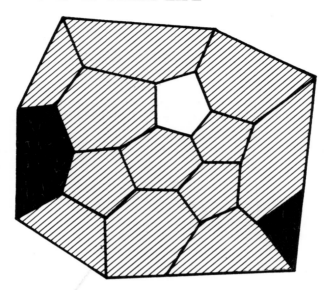

Figure 1. Snort Farm after Farmer Black's Second Purchase of Bulls.

Figure 1 shows a farm as it might look after Farmer Black's second purchase. The two black fields hold bulls, the white one holds cows and the shaded ones are still empty. To get a clear idea of what is going on let's put a dot (•) in each field that is still available to both players, a black spot (●) in one usable only for bulls, and a white spot (○) in one open to cows only. There's one field that's not available to either player since it's adjacent to both bulls and cows, and we've indicated this in Fig. 2(a) by the piebald spot (◖). These dots and spots are now joined by lines indicating adjacency of fields.

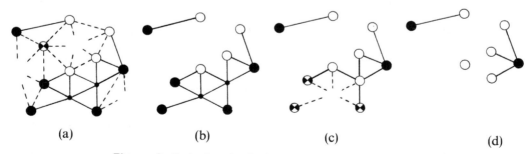

(a)   (b)   (c)   (d)

Figure 2. Reducing the Problems of Farm Management.

So Fig. 2(a) contains all the information of Fig. 1 in a more perspicuous form. We can further simplify such figures by

omitting any piebald spot,
omitting any line joining similarly colored spots,

as in Fig. 2(b), since the omitted things have no further effect on the game.

To play Snort directly on these simplified graphs, Black, when he takes a node, should add a black coloration to all neighboring ones. This is in addition to any coloration already present, so that a white node will become piebald and can therefore be omitted. Of course, similar remarks can be made for the other player; for instance if Farmer White now puts cows in the lowest field available to him we get Fig. 2(c), simplifying to Fig. 2(d).

Figure 3 contains the values of a number of Snort positions that can be found this way:

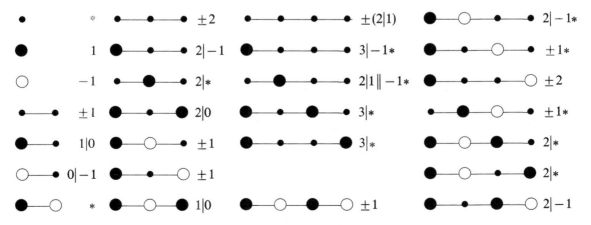

In the Extras you'll find a more extensive Snort dictionary from which many of the examples for this chapter have been taken.

Figure 3. A Short Snort Dictionary.

DON'T MOVE IN A NUMBER UNLESS THERE'S NOTHING ELSE TO DO!

When you're playing in a sum of games with values of different types, it can be quite hard to decide where your best move lies. But since if x is a number in simplest form, we have

$$x^L < x < x^R,$$

each player makes himself worse off by moving in x. So when considering which component to move in, you should always prefer the non-numbers:

> DON'T MOVE IN A NUMBER
> UNLESS THERE'S
> NOTHING ELSE TO DO!

THE NUMBER AVOIDANCE THEOREM

You'll find a more formal proof in the Extras. More generally the obvious question to ask when comparing moves in different components is

WHAT'S IN IT FOR ME?

For example, if Left makes the move from G to G^L then what's in it for him is the amount

$$G^L - G$$

by which the value is increased. On the other hand, Right, who's trying to keep things down, gains

$$G - G^R$$

by moving from G to G^R, since this is how much the value is *reduced*. So we'll call the various differences

$$G^L - G \quad \text{and} \quad G - G^R$$

the (Left and Right) **incentives** of G.

Looking at various numbers in simplest form, for example,

$$1 = \{0| \ \}, \qquad 2\tfrac{1}{2} = \{2|3\}, \qquad \tfrac{3}{4} = \{\tfrac{1}{2}|1\},$$

you can see that the incentives

$$x^L - x \quad \text{and} \quad x - x^R$$

are found among the negative numbers

$$-1, \ -\tfrac{1}{2}, \ -\tfrac{1}{4}, \ -\tfrac{1}{8}, \ \ldots$$

explaining why each player feels a *dis*incentive to move from x. But we'll see that from any *non-number*, each player has an incentive which is *almost* positive, being strictly greater than all these negative numbers.

For example, $2|-1$ *isn't* a number, but $1\frac{1}{4} = 1|1\frac{1}{2}$ *is*, and so we have

$$\{2|-1\} + 1\frac{1}{4} = 3\frac{1}{4}|\frac{1}{4},$$

since the players won't consider the moves to

$$\{2|-1\} + 1 \quad \text{and} \quad \{2|-1\} + 1\frac{1}{2}$$

because they know the Number Avoidance Theorem.

More generally we have

THE TRANSLATION PRINCIPLE

> If $G = \{G^L|G^R\}$ *isn't* a number
> and x *is*, then
> $$\{G^L|G^R\} + x = \{G^L + x \mid G^R + x\},$$

because

$$G + x = \{G^L + x, G + x^L \mid G^R + x, G + x^R\}$$

and, by the Number Avoidance Theorem, the options

$$G + x^L \quad \text{and} \quad G + x^R$$

are dominated.

The Snort position

is *hot* because Left will move to

with value 2, and Right to

with value -1, but whichever of these two positions is reached, neither player would like to move in what remains because their values are numbers. We call 2 the Left stop of G, and -1 its Right stop. And because G satisfies the equation

$$G + G = 1,$$

we might say that it has a "mean value" of $\frac{1}{2}$.

Similarly the game

$$H = \bullet\!\!-\!\!\bullet\!\!-\!\!\bullet\!\!-\!\!\bullet = 2|1\,\|-1*$$

has a Left stop of 1, a Right stop of -1, and has mean value $\frac{1}{4}$ because it satisfies

$$4 \cdot H = 1.$$

In this case the mean value is *not* the average of the Left and Right stops. How do we compute the stopping values and the mean value for an arbitrary game which doesn't seem to satisfy any convenient little equation?

THE LEFT AND RIGHT STOPS

are easily found. Let us agree to stop the play of any game when its value becomes a number. Because moving in numbers is bad for you this doesn't have any effect on intelligent play. When all the components have become numbers sensible players will stop playing altogether and just tot up the score! So the positions of a game whose values are numbers become stopping positions with this rule. The ones whose values *aren't* numbers may be called *active* positions since the players will still want to move in them.

When an active game such as

$$G = \bullet\!\!-\!\!\bullet\!\!-\!\!\bullet\!\!-\!\!\bullet\!\!-\!\!\bullet = 3|2\,\|\,0, \pm1$$

is played together with some other games that have already stopped at numerical values the play will concentrate in G until it also reaches a stopping position, x, say. Left should try to make x as large as possible, and Right to make it as small as possible. In this case, if Left starts, G will stop at value 2 with Left to move, while if Right starts, G will stop at 0, again with Left to move. We indicate this situation by writing

$$L(G) = L(2), \qquad R(G) = L(0).$$

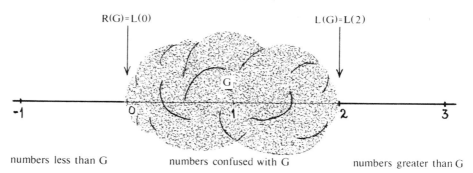

Figure 4. The Left and Right Stops and Confusion Interval of $3|2\,\|\,0, \pm1$.

By playing a general game G in this way we define the two numbers which we call the **Left stop** and **Right stop** of G, and also find who is to move when these stops are reached. We then know how G compares with all numbers, because the cloud for G in Fig. 4 crosses the axis at the Left and Right stops on the sides determined by whose turn it is to play. In our example the cloud passes to the *left* of 0 and to the *left* of 2. The region between the Left and Right stops (covered by the cloud in our figures) is called the **confusion interval**.

Figure 5 shows the confusion intervals of

$$\downarrow = 0|0\,\|\,0, \qquad\qquad * = 0|0, \qquad\qquad \uparrow = 0\,\|\,0|0$$

for which we have

$$L(\downarrow) = R(\downarrow) = L(0); \qquad L(*) = R(0), R(*) = L(0); \qquad L(\uparrow) = R(\uparrow) = R(0).$$

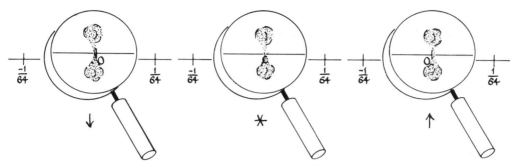

Figure 5. The Confusion Intervals of Down, Star and Up.

You can see that a confusion interval may contain just one point, or be empty, in several different ways In each of these cases, the game is *infinitesimally close* to a number.

COOLING—AND THE THERMOGRAPH

A game which is confused with a *large* interval of numbers is *hot* and both players will be eager to move in it. To find its mean value. we should try to decrease the confusion. by cooling it. To cool a game by t degrees we impose a tax of size t payable at each move. However we must take care to provide appropriate exemptions for moves to stopping positions so that our tax rules won't distort the underlying economy. Numbers are already inactive and must not be changed by additional cooling.

The game G_t (*G* **cooled by** t) is defined for increasing values of t as follows:

> $$G_t = \{G_t^L - t \mid G_t^R + t\}$$
>
> *unless* there is a smaller temperature t' for which $G_{t'}$ is infinitesimally close to a number x, in which case
>
> $$G_t = x \quad \text{for all} \quad t > t'.$$

THE COOLING FORMULA

Let's look at our Snort position

$$G = \bullet\!\!-\!\!-\!\!-\!\bullet\!\!-\!\!-\!\!-\!\bullet = 2|-1$$

as t increases. We find

$$G = G_0 = 2|-1$$
$$G_{\frac{1}{2}} = 1\tfrac{1}{2}|-\tfrac{1}{2} \quad (= 2-\tfrac{1}{2}\,|\,-1+\tfrac{1}{2})$$
$$G_1 = 1|0$$
$$G_{1\frac{1}{2}} = \tfrac{1}{2}|\tfrac{1}{2} = \tfrac{1}{2}+*$$

which is infinitesimally close to $\frac{1}{2}$ and so

$$G_t = \tfrac{1}{2} \quad \text{for all} \quad t > 1\tfrac{1}{2}.$$

So this game reduces to its mean value, $\frac{1}{2}$, when it is cooled through any temperature exceeding $1\frac{1}{2}$.

We represent this by drawing the **thermograph** of G (Fig. 6) in which, at height t above the ground, we plot the Left and Right stops of G_t. It's handy to have the numbers along the axis in *descending* order to keep Left's moves to the left and Right's moves to the right.

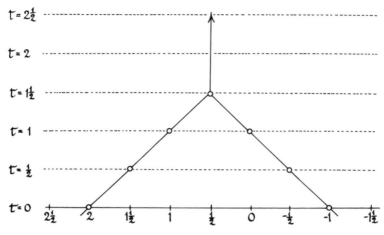

Figure 6. The Thermograph of $2|-1$.

COOLING SETTLES THE MEAN VALUE

It will be clear that cooling by a sufficiently large amount must necessarily lead to a number, m, say, so that we have

$$G_t = m \quad \text{for} \quad t > t_0.$$

This means that every thermograph is surmounted by an infinite vertical **mast**. The smallest value of t_0 for which this holds is called the **temperature**, $t(G)$, of G, and we have

$$m - t < G < m + t$$

for all $t > t(G)$. Why is m the mean value of G?

The answer is that we can prove

$$(A + B + C + \ldots)_t = A_t + B_t + C_t + \ldots$$

and in particular

$$(G + G + G + \ldots)_t = G_t + G_t + G_t + \ldots$$

so that for all $t > t(G)$ we have

$$(G + G + G + \ldots)_t = m + m + m + \ldots$$

and

$$m + m + m + \ldots - t < G + G + G + \ldots < m + m + m + \ldots + t.$$

> To within a bounded error, a lot of copies of G may be replaced by the same number of copies of its mean value.

If it were not for the tax exemptions for stopping positions, the equation

$$(A+B+C+\ldots)_t = A_t + B_t + C_t + \ldots$$

would be obvious, because the typical Left option is

$$(A+B^L+C+\ldots)_t - t = A_t + (B_t^L - t) + C_t + \ldots,$$

so that the tax on the whole move from

$$A + B + C + \ldots \quad \text{to} \quad A + B^L + C + \ldots$$

can be regarded as charged to the component move from

$$B \quad \text{to} \quad B^L.$$

Fortunately the tax exemptions on stopping positions don't affect this because if x is a number, the Translation Principle ensures that

$$(x+G)_t = x+G_t, \qquad (x-G)_t = x-G_t, \qquad x_t = x,$$

so that the equation

$$(A+B)_t = A_t + B_t$$

holds true if any one of A, B and $A+B$ is made equal to a number x.

HOW TO DRAW THERMOGRAPHS

The Snort position

has the same value

$$G = 2|1\|0$$

as the Domineering position

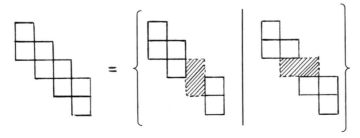

Let's draw its thermograph and find its mean value.

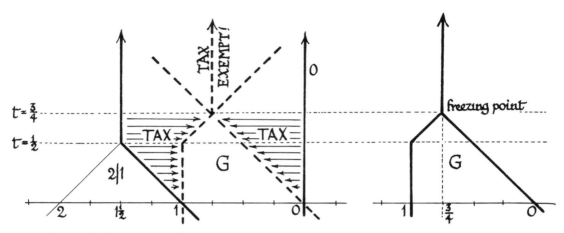

Figure 7. Drawing the Thermograph of G.   **Figure 8.** The Final Form.

The thermograph of $2|1$ is like the one we already found for $2|-1$; its Left and Right boundaries are slanting lines which start at 2 and 1 and then meet and become vertical at height $t = \frac{1}{2}$ showing that $2|1$ has temperature $\frac{1}{2}$ and mean value $1\frac{1}{2}$. Because 0 is already a number, *its* thermograph is just a vertical line.

After Left has moved from G to $2|1$ it will be *Right's* turn and so the *Right* boundary of $2|1$ is important and has been boldly drawn. We've also emphasized the *Left* boundary of 0 (which happens to coincide with its Right boundary).

Now to impose the tax! We tax Left by moving *rightwards* since this corresponds to *subtraction* of t on our reversed scale. When we move the Right boundary through a distance t at height t it yields the thick broken line which starts vertically at 1 before turning to slant to the right at height $\frac{1}{2}$. Because Right is taxed by *addition* of t we move the Left boundary of 0 to the *left* yielding the slanting thick broken line through 0.

These two thick broken lines define the Left and Right stops for G_t until they meet at a place called the **freezing point** (in this case at height $\frac{3}{4}$ above the point $\frac{3}{4}$, showing that G cooled by $\frac{3}{4}$ is infinitesimally close to $\frac{3}{4}$ and so $G_t = \frac{3}{4}$ for all $t > \frac{3}{4}$. The thermograph of G is therefore as in Fig. 8, both boundaries coinciding with the vertical mast above this point.

WHEN A PLAYER HAS SEVERAL OPTIONS

the best one to choose may depend on the cooling temperature. Figure 9 shows how to draw the thermograph in such a case, namely for the Snort position

$$G = \bullet\!\!-\!\!-\!\!\bullet\!\!-\!\!-\!\!\bullet\!\!-\!\!-\!\!\bigcirc\!\!-\!\!-\!\!\bullet\!\!-\!\!-\!\!\bigcirc = \{\{2|-1\},0\|\{-2|-4\}\}.$$

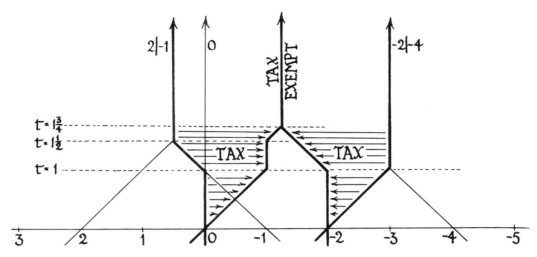

Figure 9. Drawing a Thermograph when Left has Two Options.

Which of his options $2|-1$ and 0 does Left choose? Since it will be *Right's* turn to move it is the option's *Right boundary* which is important and so

> For each temperature t,
> *Left* chooses whichever of
> his options has *leftmost*
> *Right boundary* at t.

In the example this is 0 for $t \leqslant 1$, and $2|-1$ for $t > 1$, and so we've emphasized the Right boundary of 0 below the dotted line at $t = 1$ and the Right boundary of $2|-1$ above it. We have also emphasized the Left boundary of Right's only option, $-2|-4$. The thermograph boundaries for G are therefore given by the thick lines obtained by taxing these by an amount t at each height t until they meet.

FOUNDATIONS FOR THERMOGRAPHS

You'll see that the bottoms of our thermographs are always a bit ragged because we continue their boundaries a little bit below the ground. To see why, let's look at the thermographs of $*$ and $\uparrow$. For $* = 0|0$ the relevant option boundaries are both the vertical line through 0 which are taxed into two oppositely slanting lines through 0. Since these meet at 0, the thermograph of $*$ is vertical above 0, but has two slanting lines just below 0, as in Fig. 10(a) (or Fig. 11(a) with $a = b = 0$).

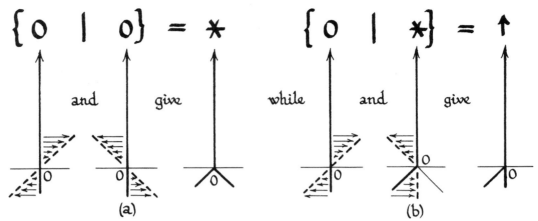

Figure 10. The Thermographs of Star and Up.

The same Left boundary serves for ↑. To find its *Right* boundary we tax the Left boundary of ∗ to obtain the broken line which is slanting above the ground, but vertical just below it, as shown in Fig. 10(b) (or Fig. 11(b), with $a = b = 0$). Once again, these meet at ground level, but diverge just below it, although this time the Right boundary remains vertical.

EXAMPLES OF THERMOGRAPHS

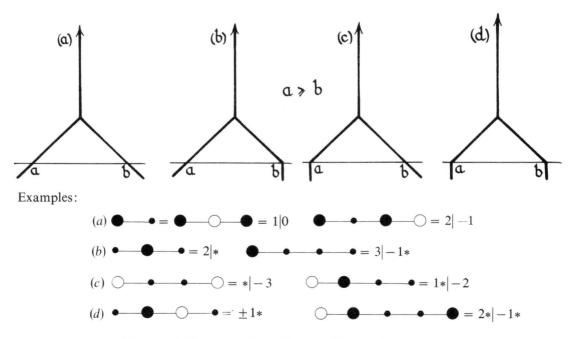

Figure 11. Thermographs of Games with Two Stops, x or $x\ast$.

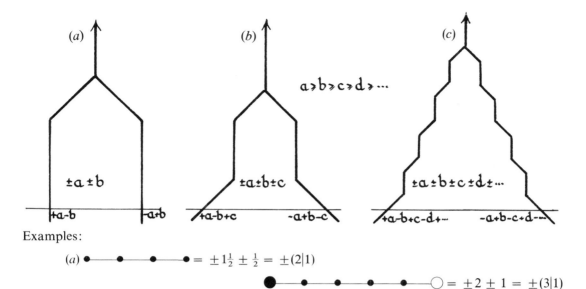

Examples:

(a) ●——————●——————●——————● $= \pm 1\frac{1}{2} \pm \frac{1}{2} = \pm(2|1)$

● ● ● ● ● ○ $= \pm 2 \pm 1 = \pm(3|1)$

(b) ●——————⬤——————●——————○——————● $= \pm 1\frac{1}{2} \pm \frac{1}{2} \pm 0 = \pm(2*|1*)$

(c) The Childish Hackenbush position with several loops of l_i blue and r_i red

edges, $i = 1, 2, 3, \ldots$

Figure 12. Saskatchewan Landscape; Thermographs of Games with Two, Three or More Switches.

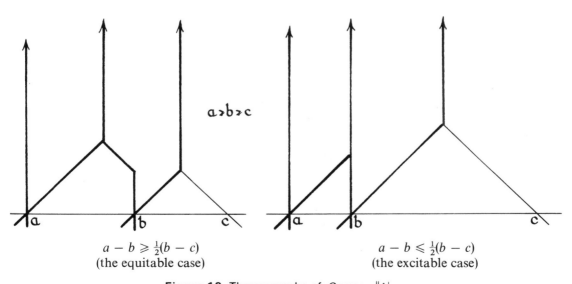

$$a - b \geqslant \tfrac{1}{2}(b - c)$$
(the equitable case)

$$a - b \leqslant \tfrac{1}{2}(b - c)$$
(the excitable case)

Figure 13. Thermographs of Games $a \| b | c$.

WHO IS TO MOVE FROM THE FINAL STOP?

This is easy to see from the thermograph, since a *vertical* line represents a stopping point reached after *equal* numbers of moves by each player, while a *slanting* line is one reached after the starting player has *also* made the last move. This means that the confusion interval of G_t includes endpoints on slanting lines but *ex*cludes ones on vertical lines. It is important to notice that where a thermograph boundary changes slope the confusion interval is determined from the *down*ward slope. Thus in Fig. 11(a) *both* endpoints are in the confusion interval, and in Fig. 11(d) *neither*. For Fig. 11(b), a is in and b is not, and conversely for Fig. 11(c).

If x is a number you can tell whether $G \geqslant x$ or $G \leqslant x$ by seeing whether the thermograph of G is entirely to the left or right of the vertical line through x. Thus the thermograph shown in Fig. 14 for the game

$$G = \;\bullet\!\!-\!\!-\!\!-\!\!\bullet\!\!-\!\!-\!\!\bullet\!\!-\!\!-\!\!\bullet\!\!-\!\!-\!\!\bullet\!\!-\!\!-\!\!\bullet\; = \; 4|3\,\|\,1*\,|-1*$$

shows that $G \leqslant 3$, but $G \not\geqslant 1$ because the thermograph has a "toenail" protruding to the right of 1. On the other hand, if x is any number less than 1, we have $G > x$ (the toenail is infinitesimally small).

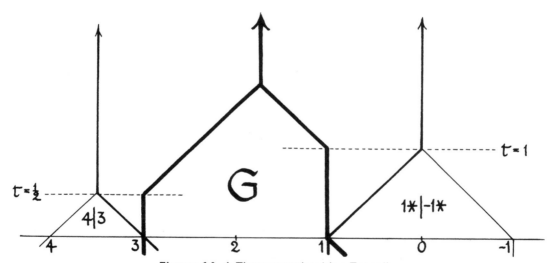

Figure 14. A Thermograph with a Toenail.

A FOUR-STOP EXAMPLE

If you're to play well in complicated situations you'll need to be familiar with thermographs and to understand the Thermostatic Strategy given later in the chapter. In the next few sections we'll discuss play in sums of 4-stop games of the form

$$H = a|b\,\|\,c|d \qquad (a \geqslant b > c \geqslant d)$$

to show you the kind of considerations that arise. By the Translation Principle this can be converted into the form

$$H = \tfrac{1}{4}s + \{x \pm y \mid -x \pm z\} = \tfrac{1}{4}s + G, \text{ say,}$$

where

$$s = a+b+c+d,$$

$$x = \tfrac{1}{4}(a+b-c-d),$$

$$y = \tfrac{1}{2}(a-b),$$

$$z = \tfrac{1}{2}(c-d).$$

The thermograph of this game has three possible forms (Fig. 15) according to the sizes of the numbers involved. The informal terms *equitable* and *excitable* refer to certain aspects of your strategy when playing sums of these games. We won't give exact definitions but the next few sections contain a heuristic discussion of these ideas.

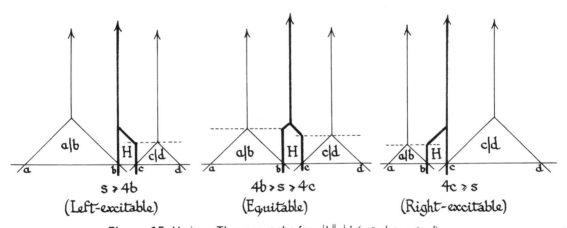

Figure 15. Various Thermographs for $a|b \| c|d$, $(a \geqslant b > c \geqslant d)$.

THE CHEQUE-MARKET EXCHANGE

In Chapter 5 we played the game of Cashing Cheques. Each cheque has a specified value in terms of some number of moves, but a blank payee. Either player may acquire any single cheque at his turn. An unclaimed cheque of amount x is the game $\pm x = \{x \mid -x\}$.

Let us now imagine a market-place for cheques in which Honest Joe offers either player an unclaimed cheque of value x in return for another unclaimed cheque of value y. If x exceeds y, then we have only a disguised form of the two-unclaimed-cheques game,

$$\{x \pm y \mid -x \pm y\} = \pm x + \pm y.$$

However if $y \geqslant x$, then neither player will ever accept Honest Joe's offer, which evidently has value 0.

More interesting variations arise when the *same* unclaimed cheque of size x is offered for sale to Left and Right at *different* prices! Suppose that x moves are offered to Left in exchange for an unclaimed cheque of value y, but that these same x moves are offered to Right in exchange for an unclaimed cheque of value z. The game represented by this pair of offers is

$$G = \{x \pm y \,|\, -x \pm z\}.$$

If x is quite large compared with y and z, then it's quite obvious how to play G, even when it's added to other games of similar type.

EQUITABLE GAMES

Indeed, play in the sum of n copies of it,

$$n.G = n.\{x \pm y \,|\, -x \pm z\},$$

proceeds in a very equable and equitable manner whenever x is large enough compared with y and z. In this case the players each view G as a bargain of largish size x and they take turns in acquiring these desirable bargains. They won't bother about the comparatively small prices $\pm y$ and $\pm z$ while there are still big bargains to be had. This short-sighted view is optimal because the unclaimed cheques of values $\pm y$ and $\pm z$ will themselves be equitably divided later on in the game. If $x > y \geqslant z \geqslant 0$ and both $x - y$ and $x - z$ are greater than $y - z$ then the Left stops of $n.G$ are:

$L(0)$	$L(G)$	$L(2.G)$	$L(3.G)$	$L(4.G)$	$L(5.G)$	$L(6.G)$	$L(7.G)$	$L(8.G)$	...
0	$x-y$	$y-z$	$x-z$	0	$x-y$	$y-z$	$x-z$	0	....

In our 4-stop example, $H = a|b\|c|d$, when

$$3b + c > s > 2b + 2c$$

the equitableness of H becomes very clear when we write the stopping positions of $n.H$ in terms of those of H:

$L(0)$	$L(H)$	$L(2.H)$	$L(3.H)$	$L(4.H)$	$L(5.H)$	$L(6.H)$	$L(7.H)$	$L(8.H)$	...
0	b	$a+d$	$a+b+d$	s	$s+b$	$s+a+d$	$s+a+b+d$	$2s$	....

In general, a very equitable game is one in which, for some sufficiently large $n = 2^j$, the value of both the Left stop and Right stop of $n.G$ is

$$\sum_i 2^{j-k(i)} a_i$$

where the a_i are all the possible stopping positions of G and $k(i)$ is the number of moves from G to the stopping position a_i. So 2^j copies of a very equitable game add up to a number when j is large enough.

EXCITABLE GAMES

If $y + z \geqslant 2x$, then the game

$$G = \{x \pm y \,|\, -x \pm z\}$$

simplifies to a number. But if G is a non-number in which just one of y and z exceeds x, then we call G excitable.

Considered as a public market offer of x free moves, the excitable game G is certainly not equitable, for it is offered to one player at a discount and to the other at a markup! And while the unlikelihood of immediate redemption allows the player of a sum of many copies of an *equitable* game to ignore the possible cost (or profit!) which he may realize later as a result of the $\pm y$ or $\pm z$ which he pays for the immediate gain of x, the player of the sum of many copies of an *excitable* game can't!

If $y > x$ and Left accepts the offer represented by G, then he must face the likelihood that Right will realize a quick profit by immediately redeeming the $\pm y$ cheque. It will cost Left about $n(y-x)$ to play n copies of the excitable game G. In fact Left plays in G primarily because he is a spoiler who realizes that if he doesn't buy up every available copy of G at a small loss, Right will later be able to buy some of them at a handsome profit. Right, on the other hand, may view Left's move from G to $x \pm y$ as a threat to move to $+y$ next time, a threat serious enough to demand an immediate response to $-y$.

In general, when playing a sum of several games, a move in an equitable component is usually followed by a reply in a different component, but a move in an excitable one usually requires a response in the same component. A *very* excitable move poses a grave threat which *must* be answered immediately; an equitable move does not. In the language of the Japanese game of Go:

> Excitable moves keep **sente**.
> Equitable ones don't.

The game $H = a|b \,\|\, c|d$, with $a \geqslant b > c \geqslant d$, is very equitable if $3b+c > s > b+3c$, and is excitable if $s > 4b$ or $4c > s$. Otherwise, the sum $n.H$ is best played equitably until about 3 turns before the stopping position, when optimum play switches to a more exciting finish. Many games, $2|1\,\|-1|-5$ for example, have non-obvious tendencies to be mildly excitable in certain circumstances, and so "equitable" and "excitable" are best thought of as informal terms.

In general the Left stop of $n.H$, when well played, is:

	$L(H)$	$L(2.H)$	$L(3.H)$	$L(4.H)$	$L(5.H)$	$L(6.H)$	$L(7.H)$	$L(8 \cdot H)$	$L(9.H)$	...	m
$s > 4b$	b	$2b$	$3b$	$4b$	$5b$	$6b$	$7b$	$8b$	$9b$	...	b
$4b > s > 3b+c$	b	$2b$	$3b$	s	$s+b$	$s+2b$	$s+3b$	$2s$	$2s+b$	...	$\frac{1}{4}s$
$3b+c > s > 2b+2c$	b	$a+d$	$a+b+d$	s	$s+b$	$s+a+d$	$s+a+b+d$	$2s$	$2s+b$	...	$\frac{1}{4}s$
$2b+2c > s > b+3c$	b	$b+c$	$a+b+d$	s	$s+b$	$s+b+c$	$s+a+b+d$	$2s$	$2s+b$	...	$\frac{1}{4}s$
$b+3c > s > 4c$	b	$b+c$	$b+2c$	$b+3c$	$s+b$	$s+b+c$	$s+b+2c$	$s+b+3c$	$2s+b$	...	$\frac{1}{4}s$
$4c > s$	b	$b+c$	$b+2c$	$b+3c$	$b+4c$	$b+5c$	$b+6c$	$b+7c$	$b+8c$	...	c

THE EXTENDED THERMOGRAPH

Let's see if we can't manage to compute the thermograph of a fairly complicated game like the Snort position

$$G = \text{○—●—○—●—●—●} = \{0, \{2|-1\}\,\|\,\{-2|-4\}\}$$

without first having to draw separate thermographs for all its options (cf. Fig. 9). For small enough t we have

$$G_t = \{0-t, \{2-t \mid -1+t\} -t \| \{-2-t \mid -4+t\} +t\}$$
$$= \{-t, \{2-2t \mid -1\} \| \{-2 \mid -4+2t\}\},$$

and we can indicate the stopping positions of this game by lines of appropriate slants as in Fig. 16.

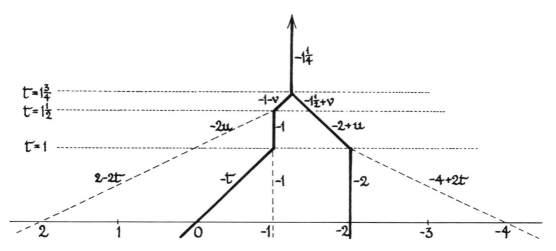

Figure 16. An Extended Thermograph.

Some of these lines meet at height $t = 1$, for which we find

$$G_1 = \{-1, \{0 \mid -1\} \| -2 + *\}.$$

If t is just greater than 1, say $t = 1+u$, the first option becomes dominated and we have

$$G_t = G_{1+u} = \{\{-2u \mid -1\} \| -2 + u\}$$

until at $t = 1\frac{1}{2}, u = \frac{1}{2}$

$$G_{1\frac{1}{2}} = \{-1+* \mid -1\frac{1}{2}\}$$

and so for $t = 1\frac{1}{2} + v$ and small enough v

$$G_t = \{-1-v \mid -1\frac{1}{2}+v\}$$

until at $t = 1\frac{3}{4}, v = \frac{1}{4}$ we reach

$$G_{1\frac{3}{4}} = -1\frac{1}{4} + *$$

and so

$$G_t = -1\frac{1}{4}$$

for all larger t.

The **extended thermograph** contains lines representing *all* the stopping positions of the simplest form of G_t, for all values of t, with the Left and Right stops emphasized.

GETTING THE RIGHT SLANT

It's fairly easy to work out the slants of all these lines directly. For instance, consider the game

$$\{a\|b|c\} \;\||\|\; \{\{d\|e|f\} \;\||\|\; g\}.$$

Begin by putting a 0 under the slash of highest "order"; then put a 1 under the principal slash (a double one) in the Left option, and a -1 under the treble one in the Right option. Then continue with successive generations of options, adding 1 to or subtracting 1 from the parent number:

$$\{a \;\|\; b \;|\; c\} \quad \||\| \quad \{\{d \;\|\; e \;|\; f\} \;\||\|\; g\}$$

```
                              0
         1                               -1
     2       0              0                 -2
         1  -1           1        -1
                              0   -2
```

and we read off the slants of the lines through

a	b	c	d	e	f	g
2	1	-1	1	0	-2	-2.

to be

When there is more than one option, treat each one similarly. Our previous example was

$$0 \;,\; 2 \;|\; -1 \;\|\; -2 \;|\; -4$$

```
                    0
    1          1              -1
       2     0        0    -2
```

giving the lines $\quad 0-1t,\; 2-2t,\; -1-0t,\; -2-0t,\; -4-(-2t).$

THE THERMOSTATIC STRATEGY

We can't always work out the thermograph of a sum of several games from the thermographs of the components. For example, if

$$G = 4|-4 \quad \text{and} \quad H = \{4, 4\pm4 \;|\; -4,\; -4\pm4\}$$

then G, H and $G+H$ all have the same thermograph. However the thermograph of $G+G$ is just a simple mast through 0, and so is different from that of $G+H$. The Left stop of the sum of two games with the same thermograph as G might be anything from 0 to 4, while the Right stop may be anything from -4 to 0. We can't hope to obtain any more precise estimates of the confusion interval without looking beyond the thermographs into the more detailed structure of the components.

Indeed, when there are many components, the optimal strategy can be very complex and you may have neither the time nor the computing power needed to find the very best move. However, our thermostatic strategy, THERMOSTRAT, gives you an easy way of finding a "good move" which is close to optimal and will be enough to ensure your victory in many situations.

THERMOSTRAT finds a good component for you to move in and then you can ignore the other components and find your proper play by just looking at the thermograph of this one. Even though the number of components may be very large, THERMOSTRAT ensures that you'll get a stopping position for the sum which differs from the optimal one by no more than the temperature of the hottest game.

Here's how to play THERMOSTRAT on

$$A + B + C + ...,$$

supposing that your name is Left and you know the thermographs of $A,B,C,...$. Draw the **compound thermograph** whose *right boundary* is the sum

$$R_t(A) + R_t(B) + R_t(C) + ...$$

of those for the components, and whose *width* at height t

$$W_t = \max\{W_t(A),W_t(B),W_t(C),...\}$$

is the largest width of any of the components at that height (Fig. 17). In other words the Left boundary of the compound thermograph is

$$R_t(A) + R_t(B) + R_t(C) + ... + W_t.$$

This is the amount that THERMOSTRAT guarantees Left if he starts with his thermostat set to give an ambient temperature of t.

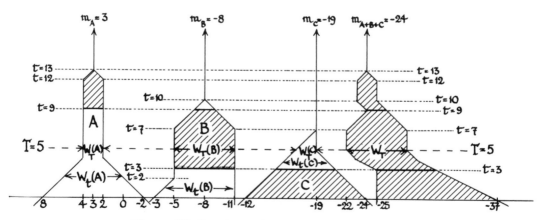

Figure 17. Drawing a Compound Thermograph.

The temperatures at which Left feels most comfortable in our example are those between 5 and 7, where the Left boundary of the compound thermograph is furthest left. Since he's a seasoned campaigner who shows only just as much heat as is absolutely necessary, he prefers an ambient temperature of $T = 5$, and will therefore move in component B, whose thermograph is the widest one at $T = 5$.

> The **ambient temperature**
> is the least T for which
> $$R_T(A) + R_T(B) + R_T(C) + ... + W_T$$
> is maximal.

> To find the THERMOSTRAT move,
> first find the ambient temperature, T,
> and then make the T-move in a
> component that's widest at T.

Left's T-**move** in a game G is a move to an option which determined the Left boundary of the thermograph of G at temperature T.

In our example, suppose that the thermograph of

$$B = \{-3, 9 \,|\, -5 \,\|\, -11 \,|\, -25\}$$

was worked out as in Fig. 18, and you'll see that $B^{L_2} = 9|-5$ was the option that determined its Left boundary at temperature $T = 5$. The THERMOSTRAT move is therefore that from

$$A + B + C \quad \text{to} \quad A + B^{L_2} + C.$$

In the Extras you'll see a proof that THERMOSTRAT does as well as we say it does.

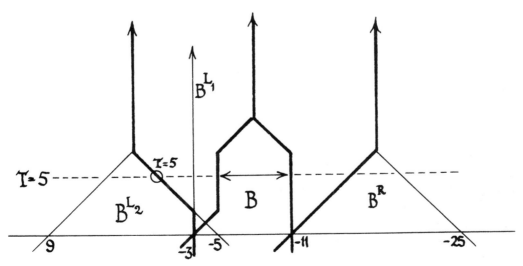

Figure 18. Thermograph of $B = \{B^{L_1}, B^{L_2} | B^R\} = \{-3, 9 \,|\, -5 \,\|\, -11 \,|\, -25\}$.

THERMOSTRAT'S NOT OFTEN WRONG!

Because the boundary lines of a thermograph are always vertical or diagonal the difference between the Left or Right stop of a game and its mean value is at most equal to the game's temperature. Moreover,

> the temperature of any sum
> is no more than the
> temperature of any component.

THERMOSTRAT achieves this bound, so

> when you're playing the sum
> of a large number of games,
> the difference between THERMOSTRAT
> and the optimal strategy is
> bounded by the largest temperature.

For example if Left is playing the sum of a million games which all have integer stopping positions and temperatures at most 10, then THERMOSTRAT guarantees that he'll come within 10 of the optimal stopping position. In fact by playing THERMOSTRAT, Left evidently makes a suboptimal move (i.e. one that decreases his final stopping position) at most 10 times, even though the compound game lasts several million moves:

> THERMOSTRAT makes millions
> of optimal moves, and only
> a few suboptimal ones!

THERMOSTRAT provides independent proofs that

> the Mast Value of a game
> is also its Mean Value,

and that

> the Mast Value of a sum of
> games is the sum of the
> Mast Values of the components,

because the value it guarantees to either player is within a bounded amount of the sum of the mast values. THERMOSTRAT might therefore be called

PLAYING THE AVERAGES.

THERMOSTRAT has the property that for sums of many components,

the action's routinely
in the hottest game.

WHERE'S THE ACTION?

But it also tells you a good move to make in the more exciting situations when this isn't so.

HEATING

The inverse of cooling is called **heating**. Formally, the result of heating G through a temperature t is the **integral**

$$\int^t G = \left\{ \int^t G^L + t \,\middle|\, \int^t G^R - t \right\},$$

unless G is a number, in which case

$$\int^t G = G.$$

As we cool a game down until it freezes at its mean value there will be certain critical temperatures at which it undergoes a phase change and "gives off" **particles**, and we can obtain the original game from the mean value by adding the heated forms of these particles.

Let's look at this for some of our examples. For the Snort position

$$G = \,\bullet\!\!-\!\!-\!\!\bullet\!\!-\!\!-\!\!\bullet\, = 2|-1$$

we found

$$G_{1\frac{1}{2}} = \tfrac{1}{2} + *$$

and

$$G_t = \tfrac{1}{2} \quad \text{for } t > 1\tfrac{1}{2}.$$

So at temperature $1\frac{1}{2}$, G gives off the particle $*$, and heating $G_{1\frac{1}{2}}$ by $1\frac{1}{2}$ we find

$$\bullet\!\!-\!\!-\!\!\bullet\!\!-\!\!-\!\!\bullet = \tfrac{1}{2} + \int^{1\frac{1}{2}} *.$$

For

$$G = \,\bullet\!\!-\!\!-\!\!\bullet\!\!-\!\!-\!\!\bullet\!\!-\!\!-\!\!\bullet\!\!-\!\!-\!\!\bullet\, = 1\|0|-2,$$

at the (only) critical temperature of 1 we find

$$G_1 = 0\|0|0 = \uparrow$$

and so

$$\bullet\!\!-\!\!\bullet\!\!-\!\!\bullet\!\!-\!\!\bullet\!\!-\!\!\bullet = \int^1 \uparrow.$$

For the example

$$G = \bullet\!-\!\circ\!-\!\bullet\!-\!\circ\!-\!\bullet\!-\!\circ\!-\!\bullet = 2|1\|0$$

there are two critical temperatures. We find

$$G_{\frac12} = \{1|1\|\tfrac12\} = \{1+*\,|\tfrac12\}$$

but for small $\delta > 0$

$$G_{\frac12+\delta} = \{1-\delta\,|\tfrac12+\delta\}$$

whose "limit" as δ tends to 0 is

$$G_{\frac12+} = 1|\tfrac12.$$

The particle given off at temperature $\tfrac12$ is the difference

$$G_{\frac12} - G_{\frac12+} = 1*|\tfrac12 + -\tfrac12|-1$$
$$= \{\tfrac12*|*, \tfrac12*|0 \| 0|-\tfrac12, *|-\tfrac12\}$$
$$= \varepsilon, \text{ say.}$$

The next and last critical temperature is $t = \tfrac34$, at the freezing point, and we find

$$G_{\frac34} = \tfrac34+*,$$

so that

$$G = \bullet\!-\!\circ\!-\!\bullet\!-\!\circ\!-\!\bullet\!-\!\circ\!-\!\bullet = \tfrac34 + \int^{\frac34} *+ \int^{\frac12} \varepsilon.$$

In general a game G has certain **critical temperatures**

$$t_0, \ t_1, \ t_2, \ \ldots$$

at which G_t differs from the limit, G_{t+}, of $G_{t+\delta}$ as δ tends to 0, so that at temperature t the cooled game changes phase and gives off the particle

$$\varepsilon_t = G_t - G_{t+}.$$

We then have Simon Norton's **thermal dissociation** of G:

$$G = G_\infty + \int^{t_0} \varepsilon_{t_0} + \int^{t_1} \varepsilon_{t_1} + \ldots$$

in which G_∞ is the mean value, the ε's are the (infinitesimal) particles given off and the largest t_i is G's own temperature.

BUT BEWARE: Although every corner on the thermograph indicates a phase change there can be *latent* phase changes as well. Several instances occur among Snort positions, for example

$$G = \bullet\!-\!\circ\!-\!\bullet\!-\!\bullet\!-\!\bullet = \{3|1*\| -1*|-2*, \ 0|-3\}$$

undergoes a phase transition from

$$G_{1\frac{1}{2}} = \tfrac{1}{2}|0,* \quad \text{to} \quad G_{1\frac{1}{2}+} = \tfrac{1}{2}|0$$

which is concealed in its thermograph (Fig. 19).

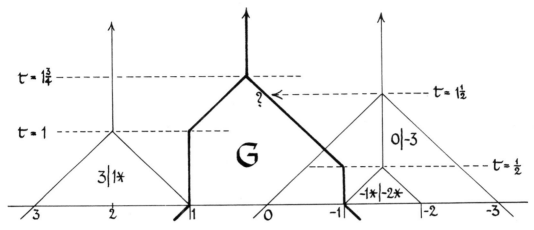

Figure 19. The Thermograph of $\{3|1*\|-1*|-2*,0|-3\}$.

A common type of example is

$$\int^{\cdot 3}\uparrow + \int^{\cdot 5}\uparrow$$

which has the same thermograph (Fig. 20) as its hotter component, obscuring the phase change at $t = 3$.

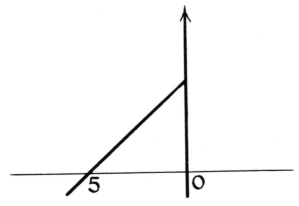

Figure 20. The Thermograph of $\int^3\uparrow + \int^5\uparrow$, or of $\int^5\uparrow$.

DOES THE EXCITEMENT SHOW?

When the Left and Right boundaries are both slanting as they meet, it's a hint that the game may be equitable, and in the simplest cases the particle given off at the freezing point will be $*$. This happens for

$$G = \bullet\!\!-\!\!\bullet\!\!-\!\!\bullet\!\!-\!\!\circ\!\!-\!\!\bullet = 2*\|0|-1,$$

whose thermograph is shown in Fig. 21.

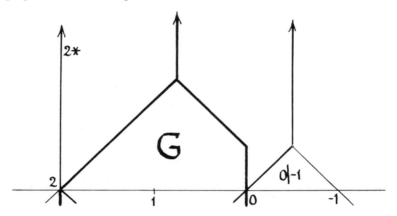

Figure 21. Thermograph of $\{2*\|0|-1\}$.

But if, say, the Right boundary is vertical at the freezing point, the game is likely to be Right-excitable and the final particle given off will be a positive infinitesimal, often a tiny. For example, the game

$$H = 5\|1|-9$$

has temperature 4 and we find

$$H_4 = 1\|1|-1 = 1+\{0\|0|-2\} = 1 + +_2.$$

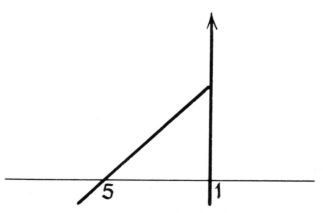

Figure 22. Thermograph of $\{5\|1|-9\}$.

Since this is the only critical temperature we have

$$H = 1 + \int^4 +_2$$

an excitable game whose thermograph is shown in Fig. 22.

However, we'll see that in some cases the behavior of a game is controlled by a particle given off just *before* its freezing point, and in these cases the opposite adjective (of excitable, equitable) may be more appropriate.

HOW TO SELL INFINITESIMAL VALUES TO YOUR PROFIT-CONSCIOUS FRIENDS

Those who think in business terms usually associate the stopping positions with money rather than with numbers of free moves. Such hard-headed business people aren't usually interested in infinitesimal games. "When there's no money in it," they ask, "why quibble about who gets the last move?" The answer is

> You can't know all about hot games
> unless you know all about infinitesimals.

This is obvious because any hot game can be built by heating up infinitesimals. Although sums of differently heated infinitesimals can be very complex, sometimes a single heated infinitesimal provides an idea which is crucial to finding the best move in a hot game.

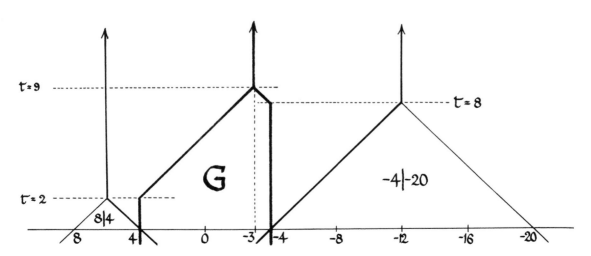

Figure 23. Thermograph of $\{8|4 \,\|\, -4| -20\}$.

For example let's consider the game

$$G + G + \{-4|-20\}$$

where

$$G = 8|4\| -4|-20$$

has the thermograph shown in Fig. 23, mean value -3, temperature 9, and whose freezing point has the two slanting lines we normally associate with equitable games. However, if you don't look too closely you won't see much difference between G and the following excitable approximation whose thermograph (Fig. 24) differs by at most 1 unit from that of G for all temperatures above 1:

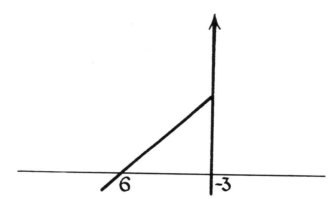

Figure 24. Thermograph of $H = -3 + \int^9 \uparrow = \{6\| -3|-21\}$.

Since the approximating game satisfies

$$H + H + \{-3|-21\} = -18 + \int^9 (\uparrow + \uparrow + *),$$

the original game behaves like

$$\uparrow + \uparrow + *,$$

in which Left should take care to move *not* to $\uparrow + *$ (which is *not* positive), but to $\uparrow + \uparrow$. So Left's best move in the original game is *not* to

$$G + \{8|4\} + \{-4|-20\}$$

but to

$$G + G - 4.$$

A Right move from

$$G + G + G$$

to

$$G + G + \{-4|-20\}$$

might not have been exciting in any strict sense, but it was bold enough to force Left to abandon his routine defence in order to get the last move in one of the hotter games (temperature greater than 2).

NIM, REMOTENESS AND SUSPENSE IN HOT GAMES

Again, if you understand the purely infinitesimal game of Nim, you'll not be too surprised to find that in the hot sum

$$\int^{100} *5 + \int^{99} *6 + \int^{98} *8$$

the only winning move is in the coolest game, to

$$98 + \int^{98} *3.$$

This won't be found by any strategy which plays the averages, because the hotter moves obscure it. But because there's a big temperature gap between 98 and 0 and only a small one between 100 and 98, the infinitesimal considerations dominate the thermal ones. In this position Left can ensure a stopping value of at least 89, but only with the above starting move. Any other starting move gives Right -89 or better.

Hot games can also be made to depend on notions such as the suspense and remoteness numbers we'll introduce in Chapter 9. Consider *asymmetrical* heating:

$$\int_x^y 0 = 0,$$

$$\int_x^y * = x | -y,$$

$$\int_x^y *2 = \left\{ x, x + \int_x^y * \,\middle|\, -y, -y + \int_x^y * \right\},$$

$$\dots\dots\dots\dots\dots\dots\dots\dots\dots\dots\dots\dots\dots\dots\dots\dots\dots\dots\dots,$$

$$\int_x^y *n = \left\{ x + \int_x^y *k \,\middle|\, -y + \int_x^y *k \right\}_{k=0,1,2,\dots,n-1}.$$

This is Nim with the condition that Left collects x points every move while Right collects y points. In a game like

$$\int_{100}^{99} *5 + \int_{100}^{99} *6 + \int_{100}^{99} *8$$

each player will try first to win the Nim game, but subject to that, Left will try to prolong the game and Right will try to shorten it. The confusion interval runs from 100 to -99, corrected by the suspense and remoteness functions of the corresponding Nim game. Evidently

> you can't know everything about hot games
> unless you know lots of things about lots of others.

OVERHEATING

Other kinds of heating sometimes turn up. If you apply the rule for heating G by an amount X without any reservations at all we get what we call **overheating**, for which we use the notation

$$\int_0^X G.$$

So we have

$$\int_0^X G = \left\{ X + \int_0^X G^L \;\middle|\; -X + \int_0^X G^R \right\},$$

even when G is a number. The most common case is $X = 1$, although X may be any positive game. Let's see what happens when we overheat by 1, using just

$$\int G \quad \text{for} \quad \int_0^1 G.$$

We find

$$0 = \{ \mid \}, \qquad \text{so} \qquad \int 0 = \{ \mid \} = 0,$$
$$1 = \{0 \mid \}, \qquad \text{so} \qquad \int 1 = \{1 + \int 0 \mid \} = 1 \mid \; = 2,$$
$$2 = \{1 \mid \}, \qquad \text{so} \qquad \int 2 = \{1 + \int 1 \mid \} = 3 \mid \; = 4,$$

and so on, all integers doubling.

$$\tfrac{1}{2} = \{0 \mid 1\}, \qquad \text{so} \qquad \int \tfrac{1}{2} = \{1 + \int 0 \mid -1 + \int 1\} = 1 \mid 1 = 1*,$$
$$\tfrac{1}{4} = \{0 \mid \tfrac{1}{2}\}, \qquad \text{so} \qquad \int \tfrac{1}{4} = \{1 + \int 0 \mid -1 + \int \tfrac{1}{2}\} = 1 \mid *,$$
$$\tfrac{3}{4} = \{\tfrac{1}{2} \mid 1\}, \qquad \text{so} \qquad \int \tfrac{3}{4} = \{1 + \int \tfrac{1}{2} \mid -1 + \int 1\} = 2* \mid 1,$$
$$\tfrac{1}{8} = \{0 \mid \tfrac{1}{4}\}, \qquad \text{so} \qquad \int \tfrac{1}{8} = \{1 + \int 0 \mid -1 + \int \tfrac{1}{4}\} = 1 \| 0 \mid -1*.$$

We can also overheat non-numbers:

$$\pm 1 = \{1 \mid -1\}, \qquad \text{so} \qquad \int \pm 1 = \{1 + \int 1 \mid -1 + \int -1\} = 3 \mid -3 = \pm 3,$$
$$* = \{0 \mid 0\}, \qquad \text{so} \qquad \int * = \{1 + \int 0 \mid -1 + \int 0\} = 1 \mid -1 = \pm 1,$$
$$\uparrow = \{0 \mid *\}, \qquad \text{so} \qquad \int \uparrow = \{1 + \int 0 \mid -1 + \int *\} = 1 \| 0 \mid -2.$$

Overheating preserves sums:

$$\int_0^X (A + B + C + \ldots) = \int_0^X A + \int_0^X B + \int_0^X C + \ldots,$$

and so must multiply mean values by a constant factor. In particular, since

$$\int_0^1 1 = 2, \text{ the mean value of } \int_0^1 x \text{ is } 2x$$

for any number x. Figure 25 illustrates this with a few thermographs. These are easily found successively; for instance, each one in the bottom row derives from the two nearest to it above. You can find the thermograph for $\int(1 - x)$ by reflecting that for $\int x$ in the vertical line through 1.

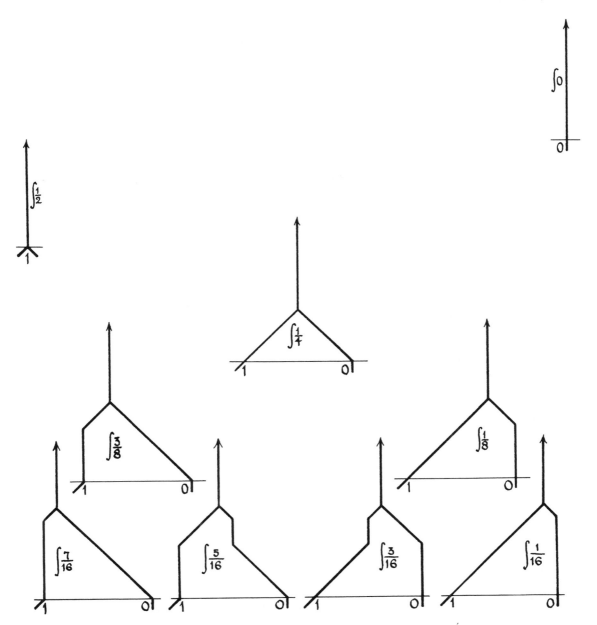

Figure 25. Thermographs of $\int_0^1 x$, $x = \frac{1}{2}, \frac{7}{16}, \frac{3}{8}, \frac{5}{16}, \frac{1}{4}, \frac{3}{16}, \frac{1}{8}, \frac{1}{16}, 0$

Figure 26 superposes all these thermographs, so that you can see how the thermograph for $\int x$ changes as x varies.

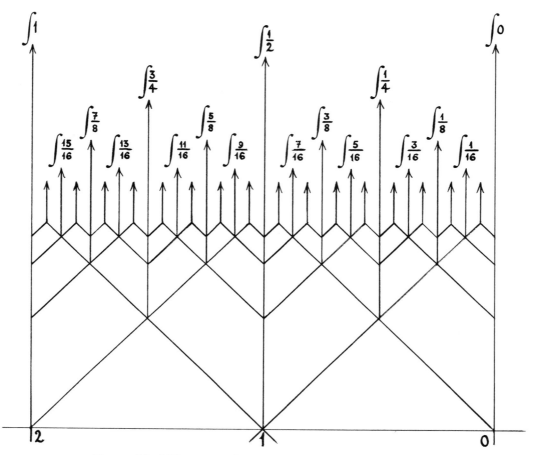

Figure 26. A Thermographic Thicket of Overheated Numbers.

Sequences like

$$\int_{\tfrac{1}{2}} = 1*,$$
$$\int_{\tfrac{3}{4}} = 2*|1,$$
$$\int_{\tfrac{7}{8}} = 3*|2\|1,$$
$$\int_{\tfrac{15}{16}} = 4*|3\|2\,\|\!\|\,1,$$
$$\ldots\ldots\ldots\ldots\ldots,$$

arise in several games. Here are some examples.

The sequence of Domineering zigzags:

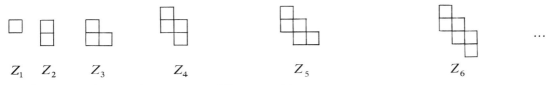

$Z_1 \quad Z_2 \quad Z_3 \qquad Z_4 \qquad\qquad Z_5 \qquad\qquad\qquad Z_6$

has the same values as the sequence of Snort positions

We have

$$Z_{2n+1} = \pm(Z_0+Z_{2n-1}, Z_2+Z_{2n-3}, Z_4+Z_{2n-5}, \ldots),$$

$$Z_{2n+2} = \{Z_0+Z_{2n}, Z_2+Z_{2n-2}, Z_4+Z_{2n-4}, \ldots \mid Z_1+Z_{2n-1}, Z_3+Z_{2n-3}, Z_5+Z_{2n-5}, \ldots\}$$

leading to the table

n	0	1	2	3	4	5	6	7	8	9	10	11	...
Z_n	0	0	1	*	1|0	± 1	2|*	± 1*	2|1||0	$\pm(2\|*, 2\|0)$	1*	Z_9+*	...

Let's compare

$$Z_8 = 2|1\|0 \quad\text{with}\quad \textstyle\int \frac{3}{8} = 2|1*\|*.$$

There is only an infinitesimal difference, so that Z_8 is just $\int\frac{3}{8}$ **infinitesimally shifted** and we write

$$Z_8 \text{ is } \textstyle\int\frac{3}{8}\text{-ish.}$$

In the same notation, we find that

$$
\begin{aligned}
Z_{8n+1} \quad\text{or}\quad Z_{8n+3} &\text{ is } 0\text{-ish,} &&\text{i.e. } \textstyle\int 0\text{-ish,}\\
Z_{8n-1} \quad\text{or}\quad Z_{8n-3} &\text{ is } \pm 1\text{-ish,} &&\text{i.e. } \textstyle\int *\text{-ish.}\\
Z_{8n+2} &\text{ is } 1\text{-ish,} &&\text{i.e. } \textstyle\int\frac{1}{2}\text{-ish,}\\
Z_{8n-2} &\text{ is } 2|0\text{-ish,} &&\text{i.e. } \textstyle\int\frac{1}{2}*\text{-ish,}
\end{aligned}
$$

while Z_{4n} gives the interesting sequence

$$Z_4 = 1|0, \qquad Z_8 = 2|1\|0, \qquad Z_{12} = \{3|2\|1\|\|0\}\text{-ish,} \qquad Z_{16} = \{4|3\|2\|\|1\|\|\|0\}\text{-ish,} \qquad \ldots .$$

Comparing these with

$$\textstyle\int\frac{3}{4} = 2*|1, \qquad \int\frac{7}{8} = 3*|2\|1, \qquad \int\frac{15}{16} = 4*|3\|2\|\|1, \qquad \int\frac{31}{32} = 5*|4\|3\|\|2\|\|\|1, \qquad \ldots$$

and noting that $\int\frac{1}{2} = 1*$ is 1-ish, we see that

$$Z_4 \text{ is } \textstyle\int\frac{1}{4}\text{-ish,} \quad Z_8 \text{ is } \int\frac{3}{8}\text{-ish,} \quad Z_{12} \text{ is } \int\frac{7}{16}\text{-ish,} \qquad Z_{16} \text{ is } \int\frac{15}{32}\text{-ish,} \qquad \ldots .$$

The Domineering position of Fig. 27 has value

$$\textstyle\frac{1}{2} + * + Z_7 + Z_{14} - Z_8 + *$$

which is

$$\textstyle\frac{1}{2} + \int(* + \frac{1}{2}* - \frac{3}{8})\text{-ish,} \qquad\text{i.e. } \frac{1}{2} + \int\frac{1}{8}\text{-ish.}$$

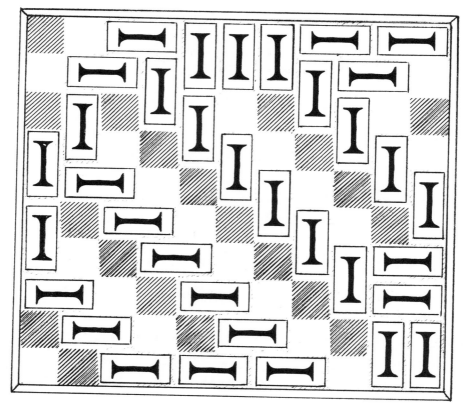

Figure 27. A Domineering Position after Left's Eighteenth Move.

Although $\int\frac{1}{8}$ is surely positive, it has a Right stop of 0 and so there are $\int\frac{1}{8}$-ish games which are *not* positive. However, in our case the $\frac{1}{2}$ outweighs the "ish", so that Left should win, even though it is not his turn. Even without the $\frac{1}{2}$, Left could win by starting, because the *Left* stop of $\int\frac{1}{8}$ is 1 and this *won't* be affected by the "ish".

COOLING THE CHILDREN'S PARTY

The children's party game that closed our previous chapter is really just Snort played on a circular graph, which after some moves gets replaced by a number of chains of the forms

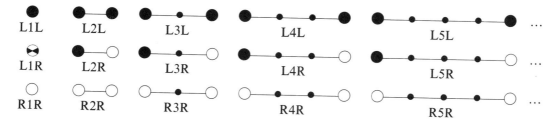

This time it's only after cooling by 1 that we see the structure. In fact

$$(LnR)_1 \text{ is } \begin{cases} 0\text{-ish for } n = 6k+1, 6k+2, 6k+3, \\ \pm 1\text{-ish for } n = 6k, 6k-1, 6k-2, \end{cases}$$

while

$$(LnL)_1 \text{ is } \begin{cases} 2\text{-ish for } n = 6k+2, \\ (3|1)\text{-ish for } n = 6k-1, \end{cases}$$

and otherwise

1-ish	(2|1)-ish	(3|2‖1)-ish	(4|3‖2⫴1)-ish	...
for $n = 1$ or 3	4 or 6	7 or 9	10 or 12	....

All these cooled values are $\int X$-ish for suitable X, as given in the table:

	1	2	3	4	5	6	7	8	9	10	11	12	13	14	...
X for $(LnL)_1$	$\frac{1}{2}$	1	$\frac{1}{2}$	$\frac{3}{4}$	1*	$\frac{3}{4}$	$\frac{7}{8}$	1	$\frac{7}{8}$	$\frac{15}{16}$	1*	$\frac{15}{16}$	$\frac{31}{32}$	1	...
X for $(LnR)_1$	0	0	0	*	*	*	0	0	0	*	*	*	0	0	...

BUT HOW DO YOU COOL A PARTY BY ONE DEGREE?

The obvious answer is to insist that each child bring a present suitable for one of the opposite sex. We suggest that each girl bring a unit blue Hackenbush stick and each boy a red one:

"blue for a boy, pink for a girl"

But a child who promises to be sociable and sit in a gap containing only 1 or 2 chairs is exempt from this requirement because the values of

L1L, L1R, R1R, L2L, L2R, R2R

are already number-ish and must not be further cooled.

EXTRAS

THREE SNORT LEMMAS

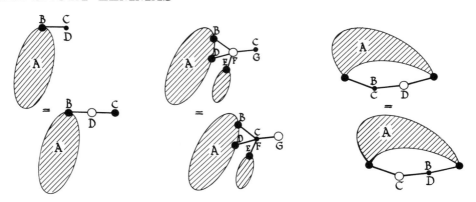

These identities are established by noting the corresponding moves indicated by letters above (Left) or below (Right) the appropriate nodes. In the middle figure the nodes D, E need not be present.

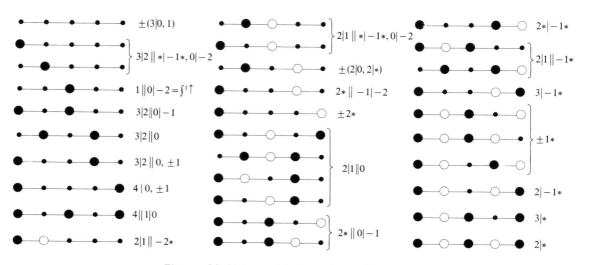

Figure 28. Values of 5-Node Snort Chains.

176

Table 1. Values of Snort Chains with Six Nodes

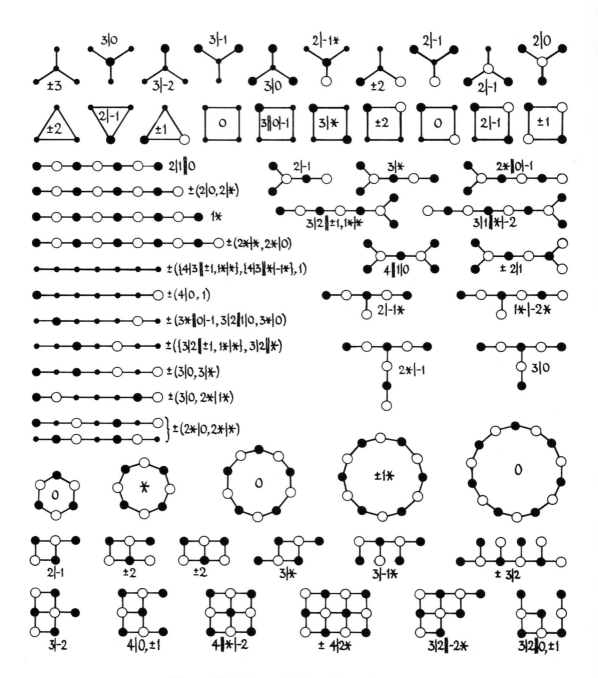

Figure 29. Values of Various Snort Positions.

A SNORT DICTIONARY

In Fig. 3 we gave the values of Snort chains with at most four nodes. Figure 28 gives values of 5-node chains and Table 1 those of chains with 6 nodes. Every such chain, or its negative, occurs. For the 6-node chains find 3 nodes at the head of a column and the remaining 3 on the right of the table; the arrowheads indicate the connexions. Figure 29 lists some miscellaneous positions.

PROOF OF THE NUMBER AVOIDANCE THEOREM

It will be enough to prove that if x is equal to a number, but G is not, and if

$$G + x \rhd 0, \quad \text{then some} \quad G^L + x \geqslant 0.$$

This statement is unaffected if we replace x by an equivalent game and so we can suppose that x is in simplest form. The good move from $G + x$ must be to $G + x^L \geqslant 0$ since otherwise some $G^L + x \geqslant 0$. If no $G^L + x \geqslant 0$, let

$$x > x^L > x^{LL} > x^{LLL} > \ldots$$

be the finite decreasing sequence of successive Left options of x. If y is the smallest of these which has

$$G + y \geqslant 0,$$

then since G is not equal to the number $-y$, we have

$$G + y > 0, \quad \text{and so some} \quad G^L + y \geqslant 0,$$

since we cannot have $G + y^L \geqslant 0$. So, for this G^L,

$$G^L + x \geqslant G^L + y \geqslant 0.$$

The result can be used repeatedly to show that if $x, y, z, \ldots$ are equal to numbers, but $G, H, K, \ldots$ are not, and if

$$x + y + z + \ldots + G + H + K + \ldots \rhd 0,$$

then we can find a good move for Left from one of the components $G, H, K, \ldots$.

WHY THERMOSTRAT WORKS

We assert that for any given T, Left can guarantee at least

$$R_T(A) + R_T(B) + R_T(C) + \ldots - T$$

if *Right* starts, and at least

$$R_T(A) + R_T(B) + R_T(C) + \ldots + W_T$$

if he starts himself.

For suppose that Right moves from

$$A + B + C + \ldots \quad \text{to} \quad A^R + B + C + \ldots.$$

Then Left is inductively guaranteed at least

$$R_T(A^R) + R_T(B) + R_T(C) + \dots + W_T(A^R)$$

and Fig. 30 shows that

$$R_T(A^R) + W_T(A^R) \geqslant R_T(A) - \dot{T},$$

no matter how T compares with the temperature of A.

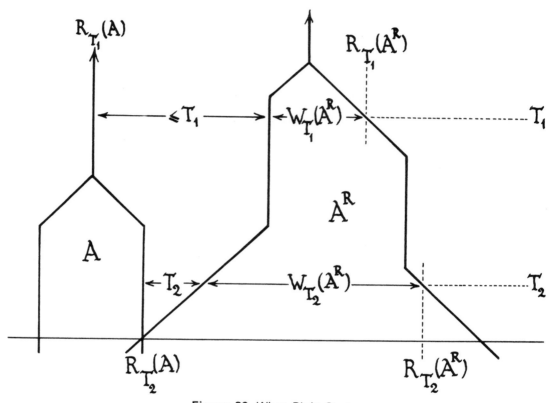

Figure 30. When Right Starts.

If it's *Left's* turn to move, we'll suppose first that some component has temperature at least T, and so the component, B, say, which is widest at T, will have temperature at least T since games of lower temperature have width 0 at T. In this case THERMOSTRAT tells Left to make the T-move in B, say from

$$A + B + C + \dots \quad \text{to} \quad A + B^L + C + \dots$$

when he is inductively guaranteed at least

$$R_T(A) + R_T(B^L) + R_T(C) + \dots - T,$$

and Fig. 31 shows that

$$R_T(B^L) - T = R_T(B) + W_T$$

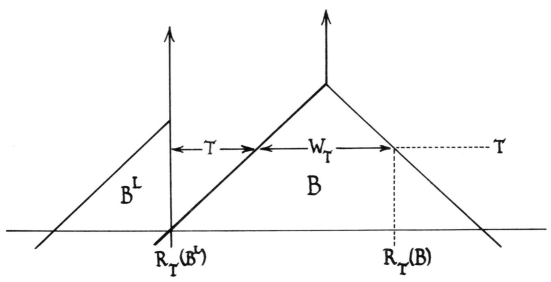

Figure 31. When Left Starts.

But, if every component has temperature strictly less than T, this argument fails. In this case Left should *reset* his thermostat to T_0, the largest temperature of any component (or possibly to an even cooler temperature) before continuing. Figure 32 shows that this will not reduce the value of

$$R_T(A) + R_T(B) + R_T(C) + \ldots + W_T.$$

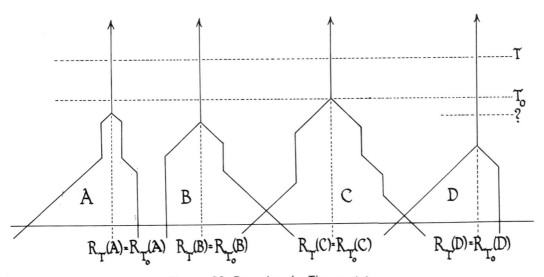

Figure 32. Resetting the Thermostat.

REFERENCES

The existence of mean values for a class of games rather like ours was first raised and proved by Milnor and Hanner. Another proof (with a constructive algorithm) is due to Berlekamp, and yet another (very short, but nonconstructive) to S. Norton. Our thermographic method is taken from ONAG.

J. H. Conway, "On Numbers and Games", Academic Press, London and New York, 1976, Chapter 9.

Olof Hanner. Mean play of sums of positional games, Pacific J. Math. **9** (1959) 81–99; MR 21 #3277.

John Milnor, Sums of positional games, in Kuhn and Tucker (eds.) "Contributions to the Theory of Games", Ann. Math. Studies #28, Princeton, 1953 291–301.

Chapter 7

Hackenbush

All things by immortal power,
Near or far,
Hiddenly
To each other linkèd are,
That thou canst not stir a flower
Without troubling of a star.

Francis Thompson, *The Mistress of Vision.*

In this chapter we'll tell you what we know about Hackenbush (except for infinite and loopy varieties that you'll find in Chapter 11) but first we'd perhaps better warn you that the arguments are rather long. For those who are eager to skip on, some of the remarks about flower gardens are repeated in Chapter 8, so that you won't need to read this chapter to understand anything else in the book.

GREEN HACKENBUSH

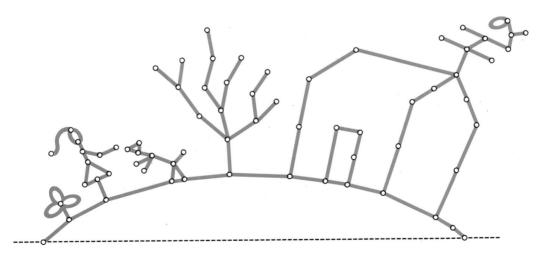

Figure 1. A Green Hackenbush Bridge.

183

In a totally grEen Hackenbush picture such as Fig. 1, any edge may be chopped by Either player, after which any edges no longer connected to the ground disappear.

Here there's a complete theory. First we observe that the Snakes-in-the-Grass argument of Chapter 2 shows that Hackenbush pictures made only of green strings are directly equivalent to Nim.

Next we use a very important tool, applicable not only in Green Hackenbush, but in Hackenbush more generally, called the **Colon Principle**.

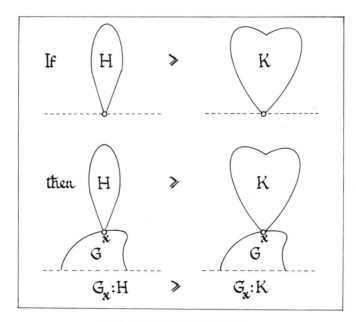

THE COLON PRINCIPLE

You can easily prove this by playing the difference of the two lower games. In particular,

$$\text{if } H = K, \text{ then } G_x:H = G_x:K$$

For a formal definition of $G:H$ see the Extras.

GREEN TREES

can now be evaluated using only the Colon Principle. For example, the tree

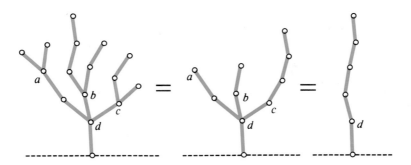

has value ∗5 because

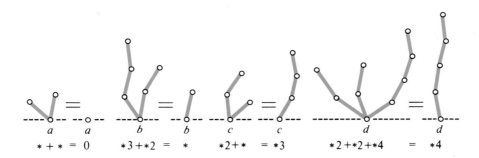

You can see that the Colon Principle often allows you to do your additions at some distance above the ground.

Observe that two kinds of addition are needed here. When moving down a branch towards the ground the nim-value is increased by adding 1 in the schoolbook way, +1, but when several branches join at a node, their values are added in the nim way, ⁺. But because *both* types of addition have the properties

odd plus odd = even plus even = even,
odd plus even = even plus odd = odd,

you can see that:

> The nim-value of any sum of
> green trees has the same parity
> as the total number of edges.

THE PARITY PRINCIPLE

The Fusion Principle below will show that this extends to all Green Hackenbush pictures.

FUSION

You **fuse** two nodes of a picture by bringing them together into a single one. Any edge joining them gets bent into a loop at the resulting node. If you fuse x and y in Fig. 2(a) you get Fig. 2(b); if you fused x and z, you'd get Fig. 2(c).

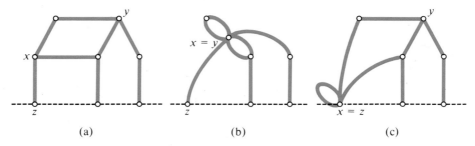

(a)   (b)   (c)

Figure 2. Fusion to Your House!

Green Hackenbush is completely solved by

THE FUSION PRINCIPLE:

you can fuse all the nodes in
any cycle of a Green Hackenbush
picture without changing its value,

and the fact that a loop at any node has the same effect as a twig there. For example the girl

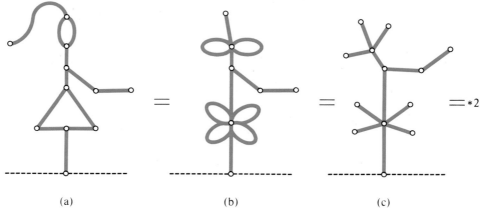

(a)   (b)   (c)

Figure 3. Sizing Up a Green Girl.

of Fig. 3(a) becomes the green shrub of Fig. 3(b) when we've fused the four nodes of her skirt and the two nodes of her head, and this becomes a tree (Fig. 3(c)) on replacing the leaves by twigs. The Colon Principle then shows the tree, and therefore the girl, to have value *2.

PROVING THE FUSION PRINCIPLE

It will take us quite a long time to prove this principle. An alternative, but equally long, proof using mating functions and the Welter function (see Chapter 15) will be found in ONAG. The proof here has the advantage of explicitly constructing the winning move. We'll omit some purely arithmetic computations which are needed for the proof, but not to find the winning move.

If there's any counter-example to the Principle, choose one with the smallest number, n, of edges, and among counter-examples with n edges choose one, G, say, with the smallest possible number of nodes (so there can be no legal fusion of any two nodes of G).

First, *G can only have one ground node* since it never affects play to fuse all ground nodes.

Next, *G can contain no pair of nodes a, b, connected by three or more edge-disjoint paths* for otherwise the game H, obtained by fusing a and b, would have to have a different nim-value and so there would be a winning move in $G + H$. Whichever of G and H this move is in, respond with the corresponding move in the other, reaching a game $G' + H'$. But since G' and H' have at most $n-1$ edges, we can fuse any cycles in them to single points without affecting their values and because there is still a cycle containing both a and b, we see that $G' + H' = 0$, dismissing the supposed winning move from $G + H$.

No cycle of G can exclude the ground for if G had such a cycle C, consider the position G' which would remain after Hackenbush moves chopping all edges of C. Then G' can't contain two distinct nodes of C, for these would be connected, in G, by three edge-disjoint paths (two in C and one in G'). So G' contains only one node, x, of C, and G looks like Fig. 4(a). Now if x were the ground we could apply the Fusion Principle to fuse all nodes of the smaller graph (Fig. 4(b)) and the Colon Principle allows us to fuse these nodes *off* the ground.

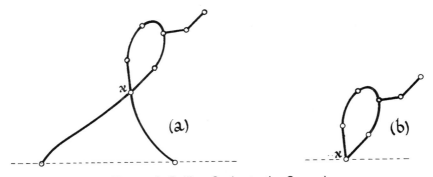

Figure 4. Pulling Cycles to the Ground.

Finally, *G contains only one cycle which includes the ground* for otherwise it would be the sum of smaller graphs, since nodes from distinct cycles can't be joined by other paths. But we could now apply the Fusion Principle to these smaller graphs.

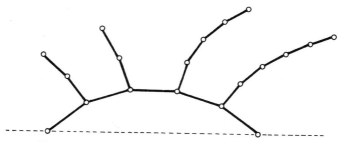

Figure 5. What a Minimal Criminal Looks Like.

We can now see that *G* must look like a bridge (Fig. 5, though officially we should identify the two ground nodes) in which, by the Colon Principle, we can suppose that the edges not in the bridge form at most one string at each node.

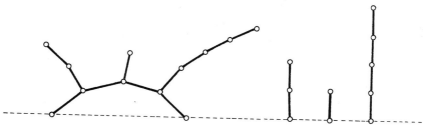

Figure 6. An Even Span Bridge with Copies of its Strings.

The number of edges in the bridge (its **span-length**) *is odd.* If a bridge has even span-length, consider the sum (Fig. 6) of this bridge with copies of all of its strings. Removing any edge of the bridge in this is bad, because the resulting nim-value is odd by the Parity Principle. A symmetry strategy therefore shows that Fig. 6 has value 0 and the Fusion Principle applies.

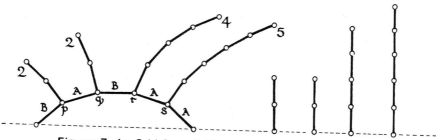

Figure 7. An Odd Span Bridge with Copies of its Strings.

The Fusion Principle for a bridge of *odd* span-length asserts that its value is found by adding * to the sum of its strings. So we must show that Fig. 7 has value *.

Certainly *no option has value* *, because moves in the bridge lead to even nim-values by the Parity Principle, and moves in the strings can be reversed to * by responding with their images (after which the Fusion Principle will apply to the smaller picture).

It will therefore suffice to find an option of value 0. To do this, label the bridge edges with *A* or *B*, giving adjacent edges the *same* label if there is an *odd* string between them, and different labels if there's an *even* string between. The edges with the (*Devil's*) label which occurs an *even* number of times (*B* occurs twice in Fig. 7) are bad moves since each of them can be seen to lead to a sum of two trees and several strings where the nim-value of the sum is congruent to 2, mod 4, and therefore non-zero. However any of the (*odd* number of) edges with the other (*Godd's*) label leads to a sum with nim-value congruent to 0, mod 4. To find a good bridge move among these, we reduce the graph to a simpler one by shrinking any edge with a Devil's label to a single point, and halving all string lengths (rounding *down* if they're odd). It can be shown that this reduction also halves the nim-value. Applying it to Fig. 7 leads to the simpler Fig. 8 because 2 halves to 1, 2∓4 halves to 3 and 5 halves to 2. A similar labelling splits the bridge edges into an even (Devil's) number labelled *D* and an odd (Godd's) number labelled *C*. Since in our case there is only one *C* edge, it is the winning move in Fig. 8, and the corresponding edge (between the 5 string and the ground) wins in Fig. 7.

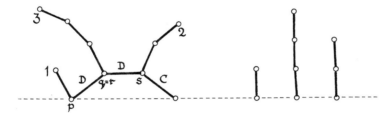

Figure 8. Half of Figure 7.

A MORE COMPLICATED PICTURE

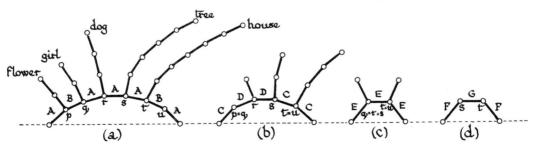

Figure 9. Simplifying and Halving Figure 1.

We'll find a winning move in our opening picture, Fig. 1. When we fuse the cycles contained in or under the girl, dog and house, and evaluate the various pieces we get Fig. 9(a). The halving process leads successively to Figs. 9(b), 9(c) and 9(d). The only good move in this last is the centre span of the reduced bridge. This corresponds to the edge between tree and house in Fig. 1.

Since edges on grounded cycles tend to split the picture up too quickly, the reader who wishes to bamboozle his opponents will verify that there are 17 other good moves in Fig. 1: the bird's tail, the top left branch of the T.V. antenna, any of the four pieces of foundation under the house, the lowest twig on the (right of the) tree, the dog's tail, his face, either hind leg, either part of the girl's head and any of the four parts of her skirt.

Green Hackenbush can be applied to the theory of

IMPARTIAL MAUNDY CAKE

which is played like ordinary Maundy Cake (Chapter 2) except that either player may divide the cake in either direction. Since the game is impartial, any even number of identical cakes cancel, while an odd number have the same value as a single cake.

If α and β are the numbers of *odd* prime divisors of a and b, counted with multiplicities, we shall say that an a by b cake has type

$$D(\alpha,\beta) \qquad \text{or} \qquad E(\alpha,\beta)$$

according as ab is

$$\text{odd} \qquad \text{or} \qquad \text{even}.$$

The moves that produce an odd number of cakes correspond just to reductions of α or β. However, a move that produces an even number of cakes is necessarily from a type $E(\alpha,\beta)$ cake and gives value 0, so

$$D(\alpha,\beta) \qquad \text{and} \qquad E(\alpha,\beta)$$

have the same values as the Green Hackenbush positions

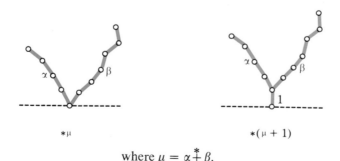

$$*\mu \qquad\qquad\qquad\qquad *(\mu + 1)$$

where $\mu = \alpha \overset{*}{+} \beta$.

We shall discuss Many-Way Maundy Cake in the Extras.

BLUE-RED HACKENBUSH

Recall that in Hackenbush

> bLue edges may be chopped by Left,
> Red edges may be chopped by Right,
> grEen edges may be chopped by Either.

We've just seen what happens when *all* edges are green. If *no* edges of a picture P are green its value is always an ordinary number. For suppose Left makes a move resulting in a picture P^L, say. Then P can be obtained from P^L by adding a blue edge which perhaps supports some other edges and it is easy to see that this has *strictly* increased the value, so

$$P^L < P < P^R \quad \text{for all options } P^L, P^R.$$

By induction, P^L and P^R are numbers, so P is a number. On the other hand, we'll see later in this chapter that it can be very hard to work out just which number it is.

HACKENBUSH HOTCHPOTCH

You'll remember from Chapter 2 that this is our name for Hackenbush when the picture may involve all three colors, bLue, Red, grEen.

Roughly how big is a Hotchpotch picture? The most important thing to look at is the part of the picture made of the red and blue edges which are connected to the ground by other red and blue edges. We call this the **purple mountain**; the rest of the picture is the **green jungle** (which may have red and blue blossoms imbedded in it).

> The value of a Hotchpotch picture is
> only infinitesimally different from
> the value of its purple mountain.

To see this, suppose that the value of the purple mountain is the number x. Then chopping any edge not in the mountain yields a smaller picture with the same mountain whose value is

$$x\text{-ish} \quad \text{(``}x \text{ infinitesimally shifted'')}$$

meaning the sum of x and something like ↑ or $*$ that is infinitesimally small. Moves in the mountain lead to values that are x^L-ish or x^R-ish, depending on who makes them. Since these are more than infinitesimally different from x,

> no sane person will chop
> an edge in the purple
> mountain while there's
> any other edge to chop.

It follows that, from the point of view of all the edges *not* in it, the purple mountain behaves exactly like the ground.

> The green jungle slides
> down the purple mountain!

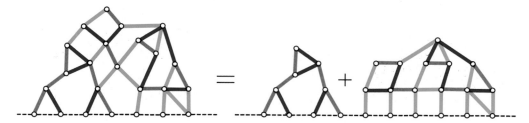

Figure 10. Sliding Jungles down Mountains.

> If you know all about
> Purple Mountains
> and Green Jungles
> you know all about
> Hackenbush Hotchpotch.

FLOWER GARDENS

The green jungles that have come nearest to being cleared are the **flower gardens** which are sums of flowers and totally green positions:

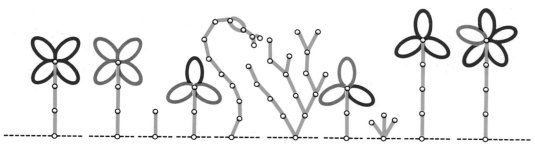

Figure 11. A Variegated Flower Garden.

A **flower** has a **stem** of green edges supporting a **blossom** of blue or red petals. Of course the *negative* of a flower is another flower of the same stem-length, but with petals of opposite colors—the first two flowers of Fig. 11 are negatives of each other. By the Colon Principle a flower with l blue petals and r red ones has the same value as an equally long one with $l-r$ blue petals or $r-l$ red ones according as $l \geqslant r$ or $l \leqslant r$. So the last flower of Fig. 11 simplifies to its neighbor. For this reason we shall assume from now on that any blossom is purely red or purely blue—a **geranium** or a **delphinium**.

As a flower game proceeds some of the blossoms may be cut right off although part of the stems remain. You can think of the resulting green strings as grass or snakes—their values are just nimbers and can be summed by the nim-addition rule to a single nimber, $*n$.

THE BLUE FLOWER PLOY

> If there are no red flowers,
> at least one blue one, and
> any amount of greenery,
> then Left has a winning move.

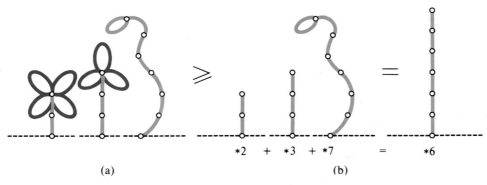

$$*2 \quad + \quad *3 \quad + \quad *7 \quad = \quad *6$$

(a)	(b)

Figure 12. Blue Petals Won't Hurt Left.

For such a position (Fig. 12(a)) is better for Left than the one (Fig. 12(b)) obtained from it by removing the blue petals, which has a nimber value $*n$, say. But if $n \neq 0$, Left can move to 0 in this (and so to a position $\geqslant 0$ in the original) while if $n = 0$ he moves to a position $\geqslant 0$ by taking a blue petal.

Moreover:

> If there are no red flowers,
> at least *two* blue ones, and
> any amount of greenery, Left
> wins even if Right begins,

THE TWO-AHEAD RULE

because Right can destroy at most one blue flower. It follows that the difference between any blue and any red flower exceeds any nimber, and so:

> In a sum of flowers and nimbers,
> Left will prefer any move which
> cuts a red flower to any move
> which cuts a blue flower.

Of course Right prefers all the moves cutting blue flowers to all the moves cutting red ones. Green edges make good Hotchpotch players more aggressive than Blue-Red Hackenbush players, who win by conserving their own resources. In the presence of green edges you should destroy your opponent's property.

ATOMIC WEIGHTS

In Blue-Red Hackenbush the basic unit of measurement $(+1)$ is the single blue edge—there is a sense in which Hotchpotch positions can be measured in terms of another sort of unit.

In any sum of flowers and nimbers either player might play aggressively and refrain from playing on any nimber until all flowers of his opponent's color are gone. This shows that

> a flower garden with at least
> two more blue flowers than red
> ones is positive—one with
> at least two more red flowers
> than blue ones is negative.

So to within a possible uncertainty of 1 or 2 flowers, the total *numbers* of blue and red flowers are all that concern us; their shapes are relatively unimportant.

We can say that all blue flowers have **atomic weight** $+1$, all red ones atomic weight -1, and purely green positions make no contribution to the atomic weight.

> If atomic weight $\geqslant 2$, then Left wins.
> If atomic weight $\leqslant -2$, then Right wins.

For other atomic weights we have to look at the position more closely.

Although the basic unit of atomic weight is the "blue flower", this is not a precise unit because different blue flowers certainly have different values. In general the longer the stem-length of a blue flower the less advantageous it is for Left, and the number of petals becomes relevant only for flowers of the same stem-length.

But to the first order of importance it doesn't matter! A thousand blue flowers is a 1000-flower advantage to Left and he can win the sum of this position with any position which is a 998-flower advantage to Right, even if the red flowers are bigger and better than the blue ones.

QUANTITY BEATS QUALITY!

> Among Hotchpotch flowers, *quantity*
> is much more important than *quality*,

except in certain cases where the *quantities* differ by at most one. Any position of atomic weight 0 is infinitesimally small compared to one of atomic weight 2 or more.

ATOMIC WEIGHTS OF JUNGLES

Recall that in a green jungle there may be red and blue edges, but only green edges touch the ground. For jungles with no red edges we have a slight generalization of the Blue Flower Ploy:

> If a jungle has no red edges
> and at least one blue one,
> Left has a winning move.

THE BLUE JUNGLE PLOY

For if we were to rub out all the blue edges we'd get a pure Green Hackenbush position which we could evaluate as $*n$ for some n, using Green Hackenbush theory. If $n \neq 0$, Left has a winning move in this and his corresponding move in the original jungle is at least as good. If $n = 0$, Left chops a blue edge.

For more general jungles we'll prove at the end of Chapter 8 that there is a whole number atomic weight, although this can be quite hard to find. However, for *parted* jungles, there *is* a way, based on "max-flow min-cut" theory.

A **parted jungle** is a green jungle in which red and blue edges never touch each other. This is how to look at a parted jungle (Fig. 13). The left set contains all nodes that belong to blue edges, the right set those belonging to red ones, and there may be other nodes in between where there are only green edges.

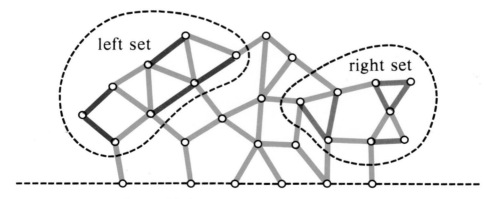

Figure 13. How to Look at a Parted Jungle.

Here's how to work out the atomic weight of a parted jungle.

> First find a *maximal flow* from the left set to the
> right set along the green edges, treating the ground
> as a single node. Then, if you can, *enlarge* the flow
> to obtain as many tracks as you can from the left or
> right set to the ground. If this enlargement has *n*
> tracks from the left set to the ground, the atomic
> weight is $+n$; if *m* tracks from right set to ground,
> the atomic weight is $-m$.

THE FLOW RULE

A **flow** between two sets of nodes consists of a number of green **tracks** (paths) from the first set to the second and is **maximal** if it contains as many such tracks as possible. No two tracks may share an edge, although they may share nodes, as in Fig. 14, showing a case of atomic weight $+3$. The maximal flow has five tracks, a,b,c,d,e; the enlargement three more tracks 1,2,3. Thin green edges are not part of the flow, nor are the red and blue edges.

Of course, in the parted jungle you're faced with, the left and right sets need not be conveni-

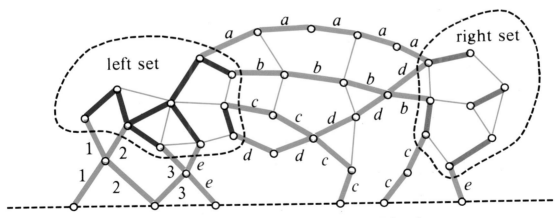

Figure 14. A Parted Jungle with Atomic Weight $+3$.

ently at the left and right of the picture. What is the atomic weight of Fig. 15? The camera we've used doesn't provide enough resolution for you to see the fine structure of those skulls, but it won't affect the answer.

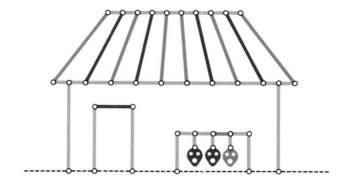

Figure 15. What Do You Find After Traversing the Tracks?

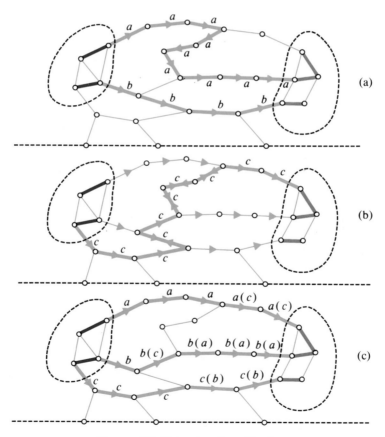

Figure 16. Retracing Your Tracks.

MAKING TRACKS IN THE JUNGLE

To find the desired maximal flow, first find as many green tracks from the left set to the right set as you can, using no green edge twice, and put arrows showing the direction of travel on all the green edges you've used (Fig. 16(a)). Even if you can't add a new track to these, you can't be sure you've found a maximal flow because you might have started badly.

Now start at the left set and try to reach the right set along green edges possibly using ones you've already used, but *only in the wrong direction*, as in Fig. 16(b). If you can do this, then by deleting any edge you have used both ways you can get a larger flow, as in Fig. 16(c). If you carry on like this until you can go no further, you've found a maximal flow between the left and right sets.

To be absolutely sure that this has happened, you can *tint* the various nodes. The nodes in the left set are already tinted blue and you tint another node blue only if you can reach it from a previously tinted node by going along a green edge *not* in the flow, or *backwards* along one that *is*. You could alternatively tint nodes red starting from the right set, but this time only allowing yourself to use the flow edges *forwards*. You can increase the size of your flow when (and only when) some node gets tinted both colors. When you *do* have a maximal flow, you've also partitioned the nodes into three separate sets: those tinted blue, those tinted red, and the rest.

> The atomic weight of the jungle is
> *positive*, *negative* or *zero*
> according as the ground node is
> *tinted blue, tinted red* or *untinted*.

If the ground is tinted you can enlarge the flow by adding more tracks between it and the appropriate set. When trying to find a new track you may, as before, use the edges of the original flow, provided you do so in the wrong direction. The Flow Rule now tells us that the atomic weight is the largest number of tracks by which you can enlarge the flow (with sign + for tracks from left set to ground, sign − for tracks from ground to right set).

Of course, the enlarged flow defines a whole new set of tints as follows:

Blue tinted nodes are those you can reach from the left set by walking along unused, or backwards along used, green edges.

Red tinted nodes are those reached from the right set along unused, or forwards along used, green edges.

But now:

Green tinted nodes are those you can reach from the ground without going in *either* direction along an edge carrying a flow *direct from blue to red*, and without going *against* the flow along an edge carrying flow from blue to ground, or *with* it along one carrying flow from ground to red.

All other nodes are **untinted**.

If the atomic weight were *negative*, of course you would pretend that the ground is blue when enlarging the flow, and in defining green tinted nodes.

TRACKING DOWN AN ANIMAL

Penetrating one particular jungle we found the fabulous beast of Fig. 17. Now let's work out those maximal flows. The two arrowed tracks are easy to find and are a maximal flow from left set to right set because we could sever the animal's head with just two cuts at the base of his neck. Ford and Fulkerson's Max-Flow Min-Cut Theorem tells us that we can always check maximality this way.

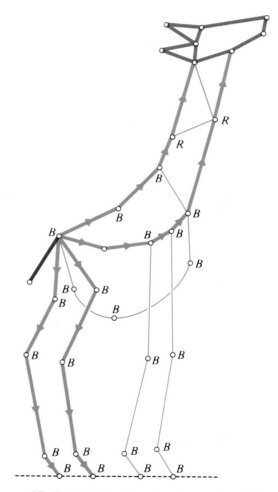

Figure 17. The *R*ed-headed b*L*ue-tailed *G*-raph (Before).

Now to enlarge the flow! The ground is tinted blue at the moment because we can get to it from the tail down either back leg. We must therefore find more tracks from the left set to the ground. The two back legs will obviously be tracks in our enlarged flow. Is this maximal?

No! By creeping rightwards along the animal's underbelly until you reach the base of the neck, back down one edge of the original flow, and then down his front leg, we find a third track (Fig. 18).

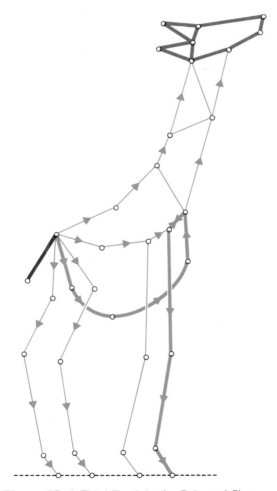

Figure 18. A Third Track in the Enlarged Flow.

The resulting triply enlarged flow (Fig. 19) is maximal, because there are only 5 green edges emerging from the monster's tail. The atomic weight is therefore $+3$, even though there are 10 red edges and only 1 blue one. The tints are shown by labels in Fig. 19, untinted nodes being unlabelled.

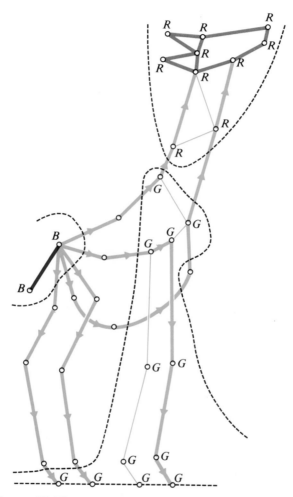

Figure 19. The *R*ed-headed b*L*ue-tailed *G*-raph (After).

AMAZING JUNGLE

What is the atomic weight of the Amazing Jungle of Fig. 20? The ground is the shaded rectangle. (Answer in the Extras.)

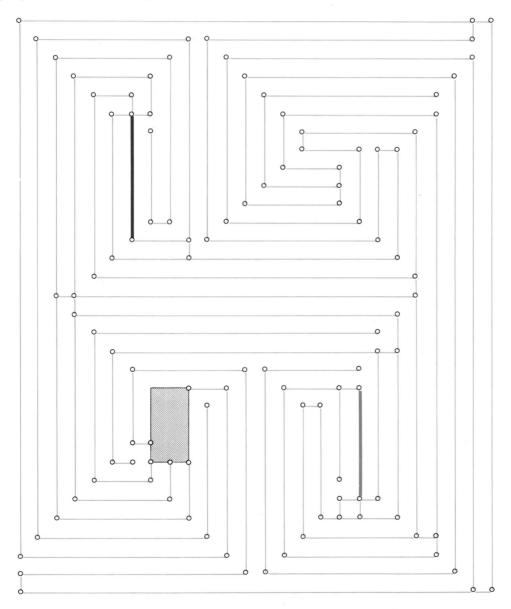

Figure 20. Make Tracks Through the Amazing Jungle.

SMART GAME IN THE JUNGLE

As experienced trackers we can advise you on good moves in the jungle. They may not always be the very best ones but they'll let you (Left) win when the atomic weight is 2 or more, or if it's 1 and you have the move.

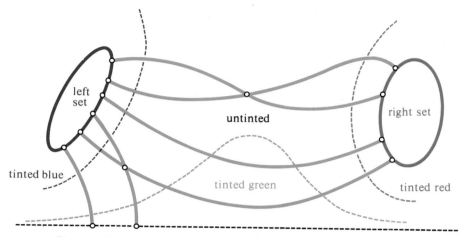

Figure 21. Parted Jungle with Enlarged Maximal Flow and Tints.

Your jungle, with the enlarged maximal flow and tints, should look something like Fig. 21, but you should see it as Fig. 22 in your mind's eye. The green tinted nodes are just an extension

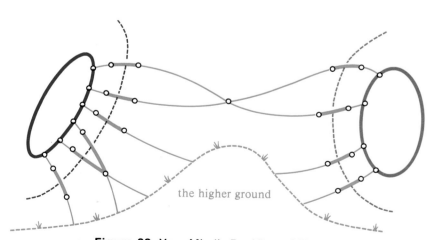

Figure 22. Your Mind's Eye View of Figure 21.

of the grassy ground and the tracks (of the flow) which join them to blue or red tinted nodes are like the tangled stems of blue or red imbedded flowers. All the other edges are more or less irrelevant, including those on any of the tracks between the left and right sets which don't have any green tinted nodes.

What move should you make?

For each imbedded flower the stem edge to chop is the one which crosses the boundary of the red or blue tinted region, and in general the players should behave just as they do in a flower garden, aggressively chopping down their opponent's flowers.

More precisely:

If you've a move leading to a Green
Hackenbush position of value 0, make it
and play Green Hackenbush thereafter.
(Can only happen when there's just 1 flower.)
Otherwise, chop down a flower
of your opponent's color, if there is one,
and if not, chop one of the track edges
where it crosses the boundary of his region.
If this is impossible, then
there's no edge of your opponent's color
and you can use the Blue Jungle Ploy
(or the Red Jungle Ploy if you're Right).

JUNGLE WARFARE TACTICS

But beware!! As you play the game the status of the various nodes will change, and you may have to blaze some new trails through the jungle.

The Jungle Warfare Tactics can be used to prove the Flow Rule. To see how they work, you must play a few games for yourself.

UNPARTED JUNGLES

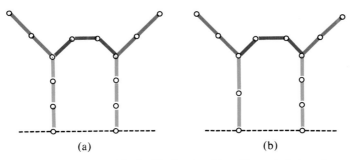

(a)   (b)

Figure 23. Deceptively Similar-Looking Unparted Jungles.

When red and blue edges touch inside a green jungle, the theory gets very complicated and we don't know the answers. The unparted jungles of Figs. 23(a) and 23(b) look very similar but (a) has atomic weight 0, while (b) has atomic weight $+2$. The more general theory of atomic weight in Chapter 8 can be used to show that *every* jungle has integral atomic weight, but there are great difficulties in extending the max-flow min-cut theory:

> ### HACKENBUSH IS HARD!

BLUE-RED HACKENBUSH CAN BE HARD, TOO!

The hardness of Hackenbush Hotchpotch arises partly from the poorly understood infinitesimal values that turn up there. The hardness of Blue-Red Hackenbush is rather different. Although the values are all ordinary numbers, it may be hard to work out exactly which ordinary number is the answer. If you're only interested in finding the values of individual pictures, don't bother with the rest of this chapter.

REDWOOD FURNITURE

A piece of **redwood furniture** is a Blue-Red Hackenbush picture in which

> no red edge touches the ground,
> each blue edge (**foot**) has one end on the ground and
> the other touching a unique red edge (called a **leg**),

for example, the bed, chair and climbing bars of Fig. 24.

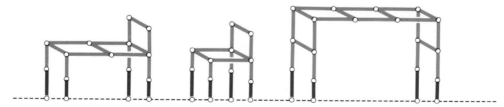

Figure 24. Some Pieces of Redwood Furniture.

Now:

> Any connected piece of redwood furniture has value
>
> $$\frac{1}{2^n}$$
>
> for some $n = 0,1,2,\ldots$.

THE REDWOOD FURNITURE THEOREM

This is proved by a reversibility argument in which Right responds to any Left move (which is necessarily to chop a foot) by chopping the corresponding leg. Let

$$G^{LRLR\ldots LR}$$

be the position obtained from G after several such pairs of moves. We assert that

$$G^{LRLR\ldots LR} \leqslant G.$$

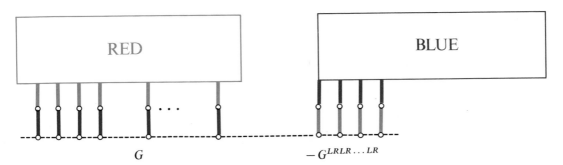

Figure 25. How Furniture Reduces in Value.

This is because Left has an obvious strategy when Right starts in Fig. 25, pairing all edges of $-G^{LRLR\ldots LR}$ with the corresponding edges in G and the remaining feet and legs in G with each other.

Since, in particular, every

$$G^{LR} \leqslant G,$$

every left option of G is reversible, showing that G simplifies to a form

$$\{G^{LRL}|G^R\}.$$

But then since every

$$G^{LRLR} \leqslant G,$$

every Left option in *this* is reversible, and so on, as long as the furniture has any legs to stand on. Eventually we conclude that

$$G = \{0 | G^R\}$$

and so its value is the first of

$$1, \tfrac{1}{2}, \tfrac{1}{4}, \tfrac{1}{8}, \dots$$

that is less then every G^R.

In the remainder of this section it will be handy to count the picture consisting of a single blue edge as a degenerate piece of redwood furniture. Since the value of this is 1, the Redwood Furniture Theorem still holds.

Now:

> If there is any move for Right
> which leaves a piece of
> redwood furniture connected,
> then one of these moves is
> a worthwhile move for Right.

THE DON'T-BREAK-IT-UP THEOREM

We'd better explain exactly what this means. Since

$$\frac{1}{2^n} = \left\{ 0 \,\middle|\, \frac{1}{2^{n-1}} \right\},$$

any move to a value $\leqslant 1/2^{n-1}$ is a move that's **worthwhile** for Right (even if he has other moves to strictly smaller values).

If there were any counter-example to the Don't-Break-It-Up Theorem, there'd be one, G say, with the smallest number of edges. Since G contains a Right move leaving it connected, it must contain a red cycle or a red twig (an edge with one end free). Now let G^R be a worthwhile option for Right, corresponding to an edge x whose removal breaks G into non-empty portions G_1, G_2. Since G_1 has fewer edges than G, the Don't-Break-It-Up Theorem is known to apply to it, and it has a worthwhile option, removing an edge x', that doesn't break it up. Let $G^{R'}$ be the Right option of G obtained by removing x'. So G looks like Fig. 26, where G_3 is what remains of G_1 when x' is removed. Let

$$G_2 = \frac{1}{2^p}, \qquad G_3 = \frac{1}{2^q},$$

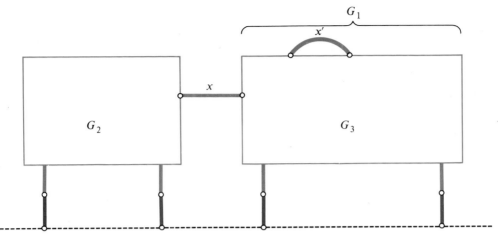

Figure 26. A Minimal Criminal for the Don't-Break-It-Up Theorem.

so that

$$G_1 = \left\{0 \middle| \frac{1}{2^q}\right\} \cdot = \frac{1}{2^{q+1}},$$

$$G = \left\{0 \middle| G^R\right\} = \left\{0 \middle| \frac{1}{2^p} + \frac{1}{2^{q+1}}\right\}$$

and

$$G^{R'} \leqslant \left\{0 \middle| \frac{1}{2^p} + \frac{1}{2^q}\right\}$$

because removing x from $G^{R'}$ leaves $\dfrac{1}{2^p} + \dfrac{1}{2^q}$. But now

$$\tfrac{1}{2}G^{R'} \leqslant \left\{0 \middle| \frac{1}{2^{p+1}} + \frac{1}{2^{q+1}}\right\} \leqslant G,$$

showing that $G^{R'}$ is an all-in-one-piece worthwhile option of G.

Now let A be a piece of redwood furniture, with a worthwhile move for Right that leaves it all in one piece, B. Then

$$A = \{0|B\} = \tfrac{1}{2}B$$

since the value of B has the form $1/2^n$ by the Redwood Furniture Theorem. Similarly, if B has a worthwhile move to C, still in one piece, then $B = \tfrac{1}{2}C$, and so on. By making m such worthwhile moves we eventually conclude that

$$A = \frac{1}{2^m}T,$$

where T is a piece of redwood furniture which is disconnected by the removal of any red edge. You should look at this upside-down (Fig. 27) because the red edges, having no cycle, now form a tree, and the blue ones touch the sky!

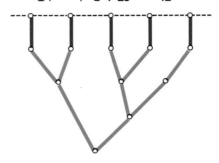

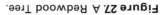

Figure 27. A Redwood Tree.

REDWOOD BEDS

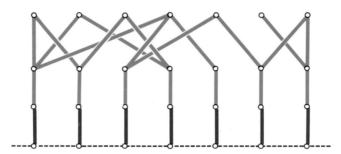

Figure 28. A Redwood Bed.

A **redwood bed** is a piece of redwood furniture in which the **mattress** edges (all red edges other than the legs) each have just one end at the top of a leg (Fig. 28). Its value will be of form

$$\frac{1}{2^n} T$$

where T is a redwood tree obtained by making a succession of worthwhile moves for Right

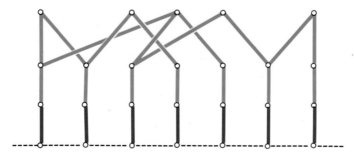

Figure 29. Redwood Tree T Used in Making the Bed.

until any further such move would disconnect the picture (Fig. 29). We assert that

$$\boxed{T \text{ has value } \frac{1}{2}.}$$

If not, let T be the smallest counter-example and let Right make any worthwhile move from T. The result is a pair of redwood trees. Either these are both smaller trees of the same type (and therefore have value 1/2) or just one of them has an extra twig (on the left of the right-hand tree in Fig. 30).

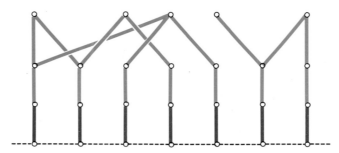

Figure 30. Two Redwood Trees of Differing Type.

But in the former case

$$T = \left\{0 \middle| \frac{1}{2} + \frac{1}{2}\right\} = \frac{1}{2}$$

and in the latter

$$T = \left\{0 \middle| \frac{1}{2} + \frac{1}{4}\right\} = \frac{1}{2}$$

since the twig must be a worthwhile move (and so halve the value) by the Don't-Break-It-Up Theorem.

HOW BIG IS A REDWOOD BED?

Make worthwhile moves from the bed B for as long as you can without disconnecting it. Since the tree T you obtain has value 1/2, we find

$$B = \frac{1}{2^m} \times \frac{1}{2} = \frac{1}{2^{m+1}},$$

where m is the number of moves you have made. How big is m?

We assert that m is the *largest* number of red edges, m', whose removal keeps the bed in one piece, T'. For, take away these edges one at a time, obtaining a sequence of pictures

$$B, C, \ldots, T'.$$

Then

$$B \leqslant \{0|C\} = \tfrac{1}{2}C, \qquad C \leqslant \{0|D\} = \tfrac{1}{2}D, \qquad \ldots$$

and so

$$B \leqslant \frac{1}{2^{m'}} T' = \frac{1}{2^{m'+1}}$$

so that $m \geqslant m'$.

> To work out the size of a redwood bed B you must know what is the smallest redwood tree in B which contains all its legs.

But it follows from the work of Karp (and see also Garey and Johnson) that this problem is "NP-complete". Now among those who know them best, such problems are universally regarded as hard. So

> EVEN BLUE-RED
> HACKENBUSH
> CAN BE HARD!

Would you like to find the value of Fig. 31?

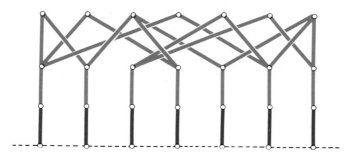

Figure 31. A Moderately Hard Bed.

WHAT'S THE BOTTLE?

Figure 32. What's the Bottle?

EXTRAS

ORDINAL ADDITION, THE COLON PRINCIPLE, AND NORTON'S LEMMA

The compound Hackenbush game $G_x : H$ at the beginning of the chapter is a generalization of the **ordinal sum**, $G : H$, which can be defined for any two games,

$$G : H = \{G^L, G : H^L \mid G^R, G : H^R\}.$$

In this kind of sum, any move in G annihilates H, while moves in H leave G unaffected. (The general Hackenbush compound is similar but there may be moves in G which do not annihilate H.)

The Colon Principle,

$$H \geqslant K \quad \text{implies} \quad G : H \geqslant G : K,$$

applies in general, and shows in particular that

$$H = K \quad \text{implies} \quad G : H = G : K,$$

so that $G : H$ depends only on the *value* of H, not on its form. Unfortunately it *may* depend on the *form* of G, because there are games $G_1 = G_2$ for which $G_1 : H \neq G_2 : H$. This defect is compensated by Norton's Lemma (Chapter 8) which implies that $G : H$ is usually almost indistinguishable in value from G. The lemma asserts, more precisely, that if

$$G < K, \qquad G \parallel K, \qquad G > K,$$

then

$$G : H < K, \qquad G : H \parallel K, \qquad G : H > K,$$

unless some position of K has the same value as G.

Most of these properties continue to hold for variations such as the general Hackenbush compound $G_x : H$.

BOTH WAYS OF ADDING IMPARTIAL GAMES

We know that nim-values are exactly what you need to work out outcomes of ordinary sums of impartial games. What else is required if you might be taking ordinal sums as well? The answer is: just the nim-values of the options.

If a game has nim-value m and options with nim-values $a, b, c, \ldots$, the possible changes in nim-value are

$$\alpha = m \overset{*}{+} a, \qquad \beta = m \overset{*}{+} b, \qquad \gamma = m \overset{*}{+} c, \ldots$$

and so we'll write

$$\{a, b, c, \ldots\} = m_{\{\alpha, \beta, \gamma, \ldots\}}$$

for such a game and call $\{\alpha, \beta, \gamma, ...\}$ the **variation set**. The Sprague-Grundy theory tells us how to "add" this information in the ordinary sense:

$$m_{\{\alpha, \beta, \gamma, ...\}} \overset{*}{+} n_{\{\delta, \varepsilon, \zeta, ...\}} = (m \overset{*}{+} n)_{\{\alpha, \beta, \gamma, ..., \delta, \varepsilon, \zeta, ...\}}$$

(nim-add the values and unite the variations). Thus, since $\{0, 1, 6\} = 2_{\{2, 3, 4\}}$ and $\{0, 3, 4\} = 1_{\{1, 2, 5\}}$ we have

$$\{0, 1, 6\} + \{0, 3, 4\} = 3_{\{1, 2, 3, 4, 5\}} = \{2, 1, 0, 7, 6\} .$$

To add them in the *ordinal* sense we can use the rule

$$\{a, b, c, ...\} : \{d, e, f, ...\} = \{a, b, c, ..., m_d, m_e, m_f, ...\}$$

where $m_0, m_1, m_2, ...$ are *all* the numbers *not* appearing in $\{a, b, c, ...\}$. For $\{0, 1, 6\}$, the missing numbers are $m_0 = 2$, $m_1 = 3$, $m_2 = 4$, $m_3 = 5$, $m_4 = 7$, $m_5 = 8$, ... and so

$$\{0, 1, 6\} : \{0, 3, 4\} = \{0, 1, 6, 2, 5, 7\} .$$

MANY-WAY MAUNDY CAKE

You can play Maundy Cake in as many dimensions as you like, with reservations of certain of the dimensions for certain players. Then the value of an

$$a \times b \times c \times ... \qquad \times r \times s \times t \times ... \qquad \times l \times m \times n \times ... \qquad \text{cake,}$$

in which the dimensions

$$a, b, c, ... \qquad\qquad r, s, t, ... \qquad\qquad l, m, n, ...$$

may be cut by

either player,   Right only,   Left only,

is

$$abc... \ M(rst...,lmn...) + *(\mu \text{ or } \mu + 1)$$

where $M(x,y)$ is the function of Chapter 2 (Extras), and

$$\mu = \alpha \overset{*}{+} \beta \overset{*}{+} \gamma \overset{*}{+} ...$$

where $\alpha, \beta, \gamma ...$ are the numbers of odd prime divisors (counting repetitions) of $a, b, c, ...$ respectively. The 1 is added just if $abc...$ is even.

The proof involves the sliding of an abstract green jungle down an abstract purple mountain, the mountain being multiplied by a factor at each stage of the slide!

SOLUTION TO FIGURE 15

The atomic weight of the door is 2. The maximum Blue to Red flow occupies all but the centre-most horizontal edges of the roof ridge and the eaves. The nodes where the walls meet the eaves are tinted Green and the atomic weight of the roof and walls is 0. The maximum Blue-Red flow occupies both Green hairs by which the shrunken Blue heads are hanging. The left post carries

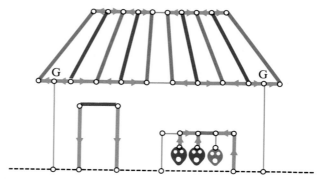

Figure 33. How to Keep Track Without Losing Your Head.

no flow to the ground, but the right one carries a flow from Ground to Red, so the atomic weight of the three shrunken heads and the bar and posts which hold them is -1. Therefore the atomic weight of the whole picture is $2+0+(-1) = +1$.

TRACKS CLEARED THROUGH THE AMAZING JUNGLE

Kimberley King, who's an experienced tracker, found two tracks (1 and 2 in Fig. 34) from Blue to Red direct, and a third one (3) from Blue to ground, and you won't be able to find any more. Therefore Blue is one up, but if he's to bag his game he'd still better go first.

HOW HARD WAS THE BED?

We have to find the smallest redwood tree in Fig. 31 which includes all the legs. Figure 35 is the adjacency matrix for the graph formed by the two top rows of nodes and the edges which

	1	2	3	4	5	6	7
1	1	1	0	1	0	0	0
2	1	0	1	0	0	0	0
3	0	0	0	0	1	1	0
4	0	1	1	0	0	0	0
5	0	0	1	0	0	0	1
6	0	0	0	1	1	0	1
7	0	0	0	0	0	1	1

Figure 35. Coverlet for the Moderately Hard Bed.

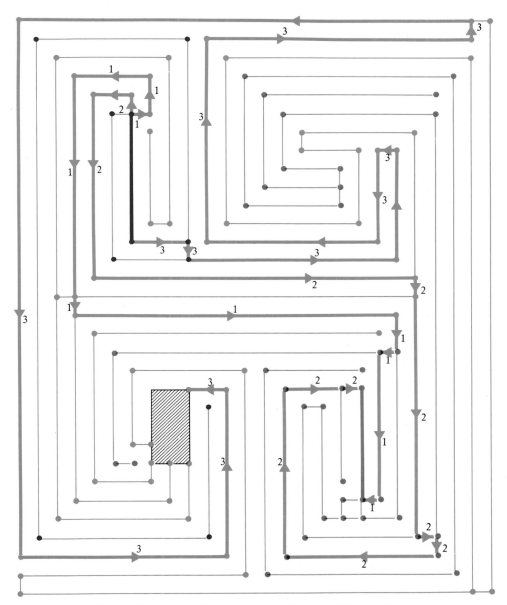

Figure 34. Tracks Cleared Through the Amazing Jungle.

connect the legs. It is not enough to include just 3 of the top nodes, since only 2 of them (columns 3 and 7) are on 3 edges, and $3+3+2 = 8$ edges are not enough to connect the 7 legs, which would need $7+(3-1) = 9$. If we use 4 top nodes, then $7+(4-1) = 3+3+2+2$ and we can manage with columns 3 and 7, just one of columns 5 and 6 (in order to connect the third leg (row 3) and just one other (column 1, 2 or 4). So, of the 16 connecting edges, only 10 are really required, and 6 can be removed, and the value of the bed is

$$\frac{1}{2^{6+1}} = \frac{1}{128}.$$

NP-HARDNESS

Throughout this book we try to help you to acquire winning ways. We consistently focus our attention on those games which have enough structure for us to help you acquire tools and technique so that you can beat your friends consistently until they've read the book too. When both sides have read it, fair competition is again possible, but with a much higher standard of play.

Many combinatorial theorists have recently made a quite different approach. Instead of studying particular games for which clever strategies can be demonstrated, they try to prove that certain classes of games are **hard** in the sense that any algorithm for playing all of them correctly must necessarily take a very large amount of computation. In some sense this approach is complementary to ours. Every positive result, consisting of a constructive strategy of the sort we seek, opens up a question of generalization: can the same techniques be used to solve some larger class of games efficiently? Every negative result, consisting of a proof that any algorithm which solves all the games in some large class must be complex in some sense or other, opens up a question of specialization: what subclasses of the large class of "hard" games are really hard, and which are "easy"? Typically the "hard" class of games contains infinitely many hard games, but it's often true that all the games of such a class which satisfy some additional conditions are "easy". Sometimes there is even a known algorithm which solves most of the games in the "hard" class very quickly and efficiently, but it requires an inordinately long time to solve a relatively small subset of the games; this small subset makes the class "hard".

There are several different definitions of what constitutes a computationally "hard" class of problems. One of the strongest definitions is those which are "complete in exponential time". This means that any algorithm which can solve all the problems in the class has the property that its running time, measured as a function of the length of the input needed to define the problem, is greater than an exponential function of this input infinitely often. Stockmeyer and Chandra have introduced a game called PEEK which they prove is hard in this sense.

Several other classes of games *appear* to be just as hard, but no one has yet been able to prove whether they really require exponential time (infinitely often) or not! The two most important such classes are problems which are "complete in PSPACE" and problems which are "NP-complete". For precise definitions, see the recent beautiful book by Garey and Johnson. Even and Tarjan have shown that Generalized Hex is PSPACE-complete and Schaefer has done the same for Generalized Geography, Generalized Kayles, Col and Snort. Problems known to be at least as hard as NP-complete problems are said to be NP-hard. Fraenkel and Yesha have shown that their annihilation games are NP-hard; Fraenkel *et al.* that $N \times N$ checkers is PSPACE-hard and

PSPACE- complete for certain drawing rules; Lichtenstein and Sipser that $N \times N$ Go is PSPACE-hard; and the analogous result for Chess has recently been obtained by Jim Storer at Bell Labs. Problems which are complete in exponential time are PSPACE-hard, and PSPACE-hard problems are NP-hard, but it's not known if the converses to either of these statements are true.

It *is* known, though, that a good algorithm for solving any NP-hard problem would solve *all* problems which are NP-complete. For example, we've seen in this chapter that any good algorithm for evaluating arbitrary Blue-Red Hackenbush positions could be modified to give a good algorithm for finding a minimum spanning tree of a bipartite graph. Moreover, if some miraculous hypothetical algorithm to evaluate Blue-Red Hackenbush positions had a running time which was bounded by a polynomial function of the length of its input, the same would be true of the derived algorithm for finding a minimum spanning tree. Since this latter problem is NP-complete, the problem of evaluating Blue-Red Hackenbush positions is NP-hard.

By following ideas pioneered by Cook and Karp, Garey and Johnson have uncovered a very wide range of combinatorial problems which are NP-complete. An asymptotically good algorithm for solving any of these problems could be modified to yield a good algorithm for solving any of the others. Many famous mathematicians and computer scientists have tried very hard to solve some of these problems, and without success. Thus:

> If you can prove that a game is
> NP-hard, you can be confident
> that, as of 1981, no one knows
> an asymptotically good algorithm
> for solving it.

Our thermography-based strategy in Chapter 6 requires only a small amount of computation to find near-optimal moves in the sum of any number of short hot games. THERMOSTRAT yields millions of optimal moves, only a few suboptimal ones. But if you always insist on finding the very best move, you will have to do a lot of computing, because Lockwood Morris has recently found a way to construct some rather short hot games whose sum is NP-hard.

In Chapter 16, we'll prove, in a formal sense, that Dots-and-Boxes is NP-hard. However, notice that this asymptotic result says little about the difficulties of calculating good strategies for playing games on boards of sizes small enough to be interesting. In fact most of Chapter 16 is devoted to exhibiting such strategies. Indeed, we consider the class of Dots-and-Boxes positions which we prove to be NP-hard to be a rather degenerate, relatively dull subclass of end-game positions. Some people consider a class of problems "finished" when it has been shown to be NP-hard. Philosophically this is a viewpoint we strongly oppose.

> Some games which are NP-hard
> are very interesting!

It may be possible to find strategies for playing such games which will enable you consistently to beat opponents who haven't read this book; Dots-and-Boxes is an excellent example.

Oh, by the way,

THE BOTTLE AT THE END OF CHAPTER SEVEN

is 7 $.\uparrow$, together perhaps
with some additives of no atomic weight.

REFERENCES

J.H. Conway, "On Numbers and Games", Academic Press, London and New York, 1976, pp. 86–91 (Blue-Red Hackenbush), 165–172 (Green Hackenbush), 188–189 (Hackenbush Hotchpotch).

Stephen A. Cook, The complexity of theorem-proving procedures, Proc. 3rd A.C.M. Sympos. Theory of Comput., 1971, 151–158; Zbl. 253.68020.

J.E. Damß and D. Markert, Strategien für ein kombinatorisches Spiel, Praxis Math. **20** (1978) 75–83.

S. Even and R.E. Tarjan, A combinatorial problem which is complete in polynomial space, J. Assoc. Comput. Mach. **23** (1976) 710–719; Zbl. 355.68041.

L.R. Ford and D.R. Fulkerson, "Flows in Networks", Princeton University Press, 1962.

A.S. Fraenkel and Y. Yesha, Complexity of problems in games, graphs and algebraic equations, Discrete Appl. Math. **1** (1979) 15–30.

A.S. Fraenkel, M.R. Garey, D.S. Johnson, T. Schaefer and Y. Yesha, The complexity of checkers on an $n \times n$ board—Prelim. Report. Proc. 19th Ann. Sympos. Foundations Comput. Sci., IEEE Comput. Soc., Long Beach, 1978, 55–64.

M.R. Garey and D.S. Johnson, Approximation algorithms for combinatorial problems: an annotated bibliography, *in* J.F. Traub (ed.) "Algorithms and Complexity; New Directions and Recent Results", Academic Press, New York and London, 1976, pp. 41–52.

Michael R. Garey and David S. Johnson, "Computers and Intractability; a Guide to the Theory of NP-completeness", W.H. Freeman, San Francisco, 1979.

M.R. Garey, D.S. Johnson and L. Stockmeyer, Some simplified NP-complete problems, Proc. 6th A.C.M. Sympos. Theory of Comput., 1974, 47–63.

M.R. Garey, D.S. Johnson and L. Stockmeyer, Some simplified NP-complete graph problems, Theor. Comput. Sci. **1** (1976) 237–267; Zbl. 338.05120.

M.R. Garey, D.S. Johnson and R. Endre Tarjan, The planar Hamiltonian circuit problem is NP-complete, SIAM J. Comput. **5** (1976) 704–714; Zbl. 346.05110.

I.J. Good, And Good saw that it was god(d), Parascience Proc. **1** #2 (Feb. 1975) 3–13.

Richard M. Karp, Reducibility among combinatorial problems, *in* R.E. Miller and J.W. Thatcher (eds.) "Complexity of Computer Calculations," Plenum, New York, 1972, pp. 85–103.

Richard M. Karp, The fast approximate solution of hard combinatorial problems, Proc. 6th SE Conf. Combinatorics, Graph Theory, Computing, Boca Raton, 1975, 15–31; Zbl. 369.05049.

R.M. Karp, On the computational complexity of combinatorial problems, Networks, **5** (1975) 45–68; Zbl. 324.05003.

David Lichtenstein and Michael Sipser, GO is P-space hard, Proc. 19th Ann. Sympos. Foundations Comput. Sci., IEEE Comput. Soc., Long Beach, 1978, 48–54; MR **80e**: 68115.

W.J. Paul and R.E. Tarjan, Time-space trade-offs in a pebble game, Acta Inform. **10** (1978) 111–115.

Wolfgang J. Paul, Robert Endre Tarjan and James R. Celoni, Space bounds for a game on graphs, Math. Systems Theory, **10** (1977) 239–251; Zbl. 366.90151. Corrections, *ibid.* **11** (1977) 85.

Stefan Reisch, Gobang is PSPACE-complete, Acta Informatica; Zbl. 401.90112.

Edward Robertson and Ian Munro, NP-completeness, puzzles and games, Utilitas Math. **13** (1978) 99–116.

Thomas J. Schaefer, On the complexity of some two-person perfect information games. J. Comput. Systems Sci. **16** (1978) 185–225.

Larry J. Stockmeyer and Ashok K. Chandra, Provably difficult combinatorial games, SIAM J. Comput. **8** (1979) 151–174; MR **80d**: 68055; Zbl. 421.68044.

Larry J. Stockmeyer and Ashok K. Chandra, Intrinsically difficult problems, Sci. Amer. **240** #5 (May 1979) 140–159.

Chapter 8

It's a Small, Small, Small, Small World!

There are many games, such as

$$* = 0|0, \qquad \uparrow = 0|*, \qquad *2 = \{0, *|0, *\}, \qquad \uparrow* = \{0, *|0\}, \qquad \dots,$$

in which *both* players have legal moves from *every* non-terminal position. This prevents numbers such as

$$1 = \{0| \ \}, \qquad -3 = \{ \ |-2\}, \qquad \dots,$$

from arising, and in fact ensures that all the positions have infinitesimal values. We'll call such games **all small**.

Figure 1. Another Flower Garder .

221

Figure 1 shows a Hackenbush Hotchpotch flower garden. Recall from earlier Chapters that although

> bLue edges may only be chopped by Left, and
> Red only by Right, any
> grEen edge may be chopped by Either,

so since the only edges which touch the ground are green, both players will have legal moves if anything at all remains of the picture. Hackenbush flower gardens are therefore all small.

You don't need to have read Chapter 7, which dealt with complicated Hackenbush positions, because the simple properties of flowers which we use now will be redeveloped as we want them.

UPPITINESS AND UNCERTAINTY

The small games that occurred in Hackenbush Hotchpotch (Chapter 7) have values that can be expressed as a whole number of flowers or an equivalent number of ups. In this chapter we'll show that every small game has a certain *atomic weight* which can also be called its *uppitiness* since it tells us what number of ups it's most nearly equal to.

Even in sums of Hackenbush Hotchpotch flowers there's a fundamental uncertainty of $\uparrow$ or $\Uparrow$ which makes a complete analysis very hard. What we *can* say is that an advantage of 2 or more flowers is enough to win even if the opponent has the next move. One or no flowers may or may not suffice because then the players must prepare to fight a Nim-like battle over stem-lengths, in addition to their main aim of weeding out the opponent's color. In fact when all earthly blooms have faded, the stars will still remain, and the outcome will depend on the resulting Nim-game value.

Much the same can be said even about the all small games that do not arise in Hackenbush. Every such game g has a definite atomic weight G, and

$$\boxed{\text{if } G \geqslant 2, \text{ then } g \geqslant 0.}$$

DOUBLE-UP TO BE SURE

On the other hand, an atomic weight G of 0 or 1 may not be enough because of the subtle Nim-like problems embedded in g.

We can reduce the amount of uncertainty, but at some cost, by adding a very large Nim-heap. Since this has value $*N$ for some large number N, we shall call it a **remote star**. Since the exact value of N doesn't matter provided it's large enough, we'll use a special symbol,

$$\text{☆} \quad (\text{"far star"})$$

for any remote enough star. It turns out that

$$\boxed{g + \text{☆} \geqslant 0 \text{ exactly when } G \geqslant 1.}$$

So if Right starts when a remote star is present, an atomic weight of at least 1 is not only sufficient, but also necessary, for Left to win.

The remote star stops us from having to worry about the exact structure of the Nim-like part of the game, since from a remote enough star we can reach any desired nimber,

$$0, *1, *2, *3, \dots .$$

To know the outcome of

$$g + \star$$

what you need is just the atomic weight of g.

In general we'll use small letters for small games and large ones for their atomic weights.

COMPUTING ATOMIC WEIGHTS

Calculating atomic weights is very like cooling by temperature 2 (Chapter 6) except that we must occasionally compare g with the remote stars.

Suppose that

$$g = \{a,b,c,\dots | d,e,f,\dots\}$$

and that we already know the atomic weights

$$A \text{ of } a, \quad B \text{ of } b, \quad C \text{ of } c, \quad \dots; \qquad D \text{ of } d, \quad E \text{ of } e, \quad F \text{ of } f, \quad \dots,$$

then:

the atomic weight G of g is

$$G_0 = \{A-2, B-2, C-2, \dots | D+2, E+2, F+2, \dots\}$$

unless G_0 is an integer *and*
either $g > \star$ or $g < \star$.
In these **eccentric** cases:

if $g > \star$, G is the largest integer for which

$$G \triangleleft| D+2, \ G \triangleleft| E+2, \ G \triangleleft| F+2, \ \dots;$$

if $g < \star$, G is the least integer for which

$$G |\triangleright A-2, \ G |\triangleright B-2, \ G |\triangleright C-2, \ \dots.$$

THE ATOMIC WEIGHT CALCULUS

We'll usually write just

$$G = \text{``}\{A-2, B-2, C-2, \dots | D+2, E+2, F+2, \dots\}\text{''},$$

the quotation marks indicating that proper care must be taken in the eccentric cases.

How remote should ☆ be?

> $*N$ will already serve as a remote star for g, provided that no position of g (including g itself) has value $*N$.

Thus $*2$ is remote enough for $\uparrow = 0|*$, and so, since

$$\uparrow > *2, \text{ we can write } \uparrow > \text{☆}.$$

Similarly $*(m+1)$ is remote enough for $*m$, and since

$$*m \parallel *(m+1), \text{ we have } *m \parallel \text{☆}.$$

This is enough to show that

> every nimber $*m$ has atomic weight 0,

for if we know this of 0, $*1$, $*2$, say, then since $*3 \parallel$ ☆, our formula gives

$$G_0 = \{0-2, 0-2, 0-2 \mid 0+2, 0+2, 0+2\} = 0$$

for the atomic weight of

$$*3 = \{0, *1, *2 \mid 0, *1, *2\}.$$

On the other hand,

> $\uparrow$ has atomic weight 1,

because although we find

$$G = \text{``}\{0-2 \mid 0+2\}\text{''} = \text{``}\{-2 \mid 2\}\text{''}$$

we have an eccentric case

$$\uparrow > \text{☆}$$

and so we must choose the *largest* integer $\lhd \; 0+2$, namely 1.

Let's check that $\downarrow * |0 = \Downarrow$ has atomic weight -2, as it should. Our calculus gives

$$G = \text{``}\{-1-2 \mid 0+2\}\text{''} = \text{``}\{-3 \mid 2\}\text{''}$$

but since

$$\Downarrow < \text{☆}$$

we must choose the *least* integer $\rhd \; -3$, namely -2.

EATCAKE

is a game due to Jim Bynum. It is the disjunctive version of Eatcakes, which we will meet in Chapter 9. A number of rectangular cakes (initially just one) are on the table, ruled into 1×1 squares. At his move Left (Lefty) must eat a vertical strip of width 1 through *just one* of these cakes, thereby probably dividing it into two smaller cakes. Right (Rita) eats horizontal strips in a similar way.

So you don't have to keep asking Mother to bake more cakes, Bynum suggests you play his game with ordinary playing cards. In Fig. 2 you see Rita making the second move of a game.

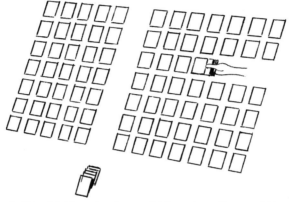

Figure 2. Rita Making the Second Move in a Game of Eatcake.

Bynum made a case by case analysis of all sufficiently small starting rectangles and empirically discovered that the outcome depends only on the parity of the two edge-lengths. This was proved in ONAG (pp. 201–204) where it is shown that the values of rectangles are as shown in

	1	2	3	4	5	6
1	$*$	$-g_1$	$*$	$-g_1$	$*$	$-g_1$
2	g_1	$*$	g_2	$g_2 - g_1 + *$	g_3	$g_3 - g_1 + *$
3	$*$	$-g_2$	$*$	$-g_2$	$*$	$-g_2$
4	g_1	$g_1 - g_2 + *$	g_2	$*$	g_3	$g_3 - g_2 + *$
5	$*$	$-g_3$	$*$	$-g_3$	$*$	$-g_3$
6	g_1	$g_1 - g_3 + *$	g_2	$g_2 - g_3 + *$	g_3	$*$

	1	2	3	4	5	6	7
1	$\|$	$-$	$\|$	$-$	$\|$	$-$	$\|$
2	$+$	$\|$	$+$	$\|$	$+$	$\|$	$+$
3	$\|$	$-$	$\|$	$-$	$\|$	$-$	$\|$
4	$+$	$\|$	$+$	$\|$	$+$	$\|$	$+$
5	$\|$	$-$	$\|$	$-$	$\|$	$-$	$\|$
6	$+$	$\|$	$+$	$\|$	$+$	$\|$	$+$
7	$\|$	$-$	$\|$	$-$	$\|$	$-$	$\|$

Table 1. (a) Values of Eatcake.　　　　　　　　(b) Outcomes of Eatcake.

Table 1(a), where the games g_i are defined by

$$g_1 = 0|* = \uparrow,$$
$$g_2 = \{g_1 + g_1 \mid *\},$$
$$g_3 = \{g_1 + g_2, g_2 + g_1 \mid *\},$$
$$g_4 = \{g_1 + g_3, g_2 + g_2, g_3 + g_1 \mid *\},$$
$$g_5 = \{g_1 + g_4, g_2 + g_3, g_3 + g_2, g_4 + g_1 \mid *\},$$

and in general

$$g_n = \{g_1 + g_{n-1}, g_2 + g_{n-2}, \ldots, g_{n-1} + g_1 \mid *\}.$$

What are the atomic weights of these? We know that

$g_1 = \uparrow$ has atomic weight 1, and so

$g_2 = \Uparrow\!|*$ has atomic weight $\{2-2\mid 0+2\} = 1$, then

$g_3 = \{g_1 + g_2 \mid *\}$ has the same atomic weight $\{2-2\mid 0+2\} = 1$,

and by induction so do $g_4, g_5, \ldots$.

When you're playing a game of Eatcake you can use Table 1 to evaluate the position in the form

$$g_a + g_b + \ldots - g_c - \ldots (+*, \text{possibly})$$

and since all the g_i have atomic weight 1,

> if there are at least 2 more
> positive g_i than negative ones,
> or at least 1 more and Left
> has the move, then Left can win.

For the further analysis, it's wise to let

$$g_n = h_1 + h_2 + \ldots + h_n.$$

The h_i are positive infinitesimals with very interesting properties (see ONAG, pp. 203–204).

SPLITTING THE ATOM

Atomic weights are usually whole numbers, but not always. For example,

$\Uparrow\!|\downarrow$ has atomic weight $\{2-2\mid -1+2\} = 0|1 = \frac{1}{2}$,

and more complicated numbers can also happen. But atomic weights needn't even be numbers:

$\Uparrow\!|\Downarrow$ has atomic weight $\{2-2\mid -2+2\} = 0|0 = *$, and

$\Uparrow\!\!\!|\,\Downarrow\!\!\!$ has atomic weight $\{3-2\mid -3+2\} = 1|-1 = \pm 1$.

But they still add up nicely:

> If $g,h,k,\ldots$ have atomic weights $G,H,K,\ldots$,
> then $g+h+k+\ldots$ has atomic weight $G+H+K+\ldots$.

For example,

$$\Uparrow|\!\downarrow \;+\; \Uparrow|\!\Downarrow \text{ has atomic weight } \tfrac{1}{2} + *.$$

In a moment we'll see that some quite interesting atomic weights arise in the game of Childish Hackenbush Hotchpotch. But first

TURN-AND-EATCAKE

This game was introduced in ONAG (pp. 199–200) where it was described as the twisted form of Bynum's Game. It is played just like Eatcake except that before eating a strip, the player must turn the appropriate cake through one right angle.

	1	2	3	4	5	6	7	8	9	10	11	12
1	$*$	$\uparrow$	$*$	$\uparrow^2$		$\uparrow^2$	$*$	$\uparrow$	$*$	$\uparrow^2$		$\uparrow^2$
2	$\downarrow$	0	$\downarrow$	0	$\downarrow_2$	0	$\downarrow$	0	$\downarrow$	0	$\downarrow_2$	0
3	$*$	$\uparrow$	$*$	$\uparrow^2$		$\uparrow^2$	$*$	$\uparrow$	$*$	$\uparrow^2$		$\uparrow^2$
4	$\downarrow_2$	0	$\downarrow_2$	0	$\downarrow_3$	0	$\downarrow_2$	0	$\downarrow_2$	0	$\downarrow_3$	0
5		$\uparrow^2$		$\uparrow^3$	$*$	$\uparrow^2$		$\uparrow^3$		$\uparrow^2$	$*$	$\uparrow^3$
6	$\downarrow_2$	0	$\downarrow_2$	0	$\downarrow_2$	0	$\downarrow_2$	0	$\downarrow_2$	0	$\downarrow_2$	0
7	$*$	$\uparrow$	$*$	$\uparrow^2$		$\uparrow^2$	$*$	$\uparrow$	$*$	$\uparrow^2$		$\uparrow^2$
8	$\downarrow$	0	$\downarrow$	0	$\downarrow_3$	0	$\downarrow$	0	$\downarrow$	0	$\downarrow_3$	0
9	$*$	$\uparrow$	$*$	$\uparrow^2$		$\uparrow^2$	$*$	$\uparrow$	$*$	$\uparrow^2$		$\uparrow^2$
10	$\downarrow_2$	0	$\downarrow_2$	0	$\downarrow_2$	0	$\downarrow_2$	0	$\downarrow_2$	0	$\downarrow_2$	0
11		$\uparrow^2$		$\uparrow^3$	$*$	$\uparrow^2$		$\uparrow^3$		$\uparrow^2$	$*$	$\uparrow^3$
12	$\downarrow_2$	0	$\downarrow_2$	0	$\downarrow_3$	0	$\downarrow_2$	0	$\downarrow_2$	0	$\downarrow_3$	0

Table 2. Most of the Values in Turn-and-Eatcake.

Except for rectangles having a side of form $6n+5$ the values have period 6 (Table 2). The games

$$\uparrow^2 = \{0\,|\,\downarrow +*\} \qquad \text{(pronounced ``up second''), and}$$
$$\uparrow^3 = \{0\,|\,\downarrow +\downarrow_2 +*\} \qquad \text{(pronounced ``up third'')}$$

behave as if they were indeed the square and cube of $\uparrow$, so that:

any number of copies of $\uparrow^2$ add to less than $\uparrow$;
any number of copies of $\uparrow^3$ add to less than $\uparrow^2$.

We've written

$$\downarrow_2 \text{ ("down second") and } \downarrow_3 \text{ ("down third")}$$

for the negatives of $\uparrow^2$ and $\uparrow^3$. These games have atomic weight 0.

In the rows corresponding to an edge-length $6n + 5$ the entries, after the third, have period 6. For the entries missing from Table 2 the other edge-length is odd and the value is

$$(\text{a multiple of } \uparrow) + *.$$

	1	3	5	7	9	11	13	15	17	19
$6n+5$	$\uparrow + *$	$*.\uparrow + *$	$*$	$\frac{1}{2}.\uparrow + *$	$\frac{1}{4}.\uparrow + *$	$*$	$\frac{1}{2}.\uparrow + *$	$\frac{1}{4}.\uparrow + *$	$*$	$\frac{1}{2}.\uparrow + *$

(*Column* entries missing from Table 2 are the negatives of these, i.e. they have $\downarrow$ in place of $\uparrow$.)

As you can see, the multipliers involve $*$'s and fractions. We'll show you how to define general multiples of $\uparrow$ later in this chapter. The only non-integer multipliers which arise in Turn-and-Eatcake are

$$*.\uparrow + * = \Uparrow|\Downarrow \text{ which has incentive } (2+*).\uparrow + *,$$
$$\tfrac{1}{4}.\uparrow + * = \Uparrow|1\tfrac{1}{2}.\downarrow \text{ which has incentive } (1\tfrac{3}{4}).\uparrow + *,$$
$$\tfrac{1}{2}.\uparrow + * = \Uparrow|\downarrow \text{ which has incentive } (1\tfrac{1}{2}).\uparrow + *.$$

You should choose between them in this order and prefer to move in one of these (or its negative) rather than elsewhere.

Beware! It is *not true* that $\uparrow^2 < \tfrac{1}{4}.\uparrow$,

and it is *not true* that $\uparrow^2 = \uparrow.\uparrow$.

ALL YOU NEED TO KNOW ABOUT ATOMIC WEIGHTS BUT WERE AFRAID TO ASK

Although it's quite hard to *prove* things about atomic weights, they're very easy to *use*, because they usually turn out to be whole numbers. Here's a complete list of properties; big letters are the atomic weights of the corresponding little ones:

If $G \geqslant 2$	then $g \geqslant 0.$
If $G \leqslant -2$	then $g \leqslant 0.$
If $G \rhd 0$	then $g \rhd 0.$
If $G \lhd 0$	then $g \lhd 0.$
$G \geqslant 1$	just if $g > ☆.$
$G \leqslant -1$	just if $g < ☆.$
$-1 \lhd G \lhd 1$	just if $g \parallel ☆.$

And remember that for

$$g = \{a,b,c,\ldots \mid d,e,f,\ldots\}$$

our Atomic Weight Calculus gives

$$G = \{A-2, B-2, C-2, \ldots \mid D+2, E+2, F+2, \ldots\}$$

except in the eccentric cases when this is an integer *and*

$$either\ g > \text{☆}; \quad G = \text{largest integer} \lhd \text{all of } D+2, E+2, F+2, \ldots:$$
$$or\ \ g < \text{☆}; \quad G = \text{least integer} \rhd \text{all of } A-2, B-2, C-2, \ldots.$$

Also

$$\boxed{\begin{array}{l} g + h + k + \ldots \text{ has atomic weight } G + H + K + \ldots, \\ \quad -g \qquad\quad \text{has atomic weight} \qquad -G. \end{array}}$$

We'll be back to prove all these results after a childish interlude.

CHILDISH HACKENBUSH HOTCHPOTCH

Like other variations on the Hackenbush theme, this game is played on a picture with colored edges. This time each edge is either red or blue or green. Just as in ordinary Hackenbush Hotchpotch, Either player may remove *any* grEen edge along with all other edges no longer connected to the ground. Alternatively, Left may remove any single bLue edge but only under the *childish* condition that its removal does not disconnect any other edge from the ground. Similarly Right may chop a Red edge only if it leaves all other edges connected to the ground. Observe that the childish condition applies *only* to the red and blue edges, *not* to the green ones.

Left and Right can't remember whose turn it is to move next in the Childish Hackenbush Hotchpotch position of Fig. 3. Does this matter?

Figure 3. Does it Matter who Gets First Lick at the Lollipops?

Except for the rightmost summand, the position is a sum of **lollipops** made of red and blue loops supported by a number of green branches each of which connects the base of the loop directly to the ground. The value of a grounded loop made of $x+2$ blue edges joined at the top to $y+2$ red ones is $\{x \mid -y\}$, good moves being as shown in Fig. 4. Each player chops his lowest edge because this allows him to play all but one of his remaining edges at leisure.

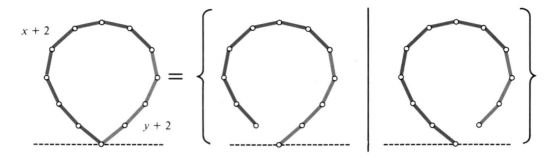

$$x + 2$$

$$y + 2$$

Figure 4. A Childish Hackenbush Loop Worth $\{x|-y\}$.

For the childish lollipop made of such a red-blue loop supported by n green edges, we'll use the symbol

$$\{x|-y\}_n.$$

From this game Left has only two plausible moves:

$$\text{to } \{x|-y\}_{n-1} \qquad \text{or } (x)_n,$$

where $(x)_n$ denotes a picture of value x supported by a sheaf of n green edges. Since Right has a similar choice of moves, we have

$$\{x|-y\}_n = \{\{x|-y\}_{n-1},(x)_n \,\|\, \{x|-y\}_{n-1},(-y)_n\},$$

and similarly

$$(x)_n = \{(x)_{n-1},(x^L)_n \,|\, (x)_{n-1},(x^R)_n\}.$$

In this notation, the six lollipops of Fig. 3 have values

$$\{1|0\}_7, \quad \{0|-2\}_5, \quad \{0|-1\}_4, \quad \{1|-1\}_4, \quad \{4|-1\}_2, \quad \{0|0\}_1$$

and you can check that the non-lollipop at the end has value $(\frac{1}{2})_1$.

ATOMIC WEIGHTS OF LOLLIPOPS

If z is an integer, the position $(z)_n$ is actually a grown-up Hackenbush Hotchpotch position whose atomic weight is

$$n, \qquad 0 \qquad \text{or} \qquad -n,$$

according as

$$z > 0, \quad z = 0 \qquad \text{or} \qquad z < 0.$$

(Work this out for yourself, or use the flow method of Chapter 7.)

We can now use the Atomic Weight Calculus to find the atomic weights of all Childish Hackenbush lollipops. When $x = y = 0$, we have

$$\{0|0\}_n \,\|\, \star \text{ for all } n, \text{ and so it has atomic weight } 0.$$

In the more interesting case $x > 0, y = 0$, we have

$$\{x|0\}_n > \star,$$

and so we can work out the atomic weights:

game	atomic weight
$\{x\|0\}_1$	"$\{1-2\|0+2\}$" $= 1$, an eccentric case,
$\{x\|0\}_2$	$\{2-2\|0+2\} = 1$,
$\{x\|0\}_3$	$\{1\|2\} = 1\frac{1}{2}$,
$\{x\|0\}_4$	$\{2\|2\} = 2*$,
$\{x\|0\}_5$	$\{3\|2\} = 2\frac{1}{2}\pm\frac{1}{2}$,
$\{x\|0\}_6$	$\{4\|2\} = 3\pm1$,
$\{x\|0\}_7$	$\{5\|2\} = 3\frac{1}{2}\pm1\frac{1}{2}$,

....

In the most common case with $x > 0$, $-y < 0$, we have

$$\{x\|-y\}_n \parallel \star$$

and so:

game	atomic weight
$\{x\|-y\}_1$	$\{1-2\|-1+2\} = 0$,
$\{x\|-y\}_2$	$\{2-2\|-2+2\} = *$,
$\{x\|-y\}_3$	$\{1\|-1\} = \pm1$,
$\{x\|-y\}_4$	$\{2\|-2\} = \pm2$,
$\{x\|-y\}_5$	$\{3\|-3\} = \pm3$,

....

From these results we can find the atomic weights of all the components in Fig. 3, respectively

$$3\frac{1}{2}\pm1\frac{1}{2} \quad -2\frac{1}{2}\pm\frac{1}{2} \quad -2* \quad \pm2 \quad * \quad 0 \quad 1$$

corresponding to the values

$$\{1\|0\}_7 \quad \{0\|-2\}_5 \quad \{0\|-1\}_4 \quad \{1\|-1\}_4 \quad \{4\|-1\}_2 \quad \{0\|0\}_1 \quad \text{and} \quad (\tfrac{1}{2})_1$$

so that the atomic weight of the whole figure is precisely

$$\pm2\pm1\frac{1}{2}\pm\frac{1}{2}.$$

If we were playing the resulting game of Cashing Cheques (Chapter 5) on these atomic weights the first player would clearly win with a full move to spare, so writing

$$g = \{a,b,c,\dots\|d,e,f,\dots\}$$

for the sum of everything in Fig. 3 we can suppose

$$A \geqslant 1 \quad \text{and} \quad D \leqslant -1.$$

Now since $A \geqslant 1$ implies $a > \star$ and $D \leqslant -1$ implies $d < \star$, the optimal strategy in the Cashing Cheques game would also ensure a win for the first player on the sum of Fig. 3 with a remote star. But what, if anything, can we deduce about the outcome of Fig. 3 alone? Since some games of atomic weight 1 are positive (e.g. ↑) but others are fuzzy (e.g. ↑*) we can't say for sure that a move to a position of atomic weight at least 1 is always good enough to win for Left.

Nevertheless we *can* assert (and prove!) that the first player can win Fig. 3 and *only* by optimizing the atomic weight. The reason is that a remote star actually *is* present! The lollipop of atomic weight 0 has value

$$\{0|0\}_1 = (*1)_1 = *2,$$

and with respect to everything else in the figure, $*2$ is remote!

PROVING THINGS ABOUT ATOMIC WEIGHTS

will take us quite a long time, so if you only want to *use* them, why not just play a few more childish games while you're waiting for the rest of us to finish the chapter? You don't *have* to follow the proofs!

We can use Hackenbush flower gardens to make the proofs look easier and prettier! To be quite precise we'll define a **flower** to have a green **stem** of at least 1 edge, topped by a completely blue or a completely red **blossom** which also must have at least 1 edge (**petal**). A **flower garden** is any position made up of such flowers and possibly some purely green grass (or snakes!) as in Fig. 1.

Recall the rules saying who can chop the various colors of edge and that after each chop we remove any edges no longer connected to the ground. So that you don't have to reread Chapter 7, we'll remind you here how to play well in flower gardens.

PLAYING AMONG THE FLOWERS

If your garden has no flowers, then each piece of grass (or snake) has some value $*n$ and you're really playing Nim (Chapter 2).

If there's a blue flower but no red ones, then Left, if he has the move, can win as follows: if there is a winning move in the Nim-position got by ignoring the blue petals, he should make it. Otherwise he should pluck a blue petal, and leave this awkward Nim-position for Right. Any blue petals that remain won't hurt Left. (This is the Blue Flower Ploy of Chapter 7.)

In more general flower gardens:

Left can win if he has the move
and is at least 1 flower ahead

$(G \geqslant 1)$,

THE ONE-UPMANSHIP RULE

Left can win without the move
if he is at least 2 flowers ahead

$(G \geqslant 2)$.

THE TWO-AHEAD RULE

These are particular cases of

THE ATOMIC WEIGHT RULES:

> if $G \rhd 0$, then $g \rhd 0$;
> if $G \geqslant 2$, then $g \geqslant 0$,

but can be proved directly, for if the position has 2 more blue flowers than red ones when Left presents it to Right, it will still have at least 1 more when the turn reverts to Left. He can then either restore his advantage by chopping down a red flower or use the Blue Flower Ploy if no red flower remains.

WHEN IS g AS UPPITY AS h?

We'll reserve the name **flowerbed** for a flower garden that has just as many blue flowers as red ones:

When your garden is BalancED
(With just as many Blue as rED)
We shall call it a flowerBED.

Since the blue and red flowers cancel, we want to say that a flowerbed has atomic weight 0. But we can't use the notion of atomic weight before we prove things about it, and so we'll define g and h to be **equally uppity** and write $g \doteq h$ exactly when there are flowerbeds f_1 and f_2 for which

$$f_1 \geqslant g-h \geqslant f_2.$$

> Two games are equally uppity just
> if we can trap their difference
> between two flowerbeds.

Obviously

$$g \doteq h \quad \text{implies} \quad g+k \doteq h+k.$$

and, because the sum of 2 flowerbeds is a flowerbed,

$$g \doteq h \quad \text{and} \quad h \doteq k \quad \text{imply} \quad g \doteq k.$$

If we can only find a *single* flowerbed f for which

$$g-h \geqslant f,$$

we'll say that g is **at least as uppity** as h and write $g \gtrdot h$.

If g is exactly as uppity as some multiple of up, say

$$g \doteq G.\uparrow$$

we'll say that G is the **uppitiness** of g. It will take us quite a long time to prove that this is just the atomic weight. Note that *any* flowerbed f has uppitiness 0 since

$$f \geqslant f - 0.{\uparrow} \geqslant f.$$

Taking g to be *any* blue flower, and h to be ↑, we have

$$g - h = f$$

for the flowerbed f of Fig. 5. This shows that:

> any blue flower has uppitiness 1.

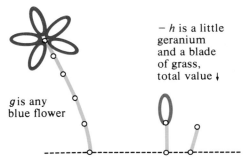

$-h$ is a little
geranium
and a blade
of grass,
total value ↓

g is any
blue flower

Figure 5. The Flowerbed f.

[Note that flowers of stem length 1, with just one petal, are **geRaniums** Red or **deLphiniums** bLue, whose values are ↓∗ or ↑∗.]

GO FLY A KITE!

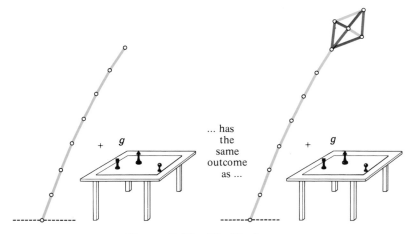

... has
the
same
outcome
as ...

$+$ g

$+$ g

Figure 6. The Kite Strategy.

We'll need to show that it doesn't matter which remote star you use when computing the atomic weight of g. In Hackenbush, a remote star is just a long piece of green string and we can in fact show that provided it's long enough it doesn't matter at all what's on top of it. You might as well go and fly any kind of kite (Fig. 6).

We'll show that Left can convert a winning strategy for

$$string + g$$

into one for

$$kited\ string + g$$

provided that the string is so long that its value is distinct from all the values of positions in g (this is the exact meaning of "remote").

Left should just ignore the kite and play his old strategy until Right moves in the kite, when, since we're ignoring the kite, it's just as if he's made no move at all. But since Left's strategy wins if we ignore the kite, the position

$$kited\ string + h$$

that Right just moved from had

$$string + h \geqslant 0$$

and therefore

$$string + h > 0$$

since

$$string \neq h.$$

Left therefore had a winning move in $string + h$, and since Right's move has affected neither $string$ nor h, this move is still available and Left can continue with his strategy.

In the colon notation introduced in the Extras to Chapter 7, the value of a kited string is $string:kite$. Our argument actually proves **Norton's Lemma** (more precisely stated there) that for any S and K, the games S and $S:K$ have the same order relations with every game that has no position of value S.

ALL REMOTE STARS AGREE

The all green kite in

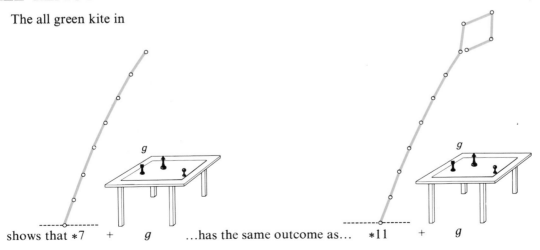

shows that $*7$ $+$ g ...has the same outcome as... $*11$ $+$ g

provided that no position of g has value $*7$. More generally,

> if neither $*m$ nor $*n$ is
> the value of any position
> in g, then the outcomes
> of $*m+g$ and $*n+g$ are
> the same.

This justifies our use of ☆ for all remote stars:

$$g > ☆ \qquad \text{means} \qquad g > *m$$
$$g < ☆ \qquad \text{means} \qquad g < *m$$
$$g \parallel ☆ \qquad \text{means} \qquad g \parallel *m$$

for *any* $*m$ which is *not* the value of *any* position in g.

LARGE AND SMALL FLOWERBEDS

Figure 7 shows that any flowerbed f is less than a 2-flower flowerbed in which one of the flowers is a very tall red one. This is because it doesn't matter what's at the top of a very long string and so we can change the tall red flower into a tall blue one, making Left two flowers ahead.

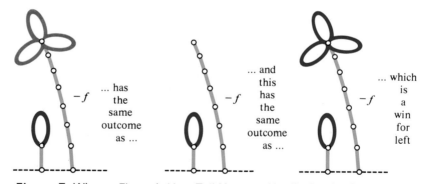

Figure 7. When a Flower's Very Tall You can Hardly See Its Petals.

> For a large flowerbed
> You need just one tall red.

And

> Your bed will be small
> When a blue flower's tall.

Since we now know the largest and smallest flowerbeds, we can simplify our uppitiness test.

The games g and h will be *equally uppity* only if

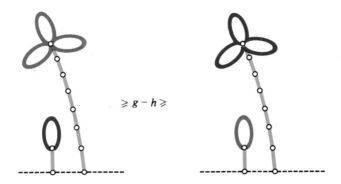

$$\geqslant g - h \geqslant$$

(for tall enough flowers) or, simpler still, if

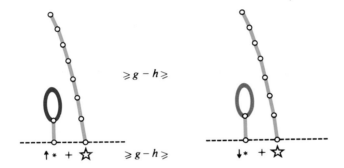

$$\geqslant g - h \geqslant$$

$$\uparrow * + \;\star \qquad \geqslant g - h \geqslant \qquad \downarrow * + \;\star$$

(for remote enough $\star$). We call this the **Remote Star Test**.

When comparing remote stars with sums of other games, it is wisest to take

$$\star = *N$$

where N is the power of 2 next greater than all the m for which $*m$ appears in the other games, because then

$$m < N, \quad n < N \quad \text{imply} \quad m \overset{*}{+} n < N.$$

PLAYING UNDER A LUCKY STAR

If you find yourself playing a sum of ordinary games and one remote star, you're lucky, because

> in the presence of a remote star,
> you can exchange a game for any
> other of the same uppitiness.

THE EXCHANGE PRINCIPLE

In symbols, if $g \doteqdot h$, then

$$g + \text{☆} \quad \text{has the same outcome as} \quad h + \text{☆}$$

It will suffice to prove that if $g \geqslant h$ and

Left can win	h + tall red flower,
then he can win	g + tall blue flower,

for the Kite Strategy shows that we can replace these tall flowers by remote stars without affecting outcomes.

But then because

$$g - h \geqslant \text{some flowerbed}, f,$$

we have

$$(g + \text{tall blue}) - (h + \text{tall red}) \geqslant f + (2 \text{ tall blues}),$$

and this is positive by the Two-Ahead Rule.

GENERAL MULTIPLES OF UP

We're now almost in a position to prove that the Atomic Weight Calculus gives the right answers. What we've got to do is to show that when the rule says that the atomic weight of g is G, then

$$g \doteqdot G.\!\uparrow$$

or, by the Remote Star Test, that

$$\uparrow\! * + \text{☆} \geqslant g - G.\!\uparrow \geqslant \downarrow\! * + \text{☆}$$

But since atomic weights need not be integers we'll have to say just what we mean by $G.\!\uparrow$ when G is a non-integer game such as

$$\{0|1\} = \tfrac{1}{2}, \qquad \{0|0\} = *, \quad \text{or} \quad \{1|-1\} = \pm 1,$$

as well as integer ones such as

$$\{1| \ \} = 2, \qquad \{ \ |-3\} = -4 \quad \text{or} \quad \{ \ | \ \} = 0.$$

Simon Norton has shown how to define such multiples $G. U$ for any positive game U. When we put $U = \uparrow$ his definition reduces to

$$G.\!\uparrow = \{G^L.\!\uparrow + \Uparrow\! * \,|\, G^R.\!\uparrow + \Downarrow\! *\}$$

But this formula must *only* be used for *non-integral* games *G*—if *G* is an integer you must use the obvious rules:

$$2.\uparrow = \uparrow + \uparrow, \qquad (-4).\uparrow = \downarrow + \downarrow + \downarrow + \downarrow, \qquad 0.\uparrow = 0$$

For the non-integral multipliers

$$\tfrac{1}{2} = \{0|1\}, \qquad * = \{0|0\}, \qquad \pm 1 = \{1|-1\}$$

we find

$$\tfrac{1}{2}.\uparrow = \{0.\uparrow + \Uparrow * \,|\, 1.\uparrow + \Downarrow *\} = \{\Uparrow * \,|\, \downarrow *\},$$
$$*.\uparrow = \{0.\uparrow + \Uparrow * \,|\, 0.\uparrow + \Downarrow *\} = \{\Uparrow * \,|\, \Downarrow *\},$$
$$(\pm 1).\uparrow = \{1.\uparrow + \Uparrow * \,|\, (-1).\uparrow + \Downarrow *\} = \{\Uparrow * \,|\, \Downarrow *\}.$$

In the Extras we'll give Norton's definition of *G.U* for all positive games *U* and show that

$$(A+B+C+...).U = A.U + B.U + C.U + ...$$

and in particular

$$(A+B+C+...).\uparrow = A.\uparrow + B.\uparrow + C.\uparrow + ...$$

PROOF OF THE REMOTE STAR RULES

One of the things we've got to prove about atomic weights is that

$$G \geqslant 1 \qquad \text{exactly when} \qquad g > *$$

from which, by symmetry,

$$G \leqslant -1 \qquad \text{exactly when} \qquad g < *,$$

and so

$$-1 \lhd G \lhd 1 \qquad \text{exactly when} \qquad g \parallel *.$$

Of course we can suppose these results for all the options of

$$g = \{a,b,c,... \,|\, d,e,f,...\}.$$

*We suppose first that g > * and show that Right has no good move in G−1 (i.e. that G ⩾ 1).* Because Right has no good move in *g + * we know that

$$d \rhd *, \quad e \rhd *, \quad f \rhd *, \quad ...$$

and so

$$D \rhd -1, \quad E \rhd -1, \quad F \rhd -1, \quad ....$$

If *G* is *not* an integer, Right won't move in the component −1 ("never move in an integer unless you have to") so his move is to one of

$$(D+2) - 1, \quad (E+2) - 1, \quad (F+2) - 1, \quad ..., \qquad \text{all} \rhd 0.$$

If *G is* an integer, it is the greatest number ⊲ all of

$$D+2, \quad E+2, \quad F+2, \quad ...$$

so that we can suppose

$$G+1 \geqslant D+2, \quad \text{say,}$$

so that

$$G \geqslant D+1 \rhd -1+1 = 0.$$

But an *integer* $\rhd$ 0 is $\geqslant 1$.

Of course we could also have shown that

$$g < \unicode{x2606} \quad \text{implies} \quad G \leqslant -1.$$

Now we suppose that $G \geqslant 1$ and we'll deduce that $g > \unicode{x2606}$. By the previous remark we cannot have $g < \unicode{x2606}$. So if our statement fails we can only have $g \parallel \unicode{x2606}$ and can therefore suppose that

$$G = \{A-2, B-2, C-2, \ldots \mid D+2, E+2, F+2, \ldots\}.$$

Because $G \geqslant 1$ we must have

$$1 \lhd \mid D+2, E+2, F+2, \ldots.$$

that is,

$$D \rhd \mid -1, \quad E \rhd \mid -1, \quad F \rhd \mid -1, \quad \ldots,$$

and so

$$d+\unicode{x2606}, \qquad e+\unicode{x2606}, \qquad f+\unicode{x2606}, \qquad \ldots$$

are all $\rhd$ 0. But since $g \parallel \unicode{x2606}$, Right has *some* good move from $g + \unicode{x2606}$. This must therefore be to

$$g + *m \text{ for some } m.$$

We'll show that this cannot be. Because $G \neq 0$ we cannot have all of

$$A-2, B-2, C-2, \ldots \lhd \mid 0$$

and so can suppose

$$A - 2 \geqslant 0, \quad \text{i.e.} \quad A \geqslant 2.$$

Left can therefore move from $g + *m$ to $a + *m$ and win by the Two-Ahead Rule.

PROOF THAT ATOMIC WEIGHT = UPPITINESS

We suppose once again that

$$g = \{a,b,c,\ldots \mid d,e,f,\ldots\}$$

where the atomic weights

$$A,B,C,\ldots,D,E,F,\ldots \quad \text{of} \quad a,b,c,\ldots,d,e,f,\ldots$$

have already been shown to coincide with their uppitinesses, or, in symbols:

$$a \doteq A.\uparrow, \quad b \doteq B.\uparrow, \quad c \doteq C.\uparrow, \quad \ldots,$$
$$d \doteq D.\uparrow, \quad e \doteq E.\uparrow, \quad f \doteq F.\uparrow, \quad \ldots.$$

We want to prove that

$$g \doteq G.\uparrow,$$

where G is the value given by the Atomic Weight Calculus.

By the Remote Star Test for uppitiness, we only have to prove

$$\uparrow* + \unicode{x2606} \geqslant g - G.\uparrow \geqslant \downarrow* + \unicode{x2606},$$

and by symmetry it will suffice to show that Right has no good move in

$$(G.\uparrow + \uparrow* + \unicode{x2606}) - g.$$

Observe that we *always* have

$$A-2, B-2, C-2, \ldots \lhd\!| \; G \; \lhd\!| \; D+2, E+2, F+2, \ldots$$

even in the eccentric cases when G is *not* defined as

$$\{A-2, B-2, C-2, \ldots \mid D+2, E+2, F+2, \ldots\}.$$

Suppose Right moves from the component $-g$, to $-a$, say. Then since we have a lucky ☆, the resulting position can be exchanged for

$$(G.\!\uparrow + \uparrow\! * + \text{☆}) - A.\!\uparrow$$

But $G \mathrel{|\!\rhd} A-2$, and so this game has the form

$$X.\!\uparrow + \downarrow\! * + \text{☆}$$

for some $X \mathrel{|\!\rhd} 0$. If X is an integer we have

$$X.\!\uparrow + \downarrow\! * + \text{☆} \geqslant \uparrow + \downarrow\! * + \text{☆} = * + \text{☆},$$

from which Left has a winning move to 0. Otherwise there is some $X^L \geqslant 0$ and Left can move to

$$(X^L.\!\uparrow + \Uparrow\! *) + \downarrow\! * + \text{☆} \geqslant \uparrow + \text{☆} \geqslant 0.$$

Now we must consider Right's other moves from

$$(G.\!\uparrow + \uparrow\! * + \text{☆}) - g,$$

namely those in the parenthesized portion. Fortunately—see the Star-Shifting Principle in the Extras—we can simplify the parenthesis to

$$\{ \; (G^L.\!\uparrow + \Uparrow\! *) + \uparrow\! * + \text{☆} \quad | \quad (G^R.\!\uparrow + \Downarrow\! *) + \uparrow\! * + \text{☆} \; \}.$$

When G is *non*-integral, this is

$$\{(A+1).\!\uparrow + \text{☆}, (B+1).\!\uparrow + \text{☆}, \ldots \mid (D+1).\!\uparrow + \text{☆}, (E+1).\!\uparrow + \text{☆}, \ldots\}$$

and when G is

…	-4	-3	-2	-1	0	1	2	…

it becomes

$$\ldots \quad \{\Downarrow + \text{☆} \mid 0\} \quad \{\downarrow + \text{☆} \mid 0\} \quad \{\text{☆} \mid 0\} \quad * + \text{☆} \quad \{0 \mid \text{☆}\} \quad \{0 \mid \uparrow + \text{☆}\} \quad \{0 \mid \Uparrow + \text{☆}\} \quad \ldots$$

There are four cases:

In the non-integral case we can suppose Right moves to

$$((D+1).\!\uparrow + \text{☆}) - g$$

from which Left should move to

$$(D+1).\!\uparrow + \text{☆} - d$$

which we can exchange for

$$(D+1).\!\uparrow + \text{☆} - D.\!\uparrow = \uparrow + \text{☆} \geqslant 0.$$

If G is a negative integer, Right can only move to

$$*m - g$$

for some $*m$ (indeed $*m = 0$ unless G is -1). But in this case we have $g < \not\approx$ and so can't have $g \geqslant *m$, so Right's move was no good.

If G is zero, Right's move takes him to

$$\not\approx - g.$$

But, unfortunately for him, we have $g \parallel \not\approx$ in this case.

If G is a positive integer, Right has moved to

$$G.\!\uparrow + \not\approx - g.$$

But in this case G was the largest integer for which

$$G \vartriangleleft\!\shortmid D+2, E+2, F+2, \ldots$$

so that we can suppose

$$G+1 \geqslant D+2, \quad \text{say}.$$

Left can now move to

$$G.\!\uparrow + \not\approx - d$$

for the appropriate d, and this can be exchanged for

$$G.\!\uparrow + \not\approx - D.\!\uparrow \geqslant \uparrow + \not\approx \geqslant 0.$$

THE WHOLENESS OF HACKENBUSH HOTCHPOTCH

Our last proof of the chapter shows that all ordinary Hackenbush Hotchpotch positions have integer atomic weights. For otherwise let

$$g = \{a,b,c,\ldots \mid d,e,f,\ldots\}$$

be a smallest counter-example in which a, obtained by chopping edge α, is the Left option of largest atomic weight A, and d, obtained by chopping edge δ, is the Right option of least atomic weight D.

Now chop *both* edges α and δ to obtain the position h, of atomic weight H. Then since either $h = a$ or h is a right option of a, we must have

$$A-2 \vartriangleleft\!\shortmid H, \quad \text{and similarly} \quad H \vartriangleleft\!\shortmid D+2,$$

showing that H is an integer for which

$$A-2, B-2, C-2, \ldots \vartriangleleft\!\shortmid H \vartriangleleft\!\shortmid D+2, E+2, F+2, \ldots$$

so that the atomic weight of g must be an integer (though it needn't be H).

PROPER CARE OF THE ECCENTRIC

You don't always need to compare g with remote stars in order to interpret the formula

$$G = \text{``}\{A-2, B-2, C-2, \ldots \mid D+2, E+2, F+2, \ldots\}\text{''}.$$

In fact you can drop the quotation marks unless there are two or more integers N that **fit**, i.e. satisfy

$$A-2, B-2, C-2, \ldots \lhd\!| \; N \; \lhd\!| \; D+2, E+2, F+2, \ldots .$$

Moreover, if only *positive* integers fit,

$$\text{``}\{A-2, B-2, C-2, \ldots | D+2, E+2, F+2, \ldots\}\text{''}$$

means the *most positive* one; and if only negative integers fit, the most negative one. The only doubtful cases are when 0 and at least one other integer fit, when G is

$$\text{\emph{most positive},} \qquad \text{\emph{zero},} \qquad \text{or} \qquad \text{\emph{most negative},}$$

according as

$$g > \text{☆} \qquad g \parallel \text{☆} \qquad \text{or} \qquad g < \text{☆}.$$

Examples:

$$\text{``}\{-\tfrac{1}{2}|1\}\text{''} = 0, \qquad \text{``}\{0|1\}\text{''} = \tfrac{1}{2}, \qquad \text{``}\{1|\!\downarrow\! 1\}\text{''} = \pm 1,$$
$$\text{``}\{0|4*\}\text{''} = 4, \qquad \text{``}\{-3|\!\downarrow\!\}\text{''} = -2,$$
$$\text{``}\{*|4\}\text{''} = 0 \text{ or } 3, \qquad \text{``}\{-2|6+\!\downarrow\!\}\text{''} = -1, 0 \text{ or } 5.$$

GALVINIZED GAMES

Atomic weight theory has a surprising application to the following peculiar kind of sum. Let Left and Right play the **galvinized sum**

$$l_1 + l_2 + l_3 + \ldots + r_1 + r_2 + r_3 + \ldots$$

just like an ordinary sum except that the winner is declared to be Left or Right according as the last game to end is an l_i or an r_j (so you win by finishing off your opponent's games quickly). A game

$$g = \{a,b,c,\ldots \,|\, d,e,f,\ldots\}$$

appearing in a galvinized sum has an **electric charge** G, defined by

$$G = \text{``}\{A-2, B-2, C-2, \ldots \,|\, D+2, E+2, F+2, \ldots\}\text{''}$$

except that now when more than one integer fits we take the

$$\text{\emph{most positive} if } g \text{ is one of the } l_i \quad \text{(positively charged)}$$

and the

$$\text{\emph{most negative} if } g \text{ is one of the } r_j \quad \text{(negatively charged)}$$

(Of course, $A,B,C,\ldots,D,E,F,\ldots$ are the charges of $a,b,c,\ldots,d,e,f,\ldots$.) If you remember the race to pick your opponent's flowers in Hackenbush Hotchpotch, you'll see that the *ordinary* sum of

$$L_1.\!\uparrow + L_2.\!\uparrow + L_3.\!\uparrow + \ldots + R_1.\!\uparrow + R_2.\!\uparrow + R_3.\!\uparrow + \ldots + \text{☆}$$

behaves just like the *galvinized* sum

$$l_1 + l_2 + l_3 + \ldots + r_1 + r_2 + r_3 + \ldots,$$

which is therefore a win for

Left,	Right,	or	the first player,

according as $X = L_1 + L_2 + L_3 + \ldots + R_1 + R_2 + R_3 + \ldots$ satisfies

$$X \geqslant 1, \qquad X \leqslant -1, \qquad \text{or} \qquad -1 \lhd\!\!\mid X \lhd\!\!\mid 1.$$

Because our electric charges are closely related to atomic weights, this simple version of the theory only applies when the games are such that a player always has a legal move in each of his opponent's games which has not yet ended. However it *does* apply to all impartial games and provides a simple proof of Fred Galvin's nice theorem that when l_1 and r_1 are the same impartial game, then their galvinized sum is a first player win.

TRADING TRIANGLES

is a simple example. Each player has a number of heaps and may reduce the size of a heap belonging to either player by any one of the triangular numbers

$$1, \; 3, \; 6, \; 10, \; 15, \; 21, \; \ldots \, .$$

Using T_n for the electric charge of a Left-owned heap of size n, we find, for instance,

$$
\begin{aligned}
T_0 &\qquad 0 \\
T_1 &\qquad \text{``}\{0-2 \mid 0+2\}\text{''} = 1, \\
T_2 &\qquad \text{``}\{1-2 \mid 1+2\}\text{''} = 2, \\
T_3 &\qquad \{2-2, 0-2 \mid 2+2, 0+2\} = 1, \\
T_4 &\qquad \text{``}\{1-2, 1-2 \mid 1+2, 1+2\}\text{''} = 2, \\
T_5 &\qquad \text{``}\{2-2, 2-2 \mid 2+2, 2+2\}\text{''} = 3, \\
T_6 &\qquad \{3-2, 1-2, 0-2 \mid 3+2, 1+2, 0+2\} = 1\tfrac{1}{2},
\end{aligned}
$$

....

T_0	0							
T_1, T_2	1	2						
T_3 to T_5	1	2	3					
T_6 to T_9	$1\tfrac{1}{2}$	2	3	2				
T_{10} to T_{14}	1	2	3	2	3			
T_{15} to T_{20}	$1\tfrac{1}{2}$	2	3	2	3	2		
T_{21} to T_{27}	1	2	3	2	2	3	2	
T_{28} to T_{35}	1	2	3	2	3	3	2	3
T_{36} to $\ldots$	$1\tfrac{1}{2}$	2	2	$\ldots$				

Is there a simple rule? The most famous entry in Gauss's diary is that for 1796 July 10 which reads

$$\text{EYPHKA! num} = \triangle + \triangle + \triangle.$$

which we know to mean that it was on that day that the Prince of Mathematicians finally established that every whole number can be expressed as the sum of at most three triangular numbers. Every triangular number we have calculated so far has charge 0 or 1 (this happens for 0,1,3,10,21, 28,...) or $1\frac{1}{2}$ (which happens for 6,15,36,...). Let's call these two classes of triangles

acute (charge 0 or 1), and
obtuse (charge $1\frac{1}{2}$).

Then we can prove that until a charge 4 first appears, the charge of a *non*-triangular number is the least number of triangles, *not all obtuse*, that are needed to represent it, and moreover that a triangular number is obtuse if and only if there is a move from it to some heap of charge 3. Although we haven't yet seen a charge of 4, because most triangular numbers are obtuse it seems likely that eventually one will appear and sometime thereafter we might expect other new charges such as $2*$, $2\frac{1}{2}$, etc. We can't even be sure that the charges don't tend to infinity!

You can play a similar game, **Squandering Squares,** in which the heap must be reduced by perfect square amounts. In this case a greater variety of charges shows itself almost immediately.

EXTRAS

MULTIPLES OF POSITIVE GAMES

The atomic weight theory is concerned with approximating games by multiples of the basic unit, $\uparrow$. In fact we can define multiples $G.U$ taking any positive game U as the unit. For *integral* multiples we can of course use the obvious definitions, for example

$$2.U = U+U, \qquad (-4).U = -U-U-U-U, \qquad \text{and} \quad 0.U = 0$$

For *non-integral* multipliers, Simon Norton's ingenious definition makes essential use of the **incentives**

$$I = U^L - U \quad \text{or} \quad U - U^R$$

of U. Recall from Chapter 6 that incentives are always $\lhd \, 0$. Norton's definition is

$$G.U = \{G^L.U + (U+I_1), G^L.U + (U+I_2), ... \,|\, G^R.U - (U+I_1), G^R.U - (U+I_2), ...\}$$

where $I_1, I_2, ...$ are the distinct incentives.

Fortunately most choices for U have a unique largest incentive I and then we can simplify Norton's formula:

$$G.U = \{G^L.U + (U+I) \,|\, G^R.U - (U+I)\}.$$

For example, for

$$U = \uparrow = 0|*$$

the incentives are

$$0 - \uparrow = \downarrow \quad \text{and} \quad \uparrow - * = \uparrow *,$$

so that $I = \uparrow *$ is the dominant incentive, and since

$$U + I = \Uparrow *$$

we recover the definition for the multiples of $\uparrow$:

$$G.\uparrow = \{G^L.\uparrow + \Uparrow * \,|\, G^R.\uparrow + \Downarrow *\}.$$

Remember, you must *only* use Norton's definition for *non-integral G*.

MULTIPLES WORK!

There are quite a lot of things about multiples to be proved:

Independence of form: If $A = B$, then $A.U = B.U$

Monotonicity: $A \geqslant B$ if and only if $A.U \geqslant B.U$

Distributivity: $(A+B).U = A.U + B.U$

Fortunately these follow easily from the trivial observation that

$$(-G).U = -G.U$$

and the remark that you can play the games

$$A + B + C + \dots \quad \text{and} \quad A.U + B.U + C.U + \dots$$

in roughly the same way, except that a sum $U + I$ changes hands with each move.

So, if, *with* the move, you can win the left-hand sum, then, again with the move, you can win the right-hand sum when $U + I$ has been subtracted:

$$A + B + C + \dots \;\triangleright\; 0 \quad \text{implies} \quad A.U + B.U + C.U + \dots - (U+I) \;\triangleright\; 0.$$

The WITH Rule

Without the move you can win the right-hand sum whenever you can win the left-hand one

---

$$A + B + C + \dots \;\geqslant\; 0 \quad \text{implies} \quad A.U + B.U + C.U + \dots \;\geqslant\; 0.$$

The WITHOUT Rule

Since multiplications by integers obviously work, it's best to concentrate on the *non-integers* among $A, B, C, \dots$. When we've made a move in any of the non-integers we'll regard the problem as simpler even when some of the integer multipliers have been increased. We suppose, of course, that all simpler cases have been established.

FIRST FOR THE "WITH" RULE:

If all of $A, B, C, \dots$ are integers, the condition $A + B + C + \dots \;\triangleright\; 0$ tells us that their sum is at least 1, and so

$$A.U + B.U + C.U + \dots \geqslant U$$

and this is $\triangleright U + I$ since incentives are always $\triangleleft 0$.

If one of them is a non-integer, then one of the good moves from $A + B + C + \dots$ is from a non-integer component, A, say, and we have

$$A^L + B + C + \dots \geqslant 0.$$

Since this is a simpler case we already know that

$$A^L.U + B.U + C.U + \dots \geqslant 0$$

by the WITHOUT Rule, and this provides us with the desired good move from

$$A.U + B.U + C.U + \ldots -(U+I)$$

to

$$A^L.U + (U + I) + B.U + C.U + \ldots - (U+I) \geqslant 0.$$

NOW FOR THE "WITHOUT" RULE:

Given that Right has no good move from

$$A + B + C + \ldots$$

we must show that he has no good move from

$$A.U + B.U + C.U + \ldots .$$

If he moves from a term $A . U$ for which A is a *non-integer*, he gets to

$$A^R.U - (U+I) + B.U + C.U + \ldots$$

which is $\vartriangleright 0$ by the WITH Rule, since we know that

$$A^R + B + C + \ldots \vartriangleright 0.$$

If A was an *integer*, then $A.U$ has the form

$$U + U + U + \ldots \quad \text{or} \quad -U - U - U - \ldots$$

according as $A \geqslant 0$ or $A \leqslant 0$, and Right's move replaces this by

$$U^R + U + U + \ldots \quad \text{or} \quad -U^L - U - U - \ldots$$

which we can rewrite as

$$(U^R - U) + A.U \quad \text{or} \quad (U - U^L) + A.U.$$

Left is therefore faced with

$$A.U + B.U + C.U + \ldots -I = (A+1).U + B.U + C.U + \ldots -(U+I)$$

for some incentive I. But since

$$A + B + C + \ldots \geqslant 0 \quad \text{implies} \quad (A+1) + B + C + \ldots > 0$$

we have

$$(A+1).U + B.U + C.U + \ldots -(U+I) \vartriangleright 0$$

by a case of the WITH Rule that we've already proved, despite the fact that the integer A has been replaced by $A+1$.

When we deduce the WITH Rule from the WITHOUT Rule we always strictly simplify at least one of the *non-integer* multipliers. When we deduce the WITHOUT Rule from the WITH Rule, we don't make the non-integer multipliers any more complicated and it doesn't matter what happens to the integer ones.

SHIFTING MULTIPLES OF UP BY STARS

Recall from Chapter 6 that every non-zero game G has some incentive $G^L - G$ or $G - G^R$ which is at least -1, and if G is non-integral both players have such incentives. We'll use this to show that the formula

$$G.\uparrow = \{G^L.\uparrow + \Uparrow* \mid G^R.\uparrow + \Downarrow*\}$$

for non-integer G can be translated by any nimber, i.e.

$$\boxed{G.\uparrow + *N = \{G^L.\uparrow + \Uparrow* + *N \mid G^R.\uparrow + \Downarrow* + *N\}}$$

THE STAR-SHIFTING PRINCIPLE

For in the difference

$$\{G^L.\uparrow + \Uparrow* + *N \mid G^R.\uparrow + \Downarrow* + *N\} - G.\uparrow + *N$$

the only moves without exact counters are those from $*N$. If Right makes such a move, Left can respond with a move to a position

$$G^L.\uparrow + \Uparrow* + *N - G.\uparrow + *N' = (G^L - G).\uparrow + \Uparrow* + *N + *N'$$

which is positive if $G^L - G \geqslant -1$.

For non-integral G, the Star-Shifting Principle gives us the formula

$$G.\uparrow + \uparrow* + \Leftstar = \{(G^L.\uparrow + \Uparrow*) + \uparrow* + \Leftstar \mid (G^R.\uparrow + \Downarrow*) + \uparrow* + \Leftstar\}$$

which we used earlier in the chapter.

If G is an integer you can read off the simplest form of $G.\uparrow + *N$ from Table 3 of Chapter 3. In particular

$$\uparrow + \Leftstar = \{0 \mid \Leftstar\}, \qquad \Uparrow* + \Leftstar = \{0 \mid \uparrow + \Leftstar\}, \qquad \text{\Lleftstar}* + \Leftstar = \{0 \mid \Uparrow + \Leftstar\}, \qquad \ldots.$$

A THEOREM ON INCENTIVES

> In an all small game g,
> other than 0, $*$, $*2,\ldots$,
> *at least one* player has
> *at least one* incentive with
> *at least one* for its atomic
> weight.

THE AT-LEAST-ONE THEOREM

For let g have atomic weight G. We again use the fact that, unless $G = 0$, it has some incentive $\geqslant -1$.

If

$$G = \{A-2, B-2, C-2, \ldots \mid D+2, E+2, F+2, \ldots\}$$

and, say,

$$(A-2) - G \geqslant -1$$

then g's incentive

$$a - g \text{ has atomic weight} \geqslant 1.$$

If G is defined as the greatest integer

$$\lhd\!\!\shortmid \; D+2, E+2, F+2, \ldots$$

then we can suppose

$$G+1 \geqslant D+2$$

and the incentive

$$g - d \text{ has atomic weight} \geqslant 1.$$

[Similarly if G was defined to be the least integer $\shortmid\!\!\rhd \; A-2, B-2, C-2, \ldots .$]

Finally, if $G = 0$ then both players have good moves from

$$g + \text{☆}.$$

If either of these is from the component g we are finished, for if, say,

$$a > \text{☆} \quad \text{then} \quad A \geqslant 1$$

and so the atomic weight of $a-g$ is at least 1. Otherwise both good moves are from ☆, to $*m$ and $*n$ say, and we have

$$*m \leqslant g \leqslant *n$$

so that g must coincide in value with both $*m$ and $*n$.

We have only restricted the theorem to the all small games so that we can use the Atomic Weight Calculus. In fact it holds for *all* games whose values are *not* of the form

$$x, \quad x+*, \quad x+*2, \quad \ldots$$

for some number x. It has a very simple consequence which doesn't even mention atomic weight:

> Every game g which isn't a number
> has an incentive $\geqslant$ one of the stars
>
> $*, *2, *3, \ldots .$

THE STAR-INCENTIVE THEOREM

For, any incentive of atomic weight $\geqslant 1$ exceeds in particular all the *remote* stars, and if $g = x+*m$, the move to x has incentive $*m$.

SEATING FAMILIES OF FIVE

After their disastrous experience in organizing the children's party at the end of Chapter 5, Left and Right thought it more prudent to invite the parents to their next children's party. Each of the families they invited consisted of 3 children, a mother and a father, and to preserve the peace the children in each family were to be seated between their parents. Left preferred to arrange his families in the order

Mother, child, child, child, Father,

while Right preferred the opposite order. But to preserve another kind of decorum, no two grown-ups of opposite sexes were to occupy adjacent chairs.

n	0	1	2	3	4	5	6	7	8	9	10	11	12	13	14
LnL	–	0	0	0	0	−1	−1	*	*	*	*	↓*	↓*	*2	↓
LnR	0	0	0	0	0	0	*	*	*	*	*	*	*2	*2	*2
RnR	–	0	0	0	0	1	1	*	*	*	*	↑*	↑*	*2	↑

Table 3. Values for Seating Families of Five.

In the analysis we use the same kind of notation as we did for Seating Couples (Chapter 2) and Seating Boys and Girls (Chapter 5). But this time (Table 3) we see Greek crosses which suggest the following identities

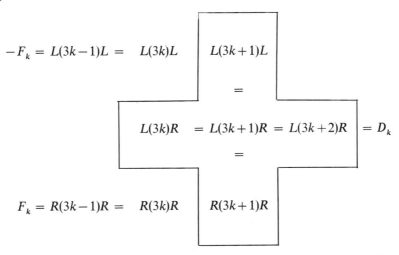

$$-F_k = L(3k-1)L = L(3k)L \qquad L(3k+1)L$$
$$=$$
$$L(3k)R = L(3k+1)R = L(3k+2)R = D_k$$
$$=$$
$$F_k = R(3k-1)R = R(3k)R \qquad R(3k+1)R$$

These can be proved to persist and indeed D_k is the Dawson's Kayles value you met in Chapter 4, so that LnR is Triplicate Dawson's Kayles. We can also show that

$$D_{k-1} \leqslant F_k \geqslant D_k.$$

k	1	2	3	4	5	6	7	8	9	10	11	12	13	14	15	16	17
F_k	0	1	*	$\uparrow_0$	$\uparrow_1$	$\uparrow_1$	$\uparrow_{02}$	*	$\uparrow_3$	$\uparrow_1$	$\uparrow_{12}$	$\uparrow_0$	$\uparrow_{03}$	$\uparrow_{13}$	$\uparrow_{12}$	$\uparrow_2$	$\uparrow_{034}$
F_{k+17}	$\uparrow_{03}$	$\uparrow_{15}$	$\uparrow_{12}$	$\uparrow_{24}$	$\uparrow_3$	$\uparrow_3$	$\uparrow_{025}$	$\uparrow_{12}$	$\uparrow_{14}$	$\uparrow_{03}$	*	$\uparrow_2$	$\uparrow_{12}$	$\uparrow_{13}:-1$	$\uparrow_0$	$\uparrow_{04}$	$\uparrow_{1235}$
F_{k+34}	$\bar{\uparrow}_{125}$	$\bar{\uparrow}_{2347}$	*	$\bar{\uparrow}_{06}$	$\bar{\uparrow}_{15}$	$\bar{\uparrow}_{125}$	$\bar{\uparrow}_{024}$	*	$\bar{\uparrow}_{36}$	$\bar{\uparrow}_{15}$	$\bar{\uparrow}_{12}$	$\bar{\uparrow}_{04}$	$\bar{\uparrow}_{03}$	$\bar{\uparrow}_{13}$	$\bar{\uparrow}_{12}$	$\bar{\uparrow}_2$	$\bar{\uparrow}_{0134}$
F_{k+51}	$\bar{\uparrow}_{034}$	$\bar{\uparrow}_{015}$	$\bar{\uparrow}_{125}$	$\bar{\uparrow}_{124}$	$\bar{\uparrow}_{34}$	*	$\bar{\uparrow}_{025}$	$\bar{\uparrow}_{125}$	$\bar{\uparrow}_{145}$	$\bar{\uparrow}_{034}$	*	$\bar{\uparrow}_{236}$	$\bar{\uparrow}_{125}$	$\bar{\uparrow}_{123}$	$\bar{\uparrow}_0$	$\bar{\uparrow}_{04}$	$\bar{\uparrow}_{1235}$

Table 4. Stars, Superstars and Other Fancy Forms Found in Seating Families of Five.

Our extended table for F_k (Table 4) shows that most of them have the form

$$\{*a, *b, *c, \dots \mid *\alpha, *\beta, *\gamma, \dots\}.$$

The value of this game is

$$\uparrow_{\alpha\beta\gamma\dots} \qquad *m = *\mu \qquad \downarrow^{abc\dots}$$

according as

$$m > \mu \qquad m = \mu \qquad m < \mu$$

where $m = \mathrm{mex}(a,b,c,\dots)$, $\mu = \mathrm{mex}(\alpha,\beta,\gamma,\dots)$.

The game $\downarrow^{abc\dots}$ is the negative of $\uparrow_{abc\dots}$. The game $\uparrow_{abc\dots}$ is the typical **superstar**; it has atomic weight 1 and simplest form

$$\uparrow_{abc\dots} = \{0, *, \dots, *(m-1) \mid *a, *b, *c, \dots\}, \qquad \text{where } m = \mathrm{mex}(a, b, c, \dots)$$

but the value does not change if Left is given arbitrarily many extra nimber options.

We have

$$\uparrow_{abc\dots} \parallel *a, \qquad \uparrow_{abc\dots} \parallel *b, \qquad \uparrow_{abc\dots} \parallel *c, \qquad \dots$$

and otherwise

$$\uparrow_{abc\dots} > *n.$$

There is a **Restricted Translation Rule**:

> If $A, B, C, \dots$ are $a \overset{*}{+} n$, $b \overset{*}{+} n$, $c \overset{*}{+} n$, $\dots$ in some order
> *and n is the least number with this property*, then
> $$\uparrow_{ABC\dots} = \uparrow_{abc\dots} + *n.$$

If there is just one subscript,

$$\uparrow_0 = \uparrow*, \qquad \uparrow_1 = \uparrow, \qquad \uparrow_2 = \uparrow + *3, \qquad \uparrow_3 = \uparrow + *2, \qquad \uparrow_4 = \uparrow + *5, \qquad \dots.$$

These properties of superstars, together with our theorems about atomic weights, dramatically simplify the calculations for Seating Families of Five. We imagine that the pattern of subscripts in Table 4 will eventually share in the general period of 102, making a complete analysis possible.

The symbols $\bar{\uparrow}_{abc\dots}$ denote games obtained from $\uparrow_{abc\dots}$ by giving Right some (unimportant) extra moves, namely

from	F_{31}	F_{33}	F_{45}	F_{48}	F_{65}	F_{67}
to	$\uparrow_{13}$	$\uparrow_{047}$	$\uparrow_{126}, \uparrow_{1235}$	$\uparrow_{135}, \uparrow_{0137}$	$\uparrow_{1235}, \uparrow_{1236}$	$\uparrow_{0457}, \uparrow_{0467}$

There's a similar game, **Seating Families of** N, for any N, with the property that either player, on seating a family, effectively reserves the two adjacent seats for his opponent. These games are cool and have mostly infinitesimal values. In Seating Families of

$$2 \qquad 5 \qquad 8 \qquad 11 \qquad \ldots$$

the values for positions LnR are those of the octal games

$$\textbf{·7} \qquad \textbf{·07} \qquad \textbf{·007} \qquad \textbf{·0007} \qquad \ldots$$

each repeated three times. The LnR values for families of

$$3, \ 4, \ 6, \ 7, \ 9, \ 10, \ 12, \ \ldots$$

are also nimbers, but the rule for generating them is more complicated.

These values can be shown to be nimbers using the easy little theorem that if

$$-a \leqslant a, \qquad -b \leqslant b, \qquad -c \leqslant c, \qquad \ldots,$$

then

$$\{-a, -b, -c, \ldots \mid a, b, c, \ldots\} = *m,$$

where m is the least number for which $*m$ is distinct from all the games $a, b, c, \ldots$.

There's another series of games in which the players seat teams of n boys or n girls, effectively reserving adjacent seats for themselves. Seating Boys and Girls is the case $n = 1$. Omar will find that the other cases provide useful exercises in thermography (Chapter 6).

REFERENCE

J. H. Conway, "On Numbers and Games", Academic Press, London and New York, 1976, Chapters 15 and 16.

Stephen Brian Grantham, "An Analysis of Galvin's Tree Game", PhD thesis, Univ. of Colorado, 1982.

Stephen Brian Grantham, "Galvin's 'racing pawns' game and a well-ordering of trees", Memoirs Amer. Math. Soc. **53**, No. 316 (1985).

CHANGE OF HEART!

New styles of architecture, a change of heart.
Wystan Hugh Auden, *Sir, no man's enemy*.

I have heard her declare, under the rose, that Hearts was her favourite suit.
Charles Lamb, *Essays of Elia*, Mrs. Battle's Opinions on Whist.

So far our compound games have been played by two players who move alternately in just one component at a time, and the rules have ensured that they always end, the last player to move being the winner. Now for a change of heart, let's see what happens when we break some of these rules.

In Chapter 9, you must move in *every* component, and in Chapter 10, you can move in whatever components you like.

In Chapter 11, there are some partizan games with infinitely many positions, and some other loopy games in which play might continue forever.

Chapter 12 deals with the rather different theory of impartial loopy games, and with some other modifications of the impartial theory, which might allow a player to make several consecutive moves.

Chapter 13 gives the theory of impartial games when the last player is declared to be the *loser*.

Chapter 9

If You Can't Beat 'Em, Join 'Em!

Remote from towns he ran his godly race.
Oliver Goldsmith, *The Deserted Village*, l. 143.

This suspense is terrible. I hope it will last.
Oscar Wilde, *The Importance of Being Earnest*, III.

ALL THE KING'S HORSES

In *sums* of games it is a move in just *one* part that counts as a move in the sum. Now we consider the **join** of several games in which we must move in *every* part.

Figure 1. How Horses Head for Home.

We shall play our first few games on the 8 by 8 chessboard illustrated in Fig. 1 with a number of horses. As his move, Left must move *every* horse he can two places West and one place North or South; Right, for his part, must move every horse he can two places North and one place East or West, as in Fig. 1. So the horses move rather like knights in Chess, but there are several differences. Each player is limited to just 2 of the possibly 8 directions a knight can move in; there may be arbitrarily many horses on the same square; and the same horse is moved by both players (the horses belong to the King, not to Left or Right). Compare the White Knight in Chapter 3.

A player will be unable to move in the game if there is any one horse which he can't move. According to the *normal play rule* he would then lose, but in this chapter we shall also give equal treatment to the *misère play rule* under which he would win.

WE CAN JOIN ANY GAMES

Our game can be regarded as made by joining together a number of one-horse games. In fact any games

$$G, \ H, \ K, \ \ldots$$

can be played simultaneously like this to obtain a compound game

$$G \wedge H \wedge K \wedge \ldots \qquad (\text{``}G \text{ and } H \text{ and } K \text{ and } \ldots\text{''})$$

called the **conjunctive compound** by Smith and in ONAG, but here, for short, their **join**. To move in the compound game you must make a move legal for you in *every* one of the component games

$$G, \ H, \ K, \ \ldots$$

rather than in just one, as in the *sum* or disjunctive compound. If you cannot do so you *lose* in normal play, but *win* in misère play.

HOW REMOTE IS A HORSE?

Everything depends on the first horse to finish, for this stops the whole game. (In this game a horse finishes when the player whose turn it is cannot move him.) If one horse—the **favorite**—seems nearer to finishing than the others you should treat it with particular care. Move it so as to win quickly if you can, and otherwise so as to postpone defeat as long as possible in the hope of bringing up a more favorable horse to finish first—in short:

The maxim holds for joins of any games. When we know who starts, a game played in this way lasts for a perfectly definite number of moves which C.A.B. Smith has called its *Steinhaus function* or *remoteness*.

We use the term **left remoteness** when Left starts, and **right remoteness** when Right starts. Since the turns alternate, we need only consider the right remotenesses of Left's options and the left remotenesses of Right's. You should try to leave an *even* remoteness (as small as possible) for your opponent, so as to ensure that when the remoteness is reduced to zero it will be his turn to move. This is because (in normal play)

> $\mathscr{P}$-positions have even remoteness
> $\mathscr{N}$-positions have odd remoteness

So remotenesses can be worked out by the rules:

> For the *left* remoteness of G in
> *normal* play, take
> 1 more than the LEAST EVEN *right* remoteness
> of any G^L which has even right remoteness,
> otherwise
> 1 more than the GREATEST ODD *right* remoteness
> if all G^L have odd right remoteness,
> and finally
> 0, if G has no left option.

Or, more concisely:

> FOR NORMAL PLAY
> Use
> 1 + LEAST EVEN
> if possible,
> 1 + GREATEST ODD
> if not, or
> ZERO
> if you've no option.

To find the *right* remoteness, use the *left* remotenesses of the *right* options, G^R, but still prefer LEAST EVEN else GREATEST ODD.

$R_L^+ R_R^+$ (normal play)

00	00	10	10	10	10	10	10
00	00	10	10	10	10	10	10
01	01	11	12	12	12	12	12
01	01	21	22	22	32	32	32
01	01	21	22	22	32	32	32
01	01	21	23	23	33	34	34
01	01	21	23	23	43	44	44
01	01	21	23	23	43	44	44

(a) First horse stuck loses.

$R_L^- R_R^-$ (misère play)

00	00	10	10	10	10	10	10
00	00	20	30	30	30	30	30
01	02	22	42	52	52	52	52
01	03	24	44	64	74	74	74
01	03	25	46	66	86	96	96
01	03	25	47	68	88	X8	x8
01	03	25	47	69	8X	XX	TX
01	03	25	47	69	8x	XT	xx

(b) First horse stuck wins.

$R_L^+ R_R^+$ (normal with pass)

00	00	12	12	34	34	56	56
00	00	12	12	34	34	56	56
21	21	11	14	34	36	56	56
21	21	41	44	44	56	56	76
43	43	43	44	44	56	56	76
43	43	63	65	65	55	58	76
65	65	65	65	65	85	88	86
65	65	65	67	67	67	68	66

(c) First horse home wins.

$R_L^- R_R^-$ (misère with pass)

00	00	12	12	45	56	56	56
00	00	23	34	34	34	67	78
21	32	22	42	42	56	56	56
21	43	24	44	54	64	74	77
54	43	24	45	66	76	86	76
65	43	65	46	67	66	98	X8
65	76	65	47	68	89	88	x9
65	87	65	77	67	8X	9x	XX

(d) First horse home loses.

R^+ (normal impartial)

0	0	1	1	2	2	3	3
0	0	1	1	2	2	3	3
1	1	1	1	3	3	3	3
1	1	1	3	3	3	3	5
2	2	3	3	4	4	5	5
2	2	3	3	4	4	5	5
3	3	3	3	5	5	5	5
3	3	3	5	5	5	5	6

(x) First horse home wins.

R^- (misère impartial)

0	0	1	1	3	4	3	3
0	0	2	3	2	2	4	5
1	2	2	2	2	4	4	4
1	3	2	3	4	5	6	5
3	2	2	4	5	4	5	6
4	2	4	5	4	7	6	7
3	4	4	6	5	6	7	6
3	5	4	5	6	7	6	7

(y) First horse home loses.

Table 1. How Remote Are All the Horses? $(X = 10, x = 11, T = 12)$

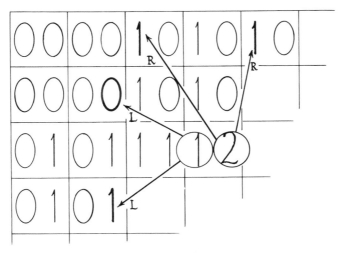

Figure 2. How Remote is a Horse?

Table 1(a) gives the left and right remotenesses (in normal play) for horses in every possible position. See how a 0 on the left side corresponds to a position from which Left cannot move. Figure 2 illustrates a case with larger remotenesses. Here Left's two options have (right) remoteness 0 and 1; of these he prefers the only even number, 0, and adds 1 to obtain 1. Right's two options have (left) remoteness 1 (not much choice!) and he adds 1 to obtain 2.

WHAT IF THE FIRST HORSE TO GET STUCK WINS?

In the *misère play* version, winner and loser are interchanged and so the players will prefer to move to *odd* rather than even. The rule for computing the misère play remotenesses is therefore, in condensed form:

> FOR MISÈRE PLAY
> Use
> 1 + LEAST ODD
> if possible,
> 1 + GREATEST EVEN
> if not, or
> ZERO
> if you've no option.

Table 1(b) gives the misère play remotenesses for our game.

Since, in either case, a join of games finishes when its *first* component does, its remoteness (of any kind) is the *least* remoteness (of the same kind) of any of the components:

$$R_L^+(G \wedge H \wedge \ldots) = \min(R_L^+(G), R_L^+(H), \ldots),$$
$$R_R^+(G \wedge H \wedge \ldots) = \min(R_R^+(G), R_R^+(H), \ldots),$$
$$R_L^-(G \wedge H \wedge \ldots) = \min(R_L^-(G), R_L^-(H), \ldots),$$
$$R_R^-(G \wedge H \wedge \ldots) = \min(R_R^-(G), R_R^-(H), \ldots).$$

In this and similar contexts we use:

L for Left starting,
R for Right starting,
$+$ for normal play,
$-$ for misère play.

> To *win*, move to a position for which
> your *opponent's* remoteness is
> EVEN in NORMAL play,
> ODD in MISÈRE play.

Let's see who wins

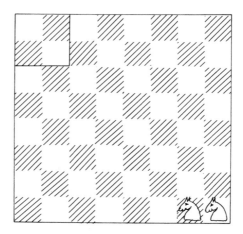

in MISÈRE play.

The left remotenesses of the two horses are 10 and 11 (X and x) so the left remoteness of the position as a whole is the least of these, 10. Since this is even, Left has a good move which changes this to the ODD number 9, but the right remotenesses of these horses are 12 and 11 (T and x), minimum 11, and so from this position Right has no good move. Left's favorite horse is the left one, but Right's is the right one, even though this seems further from finishing.

A SLIGHTLY SLOWER JOIN

We can get a more interesting game by changing the rules slightly. If one player cannot move some horse which the opponent could, we may allow him to make a *pass* move for that horse, but he must still make proper moves with all the horses he can. The game will now end as soon as the first horse reaches **home**, the top left 2 by 2 square, since then *neither* player can move this horse and passes are not allowed. The normal and misère remotenesses for this version are shown in Tables 1(c) and 1(d). They are calculated in exactly the same way, but taking account of the new pass moves. For the position whose misère remotenesses are being computed in Fig. 3, Left has a proper move to a position of right remoteness 3, so his remoteness is $1+3 = 4$. Right has no proper move, but has a pass move to the same position with Left to move, so his remoteness is $1+4 = 5$.

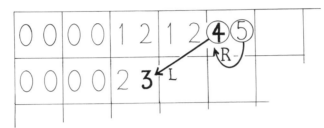

Figure 3. Right's a Bit More Remote Because He's Stuck.

MOVING HORSES IMPARTIALLY

As a further variant, we may make moves in all the four directions of Fig. 1 legal for both players, so that the game becomes an impartial one, and there is no difference between the left and right remotenesses of any position. In Tables 1(x) and 1(y) for the normal and misère versions there is therefore only one digit in each square.

For this game, the horse that seems to be ahead in

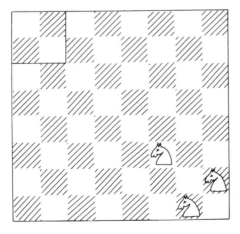

really *is* the favorite in normal play (remoteness 4 against two 5's), but the two trailing ones are joint favorites in misère play (remotenesses 6 as against 7).

All these games may be played on any size of board, or even on a quarter-infinite one. Table 5 (in the Extras) gives remotenesses for this latter case.

CUTTING EVERY CAKE

The game of Cutcake has a conjunctive version, **Cutcakes**, played with the same equipment (see Fig. 3 of Chapter 2), in which Lefty must make a vertical cut (or Rita a horizontal one), along a scored line, in *every* piece of cake. So the first player to produce the kind of strip in which his opponent has no legal move, wins in normal play, *loses* in misère. Tables 2(a) and 2(b) give the remotenesses, and Fig. 4 indicates how they were calculated.

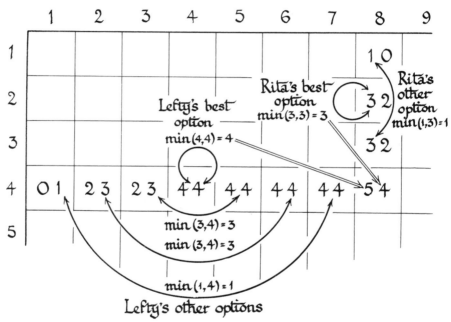

Figure 4. Lefty and Rita Ponder a 4 by 8 Cake.

In another version (Tables 2(c) and 2(d)) a player who cannot cut a particular piece of cake may pass over that piece provided his opponent can still cut it. The game ends when the *first* 1 by 1 cake appears, for this admits no cut by *either* player. So for a horizontal strip, which cannot be cut by Rita, her remoteness is one more than Lefty's.

In impartial Cutcakes (Tables 2(x) and 2(y)) the players must cut all the cakes, but each may do so in either direction.

In some of these tables, we have "writ large" some remotenesses which are the same for whole blocks of entries.

$R_L^+ R_R^+$ (normal play).

00	10 →		
01	22	32 →	
↓	23		
	↓	44	54 →
		45	
		↓	66

(a) First appropriate strip wins.

$R_L^- R_R^-$ (misère play).

00	10 →
01	
↓	22

(b) First appropriate strip loses.

$R_L^+ R_R^+$ (normal with pass).

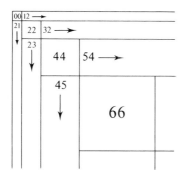

00	12 →		
21	22	32 →	
↓	23		
	↓	44	54 →
		45	
		↓	66

(c) First 1×1 cake wins.

$R_L^- R_R^-$ (misère with pass).

00	12	12	34	34	34	34	56	56	56	56	56	56	56	56	78	78
21	22		24	24	24	24	26	26	26	26	26	26	26	26	28	28
21			23 →													
43	42	32	33	43 →												
43	42		↓	34												
43	42		↓	44	45 →											
43	42															
65	62			54	55	65 →										
65	62				56											
65	62			↓	↓											
65	62					66										
65	62															
65	62															
65	62															
65	62															
87	82													77	87
87	82													78	

(d) First 1×1 cake loses.

R^+ (normal impartial).

0	1 →		
1	2	3 →	
↓	3		
	↓	4	5 →
		5	
		↓	6

(x) First 1×1 cake wins.

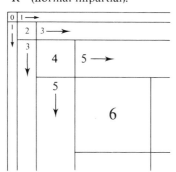

R^- (misère impartial).

0	1	1	
1	2	2	2 →
1	2	2	
2			
↓	3	4 →	
	4		
	↓	5	

(y) First 1×1 cake loses.

Table 2. How Long it Takes to Cut our Cakes.

EATCAKES

Remoteness tables for **Eatcakes**, a variant game which is more natural as a *slow* join (see later), are given in the Extras (Table 7).

WHEN TO PUT YOUR MONEY ON THE LAST HORSE

In our next variation of All the King's Horses, an apparently trivial modification of the rules produces a dramatic change in tactics. Last time we allowed you to pass for a horse you couldn't move only if your opponent could still move that horse. Now we allow you to pass provided there is *any* horse that one of you can still move, and the game only ends when *all* the horses reach home. In normal play whoever takes the last horse home is the winner; he is of course the loser in misère play.

In this game the race is not to the swift—it is the horse likely to be the *last* in the race (the **outsider**) who must be moved with special care. If you think you can win with him you should try to win *slowly*, lest your opponent hold back another horse to make the race finish in *his* favor. On the other hand if the outsider looks like he's losing for you, take him home quickly and hope to leave some more promising laggard on the course.

SLOW HORSES JOIN THE ALSO-RANS

Our game exemplifies a new way of joining several games,

$$G, \quad H, \quad K, \quad \dots$$

to produce a compound,

$$G \triangle \ H \triangle \ K \triangle \ \dots \quad (\text{``}G \text{ also } H \text{ also } K \text{ also } \dots\text{''}),$$

called the *continued conjunctive compound* in ONAG, and here, the **slow join**. Our previous kind of join may be called the *rapid join* when we need to avoid confusion. In the slow join of a number of games a player must move in every component he can, and the game ends only when he cannot move *anywhere*.

The best tactics are a travesty of those for the rapid join—move *slowly* when you're *winning*, *quickly* when you're *losing*! The winner is anxious to savor his inexorable superiority for as long as possible, while the loser wants to get it over with, but quick! Given who starts, a game lasts, when played according to these cat and mouse tactics, for a perfectly definite number of moves, called the **suspense number**.

We find these suspense numbers by a parody of the remoteness rules:

> For the *left* suspense of G in
> *normal* play, take
> 1 more than the GREATEST EVEN *right* suspense
> of any G^L which has even right suspense,
> otherwise
> 1 more than the LEAST ODD *right* suspense
> if all G^L have odd right suspense,
> and finally
> 0, if G has no left option.

In short:

> FOR NORMAL PLAY
> Use
> 1 + GREATEST EVEN
> if possible,
> 1 + LEAST ODD
> if not, or
> ZERO
> if you've no option.

And similarly:

> FOR MISÈRE PLAY
> Use
> 1 + GREATEST ODD
> if possible,
> 1 + LEAST EVEN
> if not, or
> ZERO
> if you've no option.

A handy maxim covering both cases is:

Since a slow join finishes only when its *last* component does, its suspense number (of any kind) is the *greatest* suspense number (of the same kind) of any of the components:

$$
\begin{aligned}
S_L^+(G\triangle\,H\triangle\ldots) &= \max(S_L^+(G), S_L^+(H),\ldots), \\
S_R^+(G\triangle\,H\triangle\ldots) &= \max(S_R^+(G), S_R^+(H),\ldots), \\
S_L^-(G\triangle\,H\triangle\ldots) &= \max(S_L^-(G), S_L^-(H),\ldots), \\
S_R^-(G\triangle\,H\triangle\ldots) &= \max(S_R^-(G), S_R^-(H),\ldots).
\end{aligned}
$$

$S_L^+ S_R^+$ (normal with pass)

00	00	12	12	34	34	56	56
00	00	12	12	34	34	56	56
21	21	11	12	32	34	54	56
21	21	21	22	22	34	34	56
43	43	23	22	22	34	34	56
43	43	43	43	43	33	34	54
65	65	45	43	43	43	44	44
65	65	65	65	65	45	44	44

(a) Last horse home wins.

$S_L^- S_R^-$ (misère with pass)

00	00	12	12	45	34	56	56
00	00	23	12	34	34	67	56
21	32	22	22	44	36	56	56
21	21	22	44	34	44	56	77
54	43	44	43	44	56	66	56
43	43	63	44	65	66	58	66
65	76	65	65	66	85	66	77
65	65	65	77	65	66	77	66

(b) Last horse home loses.

S^+ (normal impartial)

0	0	1	1	2	2	3	3
0	0	1	1	2	2	3	3
1	1	1	3	3	3	3	3
1	1	3	3	3	3	5	5
2	2	3	3	4	4	5	5
2	2	3	3	4	4	5	5
3	3	3	5	5	5	5	5
3	3	3	5	5	5	5	6

(x) Last horse home wins.

S^- (misère impartial)

0	0	1	1	3	2	3	3
0	0	2	1	2	2	4	3
1	2	2	4	2	4	4	4
1	1	4	3	2	3	6	5
3	2	2	2	5	4	3	4
2	2	4	3	4	3	6	5
3	4	4	6	3	6	5	6
3	3	4	5	4	5	6	7

(y) Last horse home loses.

Table 3. The Suspense of Slow Horse Racing.

Compare the two theories:

<table>
<tr><td>RAPID
REMOTENESS
MINIMUM
(favorite)</td><td>as against</td><td>SLOW
SUSPENSE
MAXIMUM
(outsider)</td></tr>
</table>

Tables 3(a) to 3(y) give suspense numbers for the four versions of All the King's Horses in which the *last* horse determines the race.

Tables 3(a) and 3(b) are for the normal and misère play of the version we have already described in which you may make a pass move for any horse you cannot move properly.

Tables 3(x) and 3(y) are for the impartial versions of the game, when left and right suspense numbers coincide.

LET THEM EAT CAKE!

Sometimes the way we play a game makes a rapid join more sensible than a slow one, or vice versa. For Cutcakes the rapid join was more natural; when we eat our cake it is less so. Tables 6 and 7, showing suspense numbers for Cutcakes and remotenesses for Eatcakes, have therefore been relegated to the Extras of this chapter.

In **Eatcakes** Lefty must eat away a vertical, or Rita a horizontal, strip of width 1 from every cake which is still on the table. This move will separate the cake into two pieces unless the eaten strip was along an edge. The last mouthful wins in normal play, loses in misère play. The disjunctive version of this game (due to Jim Bynum) is called Eatcake in Chapter 8.

Once again each cake defines a component game, but the whole game does not end when a cake is completely consumed, since nobody can see it any more. You don't have to eat a cake that isn't there! So the join is automatically a slow one—the normal and misère suspense numbers appear in Tables 4(a) and 4(b), and suspense numbers for the impartial version, in which the players eat strips in either direction, are displayed in Tables 4(x) and 4(y). For the impartial games the rows are ultimately periodic. Rows 0 through 9 of Table 4(x) have periods dividing 16, while for rows 0 through 4 of Table 4(y) the periods divide 18. In each case the first 20 entries contain a full period.

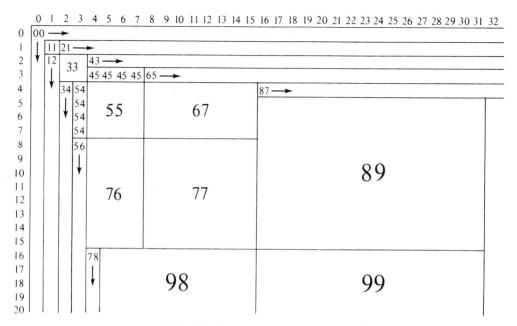

Table 4(a). Eating Cakes Normally ($S_L^+ S_R^+$).

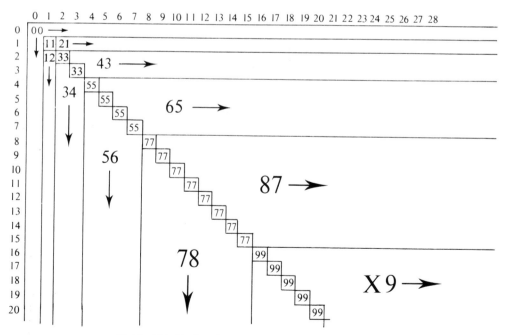

Table 4(b). Eating Cakes Miserably ($S_L^- S_R^-$). (X = 10).

270

	0	1	2	3	4	5	6	7	8	9	10	11	12	13	14	15	16	17	18	19	20	21	22	23	24	25	26	27	28	29	30	31
0	0	0	0	0	0	0	0	0	0	0	0	0	0	0	0	0	0	0	0	0	0	0	0	0	0	0	0	0	0	0	0	0
1	0	1	1	1	1	1	1	1	1	1	1	1	1	1	1	1	1	1	1	1	1	1	1	1	1	1	1	1	1	1	1	1
2	0	1	2	3	3	3	2	3	3	3	3	2	3	3	3	2	3	3	3	2	3	3	3	2	3	3	3	2	3	3	3	2
3	0	1	3	2	3	3	3	3	2	3	3	3	2	3	3	3	2	3	3	2	3	3	3	2	3	3	2	3	3	3	3	3
4	0	1	3	3	4	5	5	5	5	5	5	3	3	4	5	5	5	5	5	3	3	4	5	5	5	5	5	3	3	4	5	5
5	0	1	3	3	5	4	5	5	5	5	3	5	5	4	5	5	5	5	3	5	5	4	5	5	5	5	5	3	5	5	4	5
6	0	1	2	3	5	5	4	5	5	5	5	4	5	5	5	5	4	5	5	5	5	5	4	5	5	5	5	5	4	5	5	5
7	0	1	3	3	5	5	5	4	5	5	5	5	5	4	5	5	5	5	3	5	5	5	4	5	5	5	5	5	5	4	5	5
8	0	1	3	2	5	5	5	5	6	7	7	7	7	7	7	7	7	4	5	5	5	5	5	6	7	7	7	7	7	7	7	7
9	0	1	3	3	5	5	5	5	7	6	7	7	7	7	7	7	7	5	7	5	5	5	5	7	6	7	7	7	7	7	7	7
10	0	1	2	3	3	3	5	5	7	7	4	5	5	5	5	5	5	6	7	7	7	7	7	7	7	4	5	7	7	7	7	7
11	0	1	3	2	3	5	4	5	7	7	5	5	6	7	7	7	7	7	5	6	7	7	7	7	7	7	7	7	7	7	7	6
12	0	1	3	3	4	5	5	5	7	7	5	6	7	7	7	7	7	7	6	7	7	7	7	7	7	7	7	7	6	7	7	7
13	0	1	3	3	5	4	5	5	7	7	5	7	7	6	7	7	7	7	7	7	7	7	7	7	6	7	7	7	7	7	7	7
14	0	1	2	3	5	5	5	4	7	7	5	7	7	7	6	7	7	7	7	6	7	7	7	7	5	6	7	7	7	7	7	7
15	0	1	3	3	5	5	5	5	7	7	5	7	7	7	7	6	7	7	7	7	7	7	7	7	7	7	6	7	7	7	7	7
16	0	1	3	2	5	5	4	5	7	7	5	7	7	7	7	7	6	7	7	7	7	7	7	7	7	5	7	7	7	7	8	9
17	0	1	3	3	5	5	5	5	7	7	6	7	7	7	7	7	7	7	6	7	7	7	7	7	7	7	7	7	7	7	9	7
18	0	1	2	3	3	3	5	5	4	5	7	7	7	7	7	7	7	7	6	7	7	7	7	7	7	7	7	7	7	7	9	7
19	0	1	3	2	3	5	5	3	5	7	7	7	7	7	7	7	7	6	7	7	7	7	7	7	7	7	7	7	7	7	9	7
20	0	1	3	3	4	5	5	5	5	5	7	7	6	7	7	7	7	7	7	7	7	7	7	7	8	9	9	9	9	9	9	9
21	0	1	3	3	5	4	5	5	5	5	7	5	7	7	7	7	7	7	7	7	7	6	7	7	9	7	7	7	7	7	9	7

(x) Normal Play (S^+).

	0	1	2	3	4	5	6	7	8	9	10	11	12	13	14	15	16	17	18	19	20	21	22	23	24	25	26	27	28	29	30	31
0	0	0	0	0	0	0	0	0	0	0	0	0	0	0	0	0	0	0	0	0	0	0	0	0	0	0	0	0	0	0	0	0
1	0	1	2	2	1	2	2	1	2	2	1	2	2	1	2	2	1	2	2	1	2	2	1	2	2	1	2	2	1	2	2	1
2	0	2	3	4	4	4	3	4	4	4	2	3	4	4	4	3	4	4	4	2	3	4	4	4	3	4	4	4	2	3	4	4
3	0	2	4	3	4	4	4	4	3	4	4	4	2	3	4	4	4	4	2	4	3	4	4	4	4	3	4	4	4	4	4	2
4	0	1	4	4	5	6	6	6	6	6	6	3	4	4	3	4	6	6	6	6	6	4	5	6	6	6	6	6	3	4	4	3
5	0	2	4	4	6	5	6	6	6	6	4	6	6	5	6	6	6	6	4	6	6	4	5	6	6	6	6	6	4	6	6	6
6	0	2	3	4	6	6	5	6	6	6	6	5	6	6	6	6	5	6	6	6	6	6	5	6	6	6	6	6	5	6	6	4
7	0	1	4	4	6	6	6	5	6	6	6	6	6	3	4	6	6	6	5	6	6	6	6	5	6	6	6	6	6	4	5	6
8	0	2	4	3	6	6	6	6	7	8	8	8	8	8	8	8	8	6	7	8	8	8	8	8	8	8	8	8	6	5	6
9	0	2	4	4	6	6	6	6	8	7	8	8	8	8	8	8	8	6	8	5	6	6	6	6	7	8	8	8	8	8	8	8
10	0	1	2	4	3	4	6	6	8	8	5	6	6	6	6	6	6	7	8	8	8	8	8	8	8	6	7	8	8	8	8	8
11	0	2	3	4	4	6	5	6	8	8	6	6	6	6	5	6	6	8	6	8	6	6	7	8	8	8	8	8	8	8	8	8
12	0	2	4	4	4	5	6	6	8	8	6	6	7	8	8	8	8	8	8	8	8	8	7	8	8	8	8	8	8	8	6	7
13	0	1	4	2	3	6	6	3	8	8	6	6	8	7	8	8	8	8	8	8	8	8	8	8	7	8	8	8	8	8	8	8
14	0	2	4	3	4	6	6	4	8	8	6	5	8	6	6	6	8	7	8	8	8	8	8	8	8	8	7	8	8	8	8	8
15	0	2	3	4	6	6	6	6	8	8	6	6	8	8	6	7	8	8	8	8	8	8	8	8	7	8	8	8	8	8	8	8
16	0	1	4	4	6	6	5	6	8	8	6	6	8	8	6	7	8	8	8	8	8	8	8	8	7	8	8	8	7	8	8	8
17	0	2	4	4	6	5	6	6	8	8	7	8	8	8	8	8	8	8	7	8	8	8	8	8	8	8	9	X	X	X	X	X
18	0	2	4	4	6	6	6	5	6	6	8	8	6	8	6	7	8	8	8	8	8	8	8	8	9	X	X	X	X	X	X	X
19	0	1	2	2	6	6	6	6	7	8	8	8	8	8	8	8	8	9	X	X	X	X	X	X	X	X	X	X	X	X	X	X
20	0	2	3	4	4	6	6	6	8	5	8	6	8	8	8	8	8	7	8	X	8	8	8	8	8	X	8	8	8	8	7	8
21	0	2	4	3	4	6	5	6	8	6	8	6	7	8	8	8	8	8	8	X	8	7	8	8	8	X	8	8	8	8	8	8

(y) Misère Play (S^-). (X = 10.)

Tables 4(x) and 4(y). Eating Cakes Impartially.

271

EXTRAS

ALL THE KING'S HORSES ON A QUARTER-INFINITE BOARD

Table 1 gave remotenesses of horses on an ordinary chessboard. Some of the values near the lower and right edges of the board are affected by the horse's inability to jump off the board. Table 5 shows the values when there are no lower and right edges; the patterns indicated by the lines continue indefinitely both downwards and to the right. That in Table 5(d) is hardest to see; the rows and columns have ultimate period 4 and saltus 4, but the character of the first, second and every third is different from that of the others.

You might like to work out corresponding tables for the suspense numbers. It's most sensible to allow a player to *pass* for a given horse when he can't move it, but his opponent can.

CUTTING YOUR CAKES AND EATING THEM

Tables 6(a) and 6(b) give the normal and misère suspense numbers for the partizan game of Cutcakes, in which the rule is to cut every cake you can, so the game only ends when the cake is completely cut up. This implies that you make a pass move for a cake when you can't cut it, but your opponent can. Tables 6(x) and 6(y) are for the impartial version in which each player may cut in either direction.

Suspense numbers for Eatcakes were given at the end of the chapter. Table 7 gives the corresponding remotenesses which are appropriate for the versions in which the game ends when the *first* strip (1 by n or n by 1 cake) is eaten. Table 7(y) for R^- (misère impartial) is not shown; you can find it by adding 1 to all the entries in Table 7(x), except the one for a 1 by 1 cake. That is $R^-(1,1) = R^+(1,1) = 1$; otherwise $R^- = R^+ + 1$.

(a) $R_L^+ R_R^+$ (normal play)

00 00	10 10 →				
00 00	10 10 →				
01 01	11	12 12 →			
01 01	21	22 22	32 32 →		
↓ ↓	21	22 22	32 32 →		
	23 23	33	34 34 →		
↓	23 23	43	44 44	54 54	
		43	44 44	54 54	
↓ ↓		45 45	55	56	
		45 45	65	66	

(b) $R_L^- R_R^-$ (misère play)

00 00	10 10 →						
00 00	20	30 30 →					
01 02	22	42	52 52 →				
01 03	24	44	64	74 74 →			
↓ 03	25	46	66	86	96 96 →		
↓ 25	47	68	88	X8	x8 x8 →		
↓ 47	69	8X	XX	TX	tX	tX	
69	8x	XT	TT	FT	fT		
8x	Xt	TF	FF	SF			
↓	Xt	Tf	FS	SS			

(c) $R_L^+ R_R^+$ (normal with pass)

00	00	12	12	34		56		78		9X	
00	00	12	12								
21	21	11	14	34	36	56	58	78	7X	9X	9T
21	21	41		44		56		78		9X	
43		43									
		63		55	58	78	7X	9X	9T		
		65		65							
65		85				85		88		9X	xT
				87		87					
87		87		X7				99	9T	xT	
		X7		X9		X9		T9			
		X9				T9		T9		Tx	TT
X9		X9						Tx			
		T9									

(d) $R_L^- R_R^-$ (misère with pass)

00	00	12	12	45	56	56	56	89	9X	9X	9X
00	00	23	34	34	34	67	78	78	78	Xx	xT
21	32	22	42	42	56	56	56	86	9X	9X	9X
21	43	24	44	54	64	74	78	78	78	78	xT
54	43	24	45	66	76	86	76	96	9X	9X	9X
65	43	65	46	67	66	98	X8	98	x8	98	x8
65	76	65	47	68	89	88	xX	T8	xX	tX	xX
65	87	65	87	67	8X	Xx	XX	tT	FX	tT	fX
98	87	68	87	69	89	8T	Tt	TT	fF	ST	fF
X9	87	X9	87	X9	8x	Xx	XF	Ff	FF	sS	AF
X9	xX	X9	87	X9	89	Xt	Tt	TS	Ss	SS	aA
X9	Tx	X9	Tx	X9	8x	Xx	Xf	Ff	FA	Aa	AA

(x) R^+ (normal impartial)

0	0	1	1	2	2	3	3	4	4	5	5
0	0	1	1	2	2	3	3	4	4	5	5
1	1	1	1	3	3	3	3	5	5	5	5
1	1	1	3	3	3	3	5	5	5	5	7
2	2	3	3	4	4	5	5	6	6	7	7
2	2	3	3	4	4	5	5	6	6	7	7
3	3	3	3	5	5	5	5	7	7	7	7
3	3	3	5	5	5	5	7	7	7	7	9
4	4	5	5	6	6	7	7	8	8	9	9
4	4	5	5	6	6	7	7	8	8	9	9
5	5	5	5	7	7	7	7	9	9	9	9

(y) R^- (misère impartial)

0	0	1	1	3	4	3	3	5	6	5	5
0	0	2	3	2	2	4	5	4	4	6	7
1	2	2	2	2	4	4	4	4	6	6	6
1	3	2	3	4	5	6	5	6	7	8	7
3	2	2	4	5	4	5	6	7	6	7	8
4	2	4	5	4	7	6	7	6	9	8	9
3	4	4	6	5	6	7	6	7	8	9	8
3	5	4	5	6	7	6	7	8	9	8	9
5	4	4	6	7	6	7	8	9	8	9	X
6	4	6	7	6	9	8	9	8	9	X	x
5	6	6	8	7	8	9	8	9	X	x	X

Table 5. All The King's Horses on a Quarter-Infinite Board.
(X = 10, x = 11, T = 12, t = 13, F = 14, f = 15, S = 16, s = 17, A = 18, a = 19.)

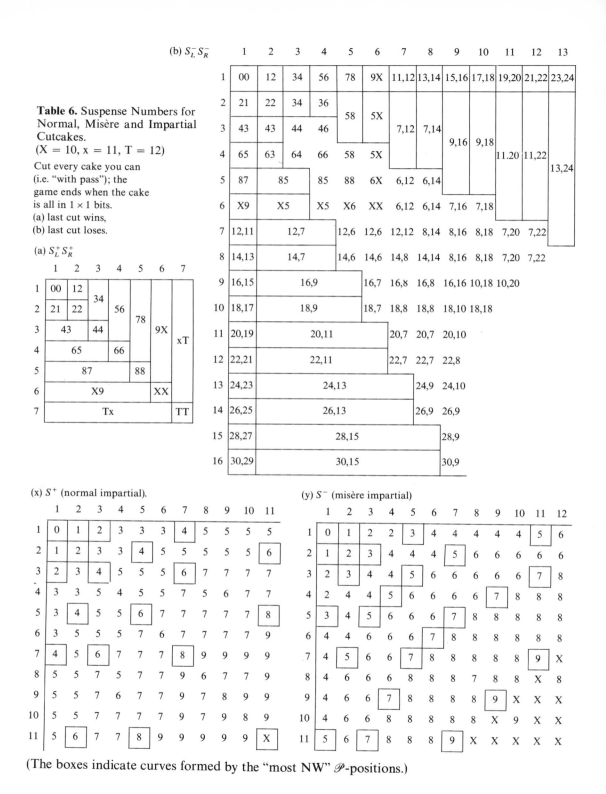

(The boxes indicate curves formed by the "most NW" $\mathcal{P}$-positions.)

(a) $R_L^+ R_R^+$ (first eaten strip wins)

	0	1	2	3	4	5	6
0	∞	∞	∞	∞	∞	∞	∞
1	∞	11	21	$\longrightarrow$			
2	∞	12					
3	∞	$\downarrow$	33				
4	∞						
5	∞						
6	∞						

(b) $R_L^- R_R^-$ (first eaten strip loses)

	0	1	2	3	4	5	6	7	8
0	∞	∞	∞	∞	∞	∞	∞	∞	∞
1	∞	11	21	$\longrightarrow$					
2	∞	12	33	43	$\longrightarrow$				
3	∞	$\downarrow$	34	55	65	$\longrightarrow$			
4	∞		56	77	87	$\longrightarrow$			
5	∞		$\downarrow$	78	99	X9	$\longrightarrow$		
6	∞			9X	xx	Tx	$\longrightarrow$		

Tables 7(a) and (b). Partizan Remoteness for Eatcakes.

(x) R^+ (normal impartial)

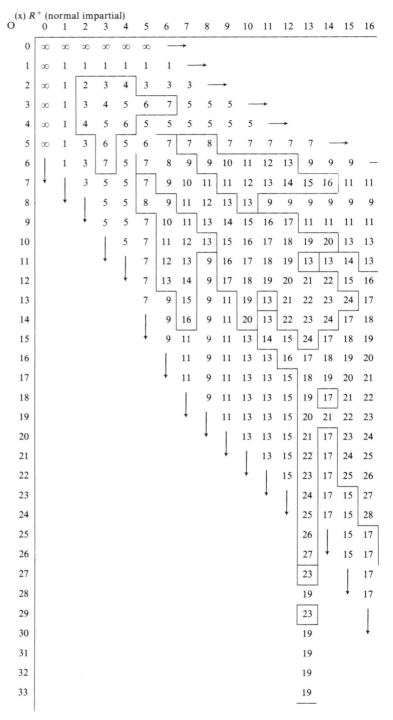

O	0	1	2	3	4	5	6	7	8	9	10	11	12	13	14	15	16
0	∞	∞	∞	∞	∞	∞	→										
1	∞	1	1	1	1	1	1	→									
2	∞	1	2	3	4	3	3	3	→								
3	∞	1	3	4	5	6	7	5	5	5	→						
4	∞	1	4	5	6	5	5	5	5	5	5	→					
5	∞	1	3	6	5	6	7	7	8	7	7	7	7	7	→		
6	↓	1	3	7	5	7	8	9	9	10	11	12	13	9	9	9	—
7	↓		3	5	5	7	9	10	11	11	12	13	14	15	16	11	11
8		↓	5	5	8	9	11	12	13	13	9	9	9	9	9	9	
9			↓	5	5	7	10	11	13	14	15	16	17	11	11	11	11
10				↓	5	7	11	12	13	15	16	17	18	19	20	13	13
11					↓	7	12	13	9	16	17	18	19	13	13	14	13
12						↓	7	13	14	9	17	18	19	20	21	22	15	16
13							7	9	15	9	11	19	13	21	22	23	24	17
14						↓		9	16	9	11	20	13	22	23	24	17	18
15						↓		9	11	9	11	13	14	15	24	17	18	19
16							↓	11	9	11	13	13	16	17	18	19	20
17							↓	11	9	11	13	13	15	18	19	20	21
18								↓	9	11	13	13	15	19	17	21	22
19								↓		11	13	13	15	20	21	22	23
20									↓		13	13	15	21	17	23	24
21										↓		13	15	22	17	24	25
22											↓		15	23	17	25	26
23												↓		24	17	15	27
24													↓	25	17	15	28
25														26	↓	15	17
26														27	↓	15	17
27														23		↓	17
28														19	↓		17
29														23			↓
30														19			↓
31														19			
32														19			
33														19			

Table 7(x). Impartial

```
17  18  19  20  21  22  23  24  25  26  27  28  29  30  31  32  33  34
─────────────────────────────────────────────────────────────────────

→

11   →

 9   9   →

11  11  11   →

13  13  13  13   →

13  13  13  13  13   →

15  15  15  15  15  15   →

18  19  20  21  22  23  24  25  26  27  [23] 19  [23] 19  19  19  19  [21]

19  [17] 21  17  17  17  17  17   →

20  21  22  23  24  25  15  15  15  15   →

21  22  23  24  25  26  27  28  17  17  17  17   →

22  23  24  25  26  27  28  29  30  31  19  19  19  19   →

23  24  25  26  27  28  29  30  31  32  33  34  35  36  37  38  23   →

24  25  26  27  28  29  30  31  32  33  21  21   →

25  26  27  28  29  30  31  32  33  34  35  36  37  38  39  40  25   →

26  27  28  29  30  31  32  33  34  35  [23] 37  23  23   →

27  28  29  30  31  32  33  34  35  36  37  38  39  40  41  42  27   →

28  29  30  31  32  33  34  35  36  37  [25] 39  40  [25] 25   →

29  30  31  32  33  34  35  36  37  38  39  40  41  42  43  44  29   →

30  31  32  33  34  35  36  37  38  39  [27] 41  42  43  [27] 27   →

31  32  33  34  35  36  37  38  39  40  41  42  43  44  45  46  47  48

19  33  21  35  [23] 37  [25] 39  [27] 41  42  43  44  45  46  47  48  49

19  34  21  36  37  38  39  40  41  42  43  44  45  46  47  48  49  50

19  35  ↓   37  [23] 39  40  41  42  43  44  45  46  47  48  49  50  51

19  36      38  23  40  [25] 42  43  44  45  46  47  48  49  50  51  52

↓   37      39  41  25  43  [27] 45  46  47  48  49  50  51  52  53

    38      40  ↓   42  44  27  46  47  48  49  50  51  52  53  54

    23      25  27  ↓   29  ↓   47  48  49  50  51  52  53  54  55
```

Remotenesses for Eatcakes.

REFERENCES AND FURTHER READING

J.H. Conway, "On Numbers and Games", Academic Press, London and New York, 1976, Chapter 14.

Martin Gardner, Mathematical games: cram, crosscram and quadraphage: new games having elusive winning strategies, Sci. Amer. **230** #2 (Feb. 1974) 106–108.

C.A.B. Smith, Graphs and composite games, J. Combin. Theory, **1** (1966) 51–81; M.R. **33** #2572.

H. Steinhaus, Definicje potrzebne do teorji gry i pościgu, Myśl Akad. Lwów, **1** #1 (1925) 13–14: reprinted as Definitions for a theory of games and pursuit, Naval Res. Logist. Quart, **7** (1960) 105–108.

Chapter 10

Hot Battles Followed by Cold Wars

And, through the heat of conflict, keeps the law
In calmness made and sees what he foresaw.
William Wordsworth, *Character of the Happy Warrior*.

When the rules of a compound game allow you to move in any desired number of component subgames, we get what has been called a **selective compound**; we shall call it the **union**. If there are any *hot* components about, both players will naturally move in all of them, and they would like this part of the game to last as long as possible. When all components are cold, they will move only in the least disadvantageous one. So a union of games, if well played, will consist of the slow join of its hot parts, followed by the ordinary sum of the residual cold games.

HOTCAKES

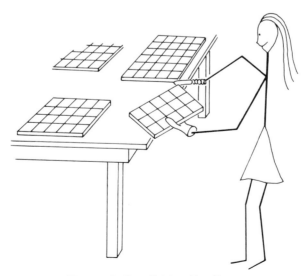

Figure 1. Rita Taking Her Turn.

279

Mother has been making cakes again and this time they are quite hot. In Cutcake (Chapter 2), Lefty made a vertical, or Rita a horizontal, cut in just one cake. In Cutcakes (Chapter 9), they made such cuts in all the cakes they could. Now they may cut whichever cakes they like, but to make it more interesting, after each cake is cut, just one of its two parts is turned through a right angle before being put back on the table. In Fig. 1 Rita has just made a horizontal cut and is seen turning one of the resulting two pieces of cake.

UNIONS OF GAMES

Hotcakes is the selective compound or union of a number of component one-cake games. More generally there is such a compound

$$G \vee H \vee K \vee \ldots \qquad (\text{``}G \text{ or } H \text{ or } K \text{ or } \ldots\text{''})$$

of any number of component games $G, H, K, \ldots$. When it is his turn to move, a player **selects** some of the components (at least one, maybe all) and then makes moves, legal for him, in each game of his selection. When a player cannot move, the game ends and that player is the loser according to the normal play rule. The selective theory (of unions) is a mixture of the disjunctive theory (of sums) and the conjuctive theory (of slow joins).

COLD GAMES—NUMBERS ARE STILL NUMBERS

Some games behave exactly like ordinary disjunctive sums. In Coldcakes we allow Lefty or Rita to cut as many cakes as they like, but we remove the new turning requirement. How does this differ from Cutcake, which they played in Chapter 2?

Not at all! Since every value in that game was a number, they were never anxious to make moves and will now be even less keen to make several moves at once. Each player will move in only one component—that which does him least harm—and the union becomes an ordinary sum. The same will happen in any game (such as Blue-Red Hackenbush) in which all the values are numbers.

HOT GAMES—THE BATTLE IS JOINED!

In a union of games there may be several hot components, in which the players want to move, and some cold ones, in which they don't. So they won't touch any cold component but will move in *all* the hot components while any such remain. We call this first part of the union the **hot battle**. Since the players make all the hot moves they can, it is a *join* of smaller hot battles for the hot components, and since it only ends when the *last* of these does, it is a *slow* join.

After the hot battle we have the **cold war**, which is just an ordinary addition sum, since all the components are numbers and the players will only move in one at a time.

TOLLS, TIMERS AND TALLIES

Table 1 shows the left and right tallies for Hotcakes. For the 2 by 3 cake the entry is

$$1_2 0_1 .$$

The **left tally**, 1_2, consists of a **toll**, 1, and a **timer**, 2, and means that if Left starts, we shall reach a cold war position of 1 after a hot battle of 2 moves. If instead Right starts we reach a cold war position of 0 after a battle of 1 move. These two little battles are illustrated in Fig. 2. It is easy to tell when the cold war begins because collections of Hotcakes only get cold when all the cakes are strips. The entry for a strip in Table 1 is therefore a single number, x, which should be regarded as an abbreviation for the pair of tallies $x_0.x_0$.

What is the fate of Fig. 3?

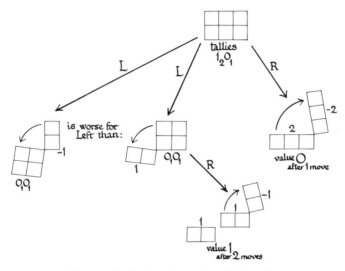

Figure 2. Battles For a Small Hotcake.

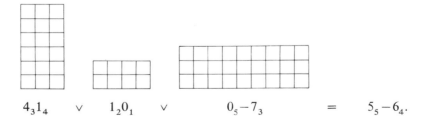

$$4_3 1_4 \quad \vee \quad 1_2 0_1 \quad \vee \quad 0_5 - 7_3 \quad = \quad 5_5 - 6_4.$$

Figure 3. A Hotcake Position.

Here the left tallies are

$$4_3, \quad 1_2, \quad 0_5$$

and so if Left moves first the value when the cold war starts will be $4 + 1 + 0 = 5$. And since the longest component battle (and therefore the whole battle) will last for 5 moves, the left tally of

	1	2	3	4	5	6	7	8	9
1	0	1	2	3	4	5	6	7	8
2	-1	$0_1 0_1$	$1_2 0_1$	$1_2 0_1$	$1_2 0_1$	$1_2 0_1$	$1_2 0_1$	$1_2 0_1$	$1_2 0_1$
3	-2	$0_1 - 1_2$	$1_3 - 1_3$	$1_4 - 2_3$	$0_4 - 3_3$	$-1_4 - 4_3$	$-1_5 - 5_3$	$0_5 - 6_3$	$0_5 - 7_3$
4	-3	$0_1 - 1_2$	$2_3 - 1_4$	$2_5 - 2_5$	$1_6 - 4_5$	$-1_6 - 6_5$	$-2_7 - 7_6$	$0_7 - 7_6$	$1_8 - 8_6$
5	-4	$0_1 - 1_2$	$3_3 0_4$	$4_5 - 1_6$	$3_7 - 3_7$	$1_8 - 6_7$	$-2_8 - 8_8$	$-2_9 - 7_8$	$1_9 - 7_9$
6	-5	$0_1 - 1_2$	$4_3 1_4$	$6_5 1_6$	$6_7 - 1_8$	$4_9 - 4_9$	$1_{10} - 8_9$	$-3_{10} - 9_{10}$	$-2_{11} - 7_{10}$
7	-6	$0_1 - 1_2$	$5_3 1_5$	$7_6 2_7$	$8_8 2_8$	$8_9 - 1_{10}$	$5_{11} - 5_{11}$	$1_{12} - 10_{11}$	$-4_{12} - 10_{12}$
8	-7	$0_1 - 1_2$	$6_3 0_5$	$7_6 0_7$	$7_8 2_9$	$9_{10} 3_{10}$	$10_{11} - 1_{12}$	$6_{13} - 6_{13}$	$1_{14} - 12_{13}$
9	-8	$0_1 - 1_2$	$7_3 0_5$	$8_6 - 1_8$	$7_9 - 1_9$	$7_{10} 2_{11}$	$10_{12} 4_{12}$	$12_{13} - 1_{14}$	$7_{15} - 7_{15}$
10	-9	$0_1 - 1_2$	$8_3 0_6$	$9_7 - 1_8$	$8_9 - 2_9$	$7_{10} - 2_{11}$	$7_{12} 2_{13}$	$11_{14} 4_{11}$	$13_{12} - 1_{16}$
11	-10	$0_1 - 1_2$	$9_3 1_6$	$11_7 0_8$	$10_9 - 2_{10}$	$8_{11} - 4_{11}$	$6_{12} - 3_{13}$	$7_{14} 2_{15}$	$12_{16} 4_{13}$
12	-11	$0_1 - 1_2$	$10_3 1_7$	$12_8 2_9$	$13_{10} - 1_{10}$	$10_{11} - 4_{11}$	$7_{12} - 5_{13}$	$6_{14} - 3_{12}$	$8_{13} 2_{17}$
13	-12	$0_1 - 1_2$	$11_3 0_7$	$12_8 1_9$	$13_{10} 1_{10}$	$13_{11} - 3_{12}$	$9_{13} - 6_{13}$	$6_{14} - 4_{12}$	$8_{13} - 3_{14}$
14	-13	$0_1 - 1_2$	$12_3 0_7$	$13_8 - 1_{10}$	$12_{11} 2_{11}$	$15_{12} - 1_{12}$	$12_{13} - 6_{13}$	$7_{14} - 4_{12}$	$9_{13} - 4_{14}$
15	-14	$0_1 - 1_2$	$13_3 0_8$	$14_9 - 1_{10}$	$13_{11} 0_{11}$	$14_{12} 2_{12}$	$16_{13} - 4_{14}$	$10_{15} - 6_{12}$	$8_{13} - 3_{14}$
16	-15	$0_1 - 1_2$	$14_3 1_8$	$16_9 0_{10}$	$15_{11} - 1_{11}$	$14_{12} 2_{13}$	$17_{14} - 1_{14}$	$14_{15} - 7_{12}$	$8_{13} - 3_{14}$
17	-16	$0_1 - 1_2$	$15_3 1_9$	$17_{10} 1_{10}$	$17_{11} - 2_{12}$	$14_{13} - 1_{13}$	$15_{14} 3_{14}$	$19_{15} - 5_{16}$	$11_{17} - 6_{14}$
18	-17	$0_1 - 1_2$	$16_3 0_9$	$17_{10} 1_{11}$	$18_{12} - 1_{12}$	$16_{13} - 3_{13}$	$14_{14} 2_{15}$	$19_{16} - 1_{16}$	$16_{17} - 8_{14}$
19	-18	$0_1 - 1_2$	$17_3 0_9$	$18_{10} 0_{11}$	$18_{12} 1_{12}$	$19_{13} - 3_{13}$	$15_{14} - 2_{15}$	$16_{16} 1_{13}$	$19_{14} - 6_{18}$
20	-19	$0_1 - 1_2$	$18_3 0_{10}$	$19_{11} 0_{11}$	$19_{13} 2_{13}$	$21_{14} - 3_{14}$	$16_{15} - 4_{15}$	$15_{16} 1_{13}$	$20_{14} - 1_{15}$
21	-20	$0_1 - 1_2$	$19_3 1_{10}$	$21_{11} 0_{12}$	$20_{13} 0_{13}$	$20_{14} - 1_{14}$	$19_{15} - 5_{15}$	$15_{16} 0_{14}$	$20_{15} 0_{15}$
22	-21	$0_1 - 1_2$	$20_3 1_{11}$	$22_{12} 1_{12}$	$22_{13} - 1_{13}$	$20_{14} 2_{14}$	$23_{15} - 5_{15}$	$16_{16} - 1_{14}$	$20_{15} - 1_{15}$
23	-22	$0_1 - 1_2$	$21_3 0_{11}$	$22_{12} 1_{13}$	$23_{14} - 2_{14}$	$20_{15} 2_{15}$	$24_{16} - 4_{16}$	$18_{17} - 1_{17}$	$21_{18} - 1_{15}$
24	-23	$0_1 - 1_2$	$22_3 0_{11}$	$23_{12} 0_{13}$	$23_{14} - 1_{14}$	$20_{15} 2_{15}$	$22_{16} - 1_{16}$	$22_{17} - 3_{14}$	$20_{15} 0_{16}$
25	-24	$0_1 - 1_2$	$23_3 0_{12}$	$24_{13} 0_{13}$	$24_{14} 1_{14}$	$25_{15} - 3_{15}$	$21_{16} 2_{16}$	$26_{17} - 4_{14}$	$20_{15} 1_{16}$

Table 1. Left and Right Tallies for Hotcakes.

the position is 5_5. The right tally is

$$(1 + 0 - 7)_4 = -6_4,$$

since the component right tallies are

$$1_4, \quad 0_1, \quad -7_3,$$

and the battle this time lasts for 4 moves.

For a union of positions with tallies

$$u_a x_i, \; v_b y_j, \; w_c z_k, \; \ldots$$

we find both left and right tallies by *adding* the tolls (which refer to an eventual *sum* of cold wars) and taking the *largest* timers (which refer to a *slow join* of hot battles), obtaining

$$(u + v + w + \ldots)_{\max(a,b,c,\ldots)} (x + y + z + \ldots)_{\max(i,j,k,\ldots)}$$

> **TOTAL TOLLS!**
> **TOPMOST TIMERS!**

WHICH IS THE BEST OPTION?

Since after Left's move it will be Right's turn, Left need only consider the *right* tallies of his options and make a shortlist of those with the largest toll. Right's shortlist consists of those *left* tallies of his options that have least toll. Both players should now choose options from their shortlists by the normal suspense rule of Chapter 9—take the largest even timer if there is one and otherwise the smallest odd timer.

Shortlist all
G^L with GREATEST RIGHT TOLL
and all
G^R with LEAST LEFT TOLL
and, from the corresponding
timers on each side, take the
LARGEST EVEN, else SMALLEST ODD.

CHOOSING BEST OPTIONS

All that remains to be explained is how to find the tallies of an arbitrary position from those of its options. Before we do this we will use what we already know to find the best options for the 9 by 3 cake. According to the rules of Hotcakes this has options as shown in

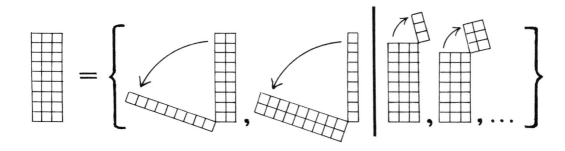

or, in symbols,

$$9 \text{ by } 3 = \left\{ 1 \text{ by } 9 \vee 9 \text{ by } 2 \atop 2 \text{ by } 9 \vee 9 \text{ by } 1 \middle| \begin{array}{l} 8 \text{ by } 3 \vee 3 \text{ by } 1 \\ 7 \text{ by } 3 \vee 3 \text{ by } 2 \\ 6 \text{ by } 3 \vee 3 \text{ by } 3 \\ 5 \text{ by } 3 \vee 3 \text{ by } 4 \\ 4 \text{ by } 3 \vee 3 \text{ by } 5 \\ 3 \text{ by } 3 \vee 3 \text{ by } 6 \\ 2 \text{ by } 3 \vee 3 \text{ by } 7 \\ 1 \text{ by } 3 \vee 3 \text{ by } 8 \end{array} \right\},$$

with tallies

$$
\left\{
\begin{array}{l}
\\
8 \quad \vee \; 0_1-1_2 = 8_1 7_2 \\
1_2 0_1 \vee \; -8 \quad = -7_2-8_1 \\
\\
\end{array}
\right.
\left|
\begin{array}{l}
6_3 0_5 \quad \vee \; -2 \qquad\;\; = \mathbf{4_3}-2_5 \\
5_3 1_5 \quad \vee \; 0_1-1_2 = \mathbf{5_3 0_5} \\
4_3 1_4 \quad \vee \; 1_3-1_3 = \mathbf{5_3 0_4} \\
3_3 0_4 \quad \vee \; 1_4-2_2 = \mathbf{4_4}-2_4 \\
2_3-1_4 \vee \; 0_4-3_3 = \mathbf{2_4}-4_4 \\
1_3-1_3 \vee \; -1_4-4_3 = \mathbf{0_4}-5_3 \quad \leftarrow \\
1_2 0_1 \quad \vee \; -1_5-5_3 = \mathbf{0_5}-5_3 \\
2 \qquad \vee \; 0_5-6_3 = \mathbf{2_5}-4_3
\end{array}
\right\}
$$

Of course, because Left only refers to right tallies and Right only to left ones, the bold-face figures are all we need. From them Left shortlists only 7_2, and Right only 0_4 and 0_5, from which she chooses 0_4. Why is this? If Right made a move to 0_5 the battle would have 5 more moves,

Left, Right, Left, Right, Left,

and Right would be forced to move first in the cold war. She therefore prefers the move to 0_4 with 4 battle moves,

Left, Right, Left, Right,

after which Left must make the first cold war move. We conclude that the players' best options have the tallies shown in

$$\{..7_2 | 0_4 ..\}.$$

HOT POSITIONS

When we know the best options, how do we find the new tallies? In the example there is no difficulty. Since $7 > 0$, this position is still hot, so the battle is not yet over. Indeed we can see just how long it will last: if Left makes the first move there will be just 2 more battle moves, while a first move by Right would be followed by 4 further battle moves. The hot battle therefore lasts for 3 or 5 moves in the two cases and the tallies are

$$7_3 0_5.$$

The same argument works for hot positions in any game when the best options have been found:

For a position
$\{..x_a | y_b ..\}$ with $x > y$,
the tallies are

$x_{a+1} y_{b+1}$

TALLY RULE FOR HOT POSITIONS

COLD POSITIONS

But if $x < y$ the position is cold and must be a number. Which number is it? We find out by a version of the Simplicity Rule. We shall discuss the cases in which Left's option has right tally $\frac{1}{2_7}$ or $\frac{1}{2_8}$ and Right's has left tally 1_3 or 1_4.

Since 7 is odd and 8 is even,

$$\frac{1}{2_8} \text{ is } better \ for \ Left \text{ than } \tfrac{1}{2} \ (\text{i.e. } \tfrac{1}{2_8} > \tfrac{1}{2}),$$

while

$$\frac{1}{2_7} \text{is } worse \ for \ Left \text{ than } \tfrac{1}{2} \ (\text{i.e. } \tfrac{1}{2_7} < \tfrac{1}{2}),$$

and for similar reasons,

$$1_4 \text{ is } better \ for \ Right \text{ than } 1 \ (\text{i.e. } 1_4 < 1),$$

while

$$1_3 \text{ is } worse \ for \ Right \text{ than } 1 \ (\text{i.e. } 1_3 > 1).$$

[Recall that "greater than" is "better for Left", "worse for Right".] We can now see from the picture

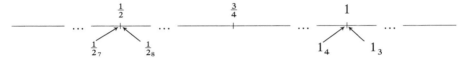

that the simplest numbers in the appropriate ranges are

$$\tfrac{3}{4} \text{ for } \{..\tfrac{1}{2_8}|1_4..\},$$
$$1 \text{ for } \{..\tfrac{1}{2_7}|1_3..\},$$
$$1 \text{ for } \{..\tfrac{1}{2_8}|1_3..\},$$
$$\text{and } \tfrac{1}{2} \text{ for } \{..\tfrac{1}{2_7}|1_4..\}.$$

For cold positions in general:

For a position
$\{..x_a|y_b..\}$ with $x < y$,
the tallies are $z_0 z_0$, where z is the
simplest number in the range
$x < z < y$ if a and b are both even,
$x \leqslant z \leqslant y$ if a and b are both odd,
$x < z \leqslant y$ if a is even and b is odd,
$x \leqslant z < y$ if a is odd and b is even.

TALLY RULES FOR COLD POSITIONS

In short:

odd timers *admit* their tolls,
even timers *exclude* their tolls,
as candidates for the simplest number.

Or, shorter still:

ODD ADMITS!
EVEN EVICTS!

Of course such positions, being cold, are really numbers, and a number z has tallies $z_0 z_0$ because it is already *in* the cold war.

TEPID POSITIONS

When Left's and Right's options both have the same toll, the rules are more delicate:

For a position
$$\{..x_a|x_b..\}$$
with equal tolls, the tallies are
$x_{a+1}x_{b+1}$ if a and b are both even,
$x_0 x_0$ if a and b are both odd,
$x_{\max(a+1,b+2)}x_{b+1}$ if a is even and b is odd,
$x_{a+1}x_{\max(b+1,a+2)}$ if a is odd and b is even.

TALLY RULES FOR TEPID POSITIONS

It is easier in practice to ask first whether the tentative tallies

$$x_{a+1}y_{b+1}$$

obey the *Lukewarmth Commandment*:

IF TOLLS BE EQUAL,
THOU SHALT NOT PERMIT AN
EVEN TIMER UNLESS THERE
BE A GREATER *ODD* ONE.

Then tallies disobeying the commandment are of two types and should be corrected as follows:

If the timers $a+1, b+1$ are both even, the correct value is x with tallies $x_0 x_0$.
If one of $a+1, b+1$ is an even number, e, and the other a smaller odd number, this odd number should be increased to $e+1$.

These rather puzzling rules must be explained in terms of battles only, since we know the value x at which the cold war will start. The important question is: who must start it? To decide when he himself wants to enter the fray, the erudite player will of course be guided by the maxim of Chapter 9:

> **GREATER GOOD!** (odd)
> **LESSER EVIL!** (even)

Let us see how this leads to the above rules by studying four simple examples.

For the battle of the example

$\{..x_8\|x_4..\}$	$\{..x_7\|x_3..\}$	$\{..x_8\|x_3..\}$	$\{..x_7\|x_4..\}$

Right sees, if he moves first, a

win	loss	short loss	short win

as against the

loss	win	longer loss	longer win

that happens if he leaves the opening move to Left. He therefore

does	does not	does	does not

want to make the first move. Left, by moving first, can guarantee a

win	loss	long win	loss of definite length;

as against the possible

loss	win	short win	indefinitely long loss

if he leaves it to Right, who may or may not respond. He therefore

does	does not	does	does

prefer to move first. The resulting tallies are

x_9x_5	x_0x_0	x_9x_4	x_8x_9

because the game is

hot	cold	(fairly hot)	both hot and cold!

More detailed explanations:

The first example $\{..x_8|x_4..\}$ is *patently* hot since $x_8 > x > x_4$, so the final timers are got by adding 1 as usual.

The second example $\{..x_7|x_3..\}$ is just as patently cold, since $x_7 < x < x_3$, and we get the number x by the Simplicity Rule.

In the third example $\{..x_8|x_3..\}$ the heat is latent. Although Left definitely wins, both players want to move: Right to take the lesser evil, and Left to ensure that his good is greater. The timers are still obtained by adding 1.

The last example $\{..x_7|x_4..\}$ is the most subtle! Right, who is sure to win the battle, has all the time in the world and would be delighted if nobody touched this game for a long time, since it might then be the last battle to end. Left, therefore, will move as soon as he can. If he is due to move, he moves to x_7, and the battle will last for 8 moves in all. But if it is Right's turn, and battles rage elsewhere, he should make a move without involving this component; and with

Left then due to move there will be 8 more moves in this battle, making 9 in all. The tallies are therefore $x_8 x_9$.

TALLY TRUTHS TOTALLY TOLD

We can now give a complete summary of all our rules for working with tallies:

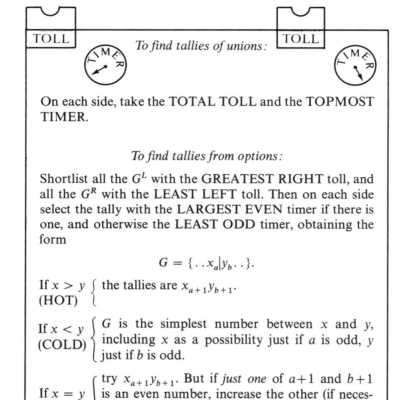

TOLL   TIMER   *To find tallies of unions:*   TOLL   TIMER

On each side, take the TOTAL TOLL and the TOPMOST TIMER.

To find tallies from options:

Shortlist all the G^L with the GREATEST RIGHT toll, and all the G^R with the LEAST LEFT toll. Then on each side select the tally with the LARGEST EVEN timer if there is one, and otherwise the LEAST ODD timer, obtaining the form

$$G = \{..x_a | y_b..\}.$$

If $x > y$ (HOT) $\left\{ \right.$ the tallies are $x_{a+1} y_{b+1}$.

If $x < y$ (COLD) $\left\{ \begin{array}{l} G \text{ is the simplest number between } x \text{ and } y, \\ \text{including } x \text{ as a possibility just if } a \text{ is odd, } y \\ \text{just if } b \text{ is odd.} \end{array} \right.$

If $x = y$ (TEPID) $\left\{ \begin{array}{l} \text{try } x_{a+1} y_{b+1}. \text{ But if } just \ one \text{ of } a+1 \text{ and } b+1 \\ \text{is an even number, increase the other (if neces-} \\ \text{sary) by just enough to make it a larger odd} \\ \text{number. If } both \text{ are even, replace each of them} \\ \text{by 0.} \end{array} \right.$

THE TALLY MACHINE

A TEPID GAME

Coolcakes is another eating game. It is the selective version of Eatcakes, which we met in Chapter 9. Across each one of as many cakes as she likes, Rita eats away a horizontal strip.

Lefty eats vertical strips in a similar way. Table 2 gives the tallies, and the displayed pattern can be shown to continue.

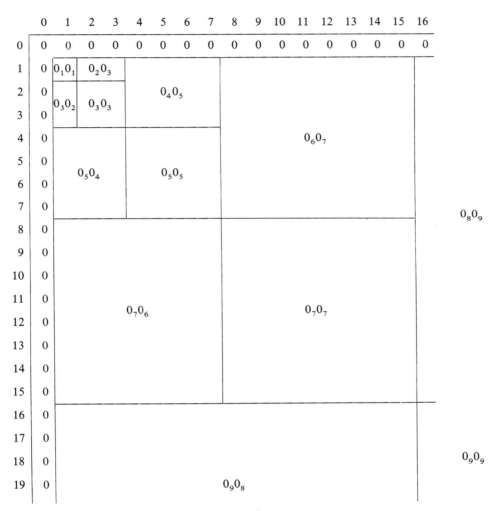

Table 2. Tallies for Coolcakes.

Why does ⬜⬜⬜ have the tallies 0_20_3? We have

$$\square\square\square = \{\boxtimes\square\square, \square\boxtimes\square \mid \boxtimes\boxtimes\boxtimes\}$$

$$0_10_1 \vee 0_10_1$$

$$0_20_3 = \{\, 0_20_3, \quad 0_10_1 \mid 0_00_0\}.$$

From the right tallies 0_3 and 0_1 Left will choose his best option, 0_1. Right sees only the left tally 0_0, so we try the tentative tallies

$$\{..0_1|0_0..\} = 0_2 0_1 ?$$

However, to avoid breaking the Lukewarmth Commandment these must be corrected:

$$\{..0_1|0_0..\} = 0_2 0_3 !$$

SELECT BOYS AND GIRLS

When Left and Right last held a children's party, at the end of Chapter 5, they took so long working out those complicated values that all hell broke loose among their hungry guests. Now the boys and girls are carefully selected and several may be seated in a single move. Left may seat any number of new boys, or Right any number of new girls, provided that, at each move, any two new arrivals are separated by a previously seated child. Once again no boy and girl may sit in adjacent seats.

The values are intriguing (Table 3). We can work them out from the equations (very like those in Chapter 5 for Seating Boys and Girls, the disjunctive form)

$$
\begin{aligned}
LnL &= \{LaL \vee LbL \mid LaR \vee RbL\} \\
(-LnL =) RnR &= \{RaL \vee LbR \mid RaR \vee RbR\} \\
(RnL =) LnR &= \{LaL \vee LbR \mid LaR \vee RbR\}
\end{aligned}
\right\} \quad a+b = n-1,
$$

$$L0R \text{ and } R0L \text{ illegal.}$$

The tolls show period 5 after some exceptions in the first two rows. The timers increase at three different speeds, as shown by the separating bars: some every period (a), some every other period (b), and the rest after steadily increasing numbers of periods (c). So, despite their latest precautions, Left and Right are sure to face hot battles of erratic lengths!

MRS. GRUNDY

When you played Grundy's Game in Chapter 4 (the move was to split a heap into any two smaller heaps of different sizes), you may have been irritated by all those unsplittable heaps of size 1 and 2 that are left at the end. **Mrs. Grundy** has a tidy mind and allows Left to remove isolated heaps of 1, and Right isolated heaps of 2, as additional moves, and, to speed the game up a little, the players may make moves in as many heaps as they like. There is a variation in which the players may split even heaps of size 4 or more into equal parts. The successive tallies are:

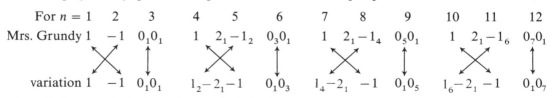

For $n = 1$	2	3	4	5	6	7	8	9	10	11	12
Mrs. Grundy 1	-1	$0_1 0_1$	1	$2_1 {-} 1_2$	$0_3 0_1$	1	$2_1 {-} 1_4$	$0_5 0_1$	1	$2_1 {-} 1_6$	$0_7 0_1$
variation 1	-1	$0_1 0_1$	$1_2 {-} 2_1 {-} 1$	$0_1 0_3$	$1_4 {-} 2_1$	-1	$0_1 0_5$	$1_6 {-} 2_1 {-} 1$	$0_1 0_7$

The tolls have period 3 in each case and the timers other than 1 increase steadily. The arrows display a remarkable coincidence: tallies for the variation are obtained by shuffling the negatives of those for the original.

LnL

Range	0		1		2		2_1	0_1	3_1	0_2
0 to 4:	0		1		2		2_1	0_1	3_1	0_2
5 to 9:	4_1	0_2	2_2	1_2	2_3	2_3	2_3	1_3	3_3	0_4
10 to 14:	4_4	0_4	3_4	1_4	2_5	2_5	2_5	1_5	3_5	0_6
15 to 19:	4_4	0_4	3_4	1_4	2_7	2_7	2_5	1_5	3_5	0_8
20 to 24:	4_6	0_6	3_6	1_6	2_9	2_9	2_7	1_7	3_7	0_{10}
25 to 29:	4_6	0_6	3_6	1_6	2_{11}	2_{11}	2_7	1_7	3_7	0_{12}
30 to 34:	4_8	0_8	3_6	1_6	2_{13}	2_{13}	2_9	1_7	3_7	0_{14}
35 to 39:	4_8	0_8	3_8	1_8	2_{15}	2_{15}	2_9	1_9	3_9	0_{16}
40 to 44:	4_{10}	0_{10}	3_8	1_8	2_{17}	2_{17}	2_{11}	1_9	3_9	0_{18}
45 to 49:	4_{10}	0_{10}	3_8	1_8	2_{19}	2_{19}	2_{11}	1_9	3_9	0_{20}
50 to 54:	4_{12}	0_{12}	3_8	1_8	2_{21}	2_{21}	2_{13}	1_9	3_9	0_{22}
$5k$ to $5k+4$:	4_b	0_b	3_c	1_c	2_a	2_a	2_{b+1}	1_{c+1}	3_{c+1}	0_{a+1}

LnR

0 to 4:	illegal		0		0_1	0_1	1_1	-1_1	2_1	-2_1
5 to 9:	2_2	-2_2	1_2	-1_2	0_3	0_3	1_3	-1_3	2_4	-2_4
10 to 14:	2_4	-2_4	1_4	-1_4	0_5	0_5	1_5	-1_5	2_6	-2_6
15 to 19:	2_4	-2_4	1_4	-1_4	0_7	0_7	1_5	-1_5	2_8	-2_8
20 to 24:	2_6	-2_6	1_6	-1_6	0_9	0_9	1_7	-1_7	2_{10}	-2_{10}
25 to 29:	2_6	-2_6	1_6	-1_6	0_{11}	0_{11}	1_7	-1_7	2_{12}	-2_{12}
30 to 34:	2_8	-2_8	1_6	-1_6	0_{13}	0_{13}	1_7	-1_7	2_{14}	-2_{14}
35 to 39:	2_8	-2_8	1_8	-1_8	0_{15}	0_{15}	1_9	-1_9	2_{16}	-2_{16}
40 to 44:	2_{10}	-2_{10}	1_8	-1_8	0_{17}	0_{17}	1_9	-1_9	2_{18}	-2_{18}
45 to 49:	2_{10}	-2_{10}	1_8	-1_8	0_{19}	0_{19}	1_9	-1_9	2_{20}	-2_{20}
50 to 54:	2_{12}	-2_{12}	1_8	-1_8	0_{21}	0_{21}	1_9	-1_9	2_{22}	-2_{22}
$5k$ to $5k+4$:	2_b	-2_b	1_c	-1_c	0_a	0_a	1_{c+1}	-1_{c+1}	2_{a+1}	-2_{a+1}

$$a = 2k+1, \quad b = 2\lfloor k/2 \rfloor + 2, \quad c = 2\lfloor \sqrt{2k-1} + \tfrac{1}{2} \rfloor.$$

Table 3. Tallies for Select Boys and Girls.

HOW TO PLAY MISÈRE UNIONS OF PARTIZAN GAMES

We have no idea how to play ordinary unions of partizan games with misère play.

URGENT UNIONS (SHOTGUN WEDDINGS?)

A union of games may be played with the additional rule that it finishes as soon as its first component does. The winner of that component is then the winner of the whole game, in either normal or misère play. A component may be called finished *either* if the mover can't move *or* if neither player can move (but if we use the latter rule, we must still declare that a player loses who cannot move in any component of an unfinished game).

This kind of compound of a number of games

$$G, H, K, \ldots$$

is called their **urgent union**

$$G \bigtriangledown H \bigtriangledown K \bigtriangledown \ldots \qquad (\text{``}G \text{ ur } H \text{ ur } K \text{ ur} \ldots \text{''}).$$

Dwight Duffus called this the *severed selective compound* (shortened selective in ONAG, and by Smith); when we wish to contrast it with the ordinary union, we call the latter the **tardy union**. The theory of urgent unions, for either normal or misère play, and with either finishing rule, follows from the more general theory given below.

PREDECIDERS—OVERRIDERS AND SUICIDERS

In this theory, certain moves in the components are special in that a player who makes one of them thereby instantly terminates the whole game. These **predeciding moves** are of two kinds, *overriding* and *suiciding*. A player who makes an **overriding move** wins immediately, while one who makes a **suiciding move** loses just as quickly. However, if a player cannot move when it is his turn to do so, and no predeciding move has been made, he must be said to lose.

This kind of game includes the urgent unions defined above, by making all finishing moves overriding in normal play and suiciding in misère play. But of course it also covers cases in which some finishing moves are overriding, some suiciding and some neither.

FALADA

"Some of the King's Horses, First Off Wins" is a very playable game. Since it is a severed selective horse game we simply called it **Falada**. In the Grimms' fairy tale, Falada was the horse whose severed head addressed the Goose Girl as she pondered her moves for the day. We play it on a quarter-infinite field with horses which move as in Chapter 9, except that at his turn a player may move however many he likes (at least one, possibly all). Horses are allowed to jump off the board and the first to do so is the winner. The game is plainly a union of component one-horse games, and it is a normal play *urgent* union because the winner of the soonest finishing component wins all.

Such games are solved by tallies in which the tolls are not restricted to be ordinary numbers, but are sometimes infinite.

	a	b	c	d	e	f	g	h	i	j	k	l	m	n	o	p	q	r	s	t	u	v	w	x
1	$\overline{\infty}_1\infty_1$	$\overline{\infty}_1\infty_1$	$\overline{\infty}_2\infty_1$	$\overline{\infty}_1\infty_1$	$\overline{\infty}_1\infty_1$	$\overline{\infty}_1\infty_1$	$\overline{\infty}_1\infty_1$	$\overline{\infty}_1\infty_1$	$\overline{\infty}_1\infty_1$	$\overline{\infty}_1\infty_1$	$\overline{\infty}_1\infty_1$	$\overline{\infty}_1\infty_1$	$\overline{\infty}_1\infty_1$	$\overline{\infty}_1\infty_1$	$\overline{\infty}_1\infty_1$	$\overline{\infty}_1\infty_1$	$\overline{\infty}_1\infty_1$	$\overline{\infty}_1\infty_1$	$\overline{\infty}_1\infty_1$	$\overline{\infty}_1\infty_1$	$\overline{\infty}_1\infty_1$	$\overline{\infty}_1\infty_1$	$\overline{\infty}_1\infty_1$	$\overline{\infty}_1\infty_1$
2	$\overline{\infty}_1\infty_1$	$\overline{\infty}_1\infty_1$	$\overline{\infty}_2\infty_1$	$\overline{\infty}_1\infty_1$	$\overline{\infty}_1\infty_1$	$\overline{\infty}_1\infty_1$	$\overline{\infty}_1\infty_1$	$\overline{\infty}_1\infty_1$	$\overline{\infty}_1\infty_1$	$\overline{\infty}_1\infty_1$	$2_1\overline{\infty}_1$	$\overline{\infty}_1\infty_1$	$\overline{\infty}_1\infty_1$	$\overline{\infty}_1\infty_1$	$2_1\overline{\infty}_1$	$3_1\overline{\infty}_1$	$3_1\overline{\infty}_1$	$2_1\overline{\infty}_1$	$3_1\overline{\infty}_1$	$3_1\overline{\infty}_1$	$3_1\overline{\infty}_1$	$4_1\overline{\infty}_1$	$3_1\overline{\infty}_1$	$4_1\overline{\infty}_1$
3	$\overline{\infty}_1\infty_1$	$\overline{\infty}_3\infty_1$	0	$\infty_3\overline{\infty}_3$	$0_3 0_2$	$0_3 0_2$	$1_1 0_2$	1	1	2	1	2	2	2	3	2	3	3	3	4	3	4	4	4
4	$\overline{\infty}_1\infty_1$	$\overline{\infty}_3\infty_1$	0	$0_2 0_3$	$0_3 0_2$	$3_3 0_2$	$1_1 0_2$	1	$1_1 0_2$	$1_3 1_2$	$1_3 1_2$	$2_1 1_2$	$2_1 1_2$	$2_1 1_2$	$2_2 2_2$	$2_3 2_2$	$3_1 2_2$	3	$3_1 2_2$	$3_3 3_2$	$4_1 3_2$	$4_1 3_2$	4	$4_1 3_2$
5	$\overline{\infty}_1\infty_1$	$\infty_3 0_1$	0	$0_1 0_1$	$0_1 0_1$	$0_3 0_1$	$0_3 0_1$	$\frac{1}{2}$	$\frac{1}{2}$	$1_1 1_1$	$1_3 1_2$	$1_3 1_1$	$1_5 1_1$	$1_1 1_2$	$2_1 2_2$	$2_3 2_2$	$2_3 2_1$	$2_1 2_2$	$2_1 2_2$	$3_1 3_1$	$3_3 3_1$	$3_3 3_1$	$3_1 2_1$	$3_2 2_1$
6	$\overline{\infty}_1\infty_1$	$\infty_3 0_1$	-1	$0_2 0_3$	0	0	0	0	0	1	1	1	2	1	2	2	2	2	2	3	3	3	2	3
7	$\overline{\infty}_1\infty_1$	$\infty_1 -1_1$	-1	$0_2 -1_1$	$0_1 0_3$	0	$0_1 0_1$	$\frac{1}{4}$	$\frac{1}{4}$	$1_1 1_2$	$1_1 1_1$	$1_1 1_1$	$1_5 1_4$	1_4	$2_1 1_2$	$1_5 1_1$	$2_5 4$	$2_5 4$	2_4	$3_1 2_1$	3	$3_1 3_1$	$3_5 4$	3_4
8	$\overline{\infty}_1\infty_1$	$\infty_1 0_1$	-1	$0_1 0_3$	0	0	$0_4 0_5$	$0_1 0_1$	0	$0_5 0_1$	$0_6 0_7$	$0_1 0_1$	$1_1 1_1$	1	$1_5 1_1$	$1_1 1_1$	$2_1 2_1$	$2_1 2_1$	$2\frac{1}{2}$	$2_5 2_1$	$2\frac{1}{2}$	$2\frac{1}{2}$	$2_7 2_1$	$2\frac{1}{2}$
9	$\overline{\infty}_1\infty_1$	$\infty_1 -1_1$	-1	-1	$-\frac{1}{2}$	-1	$-\frac{1}{4}$	0	0	0	0	0	1	1	1	1	1	1	2	1	3	2	3	3
10	$\overline{\infty}_1\infty_1$	$\infty_1 -1_1$	-1	$-1_2 -1_1$	$-1_1 -1_1$	-1	$-\frac{1}{2}$	0	0	$-\frac{1}{2}$	$-\frac{1}{4}$	$-\frac{1}{4}$	$1_1 1_2$	$\frac{1}{2}$	$1_1 1_1$	$1_7 1_6$	1_4	$2_1 1_1$	$1_9 1_8$	$2_1 2_1$	$2_1 1_1$	2_4	$3_2 2_1$	3
11	$\overline{\infty}_1\infty_1$	$\infty_1 -1_1$	-1	$-1_2 -1_3$	-1	-1	$-1_4 -1_5$	-1	-1	0	$-\frac{1}{2}$	0	1	1	1	1	1	$1_7 1_1$	$1_1 1_1$	$1\frac{1}{2}$	$1_9 1_1$	2	$2_7 2_1$	$2\frac{1}{2}$
12	$\overline{\infty}_1\infty_1$	$\infty_1 -2_1$	-2	$-1_2 -2_1$	-1	-1	$-1_1 -1_1$	$-\frac{1}{2}$	-1	$-\frac{1}{4}$	0	0	$1_1 1_2$	$\frac{1}{2}$	$\frac{1}{2}$	$1_1 1_1$	1	1	2	$1\frac{1}{4}$	2	2	2	3
13	$\overline{\infty}_1\infty_1$	$\infty_1 -1_1$	-2	$-1_2 -2_1$	$-1_1 -1_1$	-1	$-1_1 -1_1$	$-\frac{1}{2}$	-1	$-1_2 -1_1$	$-\frac{1}{4}$	0	$0_1 0_1$	$0_9 0_8$	$\frac{1}{4}$	$1_1 1_1$	$1\frac{1}{4}$	$\frac{1}{2}$	$\frac{1}{2}$	$1\frac{1}{4}$	$2_1 1_1$	$2\frac{1}{4}$	$2_1 1_1$	$2_9 2_8$
14	$\overline{\infty}_1\infty_1$	$\infty_1 -2_1$	-2	$-2_2 -2_3$	$-1_1 -1_1$	-1	$-1_2 -1_1$	$-1_4 -1_5$	-1	$-1_6 -1_7$	$-\frac{1}{2}$	-1	$0_1 0_1$	$0_1 0_1$	0	$1_1 1_1$	1	$1_1 1_1$	$1_1 1_1$	1	$1_9 1_1$	$1\frac{1}{2}$	2	$2_1 1_1$
15	$\overline{\infty}_1\infty_1$	$\infty_1 -2_1$	-2	$-2_2 -2_3$	-2	-1	$-1_4 -1_4$	$-1\frac{1}{2}$	-2	$-1\frac{1}{4}$	$-\frac{1}{2}$	-1	$0_8 0_9$	0	0	$0_9 0_1$	$-\frac{1}{2}$	0	$1_1 1_1$	1	$1_1 1_1$	$1_1 1_1$	$1\frac{1}{4}$	$2_1 1_1$
16	$\overline{\infty}_1\infty_1$	$\infty_1 -3_1$	-2	$-2_2 -3_1$	$-2_1 -2_1$	-2	$-1\frac{1}{2} -1_1$	-1	-2	$-1\frac{1}{2} -1_1$	-1	-1	$-\frac{1}{2} -1_1$	$-\frac{1}{2}$	0	$0_1 0_1$	$-\frac{1}{2}$	$-\frac{1}{4}$	$1\frac{1}{2} 1_1$	$1\frac{1}{4}$	$1_1 1_1$	$1_1 1_1$	1	$2_1 1\frac{1}{2}_1$
17	$\overline{\infty}_1\infty_1$	$\infty_1 -2_1$	-3	$-2_2 -2_1$	-2	-2	$-2_1 -2_5$	$-2_1 -2_1$	-2	$-1\frac{1}{2}_2 -2_1$	-2	-1	$-1_8 -1_9$	$-\frac{1}{2}$	-1	0	0	0	$0_{11} 0_1$	1	$-\frac{1}{2}$	$1_1 1_1$	1	$1_1 1_1$
18	$\overline{\infty}_1\infty_1$	$\infty_1 -3_1$	-3	-3	$-2\frac{1}{2}$	-2	$-2\frac{1}{4}$	-2	-2	-2	$-2\frac{1}{2}$	-2	-1	0	0	$-\frac{1}{4}$	0	0	0	1	$-\frac{1}{4}$	1	1	1
19	$\overline{\infty}_1\infty_1$	$\infty_1 -3_1$	-3	$-2_2 -3_1$	$-2\frac{1}{2}$	-2	$-2\frac{1}{4}$	-2	-2	-2	$-1\frac{1}{2}$	-2	$-1\frac{8}{9} -1_9$	$-\frac{1}{2}$	-1	$-\frac{1}{2}_1 -1_1$	$0_1 0_{11}$	0	$0_1 0_1$	$0_{13} 0_{12}$	$\frac{1}{4}$	$1\frac{1}{2}_1 1_1$	1	$1_1 1_1$

Table 4. A Filled-out Falada Field.

Table 4 shows these **unrestricted tallies** for this game. A position in which one of Left's options is already an overriding win has left tally ∞_1. Another position in which *every* right option has a left tally ∞_1 will have right tally ∞_2, and so on. In general a tally ∞_n refers to a position for which Left has a strategy which leads to an overriding move at the nth move. This will be a *left* tally if n is *odd*, a *right* one if n is *even*. A tally $-\infty_n$ (often written $\overline{\infty}_n$) is assigned to a position for which Right has an n-move overriding win strategy. It will be a *left* tally if n is even, a *right* one if n is odd. A tally ∞_0 would indicate a position that has already been (overridingly) won by Left, $\overline{\infty}_0$ one already overridingly won by Right.

Places at the very edge of the board have tallies $\infty_1, \overline{\infty}_1$ since either player has an immediate overriding win; the same is true of square b2. The tallies for b3 are ∞_1, ∞_2 since Left will win in 1 move if he starts, 2 moves if Right starts, even if Right does not move the horse on this square. But a horse on b4 can be moved by Right to c2 and so yields a 3-move win for him, corresponding to right tally $\overline{\infty}_3$. The right tally of b5 is 0_1, however, because Right will move this horse to c3, from which position neither player will voluntarily move it, lest his opponent win outright. In symbols the value of c3 is found from the equation

$$\{..\,\overline{\infty}_1\,|\,\infty_1\,..\} = 0,$$

since 0 is the simplest number between $-\infty$ and $+\infty$.

An especially interesting square is d4, from which either player has an outright win in 3 moves. The play might go along one of the lines sketched in Fig. 4, but there are other alternatives and the losing player might pass on b3 or c2 by moving some other horse.

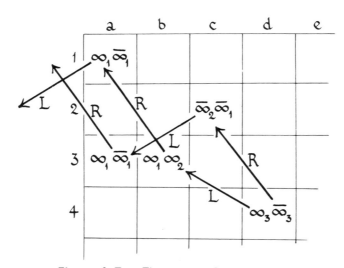

Figure 4. Two Three-move Overriding Wins.

You'll find it hard to keep your opponents interested in Falada if you make them wait while you laboriously consult Table 4, so why not play on the beautifully patterned field of Fig. 7 in the Extras?

We'll be back with some more games after a word from the makers of Unrestricted Tallies:

Frame 0

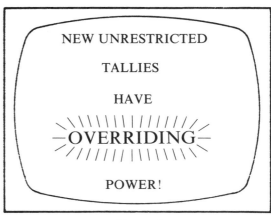

Frame 1

Timers on *infinite* tolls are *remoteness* functions, not suspense numbers. Therefore:

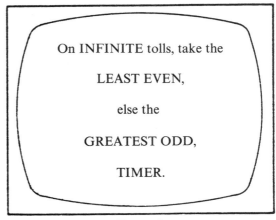

Frame 2

Frame 3

New tallies work just as in the old machine:

FOR HOT WORK:

$$\{..\infty_a|x_b..\} = \infty_{a+1}x_{b+1},$$

$$\{..x_a|\overline{\infty_b}..\} = x_{a+1}\overline{\infty_{b+1}},$$

$$\{..\infty_a|\overline{\infty_b}..\} = \infty_{a+1}\overline{\infty_{b+1}},$$

ADD ONE to TIMERS.

Frame 4

FOR COLD WORK:

$$\{..x_a|\infty_b..\} = \{..x_a|\ \},$$

$$\{..\overline{\infty_a}|x_b..\} = \{\ |x_b..\},$$

$$\{..\overline{\infty_a}|\infty_b..\} = 0, \text{ use the}$$

SIMPLICITY RULE.

Frame 5

But for the delicate games, whose two tallies have the same infinite toll, use the new program cycle:

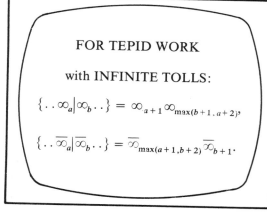

FOR TEPID WORK

with INFINITE TOLLS:

$$\{..\infty_a|\infty_b..\} = \infty_{a+1}\infty_{max(b+1,a+2)},$$

$$\{..\overline{\infty_a}|\overline{\infty_b}..\} = \overline{\infty}_{max(a+1,b+2)}\overline{\infty}_{b+1}.$$

Frame 6

NEW!
UNRESTRICTED
TALLIES
for
URGENT
UNIONS

Frame 7

When using Frame 6, treat $\{..\infty_a|\ \}$ like $\{..\infty_a|\infty_{-1}..\}$ and $\{\ |\overline{\infty_b}..\}$ like $\{..\overline{\infty}_{-1}|\overline{\infty_b}..\}$.

According to Frames 1 and 2, the tallies of

$$3_6 \overline{\infty}_3 \;\lor\; \infty_9 5_{12} \;\lor\; 2^{\frac{1}{2}}_{2,1} 0_2 \;\lor\; \overline{\infty}_8 \overline{\infty}_5$$

are

$$\overline{\infty}_8 \overline{\infty}_3,$$

since the tallies with infinite tolls on the left side are ∞_9 and $\overline{\infty}_8$, and $\overline{\infty}_8$ has the tiniest timer. On the right side $\overline{\infty}_3$ beats $\overline{\infty}_5$. On *each* side the tally with infinite toll (whether ∞ or $\overline{\infty}$) and least timer overrides the others.

The timers on infinite tolls are *remoteness* functions, not suspense numbers, since a player with an *overriding* win wants to win quickly, while his opponent tries to lose slowly.

Let's use Frame 3 to find tallies for the example

$$\{..\overline{\infty}_5, ..\infty_6, ..2_2, ..\overline{\infty}_1, ..\infty_4 \mid 1_9.., 3_8.., 1_6.., \infty_1.., 1_2..\}.$$

In this Left shortlists his options with the greatest right toll (∞) and Right those with least left toll (1), to obtain

$$\{..\infty_6, ..\infty_4 \mid 1_9.., 1_6.., 1_2..\} = \{..\infty_4 \mid 1_6..\} = \infty_5 1_7.$$

Since his timers are *remoteness* functions, Left prefers ∞_4 to ∞_6 (*least* even, else *greatest* odd), but Right, who sees *suspense* numbers, prefers 1_6 to 1_9 and 1_2 (*greatest* even, else *least* odd). Since this game is hot, its tallies $\infty_5 1_7$ are found in the obvious way (Frame 4); had it been cold we should still have used the Simplicity Rule (Frame 5).

To cover the new kind of tepid case (Frame 6), when the best options for each side have the same infinite toll, we bring you a new commandment:

The *Markworthy Commandment*:

IF *INFINITE* TOLLS BE EQUAL,
THOU SHALT NOT PERMIT AN
ODD TIMER UNLESS THERE
BE A GREATER *EVEN* ONE.

Thus,

$$\{..\infty_4 \mid \infty_7..\} = \infty_5 \infty_8,$$

since this obeys the commandment, but

$$\{..\infty_8 \mid \infty_3..\} = \infty_9 \infty_{10},$$

since the trial tallies $\infty_9 \infty_4$ would disobey it. Cases when one player has no option (or upsets the board in a fit of anger) are dealt with by adjoining the suicidal option $..\overline{\infty}_{-1}$ for Left or $\infty_{-1}..$ for Right. Thus

$$\{..\infty_6 \mid \} = \{..\infty_6 \mid \infty_{-1}..\} = \infty_7 \infty_8.$$

A detailed explanation for these rules will be found in the Extras, where we shall also explain why battles sometimes end before their time.

Here is what your new tally machine will look like:

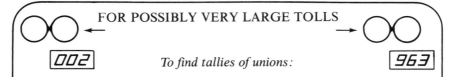

FOR POSSIBLY VERY LARGE TOLLS

002   *To find tallies of unions:*   963

On each side:
  If all tolls are FINITE, operate like old machine.
  Otherwise, take the INFINITE TOLL with the TINIEST TIMER.

To find tallies from options:

Select best options as before, using $-\infty < x < \infty$, except that among tallies with INFINITE TOLLS, prefer that with the LEAST EVEN TIMER if there is one, otherwise that with the GREATEST ODD TIMER ("no option" counts as $\overline{\infty}_{-1}$ for Left, ∞_{-1} for Right).
From the resulting form

$$\{..x_a | y_b..\}$$

compute tallies as before, *except* that if $x = y$ and both are infinite, you should (if necessary) increase the *even* timer of $x_{a+1} y_{b+1}$ by just enough to make it an even number larger than the odd one.

NEW UNRESTRICTED TALLY MACHINE

ONE FOR YOU, TWO FOR ME, NOTHING FOR BOTH OF US

This game, also called **Squares Off**, is played with several heaps of beans. The move is to take perfect square numbers (greater than 1) of beans away from any number of the heaps. Since a move removes at least 4 beans, heaps of 0, 1, 2, 3 cannot be further reduced. We declare that a move leaving 0 is an overriding win for whoever makes it (*nothing for both of us*), while one leaving 1 is an overriding win for Right (*one for you*) and one leaving 2 is an overriding win for Left (*two for me*). A move leaving 3 is not an overriding win for either player and does not terminate the game unless all other heaps are also of size 3. Table 5 gives the values.

1–10	$\overline{\infty}$	∞	0	$\infty_1\overline{\infty}_1$	$\overline{\infty}_2\overline{\infty}_1$	$\infty_1\infty_2$	$0_1 0_1$	0	$\infty_1\overline{\infty}_1$	$\overline{\infty}_3\overline{\infty}_1$
11–20	$\infty_1 0_2$	$0_1 0_1$	0	$\overline{\infty}_4\overline{\infty}_3$	$\infty_3\infty_4$	$\infty_1\overline{\infty}_1$	$0_1\overline{\infty}_1$	$\infty_1\infty_5$	$\infty_5 0_1$	1
21–30	$0_2\overline{\infty}_3$	$\infty_3 0_1$	$0_2\overline{\infty}_5$	$\infty_5 0_1$	$\infty_1\overline{\infty}_1$	$0_2\overline{\infty}_1$	$\infty_1 0_3$	$0_1 0_1$	$1_1 0_1$	$\overline{\infty}_4\overline{\infty}_3$
31–40	$\infty_3\overline{\infty}_4$	$0_2 0_3$	$0_1 0_1$	$\overline{\infty}_6\overline{\infty}_5$	$\infty_5 0_3$	$\infty_1\overline{\infty}_1$	$0_2\overline{\infty}_1$	$\infty_1\overline{\infty}_7$	$0_1\overline{\infty}_5$	$\infty_5\overline{\infty}_6$
41–50	$0_4\overline{\infty}_3$	$\infty_3 0_3$	$0_2\overline{\infty}_7$	$\infty_7 0_1$	$1_1 0_5$	$0_4\overline{\infty}_5$	$\infty_5 0_3$	$0_2 0_3$	$\infty_1\overline{\infty}_1$	$\overline{\infty}_6\infty_1$
51–60	$\infty_1 0_3$	$0_1 0_3$	$0_2 0_3$	$0_2\overline{\infty}_3$	$\infty_3\overline{\infty}_5$	$\infty_5 0_2$	$0_1 0_5$	$0_2 0_3$	$\overline{\infty}_8\overline{\infty}_7$	1
61–70	0	$0_1 0_5$	$0_4\overline{\infty}_5$	$\infty_1\overline{\infty}_1$	$\infty_7 0_1$	$\infty_1\overline{\infty}_5$	$\infty_5 0_5$	$0_2\overline{\infty}_9$	$1_1\overline{\infty}_3$	$\infty_3\overline{\infty}_7$
71–80	$0_2 0_5$	$0_3 0_5$	$0_2 0_3$	$0_4 0_5$	$0_3\overline{\infty}_7$	$\infty_7 0_2$	$0_1 0_5$	$0_2\overline{\infty}_5$	$\infty_5\infty_5$	$\infty_5 0_3$
81–90	$\infty_1\overline{\infty}_1$	$0_2\overline{\infty}_1$	$\infty_1\overline{\infty}_7$	$1_1\overline{\infty}_9$	$1_1 0_3$	$0_1\overline{\infty}_3$	$\infty_3 0_3$	$0_2 0_5$	$\overline{\infty}_7 0_3$	$0_6 0_7$
91–100	$0_4 0_5$	$0_3 0_3$	$0_2 0_3$	$0_1\overline{\infty}_5$	$\infty_5\infty_5$	$\infty_5 0_3$	$0_1 0_3$	$0_4\overline{\infty}_7$	$0_4\overline{\infty}_7$	$\infty_1\overline{\infty}_1$

Table 5. How "Squares Off" Jumbles Finite and Infinite Tolls.

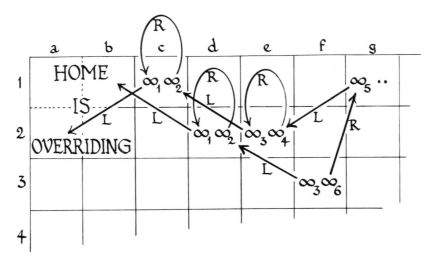

Figure 5. f3's Falada Fate.

TWO MORE FALADA GAMES

In each of these the players are forbidden to jump off the board and it is the first horse *home* that decides the game. Table 6 gives tallies for the first home *wins* version. Here there are two well-defined regions yielding overriding wins bordering a central region with finite tallies. Figure 5 forecasts the fate of a horse on the square f3 with tallies $\infty_3\infty_6$.

If the first horse home *loses* we get Table 7 in which no infinite tolls appear. In fact, whenever the only predeciding moves are suiciding ones, this always happens. In such cases we always get the same tallies as we would by passing a(n unenforceable?) law making suicide *illegal*.

Both the above games may end with a predeciding move. In this case the player unable, or unwilling, to move loses.

	a	b	c	d	e	f	g	h	i	j	k	l
1	Home is		$\infty_1\infty_2$	$\infty_1\infty_2$	$\infty_3\infty_4$	$\infty_3\infty_4$	$\infty_5\infty_6$	$\infty_5\infty_6$	$\infty_7\infty_8$	$\infty_7\infty_8$	$\infty_9\infty_{10}$	$\infty_9\infty_{10}$
2	Overriding!		$\infty_1\infty_2$	$\infty_1\infty_2$	$\infty_3\infty_4$	$\infty_3\infty_4$	$\infty_5\infty_6$	$\infty_5\infty_6$	$\infty_7\infty_8$	$\infty_7\infty_8$	$\infty_9\infty_{10}$	$\infty_9\infty_{10}$
3	$\overline{\infty}_2\overline{\infty}_1$	$\overline{\infty}_2\overline{\infty}_1$	$\infty_1\overline{\infty}_1$	$\infty_1\infty_4$	$\infty_3\infty_4$	$\infty_3\infty_6$	$\infty_5\infty_6$	$\infty_5\infty_8$	$\infty_7\infty_8$	$\infty_7\infty_{10}$	$\infty_9\infty_{10}$	$\infty_9\infty_{12}$
4	$\overline{\infty}_2\overline{\infty}_1$	$\overline{\infty}_2\overline{\infty}_1$	$\overline{\infty}_4\overline{\infty}_1$	0	0	$\infty_5\infty_6$	$\infty_5\infty_6$	$\infty_7\infty_8$	$\infty_7\infty_8$	$\infty_9\infty_{10}$	$\infty_9\infty_{10}$	$\infty_{11}\infty_{12}$
5	$\overline{\infty}_4\overline{\infty}_3$	$\overline{\infty}_4\overline{\infty}_3$	$\overline{\infty}_4\overline{\infty}_3$	0	0	1	1	$\infty_7\infty_8$	$\infty_7\infty_8$	$\infty_9\infty_{10}$	$\infty_9\infty_{10}$	$\infty_{11}\infty_{12}$
6	$\overline{\infty}_4\overline{\infty}_3$	$\overline{\infty}_4\overline{\infty}_3$	$\overline{\infty}_6\overline{\infty}_3$	$\overline{\infty}_6\overline{\infty}_5$	−1	0_10_1	1	2	2	$\infty_9\infty_{10}$	$\infty_9\infty_{12}$	$\infty_{11}\infty_{12}$
7	$\overline{\infty}_6\overline{\infty}_5$	$\overline{\infty}_6\overline{\infty}_5$	$\overline{\infty}_6\overline{\infty}_5$	$\overline{\infty}_6\overline{\infty}_5$	−1	−1	0	0	2	3	3	$\infty_{11}\infty_{12}$
8	$\overline{\infty}_6\overline{\infty}_5$	$\overline{\infty}_6\overline{\infty}_5$	$\overline{\infty}_8\overline{\infty}_5$	$\overline{\infty}_8\overline{\infty}_7$	$\overline{\infty}_8\overline{\infty}_7$	−2	0	0	1	1	3	4
9	$\overline{\infty}_8\overline{\infty}_7$	$\overline{\infty}_8\overline{\infty}_7$	$\overline{\infty}_8\overline{\infty}_7$	$\overline{\infty}_8\overline{\infty}_7$	$\overline{\infty}_8\overline{\infty}_7$	−2	−2	−1	0_10_1	1	2	2
10	$\overline{\infty}_8\overline{\infty}_7$	$\overline{\infty}_8\overline{\infty}_7$	$\overline{\infty}_{10}\overline{\infty}_7$	$\overline{\infty}_{10}\overline{\infty}_9$	$\overline{\infty}_{10}\overline{\infty}_9$	$\overline{\infty}_{10}\overline{\infty}_9$	−3	−1	−1	0	0	2
11	$\overline{\infty}_{10}\overline{\infty}_9$	$\overline{\infty}_{10}\overline{\infty}_9$	$\overline{\infty}_{10}\overline{\infty}_9$	$\overline{\infty}_{10}\overline{\infty}_9$	$\overline{\infty}_{10}\overline{\infty}_9$	$\overline{\infty}_{12}\overline{\infty}_9$	−3	−3	−2	0	0	1
12	$\overline{\infty}_{10}\overline{\infty}_9$	$\overline{\infty}_{10}\overline{\infty}_9$	$\overline{\infty}_{12}\overline{\infty}_9$	$\overline{\infty}_{12}\overline{\infty}_{11}$	$\overline{\infty}_{12}\overline{\infty}_{11}$	$\overline{\infty}_{12}\overline{\infty}_{11}$	$\overline{\infty}_{12}\overline{\infty}_{11}$	−4	−2	−2	−1	0_10_1

Table 6. Tallies for Falada, First Home Wins.

Home is		0	0	2	1	2	2	4	3	4	4	6	5	6	6
Suiciding!		1	0	1	1	3	2	3	3	5	4	5	5	7	6
0	-1	$0_1 0_1$	$0_1 0_1$	$1_1 0_1$	1	$1_1 1_1$	$1\frac12$	$3_1 2_1$	3	$3_1 3_1$	$3\frac12$	$5_1 4_1$	5	$5_1 5_1$	$5\frac12$
0	0	$0_1 0_1$	0	$0_2 0_3$	$\frac12$	$\frac12$	2	1	2	2	4	3	4	4	6
-2	-1	$0_1 -1_1$	$0_3 0_2$	0	1	0	1	1	3	2	3	3	5	4	5
-1	-1	-1	$-\frac12$	-1	$0_3 0_3$	$\frac14$	$1_1 \tfrac12_1$	1	$1_1 1_1$	$1\frac12$	$3_1 2_1$	3	$3_1 3_1$	$3\frac12$	$5_1 4_1$
-2	-3	$-1_1 -1_1$	$-\frac12$	0	$-\frac14$	0	$0_4 0_5$	$\frac12$	$\frac12$	2	1	2	2	4	3
-2	-2	$-1\frac12$	-2	-1	$-\tfrac12_1 -1_1$	$0_5 0_4$	0	1	0	1	1	3	2	3	3
-4	-3	$-2_1 -3_1$	-1	-1	-1	$-\frac12$	-1	$0_5 0_5$	$\frac14$	$1_1 \tfrac12_1$	1	$1_1 1_1$	$1\frac12$	$3_1 2_1$	3
-3	-3	-3	-2	-3	$-1_1 -1_1$	$-\frac12$	0	$-\frac14$	0	$0_6 0_7$	$\frac12$	$\frac12$	2	1	2
-4	-5	$-3_1 -3_1$	-2	-2	$-1\frac12$	-2	-1	$-\tfrac12_1 -1_1$	$0_7 0_6$	0	1	0	1	1	3
-4	-4	$-3\frac12$	-4	-3	$-2_1 -3_1$	-1	-1	-1	$-\frac12$	-1	$0_7 0_7$	$\frac14$	$1_1 \tfrac12_1$	1	$1_1 1_1$
-6	-5	$-4_1 -5_1$	-3	-3	-3	-2	-3	$-1_1 -1_1$	$-\frac12$	0	$-\frac14$	0	$0_8 0_9$	$\frac12$	$\frac12$
-5	-5	-5	-4	-5	$-3_1 -3_1$	-2	-2	$-1\frac12$	-2	-1	$-\tfrac12_1 -1_1$	$0_9 0_8$	0	1	0
-6	-7	$-5_1 -5_1$	-4	-4	$-3\frac12$	-4	-3	$-2_1 -3_1$	-1	-1	-1	$-\frac12$	-1	$0_9 0_9$	$\frac14$
-6	-6	$-5\frac12$	-6	-5	$-4_1 -5_1$	-3	-3	-3	-2	-3	$-1_1 -1_1$	$-\frac12$	0	$-\frac14$	0

Table 7. Tallies for Falada, First Home Loses.

BAKED ALASKA

This is a particularly interesting modification of Coolcakes. It is played exactly like that game, except that a person who sees a *square* cake may eat it and win the game outright. The tallies for a square cake are therefore $\infty_1 \overline{\infty}_1$ but apart from this the game behaves like an ordinary union in which it is illegal to create a square cake, so that all other tolls are finite. (Many other games with predeciding moves behave like this.)

To make Table 8 as clear as possible we've written

$$a, b, c, d, e, \quad \text{instead of} \quad 1, 2, 3, 4, 5,$$

as timers, and written simply $\mathcal{D}$ for the illegal square cakes. For a vertical strip of two squares, Left moves to 0, but Right has no (non-suicidal) move, so the value is 1. For longer vertical strips, the value is successively halved since Right's best move is to eat an end square. Other small cakes tend to be hot, but there are some surprising exceptions (61/128 for a 5 by 11 cake!). The central values are mostly cold, with a hot coating, as the name might suggest. It seems that for large enough m, the values of m by $m+1$ cakes are alternately $-1/256$ and $(2^{-8}+2^{2-m})_a 0_a$

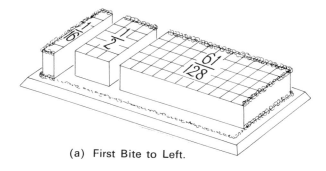

(a) First Bite to Left.

Figure 6. The Fro

	1	2	3	4	5	6	7	8
1	$\mathcal{D}$	-1	$-\frac{1}{2}$	$-\frac{1}{4}$	$-\frac{1}{8}$	$-\frac{1}{16}$	$-\frac{1}{32}$	
2	1	$\mathcal{D}$	$2_a - \frac{1}{2_a}$	$-\frac{1}{2}$	$\frac{1}{2_b} - \frac{1}{8_a}$	$\frac{1}{2_a} - \frac{1}{16_a}$	$\frac{7}{8_b} - \frac{1}{32_a}$	
3	$\frac{1}{2}$	$\frac{1}{2_a} - 2_a$	$\mathcal{D}$	-1	$-\frac{1}{2}$	$-\frac{1}{4}$	$0_a - \frac{1}{16_a}$	$\frac{1}{4_a} - \frac{1}{32_a}$
4	$\frac{1}{4}$	$\frac{1}{2}$	1	$\mathcal{D}$	$\frac{5}{4_a} - \frac{1}{2_a}$	$\frac{3}{2_a} - \frac{1}{4_a}$	$2_a 0_b$	$\frac{1}{4}$
5	$\frac{1}{8}$	$\frac{1}{8_a} - \frac{1}{2_b}$	$\frac{1}{2}$	$\frac{1}{2_a} - \frac{5}{4_a}$	$\mathcal{D}$	$0_c - \frac{5}{16_a}$	$1_a - \frac{1}{32_b}$	0
6	$\frac{1}{16}$	$\frac{1}{16_a} - \frac{1}{2_a}$	$\frac{1}{4}$	$\frac{1}{4_a} - \frac{3}{2_a}$	$\frac{5}{16_a} 0_c$	$\mathcal{D}$	$\frac{3}{4}$	$\frac{3}{4_a} 0_a$
7	$\frac{1}{32}$	$\frac{1}{32_a} - \frac{7}{8_b}$	$\frac{1}{16_a} 0_a$	$0_b - 2_a$	$\frac{1}{32_b} - 1_a$	$-\frac{3}{4}$	$\mathcal{D}$	$-\frac{1}{2}$
8	$\frac{1}{64}$	.	$\frac{1}{32_a} - \frac{1}{4_a}$	$-\frac{1}{4}$	0	$0_a - \frac{3}{4_a}$	$\frac{1}{2}$	$\mathcal{D}$
9	$\frac{1}{128}$	.	$\frac{1}{64_a} - \frac{7}{16_b}$	$-\frac{7}{16_c} - \frac{1}{2_b}$	$-\frac{1}{4}$	$-\frac{1}{4_a} - \frac{13}{16_a}$	0	$0_a - \frac{33}{64_a}$
10	$\frac{1}{256}$		.	$-\frac{15}{32_a} - \frac{3}{4_b}$	$-\frac{3}{8}$	$-\frac{1}{4}$	$-\frac{1}{8}$	0
11	$\frac{1}{512}$		.	$-\frac{31}{64_c} - 1_c$	$-\frac{61}{128}$	$-\frac{61}{128_a} - 1_a$	$-\frac{1}{4}$	$-\frac{1}{4_c} - \frac{1}{4_b}$
12	.			$-\frac{63}{128_c} - 1\frac{1}{4_a}$		$-\frac{1}{2}$	$-\frac{3}{8}$	$-\frac{5}{16}$
13	.					$-\frac{3}{4}$	$-\frac{1}{2}$	$-\frac{1}{2_a} - \frac{1}{2_a}$
14				.		$-\frac{3}{4}$	$-\frac{3}{4}$	$-\frac{1}{2}$
15						$-\frac{125}{128_b} - \frac{3}{2_a}$	$-\frac{7}{8}$	$-\frac{7}{8_a} - 1_a$
16						$-\frac{63}{64}$	$-\frac{15}{16}$	$-\frac{7}{8}$
17							$-\frac{31}{32}$	$-\frac{15}{16}$
18							$-\frac{63}{64}$	$-\frac{31}{32}$
19								-1

Table 8. Finicky Fig

(m odd), while those of m by $m+k$ cakes for

$k =$	2	3	4	5	6	7	8	9	10	11
are always	0	$\frac{1}{4}$	$\frac{3}{8}$	$\frac{7}{16}$	$\frac{1}{2}$	$\frac{3}{4}$	$\frac{7}{8}$	$\frac{15}{16}$	$\frac{31}{32}$	1

The 6 by 17 cake is hot with tallies

$$\frac{133}{128_3}\ \frac{2039}{2048_5}.$$

Figures 6(a) and 6(b) show which parts of this cake should remain after the hot battles started by Left and Right, respectively.

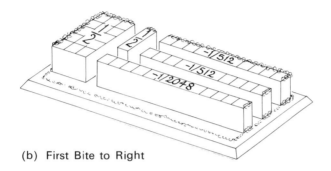

(b) First Bite to Right

...ains of Baked Alaska.

henceforth (col 9) -2^{2-n} (col 11)

henceforth $(1-2^{4-n})_b(-2^{2-n})_a$

henceforth $(\tfrac{1}{2}-2^{5-n})_b(-2^{3-n})_a$

and, for $n \geq 13$, $(\tfrac{3}{2}-2^{9-n})_d(\tfrac{1}{2}-2^{5-n})_c$

9	10	11	12	13	14	15	16	17
								$\frac{133}{128_c}\frac{2039}{2048_e}$
							$\frac{63}{64}$	$\frac{31}{32}$
							$\frac{15}{16}$	$\frac{15}{16}$
		-2^{2-n}		$\frac{3}{4}$		$\frac{3}{2_a}\frac{125}{128_b}$	$\frac{7}{8}$	$\frac{7}{8}$
		$\frac{61}{128}$	$\frac{1}{2_a}\frac{503}{1024_b}$	$\frac{1}{2}$	$\frac{7}{8}$	$\frac{7}{8}$	$\frac{3}{4}$	$\frac{3}{4}$
$\frac{7}{16_b}-\frac{1}{64_a}$		$1\frac{61}{a128_a}$	$\frac{1}{2}$	$\frac{3}{8}$	$\frac{3}{4}$	$1\frac{7}{a8_a}$	$\frac{1}{2}$	$\frac{1}{2}$
$\frac{1}{2_b}\frac{7}{16_c}$	$\frac{3}{8}$	$\frac{1}{4}$	$\frac{3}{8}$	$\frac{1}{2_a}\frac{3}{2_a}$	$\frac{1}{2}$	$\frac{1}{2}$	$\frac{7}{16}$	$\frac{7}{16}$
$\frac{1}{4}$	$\frac{1}{4}$	$\frac{1}{4}$	$\frac{5}{16}$	$\frac{3}{8}$	$\frac{7}{16}$	$\frac{7}{16}$	$\frac{3}{8}$	$\frac{3}{8}$
$\frac{13}{16_a}\frac{1}{4_a}$	$\frac{1}{8}$	$\frac{1}{4_b}\frac{1}{4_c}$	$\frac{1}{4}$	$\frac{1}{4}$	$\frac{3}{8}$	$\frac{3}{8}$	$\frac{1}{4}$	$\frac{1}{4}$
0	0	0	0	0	$\frac{1}{4}$	$\frac{1}{4}$	0	0
$\frac{33}{64_a}0_a$	$\frac{1}{128_a}0_a$	$-\frac{1}{256}$	$\frac{3}{512_a}0_a$	$-\frac{1}{256}$	$\frac{9}{2048_a}0_a$	$-\frac{1}{256}$	$\frac{33}{8192_a}0_a$	$-\frac{1}{256}$
♩	♩	♩	♩	♩	♩	♩	♩	♩
$0_a-\frac{1}{128_a}$	$\frac{1}{256}$	$0_a-\frac{3}{512_a}$	$\frac{1}{256}$	$0_a-\frac{9}{2048_a}$	$\frac{1}{256}$	$0_a-\frac{33}{8192_a}$	$\frac{1}{256}$	$0_a-\frac{129}{32768_a}$
0	0	0	0	0	0	0	0	0
$-\frac{1}{4}$	$-\frac{1}{4}$	$-\frac{1}{4}$	$-\frac{1}{4}$	$-\frac{1}{4}$	$-\frac{1}{4}$	$-\frac{1}{4}$	$-\frac{1}{4}$	
$-\frac{3}{8}$	$-\frac{3}{8}$	$-\frac{3}{8}$	$-\frac{3}{8}$	$-\frac{3}{8}$	$-\frac{3}{8}$	$-\frac{3}{8}$		
$-\frac{7}{16}$	$-\frac{7}{16}$	$-\frac{7}{16}$	$-\frac{7}{16}$	$-\frac{7}{16}$	$-\frac{7}{16}$			
$-\frac{1}{2}$	$-\frac{1}{2}$	$-\frac{1}{2}$	$-\frac{1}{2}$	$-\frac{1}{2}$				
$-\frac{3}{4}$	$-\frac{3}{4}$	$-\frac{3}{4}$	$-\frac{3}{4}$					
$-\frac{7}{8}$	$-\frac{7}{8}$	$-\frac{7}{8}$						
$-\frac{15}{16}$	$-\frac{15}{16}$							
$-\frac{31}{32}$								

Baked Alaska.

EXTRAS

A FELICITOUS FALADA FIELD

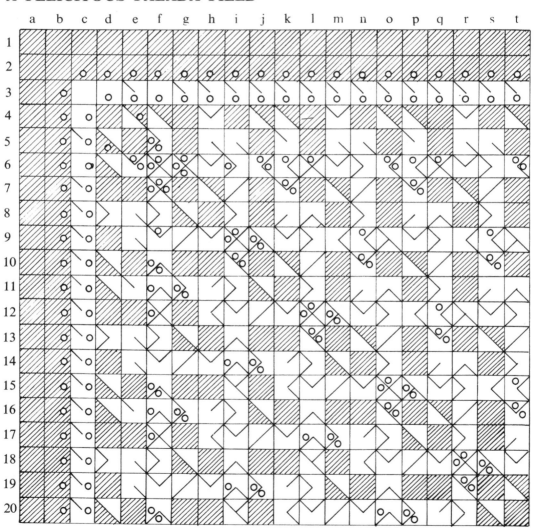

Figure 7. No Faults, Failures or Faltering on this infallible Falada Field.

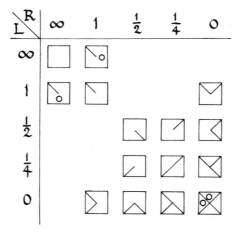

Figure 7(a). Toll Losses When Playing on Falada Field.

Each square should be considered as divided into Left and Right *halves* by the NW–SE diagonal. Make *normal* moves, 2 squares West and 1 square North for Left (2N & 1W for R), but *abnormal* ones, 2W and 1S for Left (2N & 1E for R) if there is a small circle in the S(E) of the square. Move every horse from any square which is shaded (in your half). If there is no such horse, move just one horse from an unshaded square containing a maximum number of half-diagonals, especially if there is a half-diagonal in your half. The key of Fig. 7(a) goes into more detail, indicating the loss in toll value from either player's point of view. If there is no change in toll value, then the timer changes by 1, unless there is a small circle in the W(N), in which case it changes by 3, plus 2 more for each similarly placed circle found by making NW diagonal steps of length 3. For example, Right's half of square p20 is empty, so Right should hope to find a better move. The key tells us that Right's toll worsens (increases) by 1 if he moves, but Left's toll is unchanged. If he moves from the square it should be abnormally (circle in S) and his timer changes by 3 (circle in W) + 2 × 3 (squares m17, j14 and g11 contain similarly situated circles, but d8 does not) = 9. Extrapolation of Table 4 shows that Left would move from -1 to $..-1_9$, while Right would move to 0.

THE RULES FOR TALLIES ON INFINITE TOLLS

We explain these by considering the examples

$$\{..\infty_4|\infty_7..\} \quad \text{and} \quad \{..\infty_8|\infty_3..\}$$

(in each of which Left is sure to win) in more detail. In the first example both players would like to move—Left to obtain his win at the 5th move and Right to postpone it to the 8th. It therefore behaves like a hot game, and has tallies $\infty_5\infty_8$. In the second example, Left should certainly move and reach his overriding win at the 9th move. But if Right chose to move in this component the game would only last 4 moves as against the 10 that would result if he made a pass move in this component and then allowed Left to take his 9-move win. He can make this pass move if he has a less harmful move elsewhere, and indeed by doing so he will win the whole game if in any component he has an overriding win in 9 moves or less.

In the case $\{..\infty_8|\ \}$ Right will be forced to pass since he has no option and so its tallies are again $\infty_9\infty_{10}$, just as if he had $\infty_{-1}..$ for an option.

TIME MAY BE SHORTER THAN YOU THINK!

Our timers sometimes give the wrong answer for the length of the hot battle, but this won't matter since they always get the winner right. For the example

$$\{..x_4|x_7..\} \lor y,$$

we find the tallies

$$x_9x_8 \lor y = (x+y)_9(x+y)_8,$$

which suggest that if Left starts, the battle will last for 9 moves. In fact it only last 5 moves, since to avoid moving in y he moves to

$$..x_4 \lor y$$

rather than passing in the tepid component. But since there's only one battle still being fought, and he wins it, Left doesn't care how long it lasts. The left tally x_9 indicates a battle that Left *can* drag on for 9 moves, *if he needs to.*

Chapter 11

Games Infinite and Indefinite

"I find", said 'e, "things very much as 'ow I've always found,
For mostly they goes up and down, or else goes round and round".
Patrick Reginald Chalmers, *Green Days and Blue Days*,
Roundabouts and Swings.

For ever and ever when I move.
How dull it is to pause, to make an end.
Alfred Lord Tennyson, Ulysses, l. 21.

Most of our examples in *Winning Ways* have had only finitely many positions. But a game can have infinitely many positions and still satisfy the ending condition. A few such are described in the first part of this chapter. More interesting are the games obtained by dropping the ending condition, which we call **loopy games**, since it's often possible to find oneself returning to the same position over and over again. In Chapter 12 we'll describe, amongst other things, C.A.B. Smith's complete theory for *impartial* loopy games, but in this chapter we'll see that the theory of partizan loopy games is completely different.

The ideas in this chapter are hardly used elsewhere in the book.

INFINITE HACKENBUSH

You may have wondered why numbers like $\frac{2}{3}$ don't appear as values. The answer is, they do! To see how, let's look at some Hackenbush positions that get near $\frac{2}{3}$:

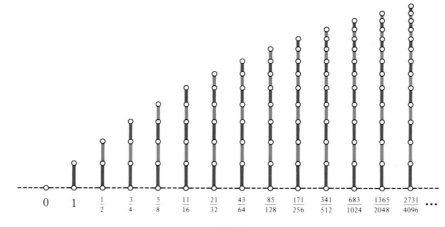

$$0 \quad 1 \quad \frac{1}{2} \quad \frac{3}{4} \quad \frac{5}{8} \quad \frac{11}{16} \quad \frac{21}{32} \quad \frac{43}{64} \quad \frac{85}{128} \quad \frac{171}{256} \quad \frac{341}{512} \quad \frac{683}{1024} \quad \frac{1365}{2048} \quad \frac{2731}{4096} \cdots$$

Maybe the value of an *infinite* alternating beanstalk will be *exactly* $\frac{2}{3}$? If so, Fig. 1 should be a second-player win, since its value is

$$\tfrac{2}{3} + \tfrac{2}{3} + \tfrac{2}{3} - 2 = 0.$$

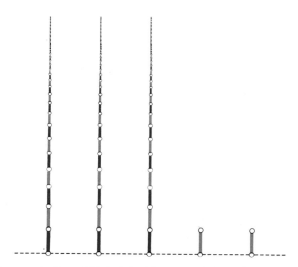

Figure 1. Two-Thirds of a Move can Take a Long Time.

After any Left opening move the value will be

$$(\tfrac{2}{3} - \varepsilon) + \tfrac{2}{3} + \tfrac{2}{3} - 2$$

and by moving one higher up in another beanstalk, Right can achieve

$$(\tfrac{2}{3} - \varepsilon) + (\tfrac{2}{3} + \tfrac{1}{2}\varepsilon) + \tfrac{2}{3} - 2.$$

If Left now responds in the remaining beanstalk, the rest of the game is finite with value

$$(\tfrac{2}{3} - \varepsilon) + (\tfrac{2}{3} + \tfrac{1}{2}\varepsilon) + (\tfrac{2}{3} - \varepsilon') - 2 < 0,$$

so Right wins. After any other Left move, Right can move from $\frac{2}{3}$ to $\frac{2}{3} + \frac{1}{2}\varepsilon$ leaving a finite game of value strictly less than

$$(\tfrac{2}{3} - \varepsilon) + (\tfrac{2}{3} + \tfrac{1}{2}\varepsilon) + (\tfrac{2}{3} + \tfrac{1}{2}\varepsilon) - 2 = 0.$$

It's just about as easy to check that Left wins if Right starts.

The argument is quite general and can be used to produce a Hackenbush string of any real value. For instance the binary expansion of π is

$$3.00100100001111110110101010001000100001011010001\ldots,$$

so the string of Fig. 2, to which Berlekamp's Rule (Extras to Chapter 3) applies, has value π.

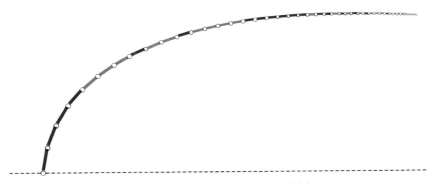

Figure 2. A Hackenbush String of Value π.

INFINITE ENDERS

But can we really make use of Hackenbush theory for infinite graphs? Is it quite safe? Do we have to worry about limiting processes?

Yes, it's quite safe, it all works, there aren't any limiting processes involved *and* we've already proved it! Although those Hackenbush strings are infinite, any Hackenbush game you play with them will come to an end in a finite time because they satisfy the *ending condition* of Chapter 1—it's not possible to have an infinite sequence of moves (even if the players don't play alternately).

In this chapter we'll use the word **ender** for a game which satisfies this strong ending condition. You can see that it's perfectly possible for a game to have infinitely many positions and still be an ender. Although most of our examples had only finitely many positions we've been careful to make the theory apply to arbitrarily large enders.

THE INFINITE ORDINAL NUMBERS

But not all infinite beanstalks have ordinary real number values. The entirely blue one marked ω in Fig. 3 has an infinite value because we can see that

$$0 < \omega, \quad 1 < \omega, \quad 2 < \omega, \quad 3 < \omega, \quad \ldots.$$

Why didn't we just call this ∞, or maybe $\aleph_0$, since it has a countably infinite number of edges? The answer is that

$$\omega + 1 > \omega$$

whereas it's usually convenient to write

$$\infty + 1 = \infty, \qquad \aleph_0 + 1 = \aleph_0.$$

Figure 3 shows how, even when you've got to the top of an infinite beanstalk, you can always add another edge to make a still higher one. The kind of numbers that arise here are the **infinite ordinal numbers** studied and named by Georg Cantor and they go on and on and on and on and on and …

$$0,1,2,\ldots,\omega,\omega+1,\omega+2,\ldots,\omega\times 2,\ldots,\omega\times 3,\ldots,\ldots,\omega\times\omega = \omega^2,\ldots,\omega^3,\ldots,\omega^4,\ldots,\omega^\omega,\ldots,\omega^{\omega^2},\ldots,\omega^{\omega^\omega},\ldots,,\ldots$$

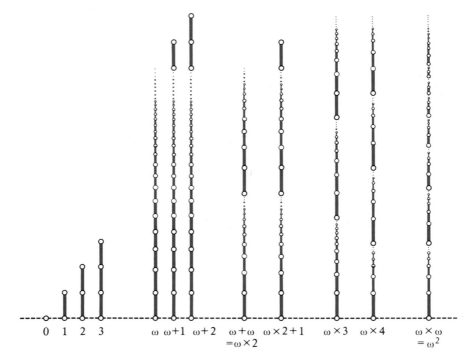

Figure 3. Beanstalks that go On and On and On and On and On and . . .:

A fairly typical infinite ordinal is

$$(\omega^{\omega^\omega} \times 5) + (\omega^{\omega^2} \times 7) + \omega^\omega + (\omega^3 \times 2) + \omega^2 + 47.$$

OTHER NUMBERS

But in our theory there are even more numbers, for instance the *negatives* of Cantor's ordinal numbers, corresponding to completely *red* beanstalks, and a much greater variety when we allow blue and red edges together (Fig. 4). You can learn how to multiply them, and divide and take square roots, from ONAG; but you can *add* and *subtract* them, just by playing the games.

Beanstalks aren't the only infinite enders in Hackenbush. Figure 5 shows the values of some infinite trees. Every Blue-Red Hackenbush position that is an ender has *some* number for its value (not necessarily real or finite).

INFINITE NIM

You can also have purely *green* infinite beanstalks (or snakes) which are *impartial* enders. If we made all the beanstalks in Fig. 3 green, their values would include *infinite nimbers*:

$$0, *1, *2, *3, \ldots, *\omega, *(\omega+1), *(\omega+2), \ldots, *(\omega \times 2), *(\omega \times 2+1), \ldots, *(\omega \times 3), \ldots, *(\omega \times 4), \ldots, *\omega^2, \ldots$$

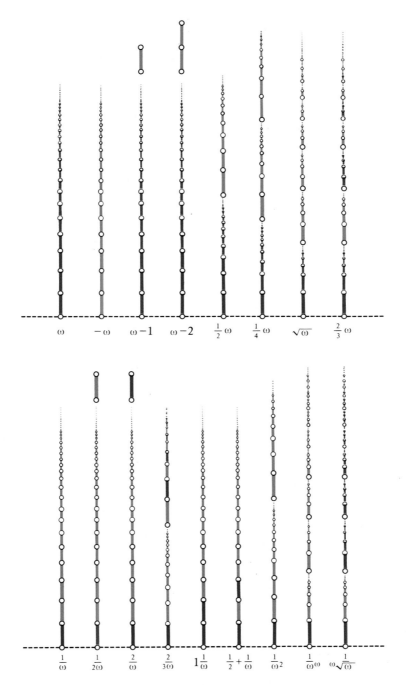

Figure 4. Brain-Baffling Bichromatic Beanstalks.

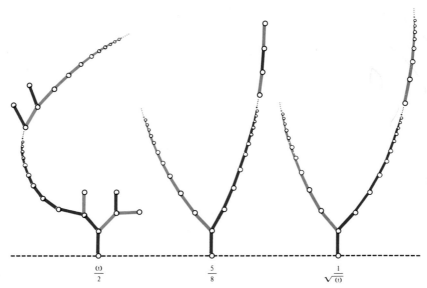

Figure 5. Some Infinite Trees (but with only *finitely* many forks).

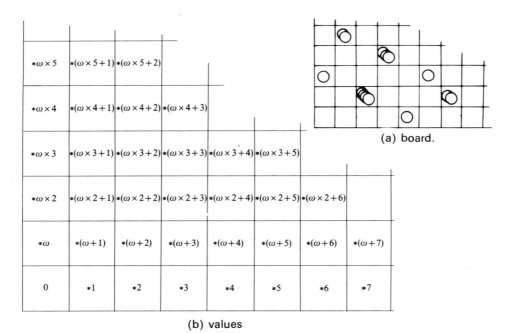

(a) board.

(b) values

Figure 6. Two-Dee Nim has Georgous Values.

The theory of Nim applies equally to these by separately nim-adding coefficients of the various powers of ω:

$$*(\omega^\omega \times 5 + \omega^2 + \omega \times 7 + 5) + *(\omega^2 \times 3 + \omega + 3) = *(\omega^\omega \times 5 + \omega^2 \times 2 + \omega \times 6 + 6).$$

This is equivalent to expanding in powers of 2 and cancelling repetitions in pairs, when we use Cantor's equations:

$$2^\omega = \omega, \qquad 2^{\omega \times 2} = \omega^2, \qquad 2^{\omega \times 3} = \omega^3, \qquad \ldots, \qquad 2^{\omega^2} = \omega^\omega, \qquad \ldots$$

(the equation $2^\omega = \omega$ is another reason for not using the cardinal name $\aleph_0$, which is (normally!) much smaller than $2^{\aleph_0}$).

Two-dimensional Nim uses a quarter-infinite board (Fig. 6(a)) and a finite number of counters of which any number can be on the same square. A counter may be moved any distance *leftwards* in its own row, or to *any* position in any *lower* row. The values shown in Fig. 6(b) are all the nimbers of the form

$$*(\omega \times a + b).$$

Of course, there is a three-dimensional version with typical value

$$*(\omega^2 \times a + \omega \times b + c).$$

Anyone for Hilbert Nim?

THE INFINITE SPRAGUE-GRUNDY AND SMITH THEORIES

Any impartial ender, G, has a value of the form

$$*\alpha$$

for some, possibly infinite, ordinal number α. The value of α is found by the Mex Rule: it is the least ordinal number different from

$$\beta, \gamma, \delta, \ldots$$

where

$$*\beta, *\gamma, *\delta, \ldots$$

are the values of the options of G.

So you can use the theory of infinite Nim to play purely green Hackenbush positions, provided they're enders.

Impartial games that need not end are handled by a similar generalization of the Smith theory, which comes in Chapter 12. Their values have the forms

$$*\alpha \quad \text{or} \quad \infty_{\beta\gamma\delta\ldots}$$

for possibly infinite ordinals

$$\alpha \quad ; \quad \beta, \gamma, \delta, \ldots .$$

SOME SUPERHEAVY ATOMS

There are some quite playable games in which there arise values such as

$$\{\ldots, -2, -1, 0, 1, 2, \ldots \mid \ldots, -2, -1, 0, 1, 2, \ldots\} = \mathbb{Z}|\mathbb{Z}, \quad \text{and} \quad \{\mathbb{Z}|\{\mathbb{Z}|\mathbb{Z}\}\} = \mathbb{Z}\|\mathbb{Z}|\mathbb{Z}.$$

(The symbol $\mathbb{Z}$ is the standard mathematical name for the collection of all integers

$$\ldots, -3, -2, -1, 0, 1, 2, 3, \ldots .)$$

In ONAG a few of these were assigned particular names and some relationships explored, e.g.

$$\infty = \mathbb{Z}\|\mathbb{Z}|\mathbb{Z},$$

$$\pm\infty = \infty| -\infty = \mathbb{Z}|\mathbb{Z},$$

$$\infty\pm\infty = \infty|0 = \mathbb{Z}|0,$$

$$\infty + \infty = 2.\infty = \mathbb{Z}\|\mathbb{Z}|0 \ (\text{``double infinity''}).$$

In many ways the games ∞ and $\pm\infty$ behave like enormously magnified versions of $\uparrow$ and $*$; there is in fact an infinitely magnifying operation defined by

$$\int^z G = \{\textstyle\int^z G^L + n | \int^z G^R - n\}_{n=0,1,2,\ldots}$$

and indeed we have

$$\int^z * = \mathbb{Z}|\mathbb{Z} = \pm\infty$$

but the integrated version of $\uparrow$ is rather smaller than $\mathbb{Z}\|\mathbb{Z}|\mathbb{Z}$.

The rest of this chapter is entirely devoted to

LOOPY GAMES

We call games that *don't* satisfy the ending condition **loopy**, because they often have closed cycles of legal moves. We will meet some impartial loopy games in Chapter 12. Now for the partizan ones!

A **play** in a loopy game G is a sequence, for example,

$$G \rightarrow G^L \rightarrow G^{LL} \rightarrow G^{LLR} \rightarrow G^{LLRL} \rightarrow G^{LLRLR} \rightarrow G^{LLRLRR} \rightarrow G^{LLRLRRR} \rightarrow \ldots$$

which may be finite or infinite and need not be alternately Left and Right. A play in a sum of several games defines plays in the individual components in an obvious way; for example

$$G+H \rightarrow G^L+H \rightarrow G^L+H^R \rightarrow G^{LL}+H^R \rightarrow G^{LLR}+H^R \rightarrow G^{LLR}+H^{RL} \rightarrow G^{LLRR}+H^{RL}$$

$$\rightarrow G^{LLRR}+H^{RLL} \rightarrow \ldots$$

has the component plays

$$G \rightarrow G^L \rightarrow G^{LL} \rightarrow G^{LLR} \rightarrow G^{LLRR} \rightarrow \ldots \text{ in } G$$

and

$$H \rightarrow H^R \rightarrow H^{RL} \rightarrow H^{RLL} \rightarrow \ldots \qquad \text{in } H.$$

Observe that when the total play is alternating, the component plays need not be.

Now when the *total* play is finite, the normal play rule tells us who wins—a player who fails to move on his turn, loses. But we must add other rules to determine the outcome when the total play is *infinite*. We shall say that

> A player *wins* the sum just if
> he wins *all* the components in
> which there is *infinite* play.
> If any infinite component play is
> *drawn*, or if two of them are won
> by *different* players, the sum is *drawn*.

FIXED, MIXED AND FREE

So, as well as the letter

$$\gamma, \text{ say,}$$

(we shall use loopy Greek letters for loopy games) that describes the structure (i.e. the *moves*) of any component game, we'll need something to tell us the *outcome* for each infinite play in γ. Certain infinite plays will be counted as wins for Left $(+)$, others as wins for Right $(-)$ and the rest as drawn games $(\pm$, or blank). A symbol

$$\gamma^{\bullet}$$

indicates a particular way of making these decisions, and the special cases

$$\gamma^{+} \qquad \text{and} \qquad \gamma^{-}$$

denote the variants of γ in which *all* infinite plays are treated alike, respectively as

$$\text{wins for Left} \quad \text{and} \quad \text{wins for Right.}$$

If **no** infinite play is drawn, we shall say that $\gamma^{\bullet}$ has been **fixed**—in particular γ^{+} and γ^{-} are the two fixed forms of γ most favorable to Left and to Right. When we omit the superscript, it will be understood that *all* infinite plays are drawn, and then we call γ **free**. Games $\gamma^{\bullet}$ in which some of the infinite plays are drawn, and some are not, may be called **mixed**.

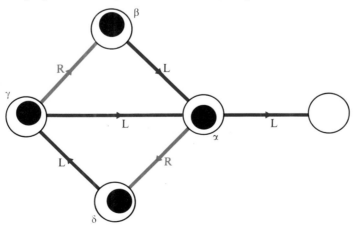

Figure 7. What's the Outcome if All Infinite Plays are Draws?

In Fig. 7, there's a counter on each of the positions α, β, γ and δ. Left moves by sliding a counter in the appropriate direction along a blue edge, Right along a red one. If all infinite plays are counted as draws, what's the outcome (a) if Left starts? (b) if Right starts?

ONSIDES AND OFFSIDES, UPSUMS AND DOWNSUMS

We're really interested in adding free games, in which all the infinite plays are counted as drawn. Let's tell you our game plan.

In general there's a way of analyzing a loopy game γ in terms of two rather less loopy ones, s and t, and we write

$$\gamma = s\&t, \qquad s = \gamma(\mathbf{on}), \qquad t = \gamma(\mathbf{off})$$

to indicate this relationship. The games s and t are called the **sides** of γ, s being the **onside** and t the **offside**. Often the sides are ordinary ending games, or *enders*, such as 1, $4\frac{1}{2}$, ↑, ∗, and in almost all other cases they are *stoppers*, which turn out to be almost as tractable. (Always $s \geqslant t$.)

Now to add games given like this you'll need to know about **upsums** $(a \curlywedge c)$ and **downsums** $(b \curlyvee d)$, because

$$
\begin{aligned}
\text{when} \quad & \gamma = a \ \& \ b \\
\text{and} \quad & \delta = c \ \& \ d \\
\hline
\text{then} \quad & \gamma + \delta = (a \curlywedge c)\&(b \curlyvee d).
\end{aligned}
$$

───── Use ─────

UPSUMS for ONSIDES!
DOWNSUMS for OFFSIDES!

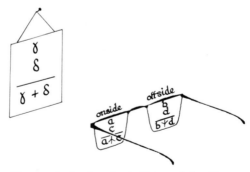

Figure 8. Seeing Both Sides of the Picture.

Onsides (and so upsums) are relevant when you intend to count draws as wins for Left, offsides (and downsums) if you count them as wins for Right. In fact loopy game theory is a sort of double-vision double-take of ending game theory (Fig. 8)!

But it's just about as easy as the ordinary theory when you know what it all means. We'll try to let you in gently ...

STOPPERS

A **stopper**, g, is a game that, when played on its own, has no ultimately *alternating* (Left and Right) infinite sequence of legal moves

$$g \rightarrow g^X \rightarrow g^{XY} \rightarrow \ldots \rightarrow g^{XY\ldots L} \rightarrow g^{XY\ldots LR} \rightarrow g^{XY\ldots LRL} \rightarrow \ldots$$

So, *no matter which position you start playing from*, play will ultimately *stop*. (But it need not have *ended* because there might still be moves available for the player whose turn it *isn't*.)

We'll use small latin letters $(a,b,\ldots,g,\ldots,s,t,\ldots)$ for stoppers, and when we write

$$\gamma(\mathbf{on}) = s, \qquad \gamma(\mathbf{off}) = t,$$

all we mean is that s and t are stoppers for which

$$\gamma^+ = s^+, \qquad \gamma^- = t^-,$$

so that γ can be replaced by s if we recount all its draws as wins for Left, and by t if we recount them as wins for Right. Since then the values of s and t completely determine that of γ, we can write

$$\gamma = s\&t.$$

Notice that if γ already *is* a stopper, say　…

$$\gamma = c,$$

then

$$\gamma(\mathbf{on}) = \gamma(\mathbf{off}) = c,$$

and so

$$\gamma = c\&c.$$

But beware! Not every game has onsides and offsides which are stoppers. See Bach's Carousel in the Extras.

on, off AND dud

Let's have a look at some of the simplest loopy games. You can't get much simpler than the games with only one position:

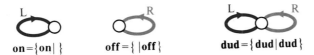

$$\mathbf{on} = \{\mathbf{on}|\ \} \qquad \mathbf{off} = \{\ |\mathbf{off}\} \qquad \mathbf{dud} = \{\mathbf{dud}|\mathbf{dud}\}$$

In **dud** either player can move, in **on** only Left and in **off** only Right. But in all cases the only legal moves are pass moves, back to the original position. It will turn out that

$$\mathbf{dud} = \mathbf{on}\ \&\ \mathbf{off}.$$

HOW BIG IS **on**?

Well, it's not hard to see that Left wins **on** − 5, say, by moving from **on** to **on** until Right has exhausted his 5 moves. In fact, since

$$\mathbf{on} > 0, \quad \mathbf{on} > 1, \quad \mathbf{on} > 2, \quad \ldots,$$

on is infinite: but by now we've met quite a few infinities— how does **on** compare with $\omega, \omega^2, \omega^\omega, \omega^{\omega^\omega}, \ldots$? The answer is:

IT'S BIGGER THAN ALL OF THEM!

For if G is *any* ender, Left can win

$$\mathbf{on} - G$$

in exactly the same way. He always moves from **on** to **on**, and since G *is* an ender there must come a day when Right cannot move in it. So **on** is a sort of super-infinite number.

In mathematical logic the name **On** is used for the Class of all

Ordinal numbers,

which is a kind of illegal ordinal larger than all the ordinary ones. We've adapted this name, and also decided to use **off** for its negative. You might think that

$$\mathbf{on} + \mathbf{off}$$

would be 0, but if you look at Left's and Right's options,

$$\mathbf{on} + \mathbf{off} = \{\mathbf{on} + \mathbf{off} \mid \mathbf{on} + \mathbf{off}\},$$

you'll see that **on** + **off** has a pass move for each player from its only position. In other words it is the game we call

$$\mathbf{dud} = \mathbf{d}\text{eathless } \mathbf{u}\text{niversal } \mathbf{d}\text{raw},$$

since no matter what other game you play it with, nobody can ever bring the game to an end:

$$\mathbf{dud} + \gamma = \mathbf{dud}.$$

> If any one component is **dud**, so's the sum!

SIDLING TOWARDS A GAME

Here's a good way to size up (or cut down to size) the values of many loopy games. Given approximations to the values from above or below, you can put them into the equations defining your games and often get better approximations. For example, putting the inequality

$$\mathbf{on} \geqslant 0$$

into the definition

$$\mathbf{on} = \{\mathbf{on} \mid \ \}$$

we can deduce

$$\textbf{on} \geqslant \{0| \ \} = 1, \quad \text{then } \textbf{on} \geqslant \{1| \ \} = 2,\dots.$$

The Sidling Process doesn't stop with the integers! It implies

$$\textbf{on} \geqslant \{0,1,2,\dots| \ \} = \omega, \quad \text{then } \textbf{on} \geqslant \{\omega| \ \} = \omega+1,\dots, \quad \textbf{on} \geqslant \omega^\omega, \dots$$

once again, but without having to consider any details of strategy.

Now let's sidle in on a more complicated example. The game in Fig. 7 has five positions, $0, \alpha, \beta, \gamma, \delta$, for which the defining equations are $0 = \{ \ | \ \}$,

$$\alpha = \{0|\delta\}, \qquad \beta = \{\alpha| \ \} \qquad \gamma = \{\alpha|\beta\} \qquad \delta = \{\gamma| \ \}.$$

How big are their values? Since we don't obviously know anything better, let us put the obvious upper bounds

$$\alpha \leqslant \textbf{on}, \qquad \beta \leqslant \textbf{on}, \qquad \gamma \leqslant \textbf{on}, \qquad \delta \leqslant \textbf{on},$$

into the defining equations. We deduce successively

$$\alpha \leqslant \{0|\textbf{on}\} = 1,$$
$$\beta \leqslant \{1| \ \} = 2,$$
$$\gamma \leqslant \{1|2\} = 1\tfrac{1}{2},$$
$$\delta \leqslant \{1\tfrac{1}{2}| \ \} = 2,$$

and then

$$\alpha \leqslant \{0|2\} = 1.$$

This is the same as we got before, so by carrying on we'll never get any better upper bounds than

$$\alpha \leqslant 1, \qquad \beta \leqslant 2, \qquad \gamma \leqslant 1\tfrac{1}{2} \qquad \delta \leqslant 2.$$

But we *could* start from the obvious *lower* bounds

$$\alpha \geqslant \textbf{off}, \qquad \beta \geqslant \textbf{off}, \qquad \gamma \geqslant \textbf{off}, \qquad \delta \geqslant \textbf{off},$$

and derive improved ones:

$$\beta \geqslant \{\textbf{off}| \ \} = 0,$$
$$\gamma \geqslant \{\textbf{off}|0\} = -1,$$
$$\delta \geqslant \{-1| \ \} = 0,$$
$$\alpha \geqslant \{0|0\} = *,$$
$$\beta \geqslant \{*| \ \} = 0,$$
$$\gamma \geqslant \{*|0\} = \downarrow,$$
$$\delta \geqslant \{\downarrow| \ \} = 0.$$

The repeated value for δ shows that the process has again converged, and won't give us any better lower bounds than

$$\alpha \geqslant *, \qquad \beta \geqslant 0, \qquad \gamma \geqslant \downarrow, \qquad \delta \geqslant 0.$$

SIDLING PICKS SIDES

What are these upper and lower bounds that the Sidling Process gives? The Sidling Theorem asserts that they are just the two sides of your game:

> Sidling in from **on** gives the *onside*.
> Sidling in from **off** gives the *offside*.

THE SIDLING THEOREM

This is proved in the Extras, but you don't have to understand the proof to be able to use the theorem. Thus in our example we found

$$\alpha \leqslant 1, \qquad \beta \leqslant 2, \qquad \gamma \leqslant 1\tfrac{1}{2}, \qquad \delta \leqslant 2,$$
$$\alpha \geqslant *, \qquad \beta \geqslant 0, \qquad \gamma \geqslant \downarrow, \qquad \delta \geqslant 0,$$

and so by the Sidling Theorem we can write

$$\alpha(\mathbf{on}) = 1, \qquad \beta(\mathbf{on}) = 2, \qquad \gamma(\mathbf{on}) = 1\tfrac{1}{2}, \qquad \delta(\mathbf{on}) = 2,$$
$$\alpha(\mathbf{off}) = *, \qquad \beta(\mathbf{off}) = 0, \qquad \gamma(\mathbf{off}) = \downarrow, \qquad \delta(\mathbf{off}) = 0,$$

or just

$$\alpha = 1\&*, \qquad \beta = 2\&0, \qquad \gamma = 1\tfrac{1}{2}\&\downarrow, \qquad \delta = 2\&0.$$

Starting with one counter at each node in Fig. 7 gives the value

$$\alpha + \beta + \gamma + \delta = \varepsilon, \quad \text{say},$$

and the Sidling Theorem tells us that ε^+ is the onside of this, namely

$$1 + 2 + 1\tfrac{1}{2} + 2 = 6\tfrac{1}{2},$$

which is positive so that when infinite plays count as wins for Left he should win no matter who starts. But if infinite plays are wins for Right, we have ε^- which is the offside

$$* + 0 + \downarrow + 0 = \downarrow*,$$

which is fuzzy, so that whoever starts should win.

If Left starts he wins no matter what decision we make about infinite play, but if Right starts the play should continue indefinitely and the outcome is,

in ε^+,	a win for Left;
in ε^-,	a win for Right;
in ε itself,	a draw.

STOPPERS HAVE ONLY ONE SIDE

We've already seen that for a stopper s the two sides are equal,

$$s = s\&s.$$

The games

over, under, upon, and upon∗

are easy examples:

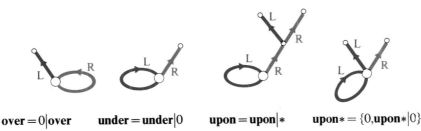

over = 0|over   under = under|0   upon = upon|∗   upon∗ = {0,upon∗|0}

For such games it doesn't matter which way you sidle. Thus for

$$\text{over} = 0|\text{over}$$

we get the upper bounds

on, $0|\text{on} = 1$, $0|1 = \frac{1}{2}$, $0|\frac{1}{2} = \frac{1}{4}$, ... $\{0|1,\frac{1}{2},\frac{1}{4},...\} = \dfrac{1}{\omega}$, $0\Big|\dfrac{1}{\omega} = \dfrac{1}{2\omega}$,...

which suggest that

$$\text{over} = \frac{1}{\text{on}}.$$

What about sidling in from below? Since **over** is obviously positive, we can start from 0 instead of **off**, getting lower bounds

$$0, \quad 0|0 = *, \quad 0|* = \uparrow, \quad 0|\uparrow = \Uparrow*, \quad 0|\Uparrow* = \Lleftarrow, \quad ...$$

which actually do tend to $\dfrac{1}{\text{on}}$ from below.

> For a *stopper*, both sidlings
> tend to the same place.

This saves a great deal of time when you're sidling towards stoppers because you can start wherever you like. For

$$\text{upon} = \text{upon}|*,$$

starting from 0, we get

$$0, \quad 0|* = \uparrow, \quad \uparrow|* = \uparrow+\uparrow^2, \quad (\uparrow+\uparrow^2)|* = \uparrow+\uparrow^2+\uparrow^3, \quad ...$$

which suggest that its value is the superinfinite sum

$$\uparrow + \uparrow^2 + \uparrow^3 + ... + \uparrow^\omega + \uparrow^{\omega+1} + ... + \uparrow^{\omega\times2} + ... + \uparrow^{\omega^2} + ...$$

(We met $\uparrow^2$ and $\uparrow^3$ in Chapter 8; $\uparrow^\alpha$ is an obvious generalization.)

Of course, since the later powers of ↑ are infinitesimal compared with ↑ itself, **upon** is still less than ⇑. We needn't do the other two examples since

$$\textbf{under} = -\textbf{over},$$

$$\textbf{upon}* = \textbf{upon} + *.$$

Exercise One. Evaluate

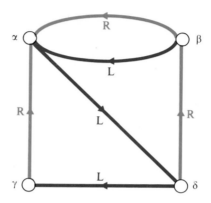

and check your answers in the Extras.

'TIS!–'TIS N!–'TIS!–'TIS N!–...

This is a well-known children's game in which Left says "'Tis!", Right says "'Tis n'!", Left says "'Tis!" and so on, with neither player allowed two consecutive moves, as shown by the graph

or, in symbols,

$$\textbf{tis} = \{\textbf{tisn}|\ \}, \qquad \textbf{tisn} = \{\ |\textbf{tis}\}.$$

Practise your sidling and prove that

$$\textbf{tis} = 1 \,\&\, 0, \qquad \textbf{tisn} = 0 \,\&\, -1.$$

Given who starts, what should be the outcome of

$$\textbf{tis} + *$$

when all infinite plays are counted as draws?

LOOPY HACKENBUSH

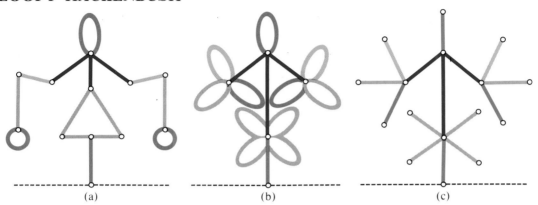

Figure 9. Girl with Yo-Yos.

This game was introduced by Bob Li, who called it Double Hackenbush. As well as the normal red and blue Hackenbush edges, we have **pink** and **pale** (= pale blue) ones (Fig. 9(a)) and the new moves:

Left may repaint any *pale* edge *pink*,
Right may repaint any *pink* edge *pale*.

Pink and pale edges may not be *chopped*.

By thinking of edges that are

red,   pink,   absent,   pale,   blue

as having labels

$$-1 \qquad -\tfrac{1}{2} \qquad 0 \qquad +\tfrac{1}{2} \qquad +1$$

we can express the rules for all four types of edge by saying that

Left may *decrease* a *positive* label by 1, while
Right may *increase* a *negative* label by 1.

DISENTANGLING LOOPY HACKENBUSH

Since the new pink and pale edges can never be chopped, it won't affect play to bring together the two ends of any such edge, so bending it into a loop (Fig. 9(b)), and then replace such loops by *twigs* (Fig. 9(c)) just as we did when applying the Fusion Principle in Green Hackenbush (Chapter 7).

So it suffices to consider Loopy Hackenbush pictures in which all the pink and pale edges are twigs. What values have these?

Because the rules provide the following moves:

the answer is

> for a *pale* twig, **tis**,
> for a *pink* twig, **tisn**.

Since

$$\textbf{tis} = 1 \,\&\, 0, \qquad \textbf{tisn} = 0 \,\&\, -1,$$

this gives us a very easy way to take sides:

> For *onsides*, replace *pale* by *blue* and delete *pink*.
> For *offsides*, replace *pink* by *red* and delete *pale*.

LI'S RULES FOR LOOPY HACKENBUSH

But beware! You must first have applied the fusion process to all pale and pink edges.

Since Li's Rules reduce Loopy Hackenbush pictures with red, pink, pale and blue edges to ordinary Blue-Red Hackenbush pictures, they show that the values have the form

number & number.

For instance Fig. 9 has value $-\dfrac{1}{64} \,\&\, -\dfrac{5}{8}$.

LOOPILY INFINITE HACKENBUSH

Infinite Hackenbush pictures can have loopy values even without pink or pale edges. For instance, let the infinite delphinium we met in Chapter 2 (Fig. 22) have value d. Then

$$d = \{0, d \,|\, 0\}$$

since removing a blue petal leaves a precisely similar delphinium.

So its value is **upon∗**.

Several values of infinite Hackenbush pictures are shown in Fig. 10. Some of these also have pale and pink edges, but this really adds no extra generality because Li's Rules continue to apply.

Don't confuse these Hackenbush pictures with the diagrams (with arrows) showing legal moves that you find elsewhere in this chapter.

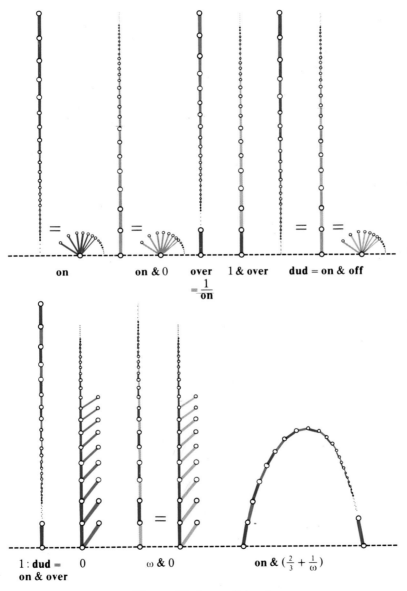

Figure 10. Large & Loopy.

SISYPHUS

> With useless endeavour
> Forever, forever
> Is Sisyphus rolling
> His stone up the mountain!

> Longfellow: *Masque of Pandora* (Chorus of the Eumenides).

Here's a game to practise your sidling with (Fig. 11).

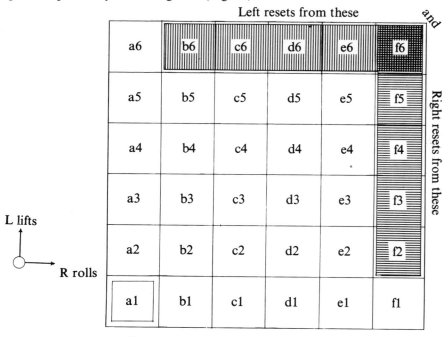

Figure 11. A Sisyphus Board.

Start with any number of stones on any of the squares. When it's his turn, Right *rolls* one stone one place to the right, Left *lifts* a stone one place upwards. Whenever there's a stone on any of the squares b6, c6, d6, e6, f6, Left has the additional option of **resetting** it to a1, and likewise a stone on one of f2, f3, f4, f5, f6 may be reset to a1 by Right.

To find the onsides we sidle down the first column:

$$\text{a6} \leqslant \mid \mathbf{on} = 0, \quad \text{a5} \leqslant 0 \mid \mathbf{on} = 1, \quad \text{a4} \leqslant 1 \mid \mathbf{on} = 2, \quad \text{a3} \leqslant 3, \quad \text{a2} \leqslant 4, \quad \text{a1} \leqslant 5,$$

and then southwest from the top right corner:

$$\text{f6} \leqslant 5 \mid 5 = 5*, \quad \text{e6} \leqslant 5 \mid 5* = 5{\uparrow}, \quad \text{f5} \leqslant 5* \mid 5 = 5{\downarrow}, \quad \text{e5} = 5{\uparrow} \mid 5{\downarrow} = 5*$$
$$\text{d6} \leqslant 5 \mid 5{\uparrow} = 5{\Uparrow}*, \quad \text{f4} \leqslant 5{\downarrow} \mid 5 = 5{\Downarrow}*, \ldots$$

leading to the *provisional* approximations of Fig. 12.

0	$5\uparrow\!\uparrow\!\uparrow*$	$5\uparrow\!\uparrow$	$5\uparrow*$	$5\uparrow$	$5*$
1	$5\uparrow\!\uparrow$	$5\uparrow*$	$5\uparrow$	$5*$	$5\downarrow$
2	$5\uparrow*$	$5\uparrow$	$5*$	$5\downarrow$	$5\downarrow\!\downarrow*$
3	$5\uparrow$	$5*$	$5\downarrow$	$5\downarrow\!\downarrow*$	$5\downarrow\!\downarrow$
4	$5*$	$5\downarrow$	$5\downarrow\!\downarrow*$	$5\downarrow\!\downarrow$	$5\downarrow\!\downarrow\!\downarrow*$
5	$5\downarrow$	$5\downarrow\!\downarrow*$	$5\downarrow\!\downarrow$	$5\downarrow\!\downarrow\!\downarrow*$	5

Figure 12. First Attempt at Onsides of Sisyphus.

But now we get

$$\boxed{a1} \leqslant 4|5{\downarrow} = 4\tfrac{1}{2}, \quad \text{and so} \quad \boxed{f6} \leqslant 4\tfrac{1}{2}|4\tfrac{1}{2} = 4\tfrac{1}{2}*$$

and all the 5s get replaced by $4\tfrac{1}{2}$s, except that the bottom row becomes

$4\tfrac{1}{4}$	$4\tfrac{1}{2}\downarrow$	$4\tfrac{1}{2}\downarrow\!\downarrow*$	$4\tfrac{1}{2}\downarrow\!\downarrow$	$4\tfrac{1}{2}$	5

since

$$\boxed{f1} \leqslant \{4\tfrac{1}{2}\downarrow\!\downarrow*| \;\} = 5, \quad \ldots, \quad \boxed{a1} \leqslant \{4|4\tfrac{1}{2}\} = 4\tfrac{1}{4}.$$

We now find ourselves successively replacing $4\tfrac{1}{2}$s by $4\tfrac{1}{4}$s, then by $4\tfrac{1}{8}$s and so on, until eventually the process converges to Fig. 13.

0	$4\tfrac{1}{32}\uparrow\!\uparrow\!\uparrow*$	$4\tfrac{1}{32}\uparrow\!\uparrow$	$4\tfrac{1}{32}\uparrow*$	$4\tfrac{1}{32}\uparrow$	$4\tfrac{1}{32}*$
1	$4\tfrac{1}{32}\uparrow\!\uparrow$	$4\tfrac{1}{32}\uparrow*$	$4\tfrac{1}{32}\uparrow$	$4\tfrac{1}{32}*$	$4\tfrac{1}{32}\downarrow$
2	$4\tfrac{1}{32}\uparrow*$	$4\tfrac{1}{32}\uparrow$	$4\tfrac{1}{32}*$	$4\tfrac{1}{32}\downarrow$	$4\tfrac{1}{32}\downarrow\!\downarrow*$
3	$4\tfrac{1}{32}\uparrow$	$4\tfrac{1}{32}*$	$4\tfrac{1}{32}\downarrow$	$4\tfrac{1}{32}\downarrow\!\downarrow*$	$4\tfrac{1}{32}\downarrow\!\downarrow$
4	$4\tfrac{1}{32}*$	$4\tfrac{1}{32}\downarrow$	$4\tfrac{1}{32}\downarrow\!\downarrow*$	$4\tfrac{1}{32}\downarrow\!\downarrow$	$4\tfrac{1}{32}\downarrow\!\downarrow\!\downarrow*$
$4\tfrac{1}{32}$	$4\tfrac{1}{16}$	$4\tfrac{1}{8}$	$4\tfrac{1}{4}$	$4\tfrac{1}{2}$	5

Figure 13. The Onsides of Sisyphus.

Of course, the offsides are found by swapping rows with columns and negating the values, for instance

$$\boxed{d1} = 4\tfrac{1}{4} \,\&\, -2, \qquad \boxed{d2} = 4\tfrac{1}{32}\Downarrow* \,\&\, (-4\tfrac{1}{32})\Downarrow*.$$

LIVING WITH LOOPS

With what you know so far you should be able to evaluate most of the loopy games you meet in practice. If you want more examples, look near the end of the chapter. Until then we'll show you some more ideas which experts can use to simplify the calculations.

COMPARING LOOPY GAMES

Because the sides of loopy games are not always enders, we need ways of comparing them. This is one problem that's best solved for *fixed* (no draw) games.

> If $\alpha^{\bullet}$ and $\beta^{\bullet}$ are *fixed* games, then
> $$\alpha^{\bullet} \geqslant \beta^{\bullet}$$
> just if Left can arrange to win or draw in
> $$\alpha^{\bullet} - \beta^{\bullet}$$
> provided that Right starts.

THE INEQUALITY RULE

So the condition is that Left **avoids loss** or **survives** in $\alpha^{\bullet} - \beta^{\bullet}$, supposing always that Right starts.

Now any play of $\alpha^{\bullet} - \beta^{\bullet}$ yields component plays in $\alpha^{\bullet}$ and $-\beta^{\bullet}$, and so a mirror-image play in $+\beta^{\bullet}$. Examination of Table 1 shows that Left's strategy must arrange that

> Left has a move after every move of Right's   (i) (REMAIN)
> and the resulting plays in $\alpha^{\bullet}$ and $\beta^{\bullet}$ have
> $$\text{sign}(\alpha^{\bullet}) \geqslant \text{sign}(\beta^{\bullet}) \qquad \text{(ii) (ON TOP)}$$

SURVIVAL CONDITIONS

$\text{sign}(\alpha^{\bullet})$	$+$	$+$	$+$	0	0	0	$-$	$-$	$-$
$\text{sign}(-\beta^{\bullet})$	$+$	0	$-$	$+$	0	$-$	$+$	0	$-$
Does Left avoid loss?	Yes	Yes	Yes	Yes	Yes, if (i)	No	Yes	No	No
$\text{sign}(+\beta^{\bullet})$	$-$	0	$+$	$-$	0	$+$	$-$	0	$+$
Is $\text{sign}(\alpha^{\bullet}) \geqslant \text{sign}(\beta^{\bullet})$?	Yes	Yes	Yes	Yes	Yes	No	Yes	No	No

Table 1. The Significance of Signs.

In the table, $+$ and $-$ denote infinite plays that are respectively wins for Left and Right, while 0 denotes a *finite* play. (Because the theory works only for *fixed* games, no infinite play is *drawn*.) For unfixed games $\alpha_1^{\cdot}$ and $\alpha_2^{\cdot}$,

$$\alpha_1^{\cdot} \geqslant \alpha_2^{\cdot}$$

means just that both

$$(\alpha_1^{\cdot})^{+} \geqslant (\alpha_2^{\cdot})^{+} \quad \text{and} \quad (\alpha_1^{\cdot})^{-} \geqslant (\alpha_2^{\cdot})^{-}$$

where $(\alpha_1^{\cdot})^{+}$ and $(\alpha_1^{\cdot})^{-}$ are the fixed games obtained from $\alpha_1^{\cdot}$ by redefining drawn plays in $\alpha_1^{\cdot}$ as wins for Left and Right respectively.

The Inequality Rule amounts to a *definition* of inequalities between loopy games and must be shown to work. For example we must show that

$$\alpha_1^{\cdot} \geqslant \alpha_2^{\cdot} \quad \text{implies} \quad \alpha_1^{\cdot} + \beta^{\cdot} \geqslant \alpha_2^{\cdot} + \beta^{\cdot},$$

where we might as well suppose that $\alpha_1^{\cdot}$, $\alpha_2^{\cdot}$ and $\beta^{\cdot}$ are fixed.

In other words, we must produce a strategy for Left in

$$\alpha_1^{\cdot} + \beta^{\cdot} - \alpha_2^{\cdot} - \beta^{\cdot}$$

that makes

$$\text{sign}(\alpha_1^{\cdot} + \beta^{\cdot})^{+} \geqslant \text{sign}(\alpha_2^{\cdot} + \beta^{\cdot})^{+}$$

and

$$\text{sign}(\alpha_1^{\cdot} + \beta^{\cdot})^{-} \geqslant \text{sign}(\alpha_2^{\cdot} + \beta^{\cdot})^{-}$$

(note that $\alpha_1^{\cdot} + \beta^{\cdot}$ and $\alpha_2^{\cdot} + \beta^{\cdot}$ need *not* be fixed).

Fortunately this happens if Left plays his given strategy in $\alpha_1^{\cdot} - \alpha_2^{\cdot}$ and the Tweedledum and Tweedledee Strategy in $\beta^{\cdot} - \beta^{\cdot}$, because each column of the Tables

	sign($\beta^{\cdot}$)					sign($\beta^{\cdot}$)		
	$-$	0	$+$			$-$	0	$+$
$-$	$-$	$-$	$+$		$-$	$-$	$-$	$-$
sign($\alpha_i^{\cdot}$) 0	$-$	0	$+$	sign($\alpha_i^{\cdot}$) 0		$-$	0	$+$
$+$	$+$	$+$	$+$		$+$	$-$	$+$	$+$

for $\text{sign}(\alpha_i^{\cdot} + \beta^{\cdot})^{+}$ and $\text{sign}(\alpha_i^{\cdot} + \beta^{\cdot})^{-}$

increases downwards.

THE SWIVEL CHAIR STRATEGY

We must also show that

$$\alpha^{\cdot} \geqslant \beta^{\cdot} \quad \text{and} \quad \beta^{\cdot} \geqslant \gamma^{\cdot} \quad \text{imply} \quad \alpha^{\cdot} \geqslant \gamma^{\cdot}$$

where once again we can suppose $\alpha^{\cdot}$, $\beta^{\cdot}$, $\gamma^{\cdot}$ to be fixed games.

In other words, Left is given surviving strategies in $\alpha^{\cdot} - \beta^{\cdot}$ and $\beta^{\cdot} - \gamma^{\cdot}$ and desires one in $\alpha^{\cdot} - \gamma^{\cdot}$. To find it he employs two tables, a swivel chair and Right's manservant, mr. read (Fig.

14). He plays his given strategies in the pairs $\alpha^{\bullet}$, $-\beta^{\bullet}$ and $\beta^{\bullet}$, $-\gamma^{\bullet}$ and instructs mr. read to play the Tweedledum and Tweedledee Strategy, responding to a Left move in $\beta^{\bullet}$ or $-\beta^{\bullet}$ with the Right mirror-image reply (read's lower case initial marks his humble status.)

Figure 14. The Swivel Chair Strategy.

If he does this the resulting plays will have

$$\operatorname{sign}(\alpha^{\bullet}) \geqslant \operatorname{sign}(\beta^{\bullet}) \quad \text{and} \quad \operatorname{sign}(\beta^{\bullet}) \geqslant \operatorname{sign}(\gamma^{\bullet})$$

(mr. read's instructions make $\operatorname{sign}(\beta^{\bullet}) = -\operatorname{sign}(-\beta^{\bullet})$), so we've certainly satisfied the ON TOP condition. Also, if the total play in the real game $\alpha^{\bullet} - \gamma^{\bullet}$ is finite, then

$$0 = \operatorname{sign}(\alpha^{\bullet}) \geqslant \operatorname{sign}(\beta^{\bullet}) \geqslant \operatorname{sign}(\gamma^{\bullet}) = 0$$

and so the play in all four components is finite and Left made the last move. This wasn't in $\beta^{\bullet}$ or $-\beta^{\bullet}$ since mr. read would have obediently replied, and so must have been in the real game $\alpha^{\bullet} - \gamma^{\bullet}$.

STOPPERS ARE NICE

We've already seen that

> a stopper s has only one side:
> $$s(\mathbf{on}) = s(\mathbf{off}) = s,$$
> $$s = s \,\&\, s,$$

and so

> for stoppers, both sidlings
> tend to the same place.

Here are some other ways in which stoppers behave like ordinary enders:

> If s and t are stoppers,
> then the inequalities
> $$s^+ \geqslant t^+, \quad s^+ \geqslant t^-, \quad s^- \geqslant t^-$$
> are all equivalent and
> any one of them implies
> $$s \geqslant t.$$

INEQUALITIES FOR STOPPERS

This means you can usually forget about those $^+$ and $^-$ signs for stoppers. In particular:

> To check an inequality
> $$s \geqslant t$$
> between stoppers, it suffices
> to show that Left can respond
> to every move in $s-t$, Right
> starting.

COMPARING STOPPERS

> You can simplify stoppers
> by omitting dominated options
> and bypassing reversible ones
> just as you do for enders.

SIMPLIFYING STOPPERS

> A stopper which has only finitely
> many positions has a unique
> **simplest form** with no dominated
> or reversible moves from any position.

THE SIMPLEST FORM THEOREM FOR STOPPERS

We only sketch the proofs.

If s and t are stoppers, and we have infinite play in $s-t$, then we must have infinite play in *both* s and t, for otherwise there'd be an ultimately alternating infinite sequence of moves in one of them. This establishes the inequality rules.

Now let s be any stopper and $\hat{s}$ be obtained by omitting some dominated Left options from various positions of s, retaining, of course, enough options to dominate them. If t is another stopper, and $s \geqslant t$, we shall show that $\hat{s} \geqslant t$.

What we shall show is that when Right makes any move from a position

$$\hat{s}_0 - t_0 \quad \text{of} \quad \hat{s} - t$$

for which we had

$$s_0 \geqslant t_0$$

then Left can reply to a position

$$\hat{s}_m - t_m, \quad \text{say,}$$

for which we still have

$$s_m \geqslant t_m.$$

If Left can keep on making just one more move like this he can keep on forever!

After Right's move from

$$\hat{s}_0 - t_0$$

we arrive at a position

$$\hat{s}_1 - t_1$$

with Left to move. What did he do from the corresponding position

$$s_1 - t_1$$

of $s-t$? The moves in $-t_1$ are still available to him, so we might as well suppose he moved to

$$s_2 - t_1$$

for some Left option s_2 of s_1; now s_2 might be one of the Left options we omitted in deriving $\hat{s}$ from s, but we certainly retained some Left option s_3 of s_1 dominating s_2, and Left can move to

$$\hat{s}_3 - t_1.$$

Since we had $s_2 \geqslant t_1$, we must have $s_3 \geqslant t_1$, and Left has survived for one more move.

This shows that $\hat{s} \geqslant s$ and it is obvious that $\hat{s} \leqslant s$. A similar argument shows that we can bypass reversible options. The remaining proofs are very like those for ordinary enders.

PLUMTREES ARE NICER!

The moves of an ordinary ender form a tree in which blue branches correspond to Left moves and red ones to Right ones, and we may use green branches for moves which may be made by either player.

We get **plumtrees** from ordinary trees by adding plums! We use blue plums to indicate pass moves for Left, red plums for pass moves for Right and green ones for pass moves available to either player. Figure 15 shows our old examples and a new pair, **tiny** and **miny**.

on

off

over

under

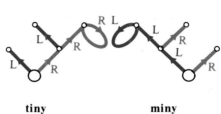

dud = on & off

upon *   upon   tiny   miny

Figure 15. Some Choice Plums.

How big is **tiny**?

We've met some *ordinary* tiny games

$$+_G = \{0\|0|-G\} \qquad (\text{"tiny } G\text{"})$$

before. A 4×2 rectangle in Domineering has value $+_2$ and in Toads and Frogs we met $+_{\frac{1}{4}}$ and $+_{1|\frac{1}{2}}$, and found them to be very small positive games. But

$$\textbf{tiny} = +_{\text{on}}$$

is no ordinary game: since **on** exceeds every other game, $+_{\text{on}}$ is smaller than any other positive game.

> **tiny** is the smallest positive value there is!

Of course,

$$\textbf{miny} = -_{\text{on}} = -\textbf{tiny}$$

is the least negative game there is.

TAKING CARE OF PLUMTREES

When all your games are plumtrees, then everything in your garden's lovely, because there are so many things you can do with them.

GATHERING. Of course you'll be keen to gather the fruits of your labors. With plumtrees this is easy because the sum of a number of plumtrees is always another plumtree, which has a pass for a given player in some position only when one of the components does.

RIPENING. We can suppose that each plumtree has at most one plum per node, since a pair of red and blue plums can be replaced by a single green one. In this form the two sides of a plumtree are easily found by ripening it:

> To find the *onside*, replace all green plums by *blue* ones.
>
> To find the *offside*, replace all green plums by *red* ones.

PRUNING. *Ripe* plumtrees (with at most one plum per node) are stoppers and so, if they have finitely many positions, can be put into simplest form by omitting dominated options and bypassing reversible ones.

GRAFTING. If g and h are ripe plumtrees with $g \geqslant h$, then $g\&h$ can be represented by a plumtree obtained by grafting g onto h as in Fig. 16. However, we must allow a Right move to **dud** from every g^L and a Left move to **dud** from every h^R to make sure the graft is not rejected.

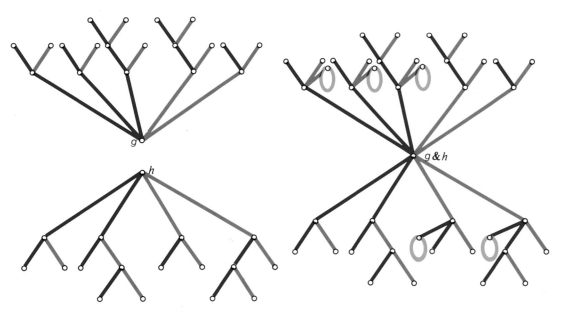

Figure 16. Grafting Two Plumtrees.

PLACING. It's often very easy to compare plumtrees with ordinary enders, using Norton's Lemma (Chapter 7, Extras), since

> g:**on** is g with a blue plum added to its initial node,
>
> g:**off** is g with a red plum added to its initial node.

For example, you can see from Fig. 15 that

$$\textbf{upon}* \quad \text{is} \quad *:\textbf{on},$$

and it therefore has the same order relation with g as $*$ does for every g not involving $*$. In fact

$$\textbf{upon}* = \uparrow *:\textbf{on}$$

(since $*:1 = \uparrow *$ and $1:\textbf{on} = \textbf{on}$) and so $\textbf{upon}*$ has the same order relation with g as $\uparrow *$ does, for every g not involving $\uparrow *$.

WORKING WITH UPSUMS AND DOWNSUMS

Let's use these ideas to add two simple plumtrees.

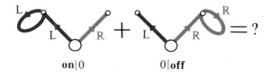

We find

$$? = \left\{ \ \textbf{on} + \{0|\textbf{off}\}, \quad \{\textbf{on}|0\} + 0 \ \middle| \ 0 + \{0|\textbf{off}\}, \quad \{\textbf{on}|0\} + \textbf{off} \ \right\}.$$

Next

$$\textbf{on} + \{0|\textbf{off}\} = \{\text{pass}, \quad \textbf{on} + 0 \ | \ \textbf{on} + \textbf{off}\}$$

where the pass indicates that Left has a pass move in the sum corresponding to his pass move in **on**. The Left option **on** in this dominates the pass move and we have

$$\textbf{on} + \textbf{off} = \textbf{dud} = \textbf{on} \,\&\, \textbf{off},$$

so that the onside of $\textbf{on} + \{\,0|\textbf{off}\}$ is

$$\textbf{on}|\textbf{on} = \textbf{on},$$

while the offside is

$$\textbf{on}|\textbf{off} = \textbf{hot}, \quad \text{say},$$

the hottest game of all! These are the *upsums* and *downsums*:

$$\textbf{on} \curlywedge \{0|\textbf{off}\} = \textbf{on}, \quad \textbf{on} \curlyvee \{0|\textbf{off}\} = \textbf{hot},$$

or, more briefly,

$$\textbf{on} + \{0|\textbf{off}\} = \textbf{on} \,\&\, \textbf{hot},$$

and similarly

$$\{\textbf{on}|0\} + \textbf{off} = \textbf{hot} \,\&\, \textbf{off}.$$

So

$$? = \{\textbf{on}\&\textbf{hot},\{\textbf{on}|0\} \,|\, \{0|\textbf{off}\},\textbf{hot}\&\textbf{off}\}$$

whose onside is

$$\{\textbf{on},\{\textbf{on}|0\} \,|\, \{0|\textbf{off}\},\textbf{hot}\} = \{\textbf{on} \,|\, \{0|\textbf{off}\}\}$$

since $\{\textbf{on}|0\}$ and $\textbf{hot} = \{\textbf{on}|\textbf{off}\}$ are dominated options.

We conclude that

$$\{on|0\} \curlywedge \{0|off\} = \{on|\{0|off\}\} = hi, \quad \text{say,}$$

and similarly

$$\{on|0\} \curlyvee \{0|off\} = \{\{on|0\}|off\} = lo, \quad \text{say.}$$

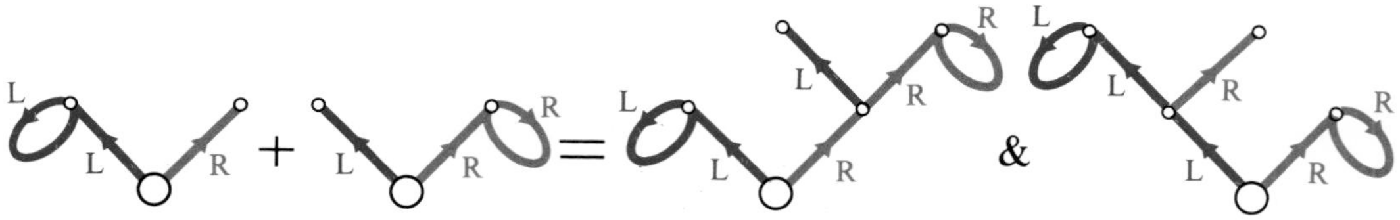

| on\|0 | + | 0\|off | = | hi | & | & | & | lo |

These answers are in simplest form.

on, off AND hot

It's easy to add these three games to any other. We call a stopper **half-on** if it has **on** as a Left option and **half-off** if it has **off** as a Right one (the half-on games are just those of the form {**on**|*a,b,c,*...}).

Both **on** and **hot** are half-on; both **hot** and **off** are half-off; **hot** is the only half-on *and* half-off game. Here's an addition table:

	on	other half-on	hot	other half-off	off
on	on	on	on & hot	on & hot	on & off
other half-on	on	on	on & hot	?	hot & off
hot	on & hot	on & hot	on & off	hot & off	hot & off
other half-off	on & hot	?	hot & off	off	off
off	on & off	hot & off	hot & off	off	off

and here's a table for some related games (**ono** = **on**|0,   **oof** = 0|**off**):

	ono	hi	lo	oof	tiny & miny
ono	on	on & ono	ono & hot	hi & lo	on|tiny & ono
hi	on & ono	on & hi	hi & lo	hot & oof	hi & on ‖ miny|off
lo	ono & hot	hi & lo	lo & off	oof & off	on|tiny ‖ off & lo
oof	hi & lo	hot & oof	oof & off	off	oof & miny|off

and here's a picture of some order relations (Fig. 17).

So

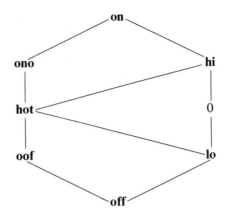

Figure 17. Higher or Lower?

A SUMMARY OF SOME SUM PROPERTIES

Upsums and downsums of stoppers have properties like ordinary sums and there are a few other relations between them and the ordering properties. Our mathematical readers might like a list:

$0 \curlywedge a = a$	$0 \curlyvee a = a$	Zero Law
$a \curlywedge b = b \curlywedge a$	$a \curlyvee b = b \curlyvee a$	Commutativity
$(a \curlywedge b) \curlywedge c = a \curlywedge (b \curlywedge c)$	$(a \curlyvee b) \curlyvee c = a \curlyvee (b \curlyvee c)$	Associativity
$-(a \curlywedge b) = (-a) \curlyvee (-b)$	$-(a \curlyvee b) = (-a) \curlywedge (-b)$	Negation
$a' \geqslant a \Rightarrow a' \curlywedge b \geqslant a \curlywedge b$	$a' \geqslant a \Rightarrow a' \curlyvee b \geqslant a \curlyvee b$	Monotonicity
	$a \curlywedge b \geqslant a \curlyvee b$	a,b Property
	$a \curlywedge b \geqslant c$ just if $a \geqslant (-b) \curlyvee c$	a,b,c Property

Some of the consequences of these are quite surprising, as we'll see later.

THE HOUSE OF CARDS

Look at this list of games:

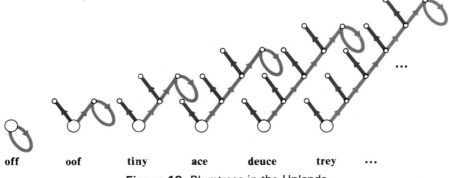

off   oof   tiny   ace   deuce   trey   · · ·

Figure 18. Plumtrees in the Uplands.

How big are they?

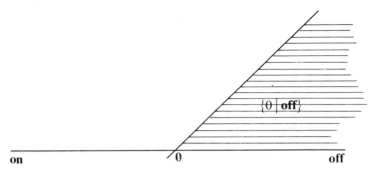

Figure 19. The Thermograph of **oof**.

We already know that **off** is the most negative game of all, and the thermograph of **oof** $= 0|$off (Fig. 19) shows it to be less than all positive numbers, but confused with all the others. We know that **tiny** is the smallest positive game of all. What about

$$\textbf{ace, deuce, trey, } \ldots?$$

It turns out that

$$\textbf{ace} + \textbf{ace} = \textbf{deuce}, \qquad \textbf{ace} + \textbf{deuce} = \textbf{trey}, \qquad \ldots$$

so that after the first three terms you only need to know about sums of **ace**s.

But when we include their negatives as well, upsums begin to differ from downsums, for example

$$\textbf{ace} \wedge (-\textbf{ace}) = \textbf{joker},$$
$$\textbf{ace} \vee (-\textbf{ace}) = -\textbf{joker},$$

where **joker** and $-$**joker** are thoroughly different games:

ace $+$ $-$ace $=$ joker   & $-$joker

Now **ace** has atomic weight 1, so by repeatedly combining **ace**s and their negatives we shall get various games whose atomic weights are all whole numbers; for example, the game

$$\textbf{deuce} = 0|\textbf{ace} \quad \text{has atomic weight 2 and is called } 2\clubsuit, \text{ and}$$
$$0|\textbf{joker} \text{ has atomic weight 1 and is called } 1\heartsuit.$$

It turns out that for most atomic weights n, we get just 4 such games

$$n\clubsuit < n\diamondsuit < n\heartsuit < n\spadesuit.$$

But for atomic weights $-1, 0, 1$ we also get

$$-\textbf{ace} < -\textbf{joker} < 0 < \textbf{joker} < \textbf{ace}$$

and their sums with **tiny** and **miny**.

Figure 20 shows you how these games are defined; Fig. 21 shows how they're compared and Fig. 22 how to add them. We use the notation

$$X+ = X \curlywedge \textbf{tiny}, \qquad X- = X \curlyvee \textbf{miny}.$$

$$A = \textbf{ace} = 0|\textbf{tiny} \qquad A- = \textbf{on}|A\,\|\,0 \qquad A+ = A$$

$$J = \textbf{joker} = 0|\overline{A}+ \qquad J- = \textbf{on}|J\,\|\,\overline{A} \qquad J+ = J$$

$$\overline{J} = -\textbf{joker} = A-|0 \qquad \overline{J}+ = A\,\|\,J\,|\textbf{off} \qquad \overline{J}- = \overline{J}$$

$$\overline{A} = -\textbf{ace} = \textbf{miny}|0 \qquad \overline{A}+ = 0\,\|\,\overline{A}\,|\textbf{off} \qquad \overline{A}- = \overline{A}$$

n	$n\clubsuit$	$n\diamondsuit$	$n\heartsuit$	$n\spadesuit$	
...	...	...	...	...	
$\overline{3}=-3$	$\overline{2}\clubsuit|0$	$\overline{2}\diamondsuit|0$	$\overline{2}\heartsuit|0$	$\overline{2}\spadesuit|0$	For all games X
$\overline{2}=-2$	$\overline{1}\clubsuit|0$	$\overline{1}\diamondsuit|0$	$\overline{1}\heartsuit|0$	$\overline{A}|0$	in this table
$\overline{1}=-1$	$\clubsuit|0$	$J|0$	$\heartsuit|0$	$0|\overline{2}\spadesuit$	$X+ = X- = X;$
0	$1\clubsuit|0$	$A|\overline{1}\diamondsuit$	$1\heartsuit|\overline{A}$	$0|\overline{1}\spadesuit$	**deuce,trey**,... are
1	$2\clubsuit|0$	$0|\diamondsuit$	$0|J$	$0|\spadesuit$	alternative names for
2	$0|A$	$0|1\diamondsuit$	$0|1\heartsuit$	$0|1\spadesuit$	$2\clubsuit, 3\clubsuit,...$
3	$0|2\clubsuit$	$0|2\diamondsuit$	$0|2\heartsuit$	$0|2\spadesuit$	(but **ace** $\neq 1\clubsuit$).
...	...	...	...	...	
	$\clubsuit = 0\clubsuit$	$\diamondsuit = 0\diamondsuit$	$\heartsuit = 0\heartsuit$	$\spadesuit = 0\spadesuit$	

Figure 20. Laying Out the Cards.

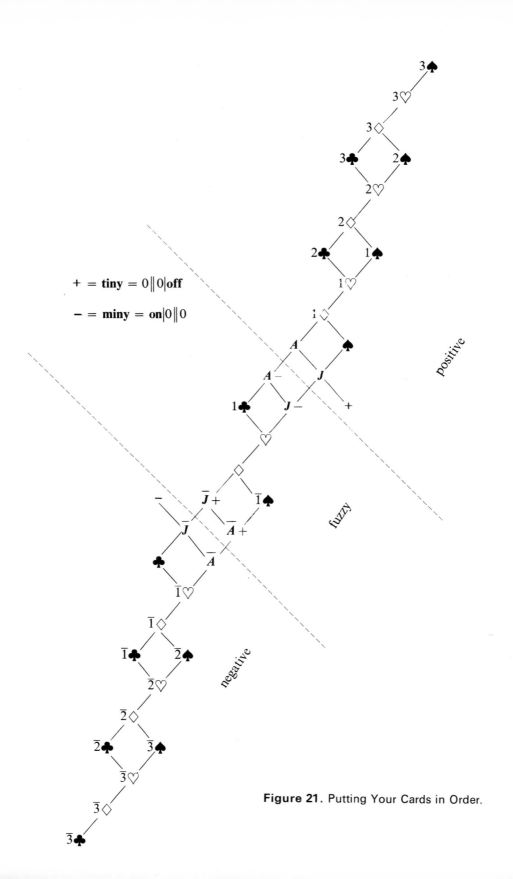

+ = **tiny** = $0 \| 0 | \text{off}$

− = **miny** = $\text{on} | 0 \| 0$

Figure 21. Putting Your Cards in Order.

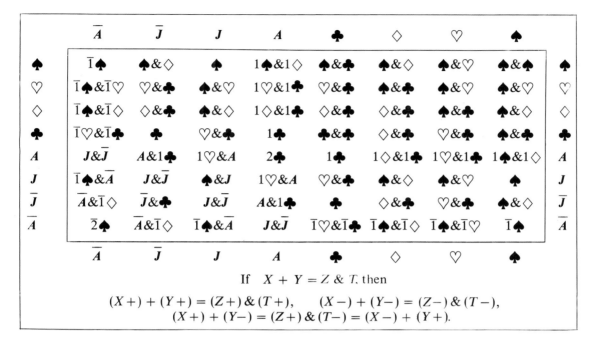

Figure 22. Adding Up Your Cards.

THE DEGREE OF LOOPINESS

Of course every ordinary ender G has

$$G + (-G) = 0.$$

But for loopy games γ we have

$$\gamma + (-\gamma) = d \,\&\, (-d),$$

where d is called the **degree of loopiness**, or just the **degree**, γ°, of γ. In symbols

$$\gamma^\circ = \gamma \curlywedge (-\gamma),$$

the upsum of γ and its negative. The a,b,c Property implies that γ° measures the downsum absorbancy of γ:

$$\gamma \curlyvee x \leqslant \gamma \quad \text{just if} \quad x \leqslant \gamma^\circ,$$

and in particular,

$$\boxed{\gamma \curlyvee x = \gamma \quad \text{for} \quad 0 \leqslant x \leqslant \gamma^\circ.}$$

THE DOWNSUM ABSORBANCY RULE

Our more mathematical readers will deduce from the properties of upsums and downsums that:

$$(-\gamma)^\circ = \gamma^\circ = \gamma^\circ \curlyvee \gamma^\circ = (\gamma^\circ)^\circ,$$

$$\gamma^\circ \curlyvee \delta^\circ \leqslant (\gamma \curlyvee \delta)^\circ \leqslant \gamma^\circ \curlywedge \delta^\circ, \qquad \gamma^\circ \curlyvee \delta^\circ \leqslant (\gamma \curlywedge \delta)^\circ \leqslant \gamma^\circ \curlywedge \delta^\circ,$$

and similarly for more complicated sums,

$$\ldots\gamma^\circ \curlyvee \delta^\circ \curlyvee \ldots \curlyvee \eta^\circ\ldots \leqslant (\ldots\gamma \curlywedge \delta\ldots \curlyvee \eta\ldots)^\circ \leqslant \ldots\gamma^\circ \curlywedge \delta^\circ \curlywedge \ldots \curlywedge \eta^\circ\ldots.$$

A most important property is that

> the degree of loopiness,
> γ°, is zero if
> γ is equal to some ender,
> and is otherwise strictly
> positive

So for genuinely loopy γ we have

$$\gamma^\circ \geqslant \textbf{tiny},$$

and therefore

$$\gamma \curlyvee \textbf{tiny} = \gamma.$$

Lots of calculations are made easier using these ideas. Let's find the degree of **tiny**:

$$\textbf{tiny}^\circ = \textbf{tiny} \curlywedge (-\textbf{tiny}).$$

Because we've added a negative quantity, this is $\leqslant$ **tiny**, but it must also be $\geqslant$ **tiny**, since **tiny** is a genuinely loopy game:

$$\textbf{tiny}^\circ = \textbf{tiny}.$$

We can now find

$$\textbf{tiny} + \textbf{tiny},$$

for since **tiny** has only red plums, **tiny** + **tiny** is a ripe plum tree and so already a stopper:

$$\textbf{tiny} \curlywedge \textbf{tiny} = \textbf{tiny} \curlyvee \textbf{tiny}.$$

But by the Downsum Absorbancy Rule

$$\textbf{tiny} \curlyvee \textbf{tiny} = \textbf{tiny},$$

and so finally,

$$\textbf{tiny} + \textbf{tiny} = \textbf{tiny}.$$

CLASSES AND VARIETIES

In the House of Cards the degrees of the various positions are

0	(for 0 only),
tiny	(for **tiny** and **miny**),
joker	(for $A, A-, J, J-, \bar{J}, \bar{J}+, \bar{A}, \bar{A}+$),
♠	(for $n\clubsuit, n\diamondsuit, n\heartsuit, n\spadesuit; \quad n = \ldots -2, -1, 0, 1, 2, \ldots$).

The positions whose degree is ♠ (unlike the others) show a striking regularity—they form themselves naturally into *classes*, one for each n, and each class exhibits all four *varieties*:

$$\clubsuit, \diamondsuit, \heartsuit, \spadesuit.$$

This seems to happen more generally for all the games of any given **stable** degree d, i.e. one that satisfies

$$d \curlywedge d = d,$$

and in this case we will write $a\langle b\rangle$ for the game of *class a* and *variety b*. Formally, the **class** of a contains all the games of degree d between

$$a\langle -d\rangle = a \curlyvee (-d) \quad \text{and} \quad a\langle d\rangle = a \curlywedge d,$$

which are the smallest and largest members of the class. Although for loopy games

$$a \curlyvee \bar{a} < 0$$

we conjecture that

$$a\langle d\rangle \curlyvee \bar{a}\langle d\rangle \geqslant 0 \quad \text{(The Stability Condition)}$$

whenever a has degree d and d is stable. We say that a is **stable to the degree** d when this condition holds. It can be proved that sums of such games enjoy the same property.

The **variety** of a is the game

$$0\langle a\rangle = a \curlyvee \bar{a}\langle d\rangle = a \curlywedge \bar{a}\langle -d\rangle.$$

In the House of Cards, for example,

$$0\langle 3\heartsuit\rangle = \heartsuit,$$

while the *class* of $3\heartsuit$ contains all four cards

$$3\clubsuit, 3\diamondsuit, 3\heartsuit, 3\spadesuit.$$

When a and b are stable to the degree d, there is a unique game

$$a\langle b\rangle = a\langle d\rangle \curlyvee 0\langle b\rangle = a\langle -d\rangle \curlywedge 0\langle b\rangle$$

which is in the same class as a, and has the same variety as b.

To add games given like this you just add the classes and add the varieties:

$$a\langle b\rangle \curlywedge c\langle d\rangle = (a+c)\langle b \curlywedge d\rangle,$$
$$a\langle b\rangle \curlyvee c\langle d\rangle = (a+c)\langle b \curlyvee d\rangle.$$

We've written $a+c$ here because it doesn't matter whether you use $a \curlywedge c$ or $a \curlyvee c$.

There is a slight extension of this theory to cover games whose degree is less than d, provided they still satisfy the Stability Condition. Such a game has both

an **upsum variety**, $\quad a \curlywedge \bar{a}\langle -d\rangle$,

and

a **downsum variety**, $a \curlyvee \bar{a}\langle d\rangle$;

you use the former when taking upsums, the latter for downsums. For example, for the game **ace**, the two varieties are

$$\clubsuit \quad \text{and} \quad \diamondsuit,$$

and so **ace** can be replaced by $1\clubsuit$ when taking upsums, and by $1\diamondsuit$ when taking downsums.

Exercise Two. Find the degree of **upon** = {pass|∗}, and investigate all sums of **upon** and its negative.

NO HIGHWAY

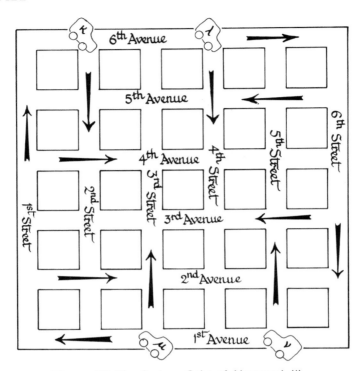

Figure 23. The Curious Cabs of Abnormal, Ill.

Figure 23 is a map of the town of Abnormal, Ill., in which you can see that all the streets and avenues are one-way. A hundred years ago this was a bustling town with tram-cars in every (N–S) street, operated by members of the Linksman's Labor Local; while the (E–W) avenues were served by elegant coaches manned by drivers of the Road Riders Regional. Sadly all this passed with the advent of the internal combustion engine, and only the two unions remain. For some time there has been an anxious truce; every cab (from the Greek Letter Cab Co.; you can see their new cab at the corner of 1st Avenue and 5th Street) has to carry one driver from each union, who takes the wheel when the cab is travelling in the appropriate direction. As there are only four cabs, competition for trips is fierce and there will always be a passenger wanting to travel one block in any legal direction (which is all the unions will allow!). The L.L.L. wants to keep the cabs running and will not allow two successive R.R.R. journeys. The R.R.R., on the other hand, are trying to wreck the system by bringing the cabs to a halt and are prepared to forego their right to make a trip on just 3 occasions.

In other words, LLL and RRR move alternately just one block in an appropriate direction, except that the RRR may have 3 pass moves. The RRR will win if the LLL cannot make a trip on their turn and the LLL win just by holding on for ever. What does this mean in loopy game terms?

Since all infinite plays win for the LLL, and

$$\gamma(\mathbf{on})^+ = \gamma^+,$$

we need only consider the onside of each position γ. So we want the onside of the sum

$$\kappa + \lambda + \mu + \nu - 3,$$

corresponding to the initial position and the 3 pass moves for the RRR.

We'll use the sidling process, starting with **on** at each intersection (Fig. 24(a)) and choosing a sensible order (Fig. 24(b)) in which to revise our estimates. We see almost immediately that the numbers in Fig. 24(c) are upper bounds, and just one more revision gives the final answers (Fig. 24(d)).

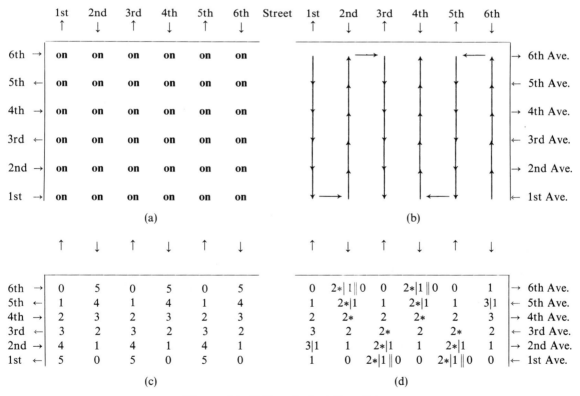

Figure 24. Sidling Grabs Idling Cabs.

	1st St. ↑	2nd St. ↓	3rd St. ↑	4th St. ↓	5th St. ↑
10th Ave. →	0	4*|3‖2‖|1‖‖|0	0	4*|3‖2‖|1‖‖|0	0
9th Ave. ←	1	4*|3‖2‖|1	1	4*|3‖2‖|1	1
8th Ave. →	2	4*|3‖2	2	4*|3‖2	2
7th Ave. ←	3	4*|3	3	4*|3	3
6th Ave. →	4	4*	4	4*	4
5th Ave. ←	5	4	4*	4	4*
4th Ave. →	5|3	3	4*|3	3	4
3rd Ave. ←	3	2	4*|3‖2	2	4|2
2nd Ave. →	3|1	1	4*|3‖2‖|1	1	2
1st Ave. ←	1	0	4*|3‖2‖|1‖‖|0	0	2|0

Figure 25. No Highway in a Town of Five Streets and Ten Avenues.

It's just as easy to solve the same kind of game in any rectangular town. Figure 25 shows the values for a 5-street, 10-avenue town, and you can guess that the value

$$9*|8\|7\||6\|||5\||||4\||\||3\|||\|2\||\|\|1\|||\||0$$

will arise in a 20-avenue town. Where have we seen such things before?

In Chapter 6 we saw that such *overheated* values arise in Domineering and in Seating Boys and Girls (though sometimes they were disturbed by infinitesimals) and that they are best expressed as integrals. We write $\int x$ for $\int_0^1 x$ and $*\int x$ for $* + \int x$, and find

$$\int 0 = 0, \qquad \int 1 = 2, \qquad \int \tfrac{1}{2} = 1*, \qquad \int \tfrac{3}{4} = 2*|1, \qquad \int \tfrac{7}{8} = 3*|2\|1, \ldots,$$

so that our previous display has value

$$-1 + \int \tfrac{1023}{1024} = *\int \tfrac{511}{1024}.$$

We also have $\int * = 1|-1$, so $\int 1* = 3|1$, etc., allowing us to rewrite Figs. 24(d) and 25 as Figs. 26 and 27.

```
 ∫0      *∫3/8    ∫0      *∫3/8    ∫0      *∫1/2
*∫1/2     ∫3/4   *∫1/2     ∫3/4   *∫1/2     ∫1*
 ∫1      *∫1      ∫1      *∫1      ∫1      *∫1½
*∫1½      ∫1     *∫1       ∫1     *∫1       ∫1
 ∫1*     *∫1/2    ∫3/4    *∫1/2    ∫3/4    *∫1/2
*∫1/2     ∫0     *∫3/8     ∫0     *∫3/8     ∫0
```

Figure 26. Overheated Cabs.

```
 ∫0      *∫15/32   ∫0      *∫15/32   ∫0
*∫1/2     ∫15/16  *∫1/2     ∫15/16  *∫1/2
 ∫1      *∫1⅜      ∫1      *∫1⅜      ∫1
*∫1½      ∫1¾     *∫1½      ∫1¾     *∫1½
 ∫2      *∫2       ∫2      *∫2       ∫2
*∫2½      ∫2      *∫2       ∫2      *∫2
 ∫2*     *∫1½      ∫1¾     *∫1½      ∫2
*∫1½      ∫1      *∫1⅜      ∫1      *∫1½*
 ∫1*     *∫1/2     ∫15/16  *∫1/2     ∫1
*∫1/2     ∫0      *∫15/32   ∫0      *∫1/2*
```

Figure 27. More Overheated Cabs.

Which union should win in Fig. 23? The four cabs are all at intersections of value $*\int_8^3$ and so have total value

$$* + * + * + * + \int(\tfrac{3}{8} + \tfrac{3}{8} + \tfrac{3}{8} + \tfrac{3}{8}) = \int_2^3 = 3*,$$

and the allowance of 3 pass moves to the RRR subtracts 3 from this, leaving $*$, so whichever union starts first should win the game.

In a well-fought game the first four moves should move all four cabs, after which

$$*\int_8^3 + *\int_8^3 + *\int_8^3 + *\int_8^3$$

will become

$$\int_4^3 + 0 + \int_4^3 + 0.$$

The next two moves should both be with the cabs that are now on 2nd or 5th Avenue, to make the sum

$$*\int 1 + 0 + *\int_2^1 + 0,$$

and the best next move is with the cab on 3rd or 4th Avenue. The cab-sum will then be

$$\int 1 + 0 + *\int_2^1 + 0 = 3,$$

making the whole game have value

$$3 - 3 = 0.$$

If RRR started, it's now LLL's turn and RRR can win by passing 3 times in succession. If LLL started, the RRR will find that their 3 passes aren't quite enough; whether they use them or not, LLL will always find a place to move.

BACKSLIDING TOADS-AND-FROGS

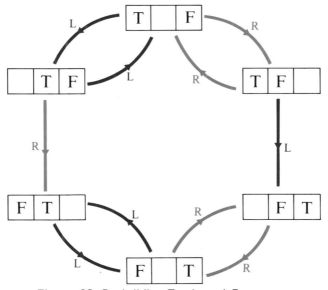

Figure 28. Backsliding Toads-and-Frogs.

This is played like ordinary Toads-and-Frogs (Chapter 1) except that the animals can *slide* backwards as well as forwards, but may not *jump* backwards. Here is the $(1,1)_1$ game (Fig. 28). Find the onsides, starting from □FT ⩽ |**on** = 0, and check that the offsides are the same, with the values of the positions $0, *, 0, *, \ldots$ alternately; so whoever starts loses.

Try analyzing the $(1,1)_2$ (one toad, one frog, two places between) and $(2,2)_1$ games and check your results in the Extras.

EXTRAS

BACH'S CAROUSEL

We tried quite hard to prove that every loopy game had stoppers for its onside and offside before Clive Bach, to whom some of the theory in this chapter is due, eventually found a game we call the Carousel (Fig. 29) which has several disturbing features:

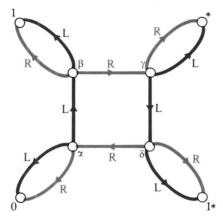

Figure 29. Bach's Carousel.

   (i) its onsides and offsides are *not* equivalent to stoppers.
  (ii) there is some dominated move that cannot be omitted,
 (iii) if, in $\alpha - \alpha$, the first player always moves round the carousel, the second player cannot afford to do anything but make the mirror image move in the other component.

Statements (i) and (ii) are proved as follows. As regards the onsides $\alpha^+, \beta^+, \gamma^+, \delta^+$, the Carousel is equivalent to

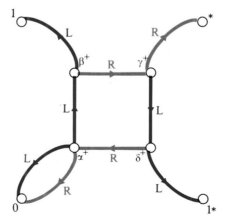

349

obtained by omitting the dominated Left option $*$ of γ and Right's options 1 of β, $1*$ of δ. This has no *reversible* options from any position and only one dominated option (0 as a Left option of α). The proof of the Simplest Form Theorem now shows that any game in simplest form equivalent to α^+ must have the structure obtained by omitting this last dominated move.

But if we omit the dominated Left option 0 of α^+, the resulting game $\hat{\alpha}$, say, is not equivalent to α^+! You can check this by showing that Right can win $\hat{\alpha} - \alpha^+$. So α^+ has no simplest form, and cannot be a stopper.

The reason why 0 cannot be omitted, even though it's dominated, is roughly that Left can always arrive at a better position by taking another trip round the Carousel than by stepping off to 0 now. But there *are* circumstances in which he can win by stepping off sometime and *won't* win by going round and round for ever!

Question: Is there an alternative notion of simplest form that works for *all* finite loopy games (in particular, for the Carousel)?

Bach also points out that the sum of the two stoppers s_0 and t_0 in Fig. 30 apparently doesn't have an onside or an offside equivalent to a stopper. (In Fig. 30, "semi-star", $\frac{*}{2}$, is $\{*,\uparrow|\downarrow*,0\}$.)

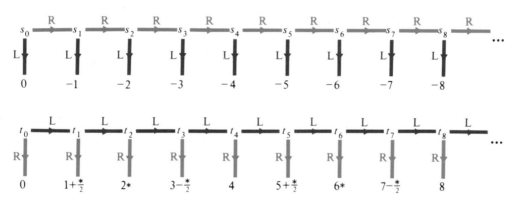

Figure 30. The Sides of the Sum of these Stoppers are not Equivalent to Stoppers.

PROOF OF THE SIDLING THEOREM

If the sidling process for a game α^+ converges when started from **on**, it produces upper bounds

$$\alpha(\mathbf{on}), \qquad\qquad \beta(\mathbf{on}), \qquad\qquad \ldots$$

or say,

$$[\alpha], \qquad\qquad [\beta], \qquad\qquad \ldots$$

for the various positions

$$\alpha^+ \qquad\qquad \beta^+, \qquad\qquad \ldots$$

of α^+, that satisfy

$$[\alpha] \leqslant \{[\alpha^L] | [\alpha^R]\}, \qquad [\beta] \leqslant \{[\beta^L] | [\beta^R]\}, \qquad \ldots$$

(in fact with equality). We show that for *any* games $[\alpha], [\beta], \ldots$ satisfying these inequalities, we have

$$[\alpha] \leqslant \alpha^+, \qquad\qquad [\beta] \leqslant \beta^+, \qquad\qquad \ldots$$

(and if $[\alpha], [\beta], \ldots$ are also upper bounds we again have equality).

We suppose therefore that Left is given survival strategies in each of the games

$$\{[\alpha^L] | [\alpha^R]\} - [\alpha], \qquad \{[\beta^L] | [\beta^R]\} - [\beta], \qquad \ldots$$

and desires one in

$$\alpha^+ - [\alpha].$$

—Since the new strategy is quite hard to find, we shall suppose that Right kindly places a potential infinity of his more mathematically inclined servants, messrs.

$$\text{rado,} \quad \text{radon,} \quad \ldots \quad \text{rademacher,} \quad \ldots$$
$$r_0, \qquad r_1, \qquad \ldots \qquad\quad r_m, \qquad\quad \ldots$$

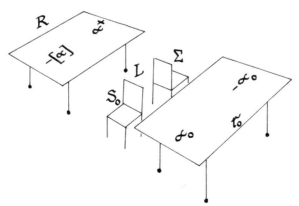

Figure 31. Sidling Strategy—Starting Seats.

at the disposal of Left, and allows him to use the Great Hall, and various furnishings, of *The Wright House*, which is rather a grand establishment.

On the far table in Fig. 31 is set up the real game $\alpha^+ - [\alpha]$ which Left is to play against his real opponent, Right. But, even before play starts, Left instructs r_0 to bring in an additional table on which is set up the difference game

$$\{[\alpha^L][\alpha^R]\} - \{[\alpha^L][\alpha^R]\} = \alpha_0 - \alpha_0, \quad \text{say},$$

and a seat labelled S_0, to be placed near the games

$$\{[\alpha^L][\alpha^R]\} = \alpha_0 \quad \text{and} \quad -[\alpha].$$

Left has, by the hypotheses of the theorem, a survival strategy, which we also call S_0, in the sum of these two games. The seat marked Σ, which was already in the Hall, is placed near the games

$$\alpha^+ \quad \text{and} \quad -\alpha_0.$$

As the game proceeds, Left occasionally instructs a new footman, r_i, to bring in a new seat, S_i, and a new table on which is set up a position of the form $\alpha_i - \alpha_i$. Footman r_i is detailed from then on to respond to a Left move in either α_i or $-\alpha_i$ with the mirror-image move in the other. In Fig. 32 we see a number of these tables, all marked with the positions in which they were originally set up.

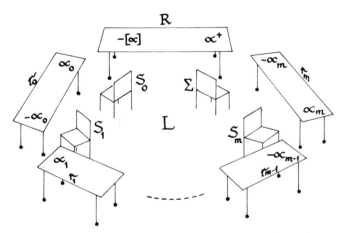

Figure 32. Right, rado, radon, . . . , round to rademacher.

The seats $S_0, S_1, \ldots, S_m$ and Σ are placed *between* adjacent tables, and each corresponds to a strategy, of sorts, for playing the two games nearest to it. The strategies S_i are easiest to describe. When seat S_i was first brought in, the games it was put next to were in a position of the form

$$\{[\beta^L][\beta^R]\} - [\beta]$$

for some position β of α; strategy S_i is Left's survival strategy for this game given by our hypotheses.

The two games nearest to seat Σ will usually have the form

$$\beta = \{\beta^L | \beta^R\} \quad \text{and} \quad -\{[\beta^L][\beta^R]\}$$

for some position β of α. The "strategy" Σ is then the following sequence of actions. If Right, or rademacher, makes a move in either of these games, Left is to make the corresponding move in the other, making the compound position have the form

$$\gamma - [\gamma]$$

for some position $\gamma = \beta^L$ or β^R of α. He then instructs a new footman, r_{m+1}, to bring in a new table on which is set up the difference game

$$\{[\gamma^L][\gamma^R]\} - \{[\gamma^L][\gamma^R]\},$$

and a new seat, S_{m+1}, to be placed near to the games

$$\{[\gamma^L][\gamma^R]\} \quad \text{and} \quad -[\gamma]$$

for whose sum he has a survival strategy of the same name, S_{m+1}. The seat Σ is then repositioned next to

$$\gamma = \{\gamma^L | \gamma^R\} \quad \text{and} \quad -\{[\gamma^L][\gamma^R]\}.$$

Left's total strategy is therefore this. To any move, whether played by his real opponent, Right, or one of the footmen $r_0, r_1, \ldots$, he replies with the response given by the strategy corresponding to the nearest seat. The strategies S_i are those for various differences $\alpha_i - \alpha_{i-1}$ with $\alpha_i \geqslant \alpha_{i-1}$ that are given us by the hypotheses, while the strategy Σ requires just one "imitation" move, and a call for a new seat and table to be inserted. It is plain that this compound strategy always gives Left a reply in a game somewhere in the Hall, but it's not entirely clear that he will eventually respond to any move in the real game with another move in that game, and perhaps even less clear that he avoids loss in that game if it continues indefinitely. We now proceed to establish these facts.

If infinitely many tables are brought in, then Left certainly makes infinitely many moves against his opponent in α^+, and since all infinite plays in α^+ are wins for Left, he avoids loss.

If not, we can imagine that no more tables are brought in than those shown in Fig. 32, say, and therefore

$$\text{sign}(\alpha^+) = \text{sign}(\alpha_m) = 0.$$

Now strategies $S_0, \ldots, S_m$ arrange that

$$\text{sign}([\alpha]) \leqslant \text{sign}(\alpha_0) \leqslant \text{sign}(\alpha_1) \leqslant \ldots \leqslant \text{sign}(\alpha_m) = 0,$$

and so $\text{sign}([\alpha]) = 0$ or $-$. If $\text{sign}([\alpha]) = -$, then Left certainly makes infinitely many moves in the real game $\alpha^+ - [\alpha]$ and satisfies the REMAIN,ONTOP survival conditions for comparing loopy games. If $\text{sign}([\alpha]) = 0$, the total play in all components is finite and Left makes the last move. This cannot be against a manservant, who always replies, so must be against his real opponent, Right. The Sidling Theorem is therefore proved.

A form of the sidling process appears in Bob Li's paper which first inspired us to attempt a general theory of loopy games. The main result of that paper is essentially the Sidling Theorem in the case when all onsides and offsides are numbers.

ANSWER TO EXERCISE ONE

It's easy to check there's no infinite alternating sequence of moves from any position of this game, so α, β, γ, δ are stoppers and we need only sidle in from one side, say from **off**.

From the defining equations

$$\alpha = \{\delta| \ \}, \qquad \beta = \{\alpha|\alpha\}, \qquad \gamma = \{ \ |\alpha\}, \qquad \delta = \{\gamma|\beta\},$$

we find successively

$$\alpha \geqslant \{\mathbf{off}| \ \} = 0,$$

$$\beta \geqslant \{0|0\} = *,$$

$$\gamma \geqslant \{ \ |0\} = -1,$$

$$\delta \geqslant \{-1|*\} = 0,$$

$$\alpha \geqslant \{0| \ \} = 1,$$

$$\beta \geqslant \{1|1\} = 1*,$$

$$\gamma \geqslant \{ \ |1\} = 0,$$

$$\delta \geqslant \{0|1*\} = 1,$$

$$\alpha \geqslant \{1| \ \} = 2,$$

$$\beta \geqslant \{2|2\} = 2*,$$

$$\gamma \geqslant \{ \ |2\} = 0,$$

$$\delta \geqslant \{0|2*\} = 1,$$

and the sidling has finished. In fact, sidling in from **on** is quicker.

tis AND tisn

The onsides of

$$\mathbf{tis} = \{\mathbf{tisn}| \ \} \quad \text{and} \quad \mathbf{tisn} = \{ \ |\mathbf{tis}\}$$

can be approximated by

$$\mathbf{tisn} \leqslant \{ \ |\mathbf{on}\} = 0,$$

$$\mathbf{tis} \leqslant \{0| \ \} = 1,$$

$$\mathbf{tisn} \leqslant \{ \ |1\} = 0$$

and the offsides by

$$\mathbf{tis} \geqslant \{\mathbf{off}| \ \} = 0,$$

$$\mathbf{tisn} \geqslant \{ \ |0\} = -1,$$

$$\mathbf{tis} \geqslant \{-1| \ \} = 0,$$

so

$$\mathbf{tis} = 1 \ \& \ 0, \qquad \mathbf{tisn} = 0 \ \& \ -1.$$

To answer the question asked earlier about the outcome of

$$\mathbf{tis} + *$$

when all infinite plays count as draws, note that Left wins by moving in *, since Right has no move in **tis**. But if Right starts he must play to **tis** $+0$ and play will now be infinite, so the game is counted a draw.

upon

The game **upon** has the stable degree

$$d = \uparrow^{\text{on}} = \{0 \mid -\textbf{upon}*\} \qquad (\text{“up-onth”}).$$

In this case by adding **upon**s and their negatives we get one class for each $n = \ldots -2, -1, 0, 1, 2, \ldots$ and each class contains just two varieties

$$(\textbf{upon} \times n)\langle -d\rangle \quad \text{and} \quad (\textbf{upon} \times n)\langle d\rangle.$$

So to add two such things you just add the n's the way you did at school and the d's like this:

$$d + d = d, \qquad (-d) + (-d) = -d,$$
$$d + (-d) = d \,\&\, (-d) = (-d) + d.$$

BACKSLIDING TOADS-AND-FROGS

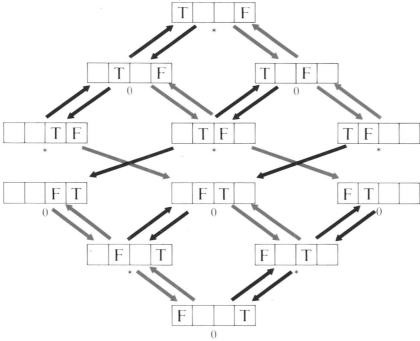

Figure 33. Latent Loopiness in Backsliding $(1,1)_2$ Toads-and-Frogs.

After sidling in on $(1,1)_2$ Toads-and-Frogs we obtain only the not very loopy looking values 0 and $*$ as in Fig. 33. However there is latent loopiness which may show itself in actual play. The sidling process for the $(2,2)_1$ game is best done in the six separate stages of Fig. 34, since then you use the fact that any jumping move takes you to an already analyzed position. You'll see that patently loopy values arise in the innermost portion (only).

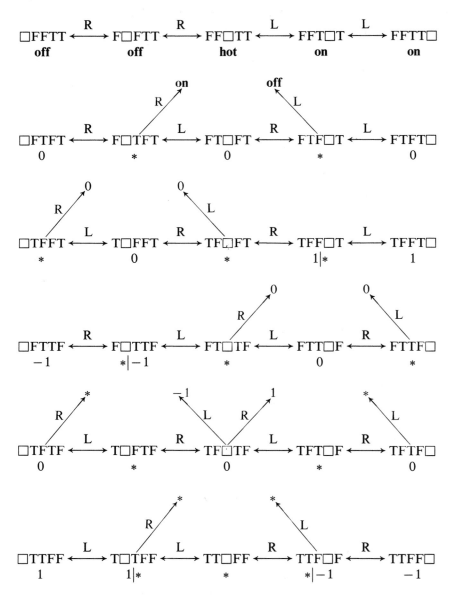

Figure 34. Patent Loopiness in Backsliding $(2,2)_1$ Toads-and-Frogs.

REFERENCES AND FURTHER READING

J.H. Conway, "On Numbers and Games", Academic Press, London and New York, 1976, Chapter 16.

J.H. Conway, Loopy games, in Béla Bollobás (ed.) "Advances in Graph Theory" (Cambridge Combinatorial Conference 1977) Ann. Discrete Math. **3** (1978) 55–74.

James Alan Flanigan, An analysis of some take-away and loopy partizan graph games, Ph.D. dissertation, UCLA, 1979.

Robert Li Shuo-Yen. Sums of Zuchswang games, J. Combin. Theory, Ser. A **21** (1976) 52–67.

Ahiezer S. Shaki, Algebraic solutions of partizan games with cycles, Math. Proc. Cambridge Philos. Soc. **85** (1979) 227–246.

Chapter 12

Games Eternal—Games Entailed

If it was not for the entail I should not mind it.
      Jane Austen, *Pride and Prejudice*, ch. 23.

The hornèd moon, with one bright star
Within the nether tip
      Samuel Taylor Coleridge, *The Ancient Mariner*, pt. iii.

What happens when you play a sum of games in a way that breaks some of the usual moving and ending conditions? The two main theories of this chapter are about *impartial* games—C.A.B. Smith's for impartial loopy games, that might last forever, and our own new theory for games with entailing or complimenting moves. The harder theories of partizan loopy games and misère play of impartial ordinary ones are treated in the neighboring chapters.

Have you noticed how the almonds at parties tend to get left in the nut-bowl because they're too hard to crack? Here's a nutty little game you can use to befuddle the other guests.

FAIR SHARES AND VARIED PAIRS

Figure 1. Anyone for Fair Shares and Varied Pairs?

359

Take up to 10 almonds and arrange them in heaps on the carpet—we suggest you start with lots of 2's and 1's. Then challenge the guest who interests you most to a game of **Fair Shares and Varied Pairs** in which the moves are:

Divide any heap into two or more *equal-sized* heaps,   **FAIR SHARES**

or

Unite any *two* heaps of *different sizes*.   **VARIED PAIRS**

You win by completely separating the almonds (into heaps of size 1) after which your opponent has no legal move. There's always at least one move from any other position, e.g. to **shatter** some heap into heaps of size 1.

The funny thing about this game is that you can often return to a position you've already seen, not always with the same player to move. In fact it can be quite hilarious to watch an accomplished player spin the game round and round in several different circles before sneaking in the win. When the winning move comes, the opponent's too giddy to work out just where they stepped off the carousel (especially if this came after another glass of wine).

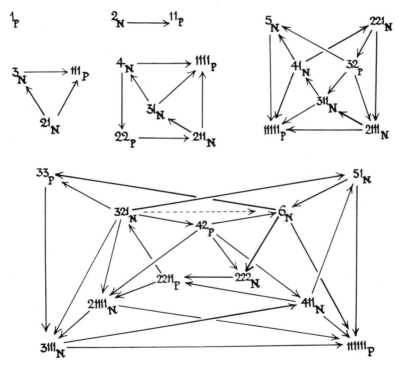

Figure 2. Fair Shares and Varied Pairs Positions with up to Six Almonds. (The dotted arrow refers to the variant Fair Shares and Unequal Partners.)

To keep your own balance in this game you'll obviously need to know the $\mathscr{P}$-positions. For instance, in the 9-almond game these are:

$$72, \quad 54, \quad 5211, \quad 4311, \quad 4221, \quad 333, \quad 321111, \quad 222111, \quad 111111111.$$

It's easy to find these on a graph of the game—mark a position $\mathscr{P}$ only if all its options have been marked $\mathscr{N}$ (in particular if it has no option) and mark a position $\mathscr{N}$ if it has an option already marked $\mathscr{P}$. We've done this in Fig. 2 for the games with up to 6 almonds.

To win, of course, you must always move to a $\mathscr{P}$-position. But if this is all you know, you might just conceivably find yourself going round and round Fig. 3 for the rest of time. You're always moving to $\mathscr{P}$-positions (in the boxes) but somehow you never seem to win. Why is this?

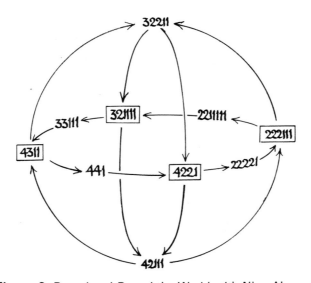

Figure 3. Round and Round the World with Nine Almonds.

HOW SOON CAN YOU WIN?

The other thing you need to know about is the *remoteness* of the positions. Recall from Chapter 9 that the remoteness is the number of moves in which the winner can force his win and recall that a position is $\mathscr{P}$ or $\mathscr{N}$ according as its remoteness is even or odd. But games with cycles can also have positions with infinite remoteness from which neither player can force a win because with best play the game continues for ever.

For such games we work out the remoteness of the positions in stages:

Stage 0.   Assign remoteness 0 to all terminal positions.

Stage 1.   Assign remoteness 1 to any position with an option of remoteness 0.

Stage 2.   Assign remoteness 2 to any new position *all* of whose options have been assigned remoteness 1.

Stage 3.   Assign remoteness 3 to any new position with an option of remoteness 2.

…   …

Stage 2n   Assign remoteness $2n$ to those new positions *all* of whose options have already been assigned smaller odd numbers (the greatest of which will be $2n-1$).

Stage 2n + 1.   Assign remoteness $2n+1$ to any new position which has an option of remoteness $2n$.

THERE MAY BE OPEN POSITIONS (𝒪-POSITIONS)

When you reach a stage where you're unable to assign any more remoteness according to these rules, all other positions have remoteness infinity and the game will continue for ever with the best play. We call these **open positions** or 𝒪-**positions**. Figure 4 shows all the 𝒫-positions (boxed) and some of the 𝒩-positions in Fair Shares and Varied Pairs played with up to 10 almonds, arranged according to their remoteness. If you want to win, remember the 𝒫-positions, especially the ones of low remoteness, but to avoid giving the show away you should not always take the shortest possible win. You can get a longer ride on the carousel by moving to 𝒫 positions of higher remoteness than necessary for a few times. Against a novice it's often a good idea to move to 𝒩-positions of high remoteness, and wait for the inevitable mistake.

It's a remarkable fact that with 10 almonds or less there are no infinite games with best play. As soon as we get to 11 almonds, the situation changes dramatically:

There is 1   𝒫-position $\boxed{11111111111}$ with remoteness 0,

         10   𝒩-positions 2111111111, 311111111, 41111111, … with remoteness 1, and

         45   𝒪-positions (all those with 2 or more splittable heaps).

So the game is rather dull—even when played between an expert and a tyro who can only see 1 move ahead, it will go on for ever.

If n is the sum of 2 primes, p and q, then in the n-almond game the "Goldbach" position $\boxed{p,q}$ has remoteness 2, but we believe that for every $n > 10$ most positions are 𝒪-positions.

In any game we expect there to be more 𝒩-positions than 𝒫-positions, because a position with a 𝒫-option is automatically 𝒩. If the game has a large number of cycles we should expect also a large number of 𝒪-positions. (Fair Shares and Varied Pairs with 10 almonds or less was atypical.) So when analyzing such a game by hand it's best to concentrate on the 𝒫-positions. You first find all the terminal positions—these are the 𝒫-positions of remoteness 0. Next you attack the 𝒫-positions of remoteness 2, which are those for which every move can be reversed to a terminal position. Continue until you have exhausted all the 𝒫-positions (or yourself). It's usually a waste of ink to write down the 𝒩- or 𝒪-positions.

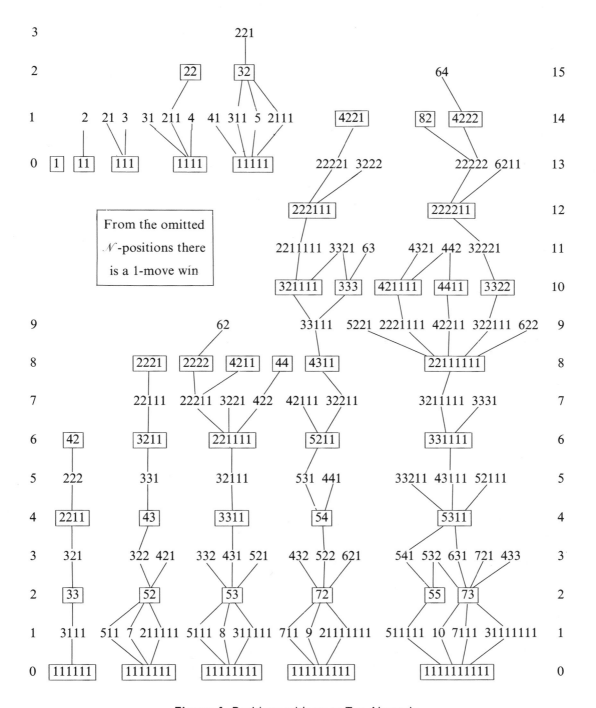

Figure 4. Positions with up to Ten Almonds.

DE BONO'S *L*-GAME

In *The Five-day Course in Thinking* Edward de Bono introduces this little game (Fig. 5).

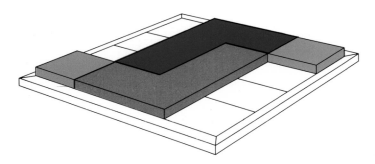

Figure 5. How to Start the *L*-Game.

It is played on a 4 × 4 board; each player has his own *L*-shaped piece which may be turned over, and there are 2 neutral 1 × 1 squares. A move has two parts:

You *must* lift up your own *L*-piece and put it back on the board in *another* position.

You *may*, if you wish, change the position of *one* of the two neutral pieces.

If you can't move, because there's only the one place for your *L*-piece, you lose.

To within symmetries of the board, there are 82 different positions for the *L*s, and therefore 82 × 28 = 2296 distinct positions in all. It's not hard to show by hand that there are just 15 $\mathscr{P}$-positions of remoteness 0; one could then look for those of remoteness 2, etc., so reducing the work to just 29 2-move backward analyses. Rather than thinking forwards or laterally, think backwards! Fortunately, however, we don't have to think at all, because V.W. Gijlswijk, G.A.P. Kindervater, G.J. van Tubergen and J.J.O.O. Wiegerink used a computer to find an optimal move from each of the 2296 positions and identified the 29 $\mathscr{P}$-positions, 1006 $\mathscr{N}$-positions and 1261 $\mathscr{O}$-positions. The $\mathscr{N}$- and $\mathscr{P}$-positions are distributed as follows:

remoteness	0	1	2	3	4	5	6	7	8	9	Total
$\mathscr{P}$-positions	15		3		3		5		3		29
$\mathscr{N}$-positions		768		27		81		11		119	1006

If you're capable of seeing just one move ahead, you don't need the complete list given in their paper. If you move to one of the 29 positions appearing in Fig. 6, and play well thereafter, you will *win*. Otherwise the game should be a *draw* by infinite repetition, unless your opponent has just left you in one of these positions with the roles reversed. In this case he probably knows what he's doing and you can expect to *lose*.

Figure 6. Remotenesses of the 29 $\mathscr{P}$-positions of De Bono's *L*-Game.

The positions in Fig. 6 have been oriented so that the red (active) *L* looks like an *L*. Try to make *your L* look like the blue (inactive) one. One of the neutral squares is printed green; the green numbers indicate possible places for the other, and tell you the remoteness of the resulting position.

In the Extras you'll find a longest sensible finishing game (remoteness 9) and N.E. Goller's elegantly simple strategy which guarantees at least a draw from the initial positon.

ADDERS-AND-LADDERS

Figure 7. A Cheap Game of Snakes-and-Ladders—Jimmy to Move.

Great-Aunt Maude gave Jimmy and Ginny a compendium of games this Christmas, but most of the games were cheaply produced and not too interesting. The Snakes-and-Ladders game, for example, was only a 5×5 card with a plastic 4-numbered die that didn't roll very well, and counters you couldn't distinguish between, as in Fig. 7. They soon found that by sliding the die along the table they could "roll" any number they liked from 1 to 4, and so they abandoned its use and just moved any counter they liked up to 4 squares onwards. They agreed that any number of counters could be on the same square and that the person who moved the last counter home was the winner.

Ginny soon noticed that when all the counters were on the top row it was what she called "that awful game with matches". In our language the game is a sum of games with one counter and the values of the top row are

$$\boxed{21} = *4, \qquad \boxed{22} = *3, \qquad \boxed{23} = *2, \qquad \boxed{24} = *1, \qquad \boxed{25} = 0.$$

When you land on $\boxed{20}$ you instantly climb the ladder to $\boxed{23}$, so

$$\boxed{20} = \boxed{23} = *2,$$

and similarly

$$\boxed{11} = \boxed{21} = *4, \qquad \boxed{9} = \boxed{25} = 0, \qquad \boxed{8} = \boxed{24} = *1$$

And because there's a snake from $\boxed{19}$ to $\boxed{7}$,

$$\boxed{19} = \boxed{7},$$

but we don't yet know the value of these two squares.

But Jimmy discovered that $\boxed{10} = \boxed{18}$ is a $\mathscr{P}$-position:

$$\boxed{10} = \boxed{18} = 0,$$

for after any Ginny move from $\boxed{18}$, Jimmy can get home in one:

Ginny's move		Jimmy's reply	
$\boxed{18} \longrightarrow$	$\boxed{19} = \boxed{7} \longrightarrow$	$\boxed{9} = $	$\boxed{25}$
$\boxed{18} \longrightarrow$	$\boxed{20} = \boxed{23} \longrightarrow$		$\boxed{25}$
$\boxed{18} \longrightarrow$	$\boxed{21} \longrightarrow$		$\boxed{25}$
$\boxed{18} \longrightarrow$	$\boxed{22} \longrightarrow$		$\boxed{25}$

Figure 8 shows the values we shall find for Adders-and-Ladders (and a simplified copy of the board for reference). A square at the foot of a ladder or head of a snake is not really a genuine position because a counter cannot stay there. Their values (red in Fig. 8) are simply copied from the other end of the (l)adder. The *loopy values* ∞_{012} and ∞_{12} will be explained later.

Because the game has cycles we are sometimes forced to compute the value of a position before we have evaluated all its options. Thus Jimmy was able to show that

$$\boxed{18} = 0,$$

despite the question mark in

$$\boxed{19} = ?, \qquad \boxed{20} = *2, \qquad \boxed{21} = *4, \qquad \boxed{22} = *3,$$

because the *questionable option is reversible* to 0:

$$\boxed{19} = \boxed{7} \longrightarrow \boxed{9} = \boxed{25} = 0.$$

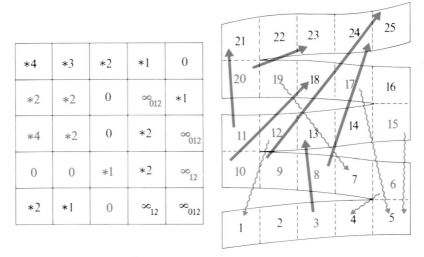

Figure 8. Adders-and-Ladders Values.

In general:

> If we have worked out the values
>
> $$*a, *b, *c, \ldots$$
>
> of *some* options of a position G and
>
> $$m = \text{mex}(a,b,c,\ldots)$$
>
> then we can assert
>
> $$G = *m$$
>
> *provided that* the *other* options of G all have reversing moves to positions already known to have value $*m$.

CALCULATING ANSWERS BY SMITH'S RULE

When the proviso is satisfied G can be replaced by $*m$ in any sum for the usual reason—it has moves corresponding to all those of $*m$, and any other move is just a delaying move which can be reversed to $*m$.

    Jimmy and Ginny didn't analyze their game much further, but *we* can, using this idea. For example the options of $\boxed{16}$ are:

$$\boxed{17} = ?, \qquad \boxed{18} = 0, \qquad \boxed{19} = ?, \qquad \boxed{20} = *2$$

and mex(0, 2)=1. So, because $\boxed{17}$ and $\boxed{19}$ have reversing moves to $*1$:

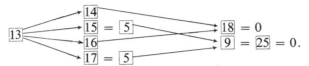

$$\boxed{17} = \boxed{5}$$
$$\boxed{8} = \boxed{24} = *1,$$
$$\boxed{19} = \boxed{7}$$

we can evaluate

$$\boxed{16} = *1.$$

Sometimes we can find the value of a position before evaluating *any* of its options. For example we could have proved that $\boxed{3} = \boxed{13} = 0$ by observing that *all* its options are reversible:

$$\boxed{13} \longrightarrow \begin{matrix} \boxed{14} \\ \boxed{15} = \boxed{5} \\ \boxed{16} \\ \boxed{17} = \boxed{5} \end{matrix} \longrightarrow \begin{matrix} \boxed{18} = 0 \\ \boxed{9} = \boxed{25} = 0. \end{matrix}$$

Here's how we justify the other non-loopy values in Fig. 8:

$$\boxed{19} = \boxed{7} = *2 \qquad \boxed{14} = *2 \qquad \boxed{2} = *1 \qquad \boxed{12} = \boxed{1} = *2$$

because

$$\boxed{8} = \boxed{24} = *1 \qquad \boxed{15} = \boxed{5} \qquad \boxed{3} = \boxed{13} = 0 \qquad \boxed{2} = *1$$
$$\boxed{9} = \boxed{25} = 0 \qquad \boxed{16} = *1 \qquad \boxed{4} \qquad \boxed{3} = \boxed{13} = 0$$
$$\boxed{10} = \boxed{18} = 0 \qquad \boxed{17} = \boxed{5} \to \boxed{7} = *2 \quad \boxed{5} \to \boxed{8} = *1 \qquad \boxed{4}$$
$$\boxed{11} = \boxed{21} = *4 \qquad \boxed{18} = 0 \qquad \boxed{6} = \boxed{4} \qquad \boxed{5} \to \boxed{7} = *2$$

and

$$\text{mex}(0,1,4) = 2 \qquad \text{mex}(0,1) = 2 \qquad \text{mex}(0) = 1 \qquad \text{mex}(0,1) = 2$$

But now there's no other position we can work out this way. In general when you've forged ahead as far as you can with Smith's Rule there often comes a stage when the analysis falters because there's no other position to which the Rule applies. All positions that are still unlabelled at this stage are called **loopy** and are *not* equivalent to Nim-heaps.

> If the non-loopy options of a loopy position G have values
>
> $$*a, *b, *c, \ldots,$$
>
> we say that G has value
>
> $$\infty_{abc\ldots}.$$

VALUES OF LOOPY POSITIONS

In particular,

$$\boxed{17} = \boxed{15} = \boxed{5} = \infty_{012}$$

$$\boxed{6} = \boxed{4} = \infty_{12}$$

as we see from their options:

$$\boxed{17} = \boxed{15} = \boxed{5} \begin{cases} \boxed{6} = \boxed{4} \\ \boxed{7} = *2 \\ \boxed{8} = *1 \\ \boxed{9} = 0 \end{cases} \qquad \boxed{6} = \boxed{4} \begin{cases} \boxed{5} \\ \boxed{6} = \boxed{4} \\ \boxed{7} = *2 \\ \boxed{8} = *1 \end{cases}$$

$$\text{mex}(0,1,2) = 3 \qquad\qquad \text{mex}(1,2) = 0$$

and the remarks:

$\boxed{5}$'s unmarked option $\boxed{4}$ has no move to an established $*3$;
$\boxed{4}$'s unmarked option $\boxed{4}$ has no move to an established 0
(although $\boxed{4}$'s other unmarked option, $\boxed{5}$, *can* be reversed to 0).

There are rules for adding these loopy games and games with ordinary nimber values. The usual Nim Addition Rule allows us to replace the non-loopy components by a single Nim-heap, $*n$, say.

$$\begin{array}{|l|}
\hline
\\
\text{With } no \text{ loopy components,} \\
\\
\qquad *n \text{ is} \begin{cases} \mathscr{P} \text{ if } n = 0, \\ \mathscr{N} \text{ if not}. \end{cases} \\
\\
\text{With } one \text{ loopy component,} \\
\\
\infty_{abc\ldots} + *n \text{ is} \begin{cases} \mathscr{N} \text{ if } n \text{ is one of } a,b,c,\ldots, \\ \mathscr{O} \text{ otherwise} \end{cases} \\
\\
\qquad \text{and has total value } \infty_{ABC\ldots} \\
\\
\qquad \text{where } A = a \overset{*}{+} n, \quad B = b \overset{*}{+} n, \ldots. \\
\\
\text{With } more \text{ loopy components,} \\
\\
\qquad \infty_{abc\ldots} + \infty_{\alpha\beta\gamma\ldots} + \ldots \text{ is always } \mathscr{O}, \\
\\
\qquad \text{and has total value } \infty. \\
\\
\hline
\end{array}$$

ADDING LOOPY VALUES

What should Jimmy do from the Adders-and-Ladders position of Fig. 7? The values of the three counters, read from Fig. 8, are

$$\boxed{1} = *2, \qquad \boxed{5} = \infty_{012}, \qquad \boxed{22} = *3,$$

so the position is really

$$\infty_{012} + *1 = \infty_{103}.$$

Jimmy's unique winning move is from $\boxed{5}$ to $\boxed{8}$ (and so up the ladder to $\boxed{24}$) since $\boxed{8} = *1$. If instead he moves from $\boxed{1}$ to $\boxed{3} = \boxed{13} = 0$, or from $\boxed{1}$ to $\boxed{4} = \infty_{12}$, the value becomes

$$\infty_{012} + *3 = \infty_{321} \quad \text{or} \quad \infty_{012} + \infty_{12} + *3 = \infty$$

and Ginny will make sure that the game continues forever (unless Jimmy makes another stupid move). Had he moved from $\boxed{1}$ to $\boxed{2} = *1$, the value would be

$$\infty_{012} + *2 \, (= \infty_{230})$$

and Ginny would instantly move from $\boxed{5}$ to $\boxed{7} = *2$.

JUST HOW LOOPY CAN YOU GET?

Loopiness may be latent, patent or even blatant!

Some positions admit circular chains of moves that need never arise in best play, even when you're adding them to other (non-loopy) games. This kind of loopiness is really illusory; unless the winner wants to take you on a trip you won't notice it. Such positions have the same kind of values $*n$ as non-loopy ones, and are only **latently loopy**.

Other positions reveal their loopiness in their values:

$$\infty_{abc\ldots}$$

and so are **patently loopy**. However if one of the subscripts is zero the loopiness only affects best play when the game arises in a sum. If the game is played by itself it should take only finitely many moves.

If no subscript is zero the position is **blatantly loopy**. The best move from such a position is to another of the same type and so a well-played game will last for ever.

Fair Shares and Varied Pairs exemplifies all three cases. Table 1 will show that with 9 almonds or less, all the loopiness is latent, while with 11 or more almonds almost all positions are blatantly loopy, often having the loopiest possible value ∞. With exactly 10 almonds there are lots of loopy positions, but none of them is blatantly so. For example 4321 with value ∞_0 is an $\mathcal{N}$-position (move to 421111) but $4321 + *1$ is an $\mathcal{O}$-position.

CORRALL AUTOMOTIVE BETTERMENT SCHEME

Figure 9 is a view of Corrall Island, which was a Charming Antipodean Beauty Spot before the Corrall Automotive Betterment Scheme, financed by the island's three wealthy landowners, built those expensive new super-highways. The island's two political parties (Left and Right) are now running for election and the gallop polls predict a walk-over for whichever party puts the last car on the scrap-heap. The parties have already enforced the one-way system indicated and each will alternately bribe a chauffeur to drive his car along one highway (in the proper direction) to the next intersection. You will see that there is no legal move away from the scrap-heap. How should we advise the ruling party, which must make the first move?

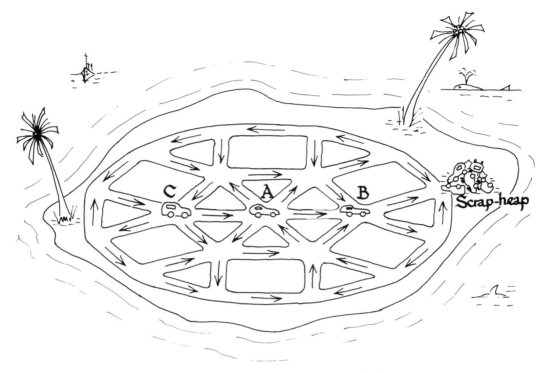

Figure 9. Corrall Automotive Betterment Scheme.

This is exactly the same kind of game as Adders-and-Ladders, but played on a rather more ingenious graph. Figure 10 shows the values, and with each non-loopy value, the **stage** at which we justified it, starting with the scrap-heap at stage 0. The C.A.B.S. Rule enables us to

> assign value $*m$ to a position G at stage k,
> *provided that G has options which have been*
> assigned values $*a$, $*b$, $*c$, ... with $\text{mex}(a,b,c,...) = m$ at earlier
> stages, *and that* all other options have moves to positions
> assigned $*m$ at stages earlier than k.

CALCULATING ASSIGNMENTS BY STAGES

For example, the node F which we labelled $*1$ at stage 5 ($*1_{@5}$) had an option E labelled 0 at stage 1, and the only other option (C, for which we later found the value $\infty_{1\,3}$) had a reversing move to D, labelled $*1$ at stage 4. This is actually the unique winning move from Fig. 9.

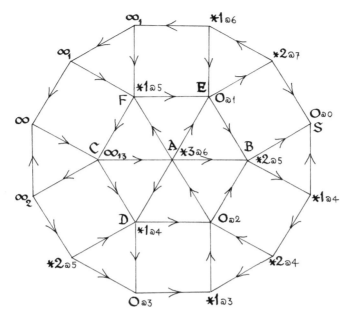

Figure 10. Graph, Values and Stages for Corrall Automotive Betterment Scheme.

So long as you label at least one node at each stage, and continue until Smith's Rule is no longer applicable, you'll get the correct values. But if you always label each node at the *earliest* stage you can (as we did for Corrall Island), you'll have a bonus:

> The number of the earliest stage
> at which you can label a position G
> with value $*n$ is half the remoteness of
> $(G$ + a Nim-heap of size n).

CELERITY ADDS BONUS STEINHAUS

SHARING OUT OTHER KINDS OF NUT

You can use these ideas to play a sum of games of Fair Shares and Varied Pairs. This time you use some heaps of Cashews, some heaps of Almonds, some heaps of Brazils, and later on we'll add a heap of Sweets. No heap may contain two different kinds of nut, but otherwise the rules are as before—you may split a heap into *equal* smaller ones or unite two heaps which contain *different* numbers of the *same* kind of nut. Table 1 contains the value and the earliest stage at which it can be assigned for each position with at most 10 nuts of one kind. You might like to practise your skill by recalculating some of these from the graphs shown in Fig. 2.

1	$0@_0$	1111111	$0@_0$	111111111	$0@_0$	1111111111	$0@_0$
		52	$0@_1$	72	$0@_1$	55	$0@_1$
11	$0@_0$	7	$*1@_1$	54	$0@_2$	73	$0@_1$
2	$*1@_1$	43	$0@_2$	5211	$0@_3$	5311	$0@_2$
		511	$*1@_2$	4311	$0@_4$	331111	$0@_3$
111	$0@_0$	3211	$0@_3$	321111	$0@_5$	22111111	$0@_4$
3	$*1@_1$	31111	$*1@_3$	333	$0@_5$	3322	$0@_5$
21	$*2@_2$	2221	$0@_4$	222111	$0@_6$	421111	$0@_5$
		22111	$0@_4$	9	$*1@_6$	4411	$0@_5$
1111	$0@_0$	211111	$*2@_4$	4221	$0@_7$	222211	$0@_6$
22	$0@_1$	331	$*2@_4$	711	$*1@_7$	4222	$0@_7$
4	$*1@_2$	421	$*1@_5$	51111	$*1@_8$	82	$0@_7$
211	$*1@_3$	322	$*2@_5$	3111111	$*1@_9$	22222	$*1@_7$
31	$*2@_3$	4111	$*2@_5$	441	$*1@_9$	10	$*2@_8$
		61	$*3@_5$	2211111	$*1@_{10}$	622	∞_{0_1}
11111	$0@_0$			42111	$*1@_{10}$	64	∞_{0_2}
32	$0@_1$	11111111	$0@_0$	21111111	$*2@_{10}$	91	∞_{0_2}
5	$*1@_1$	53	$0@_1$	33111	$*2@_{10}$		
311	$*1@_2$	3311	$0@_2$	3222	$*1@_{11}$		
221	$*1@_3$	221111	$0@_3$	3321	$*1@_{11}$		
2111	$*2@_3$	2222	$0@_4$	32211	$*2@_{11}$		
41	$*2@_4$	4211	$0@_4$	411111	$*2@_{11}$		
		44	$0@_4$	522	$*2@_{11}$		
111111	$0@_0$	8	$*1@_5$	6111	$*3@_{11}$		
33	$0@_1$	422	$*1@_6$	22221	$*2@_{12}$		
2211	$0@_2$	71	$*2@_6$	63	$*2@_{12}$		
42	$0@_3$	22211	$*1@_7$	432	$*3@_{13}$		
222	$*1@_3$	5111	$*1@_8$	81	$*3@_{13}$		
51	$*1@_4$	611	$*3@_8$	531	$*4@_{14}$		
6	$*2@_4$	311111	$*1@_9$	621	$*4@_{14}$		
3111	$*1@_5$	332	$*1@_9$				
411	$*2@_5$	41111	$*2@_9$				
21111	$*2@_6$	2111111	$*2@_{10}$				
321	$*3@_7$	3221	$*2@_{11}$				
		32111	$*3@_{11}$				
		521	$*3@_{11}$				
		62	$*4@_{11}$				
		431	$*3@_{12}$				

The 25 partitions of 10 not listed here each have value ∞_0.

Table 1. Values and Stages for Fair Shares and Varied Pairs.

FAIR SHARES AND UNEQUAL PARTNERS

In this variation you are also allowed to combine three or more heaps, all of different sizes (the dotted arrow in Fig. 2 represents such a move). This alters only a few of the values; you can find the details in the Extras.

SWEETS AND NUTS, AND MAYBE A DATE?

But let's imagine that the guest you're interested in has another game in mind, and promises to make a date if you win the following variation. You play an ordinary game of Fair Shares and

Varied Pairs with 9 almonds, but as an alternative to moving, either player may eat a number of the toffees you can also see in Fig. 1. What result should you expect if you're to start from the position of that figure?

THE ADDITIONAL SUBTRACTION GAMES

Remember that in the Subtraction Game $S(a,b,c,\ldots)$ you are allowed to take away a or b or c or ... beans from any non-empty heap. What happens if some of $a, b, c, \ldots$ are negative? Since we then find ourselves adding beans to a heap, such a game might go on forever, and we need the Smith Theory to analyze it. Table 2 gives some typical values.

n	0	1	2	3	4	5	6	7	8	9	10	11	12	13	14	15
$S(-1,2,5)$	$0_{@0}$	$0_{@1}$	$2_{@3}$	$1_{@2}$	$0_{@1}$	$3_{@5}$	$2_{@4}$	$1_{@3}$	$0_{@2}$	$3_{@6}$	$2_{@5}$	$1_{@4}$	$0_{@3}$	$3_{@7}$	$2_{@6}$	$1_{@5}$
$S(-2,4,5)$	$0_{@0}$	$1_{@2}$	$0_{@1}$	$0_{@1}$	$1_{@3}$	$2_{@5}$	$3_{@7}$	$1_{@4}$	$2_{@6}$	∞_{12}	∞_{23}	∞_{13}	∞_{12}	∞_{2}	∞	∞
$S(-1,3,8)$	$0_{@0}$	$1_{@2}$	$0_{@1}$	$1_{@3}$	$0_{@2}$	$1_{@4}$	$0_{@3}$	$1_{@5}$	$2_{@7}$	$3_{@7}$	$2_{@6}$	$0_{@3}$	$1_{@5}$	$0_{@4}$	$1_{@6}$	$0_{@5}$
$S(-2,3,8)$	$0_{@0}$	$0_{@1}$	$0_{@2}$	$2_{@4}$	$1_{@2}$	$1_{@3}$	$0_{@1}$	$0_{@2}$	$2_{@4}$	$2_{@5}$	$1_{@3}$	$1_{@4}$	$0_{@2}$	$0_{@3}$	$2_{@5}$	$2_{@6}$
$S(-2,4,10)$	$0_{@0}$	∞	$0_{@1}$	∞	$2_{@3}$	∞	$1_{@2}$	∞	$0_{@1}$	∞	$3_{@5}$	∞	$2_{@4}$	∞	$1_{@3}$	∞

Table 2. Values and Stages for some Additional Subtraction Games.

HORSEFLY

A **Horsefly**'s moves are 6 of the 8 possible moves of a knight in Chess (see Fig. 11) but there's another restriction: it can never exactly reverse the last move it made (even if other horseflies have moved meanwhile). The game shown in Fig. 11 is won by whoever lands the first horsefly at a winning post. Would you like to play first?

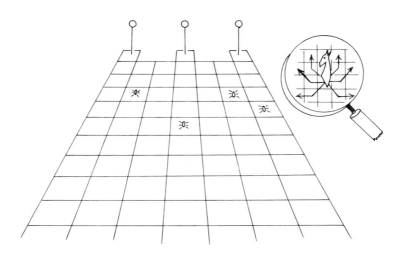

Figure 11. A Game of Horsefly.

SELECTIVE AND SUBSELECTIVE COMPOUNDS OF IMPARTIAL GAMES

In the same paper that deals with loopy impartial games, C.A.B. Smith discusses selective compounds in the impartial case. The answers are very easy. In the normal play case,

$$G \lor H \lor \dots$$

is a $\mathscr{P}$-position only when all of

$$G, H, \dots$$

are. The misère play outcome coincides with the normal outcome unless there is only one game that has not yet ended.

Smith has also discussed what we shall call **subselective compounds** in which the legal move is to move in any selection of components *except* the whole set. Such a compound is a $\mathscr{P}$-position only when the nim-values of all its components are equal. (If they're *not* all equal, you should find the lowest and reduce the rest to coincide with it.)

ENTAILING MOVES

Top Entails is a new type of heap game, played with stacks of coins. You must either split a stack into two smaller ones or remove the top coin from a stack. In the latter case your opponent's next move must use the same stack. Don't leave a stack of 1 on the board, because your opponent can remove it and then demand that you follow with a move in the resulting empty stack!

The theory of sums of games when such **entailing moves** are allowed appears for the first time in *Winning Ways*. In such sums

$$A + B + C + \dots$$

you may make a move in any component, unless your opponent has just made an *entailing move* somewhere, when you are required to follow him with a move in the same component. Often the best reply to one entailing move is another, and we might have a sustained rally of entailing moves in the same component.

The theory of such games reduces to Nim in a new way. The typical component A has a whole collection

$$a_0 < a_1 < a_2 < a_3 < \dots$$

of nim-values, only the *least* of which, a_0, is **relevant**, unless the component has just been reached by an entailing move, when *all* are relevant. To compute new values:

> The complete set of nim-values for G
> consists of *all* numbers
>
> $$g_0 < g_1 < g_2 < \dots$$
>
> *not* among the relevant values for options of G.
> Only g_0 is relevant
> unless the move to G is entailing.

And to find good moves:

A move to

$$A + B + C + \ldots$$

that *entails* a reply in component A
is good whenever there is *any* a_i for which

$$*a_i + *b_0 + *c_0 + \ldots = 0$$

while a *non*-entailing move to this position
is good, as usual, just when

$$*a_0 + *b_0 + *c_0 + \ldots = 0.$$

To see that these rules work, if the current position

$$A + B + C + \ldots = G,$$

of total value

$$*a_0 + *b_0 + *c_0 + \ldots = *g_0,$$

is not entailed, then, much as in the ordinary theory, the nim-values of its options include every number less than g_0, but not g_0 itself. If the move to A was entailing, the total values after possible moves are precisely those nimbers *not* of the form

$$*a_i + *b_0 + *c_0 + \ldots .$$

Here is a table of values for Top Entails:

0	◉	10	$*1,4\rightarrow$	20	$*2,5,8\rightarrow$	30	$*2,7\rightarrow$	40	$*1,4,8,9,12\rightarrow$
1	꒰	11	$*3.$	21	$*0,1,7.$	31	$*0,5.$	41	$*6,7,11.$
2	◉	12	$*4\rightarrow$	22	$*3,4,6,8\rightarrow$	32	$*8\rightarrow$	42	$*2,5,8,10,12\rightarrow$
3	꒰	13	$*0,2.$	23	$*2,5.$	33	$*1,6.$	43	$*9.$
4	$*1\rightarrow$	14	$*3,5\rightarrow$	24	$*7\rightarrow$	34	$*5,9\rightarrow$	44	$*3,6,7,8,11,13\rightarrow$
5	$*0.$	15	$*4.$	25	$*3.$	35	$*0,7,8.$	45	$*0,2,4,10,12.$
6	$*2\rightarrow$	16	$*2,6\rightarrow$	26	$*1,4,6,8\rightarrow$	36	$*1,6,10\rightarrow$	46	$*5,7,8,9,13\rightarrow$
7	$*1.$	17	$*5.$	27	$*7.$	37	$*4,5,9.$	47	$*3,6,10,11.$
8	$*3\rightarrow$	18	$*1,3,4,7\rightarrow$	28	$*3,5,8\rightarrow$	38	$*7,8,11\rightarrow$	48	$*4,8,12\rightarrow$
9	$*0,2.$	19	$*6.$	29	$*4,6.$	39	$*10.$	49	$*2,7,9,10.$

SUNNY AND LOONY POSITIONS

In our tables

$$*n\rightarrow$$

denotes all nimbers from $*n$ onwards, and

$$\overline{*n}$$

all nimbers other than $*n$.

So

$$*5 \rightarrow \text{ means } *5, *6, *7, *8, *9, \ldots$$
$$*\overline{5} \text{ means } 0, *1, *2, *3, *4, *6, *7, *8, \ldots$$
$$*0,1,7 \cdot \text{ means } 0, *1, *7$$

and

$$*3,4,6,8 \rightarrow \text{ means } *3, *4, *6, *8, *9, *10 \ldots.$$

But we'll often use

⬤ ("sunny")

instead of $*0 \rightarrow$ for the collection

$$0, *1, *2, *3, *4, \ldots$$

of *all* nimbers, and

🌙 ("loony")

for the empty collection, of *no* nimbers. What do these mean in practice?

When we defined Top Entails we warned you not to leave a stack of 1 because your opponent could remove it and demand that you follow with a move in the resulting empty stack. Your move would be *loony*, his *sunny*. In general:

> A **sunny move** in a component is one that
> wins for its maker, and
> a **loony move** is one that loses for him,
> *no matter what other components there are.*

In Top Entails both possible moves from a stack of 2 leave at least one stack of 1, so a move which entails your opponent to move from a stack of 2 is sunny. It's therefore loony to leave a stack of 3 (entailed or not) because your opponent can reply with this sunny move.

Remember that

⬤ means $0, *1, *2, *3, \ldots$,

and that only the *earliest* value is relevant for *non*-entailing moves, so a stack of 2 reached by an ordinary move has the ordinary value 0.

CALCULATING WITH ENTAILED VALUES

Figure 12 shows how we found the values for Top Entails. The Grundy scale is set to compute the values for a 14-stack, S_{14}. For the non-entailing moves to

$$S_1 + S_{13}, \quad S_2 + S_{12}, \quad S_3 + S_{11}, \quad S_4 + S_{10}, \quad S_5 + S_9, \quad S_6 + S_8, \quad S_7 + S_7$$

only the earliest values are relevant:

$$🌙 + 0, \quad 0 + *4, \quad 🌙 + *3, \quad *1 + *1, \quad 0 + 0, \quad *2 + *3, \quad *1 + *1,$$

yielding

$$🌙, \quad *4, \quad 🌙, \quad 0, \quad 0, \quad *1, \quad 0,$$

while the entailed option S_{13} has two values:

$$0, \quad *2.$$

The values for S_{14} are the remaining nimbers

$$*3, *5, *6, *7, *8, \ldots$$

and so we should write $3,5\rightarrow$ in the next place on the lower scale, and 3 on the upper one.

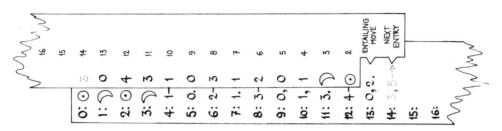

Figure 12. Grundy Scale Set to Calculate S_{14}'s Values.

The position

$$S_2 + S_6 + S_{14}$$

has value

$$0 + *2 + *3 = *1,$$

so there should be a good move reducing S_{14} to value $*2$. Our analysis shows that this must be the entailing move to S_{13}. If we make this, our opponent is forced to replace S_{13} by one of

$$S_1 + S_{12}, \quad S_2 + S_{11}, \quad S_3 + S_{10}, \quad S_4 + S_9, \quad S_5 + S_8, \quad S_6 + S_7 \quad \text{and } S_{12} \text{ (entailing)}$$

whose values

$$\text{ᗀ}, \qquad 0 + *3, \qquad \text{ᗀ}, \qquad *1 + 0, \qquad 0 + *3, \quad *2 + *1, \quad *4, *5, *6, \ldots$$

do not include $*2$, so the values for the whole position will not include 0.

Of course, since ᗀ represents the empty set, we have the obvious addition rules

$$\boxed{\begin{array}{c} \text{ᗀ} + *n = \text{ᗀ} \quad (n = 0,1,2,\ldots), \\ \text{ᗀ} + \text{ᗀ} = \text{ᗀ}. \end{array}}$$

We don't know if Top Entails contains a loony stack of more than 3 coins. The first few single-stack $\mathcal{P}$-positions are

$$S_0, S_2, S_5, S_9, S_{13}, S_{21}, S_{31}, S_{35}, S_{45}, S_{57}.$$

NIM WITH ENTAILING MOVES

It's easy to analyze any version of Nim in which we declare that some of the moves are to be entailing. As our first example we'll suppose that a move is entailing only when it decreases a heap by exactly 1. Even the move that replaces a heap of size 1 by the empty heap is entailing; since the other player cannot follow it, such a move is an outright win.

The values have an obvious pattern:

$$
\begin{array}{ccccccccccc}
0 & & 1 & 2 & & 3 & 4 & & 5 & 6 & & 7 & 8 & \cdots \\
(\odot=)*0\to & \text{☽} & *1\to & \text{☽} & *2\to & \text{☽} & *3\to & \text{☽} & *4\to & \cdots.
\end{array}
$$

To see why this pattern continues, observe that a heap of size 9 is loony because we have non-entailing moves to heaps of sizes 0, 2, 4 and 6, values 0, *1, *2 and *3, and an entailing move to a heap of size 8, values *4→, covering every possibility. And a heap of size 10 has values *5→ because the only non-loony moves are non-entailing, to heaps of sizes 0, 2, 4, 6 or 8, values 0, *1, *2, *3 or *4.

When the move which empties a heap of size 1 is declared *non*-entailing, it's no longer loony to leave a 1-heap, and the rest of the pattern shifts, making the *even* heaps loony:

$$
\begin{array}{ccccccccccccccc}
0 & 1 & 2 & 3 & 4 & 5 & 6 & 7 & 8 & 9 & 10 & 11 & 12 & \cdots \\
*0\to & *1\to & \text{☽} & *2\to & \text{☽} & *3\to & \text{☽} & *4\to & \text{☽} & *5\to & \text{☽} & *6\to & \text{☽} & \cdots
\end{array}
$$

We might instead play the game $N(a,b,c,\ldots)$ which is Nim in which moves that reduce the size of a heap by a or b or c or ... are declared entailing (even when the next player is unable to move in the reduced heap). The theory is easily deduced from that of the corresponding Subtraction Game $S(a,b,c,\ldots)$ (see Chapter 4).

Here are the value sequences for $S(2,5,7)$ and $N(2,5,7)$:

$$
\begin{array}{l|cccccccccccccccccccccc}
S(2,5,7) & \dot0 & . & 0 & 1 & 1 & 0 & 2 & 1 & 3 & 2 & 2 & 0 & 3 & 1 & 0 & 0 & 1 & 1 & 2 & 2 & 3 & 3 & \dot2 \\
n & 0 & 1 & 2 & 3 & 4 & 5 & 6 & 7 & 8 & 9 & 10 & 11 & 12 & 13 & 14 & 15 & 16 & 17 & 18 & 19 & 20 & 21 \\
N(2,5,7) & *0\to & *1\to & \text{☽} & \text{☽} & *2\to & \text{☽} & \text{☽} & \text{☽} & \text{☽} & \text{☽} & *3\to & \text{☽} & \text{☽} & *4\to & *5\to & \text{☽} & \text{☽} & \text{☽} & \text{☽} & \text{☽} & \text{☽} & \text{☽}
\end{array}
$$

$$
\begin{array}{l|cccccccccccccccccccc}
n & 22 & 23 & 24 & 25 & 26 & 27 & 28 & 29 & 30 & 31 & 32 & 33 & 34 & 35 & 36 & 37 & 38 & 39 & 40 & 41 & \cdots \\
N(2,5,7) & *6\to & *7\to & \text{☽} & \text{☽} & *8\to & \text{☽} & \text{☽} & \text{☽} & \text{☽} & \text{☽} & \text{☽} & *9\to & \text{☽} & \text{☽} & *10\to & *11\to & \text{☽} & \text{☽} & \text{☽} & \text{☽} & \text{☽} & \cdots.
\end{array}
$$

You will see that every non-zero value of $S(2,5,7)$ becomes loony in $N(2,5,7)$ and that the remaining values for $N(2,5,7)$ are just

$$
*0\to*1\to \qquad *2\to \qquad\qquad *3\to \qquad *4\to \quad \cdots
$$

in order.

For a heap H in such a game, if the non-loony values of smaller heaps are

$$
*0\to, *1\to, *2\to, \ldots, *(n-1)\to,
$$

then

$$
*0, *1, *2, \ldots, *(n-1)
$$

certainly appear among the options of H. If none of the corresponding moves is entailing, the values of H are therefore $*n\to$, but if any of these moves *is* entailing, then *all* nimbers appear among the option values, so H will be loony.

For example, the non-loony option values for a heap of size 27 in $N(2,5,7)$ are

$$*0, *1, *2, *3, *4, *5, *6\rightarrow, *7, *8$$

(since the move to a heap of size 22 is entailing), so this heap is loony.

In general

> in a Nim game with any collection of moves declared entailing, the values are
>
> $$*0\rightarrow, *1\rightarrow, *2\rightarrow, *3\rightarrow, \quad \ldots$$
>
> in order, interspersed with blocks of loony positions.

If we modify $N(2,5,7)$ by *dis*entailing the moves to 0-heaps we obtain

n	0	1	2	3	4	5	6	7	8	9	10	11	12	...
	⊙	*1→	*2→	☽	☽	*3→	☽	☽	☽	☽	☽	*4→	☽	...

and if we also disentail moves to 1-heaps:

n	0	1	2	3	4	5	6	7	8	9	10	11	12	...
	⊙	*1→	*2→	*3→	☽	☽	*4→	☽	☽	☽	☽	☽	*5→	....

After their initial terms these patterns are obtained by displacing that for $N(2,5,7)$ (and increasing the nimbers by 1 or 2).

GOLDBACH'S NIM

The same kind of argument works no matter what exotic conditions are required for a move to be entailing. **Goldbach** declares that a move is entailing just when it both takes a prime and leaves a prime. If we don't count 1 as a prime, the first few non-loony values are, for $n =$

0	1	2	3	11	12	17	23	27	29	35	37	38	...
⊙	*1→	*2→	*3→	*4→	*5→	*6→	*7→	*8→	*9→	*10→	*11→	*12→	...

But Goldbach considered 1 to be prime and so for his form of the game we find that the only non-loonies are

0	1	5	9	11	15	17	21	23	27	29	33	35	37	...
⊙	*1→	*2→	*3→	*4→	*5→	*6→	*7→	*8→	*9→	*10→	*11→	*12→	*13→	...

For this game we can prove that an odd number $n>7$ is loony just if $n-2$ is prime and $n-4$ is not. We are sure that Goldbach believes that all even numbers are loony: an even number n is non-loony only if for *every* expression

$$n = p + q$$

of n as the sum of 2 primes, each of p and q is either 3 or the larger member of a prime pair. A near miss was 122; can you find its unique entailing move to a non-loony position?

WYT QUEENS WITH TRAINS

If you don't remember the game of Wyt Queens, look at Fig. 5 on p. 61 in Chapter 3. The Queens moved either orthogonally or diagonally towards the corner of the board. Let's see what happens when some of the moves are declared entailing. Table 3 shows the values when we declare that just the orthogonal moves are entailing. The zeros are in the same places as in the ordinary game and each begins a diagonal trail, 0,1,2,3,…,; apart from these the values are loony.

	0	1	2	3	4	5	6	7	8	9	10	11
0	0→											
1		1→	0.									
2		0.	2→	1.						☽		
3			1.	3→	2.	0.						
4				2.	4→	3.	1.	0.				
5				0.	3.	5→	4.	2.	1.			
6		☽			1.	4.	6→	5.	3.	2.	0.	
7					0.	2.	5.	7→	6.	4.	3.	1.

Table 3. Entailing Orthogonally and Trailing Diagonally.

If instead we declare that just the diagonal moves are entailing we get a much more interesting game, **Off-Wyth-Its-Tail**!, whose values appear in Table 4. This time the non-loony values except zero form corridor-like trails in the two orthogonal directions. The zero values would begin the corridors if they were displaced one diagonal place.

There are lots of changes you can make to the entailing rules in this game which don't affect the values. So long as you

> *don't* entail orthogonal moves *along* the boundary, and
> *do* entail diagonal moves *onto* the boundary,

the other moves may be entailing or not, and the values will stay the same.

nim-value	k:	0	1	2	3	4	5	6	7
difference d:	0	(0,0)							
	1	(1,2)	(0,1)						
	2	(3,5)	(2,4)	(0,2)					
	3	(4,7)	(3,6)	(1,4)	(0,3)				
	4	(6,10)	(5,9)	(3,7)	(1,5)	(0,4)			
	5	(8,13)	(7,12)	(5,10)	(2,7)	(1,6)	(0,5)		
	6	(9,15)	(8,14)	(6,12)	(4,10)	(2,8)	(1,7)	(0,6)	
	7	(11,18)	(10,17)	(8,15)	(6,13)	(3,10)	(2,9)	(1,8)	(0,7)
	8	(12,20)	(11,19)	(9,17)	(8,16)	(5,13)	(3,11)	(2,10)	(1,9)

Table 5. Coordinates of Values in Table 4.

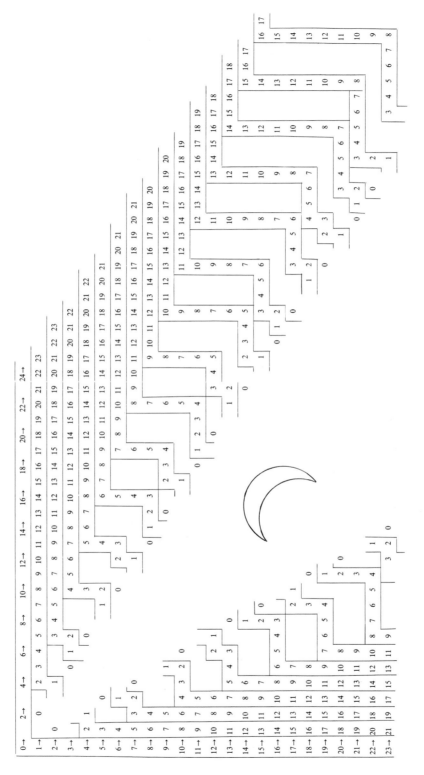

Table 4. Entailing Diagonally and Trailing Orthogonally.

The Difference Rule that we gave in the Extras to Chapter 3 for the $\mathscr{P}$-positions in Wythoff's game extends to a rule for all non-loony values in Off-Wyth-Its-Tail! Any desired k is the nim-value of infinitely many positions (x, y), one for each difference $d \geqslant k$, as in Table 5. The pair with difference d in any column of this table is found as $(x, x + d)$ where x is the smallest number that doesn't appear in the higher pairs of that column. Write to us if you can prove all our statements about this game in a few lines—our proofs are longer.

ADDING TAILS TO PRIM AND DIM

We met Prim and Dim in Chapter 4. In Prim you may remove m beans from a heap of n provided m and n have no common factor bigger than 1 ("provided m and n are *coprime*"). We shall now add the condition that when one player reduces a heap by 1, his opponent must follow in the same heap. In other words, *reduction by 1 is an entailing move*.

There are several cases: in the first version, reducing 1 to 0 is a *legal* move. If this move is declared *entailing* we obtain rather trivial nim-values:

$n =$	0	1	2	3	4	5	6	7	8	9	10	...
	◉	☾	◉	☾	◉	☾	◉	☾	◉	☾	◉	....

If 1 to 0 is *legal* but *not* entailing we find:

$n =$	0	1	2	3	4	5	6	7	8	9	10	11	12	13	14
	*0	*1→	*0	*2→	*0	*3→	*0,2	*4→	*0	*2,5·→	*0,3	*5→	*0,2	*6→	*0,4

$n =$	15	16	17	18	19	20	21	22	23	24	25	...
	*2,3,7→	*0	*7→	*0,2	*8→	*0,3	*2,4,9→	*0,5	*9→	*0,2	*3,10→	...

while if 1 to 0 is *illegal* and the move 2 to 1 is entailing:

$n = 0$	1	2	3	4	5	6	7	8	9	10	11	12	13	14	15	16	17
—	◉	☾	*1→	☾	*2→	*1	*3→	☾	*1,4→	*2	*4→	*1	*5→	*3	*1,2,6→	☾	*6→

$n =$	18	19	20	21	22	23	24	25	26	27	28	29	30	31	32	33	...
	*1	*7→	*2	*1,8→	*4	*8→	*1	*2,9→	*5	*1,9→	*3	*9→	*1,2	*10→	☾	*1,4,11→	...

In **Dim**, the move is to take a divisor off any heap, and now we shall add the condition that reduction by 1 is an entailing move. The values are:

$n =$	0	1	2	3	4	5	6	7	8	9	10	11	12	13	14
	◉	☾	*1→	☾	*2→	*1	*3→	*1,2	*4→	*1,2	*3,5→	*1,2,4	*5→	*1,2,3,4	*6→

$n =$	15	16	17	18	19	20	21	22	23	24
	*1,2,4	*3,7→	*1,2,4,5,6	*7→	*1,2,3,4,5,6	*8→	*1,2,3,4,5	*6,7,9→	*1,2,3,4,5,8	*9→

$n =$	25	26	27	28	29	30	31	32	...
	*1,2,3,4,5,6,7	*8,10→	*1,2,3,4,5,6	*7,10→	*1,2,3,4,5,6,8,9	*10→	*1,2,3,4,5,6,7,8,9	*11→	...

If the move n to 0 is made illegal and that from 2 to 1 is not entailing, *0 is adjoined to the values of all *odd* heaps.

COMPLIMENTING MOVES

In some games there are special **complimenting moves**, after which the same player has an extra **bonus move**. This happens in Dots-and-Boxes (Chapter 16) when a box is completed and in many children's board games when a double-six is thrown (to him that hath shall be given). The bonus move is quite free and can even be another complimenting move. One player may be twiddling his thumbs for quite a while while his opponent takes a whole string of consecutive moves. We can think of these thumb-twiddles as entailed pass moves whose only function is to make the turn alternate.

Let's cook up an example. **All Square** is a heap game in which the move is to split any heap into two smaller ones, and the complimenting moves are just those for which the heap sizes of these smaller ones are both perfect squares. When you've made a complimenting move you *must* move again—if you can't do so you lose—a *back-handed* compliment! Here are the values for All Square:

$n =$	1	2	3	4	5	6	7	8	9	10	11	12	13	14	15	16	17
	[0]	0	*1	[*2]	*2	*1	0	☽	[*1]	☽	0	*1	*3	*2	*1	[0]	0

$n =$	18	19	20	21	22	23	24	25	26	27	28	29	30	31	32	33	34
	☽	*4	*2	*1	*3	*2	*1	[☽]	☽	*3	*4	☽	*1	0	☽	*4	☽

$n =$	35	36	37	38	39	40	41	42	43	44	45	46	47	48	49	50	51
	*5	[*3]	*3	*2	*1	☽	☽	*3	*4	*1	☽	*3	*2	*1	[*6]	☽	*3

$n =$	52	53	54	55	56	57	58	59	60	61	62	63	64	65	66	67	68
	☽	*4	*6	*3	*2	*4	☽	*2	*3	☽	*2	*8	[*6]	☽	*4	*1	☽

$n =$	69	70	71	72	73	74	75	76	77	78	79	80	81	...
	*3	*5	*4	☽	☽	☽	0	*1	*7	*3	*5	☽	[*4]	...

To help you to recognize the complimenting moves, we've put square boxes round the values for square numbers. We found the values by using the following principle:

A complimenting move
to a position of value *n*
is really a move to

$$*\bar{n} = *0, *1, \ldots, *(n-1), *(n+1) \to,$$

i.e., every nimber *other* than *n*.

THE COMPLIMENTING EFFECT OF COMPLIMENTING MOVES

For after such a move, the opponent's move is entailed—he must twiddle his thumbs and then leave a position of value *n*. Our rules for entailing moves now show that what we left him had all values *n̄*.

In Figure 13 we see a Grundy scale for All Square, set for a heap of 13; and below it we have written the values of the various options. Since the move to $9+4$ is complimenting, it alone

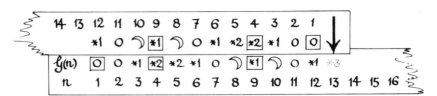

Figure 13. What's a Heap of 13 Worth?

accounts for all nimbers other than *3, and since *3 does not appear elsewhere it is the answer.
  Why is 58 a loony? We can see this using only the values

$$9: \boxed{*1}, \qquad 49: \boxed{*6}, \quad 23: *2, \quad 35: *5.$$

The complimenting move to $9 + 49$ accounts for all nimbers other than *7, which is catered for by the ordinary move to $23 + 35$. What does this mean in practice? If your opponent leaves you a position

$$58 + A + B + ...,$$

move to

$$9 + 49 + A + B + ...$$

unless the value of $A + B + ...$ is *7. The total position then has non-zero value and you can use your bonus move to correct it. If the value of $A + B + ...$ *is* *7, move instead to

$$23 + 35 + A + B + ...$$

This is a kind of strategy stealing. We find out who has the winning strategy in

$$*7 + A + B + ...$$

and make arrangements to appropriate it for ourselves.

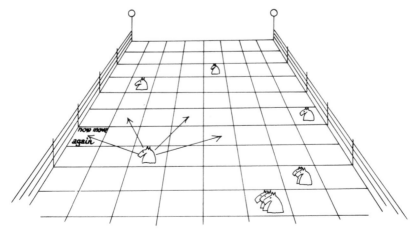

Figure 14. Horse Moves for On-The-Rails.

ON-THE-RAILS

On-The-Rails is a racecourse game with complimenting moves. The horses move as shown in Fig. 14, there can be several on a square; and the player who first moves a horse across the finishing line is the winner.

But this time there's a new twist—if you put a horse against the rails you take an extra move (which need not involve the same horse). In other words a move onto a square in either the left-most or rightmost column is a complimenting move.

The values are easy to analyze and ultimately have period 7 as shown in Table 6. In each square we show the immediate value(s) of a move onto that square. If the horse is left on the rails after the corresponding bonus move, its value is found by dropping the bar.

⊙	☽	☽	☽	☽	☽	☽	⊙
⊙	☽	☽	☽	☽	☽	☽	⊙
$*\bar{0}$	☽	☽	$*0$	$*0$	☽	☽	$*\bar{0}$
$*\bar{0}$	☽	☽	$*0$	$*0$	☽	☽	$*\bar{0}$
$*\bar{0}$	☽	☽	$*1$	$*1$	☽	☽	$*\bar{0}$
$*\bar{0}$	$*0$	☽	$*1$	$*1$	☽	$*0$	$*\bar{0}$
$*\bar{0}$	$*0$	$*0$	$*2$	$*2$	$*0$	$*0$	$*\bar{0}$
$*\bar{1}$	$*0$	☽	$*2$	$*2$	☽	$*0$	$*\bar{1}$
$*\bar{1}$	☽	$*1$	$*1$	$*1$	$*1$	☽	$*\bar{1}$
$*\bar{2}$	☽	☽	$*0$	$*0$	☽	☽	$*\bar{2}$
$*\bar{0}$	☽	$*2$	$*0$	$*0$	$*2$	☽	$*\bar{0}$
$*\bar{0}$	$*2$	☽	$*1$	$*1$	☽	$*2$	$*\bar{0}$
$*\bar{0}$	$*0$	☽	$*1$	$*1$	☽	$*0$	$*\bar{0}$
$*\bar{0}$	$*0$	$*0$	$*2$	$*2$	$*0$	$*0$	$*\bar{0}$
$*\bar{1}$	$*0$	☽	$*2$	$*2$	☽	$*0$	$*\bar{1}$
$*\bar{1}$	☽	$*1$	$*1$	$*1$	$*1$	☽	$*\bar{1}$
$*\bar{2}$	☽	☽	$*0$	$*0$	☽	☽	$*\bar{2}$
$*\bar{0}$	☽	$*2$	$*0$	$*0$	$*2$	☽	$*\bar{0}$
$*\bar{0}$	$*2$	☽	$*1$	$*1$	☽	$*2$	$*\bar{0}$

Table 6. Values for On-The-Rails.

EXTRAS

DE BONO'S *L*-GAME

N.E. Goller has found a simple and elegant strategy by which either player can guarantee to draw (at least) from the initial position of Fig. 5 (and from many others). Place your *L*-piece

either so that it occupies *three* of the central four squares (Fig. 15(a))
or so that it occupies *two* of those squares, *and* no neutral piece
occupies any other squares marked *X* in Fig. 15(b).

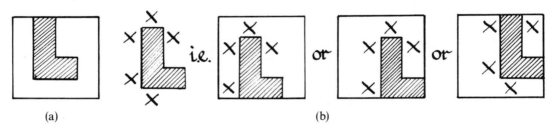

(a)   (b)

Figure 15. Nick Goller's Drawing Strategy for the *L*-Game.

Figure 16 shows a longest sensible finishing game, assuming that both players are playing well.

PROVING THE OUTCOME RULES FOR LOOPY POSITIONS

For the **closed** ($\mathcal{N}$ or $\mathcal{P}$) positions, this is easy. The only closed case not covered by the Nim theory is the assertion that

$$\infty_{abc\ldots} + *n \text{ is } \mathcal{N} \text{ if } n \text{ is one of } a,b,c,\ldots.$$

However, from this position the next player can move to

$$*n + *n = 0.$$

The other positions are of two types:

(i) $\infty_{abc\ldots} + *n$ with n *not* one of $a,b,c,\ldots$,
(ii) $\infty_{abc\ldots} + \infty_{\alpha\beta\gamma\ldots} + \ldots$.

Because we don't yet know if these are open or closed, we'll call them **ajar** for the moment. We need only show that such a position has an option which is still ajar.

388

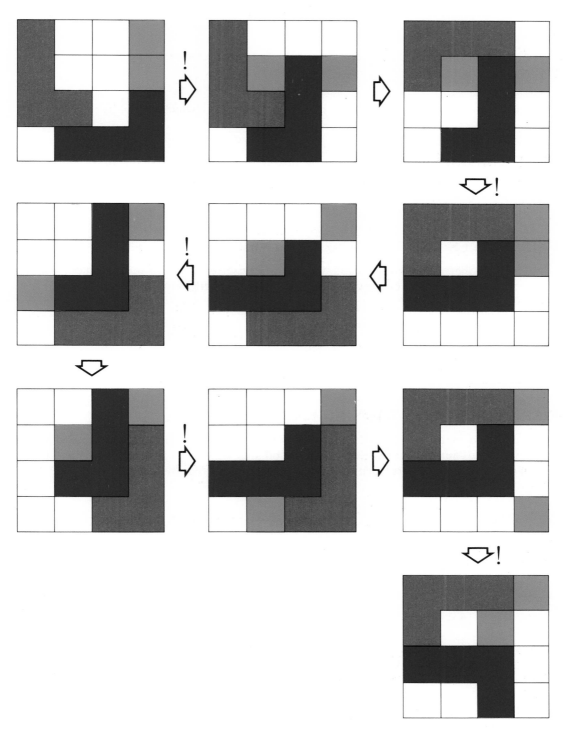

Figure 16. A Longest Sensible Finishing Game.

For (i), let $m = \text{mex}(a,b,c,\ldots)$ and observe that $n \geqslant m$ because n is not one of $a,b,c,\ldots$. If $n > m$, the position

$$\infty_{abc\ldots} + *m \text{ is ajar.}$$

If $n = m$, the position of value $\infty_{abc\ldots}$ has a loopy option $\infty_{\alpha\beta\gamma\ldots}$ which cannot be reversed to $*n$, so

$$\infty_{\alpha\beta\gamma\ldots} + *n \text{ is ajar.}$$

We can keep positions of type (ii) ajar by moving to a loopy option of one of the loopy components.

So when a position is ajar, either player can keep it ajar. A door that's always kept ajar may as well be called *open*.

FAIR SHARES AND UNEQUAL PARTNERS

If, in Fair Shares and Varied Pairs, you allow yourselves the extra moves which combine three or more heaps, then you need to make the following changes to Table 1:

421	32111	3321	42111	4221	441	4321	532	541	631	721
$*4_{@6}$	$*4_{@11}$	$*1_{@10}$	$*4_{@12}$	$*5_{@15}$	$*1_{@11}$	∞_{02}	∞_{02}	∞_{02}	∞_{02}	∞_{02}.

There are also two changes in Fig. 4: the remotenesses of 4221 and 4321 are reduced to 3, since there are now the good moves to 72 and 73. In Fair Shares and Varied Pairs, the remoteness of 4221 was 14, so this changes from a $\mathscr{P}$-position into an $\mathscr{N}$-position.

WERE YOUR WAYS WINNING ENOUGH?

You should make the date, of course, since the almond position 22221 is labelled $*2_{@12}$ in Table 1. But your prospective date might cry off after watching you swallow all but 2 of the toffees at your first move, and then dragging the game out to 25 moves in all:

(This is your only way to force a win so quickly.) There are times when your *Winning Ways* should not be used too blatantly!

DID YOU MOVE FIRST IN HORSEFLY?

You should have chosen *not* to move first, since the position of Fig. 11 is a $\mathscr{P}$-position, no matter which way those horseflies last moved. In Fig. 17 the usual value of a square is printed at its centre. However, if you've just arrived in the third or fifth column by a knight's move from the other, then you should use the small print value in the corner nearest to where you came from.

⊙			⊙			⊙
0	𝒟	𝒟	0	𝒟	𝒟	0
0	𝒟	𝒟	0	𝒟	𝒟	0
0	*1	*2	0	*2	*1	0
0	*1	∞_{01}	0	∞_{01}	*1	0
0	*1	∞_{012}	0	∞_{012}	*1	0
0	*1	∞_{013}	0	∞_{013}	*1	0

*(small-print corner values: below *2 row — *1, *1; in the ∞_{01} row — above: *1, *1; below: *2, *2; in the ∞_{012} row — above: ∞_{01}, ∞_{01}; below: *3, *3; in the ∞_{013} row — above: ∞_{01}, ∞_{01}; below: *2, *2)*

Figure 17. Values for Horsefly.

We've used

⊙ for the three winning posts,
𝒟 for squares from which there is a move to ⊙,

and to follow the later analysis you should fill in the remaining values in the order

$$0, *1, *2, *3, \infty_{01}, \infty_{012}, \infty_{013},$$

proceeding row by row for each value. The last two rows repeat indefinitely.

REFERENCES AND FURTHER READING

Edward de Bono, "The Five-day Course in Thinking—Introducing the L-game", Pelican, London 1969.

Edward de Bono, "The Use of Lateral Thinking", Pelican, London 1967; Basic Books, N.Y., 1968.

A.S. Fraenkel and U. Tassa, Strategy for a class of games with dynamic ties, Comput. Math. Appl. **1** (1975) 237–254; MR **54** #2220.

V.W. Gijlswijk, G.A.P. Kindervater, G.J. van Tubergen and J.J.O.O. Wiegerinck, Computer analysis of E. de Bono's L-game, Report #76–18, Dept. of Maths., Univ. of Amsterdam, Nov. 1976.

Cedric A.B. Smith, Graphs and composite games, J. Combin. Theory, **1** (1966) 51–81; MR **33** #2572.

Chapter 13

Survival in the Lost World

"The game," he said, "is never lost till won."
George Crabbe, *Tales of the Hall*, xv, "Gretna Green", 334.
The genius of you Americans is that you never make clear-cut
stupid moves, only complicated stupid moves which make us
wonder at the possibility that there may be something to them
we are missing.
Gamel Abdel Nasser

'Tis better to have fought and lost
Than never to have fought at all.
Arthur Hugh Clough, *Pescheria*

We've spent a lot of time teaching you how to win games by being the last to move. But suppose you are baby-sitting little Jimmy and want, at least occasionally, to make sure you *lose*? This means that instead of playing the normal play rule in which whoever can't move is the *loser*, you've switched to the **misère play** rule when he's the *winner*. Will this make much difference? Not *always...*

MISÈRE NIM

In **Misère Nim** you have a number of heaps and your move must reduce the size of any one heap, but whoever eliminates the last heap is now the *loser*. This will only affect play in the **fickle** positions when all the non-empty heaps are **singletons** (size 1) and the game gets rather boring and mechanical. You and Jimmy will take the singletons alternately and you would win in normal play by always presenting him with an even number of them. Obviously, to play in misère fashion, you should instead arrange to present Jimmy with an *odd* number of singletons. All other positions (some heaps ⩾2) are **firm** and behave alike in both normal and misère play.

Whoever first reduces the game to the fickle state does so by reducing the last heap of size 2 or more. He can therefore win in either Normal or Misère Nim by choosing whether to reduce this heap to a singleton or remove it altogether.

> Play Misère Nim exactly as you would
> play Normal Nim unless your move
> would leave an even number of
> singleton heaps and no other heap.
> Then leave an odd number instead.

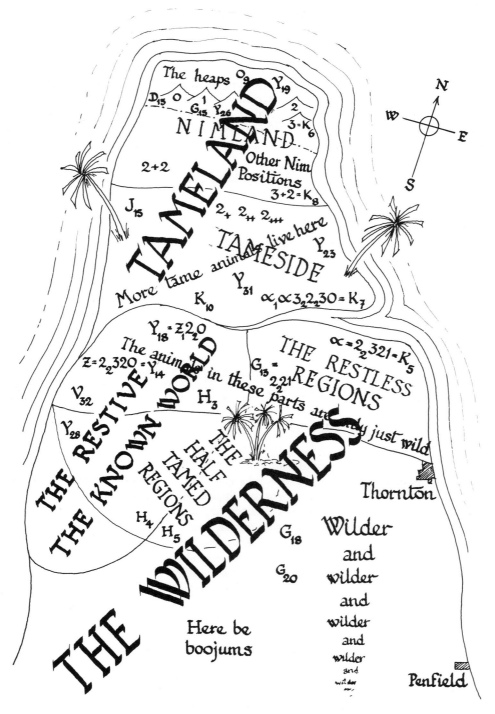

Figure 1. Game Reserves in the Lost World.

REVERSIBLE MOVES

We can still throw out all reversible moves in the misère theory, provided we take special care when we throw *all* moves out. Figure 2, illustrating reversibility for misère play, is rather like Fig. 6 in Chapter 3, but *all* branches are now available to *either* player. The game G has all the options A, B, C of the simpler game H, and additional options D, E from each of which there is a legal move to H. We say that D and E are **reversible moves** from G.

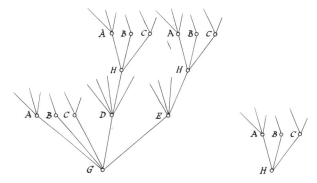

Figure 2. Reversible Moves in Misère Play.

We assert that the outcome of a sum of games will never be affected if we replace a component G by the simpler game H, provided H has at least one option. For, whoever has the winning strategy in

$$H + X + Y + Z + \ldots$$

can play

$$G + X + Y + Z + \ldots$$

with essentially the same strategy, not himself making use of the new moves from G to D or E. If his opponent uses them he can expect to reverse their effect by moving back from

$$(D \text{ or } E) + X + Y + Z + \ldots$$

to

$$H + X + Y + Z + \ldots.$$

> If G is obtainable from H
> by adding reversible moves,
> then G is equivalent to H,
> *provided* that
> if H has no option,
> then G and H have the same
> outcome.

PRUNING REVERSIBLE MOVES

Since then we can substitute H for G in any sum of games we shall simply write G=H. For example,

$$\{0,1,2,5,6,9\} = \{0,1,2\} = 3,$$

since 5, 6 and 9 have 3 as an option and 3 is not 0.

THE ENDGAME PROVISO

But this pruning process requires care when H has no legal option, i.e. is the **Endgame**, 0 (see Fig. 3). The trouble is that the argument might not even get off the ground.

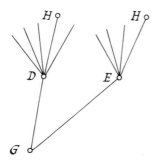

$$Ho = O$$
is the Endgame

Figure 3. The Endgame Proviso.

For if H, X, Y, Z, ... are each the Endgame, you have already won

$$H + X + Y + Z + ...\,(= 0)$$

by definition, but this doesn't help you to win

$$G + X + Y + Z + ...\,(= G).$$

So in this case we are compelled to lay down the **proviso** that G has the *same outcome as* 0, when H *is* 0.

THE AWFUL TRUTH

Since all impartial games reduce to Nim in normal play, and since misère play Nim is only a trivial modification of normal Nim, it has often been thought that misère impartial games must be almost as easy. Perhaps you play any sum of impartial games in misère play just as in normal play until very near the end, when ...?

Unfortunately not!

For example, in the normal play version of Grundy's game (Chapter 4) the single heap $\mathscr{P}$-positions with less than 50 beans are

$$G_1, G_2, G_4, G_7, G_{10}, G_{20}, G_{23}, G_{26}.$$

None of these is $\mathscr{P}$ in misère play, for which the first few single heap $\mathscr{P}$-positions are

$$G_3, G_6, G_9, G_{12}, ..., G_{42}, G_{45},$$

exactly the first fifteen multiples of 3. It seems a coincidence that G_{50} is a $\mathscr{P}$-position in both kinds of play. Many authors have made mistakes in this and similar games by riding roughshod over the subtleties of misère play.

In ONAG it is proved that the *only* way a game can be simplified in misère play is by eliminating reversible moves, observing the Endgame Proviso when appropriate. If two games have no reversible moves and *look* different, they really *are* different, because there will always be some other game whose addition yields distinct outcomes.

The complications that arise are illustrated in Fig. 4 which shows the tree structure of the game of Kayles with 7 pins, simplified as much as possible.

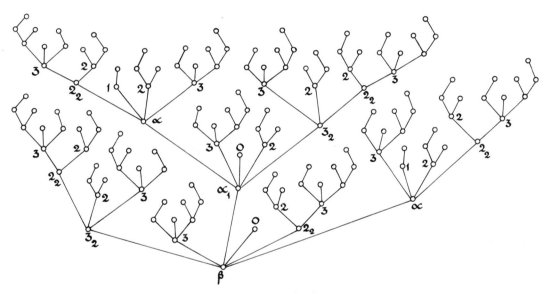

Figure 4. The Kayles Position K_7. Structure $\beta = \alpha_1 \alpha 3_2 2_2 30$, where $\alpha = 2_2 321$.

Grundy and Smith showed that there was 1 game born on day 0, 2 by day 1, 3 by day 2, 5 by day 3, 22 by day 4 and 4171780 by day 5. So there are at most

$$2^{4171780}$$

games by day 6. Removal of reversible moves reduces this huge number, but by such a small fraction that the first 625140 of its 1255831 decimal digits are not affected! The exact number is given on p.140 of ONAG.

We salvage what we can with our notion of **tame game**, but that's not too much. If you think the rest of the chapter looks rather complicated, that's because it is!

WHAT'S LEFT OF THE OLD RULES?

Here, and for the rest of the chapter, we omit the stars from the notation for Nim-heaps, so that numbers will usually mean *nimbers*.

In normal play the mex rule could be used to reduce *every* position to a Nim-heap. Although we've just seen that this no longer happens, the rule still has some force:

> If $m = \text{mex}(a,b,c,...)$ then
>
> $\{a,b,c,...\} = m,$
>
> *provided* that at least
> one of $a,b,c,...$ is 0 or 1.

THE MISÈRE MEX RULE

The Nim-addition rule in misère play is:

> *Provided*
> one of a and b is 0 or 1,
> *then*
>
> $a + b = a \overset{*}{+} b.$

THE MISÈRE NIM RULE

The Misère Mex Rule shows that

$$\{0,2,5\} = \{0\} = 1$$

and

$$\{1,3,4\} = \{\ \} = 0$$

both reduce to Nim-heaps, but positions such as

$$\{2,3\}$$

which *do* have options but *don't* have options 0 or 1, do not.

The Misère Nim Rule is easily proved by induction. For example,

$$4 + 1 = \{0+1, 1+1, 2+1, 3+1, 4+0\}$$
$$= \{\ 1, \quad 0, \quad 3, \quad 2, \quad 4\ \} = 5,$$
$$5 + 1 = \{0+1, 1+1, 2+1, 3+1, 4+1, 5+0\}$$
$$= \{\ 1, \quad 0, \quad 3, \quad 2, \quad 5, \quad 5\ \} = 4,$$

using the Misère Mex Rule.

AS EASY AS TWO AND TWO?

What do 2 and 2 make? The common man thinks 4, the *normal* Nim player says 0, but the *misère* answer is the $\mathscr{P}$-position

$$2+2 = \{2+1, 2+0\} = \{3,2\}$$

which can't be simplified any further. The only Nim-heap which is a misère $\mathscr{P}$-position is 1, but

$$1 + 1 \quad \text{and} \quad (2+2) + (2+2)$$

have different outcomes. so that certainly we can't simplify $2+2$ to 1.

If addition sums like this had had more satisfactory answers, the misère theory would be easy. Because it isn't, the games grow very complicated and we need our patent collapsing notation to record them.

When several positions have been given names, such as

$$a, b, c, \ldots$$

we shall write

$$a_n \text{ for } a+n, \text{ etc.}$$

and, for example,

$$a_m b_n cd$$

for the game

$$\{a+m, b+n, c, d\}.$$

However, to avoid ambiguity when there's a single option, we'll write

$$a_+ \text{ for } \{a\}.$$

THE MISÈRE FORM OF GRUNDY'S GAME

Recall from Chapter 4 that in Grundy's Game the move is to divide any heap into two non-empty heaps of different sizes. Let's begin its analysis in misère play, using the misère nim-addition and mex rules, and writing G_n for a Grundy heap of size n:

$$
\begin{aligned}
G_1 &= \{\ \} = 0 \\
G_2 &= \{\ \} = 0, \\
G_3 &= \{G_2+G_1\} = \{0\} = 1, \\
G_4 &= \{G_3+G_1\} = \{1\} = 0, \\
G_5 &= \{G_4+G_1, G_3+G_2\} = \{0,1\} = 2, \\
G_6 &= \{G_5+G_1, G_4+G_2\} = \{2,0\} = 1, \\
G_7 &= \{1+0, 2+0, 0+1\} = \{1,2,1\} = 0, \\
G_8 &= \{0+0, 1+0, 2+1\} = \{0,1,3\} = 2, \\
G_9 &= \{2+0, 0+0, 1+1, 2+0\} = \{2,0,0,2\} = 1, \\
G_{10} &= \{1+0, 2+0, 0+1, 1+0\} = \{1,2,1,1\} = 0, \\
G_{11} &= \{0+0, 1+0, 2+1, 0+0, 1+2\} = \{0,1,3,0,3\} = 2, \\
G_{12} &= \{2+0, 0+0, 1+1, 2+0, 0+2\} = \{2,0,0,2,2\} = 1.
\end{aligned}
$$

But number 13 is unlucky! We find

$$G_{13} = \{1+0, 2+0, 0+1, 1+0, 2+2, 0+1\} = \{1,2,1,1,2+2,1\}$$

so that

$$G_{13} = \{2+2, 2, 1\},$$

or, in the collapsed notation,

$$G_{13} = 2_2 21.$$

Since $2+2$ won't reduce to a Nim-heap, we're stuck! The authors don't even know how to play the misère sum of G_{13} with three arbitrary Nim-heaps. From Table 1 you can see that the triples of Nim-heaps x,y,z for which

$$G_{13} + x + y + z$$

is a $\mathscr{P}$-position are quite chaotic. You mustn't expect any magic formula for dealing with such positions.

x =	0	1	2	3	4	5	6	7	8	9	10	11	12	13	14	15	16	17	18	19	20	21	22	23
y																								
0	1	0	4	5	2	3	8	9	6	7	12	13	10	11	16	17	14	15	20	21	18	19	24	25
1	0	1	5	4	3	2	9	8	7	6	13	12	11	10	17	16	15	14	21	20	19	18	25	24
2	4	5	3	2	0	1	7	6	9	8	11	10	13	12	15	14	17	16	19	18	21	20	23	22
3	5	4	2	3	1	0	6	7	8	9	10	11	12	13	14	15	16	17	18	19	20	21	22	23
4	2	3	0	1	4	5	10	11	15	14	6	7	16	17	9	8	12	13	24	25	22	23	20	21
5	3	2	1	0	5	4	11	10	14	15	7	6	17	16	8	9	13	12	25	24	23	22	21	20
6	8	9	7	6	10	11	3	2	0	1	4	5	14	15	12	13	18	19	16	17	24	25	26	27
7	9	8	6	7	11	10	2	3	1	0	5	4	15	14	13	12	19	18	17	16	25	24	27	26
8	6	7	9	8	15	14	0	1	3	2	16	17	18	19	5	4	10	11	12	13	26	27	29	28
9	7	6	8	9	14	15	1	0	2	3	17	16	19	18	4	5	11	10	13	12	27	26	28	29
10	12	13	11	10	6	7	4	5	16	17	3	2	0	1	18	19	8	9	14	15	29	28	31	30
11	13	12	10	11	7	6	5	4	17	16	2	3	1	0	19	18	9	8	15	14	28	29	30	31
12	10	11	13	12	16	17	14	15	18	19	0	1	3	2	6	7	4	5	8	9	30	31	32	33
13	11	10	12	13	17	16	15	14	19	18	1	0	2	3	7	6	5	4	9	8	31	30	33	32
14	16	17	15	14	9	8	12	13	5	4	18	19	6	7	3	2	0	1	10	11	32	33	34	35
15	17	16	14	15	8	9	13	12	4	5	19	18	7	6	2	3	1	0	11	10	33	32	35	34
16	14	15	17	16	12	13	18	19	10	11	8	9	4	5	0	1	3	2	6	7	34	35	36	37
17	15	14	16	17	13	12	19	18	11	10	9	8	5	4	1	0	2	3	7	6	35	34	37	36
18	20	21	19	18	24	25	16	17	12	13	14	15	8	9	10	11	6	7	3	2	0	1	38	39
19	21	20	18	19	25	24	17	16	13	12	15	14	9	8	11	10	7	6	2	3	1	0	39	38

Table 1. Values of z for which $G_{13} + x + y + z$ is a $\mathscr{P}$-position.

But you probably don't want to play sums of G_{13} with *Nim*-heaps—after all in Grundy's game you only need play it with other *Grundy* heaps. Even if G_{13} *isn't* a Nim-position, it's still a game; let's call it a and carry on:

$$G_{14} = \{a+0, 1+0, 2+1, 0+0, 1+2, 2+1\} = a310$$

which reduces to $2 = \{1,0\}$ since both $a = 2_2 21$ and $3 = 210$ have this as an option. Even though G_{13} wasn't a Nim-heap, G_{14} is!

Carrying on still further we find two more Nim-heaps, two games which reduce to a and two new values:

$$G_{15} = \mathbf{a}20 = 1,$$
$$G_{16} = \mathbf{a}_1 2_2 21 = a,$$
$$G_{17} = \mathbf{a}310 = 2,$$
$$G_{18} = a_2 a20 = b,$$
$$G_{19} = \mathbf{b}a_1 2_2 21 = a,$$
$$G_{20} = ba3 = c,$$
$$G_{21} = \mathbf{c}\mathbf{b}_1 a_2 a20 = b,$$

where reversible options are in bold type. From now on all the positions are different. The next is

$$G_{22} = cba_1 2_2 1 = d,$$

which, however, usually behaves in much the same way as a.

Grundy's Game only reduces to Nim when all the Grundy heaps have sizes

$$1, 2, 3, 4, 5, 6, 7, 8, 9, 10, 11, 12, 14, 15, 17.$$

You can also throw in some heaps of size 13, 16 and 19 by *pretending* that $a+a = 0$ and using the rule:

> If $x,y,z,\ldots$ are Nim-heaps of size at most three, then
>
> $$a + x + y + z + \ldots$$
>
> is a $\mathscr{P}$-position just if
>
> $$x \overset{*}{+} y \overset{*}{+} z \overset{*}{+} \ldots = 1 \text{ or } 3$$
>
> *and* the number of 2- and 3-heaps is exactly
>
> $$0 \text{ or } 3 \text{ or } 5 \text{ or } 7 \text{ or } 9 \text{ or } \ldots$$

If you want to know more, look in the last section of the chapter.

ANIMALS AND THEIR GENUS

In later sections we shall show that the Misère Nim strategy extends to a large class of games we shall call **tame**, and that we can say a fair amount about some more games called **restive**, and a little bit about some **restless** games. The **genus** will help to classify these.

Recalling that the normal nim-value $\mathscr{G}^+(G)$ is the unique size of Nim-heap n for which $G+n$ is a $\mathscr{P}$-position in normal play, we now define the **misère nim-value** $\mathscr{G}^-(G)$ to be the unique n which makes $G+n$ a $\mathscr{P}$-position in misère play. You can work out these values by:

$$\mathscr{G}^+(G) = 0 \text{ if } G \text{ has no option,}$$
$$\mathscr{G}^+(G) = \operatorname{mex} \mathscr{G}^+(G') \text{ otherwise,}$$

$$\mathscr{G}^-(G) = 1 \text{ if } G \text{ has no option,}$$
$$\mathscr{G}^-(G) = \operatorname{mex} \mathscr{G}^-(G') \text{ otherwise,}$$

where G' ranges over all options of G.

Unfortunately $\mathscr{G}^-(G)$ does *not* enable us to compute $\mathscr{G}^-(G+2)$. So we shall define a more complicated symbol, the **genus** ($\mathscr{G}$-ness)

$$g^{\gamma_0\gamma_1\gamma_2\gamma_3\dots}$$

of G, where

$$g = \mathscr{G}^+(G),$$

$$\gamma_0 = \mathscr{G}^-(G), \qquad \gamma_1 = \mathscr{G}^-(G+2), \qquad \gamma_2 = \mathscr{G}^-(G+2+2), \qquad \gamma_3 = \mathscr{G}^-(G+2+2+2), \dots.$$

We shall abbreviate this symbol in various ways.

g denotes a Nim-heap of size g.

g^γ denotes a tame or restive game.

       (In these cases the full genus can be recovered from Table 2).

$g^{\alpha\beta\dots\lambda\mu}$ abbreviates the genus $g^{\alpha\beta\dots\lambda\mu\lambda\mu\lambda\mu\dots}$

It turns out that *every* genus ends up alternating between two numbers like this.

Nim-heaps	and	Tame Games	Restive Games			
g	g^γ	Genus	g^γ	Genus	g^γ	Genus
0	0^1	$0^{12020\dots}$				
1	1^0	$1^{03131\dots}$				
	0^0	$0^{02020\dots}$				
	1^1	$1^{13131\dots}$				
2	2^2	$2^{20202\dots}$	0^2	$0^{20202\dots}$	1^2	$1^{20202\dots}$
3	3^3	$3^{31313\dots}$	0^3	$0^{31313\dots}$	1^3	$1^{31313\dots}$
4	4^4	$4^{46464\dots}$	0^4	$0^{42020\dots}$	1^4	$1^{43131\dots}$
5	5^5	$5^{57575\dots}$	0^5	$0^{52020\dots}$	1^5	$1^{53131\dots}$
6	6^6	$6^{64646\dots}$	0^6	$0^{62020\dots}$	1^6	$1^{63131\dots}$
7	7^7	$7^{75757\dots}$	0^7	$0^{72020\dots}$	1^7	$1^{73131\dots}$

Table 2. Abbreviations for the Genus of Certain Games.

For Grundy's Game the genus sequence with these abbreviations is

$$.0\ 0\ 1\ 0\ 2\ 1\ 0\ 2\ 1\ 0\ 2\ 1\ 3^{1431}\ 2\ 1\ 3^{1431}\ 2\ 4^{0564}\ 3^{1431}\ 0^{20}\ 4^{0564}\ 3^{1431}\ \ldots$$

and for Kayles,

K_0	K_1	K_2	K_3	K_4	K_5	K_6	K_7	K_8	K_9	K_{10}	K_{11}	K_{12}	K_{13}	K_{14}	K_{15}	K_{16}	K_{17}	
0.	1	2	3	1	4^{146}	3	2^2	1^1	4^{046}	2^2	6^{46}	4^{046}	1^1	2^2	7^{57}	1^{13}	4^{64}	$\ldots$

The single superscript form is reserved for tame or restive games. The games K_{13} and K_{16} have the same genus

$$1^{1313\ldots}$$

but our displayed sequence abbreviates them differently since only the former is tame.

WHAT CAN WE DO WITH THE GENUS?

The genus is a very useful tool in misère play calculations, because, as we shall gradually come to understand:

1. We can find the misère outcome of a single game. The outcome is $\mathscr{P}$ if and only if the first superscript is 0.

2. If each of our games is *tame* and of known genus, we can work out the genus—and therefore the outcome—of their sum, which is also tame.

3. If $a,b,c,\ldots$ are Nim-heaps of sizes 0,1,2,3, then, from the genus of an arbitrary G, we can find the genus and outcome of

$$G + a + b + c + \ldots.$$

4. We can allow *one* of these Nim-heaps to have size 4 or more and still compute the outcome.

5. If $a,b,c,\ldots$ are *any* Nim-heaps and R is *restive* with given genus, we can find the genus and outcome of

$$R + a + b + c + \ldots.$$

6. For many restive games, R, our Noah's Ark Theorem shows that

$$R + R, \quad R + R + R, \ldots$$

are tame and of known genus and outcome.

7. And there are many more *half-tame* games, H, for which $H + H$ is tame; again of known genus and outcome.

8. For a suitably restrained *restless* game, R, an even number of copies of R will not affect the genus or outcome in suitable circumstances, again by the Noah's Ark Theorem.

FIRM, FICKLE AND TAME

In Nim only the following combinations arise:

$0^1, 1^0$	(the **fickle units**)
$0^0, 1^1$	(the **firm units**)
$2^2, 3^3, 4^4, 5^5,\ldots$	(the **big firms**)

and they can be combined according to the following rule, which works for all tame games.

If *any* component is firm, so is the sum, and
$$a^\alpha + b^\beta + \ldots = (a \overset{*}{+} b \overset{*}{+} \ldots)^{a \overset{*}{+} b \overset{*}{+} \ldots}.$$
If *all* components are fickle, so is the sum, and
$$a^\alpha + b^\beta + \ldots = (a \overset{*}{+} b \overset{*}{+} \ldots)^{1 \overset{*}{+} a \overset{*}{+} b \overset{*}{+} \ldots}.$$

COMBINING TAME GAMES

Thus
$$0^1 + 2^2 + 7^7 = 5^{?},$$
having two firm components, must be firm of genus 5^5, but
$$0^1 + 1^0 + 1^0 = 0^{?},$$
a completely fickle sum, has genus 0^1.

Let's look at the Kayles position

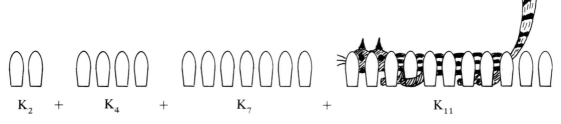

$$K_2 \quad + \quad K_4 \quad + \quad K_7 \quad + \quad K_{11}$$

Our sequence indicates that K_2, K_4 and K_7 are tame; in fact K_2 and K_4 are *very* tame, being Nim-heaps. The three tame components together make a tame game of genus 1^1,
$$2^2 + 1^0 + 2^2 = 1^1.$$

But K_{11} is a really wild animal of genus $6^{4646\cdots}$. What shall we do? Luckily we spot K_{11}'s tame option
$$K_3 + K_7$$
of genus $3^3 + 2^2 = 1^1$,

leading to
$$K_2 + K_4 + K_7 + K_3 + K_7,$$

whose genus
$$2 \quad + 1 \quad + 2^2 + 3 \quad + 2^2 = 0^0$$

shows it to be a $\mathscr{P}$-position.

WHICH ANIMALS ARE TAME . . .

Roughly speaking, those we can pretend are Nim-positions. In this book we have managed to tame many more animals than were regarded as tame in ONAG (**hereditarily tame**). But see the end of the Extras for the even larger family of **tameable games**.

For a game G to be **tame** its nim-values g^γ must certainly form one of the **tame pairs**

$$0^0, 1^1, 2^2, 3^3, 4^4, \ldots \text{ or } 0^1, 1^0$$

that arise for Nim-positions. There is no further condition if all the options of G are tame, but *wild* options of G are also allowed provided they aren't needed to determine the nim-values of G, and provided they each have **reverting** moves to *tame* games with nim-values $g^?$ and $?^\gamma$.

More precisely, if the tame options have genus

$$a^\alpha, b^\beta, \ldots$$

we must have

$$g = \text{mex}(a,b,\ldots)$$
$$\gamma = \text{mex}(\alpha,\beta,\ldots)$$

and, from any wild option, there must be moves to two (possibly equal) tame games with genus
$$g^? \quad \text{and} \quad ?^\gamma.$$

For example, the Kayles position

$$K_7 = \{K_6, K_5 + K_1, K_4 + K_2, K_3 + K_3, K_5, K_4 + K_1, K_3 + K_2\}$$
$$= \{3, \quad K_5 + 1, \quad 1 + 2, \quad 3 + 3, \quad K_5, \quad 1 + 1, \quad 3 + 2\}$$

has tame options

$$3^3, \quad\quad\quad 3^3, \quad\quad 0^0, \quad\quad\quad 0^1, \quad\quad 1^1$$

which suffice to determine the genus 2^2. The two wild options have reverting moves to tame games with this genus.

$$K_5 + 1 \rightarrow K_3 + 1, \quad \text{genus } 2^2,$$
$$K_5 \rightarrow K_3 + K_1, \quad \text{genus } 2^2,$$

and so K_7 is itself tame of genus 2^2.

To win a sum of tame games make sure that after each of your moves every component is tame and the total genus is

$$0^0 \quad \text{if } any \text{ component is } firm,$$
$$1^0 \quad \text{if } every \text{ component is } fickle.$$

If your opponent ever plays a wild card there will always be a suitable reverting move for you to respond with. Otherwise the strategy is exactly as in Misère Nim.

. . . AND WHICH ARE RESTIVE?

Once again we have a wider class than was treated in ONAG. For G to be **restive**, its nim-values g^γ have to be one of the **restive pairs** in which g is 0 or 1 and γ is 2 or more:

$$0^2, 0^3, 0^4, 0^5, \ldots \quad \text{or} \quad 1^2, 1^3, 1^4, 1^5, \ldots.$$

There is no further condition if all the options of G are tame, but wild options are also allowed provided they are not needed to determine the nim-values of G, and each has *reverting* moves to *tame or restive* games of genus

$$g^? \quad \text{and} \quad ?^\gamma$$

where each ? must be one of

$$0, 1, \gamma, \gamma \overset{*}{+} 1.$$

More precisely, if the tame options have genus

$$a^\alpha, b^\beta, \dots$$

we must have

$$g = \text{mex}(a,b,\dots) = 0 \text{ or } 1,$$
$$\gamma = \text{mex}(\alpha,\beta,\dots) \geqslant 2,$$

and, from any wild option there must be moves to two (possibly equal) tame or restive games of genus

$$g^? \quad \text{and} \quad ?^\gamma \quad (\text{each } ? = 0, 1, \gamma, \text{ or } \gamma \overset{*}{+} 1).$$

The situation can get quite awkward when you put restive animals together. We wouldn't even like to have to predict the outcome when a restive animal is put among certain tame ones but at least they behave well with Nim-positions.

Question:
Suppose R is a restive game of genus g^γ
and $m, n, \dots$ are Nim-heaps;
when is $R + m + n + \dots$ a $\mathscr{P}$-position?
Answer:
This happens when $m \overset{*}{+} n \overset{*}{+} \dots = \gamma$,
if each of $m, n, \dots$ is 0, 1, γ or $\gamma \overset{*}{+} 1$;
and when $m \overset{*}{+} n \overset{*}{+} \dots = g$, otherwise.

RESTIVE GAMES ARE AMBIVALENT NIM-HEAPS

Moreover,

If
$$0, 1 < n < \gamma, \gamma \overset{*}{+} 1$$

then

$$R + n$$

is tame of genus $(g \overset{*}{+} n)^{g \overset{*}{+} n}$.

THE INTERMEDIATE VALUE THEOREM

SOME TAME ANIMALS IN THE GOOD CHILD'S ZOO

MISÈRE WYT QUEENS

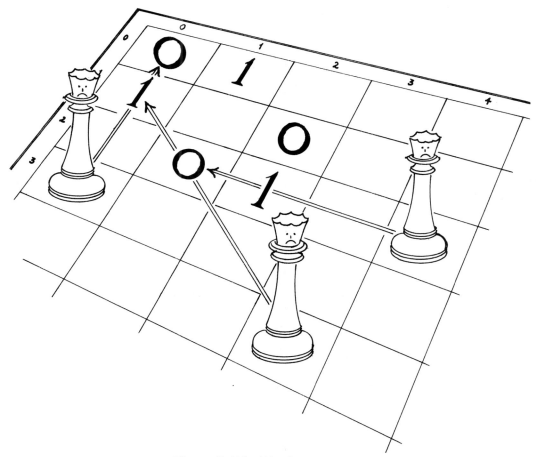

Figure 5. Why Wyt Queens are Tame.

We met the normal play version of Wyt Queens in Chapter 3, and you'll find by trial that the misère version has a genus table which appears to be entirely tame (Table 3). Figure 5 shows how every Queen outside the leading 3×3 square which can "see" a 0 or 1 in this square can also see the other, and using this we can prove that every entry outside this square is both firm and tame. Welter's Game and Moore's Nim$_k$ are also tame (see Chapter 15). Yamasaki independently gives the misère analysis of all these games. Wythoff's Game is also known as Chinese Nim or Tsyan-shizi, and Welter's Game as Sato's Maya Game.

	0	1	2	3	4	5	6	7	8	9	10	11	12	13	14	15
0	0	1	2	3	4	5	6	7	8	9	10	11	12	13	14	
1	1	2	0	4	5	3	7	8	6	10	11	9	13	14	12	
2	2	0	1	5	3	4	8	6	7	11	9	10	14	12	13	
3	3	4	5	6	2	0^0	1^1	9^9	10^{10}	12^{12}	8^8	7^7	15^{15}	11^{11}	16^{16}	
4	4	5	3	2	7	6	9^9	0^0	1^1	8^8	13^{13}	12^{12}	11^{11}	16^{16}	15^{15}	
5	5	3	4	0^0	6	8^8	10^{10}	1^1	2^2	7^7	12^{12}	14^{14}	9^9	15^{15}	17^{17}	
6	6	7	8	1^1	9^9	10^{10}	3	4	5^5	13^{13}	0^0	2^2	16^{16}	17^{17}	18^{18}	
7	7	8	6	9^9	0^0	1^1	4	5	3	14^{14}	15^{15}	13^{13}	17^{17}	2^2	10^{10}	
8	8	6	7	10^{10}	1^1	2^2	5^5	3	4	15^{15}	16^{16}	17^{17}	18^{18}	0^0	9^9	
9	9	10	11	12^{12}	8^8	7^7	13^{13}	14^{14}	15^{15}	16^{16}	17^{17}	6^6	19^{19}	5^5	1^1	
10	10	11	9	8^8	13^{13}	12^{12}	0^0	15^{15}	16^{16}	17^{17}	14^{14}	18^{18}	7^7	6^6	2^2	
11	11	9	10	7^7	12^{12}	14^{14}	2^2	13^{13}	17^{17}	6^6	18^{18}	15^{15}	8^8	19^{19}	20^{20}	
12	12	13	14	15^{15}	11^{11}	9^9	16^{16}	17^{17}	18^{18}	19^{19}	7^7	8^8	10^{10}	20^{20}	21^{21}	
13	13	14	12	11^{11}	16^{16}	15^{15}	17^{17}	2^2	0^0	5^5	6^6	19^{19}	20^{20}	9^9	7^7	
14	14	12	13	16^{16}	15^{15}	17^{17}	18^{18}	10^{10}	9^9	1^1	2^2	20^{20}	21^{21}	7^7	11^{11}	

Table 3. The Genus of Wyt Queens.

JELLY BEANS AND LEMON DROPS

The **Jelly Bean Game**, ·52, may be played with rows of jelly beans. We may take away 1 bean, provided it is strictly internal to its row, or forms the whole of its row; or 2 adjacent beans in precisely the opposite case, when they are at the end of the row but are *not* the whole row. Using J_n for a row of n jelly beans we find

$$J_1 = 1, \qquad J_2 = 0, \qquad J_3 = 2, \qquad J_4 = 2, \qquad J_5 = 1,$$

$$J_6 = \{2,3\} = 2_2 \text{ (genus } 0^0), \qquad J_7 = 3,$$

$$J_8 = 3_2 2_2 1 \text{ (genus } 2^2), \qquad J_9 = 2_2 3 2 \ (1^1).$$

Continuing the calculation,

$$J_{10} = \{J_8+J_1, \quad J_7+J_2, \quad J_6+J_3, \quad J_5+J_4, \quad J_8\},$$
$$\text{genus } \{ \quad 3^3, \qquad 3^3, \qquad 2^2, \qquad 3^3, \qquad 2^2\} = 0^0,$$

$$J_{11} = \{J_9+J_1, \quad J_8+J_2, \quad J_7+J_3, \quad J_6+J_4, \quad J_5+J_5, \quad J_9\},$$
$$\text{genus } \{ \quad 0^0, \qquad 2^2, \qquad 1^1, \qquad 2^2, \qquad 0^1, \qquad 1^1\} = 3^3$$

This is the last case which has a fickle option, $J_5+J_5=0^1$. From now on every J_n will be both firm and tame since all its options are, and the genus sequence

$$.1\ 0\ 2\ 2\ 1; 0^0\ 3\ 2^2\ 1^1\ 0^0\ 3^3\ 2^2\ 1^1\ 0^0\ 3^3 \dots$$

has period 4 after the semi-colon.

When we also allow 2 adjacent beans to be taken from *inside* a longer row we have the game of **Lemon Drops**, **·56**, with typical position L_n. The complete analysis of **·56** for normal play still eludes us, despite computations for rows of up to 50 000 drops. But at least it's no harder to play the misère version, since after $L_6=1$ every position is firm and tame:

$$.1\ 0\ 2\ 2\ 4\ 1\ 1^1\ 3\ 2\ 4^4\ 4^4\ 6^6\ 6^6\ 2^2\ 1^1\ 1^1\ 7^7\ 6^6\ 8^8\ 4^4\ 1^1\ 1^1 \dots .$$

STALKING ADDERS AND TAKING SQUARES

For **Stalking**, **·31**, the reduced forms are

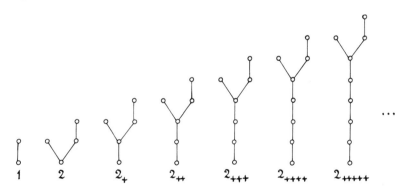

$$1 \qquad 2 \qquad 2_+ \qquad 2_{++} \qquad 2_{+++} \qquad 2_{++++} \qquad 2_{+++++}$$

showing that the game is tame with genus sequence

$$.1\ 2\ 0^0\ 1^1\ 0^0\ 1^1\ 0^0\ 1^1\ 0^0 \dots$$

while for **Adders**, **·73**, the reduced forms are

$$1 \qquad 2 \qquad 3 \qquad 2_2 \qquad 3_2 \qquad 2_{22} \qquad 3_{22} \qquad 2_{222} \qquad 3_{222} \qquad 2_{2222} \qquad 3_{2222} \dots$$

again tame, with genus sequence

$$.1 \qquad 2 \qquad 3 \qquad 0^0 \qquad 1^1 \qquad 2^2 \qquad 3^3 \qquad 0^0 \qquad 1^1 \qquad 2^2 \qquad 3^3 \dots$$

Of course, 2_{++} and 3_{22} are merely the collapsed notations for

$$(2_+)_+ = \{\{2\}\} \text{ and } (3_2)_2 = 3 + 2 + 2$$

Take-A-Square is another heap game. Each player in turn chooses a heap and takes

1 or 4 or 9 or 16 or ...

beans from it. If S_n is a heap of size n,

$$S_n = \{S_{n-1}, S_{n-4}, S_{n-9}, \ldots\}$$

and the first few S_n reduce to Nim-heaps:

n	0	1	2	3	4	5	6	7	8	9	10	11	12	13	14	15	16	17	18	19	20	21	22	23	24	25	...
S_n	0	1	0	1	2	0	1	0	1	2	0	1	0	1	2	0	1	0	1	2	0	1	0	1	2	3	...

Although 2 and 3 appear we'll never get any positions like {2,3} which don't reduce to Nim-heaps. In the Extras we'll give T.S. Ferguson's proof that *all* subtraction games reduce to Nim, and so are tame. Yamasaki has independently reached the same conclusion. His terms "flat" and "projective" both imply our "tame".

"BUT WHAT IF THEY'RE WILD?" ASKS THE BAD CHILD

She'll need to know how to compute the genus:

> For a non-empty game
>
> $$G = \{A, B, \ldots\}$$
>
> where
>
> A has genus $a^{\alpha_0 \alpha_1 \alpha_2 \cdots}$
> B has genus $b^{\beta_0 \beta_1 \beta_2 \cdots}$
> $$\cdots\cdots\cdots\cdots\cdots\cdots\cdots,$$
>
> the genus
>
> $$g^{\gamma_0 \gamma_1 \gamma_2 \cdots}$$
>
> is found from
>
> $$g = \operatorname{mex}(a, b, \ldots),$$
> $$\gamma_0 = \operatorname{mex}(\alpha_0, \beta_0, \ldots),$$
> $$\gamma_1 = \operatorname{mex}(\gamma_0, \gamma_0 \overset{*}{+} 1, \alpha_1, \beta_1, \ldots),$$
> $$\gamma_2 = \operatorname{mex}(\gamma_1, \gamma_1 \overset{*}{+} 1, \alpha_2, \beta_2, \ldots),$$
> $$\cdots\cdots\cdots\cdots\cdots\cdots\cdots\cdots,$$
> $$\gamma_{n+1} = \operatorname{mex}(\gamma_n, \gamma_n \overset{*}{+} 1, \alpha_{n+1}, \beta_{n+1}, \ldots).$$

and how to add small Nim-heaps:

> If G has genus $g^{\gamma_0\gamma_1\gamma_2\gamma_3\cdots}$
>
> then $G+1$ has genus $(g\overset{*}{+}1)^{\delta_0\delta_1\delta_2\delta_3\cdots}$
>
> $G+2$ has genus $(g\overset{*}{+}2)^{\gamma_1\gamma_2\gamma_3\cdots}$
>
> $G+3$ has genus $(g\overset{*}{+}3)^{\delta_1\delta_2\delta_3\cdots}$
>
> $G+2+2$ has genus $g^{\gamma_2\gamma_3\cdots}$
>
> $G+3+2$ has genus $(g\overset{*}{+}1)^{\delta_2\delta_3\cdots}$
>
> $\cdots\cdots\cdots\cdots\cdots\cdots\cdots\cdots\cdots\cdots\cdots\cdots,$
>
> where $\delta_0=\gamma_0\overset{*}{+}1,\quad \delta_1=\gamma_1\overset{*}{+}1,\quad \delta_2=\gamma_2\overset{*}{+}1,\ldots$

Here's how we find the genus for four of Grundy's wild animals ($a=2_2 21,\quad b=a_2 a20,$ $c=ba3,\quad d=cba_1 2_2 1$):

						c	$0^{2020\ldots}$		
		a_2	$1^{4313\ldots}$			b	$4^{0564\ldots}$		
2_2	$0^{0202\ldots}$	a	$3^{1431\ldots}$	b	$4^{0564\ldots}$	a_1	$2^{0520\ldots}$		
2	$2^{2020\ldots}$	2	$2^{2020\ldots}$	a	$3^{1431\ldots}$	2_2	$0^{0202\ldots}$		
1	$1^{0313\ldots}$	0	$0^{1202\ldots}$	3	$3^{3131\ldots}$	1	$1^{0313\ldots}$		
a	$3^{1431\ldots}$	b	$4^{0564\ldots}$	c	$0^{2020\ldots}$	d	$3^{1431\ldots}$		

Because Grundy's Game was extensively analyzed in ONAG, we'll leave further analysis until later and use Kayles as our next example.

MISÈRE KAYLES

For the tame animals in our good child's zoo we didn't need reverting moves since no wild game crossed our path. Although several tame games arise in Kayles (see Chapter 4), wild game's abounding and we'll need all our resources to tackle it. Table 4 pushes the genus analysis to heaps of size 20, and with increasing difficulty we find the next few terms:

K_{21}	K_{22}	K_{23}	K_{24}	K_{25}	$\cdots$
4^{64}	6^{46}	7^{57}	4^{64}	1^{731}	$\cdots$

The options of each game are found on the preceding two lines of the table. Thus

$$K_{10}=\delta=\{\gamma,\ \beta+2,\ \beta+1,\ \alpha+3,\ \alpha+1,\ 3+2,\ 2+2,\ 0\},$$

whose tame options: $\downarrow$ $0^0,$ $3^3,$ $\downarrow$ $\downarrow$ $1^1,$ $0^0,\ 0^1$ yield $2^2,$

while others revert to: $2,$ $2,$ $2,$

proving that K_{10} is tame with genus 2^2. In normal Kayles, no single row other than 0 can be a $\mathcal{P}$-position (take out the middle 1 or 2 pins), but the table shows that in misère play,

$$K_1,\ K_4,\ K_9,\ K_{12},\ K_{20}$$

are $\mathcal{P}$-positions. It is not hard to justify enough $\mathcal{P}$-positions:

n	K_n	$K_{n-1}+K_1$	$K_{n-2}+K_2$	$K_{n-3}+K_3$	$K_{n-4}+K_4$	$K_{n-5}+K_5$	$K_{n-6}+K_6$	$K_{n-7}+K_7$	$K_{n-8}+K_8$	$K_{n-9}+K_9$
0	0									
1	1									
2	2	0								
3	3	3								
4	1	2	$0^0(2_2)$							
5	$4^{146}(\alpha)$	0	$1^1(3_2)$							
6	3	$5^{057}(\alpha_1)$	3	$0^0(2_2)$						
7	$2^2(\beta)$	2	$6^{46}(\alpha_2)$	2						
8	$1^1(3_2)$	$3^3(\beta_1)$	$1^1(3_2)$	$7^{57}(\alpha_3)$	0					
9	$4^{046}(\gamma)$	0^0	0^0	0^0	5^{057}					
10	$2^2(\delta)$	5^{157}	3^3	1^1	2	0^{120}				
11	6^{46}	3^3	6^{46}	2^2	3^3	7^{57}				
12	4^{046}	7^{57}	0^0	7^{57}	0^0	6^{46}	0^0			
13	1^1	5^{157}	4^{64}	1^1	5^{157}	5^{75}	1^1			
14	2^2	0^0	6^{46}	5^{75}	3^3	0^{02}	2^2	0^0		
15	7^{57}	3^3	3^3	7^{57}	7^{57}	6^{46}	7^{57}	3^3		
16	1^{13}	6^{46}	0^0	2^2	5^{157}	2^{20}	1^1	6^{46}	0^0	
17	4^{64}	0^{02}	5^{75}	1^1	0^0	0^{02}	5^{75}	0^0	5^{75}	
18	3^{31}	5^{75}	3^{31}	4^{64}	3^3	5^{75}	7^{57}	4^{64}	3^3	0^{120}
19	2^{20}	2^{20}	6^{46}	2^{20}	6^{46}	6^{46}	2^2	6^{46}	7^{57}	6^{46}
20	1^{031}									

$$\alpha = 2_2321$$
$$\beta = \alpha_1\alpha3_22_230$$
$$\gamma = \beta_1\beta\alpha_3\alpha_23_220$$
$$\delta = \gamma\beta_2\beta_1\alpha_3\alpha_13_22_20$$

Table 4. Genus Analysis of Misère Kayles.

$$K_{20}, \qquad K_{11}+K_{11},\ K_8+K_{16},\ K_{13}+K_{13}, K_{14}+K_{14},\ K_{15}+K_{15},\ K_{16}+K_{16},$$

to provide good replies to

$$K_{21}, K_{22}. \qquad K_{23}, K_{24},\quad K_{25}, K_{26},\quad K_{27}, K_{28},\quad K_{29}, K_{30},\quad K_{31}, K_{32},\quad K_{33}, K_{34}.$$

Is there a larger single-row $\mathscr{P}$-position?

THE NOAH'S ARK THEOREM

Any wild game that's only just gone wild, i.e. has only tame options, must have among its options one, but not both, of the two kinds $(0^1, 1^0)$ of fickle unit and one, but not both, of the two kinds $(0^0, 1^1)$ of firm unit. If the options include both kinds of 0 or both kinds of 1:

$$0^1, 0^0, a^a, b^b, \ldots \text{ or } 1^0, 1^1, a^a, b^b, \ldots \qquad (2 \leqslant a, b, \ldots)$$

the game is restive. If one of each:

$$1^0, 0^0, a^a, b^b, \ldots \text{ or } 0^1, 1^1, a^a, b^b, \ldots \qquad (2 \leqslant a, b, \ldots)$$

we call it **restless**.

Usually two copies of a restive game make a firm zero, while two copies of a restless game can be treated as a fickle zero. So (look at Fig. 6) we can allow some restive and restless animals into our ark of tame creatures provided that they come in pairs and are suitably restrained:

Figure 6. The Noah's Ark Theorem.

Suppose that

$T_1, T_2, \ldots$ are tame,
$R_1, R_2, \ldots$ are restive, and the game
R is restless of genus $g^{\gamma \cdots}$,

and that $R_1, R_2, \ldots, R$ have only just gone wild.
   Then you can find the outcome of

$$T_1 + T_2 + \ldots + (R_1 + R_1) + (R_2 + R_2) + \ldots + (R + R) + (R + R) + \ldots$$

by noting that each pair

$$R_1 + R_1, \quad R_2 + R_2, \ldots$$

is a tame game of genus 0^0 and *neglecting* each pair

$$R + R,$$

provided that
when there is any pair $R + R$,
   (i) the only fickle tame positions of
   $T_1, T_2, \ldots, R_1, R_2, \ldots, R$ are 0 and 1, and
   (ii) for each option a^a $(a \geqslant 2)$ of R,
      either a^a has an option $\gamma \overset{*}{+} 1$,
      or R has an option $(a \overset{*}{+} 1)^{a \overset{*}{+} 1}$.

THE NOAH'S ARK THEOREM

   The complicated sounding conditions are usually satisfied automatically, because the options a^a in condition (ii) are often Nim-heaps a, and we rarely see a fickle tame position other than 0 or 1.
   The strategy showing why $R + R$ can be neglected is given in the Extras. It also proves that when (i) and (ii) are satisfied

$$T_1 + T_2 + \ldots + (R_1 + R_1) + (R_2 + R_2) + \ldots + (R + R) + \ldots + (R + R) + R$$

has the same outcome as

$$T_1 + T_2 + \ldots + (R_1 + R_1) + (R_2 + R_2) + \ldots + R.$$

In particular, all even multiples of R have genus

$$0^{1202 \ldots}$$

and all odd ones have the same genus as R.
   Thus Grundy's Game first goes wild at $G_{13} = 2_2 21$, which is restless of genus 3^{1431}, and so the sum of any odd number of copies of G_{13} will have the same genus, while the sum of any even number has the same genus 0^{120} as 0. Similar remarks hold for $K_5 = 2_2 321$ of genus 4^{146}, in Kayles.

To show that $R_1 + R_1$ is tame of genus 0^0, we exhibit a reverting move to 0^0 from *every* option:

$$R_1 + n^n \longrightarrow n^n + n^n = 0^0,$$

$$R_1 + R_1 \begin{cases} R_1 + 0^1 \longrightarrow 0^0 + 0^1 = 0^0, \\ \quad\text{or} \\ R_1 + 1^0 \longrightarrow 1^1 + 1^0 = 0^0. \end{cases}$$

Moreover if r^ρ is the genus of R_1, then $R_1 + R_1 + R_1$ is tame of genus r^r, because all options are tame and firm:

$$R_1 + R_1 + n^n = n^n,$$

$$R_1 + R_1 + R_1 \begin{cases} R_1 + R_1 + 0^1 = 0^0, \\ \quad\text{or} \\ R_1 + R_1 + 1^0 = 1^1. \end{cases}$$

This means that we can allow some pairs of restive animals to bring their children into the ark.

THE HALF-TAME THEOREM

We call a wild animal H **half-tame** if $H + H$ is tame of genus 0^0. The argument we used to prove that $R_1 + R_1$ is tame generalizes to show that:

A wild game is half-tame
provided that
all options of H are tame or half-tame,
and
if H has an option 0^1, it has an option 0^0,
if H has an option 1^0, it has an option 1^1.

THE HALF-TAME THEOREM

It is not actually necessary for the truth of the Noah's Ark Theorem that the games of each restive or restless pair be identical. It will suffice if they are merely of the same **species**. The following operations will not change the species:

(a) replacing a tame option by another tame game of the same genus (observing conditions (i) and (ii) of the Noah's Ark Theorem in the restless case),

(b) adding a new option from which there is a reverting move to a game already known to be of the same species.

GUILES

is the octal game $\cdot 15$ played with rows Y_n of n beans from which 2 adjacent beans may be removed provided neither is the end of a row and a complete row that contains 1 or 2 beans may also be removed. The genus sequence is remarkable for its repetitions:

$$0.110112212211011^41^4221^222^{1420}1^41^40^11^41^422^{1420}12^{21420}2^{1420}1^11^{631}\ldots.$$

All the occurrences of 1^4 refer to the same restive game

$$Y_{14} = Y_{15} = Y_{21} = Y_{22} = Y_{24} = Y_{25} = 2_2320 = z, \text{ say,}$$

which arises in many other contexts ($\cdot$**57**, .**72**, $\cdot$**75** and **4·7**). In terms of this

$Y_{18} = z_12_20;$	*restive,* genus 1^2,
$Y_{20} = z_1z2_231;$	*wild,* genus 2^{1420},
$Y_{23} = \{Y_{20}+1, Y_{18}, z+2, 3, 1\};$ *tame,*	genus 0^1.

Y_{19} and Y_{26} both reduce to the Nim-heap of size 2!
    Why is $Y_{28} = \{Y_{23}, Y_{20} + 2, Y_{18}+1, z+1, 2+2, 0\}$ restive? Its tame options

$$Y_{23}, 2+2, 0$$

with values

$$0^1, \quad 0^0, \quad 0^1$$

suffice to compute the value 1^2.

From $Y_{20}+2$ there are reverting moves to $3+2(1^1)$ and $2+2+2(2^2)$.
From $Y_{18}+1$ there is a reverting move to $Y_{18}(1^2)$.
From $z+1$ there are reverting moves to $0+1(1^0)$ and $3+1(2^2)$.

Y_{31} is tame of genus 1^1. It has all the options

$$2+2, 3, 2$$

of $3+2$, and from every other option except $z+z$ (which is tame of genus 0^0 by the Noah's Ark Theorem) there is a reverting move to $3+2$, so that Y_{31} is "nearly equal to" $3+2$.

DIVIDING RULERS

is the name for our next game because the positions (Fig. 7) repeat like those of the Ruler Game (Fig. 7 in Chapter 14). The move is to split any heap into two smaller heaps or to halve the size of any even heap. Writing R_n for a heap of n we have, if $n=2^kd$ and d is odd,

$$R_n = H_k, \quad \text{where} \quad H_0 = 0, \quad H_1 = 1, \quad H_2 = 2, \quad H_3 = 2_220,$$

and in general

$$H_{k+1} = \{H_0+H_0, H_1+H_1, H_2+H_2, \ldots, H_k+H_k, H_k\}.$$

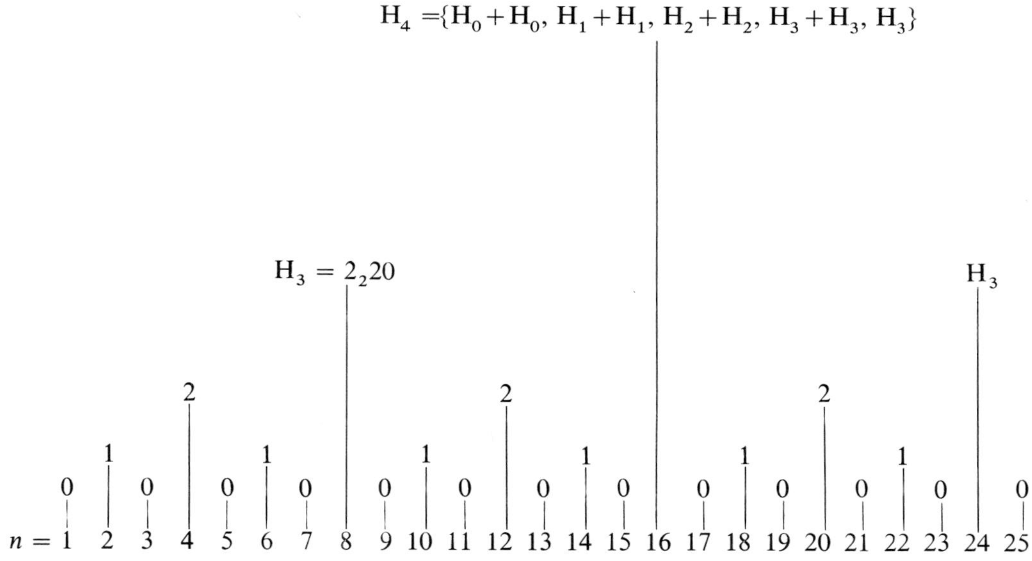

$$H_4 = \{H_0 + H_0, \; H_1 + H_1, \; H_2 + H_2, \; H_3 + H_3, \; H_3\}$$

Figure 7. Positions in Dividing Rulers.

This is because the options of R_n have the forms

$$R_{2^{k-1}d} \qquad R_{2^j a} + R_{2^j b} \qquad R_{2^k a} + R_{2^l b}$$

where a,b are odd and $j < k < l$. By induction these are

$$H_{k-1} \qquad H_j + H_j \qquad H_k + H_l.$$

The first two cases are the options defining H_k, and from the third there is a reverting move to $H_k + H_0 + H_0 = H_k$.

Because H_3 is restive and only just wild we know the genus of all its multiples:

H_3	$H_3 + H_3$	$H_3 + H_3 + H_3$	$H_3 + H_3 + H_3 + H_3$	$H_3 + H_3 + H_3 + H_3 + H_3$	$\cdots$
genus 1^3	0^0	1^1	0^0	$1^1 \ldots$	

and we can therefore predict the outcome of any position in which no heap has size divisible by 16. Also, because $H_3, H_4, \ldots$ are half-tame it is easy to find their genus:

$$H_3, H_5, H_7, \ldots \quad \text{have genus } 1^{31},$$
$$H_4, H_6, H_8, \ldots \quad \text{have genus } 2^{20}.$$

But positions where they don't occur in even numbers can be more complicated; for example

$$H_3 + H_4 \qquad\qquad \text{has genus } 3^{46}$$

but

$$H_3 + H_3 + H_3 + H_4 \quad \text{has genus } 3^{31}.$$

There is a variant in which the division of a heap into two *equal* heaps is *not* allowed. Using V_n for a heap of size n in the variant, we find that some of the theory still goes through:

$$V_d = 0, \quad V_{2d} = 1, \quad V_{4d} = 2, \quad \text{if } d \text{ is odd,}$$

but $V_8, V_{16}, V_{24}, \ldots$ are all distinct:

n	8	16	24	32	40	48	56	64	72	80	88	96	104	...
V_n	1	2	z	y	x	w	v	u	t	s	r	q	p	...
genus	1	2	1^4	1^3	1^4	2^{20}	1^4	2^{20}	1^4	2^{20}	1^4	1^{31}	1^4	...

In fact $z = 2_1 2_2 320$ is the restive game we met in Guiles and the alternate terms thereafter, $x, v, t, \ldots$ are restive of the same species. We show the tame options and reverting moves for the case

$$t = \{u+1, \quad v+2, \quad w+z, \quad x+y, \quad 2+2, \quad 0, \quad 2\}$$

tame options: 3^3 0^0, 0^1, 2^2,

reverting moves: $(v+1)+1$, $0+z$, $x+0$.

The tame options have the same genus as those of z ($v+2$ is tame of genus 3^3 by the Intermediate Value Theorem) and v, z, x are already known to have the same species. The sum of two or any larger even number of these is therefore tame of genus 0^0, while three or any larger odd number make a tame game of genus 1^1.

The game $V_{32} = y = z_1 2_2 20$ is also restive, but of a different genus, 1^3. These games $z, y, x, w, \ldots$ are still half tame, but their analysis is much more difficult than that for the first version:

$$
\begin{aligned}
y + z, y + x, y + v &\quad \text{have genus } 0^{20}, \\
z + w, z + u &\quad \text{have genus } 3^{31}, \\
y + w, y + u &\quad \text{have genus } 3^{13}, \\
z + y + z, z + y + x &\quad \text{have genus } 1^{31}, \\
\end{aligned}
$$

while $z + y + y$ is tame of genus 1^1.

DAWSON, OFFICERS, GRUNDY

For these three well known wild dogs we have made extended calculations and present you with the resulting D, O, G sequences. Shorter tables covering all the two-digit octal games will be found in the Extras.

For **Dawson's Kayles** the genus sequence for the positions D_n with n pins is:

n	1	2	3	4	5	6	7	8	9	10	11	12	13	14
D_n	0	1	1	2	0	3	1	1	0	3^{1431}	3	2^{0520}	2	4^{146}
D_{n+14}	0	5^{057}	2^{0520}	2	3^{1431}	3	0^{02}	1^{031}	1^{13}	3^{1431}	0^{31}	2^{0520}	1^{431}	1^{13}
D_{n+28}	0^{120}	4^{0564}	5^{057}	2^{20}	7^{14875}	4^{57}	0^{02}	1^{031}	1^{13}	2^{1420}	0^{31}	3^{0631}	1^{431}	1^{13}

and here is a short table for sums of two such positions:

+	A	B	C	D	D_{21}	D_{22}	D_{23}	D_{24}	D_{25}	D_{26}
$D_{10} = D_{17} + 1 = 2_221$ = A	0^{120}	1^{031}	7^{175}	6^{064}	3^{31}	2^{0520}	2^{20}	0^{120}	3^{564}	1^{031}
$D_{12} = D_{19} + 1 = A3_20$ = B	1^{031}	0^{120}	6^{064}	7^{175}	2^{20}	3^{1431}	3^{31}	1^{031}	2^{431}	0^{120}
$D_{14} = \quad BA_12_231$ = C	7^{175}	6^{064}	0^{120}	1^{031}	4^{5864}	5^{057}	5^{4975}	7^{175}	4^{5864}	6^{064}
$D_{16} = \quad CB_1A_220$ = D	6^{064}	7^{175}	1^{031}	0^{120}	5^{4975}	4^{146}	4^{5864}	6^{064}	5^{20}	

The genus of any sum of terms A,B,C,D, is correctly evaluated by *pretending* that

$$A+A = B+B = C+C = D+D = 0,$$

$$A+1 = B, \qquad C+1 = D.$$

Dawson, whose original game *was* the misère play version, found a tendency to period 14 in the outcomes of D_n which our table verifies up to $n=42$. But (unlike D_2, D_{16} and D_{30}) D_{44} is a misère $\mathcal{N}$-position because there is a move to $D_{21}+D_{21}$ which has genus 0^{02}, since every option has a reverting move into this genus:

$$D_{21} + D_{21} = \{D_{21}+D+1, \; D_{21}+C, \; D_{21}+B+1, \; D_{21}+A, \; D_{21}+3+2, \; D_{21}+2\}$$

$$D_{21}+A+3 \qquad\qquad D_{21}+2+2 \qquad\qquad 2+2.$$

For **Officers** (.6, Chapter 4) the genus sequence O_n for officers of rank n, directly responsible for $n+2$ other officers and men, is:

n	0	1	2	3	4	5	6	7	8	9	10	11
O_n	0	0	1	2	0	1	2	3^{1431}	1	2	3^{1431}	4^{0564}
O_{n+12}	0^{20}	3^{1431}	4^{0564}	2^{20}	1^{13}	3^{0531}	2^{20}	1^{13}	0^{02}	2^{20}	1^{13}	4^{0564}
O_{n+24}	5^{475}	1^{13}	4^{0564}	5^{475}	1^{13}	2^{20}	0^{02}	1^{13}	...			

For the single heap positions G_n in **Grundy's Game** the genus sequence was computed to 50 terms in ONAG:

n	1	2	3	4	5	6	7	8	9	10
G_n	0	0	1	0	2	1	0	2	1	0
G_{n+10}	2	1	3^{1431}	2	1	3^{1431}	2	4^{0564}	3^{1431}	0^{20}
G_{n+20}	4^{0564}	3^{1431}	0^{20}	4^{0564}	3^{1431}	0^{20}	4^{0564}	1^{13}	2^{20}	3^{02}
G_{n+30}	1^{13}	2^{20}	4^{02}	1^{13}	2^{475}	4^{02}	1^{13}	2^{475}	4^{0564}	1^{13}
G_{n+40}	5^{475}	4^{0564}	1^{13}	5^{475}	4^{0520}	1^{13}	5^{475}	4^{20}	1^{13}	0^{0431} ...

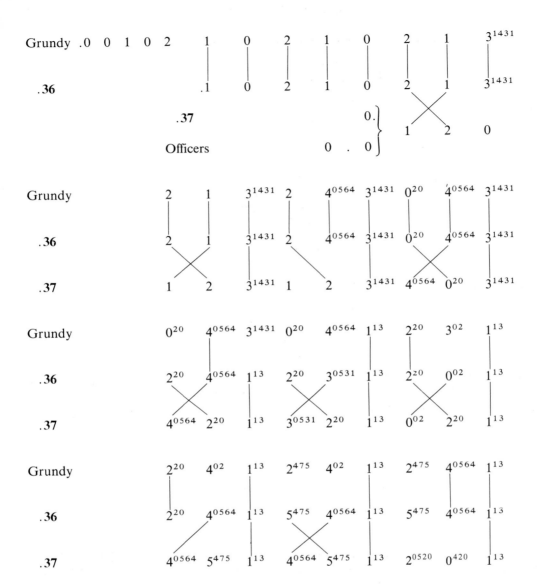

When there are no heaps of 28 or more we can *pretend* that

$$G_{13} = G_{16} = G_{19} = G_{22} = G_{25} = a,$$
$$G_{18} = G_{21} = G_{24} = G_{27} = b,$$
$$G_{20} = G_{23} = G_{26} = c,$$

and that

$$a+a = b+b = 0, \qquad c+c+c = c+c.$$

When adding these, use the table:

number of copies of c: together with:	none	one	two or more
0	0^{120}	0^{20}	0^{02}
a	3^{1431}	3^{431}	3^{31}
b	4^{0564}	4^{564}	4^{46}
$a+b$	7^{05875}	7^{5875}	7^{75}

The following equalities show that this table is also useful when playing Officers:

$$G_{13} = G_{16} = G_{19} = a = O_7 = O_{10}.$$
$$G_{18} = G_{21} = b = O_{11},$$
$$G_{20} = c = O_{12},$$
$$G_{22} = d = O_{13}.$$

In the sense of the Extras to Chapter 4, Officers is a first cousin to .**37**. The game .**36** is even more closely related to Grundy's Game, as shown in the scheme opposite.

Solid lines indicate equalities of genus which in the first two blocks are identities.

The misère theory of impartial games is the last and most complicated theory in this book. Congratulations if you've followed us this far. In the second part of the book you can relax while learning to play some particular games.

EXTRAS

ALL SUBTRACTION GAMES REDUCE TO NIM

Take-A-Square, the last game in the good child's zoo, is the subtraction game corresponding to the set
$$\{1,4,9,16,...\}.$$
Although its values will never become periodic we do know that they will always reduce to Nim-heaps.

T.S. Ferguson proved from his Pairing Property that a heap of size n in the subtraction game corresponding to *any* subtraction set

$$\{s_0,s_1,s_2,...\} \qquad (0<s_0<s_1<s_2<...)$$

reduces to a Nim-heap of size $\mathcal{G}(n)$, its (normal) nim-value.

Certainly

$$\mathcal{G}(n) = \text{mex}(\mathcal{G}(n-s_0),\mathcal{G}(n-s_1),\mathcal{G}(n-s_2),...)$$

so we need only show that if $\mathcal{G}(n)=0$, then $\mathcal{G}(n-s_k)=1$ for some s_k. But if $\mathcal{G}(n)=0$ and there is *any* legal move, it is legal to take the *least* number, s_0, so $\mathcal{G}(n-s_0)>0$. Hence there is *some* s_k with $\mathcal{G}(n-s_0-s_k)=0$. But we showed in the Extras to Chapter 4 that every nim-value 0 in a sub-traction game is accompanied by a nim-value 1 that occurs s_0 places later, so

$$\mathcal{G}(n-s_0-s_k+s_0) = \mathcal{G}(n-s_k) = 1,$$

as desired.

You can now use the tables in Chapter 4 to play the misère forms of all the subtraction games dealt with there.

PRIM AND DIM

These games from Chapter 4 are rather like subtraction games. For $Prim^+$, $Prim^-$, and Dim^+, every heap has an option 0 or 1 and so reduces to a Nim-heap. But for Dim^- (remove from n a divisor less than n) the genus sequence is

$$.0\ 1\ 0\ 2\ 0^0\ 1^3\ 0^0\ 3^{13}0^0\ 1^{20}0^0\ 1^{46}0^0\ 2^{13}0^0... .$$

For $n>5$ it can be shown that the genus is
$$g^{\gamma\delta\gamma\delta}...$$
where $n=2^g d$ (d odd) and

$$\gamma = g - 2 \quad \text{if } d = 1,$$
$$\gamma = g + 2 \quad \text{if } d = 3,$$
$$\gamma = g + 1 \quad \text{if } d = 5,$$
$$\gamma = g \qquad \text{if } d \geqslant 7,$$

and

$$\delta = \gamma \overset{*}{+} 2.$$

PROOF OF THE NOAH'S ARK THEOREM

It remains to show that, in the conditions of the theorem, if

$$R = \{\gamma, \delta^o, a^a, b^b, \ldots\}$$

is a restless game with genus $g^{\gamma \cdots}$, where γ, δ are 0,1 in some order and $2 \leqslant a < b < \ldots$, then pairs $R + R$ may be neglected in calculating the outcome of

$$R + R + R + \ldots + T$$

where T is a tame game. We prove the result by induction. If the number of copies of R is odd, we note that the options of $(2n+1).R + T$,

$$2n.R + R' + T \quad \text{and} \quad (2n+1).R + T'$$

have the same outcomes as

$$R' + T \quad \text{and} \quad R + T',$$

the options of $R + T$. In particular $(2n+1).R + \gamma$ is a $\mathscr{P}$-position.

If the number of copies of R is even, it suffices to prove that $(2n+2).R + T$ is a $\mathscr{P}$-position when T is. If T has genus 1^0 it must be 1, and the options of $(2n+2).R + 1$ can be reverted to $\mathscr{P}$-positions:

$$(2n+2).R + 1 \begin{cases} (2n+2).R & \longrightarrow (2n+1).R + \gamma, \\ (2n+1).R + \gamma + 1 & \longrightarrow (2n+1).R + \gamma, \\ (2n+1).R + \delta^o + 1 & \longrightarrow 2n.R + \gamma + \delta^\delta + 1 = 2n.R + 0^0, \\ (2n+1).R + a^a + 1 & \searrow \begin{cases} \text{or} & (2n+1).R + \delta + 1 = (2n+1).R + \gamma, \\ & 2n.R + a^a + (a \overset{*}{+} 1)^{a \overset{*}{+} 1} + 1 = 2n.R + 0^0, \end{cases} \end{cases}$$

according to which part of condition (ii) of the theorem is satisfied.

The options of $(2n+2).R + T$, where T has genus 0^0, can be similarly reverted:

$$(2n+2).R + T \begin{cases} (2n+1).R + R' + T & \longrightarrow 2n.R + R' + R' + T = 2n.R + 0^0, \\ (2n+2).R + T' & \longrightarrow (2n+2).R + T'', \end{cases}$$

where T'' is a $\mathscr{P}$-position.

MISÈRE OCTAL GAMES

Table 5 gives the genus sequence for a number of 2-digit octal games. Use the guide below for games that do not appear in the main table (M). An entry in the guide is then an equivalent game (subscript 1 denotes "first cousin of") that *does* appear, or the complete value sequence when all positions are Nim-heaps.

	0	1	2	3	4	5	6	7
·0	.0̇	.010̇	.0011̇	.0110̇	M	.01̇	M	M
·1	.10̇	.110̇	.1001̇	.1100̇	M	M	M	M
·2	.01̇	.01̇	.012̇	.012̇	.01̇	.01̇	M	·26
·3	.10̇	M	.102̇	.120̇	M	M	M	M
·4	·07$_1$	·17$_1$	·07$_1$	·17$_1$	M	M	·44	·45
·5	.10̇	.1̇	M	M	M	.1̇	M	M
·6	·37$_1$	·37$_1$	·37$_1$	·37$_1$	M	·64	·64	·64
·7	.10̇	M	M	M	M	M	M	M
4·	.01̇	.1̇	.01̇	M	·77$_1$	.1̇	·77$_1$	M

Guide to Table 5.

In Table 5, $a,b,c,\ldots$ refer to the first, second, third,... entries that are not single digits. The letters A,D,T,H,F in the last column refer to the following

Notes

A   Additional information is to be found in the text.
     ·07 = Dawson's Kayles,   ·15 = Guiles,   ·31 = Stalking,
     ·36   (cf Grundy and)   ·37 = Officers,   ·52 = Jelly Beans,
     ·56 = Lemon Drops,   ·73 = Adders,   ·77 = Kayles,

D   Every entry is duplicated. For ·44 the duplicated values are those of Kayles, while ·57 duplicates 4·7.

T   Every position is tame. For ·73 and 4·3 every position is a Nim-position. T.S. Ferguson observed that ·73 and ·333 do *not* have the same misère play (cf. entry ·26 in Table 6(b) of Chapter 4).

H   Every position is half-tame. The first few values for the three games ·26, ·57 and 4·7 are closely related and contain increasing numbers of genus superscripts before settling down. Does this continue?

F Jim Flanigan has worked out a complete analysis:
After its first 6 values, ·34 has the exact period

$$0 \quad 3 \quad 1 \quad 2_21 \quad 1 \quad 2 \quad 0 \quad (2_21)+1$$

of eight terms. Two copies of 2_21 can be neglected by the Noah's Ark Theorem.

After its first 2 terms, the genus sequence for ·71 exhibits period 6:

$$1 \quad 0 \quad 1^{20} \quad 0 \quad 1 \quad 0^{1420}.$$

Although the various games of genus 1^{20} and 0^{1420} are distinct we obtain a correct analysis by *pretending* they are equivalent to r and s and using the genus table:

+	0	r	2r	3r,5r,7r,...	4r,6r,8r,...
0,2s,4s,...	0^{120}	1^{20}	0^{02}	1^{13}	0^{02}
s,3s,5s,...	0^{1420}	1^{02}	0^{20}	1^{13}	0^{02}

Game	Genus-sequence		Notes
·04	.00011 12203 31110 $4^{146}3^{1431}332^{0520}$ $224^{146}4^{146}0^{120}$	$a=2_2321\ b=2_221$	
·06	.00112 20311 $22^{1420}3^{1431}340^{564}$ $40^{564}0^{205}14753^{1431}$	$a=2_231\ b=2_221$	
·07	.01120 31103^{1431} $32^{0520}24^{146}0$ $50^{57}2^{0520}23^{1431}3$ 0^{02}	$a=2_221\ b=a3_20$	A
·14	.10010 21221 $0414^{146}4$ $1^{3}2^{1420}21^{3}2^{1720}$ $0^{02}1^{03}1^{0}0^{120}$	$a=2_2321\ b=2_2420$	
·15	.11011 22122 $1101^{4}1^{4}$ $221^{2}22^{1420}$ $1^{4}1^{4}0^{1}1^{4}1^{4}$	$a=b=2_2320\ c=a_12_20$	A
·16	.10012 21401 $42^{1420}1^{2}4^{2046}0^{1}$ $1^{0}4^{031}2^{1}16^{57}25^{720}420$	$a=2_2431\ b=2_240$	
·17	.11021 30113^{1431} $22^{0520}34^{146}1$ $50^{57}3^{1431}22^{0520}3$ 1^{13}	$a=2_221\ b=a3_20$	
·26	.01230 $1230^{4}1^{5}$ $2^{0420}3^{3}1^{0}2^{0420}1^{5}3_12020420$ 3^{1431}	$a=3_2321\ b=a+1\ c=a_1a3$	H
·31	$.120^{0}1^{1}0^{0}$ $1^{1}0^{0}1^{1}0^{0}1^{1}$ $0^{0}1^{1}0^{0}1^{1}0^{0}$	$a=2_+\ b=2_{++}$	AT
·34	.10120 10312^{1420} $1203^{0531}0$ $312^{1420}12$ 03^{0531}	$a=c=2_21\ b=d=a+1$	F
·35	$.120^{0}1^{2}0^{0}$ $2^{2}1^{02}2^{2}0^{0}1^{2}$ $0^{0}2^{2}1^{02}2^{2}0^{0}$ $1^{20}0^{0}2^{2}$	$a=2_+\ b=2_+0$	H
·36	.10210 $213^{1431}21$ $3^{1431}24^{0564}3^{1431}0^{20}$ $40^{564}3^{1431}220$	$a=b=d=2_221\ c=f=a_2a20$	A
·37	.12012 $3^{1431}123^{1431}40^{564}$ $0^{203}1^{431}40^{564}220^{1}1^{13}$ 3^{0531}	$a=b=2_221\ c=a_2a20$	A
·44	.00112 23311 $4^{146}4^{146}3332^{2}$ $2^{2}1^{1}1^{4}0^{46}4^{046}$	$a=b=2_2321\ c=d=a_1a3_22_230$	D
·45	.01122 $3114^{146}4$ $32^{2}2^{2}1^{1}1^{0}$ $40^{57}2^{2}$	$a=2_2321\ b=2_23210$	
·52	.10221 $0^{0}32^{2}1^{1}0^{0}$ $3^{3}2^{2}1^{1}0^{0}3^{3}$ $2^{2}1^{1}0^{0}$	$a=2_2\ b=3_22_21\ c=3_2\ d=b_1b2_22_33$	AT
·53	.11221 $0^{0}22^{4}4^{0}0^{0}$ $1^{6}2^{2}2^{2}1^{031}1^{1}$ $2^{2}2^{2}4^{4}1^{1}1^{631}$	$a=2_2\ b=3_22_20\ c=3_22_232$	H
·54	.10122 $2411^{1}1^{6}$ $222^{2}4^{1}5^{7}1^{1}$ $1^{1}1^{431}2^{2}2^{2}$	$a=2_2532\ b=2_254320$	H
·56	.10224 $11^{1}324^{4}$ $4^{4}6^{6}6^{2}2^{1}1^{1}$ $1^{1}7^{7}6^{6}8^{8}4^{4}$ $1^{1}1^{1}$	$a=2_25432\ b=a_1a4_22_2321$	AT
·57	.11221 $1221^{4}1^{4}$ $2^{20}2^{20}1^{431}1^{431}2_11^{1420}$ $2^{1420}1^{20431}$	$a=b=2_2320\ c=d=a_1a2_230$	DH
·64	.01234 $15^{146}3^{3}21^{431}$ $51^{40}4^{057}27^{8466}4^{657}$	$a=2_24321\ b=a3_22_25421$	
·71	$.12101^{2}$ $010^{1420}10$ $1^{20}010^{1420}1$ $01^{20}010^{1420}$	$a=2_20\ b=a_21$	F
·72	.10231 $0231^{4}0^{0}$ $2^{20}3^{3}11^{431}0^{0}2^{1420}$	$a=2_2320\ b=2_2\ c=a_2a2_230$	H
·73	$.1230^{0}1^{1}$ $2^{2}3^{3}0^{0}1^{1}2^{2}$ $3^{3}0^{0}1^{1}2^{2}3^{3}$ $0^{0}1^{1}2^{2}$	$a=2_2\ b=3_2\ c=2_{22}\ d=3_{22}$	AT
·74	.10123 $2414^{146}6^{657}$ $232^{2}1^{1}5^{857}$ $1^{1}7^{657}$	$a=2_25321\ b=a3_22_254320$	
·75	$.12121^{4}$ $2^{20}1^{431}220^{1}1^{220}$ $1^{13}2^{20}1^{13}2^{20}$	$a=2_2320\ b=a2_230$	H
·76	.10234 $16^{146}234^{46}$ $15^{3}16^{146}7657^{3}3^{2}2^{20}$ $15^{3}16^{746}$	$a=2_254321\ b=a_1a4_34_22_2321$	
·77	$.12314^{146}$ $32^{2}1^{4}0^{46}2^{2}$ $6^{46}40^{46}1^{1}2^{2}7^{57}$ $1^{13}4^{64}3^{31}2^{20}$	$a=2_2321\ b=a_1a3_22_230$	A
4·3	$.120^{0}2^{2}0^{0}$ $2^{2}0^{0}2^{2}0^{0}2^{2}$ $0^{0}2^{2}0^{0}2^{2}0^{0}$ 2^{2}	$a=2_2\ b=2_{22}\ c=2_{222}$	T
4·7	$.12121^{4}$ $2^{20}1^{431}2^{1420}1^{20431}2^{131420}$ $1^{2020431}2^{13131420}$	$a=2_2320\ b=a_1a2_230$	H

Table 5. Genus Sequences of Two-Digit Octal Games.

STOP PRESS: EVEN MORE GAMES ARE TAMEABLE!

A *single* tameable game can be added to any number of tame ones by the usual rules. If

$$G = \{T_1, T_2, ..., U_1, U_2, ...\}$$

where $T_1, T_2, ...$ are games we already know to be tameable, while $U_1, U_2, ...$ may be wild, then the three conditions for G to be **tameable** are:

(i) its nim-values g^γ must be one of the tame pairs

$$0^0, 1^1, 2^2, 3^3, 4^4, ... \quad \text{or} \quad 0^1 \text{ or } 1^0$$

(ii) g^γ must also be the nim-values of the **reduced game**

$$H = \{T_1, T_2, ...\}$$

(except that when H is empty, g^γ may be 0^1 *or* 0^0)

(iii) from each of the wild or unknown options $U_1, U_2, ...$ there must be reverting moves to two (possibly equal) tameable games of genus

$$g^? \quad \text{and} \quad ?^\gamma$$

For example, all the entries

$$0^{02}, 1^{13}, 2^{20}, 3^{31}, 0^{120}, 1^{031}$$

for the Kayles positions in Table 4 are tameable, of genus

$$0^{0/}, 1^{1/}, 2^{2/}, 3^{3/}, 0^{1/}, 1^{0/}$$

(/ being our way of distinguishing TAMEABLE from TAME). We have TAMEABLE + TAME = TAMEABLE, but TAMEABLE + TAMEABLE may be WILD. In fact TAME is the largest class of games that can be added like Nim-positions, and in which one player has a winning strategy which always returns to the class.

REFERENCES AND FURTHER READING

Charles L. Bouton, Nim a game with a complete mathematical theory, Ann. of Math., Princeton (2), **3** (1901–02) 35–39.

J.H. Conway, "On Numbers and Games", Academic Press, London and New York, 1976, Chapter 12.

T.S. Ferguson, On sums of graph games with the last player losing, Internat. J. Game Theory, **3** (1974) 159–167; MR **52** #5046.

P.M. Grundy and C.A.B. Smith, Disjunctive games with the last player losing, Proc. Cambridge Philos. Soc. **52** (1956) 527–533; MR **18**, 546.

T.H. O'Beirne, "Puzzles and Paradoxes", Oxford University Press, London, 1965, pp. 131–150.

Yōhei Yamasaki, On misère Nim-type games, J. Math. Soc. Japan, **32** (1980) 461–475.

Yōhei Yamasaki, The projectivity of Y-games, Publ. RIMS, Kyoto Univ. **17** (1981) 245–248.

numbers
2 dimensional Nim
White Knight
Theory of Join, Unions
slow Horses
Cutcake
Hotcakes
Games without perfect Info.   9817
Prisoners Dilema
Zero Sum Games
Zwickers Hypergame
              supergame

Berry's Paradox
Sprouts, Brussel sprouts
Sylver Coinage

J.P. - 40 010
40-40-JC
25 Hbl
Soccer
29 C
83

Index

GLOSSARY OF SYMBOLS

See also the Appendix (pp. 225–228) to ONAG (reference on p. 24).

$\mathbf{A} = \mathbf{ace} = \{0 \mid \mathbf{tiny}\}$, 337

$\overline{\mathbf{A}} = -\mathbf{ace} = \{\mathbf{miny} \mid 0\}$, 339

$\mathbf{A}- = \{\mathbf{on} \mid \mathbf{A} \parallel 0\}$, 339

$\overline{\mathbf{A}}+ = \{0 \parallel \overline{\mathbf{A}} \mid \mathbf{off}\}$, 339

$\aleph_0$, aleph-zero, 309

$\triangle$, also, slow join, 266

$\wedge$, and, join, 258

$\lceil \ \rceil$, "ceiling", least integer not less than, 453

$(x)_n$, $\{x \mid -y\}_n$, Childish Hackenbush values, 230

$a\langle b\rangle$, class a and variety b, 343

$\overline{1}\clubsuit = \{\clubsuit \mid 0\}$

$\clubsuit = 0 \clubsuit = \{1\clubsuit \mid 0\}$, clubs, 339

$1\clubsuit = \{\mathbf{deuce} \mid 0\}$

$\bullet\ \blacklozenge\ \bigcirc\ \textcircled{D}$, Col and Snort positions, 49, 142

γ°, degree of loopiness, 341

$2\clubsuit = \{0 \mid \mathbf{ace}\} = \mathbf{ace} + \mathbf{ace} = \mathbf{deuce}$, 337

$\overline{1}\diamondsuit = \{\overline{\mathbf{J}} \mid 0\}$

$\diamondsuit = 0 \diamondsuit = \{\mathbf{ace} \mid \overline{1}\diamondsuit\}$, diamonds, 339

$1\diamondsuit = \{0 \mid \diamondsuit\}$

$\Downarrow = \{\downarrow* \mid 0\} = \downarrow+\downarrow$, double-down, 70, 71, 73

$\Uparrow = \{0 \mid \uparrow*\} = \uparrow+\uparrow$, double-up, 70, 71, 73

$\Uparrow* = \{0 \mid \uparrow\} = \uparrow+\uparrow+*$, double-up-star, 73

$\downarrow = \{* \mid 0\}$, down, 66

$\downarrow_2 = \{\uparrow* \mid 0\}$, down-second, 227, 228

$\downarrow_3 = \{\uparrow+\uparrow^2+* \mid 0\}$, down-third, 227, 228

$\downarrow_{abc...}$, $\downarrow_{abc...}$, 252

Ψ, downsum, 316, 337

$\mathbf{dud} = \{\mathbf{dud} \mid \mathbf{dud}\}$, deathless universal draw, 317

$e = 2.7182818284\ldots$, base of natural logarithms, 576

ε, epsilon, small positive number, 308

$\doteqdot$, equally uppity, 233, 238, 240

$\lfloor \ \rfloor$, "floor", greatest integer not greater than, 53, 291

$\parallel 0$, fuzzy, 31, 34, 35

G, general game, 30–33

$G \parallel 0$, G fuzzy, 2nd player wins

$G < 0$, G negative, R wins

$G > 0$, G positive, L wins ⎬, 31

$G = 0$, G zero, 1st player wins

$G + H$, sum of games

G^L, (set of) L option(s), 33

G^R, (set of) R option(s)

$\mathscr{G}(n)$, nim-value, 82

$G.\uparrow = \{G^L.\uparrow + \Uparrow* \mid G^R.\uparrow + \Downarrow*\}$, 238, 246, 249

$>$, greater than, 34

$\geqslant$, greater than or equal, 34

$\triangleright$, greater than or incomparable, 34, 37

$\gtrsim$, at least as uppity, 233, 238

$\frac{1}{2} = \{0 \mid 1\}$, half, 9, 22

$\overline{1}\heartsuit = \{\heartsuit \mid 0\}$

$\heartsuit = 0\heartsuit = \{1\heartsuit \mid \overline{\mathbf{A}}\}$, hearts, 339

$1\heartsuit = \{0 \mid \mathbf{joker}\}$

$\mathbf{hi} = \{\mathbf{on} \parallel 0 \mid \mathbf{off}\}$, 335

$\mathbf{hot} = \{\mathbf{on} \mid \mathbf{off}\}$, 335

$\parallel$, incomparable, 37

$\infty = \mathbb{Z} \parallel \mathbb{Z} \mid \mathbb{Z}$, infinity, 309, 314, 371

$\pm\infty = \infty \mid -\infty = \mathbb{Z} \mid \mathbb{Z} = \int^{\mathbb{Z}} *$, 314

$\infty \pm \infty = \infty \mid 0 = \mathbb{Z} \mid 0$, 314

$\infty + \infty = 2.\infty = \mathbb{Z} \parallel \mathbb{Z} \mid 0$, double infinity, 314

∞_0, $\overline{\infty}_2$, unrestricted tallies, 294

$\infty_{abc...}$, 367–375

$\infty_{\beta\gamma\delta...}$, 313

$\int$, integral, 163–176, 314, 346, 347

$\mathbf{J} = \{0 \mid \overline{\mathbf{A}}+\} = \mathbf{ace} \curlywedge (-\mathbf{ace}) = \mathbf{joker}$, 338

$\overline{\mathbf{J}} = \{\mathbf{A}- \mid 0\} = \mathbf{ace} \curlyvee (-\mathbf{ace}) = -\mathbf{joker}$, 339

L, Left, 4

LnL, LnR, RnR, positions in Seating games, 46, 130, 251

$<$, less than, 34

$\leqslant$, less than or equal, 34

$\triangleleft$, less than or incomparable, 34, 37

$\mathbf{lo} = \{\mathbf{on} \mid 0 \parallel \mathbf{off}\}$, 335

$\mathcal{D}$, loony, 377–387

$\gamma, \gamma', \gamma^+, \gamma^-$, loopy games, 315

$s\&t$ loopy game, 316

$-1 = \{\mid 0\}$, minus one, 21

$-_{\mathbf{on}} = \{\mathbf{on} \mid 0 \parallel 0\}$, miny, 333

$-_{\frac{1}{4}} = \{\frac{1}{4} \mid 0 \parallel 0\}$, miny-a-quarter, 133

$-_x = \{x \mid 0 \parallel 0\}$, miny-x, 124

$\overset{*}{\times}$, nim-product, 443

$\overset{*}{+}$, nim-sum, 60, 75, 82, 108

$\mathbf{off} = \{\mid \mathbf{off}\}$, 316–320, 337

$\omega = \{0, 1, 2, \ldots \mid\}$, omega

$\omega+1 = \{\omega \mid\}$, omega plus one

$\omega \times 2 = \{\omega, \omega+1, \omega+2, \ldots \mid\} = \omega+\omega$, 309–313

$\omega^2 = \{\omega, \omega \times 2, \omega \times 3, \ldots \mid\} = \omega \times \omega$

$\mathbf{on} = \{\mathbf{on} \mid\}$, 316–321

$1 = \{0 \mid\}$, one, 9, 21

$\mathbf{ono} = \{\mathbf{on} \mid 0\}$, 335–336

$\mathbf{oof} = \{0 \mid \mathbf{off}\}$, 335–337

$\mathbf{over} = \{0 \mid \mathbf{over}\} = \dfrac{1}{\mathbf{on}}$, 321

$\pi = 3\cdot141592653\ldots$, pi, 308–309, 576

$\pm 1 = \{1 \mid -1\}$, plus-or-minus one, 118–120

I

$(\pm 1).\uparrow = \{\Uparrow\!\ast \mid \Downarrow\!\ast\}$, 239

$\Downarrow\!\!\Downarrow = \{\Downarrow\!\ast \mid 0\} = 4.\downarrow$, quadruple-down, 327

$\Uparrow\!\!\Uparrow = \{0 \mid \Uparrow\!\ast\} = 4.\uparrow$, quadruple-up, 73, 327

$\frac{1}{4} = \{0 \mid \frac{1}{2}\}$, quarter, 8, 22

$\hat{\tfrac{1}{4}} = \frac{1}{4}.\uparrow = \{\Uparrow\!\ast \mid 1\frac{1}{2}.\downarrow + \ast\}$, quarter-up, 228

$\hat{\tfrac{1}{4}}\ast = \frac{1}{4}.\uparrow + \ast = \{\Uparrow \mid 1\frac{1}{2}.\downarrow\}$, quarter-up-star, 228

R, Right, 4

$\frac{\ast}{2} = \{\ast, \uparrow \mid \downarrow\ast, 0\}$, semi-star, 350

$\hat{\tfrac{1}{2}} = \frac{1}{2}.\uparrow = \{\Uparrow\!\ast \mid \downarrow\ast\}$, semi-up, 228, 239

$\hat{\tfrac{1}{2}}\ast = \frac{1}{2}.\uparrow + \ast = \{\Uparrow \mid \downarrow\}$, semi-up-star, 228

$\hat{\tfrac{3}{2}} = 1\frac{1}{2}.\uparrow = \{\Uparrow\!\ast \mid \ast\}$, sesqui-up, 228

sign( ), 328–330

$|, \|, \interleave, \ldots$, slash, slashes, … separate L and R options, 8, 127, 346

$\overline{2\spadesuit} = \{\overline{A} \mid 0\}$

$\overline{1\spadesuit} = \{0 \mid \overline{2\spadesuit}\}$

$\spadesuit = 0\spadesuit = \{0 \mid \overline{1\spadesuit}\}$ }, spades, 339

$1\spadesuit = 0 \mid \spadesuit$

$\star$, far star, remote star, 222–224, 236–243

$\ast = \{0 \mid 0\}$, star, 40

$\ast2 = \{0, \ast \mid 0, \ast\}$ star-two, 43

$\ast n = \{0, \ast, \ldots, \ast(n-1) \mid 0, \ast, \ldots, \ast(n-1)\}$, star-$n$, 43

$\ast\alpha$, star-alpha, 313

$\hat{\ast} = \ast.\uparrow = \{\Uparrow\!\ast \mid \downarrow\ast\}$, starfold-up, 228, 239

$\ast\bar{n}$, all nimbers except $\ast n$, 377

$\ast n\rightarrow$, all nimbers from $\ast n$ onwards, 377

$\odot = 0\ast\rightarrow$, sunny, 377–381, 384

$\uparrow_{abc\ldots} = -\downarrow^{abc\ldots}$, superstars, 252

$2_1 3_0$, tallies, 280–306

$\frac{3}{4} = \{\frac{1}{2} \mid 1\}$, three-quarters, 18

$+_{\mathbf{on}} = \{0 \mid \mathbf{oof}\} = \{0 \| 0 \mid \mathbf{off}\} = $ tiny, 333, 337

$+_{\frac{1}{4}} = \{0 \| 0 \mid -\frac{1}{4}\}$, tiny-a-quarter, 124

$+_2 = \{0 \| 0 \mid -2\}$, tiny-two, 124

$+_x = \{0 \| 0 \mid -x\}$, tiny-x, 124

tis $= \{\mathbf{tisn} \mid \ \} = 1\&0$, 322, 354

tisn $= \{\ \mid \mathbf{tis}\} = 0\&-1$, 322, 354

$(l, r), (l, r)_c$, Toads-and-Frogs positions, 125, 135, 348, 355, 356

$\Downarrow = \{\Downarrow\!\ast \mid 0\} = 3.\downarrow$, treble-down, 73, 327

$\Uparrow = \{0 \mid \Uparrow\!\ast\} = 3.\uparrow$, treble-up, 73, 327

$3\spadesuit = \{0 \mid \mathbf{deuce}\} = \mathbf{trey} = \mathbf{ace} + \mathbf{deuce}$, 337

$\triangle$, triangular number, 244

$\circlearrowleft$, uggles, ugly product, 451–455

$2 = \{1 \mid \ \}$, two, 9, 21

under $= \{\mathbf{under} \mid 0\} = -\mathbf{over}$, 321

$\vee$, union, or, 280

$\uparrow = \{0 \mid \ast\}$, up, 66, 73, 252

$\uparrow^\alpha$, up-alpha, 321

$\uparrow^2 = \{0 \mid \downarrow\ast\}$, up-second, 227, 228, 321

$\uparrow\ast = \{0, \ast \mid 0\}$, up-star, 67, 221

$\uparrow^3 = \{0 \mid \downarrow + \downarrow_2 + \ast\}$, up-third, 227, 321

$\uparrow_{abc\ldots}$, 252

upon $= \{\mathbf{upon} \mid \ast\}$, 321, 355

upon$\ast = \{0, \mathbf{upon}\ast \mid 0\}$, 321

$\curlywedge$, upsum, 316, 337

∇, ur, urgent union, 292

$[a \mid b \mid c \mid \ldots]_k$, Welter function, 472

$\mathbb{Z} = \{\ldots, -2, -1, 0, 1, 2, \ldots\}$, the set of integers, 314

$0 = \{\ \mid \ \} = 0\ast = 0.\uparrow$, zero, 9, 43

absorbancy, downsum, 340
accounts-payable, 125
ace, 337
action, in hottest game, 163
active position, 146
acute triangle, 245
Adams, E.W., 116
Adders = ·73, 409, 424
Adders-and-Ladders, 366
addition
  of games, 32–34
  of loony games, 379
  of loopy games, 370
  misère, 120
  nim-, 60–61, 75–76, 101, 108–109, 115, 370, 398
    ordinal, 214
  of switches, 120
Additional Subtraction Games, 375
additives of no atomic weight, 220
adjacency matrix, 216

Air on a $\mathscr{G}$-string, 96
ajar, 388–390
Alice in Wonderland, 3, 59, 221
all small games, 221
All Square, 385
All the King's Horses, 257–263, 266–269, 272–273
almonds, 359, 373
also-ran, 266
alternating moves, 48–49
amazing jungle, 203, 216–217
ambient temperature, 160–161
ambivalent Nim-heaps, 406
anatomy of Toads-and-Frogs, 65
Andersson, Göran, 117
anger, fit of, 297
animals
  dead, 133
  Grundy's wild, 411
  tame, 405–410
  tracking, 200

annihilation games, 218
Argument, Tweedledum and Tweedledee, 5, 37, 329–330
arithmetic periodicity, 99, 112–116, 140
asymmetrical heating, 169
atomic weight = uppitiness, 195–196, 220, 222–234, 236–243, 246, 249
  calculus, 223, 240, 250
  of lollipops, 230
  of nimbers, of up, 224
  rules, 233
atomic weight,
  eccentric, 223–224, 231, 242–243
  fractional, 226–227
  properties of, 228
atoms, superheavy, 313
Austin, Richard Bruce, 54, 95, 101, 116
average versus value, 12
averages, playing the, 163, 169

baby-sitting, 393
Bach, Clive, 349
back-handed compliment, 385
Backgammon, 16
Backsliding Toads-and-Frogs, 347, 355–356
bad child, 410
Baked Alaska, 301–303
balance, 361
ball, officers', 95
Ball, W.W. Rouse, 116
bargain, 156
Baseball, Basketball, 17
Battle, 255
battle, 5
  hot, 141, 279–288, 303
Battleships, 16
bed, redwood, 206, 210–212, 216
Benson, D.C., 116
Berge, Claude, 80
Berlekamp, Elwyn Ralph, 79–80, 121, 182, 298
Berlekamp's Rule, 79–80
Bicknell-Johnson, Marjorie, 80
big firms, 403
big game, 67, 200, 204, 216, 397
bipartite graph, 212, 219
birthday, 298, 397
Black, Farmer, 141
blatantly loopy, 371
blatantly winning ways, 390
blossom, 191, 193, 232
bLue edge, 4, 191
Blue Flower Ploy, 193, 232
Blue Jungle Ploy, 196
blue tinted nodes, 199
Blue-Red Hackenbush, 3–8, 22, 31, 33, 38, 44, 206–212, 220
Blue-Red-Green Hackenbush, see Hackenbush Hotchpotch
bogus Nim-heap, 57–58
Bond, James = ·007, 94
Bono, Edward de, 364, 388, 392
bonus move, 385
Borosh, I., 80
bottle, 213, 220
boundary
  left, 150
  right, 150, 160
Bouton, Charles L., 44, 54, 80, 426
brazils, 373
Bridge, 17
bridge, 183, 188–190
bulls, 141
Bynum's Game = Eatcake, 134, 225, 269
Bynum James, 134, 225, 269
bypassing reversible options, 62–66, 72–73, 78
Byrom, John, 55

Byron, Henry J., 81

CABS, 368–373
cabs, 344–346
cake, 28, 53, 190, 215, 264–266, 269–272, 275–277, 279–284, 288–290, 301–303
Calculus, Atomic Weight, 223, 240, 250
canonical form for numbers, 24
Cards, House of, 337–341
carousal, 360
carousel, 349, 360, 362
cash flow, 124
cashews, 373
Cashing Cheques, 120–122, 141, 155, 231
Celoni, James R., 220
centralizing switches, 121
chain
  green, 42
  Snort, 174–179
chair
  redwood, 206
  swivel, 329
chalk-and-blackboard game, 3
chance moves, 16
Chandra, Ashok K., 218, 220
change of heart, 255
change, phase, 164–165
charge, electric, 243–245
Charming Antipodean Beauty Spot, 371
Checkers = Draughts, 218, 220
cheque-market exchange, 155
Chess
  complete analysis, 16
  Dawson's, 88–91, 100–101
child
  bad, 410
  good, 407
Childish Hackenbush, 45, 54, 153, 229–232
childish lollipops, 229–232
childish picture, 45
children's party, 130, 174
Chinese Nim = Wythoff's Game, 407
class and variety, 342–343
class, outcome, 30, 83
closed, 388–390
cloud, 32, 38, 119, 146
clubs, 339
coalitions, 17
code digits, 91–92, 98–100, 102–107, 112
coins, 121–122
Coinage, Sylver, 17
Col, 39–41, 49–53, 69–70, 77, 141, 218

cold game, 279–280, 287
cold position, 285–286, 302
cold war, 280–282, 284, 286
cold work, 296
Coldcakes, 280
Colon Principle, 184, 185, 214, 335
coloring, 39, 141
Commandment,
  Lukewarmth, 286, 290
  Markworthy, 297
common cosets, 109
comparing games, 37, 328
compendium, 101, 367
complementing effect, 385
complete in Pspace, 218
complete information, 16
complimenting moves, 359, 385–387
component, 32–34, 37, 255, 258, 261, 266, 268–269, 279–282, 287, 292, 305–306, 376–378, 395
  cold, 279
  hot, 279–280
  loopy, 390
  tepid, 306
compound
  conjunctive, 258, 266
  continued conjunctive, 266
  disjunctive, 258
  impartial, 376
  selective, 279
  severed selective, 292
  shortened selective, 292
  subselective, 376
compound game, 32, 255
compound thermograph, 160
computing power, 159
confused, 32, 71
confusion interval, 119, 146, 154, 159
conjecture, 111
conjunctive compound, 258, 266
Connell, Ian G., 80
constructive, 182
continued conjunctive compound, 266
contract, 124
convention, normal play, 16
Conway, John Horton, 19, 24, 54, 80, 116, 121, 140, 182, 220, 253, 278, 357, 426
Cook, Stephen A., 219, 220
Coolcakes, 288–289
cooling, 147–148, 174–175
  formula, 147
coprime, 384
Corinthians I, 13.12, 71
cork-screw, left-handed, 359
cosets, common, 109
cost, 157
counters, heaps of, 43
Couples, Seating, 46–47, 94
cousin, 101–106, 113, 115, 420

coverlet, 216
cows, 141
Coxeter, Harold Scott Macdonald, 80, 116
Cram = Impartial Domineering, 139–140, 278
Cricket, 17
criminal, minimal, 188, 209
critical temperature, 163–167
Crosscram = Domineering, 117, etc.
Cutcake, 26–27
    Hickerson's, 53
Cutcakes, 264–265, 272–274, 280
cutting, 264, 272
cycles, 186–188, 209, 296

D.A.R., 341
Damß, J.E., 220
Date, 374, 390
Dawson's Chess = ·137, 88–91, 100–101
Dawson's Kayles = ·07, 17, 92, 94, 100–101, 251, 418, 424
Dawson, Thomas Rayner, 88, 116
dead animals, 133
Death Leap Principle, 125–127, 133
degree of loopiness, 341
degree of upon, 355
degree, cooling by one, 175
deleting dominated options, 64, 78
delphinium, 49, 193, 234, 324
Descartes, Blanche, 96, 116
deuce, 337
devil's label, 189
diamonds, 339
Difference Rule, 76, 384
digits, code, 91–92, 98–100, 102–107, 112
Dim, 97, 422
    with Tails, 384
disarray, 94
discount, 157
disentailing, 381
disguise, 94
disjunctive compound, 258
dissection, 126, 132
dissociation, thermal, 164
Dividing Rulers, 416–417
dog with leftward leanings, 6
dominated option, 64, 78
Domineering = Crosscram, 117–120, 137–140, 149, 173–174, 346
Domineering, Impartial = Cram, 139–140, 278
Dominoes, 117
Don't-Break-It-Up Theorem, 208–209, 211
Dots-and-Boxes, 17, 219
Double Duplicate Nim, 113

Double Hackenbush, 323
Double infinity, 314
Double Kayles, 98
double-down, ⇓, 70–71, 73
double-six, 385
double-up, ⇑, 70–71, 73, 222
doubling of nim-values, 93
down, ↓, 65–66
down-second, 227–228
downsum, 316, 335, 337, 340
drawn, 16, 315
dud = deathless universal draw, 317–318, 333
Dudeney, Henry Ernest, 82, 116
Duffus, Dwight, 292
Duplicate Kayles, 98, 424
Duplicate Nim 113, 115
duplication of nim-values, 93, 97, 113, 115, 424–425

Eatcake = Bynum's Game, 134, 225, 269
Eatcakes, 266, 269–272, 275–277
eccentric cases of atomic weights, 223–224, 231, 242–243
economy, underlying, 147
edges, 42, 45, 325
edges,
    bLue and Red, 4–8, 31, 79, 191, 229, 242, 309, 323
    grEen, 31, 42, 184–191, 229, 242, 310
    pink and pale, 323–324
electric charge, 243
empty set, 82, 379
ender, 309–310
Endgame, 396
ending condition, 16, 48–49, 309
enlarged flow, 291
Enough Rope Principle, 17
entailing, 359, 376–385
equally favorable, 37
equally uppity, 233, 238, 240
equitable, 153, 155–157, 166
eternal games, 48, 359
even, 259, 261
    evicts!, 286
    timers, 285
Even, Shimon, 218, 220
evil = even, 267, 287
evil numbers, 109
exactly periodic, 85
exceptional values, 89–91, 100, 107
excitable, 153, 155–157, 166–168
excluded tolls, 285
excluded values, 110
exemptions, tax, 147
Ex-Officers Game = ·06, 102, 425, 470

explosive nodes, 51
exponential-time algorithms, 218–219
extended thermograph, 157–159
Extras, 16, 48, 75, 100, 132, 176, 214, 246, 272, 304, 349, 388, 422

Fair Shares and Unequal Partners, 360, 374
Fair Shares and Varied Pairs, 359, 390
fairy chess, 116, 607
fairy tale, 292
Falada, 292–294, 299–301, 304–305
far star = remote star, ☆, 222
favorite, 253, 258, 262
Ferguson, Thomas S., 86, 116, 410, 422, 426
fickle, 393, 403–405, 409, 412, 414
field, 292–293, 304
fifth column, 391
fine print, 124
finicky figures, 88, 303
finishing line, 387
firm, 393, 403–405, 409, 412
first
    bite, 302–303
    cousin, 101–102, 104–106, 113, 115
    eaten strip, 275
    home, 260, 300–301
    horse stuck, 260
    off, 292
    one-by-one cake, 265
    player wins, 30
    strip, 275
fit, 24, 243
fixed, 315
Flanigan, James Allen, 357, 425
flat, 410
floor, 53, 291
flow, 197–205, 220
flow, cash, 124
Flow Rule, 197, 199, 205
flower, 31, 38, 49, 68–69, 183, 189, 192–195, 205, 222, 232–234, 236–238, 324
flower garden, 183, 192, 221–222, 232
flowerbed, 233–234, 236, 238
flowerstalk = stem, 38
foot, 206
Ford, Lester R., 200, 220
forging, 369
form,
    canonical, 24
    simplest, 24
    standard, 100–106
Formula, Cooling, 147
foundations for thermographs, 151
Fox-and-Geese, 17
fractional atomic weights, 226
    multiples, 246

Fraenkel, Aviezri S. 80, 218, 220, 392
free, 315
freezing point, 150, 166
French Military Hunt, 17
Frogs, *see* Toads,
Fulkerson, Delbert Ray, 200, 220
function
   ruler, 97
   Steinhaus, 259
furniture, redwood, 206–212, 216
fusion, 186–188
fuzzy flowers, 31
fuzzy games, 32
fuzzy positions, 30, 34–35

$\mathscr{G}$-sequence = nim-sequence, 82, etc.
$\mathscr{G}$-value = nim-value, 82, etc.
Gale, David, 116
gallimaufry, 69–70, 77
Galvin, Fred, 244
galvinized games, 243–245
game
   birthdays, 397
   identification, 67
   in the jungle, 204
   locator, 101, 103, 424
   of pursuit, 17
   reserves, 394
   tracking, 67
   trees, 42
   with cycles, 356
Game, Additional Subtraction, 375
   big, 67, 200, 204, 216
   Bynum's = Eatcake, 134, 225, 269
   cheap, 367
   cold, 141, 280
   coolest, 169
   comparisons of, 37
   compendium, 101, 367
   compound, 32
   eating, 134, 225, 266, 269–272, 275–277
   entailed, 359, 376–385
   equitable, 153, 155–157, 166
   eternal, 48, 359
   excitable, 153, 155–157, 166–168
   Falada, 300–301
   finite, 48, 114
   fuzzy, 32
   galvinized, 243–245
   Grundy's 17, 96, 111, 414, 419–420, 424
   half-tame, 403, 415–417, 424–425
   hard, 206, 212, 218–219
   hexadecimal, 115–116
   hot, 123, 131, 141–182, 219, 279–288, 296, 303
   impartial, 17, 42, 82, 190, 214, 271, 310, 359, 376
   impartial loopy, 255, 359–392

impartial misère, 255, 393, 426
   Kenyon's, 115
   L-, 364, 388, 392
   loopy, 255, 307, 314–357, 376
   map-coloring, 39, 141
   misère Grundy's, 396–400
   misère octal, 423–425
   negative of, 35–37
   Northcott's 56
   octal, 101–115, 423–425
   ordinal sum, 214
   partizan, 17, 67, 255, 275, 292, 356, 359
   reduced, 426
   restive, 405–406, 412–418
   restless, 412–415, 423
   Sato's Maya, 407
   short hot, 219
   simplifying, 62–65, 78–79
   subtraction, 83–86, 97, 375, 410, 422
   switch, 119–123, 153
   take-and-break, 82, 91–92, 95, 109
   take-away, 82, 87, 100
   tame, 397, 402–418, 423–426
   tameable, 405, 426
   tepid, 286, 288, 296, 306
   tiniest, 123–124
   tracking, 67, 216–217
   Welter's, 407
   wild, 410
   Wythoff's, 17, 62, 76, 407
   zero, 4, 9, 43
garden, 35, 192, 221, 232
Gardner, Martin, 19, 54, 140, 278
Garey, Michael R., 212, 218–219, 220
gathering, 334
Gauss, Karl Friedrich, 244
gee-up, 238
Generalized Geography, 218
Generalized Hex, 218
Generalized Kayles, 218
genus, 402–426
geranium, 49, 193, 234
gift horse, 74, 79
Gift Horse Principle, 74, 79
Gijlswijk, V.W., 364, 392
Ginny, 367–371
giraffe, 200–202
glass of wine, 359–360
glass, magnifying, 147
Go, 17, 157, 219
Go-moku, 16
Göbel, Fritz, 116
godd, 189, 220
Goldbach position, 362
Goldbach's Nim, 381
golden number, 77
Goller, Nicholas E., 366, 388
good = odd, 267, 287
good child, 407

good move, 17, 377
Good, Irving John, 220
Goose Girl, 292
grafting plumtrees, 334
Grantham, Stephen Brian, 253
graph, 142–143
   bipartite, 212, 219
   spanning tree of, 212, 219
graphic picture of farm life, 142
grass, 42
Great Hall, 352
Great-Aunt Maude, 367
Greek letters, loopy, 315, 344
green
   chain, 42
   edges, 31, 42, 184–191, 229, 242, 310
   girl, 186
   Hackenbush, 40, 42, 44, 183–190, 220
   jungle, 191–192, 196
   snake, 42
   tinted nodes, 199
   tracks, 197
   trees, 184–187
greenwood trees, 36
grounding cycles, 187
grown-up picture, 45
Grundy
   scale, 87, 89, 93, 96, 100, 378–379, 386
   Skayles, 90
Grundy, Mrs., 290
Grundy, Patrick Michael, 44, 54, 58, 80, 116, 215, 313, 397, 424, 426
Grundy's Game, 17, 96, 111, 414, 419–420, 424
   misère, 396–400
   wild animals, 411
Guiles = ·15, 93, 102, 416, 424
Guy, Richard Kenneth, 88, 98, 101, 116

Hackenbush, 3–8, 21–22, 29, 44–45, 77, 183–220
   Hotchpotch, 31, 39, 49, 68–70, 191–206, 220, 222, 229, 242
   is hard!, 206, 212
   number system, 80
   picture, 3–4
   string, 25, 79, 309
Hackenbush, Blue-Red, 3–8, 22, 31, 33, 38, 44, 191, 206–212, 220
   Childish, 45, 54, 153, 229
   Double, 323
   Green, 40, 42, 44, 183–190, 220
   Infinite, 307, 312, 324
   Loopy, 323–324
half-move, 6, 9, 22
half-off, 336
half-on, 336

half-tame, 394, 403, 415, 424
halving nim-values, 189
Hanner, Olof, 182
hard problems, 218–220
hard redwood bed, 212, 216
hard-headed, 167
hardness, 206, 212, 218–220
Harry Kearey, 298
head,
   losing your, 216
   severed, 292
heaps, *see also* Nim-heaps, 43, etc.
heart, change of, 255
hearts, 339
heat, 123, 130, 141, 160, 279
heating, 163, 169
hereditarily tame, 405
heuristic discussion, 155
hexadecimal games, 115–116
hi, 335–336
Hickerson, Dean, 53
hierarchy, 95
highway, 344, 371
hilarity, 360
Hilbert Nim, 313
Hillman, A.P., 80
Hockey, 17
Holladay, John C., 116
hollyhocks, 38
home, 257, 260, 263, 266, 268, 299–301,
   366–367
Honest Joe, 155
horse, 29, 74, 257–258, 260–264, 266,
   272–273, 292, 299–301
   also-ran, 266
   favorite, 258, 262
   gift, 74, 79
   outsider, 266
   racing, 268
   slow, 266, 268
   working out a, 30
Horsefly, 375, 391
hot, 335–336
hot, 123, 131, 141, 145, 147, 167, 169,
   219, 280, 284, 287, 296
   battle, 141, 279–288, 303
   component, 279–280
   game, 169, 219, 287
   position, 145, 284
   work, 296
Hotcakes, 279–284
Hotchpotch, Hackenbush, 31, 39, 49,
   68–70, 191–206, 220, 222, 229, 242
house and garden, 35
House of Cards, 337–341

illegal, 300, 302, 384
imminent jump, 11

impartial, 17, 42, 82, 190, 214, 271,
   310, 359, 376
   Cutcakes, 273
   Domineering = Cram 139–140, 278
   horse-moving, 263
   loopy games, 255
   remoteness, 276
incentive, 144, 246, 249
incomparable, 37
induction, 114
inequalities for stoppers, 331
Inequality Rule, 328–329
infinite
   delphinium, 49
   ender, 309
   geranium, 49
   Hackenbush, 307, 312, 324
   Nim, 310
   ordinal numbers, 309
   repetition, 16, 364
   Smith theory, 313
   tolls, 295–300, 305–306
infinitesimal, 38, 164–169
infinitesimally close, 147
infinitesimally shifted, 173–175, 191
infinity, 309, 314, 371
Inglis, Nick, 53
ink, waste of, 362
integral, 163–176, 314, 346–347
Intermediate Value Theorem, 406, 418
interval, confusion, 119, 146, 154, 159
invoices and cheques, 124
irregular values, 89–91, 100, 107
ish = Infinitesimally·SHifted, 173–175,
   191

Jelly Beans = **·52**, 408, 424
Jimmy, 367–371, 393
Johnson, David S., 212, 218–219, 220
join, 257–278, 280
   rapid, 266
   slightly slower, 263
   slow, 266–271, 280
joker, 338
jumpee, 13
jumper, 10
jungle warfare tactics, 205
jungle
   clearing, 216–217
   parted, 196
   sliding, 192
   smart game in, 204
   tracking, 199
   unparted, 205

Karp, Richard M., 212, 219
Kayles = **·77**, 81–82, 88, 90, 92, 94,
   109–111, 218, 397, 424

Kayles
   Dawson's = **·07**, 17, 92, 94, 251,
   418, 424
   Double, 98
   Misère, 411–412
   Quadruple, 98
   Triplicate Dawson's, 251
Kenyon's Game, 115
Kenyon, John Charles, 101, 114, 116
Kindervater, G.A.P., 364, 392
King's Horses
   All the, 257–263, 266–269, 272–273
   Some of the = Falada, 292
King, Kimberley, 216
kite strategy, 234, 238
knight, 258
Knight, White, 58–61, 258
Knuth, Donald, 19, 53
Kriegspiel, 16

L-game, 364, 388, 392
Lacrosse, 17
Lasker, Edward, 99, 116
Lasker's Nim, 99, 112–113
last cut, 274
last home, 268
last horse, 266
last move, 167
last player losing, 255, 426
last player winning, 4, 10, 14, 16, 255
latent heat, 130, 287
latent loopiness, 355, 371
latent phase change, 164
lateral thinking, 364, 392
Left, 4
   boundary, 150
   excitable, 155
   remoteness, 259, 261
   stop, 145–146
   tally, 281
Lefty, 26, 264, 279
leg, 206
Lemma
   Norton's, 214, 235, 334
   Snort, 176
Lemon Drops = **·56**, 408, 424
Let them eat cake!, 269
Li Shuo-Yen, Robert, 323, 353, 357
Li's Rules, 324
Lichtenstein, David, 220
Life, 17, 55
lightning bolts, 52
line, real number, 25
lo, 335–336
lollipops, 229–230
long periods, 108
loony, 302, 377–387
loopiness, 341–343

loopiness
    blatant, 371
    degree of, 340
    latent, 355, 371
    patent, 356, 371
loopy component, 370, 390
loopy game, 255, 307, 314–357, 376
loopy Hackenbush, 323–325
loopy option, 390
loopy position, 369, 388
loopy value, 367, 369–371
Lose slowly!, 258
losing, last player, 255, 393–426
Lost World, 393–394
Loyd, Sam, 82, 116
lucky star, 237
Ludo, 16
Lukewarmth Commandment, 286, 290

m-plicate, 97
making tracks, 199
management of cash flow, 124
many-way Maundy Cake, 215
map, 39, 141, 394
Mark, 4.24; Matthew 13.12, 385
markup, 157
Markworthy Commandment, 297
mast, 148
mast value = mean value, 162
mattress, 210
Mauhin, Patrick, 29
Maundy Cake, 28–29, 53, 190, 215
max, 268
maxim, 259, 267
maximal flow, 197
Maya Game, Sato's = Welter's Game, 407
mean value, 145, 147–150, 162
mex = minimum-excludant, 57, 82, 398
Milnor, John, 182
minimal criminal 188, 209
minimal spanning tree, 212, 219
miny, 124, 126, 133
miny, 333
misère
    birthdays, 397
    Cutcakes, 273
    Grundy's Game, 396–400
    Kayles, 411–412
    Nim, 393
    octal games, 423–425
    play, 17, 258, 261, 393
    remoteness, 261
    theory, 395–399
    unions, 292
    Wyt Queens, 407
mistake, inevitable, 362
mixed, 315

money, 167
Monopoly, 17
Moore, Eliakim Hastings, 407
Moore's Nim_k, 407
Morra, Three-Finger, 16
Morris, Lockwood, 219
mountain, purple, 191–192
moves, 16, 42
    abnormal, 305
    alternating, 48
    bonus, 385
    chance, 16
    complimenting, 359, 385–387
    consecutive, 255, 385
    entailing, 359, 376–385
    equitable and excitable, 157
    five-eighths of a, 22
    good, 17, 377
    half, 6
    horse, 386
    hotter, 169
    illegal, 300–302, 384
    legal, 384
    loony, 377–387, 391
    non-entailing, 377–378, 380
    non-suicidal, 302
    normal, 305
    overriding, 292, 294, 297, 299, 300, 306
    pass, 263, 266, 318, 332, 335
    predeciding, 292, 300
    quarter, 8
    repainting, 323
    reversible, 56, 62, 72, 78, 208, 395
    reversible misère, 395
    reverting, 405
    suiciding, 292, 300
    sunny, 377–381, 384, 387, 391
    temperature-selected, 129
    three-quarter, 17
    trailing, 382
    worthwhile, 208–211
Mrs. Grundy, 290
multiples of up, 73, 238, 249
multiples, fractional and non-integral, 246
Munro, Ian, 220
musical series, 116

$\mathcal{N}$-positions, 83, 259, 361–364, 388, 390, 419
negative
    charge, 243
    numbers, 21, 310
    of a game, 35–37
    positions, 30–31, 70
Neyman, A., 116
Nim, 17, 42, 55–56, 113, 169, 367, 426
    Chinese = Wythoff's Game, 407
    Double Duplicate, 113

    Duplicate, 113, 115
    Entailing, 380
    Goldbach's, 381
    Hilbert, 313
    in hot games, 169
    infinite, 310
    Lasker's, 99, 112–113
    misère, 393
    Poker, 55
    Triplicate, 113, 115
    two-dimensional, 312–313
    Welter's, 407
nim-addition, 60–61, 75–76, 101, 108–109, 115, 370, 398
Nim-heaps, 43–44, 57–61, 82, 369, 373, 393, 398–404, 406, 410, 414, 416,
    addition, 61, 75–76
    ambivalent, 406
    bogus, 57–58
Nim-position, 43, 368, 393, 405–406, 426
nim-sequence, 82–87, 93, 97–100, 102, 104–108, 112–113, 115
nim-sum, 61, 75–76, 82, 89–90, 108–111
nim-values, 82–87, 89–98, 109–116, 185–190, 367–388, 390–391, 405–406, 422
    addition, 89, 101, 108–109, 185, 190, 370
    doubling, 93
    duplication, 93, 97, 113, 115, 424–425
    halving, 189
    periodic, 83–85, 90–91, 93, 97, 99–108, 111–116
    reflected, 108
    relevant, 376
    replication, 97
nimbers, 42–43, 58, 76, 117, 193–194, 253, 377–381, 385–386, 398
    adding, 44, 60
    infinite, 310
Nim_k, Moore's, 407
No Highway, 344–347
Noah's Ark Theorem, 403, 412–415, 423
nodes
    Col, 49–53
    explosive, 51–52
    game positions, 42, 321–323, 334–338, 349–350
    Hackenbush, 185–188, 196–199, 216–218
    Snort, 142–143, 176–179
    tinted, 199, 202–205, 217
    untinted, 199, 204
non-number, 144, 156
normal move, 305
normal play, 14, 16, 258
Northcott's Game, 56

Norton, Simon P., 141, 164, 182, 214, 235, 238, 246, 334
Noughts-and-Crosses = Tic-Tac-Toe, 16
novice, 362
NP-complete, 212, 218–220
NP-hard, 218–219
Number Avoidance Theorem, 144, 179
number system
  Hackenbush, 80
  tree and line, 25
numbers, 24, 117, 280
  canonical form, 24
  infinite ordinal, 309
  overheated, 172
  simplest, 21, 24, 285, 288
  Surreal, 19
  suspense, 266, 273
  thermographic thicket of, 172
  triangular, 244
  whole, 21
nut crackers, impossible, 359

$\mathcal{O}$-positions, 362, 364, 370–371, 388, 390
O'Beirne, Thomas H., 80, 426
obtuse triangle, 245
octal games, 101–115, 423–425
odd, 259, 261, 267, 285–287
odd admits!, 285
odious numbers, 109
off, 316–320, 333, 335–338
Off-Wyth-Its-Tail!, 382
Officers = ·**6**, 94, 419–420, 424
offside, 316–317, 320, 324–325, 328, 334–335, 349–350
Omar, 44, 74, 108, 136, 253
on, 316–318, 333
On-the-Rails, 386–387
ONAG = *On Numbers and Games*, 19, 24, 116, 137, 140, 182, 253, 278, 357, 397, 411, 426
One-for-you, Two-for-me, . . ., 299
One-upmanship Rule, 232
ono, 335–337
onside, 316–317, 320, 324–327, 334–335, 349–350
oof, 335–338
open, 362, 364, 370–371, 388, 390
option, 16, 151
  best, 283
  dominated, 64, 78
  Left, 33
  loopy, 388
  non-loopy, 369
  questionable, 367
  reversible, 62–66, 72–73, 78, 367
  Right, 33

suicidal, 297
  worthwhile, 208–211
optional extras, 84
ordinal numbers, 309
ordinal sum, 214
outcome, 30
  classes, 30, 83
  of sum, 33–34
outsider, 266
over, 321, 333
overheating, 170, 172, 346
overriding, 292, 294–297, 306

$\mathscr{P}$-positions, 83, 259, 361–365, 388, 390–391, 396–397, 399–404, 406, 411–412, 423
Pairing Property, Ferguson's, 86, 422
pairs, restive and tame, 405
pale twig, 324
Parity Principle, 185
parody, 266
parted jungle, 196
particles, 163, 666
partitions, 374
partizan, 17, 67, 255, 275, 292, 356, 339
pass, 263, 266, 318, 332, 335
patently cold and hot, 287
patently loopy, 356, 371
paths = tracks, 197, 199, 216–217
Patience = Solitaire, 17
Paul, Wolfgang J., 220
pawns, 88
Peek, 218
Peg Solitaire, 17
pencil-and-paper game, 3
Penfield, Wilder, 394
periodicity, 89–93, 99–101, 108, 112–114, 116
  arithmetic, 99, 112–116, 140
  Dawson's Chess, 89–90
  Domineering, 140
  Eatcakes, 269, 271
  Guiles, 93
  Kayles, 90–91
  octal games, 102–108, 112–114
  subtraction games, 83–85
  ultimate, 111, 269
petal, 49, 68–69, 193, 232, 324
phase change, 163–165
phase change, latent, 164
picture, 3, 45, 186
  of farm life, 142
piebald spot, 142
pink twig, 324
placing plumtrees, 334
play, 314

play
  misère, 17, 258, 261, 393
  normal, 16, 258
player
  first, 30, 31
  second, 30, 31
playing the averages, 163
Ploy
  Blue Flower, 193, 232
  Blue Jungle, 196
plumtrees, 332, 334, 337
Poker, 17
Poker-Nim, 55
Policy, Temperature, 122–123, 128–130
polyominoes, 137–138
position
  active, 146
  ajar, 388–390
  closed, 388–390
  cold, 285–286, 302
  Domineering, 118, 137–140, 149, 173–174
  fickle, 393, 403–405, 409, 412, 414
  firm, 393, 403–405, 409, 412
  fuzzy, 30, 34–35
  Goldbach, 362
  hot, 145, 284
  loony, 302, 377–387
  loopy, 369, 388
  $\mathcal{N}$-, 83, 259, 361–364, 388, 390, 419
  negative, 30–31, 70
  $\mathcal{O}$-, 362, 364, 370–371, 388, 390
  $\mathscr{P}$-, 83, 259, 361–365, 388, 390–391, 396–397, 399–404, 406, 411–412, 423
  positive, 30, 70
  starting, 16
  sunny, 377–378, 381, 384
  tepid, 286
  terminal, 4, 9, 30, 43
positive
  charge, 243
  house, 39
  house and garden, 35
  positions, 30, 70
  posy, 31
predecider, 292
pretending, 401, 419, 425
Prim, 97, 384, 422
Principle
  Bogus Nim-heap, 58
  Colon, 184–185, 214, 335
  Complimenting Move, 385
  Death Leap, 125–127, 133
  Enough Rope, 17
  Fusion, 186–188
  Gift Horse, 74, 79
  Parity, 185

Star-Shifting, 241, 249
Translation, 145, 149, 154
Uppitiness Exchange, 238
problems, hard, 218–220
profit, 157
profit-consciousness, 167
program cycle, 296
projective, 410
proof, 114, 144, 179, 196, 207–209, 211–212, 239–242, 246–250, 320, 328–330, 350–353, 388, 415, 422–423
Proviso, Endgame, 396–397
pruning plumtrees, 334
PSPACE-complete, 218–220
PSPACE-hard, 218–220
purchasing contract, 125
purple mountain, 191–192
pursuit, 17,278

Quadruple Kayles, 98
quantity beats quality!, 195
quarter-infinite board, 264, 272, 292, 313
quarter-move, 8, 22
quotation marks = eccentric cases, 223

rademacher, rado, radon, 351
rapid join, 266
rare values, 109–111
reader, assiduous, 44
    more mathematical, 342
    persevering, 89
    skeptical, 127
real number line, 25
rectangles, 26–29, 139, 225
Red edges, 4, 191
Red tinted nodes, 199
Red twig, 208
Red-Blue Hackenbush, see also Blue-Red, 3–8, etc.
reduced game, 426
redwood
    bed, 206, 210–212, 216
    furniture, 206–210
    tree, 209–210
    twig, 208, 211
References, 19, 54, 80, 116, 140, 182, 220, 253, 278, 357, 392, 426
reflexion of Nim-values, 108
Reisch, Stefan, 220
Remote Horse, 258
remote star, 222–224, 229–232, 235–243, 249–250
Remote Star Test, 237–238, 240
remoteness, 169, 258–266, 269, 272–273, 275–277, 295, 297, 361–366
    rules, 259, 261

even, 259, 261, 361
horse's, 260–264, 272–273
infinite, 361–362
Left, 259, 261
misère, 261–265, 272–273, 275
normal, 259
odd, 259, 261, 361
Right, 259, 261
replication of nim-values, 97
resetting the thermostat, 181
restive, 394, 405–406, 412–418
restless, 394, 412–415, 423
Restricted Translation Rule, 252
reversible moves, 56, 62, 72, 78, 208, 395
reverting moves, 405
Right, 4
    boundary, 150
    excitable, 155
    remoteness, 259, 261
    slant, 159
    stop, 145–146
    tally, 281
Rip Van Winkle's Game = Kayles, 82
ripening plums, 334
Rita, 26, 264, 279
Robertson, Edward, 220
round the world, 361
roundabout, 307, 349, 360
Rule
    Atomic Weight, 233
    Berlekamp's, 79–80
    C.A.B.S., 368–373
    Difference, 76, 384
    Downsum Absorbancy, 341
    Flow, 197, 199, 205
    Inequality, 328–329
    loony addition, 379
    Mex, 57, 398
    Misère Mex, 398
    Misère Nim, 398
    Misère Play, 17, 258, 261, 393
    misère remoteness, 261
    Nim-Addition, 61, 75–76, 370, 398
    Normal Play, 14, 16, 258
    One-upmanship, 232
    remoteness, 259, 261
    Restricted Translation, 252
    Simplicity, 23–27, 29, 40, 47, 50, 285, 287, 296–297
    Smith's, 368–369, 372–373
    suspense, 267, 283
    Tally, 284–285, 288, 305–306
    Two-ahead, 194, 232
    With, 247
    Without, 247
    Wythoff's Difference, 76, 384
ruler function, 97
rules, 16
rules, Li's Loopy Hackenbush, 324

saltus, 99, 113, 116, 140
Sarsfield, Richard, 80
Saskatchewan landscape, 153
Sato's Maya Game = Welter's Game, 407
scale, Grundy, 87, 89, 93, 96, 100, 378–379, 386
Schaefer, Thomas J., 108, 116, 218
Schaer, Jonathan, 45
Schuh, Fred., 116
Scissors-Paper-Stone, 16
scrap-heap, 371–372
seasoned campaigner, 160
Seating Boys and Girls, 130–131, 174–175, 253, 346
Seating Couples, 46–47, 130–131, 253
Seating Families, 94, 251–253
second cousin, 101–102, 104, 106, 113
second player wins, 30
Select Boys and Girls, 290
selective compound, 279–280, 292, 376
selective compound, shortened, = severed, 292
sente, 157
set
    empty, 82, 379
    subtraction, 84–86, 422
    variation, 215
Seven-up, 213, 220
severed head, 200, 292
severed selective compound, 292
sex, opposite, 130
Shaki, Ahiezer S., 357
shatter, 360
She-Loves-Me-Constantly, e.g. ·51, 102
She-Loves-Me, She-Loves-Me-Not, e.g. ·05, 101, 113, 115, 253
shifting
    by stars, 241, 249
    infinitesimally, 173, 191
short hot games, 219
shortened selective = severed, 292
short-sighted view, 156
shortlist, 283–284
side, 316–317, 320–321, 324–328, 330, 334–336, 349
sidling, 318–322, 326, 330, 345, 351–355
Sidling Theorem, 320, 351–353
sign, 328–331, 353
Silber, Robert, 80
simplest form, 21, 24, 73, 350
simplest number, 21, 24, 285, 288
Simplicity Rule, 23–27, 29, 40, 47, 50, 285, 287, 296–297
simplifying games, 62–65, 78–79
singleton, 393
Sipser, Michael, 219–220
Sisyphus, 326–328

Ski-Jumps, 9–13, 21, 29
skittles, 81
slant, right = correct, 159
slash, 8, 159, 346
slashes, 127, 346
sliding jungles, 192
slipper, 10
slow horses, 266, 268
slow join, 266–271, 280
small, 38, 221–253
Smith Theory, 313, 375
Smith's Rule, 368–369, 372–373
Smith, Cedric Austen Bardell, 88, 96,
    98, 101, 116, 258, 278, 292, 368–
    369, 371–373, 397, 426
snakes, 42–44, 232
Snakes-and-Ladders, 16, 366
Snort, 49, 141–143, 145–154, 157, 163–
    166, 173–179, 218
  dictionary, 176–179
  lemmas, 176
Solitaire, 17
spades, 1, 339
span-length, 188
spanning tree of graph, 212, 219
sparse space, 109–112
species, 415
splitting the atom, 226–227
spoiler, 157
spot, 142, 371
Spots and Sprouts, 94
Sprague–Grundy Theory, 58, 215, 313
Sprague, Roland Percival, 44, 58, 80,
    116, 215, 313
Squandering Squares, 245
Squares Off, 299
Stability Condition, 343
stage, 372–375
stalemate = tie, 16
stalk = stem, 69
Stalking = ·31, 409, 424
standard form, 100, 102, 104–107,
    113
star, 36, 40, 118, 123, 183
  far, 222
  lucky, 237
  remote, 222–224, 229–232, 235–243,
    249–250
  thermograph of, 152
Star-Incentive Theorem, 250
Star-Shifting Principle, 241, 249
starting position, 16
startling value, 40
Steinhaus function = remoteness, 259
Steinhaus, Hugo, 278, 373
stem, 38, 49, 69, 193, 205, 232
Stockmeyer, Larry, 218
stop, Left and Right, 145–146
stopper, 317, 320–321, 331–332, 334,
    336–337, 342, 349–350

stopping position, 145–162
  value, 145, 149, 169
Storer, James, 219
strategy, 169
  Goller's, 388
  kite, 234
  stealing, 386
  survival, 351–353
  Swivel Chair, 329
  symmetry, 5
  Thermostatic, 154, 159–163, 179–
    181, 219
  Tweedledum and Tweedledee, 5, 37,
    329–330
  winning, 48
string, Hackenbush, 25, 79–80, 309
structure of periods, 101, 108
subperiods of nim-values, 108
subselective compounds, 376
subtraction game, 83–86, 97, 375, 410,
    422
subtraction set, 84–86, 422
suicider, 292, 297
sums
  eternal, 48
  galvinized, 243
  of games, 32, 118, 214, 257
  of nimbers, 44
  NP-hard, 219
  ordinal, 214
sunny positions, 377–381, 384
superheavy atoms, 313
superstars, 252
Surreal Numbers, 19
survival, 328, 351–353, 393
suspense, 169, 268
  numbers, 266–272, 274, 295, 297
  rule, 267, 283
Sweets and Nuts, 373–374, 390
switches, 119–123, 153
Swivel Chair Strategy, 329
Sylver Coinage, 17

T-move, 161
tails, 376, 382, 384
Tait, Hilary, 290
Take-A-Square, 410, 422
take-and-break games, 81–116
take-away games, 82–87, 97, 100, 375,
    410, 422
tally, 280–306
  machine, 288, 298
  rules, 284–285, 288, 305–306
tame, 397, 402–418, 423–426
tameable, 405, 426
tardy union, 292
Tarjan, Robert Endre, 218
tax exemption, 147, 149–152

temperature, 122–123, 148–151, 160–
    169, 180
  ambient, 160–161
  critical, 163–167
  policy, 122–123, 128–130
Tennis, 17
tentative tally, 286
tepid component, 306
tepid game, 288
tepid position, 286
tepid work, 296
terminal position, 4, 362, 396
Test
  Remote Star, 237
  Uppitiness, 236
Theorem
  At-least-one, 249
  Don't-Break-It-Up, 208–209, 211
  Half-Tame, 415
  Intermediate Value, 406, 418
  Max-Flow, Min-cut, 196, 200
  Noah's Ark, 403, 412–415, 423
  non-arithmetic periodicity, 114
  Number Avoidance, 144, 179
  on simplifying games, 78–79
  Redwood Furniture, 207–209
  Sidling, 320, 351–353
  Simplest Form, 350
  Star-Incentive, 250
theory, Green Hackenbush, 183–190,
    196
Theory, Smith, 313, 375
thermal dissociation, 164
thermograph, 147–155, 157–162, 164–
    168, 170–172, 180–181, 338
  compound, 160
  extended, 157–158
  four-stop 154–155
  of **oof**, 338
thermographic thicket, 172
thermographs of star and up, 152
thermography, 17, 147–175, 219
thermostat, 160, 181
THERMOSTRAT = Thermostatic
    Strategy, 154, 159–163, 179–181,
    219
thinking
  backwards, 364
  forwards, 364
  laterally, 364, 392
third cousin, 113
thirteen's unlucky!, 400
Three-Color Hakcenbush, *see also*
    Hackenbush Hotchpotch, 31, etc.
Three-Finger Morra, 16
three-quarters, 17–18
thumb-twiddling, 385
Thursday, Maundy, 28
Tic-Tac-Toe, 16, 93
Tie, 16

time, complete in exponential, 218–219
timer, 280–283, 285, 287–288, 290, 295–298, 305–306
tinted, 39–40, 49–51, 53, 199, 201–202, 204–205
tiny, 333, 337
tiny, 124, 166
  -a-quarter, 129
  -two, 124, 166
  -x, 124
tis, tisn, 322, 324, 354
Toads-and-Frogs, 14–15, 65–66, 70, 72, 77, 125–129, 132–136, 347–348, 355–356
toenail, 154
toll, 280–283, 285–286, 288, 292, 295–299, 305
toll, infinite, 292–300, 305–306
Top Entails, 376
tracking, 67, 200, 216
track = path, 197, 199, 216–217
Trading Triangles, 244, 245
trailing, 382–383
trains, 382
transition, phase, 165
translation
  of four-stop games, 154–155
  by nimbers, 249, 252
  by numbers, 145, 159, 154
  of switches, 121
travesty, 266
Treblecross, 93–94
tree
  Australian, 25, 210
  binary, 25
  game, 42, 397
  green, 184–187
  greenwood, 36
  infinite, 312
  redwood, 209–211
  spanning, 212, 219
  with extra twig, 211
trey, 337
Triangles, Trading, 244, 245
triangular numbers, 244
Triplicate Dawson's Kayles, 251
Triplicate Nim, 113, 115
truth, awful, 396
Tschantz, Steve, 54
Tsyan-Shizi = Wythoff's Game, 407
Tubergen, G.J. van, 364, 392
Turn-and-Eatcake, 227
Tweedledum and Tweedledee, 4, 5, 37, 329–330
twig, 186–187, 190

twigs
  pale and pink, 324
  redwood, 208, 211
Twisted Bynum, 227
two and two, 399
Two-Dimensional Nim, 312–313

ultimate periodicity, 99–100, 269
uncertainty, 222
under, 321, 333
underlying economy, 147
union, 279–306
  misère partizan, 292
  tardy, 292
  urgent, 292, 296
units, fickle and firm, 403
unparted jungles, 205
unruly, 115
unrestricted tallies, 294–298
untinted nodes, 199, 204
up, ↑, 65–74, 152, 222, 224, 238, 249
up-second, 227–228, 321
up-onth, 355
upon, 321, 333, 355
upon∗ = delphinium, 321, 324, 333
uppitiness = atomic weight, 222, 233, 236–238, 240–242
uppity, equally, 233
upset board, 297
upstart equality, 73
upsum, 316, 335, 337
urgent unions, 292, 296

value, 6–15, 18, 21–30, 38–41, 45–47
  mast, 145, 147–150, 162
  mean, 145, 147–150, 162
  startling, 40
value versus average, 12, 145
values
  Childish Hackenbush, 45, 54
  Col, 39–41, 52
  Cutcake, 27
  Domineering, 118, 137–140
  entailed, 377–384
  exceptional, 89–91, 100, 107
  Hackenbush, 6–8, 21–22, 29–30
  irregular, 89–91, 100, 107
  loopy, 367, 369–371
  Maundy Cake, 28
  nim-, 82–87, 89–98, 109–116, 185–190, 367–388, 390–391, 405–406, 422

non-loopy, 369
rare, 109–111
redwood bed, 211
regular, 89–90
Seating Boys-and-Girls, 131
Seating Couples, 47
Ski-Jumps, 10–13
small, 38, 167, 221–253
Snort, 143, 175–179
switch, 119–123
Toads-and-Frogs, 14–15, 128, 132–136
variations, 93
variation set, 215
varieties, 342
victory, 159
Vout, Colin, 39

waltz, ·**6**, 95–96
war, cold, 279–280
warfare, jungle, 205
weight, *see* atomic weight
Welter's Game, 407
Whist, 255
White Knight, 58–61, 258
White, Farmer, 141
whole numbers, 21
wholeness of Hackenbush Hotchpotch, 242
width, 160, 179–181
wild animals, 410–411
wild games, 410–411, 414–415, 417–418
Wilder, Thornton, 394
Wilson, Neil Y., 116
win quickly!, 258
winning post, 375, 391
wonders, numberless, 117
working out a horse, 30
world
  lost, 393–394
  small, 221
worthwhile move, option, 208–211
Wright House, 352
Wyt Queens, 61, 76, 382, 407–408
Wythoff's Difference Rule, 76, 384
Wythoff's Game, 17, 62, 76, 407
Wythoff, W.A., 80

Yamasaki, Yōhei, 407, 410
Yes!, 55, 111, 328

zero, 4, 9, 30, 43
zigzag, 173
zoo, Good Child's, 407